# THE FILM COMEDY READER

# THE
# FILM
# COMEDY
## READER

Edited by
## GREGG RICKMAN

**LIMELIGHT EDITIONS**
New York

**To the memory of
Mike Vanderlan**

First Limelight Edition  December 2001

Library of Congress Cataloging-in-Publication Data

The film comedy reader / edited by Gregg Rickman.
    p. cm.
  Includes bibliographical references.
  ISBN 0-87910-295-0
1. Comedy films—United States—History and criticism.   I. Rickman, Gregg.

PN1995.9.C55 F55 2001
791.43'617—dc21

                           2001046184

Interior design by Jeffrey H. Fischen

The editor is grateful for permission to reprint copyrighted material as detailed in the
Acknowledgments.

# Contents

# vi CONTENTS

# Acknowledgments

Apart from this book's contributors, I'd like to thank many friends, contributors, and colleagues for their support, interest, and assistance with the text and with visual illustrations: Andrea Agee, Ken Bowers, Claire Brandt of Eddie Brandt's Hollywood Matinee, Larry Chadbourne, Aneta Chapman, Renée R. Curry, Eleanor Knowles Dugan, John Fairchild, Tony Guzman, Jim Kitses, Blake Lucas, Chon Noriega, Lee Sanders, Ben Schwartz, Bob Stephens and Laurel Wellman.

David Chierichetti deserves particular praise for his liberality with his beautiful collection of stills. His book on the very fine Hollywood director Mitchell Leisen is available from Photoventures Press, 3700 Eagle Rock Blvd., Los Angeles CA 90065.

Certain individuals at various university presses have been very helpful; they include Michelle Provorny of the University of California Press and Jeff Moen of the University of Minnesota Press. Bruce Long of the on-line magazine *Taylorology* (http://www.public.asu.edu/~bruce/Taylor) provided access to the archives of his splendid on-line journal from which I've pulled the essays by Parsons and Oettinger.

I'm particularly grateful to Mel Zerman for his continued support for the project.

Essays are published as originally written, with the exception of a few silently corrected errors and also emendations by the authors on a few of the reprinted pieces. Frank Krutnik

and Jonathan Rosenbaum graciously allowed me editing privileges on their work. For stylistic reasons previously published essays have been brought into line with the same forms of punctuation and referencing. Captioning on the stills is mine.

Frank Krutnik, "Jerry Lewis: The Deformation of the Comic," *Film Quarterly* vol. 48, no. 1, Fall 1994. Copyright ©1994 by the Regents of the University of California. Reprinted by permission of University of California Press.

William Ian Miller, "'I Can Take a Hint': Social Ineptitude, Embarrassment, and *The King of Comedy*," from *The Movies: Texts, Receptions, Exposures*, edited by Laurence Goldstein and Ira Konigsberg. Copyright ©1996 by the author. Reprinted by permission of the author.

Richard Combs, "Blake Edwards: 'Weather's fine. Having a little party. Wish you were here.'" Copyright ©2001. Printed by permission of the author.

Jonathan Rosenbaum, "Bridge Over Troubled Water: *The Graduate*," *Chicago Reader* March 28, 1997. Copyright ©1997 the *Chicago Reader*. Reprinted by permission of the *Chicago Reader*.

Gregg Rickman, "*The Producers*." Copyright ©2001. Printed by permission of the author.

Aneta Chapman, "Let Life Begin: *Harold and Maude*." Copyright ©2001. Printed by permission of the author.

Brian Henderson, "Romantic Comedy Today: Semi-Tough or Impossible?," *Film Quarterly* vol. 31, no. 4, Fall 1979. Copyright ©1979 by the Regents of the University of California. Reprinted by permission of University of California Press.

Gregg Rickman, "Runaway Brides." Copyright ©2001. Printed by permission of the author.

Aneta Chapman, "'My Goal Was to Make Him Cary Grant': Eddie Murphy and *Boomerang*." Copyright ©2001. Printed by permission of the author.

Doug Williams, "Introspective Laughter: Nora Ephron and the American Comedy Renaissance." Copyright ©2001. Printed by permission of the author.

Gregg Bachman, "Neither Here nor There," from *Perspectives on Woody Allen*, edited by Reneé R. Curry and Terry Allison. Copyright ©1996 G.K. Hall. Reprinted by permission of G.K. Hall.

Christine List, "Self-Directed Stereotyping in the Films of Cheech Marin," from *Chicanos and Film*, edited by Chon Noriega. Copyright ©1994 the University of Minnesota Press. Reprinted by permission of the University of Minnesota Press.

Gregg Rickman, "Notes on *Bamboozled*." Copyright ©2001. Printed by permission of the author.

David Thomson, "Shoot the Actor," *Film Comment* March-April 1998. Copyright ©1998. Reprinted by permission of the author.

Dan Sallitt, "Notes on David O. Russell." Copyright ©2001. Printed by permission of the author.

Jonathan Rosenbaum, "In a World of His Own: *Rushmore*," *Chicago Reader* Feb. 12, 1999. Copyright ©1999 the *Chicago Reader*. Reprinted by permission of the *Chicago Reader*.

Robin Wood, "'I Just Went Gay, All of a Sudden': Gays and '90s Comedy." Copyright ©2001. Printed by permission of the author.

*Tickets please. The carnival's about to start.*

# Introduction

This is an anthology of essays about American screen comedy from the 1910s through the year 2000. Since at least the 1910s, with the ascendancy of Mack Sennett, comedies from Hollywood have enjoyed unrivaled worldwide popularity, and this anthology reflects that fact.

This book has no ax to grind, does not exist to prove a thesis. No single overarching theory of comedy is posited or assumed—beyond that comedies should be funny. (This is not a universally agreed upon proposition, but does underlie all the essays in this book!) While this is not a book of film theory, some competing theories of comic cinema are commented on below. Not everyone agrees with everyone else in this volume; but then, this book is hopefully "polyphonic," many-voiced, to borrow a term popularized by the influential Russian theorist Mikhail Bakhtin. Several schools of thought contend on this subject, and they inflect and influence some of this volume's best pieces.

Given the number of great comic films that have been made, and the many fine essays that have been written about them, it has been very difficult to include everything of note, and there are many regrettable gaps. A few key essays aside, this anthology focuses on the specific historical moment of a film's creation rather than the sociology of its reception. A glance at our table of contents reveals that this book is not organized in strict chronological order, but rather in a series of thematic groupings loosely organized by era. The opening section is devoted to five foundational essays, the first of which, "What Are the Six Ages of Comedy," while credited to Buster Keaton, was probably written by one of Keaton's gagmen for a 1924 book, *The Truth About the Movies*, edited by Lawrence A. Hughes. Assuming Keaton didn't write the piece—or indeed, didn't even dictate it as he claims in the opening paragraph—it's still an amusing look back at early film comedy, emphasizing as it does its shift from Keystone-era slapstick to the ambitious, epic-scale quality of mid-1920s feature filmmaking. Harold Lloyd's 1919 interview with Louella Parsons—given just as Lloyd was making the leap to stardom with his new "glasses" character—captures some of the spirit of this age, as does Ruth Waterbury's 1925 interview with W.C. Fields, "The Old Army Game," made just when the stage comedian was transferring his talents to film.

Malcolm H. Oettinger's 1923 interview with Keaton, "Low Comedy as a High Art," originally published in *Picture-Play*, includes some interesting comments by Oettinger on the top comics of the era (Charlie Chaplin, Keaton, and Lloyd), demonstrating that the pantheon discussed by James Agee in his seminal essay "Comedy's Greatest Era" (1949), which follows, was already in place at that earlier date. The interview also emphasizes Keaton's modesty about his work ("It's hokum") in marked contrast to the beauty Agee and so many other critics would perceive in Keaton's films in 1949 and since.

Buster Keaton is just one of the great star comedians of cinema's early years, and the next section of this book, Part II, offers modern perspectives on Keaton and his contemporaries Chaplin, Lloyd, the Three Stooges and Laurel and Hardy. Rick Levinson's essay on "Comic Play" emphasizes the joy of performance to be found in their work and that of their modern successors: "Laughter is an echo of that joy." J. Hoberman's contempo-

• • • • • • • • • • • • • • • • • • • • • • • • • • • • • • • • • • • • • • • • • • • • • • • •

rary rethinking of the Chaplin Tramp in modern times is neatly balanced by Charles Barr's suggestion in his essay that Laurel and Hardy's *Big Business* can fairly represent the human condition for all eternity. Ken Bowers and Kathleen Chamberlain's pieces, meanwhile, respectively discuss the development of Harold Lloyd's screen character in his neglected short subjects of 1917-20, and relate the Stooges' work to classic comic archetypes of the *commedia dell' arte*. Both essays are grounded in the specific historical context in which these films were made.

As are the essays in Part III, on the gagmen who created much of the material these and other comedians performed. Frank Capra's essay detailing the work of "The Gag Man" (1927), drawing from his own early work for Mack Sennett and Harry Langdon, defines the role of "this newly conceived specialist." Ben Schwartz's groundbreaking survey of the career of Hollywood gagman Al Boasberg follows. Schwartz's history places its protagonist against the transition from silent films to sound and the accompanying shift from visual humor to the verbal gags that have dominated Hollywood comedy from the 1930s on. Schwartz traces in detail how this forgotten figure helped create the personas of such legendary comedians as Jack Benny, Bob Hope, George Burns, and Gracie Allen, and also how he helped recreate the screen characters of such disparate clowns as Buster Keaton and the Marx Brothers. Schwartz's densely researched study redraws the map of American comedy and provides reason enough for this book's existence.

Schwartz digs deep to uncover Boasberg's submerged career. A care for how films are actually made underlies many of this book's best pieces, in particular the four pieces on the performing styles of Mae West, Irene Dunne, Edgar Kennedy and Cary Grant that comprise Part IV. The late Andrew Britton's monograph on Grant is a superb look at a film persona central to the history of Hollywood comedy, while Donald Phelps' lively appreciation of Kennedy stands in for a necessary close look at all of Hollywood's many superb character actors. Richard Schickel's appreciation of Irene Dunne calls attention to the central part women played in the great screwball comedies of the 1930s, as does director Leo McCarey's 1935 appreciation of the incomparable Mae West, whom he had directed the previous year in *Belle of the Nineties*. McCarey's brilliant handling was in fact central to the careers of all the actors discussed in this section.

Readers interested in the full sweep of romantic comedy might wish to look ahead to Part X, which takes up some key films of the 1930s by Ernst Lubitsch and Frank Capra in the context of their contemporary equivalents. Part V looks at that era from another perspective, from that of the filmmaker. Dan Sallitt opens with some brief, penetrating remarks on the acting in Lubitsch's films, which is followed by Chris Fujiwara's essay on a little-known film, *5th Ave Girl*, by the forgotten but vital Gregory La Cava. Matty Roth's critique of Howard Hawks' *His Girl Friday* fills out this section, Fujiwara and Roth making quite different use in their pieces of Stanley Cavell's ideas on the "comedy of remarriage" as put forward in his 1981 landmark study *Pursuits of Happiness* (ideas further taken up in Part X).

Comedy is not a single, discrete genre. Part VI looks at the overlap of comedy and horror in films as disparate as *The Old Dark House* and *Abbott and Costello Meet Frankenstein*, in the essays by Jim McCaffery and Bob Stephens. A justly celebrated essay by Manny Farber and W.S. Poster on writer-director Preston Sturges opens Part VII. Particular attention is paid in this section to a filmmaker more associated with musicals than with comedies, Vincente Minnelli, director of both *Father of the Bride* and *Bells Are Ringing*, the former film commemorated for its delicacy in Blake Lucas' sensitive reading, the latter discussed in an essay by Raymond Durgnat that reminds us of the comic nature of certain musicals. One common theme of the section is the way the intimate bond of romance and marriage mirrors a larger community—the wedding party of *Father of the Bride*, the telephonic community of *Bells Are Ringing*, the mob scenes of Sturges and of Billy Wilder, director of the classic *Some Like It Hot*, discussed in a brief essay by the present writer.

Many of the films discussed here appeared in the immediate postwar era of 1945-65. A second group of key figures associated with this period is discussed in Part VIII, which opens with Paul Willemen's assessment of director Frank Tashlin, "Tashlin's Method: An Hypothesis" (1973), a brief but highly influential essay here revised by its author for the first time since its publication. Frank Krutnik, like Willemen a major figure in film studies, continues his career-long interest in the subgenre of "comedian comedy" (films built around the personality of a particular comic), in his "Jerry Lewis: The Deformation of the Comic," which follows. William Ian Miller's "'I Can Take a Hint': Social Ineptitude, Embarrassment, and *The King of Comedy*" amplifies the themes of humiliation and disgust always latent in Lewis' work as they appeared in Martin Scorsese's 1982 vehicle for Lewis and Robert DeNiro. It's a major contribution to comic film theory, by an historian outside the field of academic film studies (as are indeed many of the essayists in this book). Lewis, interestingly, joins Buster Keaton (in Parts I and II), Leo McCarey (central to the careers of each of the actors discussed in Part IV), Vincente Minnelli (in Part VII) and Woody Allen (in Parts XI and XII) as key figures in their respective eras of film comedy, individuals worthy of extensive analysis from several angles. The comic-romantic star Cary Grant also serves as a multiply-referenced touchstone for many writers.

Essays in Part IX, X, and XI address the radical shifts suffered by comedy (along with much else) in the Vietnam era and since. The dark comedy of Blake Edwards, Mike Nichols' *The Graduate*, Mel Brooks' decidedly unromantic *The Producers*, and Hal Ashby's *Harold and Maude*, all discussed in Part IX, are rooted in that era of dislocation. Part X takes up the shift between the great "screwball" and other romantic comedies of the 1930s and more recent times with Brian Henderson's seminal essay "Romantic Comedy Today: Semi-Tough or Impossible?" (1979), which looks back to the 1930s in its sorrowing examination of that beleaguered subgenre in the 1970s. It's followed by my own piece comparing Frank Capra's *It Happened One Night* (1934) with Garry Marshall's *Runaway Bride* (1999), an essay which also briefly surveys commentary on romantic comedy since Henderson's pathbreaking work. Aneta Chapman's essay on the Eddie Murphy vehicle *Boomerang*, and Doug Williams' essay on the films of Nora Ephron, which follow, together help show how romantic comedy has transformed itself in the two decades since Brian Henderson's essay.

Part XI takes up the work of some contemporary comic performers, some of them who extensively employ their ethnicity in their work, as for example Woody Allen, whose confrontation with Judaism is discussed in Gregg Bachman's thoughtful, personal piece. Ethnicity as handled by the 1970s-80s team of Cheech Marin and Tommy Chong is then examined in Christine List's important essay "Self-Directed Stereotyping in the Films of Cheech Marin" (of which more below), while my essay on Spike Lee's *Bamboozled* addresses blackface minstrelsy as perceived in a controversial film of the year 2000.

The book's final section, Part XII, touches on some of the major comic trends and filmmakers of the 1990s, including Allen, whose work of that decade is cooly assessed by David Thomson. The remaining essays forecast perhaps the great careers and films we

•  •  •  •  •  •  •  •  •  •  •  •  •  •  •  •  •  •  •  •  •  •  •  •  •  •  •  •  •  •  •  •  •  •  •  •  •  •  •  •  •

can expect in the new century from such newcomers as Wes Anderson, Greg Mottola, David O. Russell and others, with Jonathan Rosenbaum's review of Anderson's *Rushmore* (a film, he notes, containing something of the spirit of Buster Keaton), and original essays by Dan Sallitt and Robin Wood.

Now as to this volume's gaps. This anthology has eschewed republication of any of the several excellent essays in the anthologies *Comedy /Cinema/Theory*, edited by Andrew S. Horton for the University of California Press in 1991, or from *Classical Hollywood Comedy*, edited by Kristine Brunovska Karnick and Henry Jenkins for the American Film Institute in 1995. Those fine books broke new ground with entirely new work. This anthology is, however, intensely interested in how ideas develop over time, and so readers will find in these pages many important essays from the past—several pieces from the teens and 1920s, James Agee's 1949 "The Golden Age of Comedy," and more recent landmarks by Manny Farber and W.S. Poster (1954), Charles Barr (1968), Raymond Durgnat (1973), Paul Willemen (1973) and Brian Henderson (1979).

Agee's essay is worth dwelling on. No one has ever done more than Agee does here to set the agenda for the critical study of a film genre, in three crucial ways.

—Agee's essay argued that silent comedy, with its strong emphasis on the visual, was purer, and funnier, than sound comedies could possibly be. Agee's argument has underpinned many of the studies of film comedy written since, including such influential work as Gerald Mast's *The Comic Mind* (1973) and Walter Kerr's *The Silent Clowns* (1975).

—For years to come Agee also established a starring comedian's talents and personality as the major factor by which to judge screen comedy. A contemporary film such as *The Paleface* (1948), a Bob Hope vehicle, served as Agee's example of a film that fell short of greatness due in large part to its failure to meet the standards of the silent film classics built around such non-verbal comics as Chaplin or Keaton. (Only in retrospect can we see *The Paleface* as less a shadow of *The Navigator*, Agee's specific counter-example, than a precursor of the animated cartoon-inflected comedy co-scenarist Frank Tashlin would make his own, quite influentially, in the 1950s.)

—Similarly, Agee's praise of his beloved Charlie Chaplin as the greatest of all the silent clowns, and his elevation of Buster Keaton, Harold Lloyd, and Harry Langdon to near-equal status as the other three members of silent cinema's Mount Rushmore, has affected reception of their work and other silent comedians since. Singlehandedly Agee resurrected the reputations of the nearly forgotten Keaton and Langdon, while significantly burnishing Harold Lloyd's fame as well. Despite some factual errors (Keaton did not apprentice under Sennett, as Agee claims), for years to come later writers took Agee's perspective as their own in discussion of these comedians, as can be seen in the work of Mast, Kerr, and others, such as Donald McCaffery in his *4 Great Comedians* (1968). Silent comedians dismissed by Agee, meanwhile, such as Roscoe "Fatty" Arbuckle and Charley Chase, have taken years to find new partisans.

Thanks in large part to Agee, the personalities of comedians like Lloyd and W.C. Fields, even when they didn't direct, came to be seen as making them the dominant creative figures of the films Agee most admires; two decades after Agee's essay, American auteurist critic Andrew Sarris made four comedians (Lloyd, W.C. Fields, the Marx Brothers, Mae West) the only non-directing entries in his booklength discussion of Hollywood auteurs, *The American Cinema* (1968). (Keaton and Jerry Lewis' non-directing credits were also sandwiched into their filmographies.) Agee's emphasis lies behind the

*Charles Chaplin, with Merna Kennedy in* The Circus. *"Greatest of all the silent clowns."*

concept of "comedian comedy," comedies built around individual personalities, developed by Steve Seidman in the 1970s and referenced here by Krutnik and others. Seidman and those who have followed him have generally not emphasized a particular comedian's agency in the creation of his films, however, preferring a structuralist approach that equated Agee's demigods with such lowly figures as Bob Hope and Abbott & Costello—even the Three Stooges. Their interest has been in the shared narrative patterns of "comedian comedies" from the teens on. These points are taken up in Frank Krutnik's essay on Jerry Lewis' multiple personas. David Thomson's argument in his piece on Woody Allen ("Shoot the Actor") that Allen is a better director than performer takes this argument full circle, and might be said to be confirmed by Sean Penn's strong work in *Sweet and Lowdown* (1999).

Agee was disinterested in the prehistory of comedy, but a great deal of new work has been done in this field over the past twenty years and harvested in the fine scholarship of Tom Gunning and Donald Crafton (published in the Karnick-Jenkins anthology *Classical Hollywood Comedy*), and also by Noel Carroll in his contribution to Horton's *Comedy/Cinema/Theory*, fascinating essays on how early gag films evolved into narratives. Feminist theory has contributed some important readings to the field, among them Lucy Fischer's "Sometimes I Feel Like a Motherless Child" in the Horton anthology, later reprinted in her collection *Cinematernities*; and Kathleen Rowe's book on women in comedy, *The Unruly Woman*, whose comments on *It Happened One Night* are glossed in my essay "Runaway Brides." Other issues of gender are brought out in this volume in Andrew Britton's monograph on Cary Grant and in Robin Wood's characteristically acute discussion of homosexuality in recent Hollywood comedies.

It is interesting, however, how many of this book's new essays discuss comedies that are built around the difficulties of making *heterosexual* romantic relationships work— Chris Fujiwara's on *5th Ave Girl*, Blake Lucas' on *Father of the Bride*, Aneta Chapman's two essays, and Doug Williams' essay on the oeuvre of Nora Ephron, whom he sees, quite originally, as the dominant figure of 1990s romantic comedy. This trend may mark a reaction to the carnivalesque excess (and sometimes brutality) of much 1990s comedy: *Ace Ventura*, *South Park*, Howard Stern, and the sexually graphic humor of *Happiness*, *There's Something About Mary*, *American Pie* et al. Many of this book's writers, consciously or not, seem to be reacting against this trend, so omnipresent in contemporary culture thanks in part to the carnivalesque Clinton-Lewinsky scandal of 1998 (which *Mary's* great success in the summer of 1998 so eerily paralleled). For all that, the darker psychological aspects of humor are hardly absent from this book—pace William Ian Miller's essay on the comedy of humiliation.

Christine List's 1994 essay on the films of Cheech and Chong, reprinted here, has already been recognized as a key contribution to the literature of race and ethnicity in American culture. A separate anthology of equal length to this one could be edited from the excellent work that's been done on this fraught subject, an anthology that would include among others Mark Winokur's study of the Marx Brothers as ethnic comedians (in his 1996 book *American Laughter*), the careful historical studies done by Eileen Bowser on "Racial/Racist Jokes in American Silent Slapstick Comedy" (1995), and Charlene Regester's exhaustive survey of the response of the black press of his time to Stepin Fetchit's stereotyped character. Their key point ("not all the jokes we think of as racist were necessarily received that way by contemporary spectators"—Bowser, 43) is echoed in more theory-based essays by Mark A. Reid and Harriet Margolis which discuss the "reading strategies" audiences may have used on these films (Reid) and the "self-directed stereotypes" employed by contemporary black filmmakers Robert Townsend and Keenan Ivory Wayans while making their films *Hollywood Shuffle* and *I'm Gonna Git You Sucka* (Margolis). Margolis defines her term as "the deployment of stereotypes by the people being stereotyped in order to undermine those stereotypes by exposing their ridiculous underpinnings" (53), an approach developed by List (whom Margolis acknowledges) in relationship to the Hispanic-American response to the Cheech and Chong comedies of the 1970s-80s. My essay "Notes on *Bamboozled*" addresses blackface minstrelsy as perceived by Spike Lee in his controversial recent film.

On the whole, however, this anthology eschews questions of audience response in favor of explications of the films themselves, and studies of the individuals who made them. Some further background on the different schools of film theory which inflect our readings of cinema follows. To briefly summarize, a divide exists between those who define the comic film in terms of its narrative pattern, and those who define it in terms of its goal, the physical act of laughter. Dirk Eitzen's essay "Comedy and Classicism," in the 1997 anthology *Film Theory and Philosophy*, usefully summarizes this debate using examples from the Karnick and Jenkins anthology *Classical Hollywood Comedy*. Eitzen located in these essays "a spectrum between the view that comedy and narrative are wholly incompatible impulses [and] the view that they are different but complementary" (Eitzen, 401). Donald Crafton's aforementioned essay "Pie and Chase," from that collection, speaks of the separation between the domains of slapstick and story as "a calculated rupture, designed to keep the two elements antagonistically apart" (Crafton, 107), while others argue that comic situations are dependent on narratives to be understood. This emphasis on narrative dominates literary theorists of comedy as well, Suzanne Langer, Northrop Frye and others "find(ing) that the action of comedy is basically the action of a sympathetic figure meeting and overcoming every obstacle, thus becoming heroic" even as "other critics, like Bergson and Meredith, define the action of comedy as the unmasking of a villain or of a humorous character, resulting in a healthy restoration of society and its values" (Grave, 14).

Frye's work—in particular his essay "The Mythos of Spring: Comedy" in *The Anatomy of Criticism* (1957)—has influenced many studies of comedy since it was written, particularly the philosopher Stanley Cavell's highly influential book on screwball comedy *Pursuits of Happiness: The Hollywood Comedy of Remarriage* (1981), cited in this book by more than one writer. Cavell took Frye's concept of "the green world," the "place where the action moves after an opening in a big city; the place within which the plot complicates and then resolves itself; a place beyond the normal world, where the normal laws of the world are interfered with; a place of perspective and education" (Cavell, 172) and applied it to such films as *Bringing Up Baby* and *The Philadelphia Story*. Cavell's concerns, however, are different from those of the feminist/psychoanalytic strain of film theory prominent since the 1970s, as suggested by the critique of Cavell's work in Matty Roth's essay on *His Girl Friday*, reprinted here.

Eitzen himself eschews a study of comic film narrative in favor of an emphasis on the strong emotional response comedies can draw—an emotional response evident in the act of laughter itself.

> Psychoanalytic theorists have written a great deal about the desire attached to movies, but that is something different from emotions. When we speak of emotional impulses, we are talking not about libidinal urges, but about conscious gratification. We like comedy because it makes us laugh. We like melodrama because it makes us cry. We like sex and violence because they arouse and excite us. And so on . . . . (T)hese manifestations are a topic that film theorists have scarcely broached. (Eitzen, 409.)

Eitzen here breaks not only with psychoanalytic film theory but also with the narrative-oriented model of classical Hollywood cinema associated with such theorists as David Bordwell, Kirsten Thompson and Noel Carroll, among others. To Eitzen, an emphasis on the raw emotional states aroused by comedy helps align "the Hollywood cinema more closely with amusement park attractions, variety shows, video games, nonfiction television, and other popular nonnarrative entertainments" rather than with the narrative structures emphasized by Bordwell et al.

As such, Eitzen's ideas link up with the notion that comedy originated in the experience of carnival, expressed by Mikhail Bakhtin in his *Rabelais and His World* (first English translation 1965), and many of his modern followers. To quote Robert Stam's gloss in his book on Bakhtin and film theory:

> Carnival, for Bakhtin, refers to the pre-Lenten revelry whose origins can be traced back to the Dionysian festivities of the Greeks and the Saturnalia of the Romans, but which enjoyed its apogee of both observance and symbolic meaning in the High Middle Ages. In that period, Bakhtin points out, carnival played a central symbolic role in the life of the community ( . . . ) characterized by the ludic undermining of all norms. The carnivalesque principle abolishes hierarchies, levels social classes, and creates another life free from conventional rules and restrictions. In carnival, all that is marginalized and excluded—the mad, the scandalous, the aleatory—takes over the center in a liberating explosion of otherness. The principal of material body—hunger, thirst, defecation, copulation—becomes a positively corrosive force, and festive laughter enjoys a symbolic victory over death, over all that is held sacred, over all that oppresses and restricts. (Stam, 86.)

Bakhtin's ideas became dominant in film comedy theory in the 1980s and 1990s, succeeding such earlier theorists of comedy as Henri Bergson and Sigmund Freud. (As William Paul points out, "Bergson and Freud considered laughter chiefly in terms of its purpose," a teleological approach he feels emphasizes comedy's social aspects at the expense of its full range, "a great tradition of vital art generally decried for its vulgarity." Paul, 49.) Such key recent studies as Paul's *Laughing Screaming* (1994) and Andrew Horton's aforementioned anthology *Comedy/Cinema/Theory* are animated in large part by Bakhtin's notion of comedy as at once corrosive and liberating, an idea reflected in two dominant trends in comedy scholarship today: 1) carnival excess, as discussed by Stam and Paul; 2) the emphasis on the vaudevillian roots of film comedians in work by Henry Jenkins and others. As Horton writes in the introduction to his collection, "Bakhtin's perspective allows us to see the carnivalesque backgrounds of Chaplin (vaudeville), Keaton (vaudeville acrobat), and W.C. Fields (vaudeville juggler). . . ."

> The Keystone Kops, after all, lived and romped in the street, receiving their sanctioned freedom not from the Catholic church feast day calendar but from Mack Sennett himself, who, like those practitioners of another carnivalesque form, *commedia dell' arte*, raised improvisation to an artistic peak. Clearly the Marx Brothers work, joke, and "destroy" in a carnivalesque freedom and frenzy as well. For them, every day is a holiday, uncontrolled by society's schedules and norms. (35)

Kathleen Chamberlain's essay in this book, "The Three Stooges and the *Commedia dell' Arte*," reflects this new historical interest in the theatrical roots of screen comedy.

Jenkins, most notably in his book *What Made Pistachio Nuts?* (1992), has made vaude-villian aesthetics the center of an important new school's analyses of screen comedy. An awareness of the importance of comedians' vaudeville (or other theatrical) training, cred-itable above all to Jenkins, underlies much recent scholarship on the history of comedy, as for example Robert Knopf's *The Theater and Cinema of Buster Keaton* (1999). Ben Schwartz's essay in this book on the vaudeville roots of Al Boasberg's career further grounds the historical record. Schwartz's piece shows us a gagwriter moving freely back and forth between all the comic venues of his time—vaudeville, silent films, talkies, radio, and the stage, marking a zigzag path taken by many performers as well.

While most theorists generally associate comedy with the act of laughter, Paul H. Grave, in his *Comedy in Space, Time, and the Imagination* (1983) argues that the equa-tion of comedy with laughter is "an almost universal mistake" (4), saying instead that a work must "assert a faith in human survival" to qualify as comedy (17). Grave's human-ism sounds very old fashioned these days, given the contemporary emphasis on carniva-lesque transgression. To Grave, laughter was a "highlighting device" (65) not fundamentally important to either the formal or the emotional definition of comedy as offered by such older theorists as Bergson and Langer. "Comedy is the celebration of ongoing life . . . comedy's emotional power is the power to evoke any emotional response people may have to a remembrance of the faith that the human race is destined to sur-vive" (62).

This is a far cry from the dark comedy on offer in many contemporary films. Today, the success of films like *There's Something About Mary* and *Happiness* has placed what was once marginalized in society—bathhouse, slaughterhouse, and outhouse alike—on public display with floodlights in the town square. Yet, with James Agee, we can wonder why we're not laughing as we used to. The spirit of carnival can be liberating—but it can also be scary. While a theorist such as William Paul uses Bakhtin's notions to define the "festive art" of carnival as "an art that ultimately celebrates communality . . . always inclusionary" (Paul, 71), when one thinks of carnivals in the history of American cinema, one thinks of isolated, wandering con artists like those played by W.C. Fields, misanthropes exiled from the community, and also the violence and disruption associat-ed with the circuses and carnivals of *He Who Gets Slapped*, *Nightmare Alley*, *Strangers on a Train*, *Carnival of Souls*, *The Funhouse*, and *Killer Klowns from Outer Space*. As Paul himself has demonstrated, the slide from comedy to horror is very easy.

It follows that even in mainstream comedies, with their marking off of the carnival as something other than society, carnivalesque scenes are as likely to be sites of terror, death and oppression as they are of liberation. Thus *Convict 13* (1920), with its crowd of prison-ers eagerly anticipating Buster Keaton's execution, as peanuts and ice cream are sold. The gag's repeated in the 1941 Three Stooges short *In the Sweet Pie and Pie*, and is only slight-ly varied with "the big carnival" of Billy Wilder's *Ace in the Hole* (1951), as hordes of people gather to witness Leo Minosa's living death. The nightmarish escapades of Todd Browning's *Freaks* (1932), for which gagman supreme Al Boasberg contributed jokes, are also carnivalesque in the fullest sense. Its famous banquet scene, with the carnival freaks chanting "One of us, one of us," was quoted knowingly by Robert Altman in *The Player* exactly sixty years later. That film's murderer, played by Tim Robbins, makes a fine Capraesque speech about his innocence—and the police, led by Whoopi Goldberg, laugh at him. "One of us, one of us" bubbles up on the soundtrack. Who's the freak?

*"The spirit of carnival can be liberating." Charles Laughton in* Ruggles of Red Gap.

What makes some of these films comedies, though, is that Keaton is not executed — the rope used on him is made of rubber, and he bounces. The Three Stooges collapse their scaffold, and they are pardoned. Wilder's crowd is anxious to see Leo Minosa escape, to rise from the dead like a modern Lazarus. They sullenly break up when Leo dies. (*Ace in the Hole* is thus finally a drama, not a comedy, despite its bitter humor.) *The Player*, however, successfully inverts the old morality by having its anti-hero get away with murder. Keaton was ahead of his time in his black humor — while he experimented with it in his shorts (*Convict 13*, *The Frozen North*, the deadly ending of *Cops*), he played that aspect of his creativity down in his features. When he didn't, with his battle-field jokes in *The General*, he was spanked by the critics for "bad taste." *Ace in the Hole* suffered similar rejection. It was too dark for its time, what with its circus trucks painted with the legend "The Great S&M Amusement Corp." But *The Player*, in its witty amorality, is a quintessential film of the 1990s.

So too is the black comedy of the Coen Brothers, Todd Solondz, Neil La Bute or in a somewhat different key David O. Russell. Films such as *Barton Fink* and *Fargo* (the Coens), *Welcome to the Dollhouse* and *Happiness* (Solondz), *Nurse Betty* (La Bute) or *Spanking the Monkey* (Russell) revel in the punishment meted out to their protagonists. Solondz reserves his most humiliating experiences for the one adult character in

*Happiness,* Joy (Jane Adams), who's not either numbed or a predator; La Bute suggests amnesia is the only way to deal with trauma. Ironists of the past such as Billy Wilder were seldom so cruel. Stanley Kubrick originally ended *Dr. Strangelove* with a pie fight in the War Room. (So much for comedies needing to be life-affirming!) Jonathan Rosenbaum has written that both he and a friend were put off by that film's misanthropy upon the film's release in 1964.

> For her [Kathy Stein], seeing the end of the world as comic was not only frightening but morally hateful, and her passionate response made a permanent impression on me. The unlikelihood of anyone of college age having that sort of reaction to *Dr. Strangelove* today tells us something important, I suspect, about what's happened to our sensibilities since then—not only in relation to the idea of nuclear holocaust, but also in relation to comedy. I think it's possible that we've lost something. (Rosenbaum, 4.)

Just what has been lost is one running theme of this book. But then James Agee makes a nostalgic sense of loss a key refrain in "Comedy's Greatest Era." We are cautioned by rigorous modern analysts of the genre not to let nostalgia blind us to the realities of comedy past. But we should not let our interest in the transgressive forget what it is that is being transgressed—the social contract comedy thrives upon by ripping up, as Groucho and Chico Marx rip up a contract in *A Night at the Opera,* always assuming it can be magically pasted together again for the next show.

The sum total of this anthology should amount to a fresh look at the dawn of a new century at the vital field of Hollywood comedy—all things considered, one of the twentieth century's more unambiguously positive gifts to its successor.

GREGG RICKMAN
SAN FRANCISCO, CALIFORNIA
JULY, 2001

## Works Cited

Eileen Bowser, "Racial/Racist Jokes in American Silent Slapstick Comedy," *Griffithiana* No. 5 (1995), 35-43.

Stanley Cavell, *Pursuits of Happiness: The Hollywood Comedy of Remarriage* (Cambridge: Harvard University Press, 1981).

Donald Crafton, "Pie and Chase," in Kristine Brunovska Karnick and Henry Jenkins, eds., *Classical Hollywood Comedy* (American Film Institute, 1995), 106-19.

Dirk Eitzen, "Comedy and Classicism," in Richard Allen and Murray Smith, eds., *Film Theory and Philosophy*(Oxford: Oxford University Press, 1997), 394-411.

Paul H. Grave, *Comedy in Space, Time, and the Imagination* (Chicago: Nelson-Hall, 1983).

Andrew Horton, "Introduction," to Horton, ed., *Comedy/Cinema/Theory* (Berkeley: University of California Press, 1995).

Harriet Margolis, "Stereotypical Strategies: Black Film Aesthetics, Spectator Positioning, and Self-Directed Stereotypes in *Hollywood Shuffle* and *I'm Gonna Git You Sucka*," *Cinema Journal* 38:3 (Spring 1999), 50-66.

William Paul, *Laughing Screaming: Modern Hollywood Horror and Comedy* (New York: Columbia University Press, 1994).

Charlene Regester, "Stepin Fetchit: The man, the image, and the African American press," *Film History* No. 6 (1994), 502-21.

Mark A. Reid, "African-American Comedy Film," Chapter 2 of *Redefining Black Film* (Berkeley: University of California Press, 1993).

Jonathan Rosenbaum, *Placing Movies: The Practice of Film Criticism* (Berkeley: University of California Press, 1995).

Robert Stam, *Subversive Pleasures: Bakhtin, Cultural Criticism, and Film* (Baltimore: Johns Hopkins University Press, 1989).

JOSEPH M. SCHENCK
PRESENTS
# BUSTER KEATON
IN
# THE GOAT
Written and Directed By
BUSTER KEATON & EDDIE CLINE

Exclusive METRO Distributors

# What Are the Six Ages of Comedy

**Buster Keaton** (1924)

In compiling the history of motion picture comedies it is hard to keep from laughing. If we laugh it will spoil our reputation. So, therefore, we will dictate, and not write this article.

**CHAPTER ONE—EXPLOSION AGE:** Many years ago a man with a camera happened to pass by a mining camp; while he was there several explosions took place, ruining not only the camp but most of the people in it. He had a very peculiar sense of humor so he decided to make motion picture comedies using explosions for the base of the comedy. This accounts for many of the eruptions heard around the world during that period, for which many first class volcanoes were blamed, thereby ruining good reputations that were built up through years of hard burning. After the dynamite trust had become wise to the reason of the shortage of dynamite, the pioneers of this industry decided to dispense with this form of comedy. This age is also responsible for so many of the stars using "doubles" to take their places when about to be thrown into the air to flirt with the angels. This is also the way they got "angels" to back motion picture companies. Some of them got so far back that they never caught up with their bank rolls. When the public tired of the explosions the "angels" tired of the deficits and thus ended the first period.

**CHAPTER TWO—COMEDY-COP AGE:** The second period of motion picture comedies is known as the Comedy-Cop Age. So many men look funny in police uniforms that we can safely say that this idea was taken from life. The first ambition of every young man when he reaches the unreasonable age of seven is to see something awful happen to a policeman. What more awful could happen to him than to see himself portrayed in a motion picture? The screams of delight that greeted these photographed catastrophes that happened to the keepers of the peace made all comedy manufacturers impatient to outdo each other in finding new ways to make a policeman look ridiculous—or natural. The so-called happenings became so dangerous that it discouraged men from becoming minions of the law, and filled up the hospitals in Los Angeles with maimed and wounded policemen who risked their lives for $7.00 a day.

**CHAPTER THREE—THE FLIVVER AGE:** Outside of the invention of the camera nothing has done more for the motion picture comedy business than the invention of the automobile—we should have said the flivver. If the manufacturer of a certain brand of car (we cannot mention his name on account of the advertising he would receive) would receive a royalty of one-tenth of a cent per mile, or one-fifth of a cent per rattle for every time they photographed his automobile, he would be able to pay all the soldiers off with a weekly bonus.

The flivver proved so popular that it made a city out of Detroit, Mich., while the flivvers made a wreck out of the streets of Hollywood and Los Angeles. Thus ended the third period.

*Comedy cops and bathing girls: Buster Keaton in* Daydreams *(1922) and*
The Cameraman *(1928).*

CHAPTER FOUR—PIE THROWING AGE: During the pie throwing age the slogan of the comedy motion picture directors was "Say it with flour." The joke about the biscuits made by the bride was soon forgotten and pies filled the air all through Hollywood, in places where only the oranges had dared to tread. So much flour littered the streets and lanes of Southern California that many nearsighted natives thought the climate had suddenly changed and that their properties were covered with snow. Blackberry, huckleberry, cranberry, apple, peach and custard, they played no favorites; their only object in life was to hit their object with a pie. This period might still be in vogue if Mr. Hoover hadn't stepped into the breach and put a ban on the use of these weapons.

CHAPTER FIVE—BATHING GIRL AGE: The bathing girl age found the comedy making business in good shape. Things began to take form in a different manner. It is believed that Annette Kellerman is the one who can be blamed for this wave of re-form. It seems as though girls' homes, girls' colleges, stenographic courses and department stores were forgotten. Every little girl who was a nice little girl got herself a bathing suit and a railroad ticket marked "California." Many of them didn't bother about the ticket. The Los Angeles railroad stations looked like commencement day at Vassar. The only difference was in the dressing. The cap and gown were replaced by bathing cap and bathing suit. Swimming teachers were at a premium, the majority of the girls being under the impression that a motion picture girl really had to go into the water. Instead of laying out schedules according to the light and sun, directors were now taking their time to suit the tides. A scarcity of fish was noticed off the Atlantic Coast, as the word was passed along that the Pacific Ocean was full of bathing girls. Thus originated the saying, "You poor fish," meaning a fish who did not know enough to follow Horace Greeley's advice to "Go West." The favorite quotation of those days was, "Mother may I go out to swim? Yes, my dearest daughter, but don't go into moving pictures."

CHAPTER SIX—PRESENT: This is the age of "Bigger and Finer" things in comedy—out West in the big open spaces, where a man's a comic—the midnight oil is burning in an effort to give the public something bigger and, better. The confidence-within-the-industry has spread from the smallest extra to the biggest-headed director. Comedians who formerly were satisfied to fall off a four-story house to make the public laugh have now doubled their efforts and are falling off eight-story buildings. Not being satisfied to have one eye blackened in a comedy fight, comics are now doing their best to blacken two eyes. A black eye now-a-days is a mark of honor and shows the wearer is striving to please his public. A comedian today no longer finds his dressing room filled with slapstick, property bricks, stuffed clubs and exploding cigars. Comic situations have taken the place of these veteran laugh getters and the best brains of the best humorists of America are getting money under false pretenses in every comedy studio in California.

This is a move in the right direction as a big earthquake is expected any day and the country may get rid of a lot of old joke writers, proving again that the motion picture industry is always striving to please, to improve conditions within the industry, and make the world a bigger and finer and funnier place to live in.

—*The Truth About the Movies* (1924), edited by Lawrence A. Hughes

# Harold Lloyd

**Louella Parsons** (1919)

Whenever the name Harold Lloyd is mentioned, everyone says in one breath: "Oh, yes, he is the young man with the glasses!"

And just as Theda Bara's name has become the synonym for vampire, and curls have entwined themselves indelibly with every thought of Mary Pickford, so have spectacles become a part of Harold Lloyd. They are his great stock in trade. Not so much of a stock in the telling, but worth an evening full of laughs in the seeing.

So when this youthful comedian walked into my office the other afternoon sans his tortoise-shell specs, the first question was a natural one.

"Where are your glasses?"

"In the studio on the Coast," he answered. "You don't expect me to wear my trade mark when I am vacationing?"

"Oh, then your specs are not donned for seeing purposes, just to help you get a laugh?"

"Solely for the purpose of making me look owlish and wise. This camouflage is the only invention I can think of which can be used successfully in more than one picture."

This spectacled young man has, indeed, become singularly successful within the last few years. He has jumped—and jumped is the word I am using advisedly—into public favor with an amazing rapidity. Likewise, his worldly goods took the same leap. From a comedian of several hundred dollars a week he became a stock owner in his company with a drawing account in lieu of a salary of enough dollars to warrant buying all the clothes he wants.

Our conversation was held in sections. He came to the office to pay his respects and between whizzing telephone bells and other numerous interruptions decided that conversation held under these circumstances was too much like trying to talk in an engine room, so he suggested we postpone our visit to luncheon the next day.

And so it was finally over the luncheon table at the Claridge that we talked of Mr. Lloyd and his picture-making ventures.

In the beginning, Harold Lloyd is a very surprising young man. He looks more like he might be a college student than an actor. In fact, he looks more like anything else in the world than an actor. He says he is 25, but he looks 19. And he doesn't think he has discovered the only receipt in the world for making folks laugh. He believes there are other young men just as capable of rising to the top, and that he cannot make good pictures alone. He believes he must have a leading woman with beauty and brains, a first-class director, a first-class camera man and an adequate supporting cast.

"It's bunk for any actor to think he is the whole show," said Mr. Lloyd. "For every man or woman in the cast who gets attention the star is building up just that much more for himself. It's the most foolhardy thing in the world to stifle another player's act in a picture. In the end it's bound to react on the star, for the public is fickle and if he tries to be the whole show the world is going to sicken of him in a twelve-month."

And best of all, young Lloyd was not talking to the grandstand. He is quite sincere,

**5**

*"The young man with the glasses."*

and actually is as square in his dealings with his company as the above sounds. How do I know? Well, a little bird whispered to me.

New York to Harold Lloyd is a joy. He hasn't had a playtime in years and this, despite the fact that he is in New York on a rather serious mission, is one wonderful vacation.

"I made five shows in one day," he said.

"Five?" I gasped. "Weren't you ready for an ambulance?"

"I was ready to see five more. I love the theatre, the cabarets, and all the dazzling lights along Broadway. I don't mean to live here or for a steady diet, but just for a recreation." ( . . . )

We spoke of prohibition, and Mr. Lloyd said it had not hurt him very much.

"Didn't you need to reform?"

"I never drank," he said. "All my friends drink, but I was afraid if I started I wouldn't know where to stop, and so I decided never to give old Johnny Barleycorn a chance to get the best of me. I intend to always keep ahead of him, and the best way to do this is to stay out of his way."

In some young men a temperance lecture of this sort would sound prudish. In Harold Lloyd it meant just one more thing in his favor. It made his common sense stock go up 100 per cent.

Mr. Lloyd has one ideal in pictures. He takes Cecil De Mille's work for a pattern, a regular cinematic textbook.

"I see Mr. De Mille's pictures again and again," he said. "It sounds funny, but after I see a De Mille production I try to pattern my comedies along the same lines. The same smooth story continuity and motive for every action."

And when we discussed Cecil De Mille it was the most natural thing in the world to speak of Bebe Daniels. She is the little dark-eyed, dark-haired girl who has played with Mr. Lloyd for so many years. There wasn't a thought of what he might be missing in losing his leading lady in the genuine ring of pleasure in Mr. Lloyd's voice when he spoke of how well Bebe Daniels is doing and what it means for her to have Cecil De Mille for a director. "She has one of the big parts in *Why Change Your Wife?*" he said; "and I am told she has done some exceptionally fine work."

The new Lloyd leading woman is a petite blonde, Mildred Davis, chosen, the creator of these comedies says, because of her fresh good looks and talent. He expects to keep her in all of his pictures, refusing to believe a constant companion in his films can deprive him of any of his merited attention.

I have heard so many stars speak of the bad judgment in having the same lead, it was refreshing to have young Lloyd speak up and say he expected the public to want to see Miss Davis just as much as they want to see him.

His success on the screen young Lloyd attributes to fate. Fate may have had a hand though I am rather inclined to the belief it is his own good common sense which has played a large part in getting his name in the electric signs in front of the Strand and Rialto. And speaking of these signs, Mr. Lloyd admits he had the thrill of his life when he saw the name Harold Lloyd twinkling merrily at him on Broadway.

"It is the most wonderful thing that every happened to me in New York or anywhere else," he confessed.

Remarks like the above and the refreshing freedom from boredom and blase mannerisms makes the youthful Mr. Lloyd a very pleasant young man indeed. ( . . . )

—*New York Telegraph*, Nov. 16, 1919

# Low Comedy as a High Art

**Malcolm H. Oettinger** (1923)

For a long time it was considered a breach of critical etiquette, if there be such a thing, to write of any one engaged in such a lowly sphere as that of comedy. It was little short of lese majesty to strum one's lyre in praise of such funny fellows as Fred Mace, John Bunny, Mack Swain, and the then blooming Chaplin. Some few did it: venturesome souls, but as a general thing it was discouraged.

Times, capriciously enough, have changed. Today Charlot is hymned by the literati and the cognoscenti, the beautiful and the damning. The mere mention of his name is sufficient to start a feverish discussion in the highest circles, even including the well-known vicious one at the Algonquin. The critics have decided that the abominable movies have produced something worth while in this harlequin of the mustachios and baggy trousers.

Five years hence they will discover Buster Keaton.

In writing of the leading drolls of the flittering photos, it is tempting to take a leaf from Eugene Field's "Wynken, Blynken, and Nod," for it is conceded, almost without question, that the preeminent names today are Chaplin, Keaton, and Lloyd. The methods of the three are utterly unlike. Each leads an individual School of the Snicker.

The comedy of Chaplin is most often elusive, bordering on the serious if not the tragic. Nothing more typical can be instanced than his moment of contemplation beside the manhole, in *The Kid*—an amazing commingling of pathos and humor. In an earlier two-reeler, *The Bank*, the great comedian also officiated at the wedding of smile and tear. It is characteristic of Chaplin to appeal to philosophers as well as to flappers.

We laugh with Lloyd, but we laugh at Keaton. These two may better be compared than Lloyd and Chaplin or Keaton and Chaplin, because Charlie is so infinitely superior, amusing though the other pair are. Neither Keaton nor Lloyd attempt to reach your funny bone through your heart: they openly tickle you. For this reason, most of all, perhaps they are not in Chaplin's class. For Chaplin has always stood alone.

Many of Harold Lloyd's pictures have whole slices played in straight comedy vein. Keaton is rarely heroic; at such fleeting times he invariably makes a swift and laughter-grafting turn to grotesquerie. Buster's stuff borders on the realm of burlesque; Lloyd at times suggests a Willie Collier of the shadow stage. His is the school sponsored by Sidney Drew, embellished with quips and quirks and occasional stunts that are solely Lloyd's. Originality marks the method of all leaders, and certainly this is true of Chaplin, Keaton, and Lloyd.

"That's the one thing that I dread," Buster told me sadly. "I dread the day when we won't find another new wheeze to wrap up, when all the gags will have been sprung, when we're stumped for something new. That's what a comedian has to guard against: running out. That is why Charlie Chaplin makes his pictures so slowly. I know as a matter of fact that he takes thousands of feet of film on every picture, only to destroy it when he sees it in the projection room. And this carefulness is just what helps to make him a great artist."

Keaton is master of snicker and guffaw technique. His art is to work up a situation deliberately, to build it as logically and as systematically as a carpenter builds a house. Gags, Buster told me, are natural or mechanical. "Both get laughs," he explained, "but the natural gag is the one we lay awake nights trying to dream of." And it is the mechanical gag that Keaton has mastered.

Take the situation in *The Boat*, where, after having built a boat, he finds that he has not made the doorway large enough, and consequently, as the boat slides to the water, it pulls the shed down with it. Take the situation in *One Week*. Buster has ordered a Sears-Roebuck bungalow for his bride-to-be. The wicked rival mixes the numerals on the various parts, and the comedy ensues when Buster attempts to assemble the jazzed sections.

This is mechanically perfect giggle material. But though one of the most adroit technicians of comedy, Buster fails to reach the heart, his pictures elude the sympathy.

It seems consistent to endow Chaplin with massive intellect, to read sermons into his capering feet. It is fairly simple to sympathize with the lovesick Harold Lloyd, upon occasion. But Keaton alone stands forth as the Trouper unabashed, unaffected, unassuming, and—very like Shaw's Undershaft—unashamed!

"We just wrap up a little hokum," he will tell you. "We build up a little story on some sure-fire idea, throw in a dozen gags, if we can think of 'em, and let 'er ride. The scenario we use is written on the correspondence end of a picture post card. If it's lost it's no great matter."

*"Mechanically perfect giggle material"*: Buster Keaton in The Boat.

You cannot read hidden motifs into the Keaton spoolings. You cannot persuade him that there was a hint of satire concealed in his last comedy, or the one before that. You cannot coerce him into admitting that he planned an unique characterization which he has steadfastly maintained. He will take credit for nothing. Not even his make-up.

"The pancake hat and the oversized collar and the misfit suit and the slapstick shoes are my old vaudeville stand-bys. My father rigged me out as a third of The Three Keatons, when I was too young to 'originate' anything but a yowl! I've kept the same make-up ever since—guess I always will."

Solemnity is more than a habit with Keaton; it's ingrown. Throughout our conversation his face was stony. Nor was this an exception to his usual attitude. I have seen him in the turmoil of a comic sequence, a business of break-away ladders, swinging ropes, and trapdoor scaffoldings; I have seen him eyeing the proceedings at one of Manhattan's most energizing nights clubs; I have seen him purring at his baby in father-like fashion; I have seen him casually viewing the day's rushes, and upon not one but all of these occasions Buster wore an expression that was infinitely more sphinxlike than the Sphinx ever thought of being. His is an entirely emotionless face, suggesting most of all, a mask. It is the ideal phiz for a droll pantaloon.

"You originated the idea of never smiling," I supposed.

But Buster refused to take credit for it. In the days of The Three Keatons, it seems, his father taught him never to crack a smile. The habit grew on him. Now it is so deeply rooted that it is almost impossible for him to grin.

It has long been one of the beliefs of the American Credo that all comedians are, off stage, lugubrious fellows, and never was a truth more apparent than in the appearance and behavior of Buster Keaton. His countenance is little short of funereal, his speech laconic, his outlook none too sanguine.

"Next I'm going back to the Coast to do a five-reel picture. No plots, you know. Just gags. But we'll space our laughs. If we ran five reels of the sort of stuff we cram into two, the audience would be tired before it was half over. So we'll plant the characters more slowly, use introductory bits, and all that.

"It'll be just as easy to make a five-reeler, because we always take about fifteen reels, anyway. Now we'll cut to five instead of two."

Buster thinks *One Week* his best comedy, but he admits he had hoped to make *The Playhouse* his best. In that clever picture, he essayed a dozen or more roles. He had intended doing all of the parts, but his ego failed him at the crucial moment.

Despite the fact that he is one of the big drawing cards, often featured in the lights and billed above the longer picture of the program, Keaton has assumed no airs, adopted no pose. He denied that he made a preparation for a picture. He denied that he planned his plots. Try as you will, you cannot convince him that he is anything more than a trouper who manages to give 'em what they like. It is useless to talk to him of psychological effects.

"It's hokum," said Buster definitely and positively. "And by draping it in different styles you disguise it and bring results each time."

According to his lights, it is simply a case of old gags in new clothing. But if this were so, there would be more Keatons. Unfortunately enough, there aren't.

—*Picture-Play Magazine*, March 1923

# The Old Army Game: W.C. Fields, the overnight comedy sensation of *Sally of the Sawdust,* knows his stuff

**Ruth Waterbury** (1925)

"My ambition is to bring back slapstick two dollared up."

Mr. W.C. Fields speaking, Mr. Fields, the newest comedian of the silver screen, a gentleman long of the Follies and the overnight movie sensation in *Sally of the Sawdust*, which Griffith made.

A unique character this, very simple, very direct, very charming. Most unexpected back stage at the Follies. Since *Sally of the Sawdust* was released the Eastern studios have been calling him the coming comedian of filmdom. He has been offered his own production unit with three major companies. On the speaking stage, two managers are claiming contracts for his services and four others are trying to outbid one another for his signature.

All of which pleases Mr. Fields but causes him no need to change his hatter.

It has taken him more than ten years to break into the movies. "That is because I am a pantomimist," he says with a smile.

"Movie directors, as a whole, think of comedy in terms of stage comedy with the words left out," explains. "Griffith doesn't. Chaplin doesn't. I'm convinced the others do. They recognize comedy through their ears, not through their eyes.

"I've been here in the Follies since 1914 and constantly during that time I have been trying for a movie chance. I never got a look-in until *Janice Meredith* [1924]. The bit I did in that was very small in the actual filming and much smaller in release. But it gave me my opportunity."

No heartbroken clown hiding his sorrow behind a mask of laughter. Not on your life. Fields would call that the old hoke, the old army game. He has spent so many years in the land of hokum he is not even to be kidded into taking himself with undue seriousness. He is very interested in his own career, but it is the same sort of balanced interest a bank president has in the bonding department . . . .

"I prefer pantomime (over dialogue)," Fields insists. "It's the better medium, much funnier than speech can ever be. The laughs can come quicker. In spoken comedy, you must wait for the laugh. Follow one line too quickly with another and you kill both laughs, the one that should have come and the one you're working toward. In pantomime, the laughs can come as fast as an audience can shake them out of their throats.

"That's why I believe so firmly in the great future for the movies. There are no racial, language, time or distance barriers for them. That's why I'm so excited about having landed in them at last—that and the fact they'll let me travel again.

*"Slapstick two-dollared up"*: W.C. Fields.

"The character I want to portray is the American husband, the boy of the newspaper cartoons. He's so comic he's pathetic and pathos is the true base of all laughter.

"At least," Mr. Fields smiles again, "that's what I think. But take all this with sufficient salt. After all in this movie game I'm only a neophyte."

Imagine a man eleven years in the Follies and six months in the studios calling himself a name like that!

Real intelligence? Well, rather.

—*Photoplay*, October 1925

# Comedy's Greatest Era

**James Agee** (1949)

In the language of screen comedians four of the main grades of laugh are the titter, the yowl, the bellylaugh and the boffo. The titter is just a titter. The yowl is a runaway titter. Anyone who has ever had the pleasure knows all about a bellylaugh. The boffo is the laugh that kills. An ideally good gag, perfectly constructed and played, would bring the victim up this ladder of laughs by cruelly controlled degrees to the top rung, and would then proceed to wobble, shake, wave and brandish the ladder until he groaned for mercy. Then, after the shortest possible time out for recuperation, he would feel the first wicked tickling of the comedian's whip once more and start up a new ladder.

The reader can get a fair enough idea of the current state of screen comedy by asking himself how long it has been since he has had that treatment. The best of comedies these days hand out plenty of titters and once in a while it is possible to achieve a yowl without overstraining. Even those who have never seen anything better must occasionally have the feeling, as they watch the current run or, rather, trickle of screen comedy, that they are having to make a little cause for laughter go an awfully long way. And anyone who has watched screen comedy over the past ten or fifteen years is bound to realize that it has quietly but steadily deteriorated. As for those happy atavists who remember silent comedy in its heyday and the bellylaughs and boffos that went with it, they have something close to an absolute standard by which to measure the deterioration.

When a modern comedian gets hit on the head, for example, the most he is apt to do is look sleepy. When a silent comedian got hit on the head he seldom let it go so flatly. He realized a broad license, and a ruthless discipline within that license. It was his business to be as funny as possible physically, without the help or hindrance of words. So he gave us a figure of speech, or rather of vision, for loss of consciousness. In other words he gave us a poem, a kind of poem, moreover, that everybody understands. The least he might do was to straighten up stiff as a plank and fall over backward with such skill that his whole length seemed to slap the floor at the same instant. Or he might make a cadenza of it—look vague, smile like an angel, roll up his eyes, lace his fingers, thrust his hands palms downward as far as they would go, hunch his shoulders, rise on tiptoe, prance ecstatically in narrowing circles until, with tallow knees, he sank down the vortex of his dizziness to the floor, and there signified nirvana by kicking his heels twice, like a swimming frog.

Startled by a cop, this same comedian might grab his hatbrim with both hands and yank it down over his ears, jump high in the air, come to earth in a split violent enough to telescope his spine, spring thence into a coattail-flattening sprint and dwindle at rocket speed to the size of a gnat along the grand, forlorn perspective of some lazy back boulevard.

Those are fine clichés from the language of silent comedy in its infancy. The man who could handle them properly combined several of the more difficult accomplishments of the acrobat, the dancer, the clown and the mime. Some very gifted comedians, unforgettably Ben Turpin, had an immense vocabulary of these clichés and were in part

**14**

so lovable because they were deep conservative classicists and never tried to break away from them. The still more gifted men, of course, simplified and invented, finding out new and much deeper uses for the idiom. They learned to show emotion through it, and comic psychology, more eloquently than most language has ever managed to, and they discovered beauties of comic motion which are hopelessly beyond reach of words.

It is hard to find a theater these days where a comedy is playing; in the days of the silents it was equally hard to find a theater which was not showing one. The laughs today are pitifully few, far between, shallow, quiet and short. They almost never build, as they used to, into something combining the jabbering frequency of a machine gun with the delirious momentum of a roller coaster. Saddest of all, there are few comedians now below middle age and there are none who seem to learn much from picture to picture, or to try anything new.

To put it unkindly, the only thing wrong with screen comedy today is that it takes place on a screen which talks. Because it talks, the only comedians who ever mastered the screen cannot work, for they cannot combine their comic style with talk. Because there is a screen, talking comedians are trapped into a continual exhibition of their inadequacy as screen comedians on a surface as big as the side of a barn.

At the moment, as for many years past, the chances to see silent comedy are rare. There is a smattering of it on television—too often treated as something quaintly archaic, to be laughed at, not with. Some two hundred comedies—long and short—can be rented for home projection. And a lucky minority has access to the comedies in the collection of New York's Museum of Modern Art, which is still incomplete but which is probably the best in the world. In the near future, however, something of this lost art will return to regular theaters. A thick straw in the wind is the big business now being done by a series of revivals of W. C. Fields's memorable movies, a kind of comedy more akin to the old silent variety than anything which is being made today. Mack Sennett now is preparing a sort of pot-pourri variety show called *Down Memory Lane* made up out of his old movies, featuring people like Fields and Bing Crosby when they were movie beginners, but including also interludes from silents. Harold Lloyd has re-released *Movie Crazy*, a talkie, and plans to revive four of his best silent comedies (*Grandma's Boy*, *Safety Last*, *Speedy* and *The Freshman*). Buster Keaton hopes to remake at feature length, with a minimum of dialogue, two of the funniest short comedies ever made, one about a porous homemade boat and one about a prefabricated house.

Awaiting these happy events we will discuss here what has gone wrong with screen comedy and what, if anything, can be done about it. But mainly we will try to suggest what it was like in its glory in the years from 1912 to 1930, as practiced by the employees of Mack Sennett, the father of American screen comedy, and by the four most eminent masters: Charlie Chaplin, Harold Lloyd, the late Harry Langdon and Buster Keaton.

Mack Sennett made two kinds of comedy: parody laced with slapstick, and plain slapstick. The parodies were the unceremonious burial of a century of hamming, including the new hamming in serious movies, and nobody who has missed Ben Turpin in *A Small Town Idol*, or kidding Erich von Stroheim in *Three Foolish Weeks* or as *The Shriek of Araby*, can imagine how rough parody can get and still remain subtle and roaringly funny. The plain slapstick, at its best, was even better: a profusion of hearty young women in disconcerting bathing suits, frisking around with a gaggle of insanely incompetent policemen and of equally certifiable male civilians sporting museum-piece mustaches. All these people zipped and caromed about the pristine world of the screen as jazzily as a convention of water bugs. Words can hardly suggest how energetically they collided and bounced apart, meeting in full gallop around the corner of a house; how hard and how often they fell on their backsides; or with what fantastically adroit clumsiness they got themselves fouled up in folding ladders, garden hoses, tethered animals and each other's headlong cross-purposes. The gestures were ferociously emphatic; not a line or motion of the body was wasted or inarticulate. The reader may remember how splendidly upright wandlike old Ben Turpin could stand for a Renunciation Scene, with his lampshade mustache twittering and his sparrowy chest stuck out and his head flung back like Paderewski assaulting a climax and the long babyish back hair trying to look lionlike, while his Adam's apple, an orange in a Christmas stocking, pumped with noble emotion. Or huge Mack Swain, who looked like a hairy mushroom, rolling his eyes in a manner patented by French Romantics and gasping in some dubious ecstasy. Or Louise Fazenda, the perennial farmer's daughter and the perfect low-comedy housemaid, primping her spit curl; and how her hair tightened a good-looking face into the incarnation of rampant gullibility. Or snouty James Finlayson, gleefully foreclosing a mortgage, with his look of eternally tasting a spoiled pickle. Or Chester Conklin, a myopic and inebriated little walrus stumbling around in outsize pants. Or Fatty Arbuckle, with his cold eye and his loose, serene smile, his silky manipulation of his bulk and his satanic marksmanship with pies (he was ambidextrous and could simultaneously blind two people in opposite directions).

The intimate tastes and secret hopes of these poor ineligible dunces were ruthlessly exposed whenever a hot stove, an electric fan or a bulldog took a dislike to their outer garments: agonizingly elaborate drawers, worked up on some lonely evening out of some Godforsaken lace curtain; underpants with big round black spots on them. The Sennett sets — delirious wallpaper, megalomaniacally scrolled iron beds, Grand Rapids *in extremis* — outdid even the underwear. It was their business, after all, to kid the squalid braggadocio which infested the domestic interiors of the period, and that was almost beyond parody. These comedies told their stories to the unaided eye, and by every means possible they screamed to it. That is one reason for the India-ink silhouettes of the cops, and for convicts and prison bars and their shadows in hard sunlight, and for barefooted husbands, in tigerish pajamas, reacting like dervishes to stepped-on tacks.

The early silent comedians never strove for or consciously thought of anything which could be called artistic "form," but they achieved it. For Sennett's rival, Hal Roach, Leo McCarey once devoted almost the whole of a Laurel and Hardy two-reeler to pie-throwing. The first pies were thrown thoughtfully, almost philosophically. Then innocent bystanders began to get caught into the vortex. At full pitch it was Armageddon. But everything was calculated so nicely that until late in the picture, when havoc took over, every pie made its special kind of point and piled on its special kind of laugh.

Sennett's comedies were just a shade faster and fizzier than life. According to legend (and according to Sennett) he discovered the speed tempo proper to screen comedy when a green cameraman, trying to save money, cranked too slow.* Realizing the tremendous drumlike power of mere motion to exhilarate, he gave inanimate objects a mischievous

---

* Silent comedy was shot at 12 to 16 frames per second and was speeded up by being shown at 16 frames per second, the usual rate of theater projectors at that time. Theater projectors today run at 24, which makes modern film taken at the same speed seem smooth and natural. But it makes silent movies fast and jerky.

life of their own, broke every law of nature the tricked camera would serve him for and made the screen dance like a witches' Sabbath. The thing one is surest of all to remember is how toward the end of nearly every Sennett comedy, a chase (usually called the "rally") built up such a majestic trajectory of pure anarchic motion that bathing girls, cops, comics, dogs, cats, babies, automobiles, locomotives, innocent bystanders, sometimes what seemed like a whole city, an entire civilization, were hauled along head over heels in the wake of that energy like dry leaves following an express train.

"Nice" people, who shunned all movies in the early days, condemned the Sennett comedies as vulgar and naive. But millions of less pretentious people loved their sincerity and sweetness, their wild-animal innocence and glorious vitality. They could not put these feelings into words, but they flocked to the silents. The reader who gets back deep enough into that world will probably even remember the theater: the barefaced honky-tonk and the waltzes by Waldteufel, slammed out on a mechanical piano; the searing redolence of peanuts and demirep perfumery, tobacco and feet and sweat; the laughter of unrespectable people having a hell of a fine time, laughter as violent and steady and deafening as standing under a waterfall.

Sennett wheedled his first financing out of a couple of ex-bookies to whom he was already in debt. He took his comics out of music halls, burlesque, vaudeville, circuses and limbo, and through them he tapped in on that great pipeline of horsing and miming which runs back unbroken through the fairs of the Middle Ages at least to ancient Greece. He added all that he himself had learned about the large and spurious gesture, the late decadence of the Grand Manner, as a stage-struck boy in East Berlin, Connecticut and as a frustrated opera singer and actor. The only thing he claims to have invented is the pie in the face, and he insists, "Anyone who tells you he has discovered something new is a fool or a liar or both."

The silent-comedy studio was about the best training school the movies have ever known, and the Sennett studio was about as free and easy and as fecund of talent as they came. All the major comedians we will mention worked there, at least briefly. So did some of the major stars of the twenties and since—notably Gloria Swanson, Phyllis Haver, Wallace Beery, Marie Dressler and Carole Lombard. Directors Frank Capra, Leo McCarey and George Stevens also got their start in silent comedy; much that remains most flexible, spontaneous and visually alive in sound movies can be traced, through them and others, to this silent apprenticeship. Everybody did pretty much as he pleased on the Sennett lot, and everybody's ideas were welcome. Sennett posted no rules, and the only thing he strictly forbade was liquor. A Sennett story conference was a most informal affair. During the early years, at least, only the most important scenario might be jotted on the back of an envelope. Mainly Sennett's men thrashed out a few primary ideas and carried them in their heads, sure the better stuff would turn up while they were shooting, in the heat of physical action. This put quite a load on the prop man; he had to have the most improbable apparatus on hand—bombs, trick telephones, what not—to implement whatever idea might suddenly turn up. All kinds of things did—and were recklessly used. Once a low-comedy auto got out of control and killed the cameraman, but he was not visible in the shot, which was thrilling and undamaged; the audience never knew the difference.

Sennett used to hire a "wild man" to sit in on his gag conferences, whose whole job was to think up "wildies." Usually he was an all but brainless, speechless man, scarcely able to communicate his idea; but he had a totally uninhibited imagination. He might say nothing for an hour; then he'd mutter "You take . . . " and all the relatively rational others would shut up and wait. "You take this cloud . . . " he would get out, sketching vague shapes in the air. Often he could get no further; but thanks to some kind of thought-transference, saner men would take this cloud and make something of it. The wild man seems in fact to have functioned as the group's subconscious mind, the source of all creative energy. His ideas were so weird and amorphous that Sennett can no longer remember a one of them, or even how it turned out after rational processing. But a fair equivalent might be one of the best comic sequences in a Laurel and Hardy picture. It is simple enough—simple and real, in fact, as a nightmare. Laurel and Hardy are trying to move a piano across a narrow suspension bridge. The bridge is slung over a sickening chasm, between a couple of Alps. Midway they meet a gorilla.

Had he done nothing else, Sennett would be remembered for giving a start to three of the four comedians who now began to apply their sharp individual talents to this new-born language. The one whom he did not train (he was on the lot briefly but Sennett barely remembers seeing him around) wore glasses, smiled a great deal and looked like the sort of eager young man who might have quit divinity school to hustle brushes. That was Harold Lloyd. The others were grotesque and poetic in their screen characters in degrees which appear to be impossible when the magic of silence is broken. One, who never smiled, carried a face as still and sad as a daguerreotype through some of the most preposterously ingenious and visually satisfying physical comedy ever invented. That was Buster Keaton. One looked like an elderly baby and, at times, a baby dope fiend; he could do more with less than any other comedian. That was Harry Langdon. One looked like Charlie Chaplin, and he was the first man to give the silent language a soul.

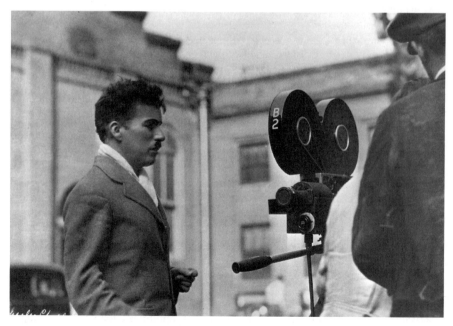

*Charlie Chaplin, director at work.*

When Charlie Chaplin started to work for Sennett he had chiefly to reckon with Ford Sterling, the reigning comedian. Their first picture together amounted to a duel before the assembled professionals. Sterling, by no means untalented, was a big man with a florid Teutonic style which, under this special pressure, he turned on full blast. Chaplin defeated him within a few minutes with a wink of the mustache, a hitch of the trousers, a quirk of the little finger.

With *Tillie's Punctured Romance,* in 1914, he became a major star. Soon after, he left Sennett when Sennett refused to start a landslide among the other comedians by meeting the raise Chaplin demanded. Sennett is understandably wry about it in retrospect, but he still says, "I was right at the time." Of Chaplin he says simply, "Oh well, he's just the greatest artist that ever lived." None of Chaplin's former rivals rate him much lower than that; they speak of him no more jealously than they might of God. We will try here only to suggest the essence of his supremacy. Of all comedians he worked most deeply and most shrewdly within a realization of what a human being is, and is up against. The Tramp is as centrally representative of humanity, as many-sided and as mysterious, as Hamlet, and it seems unlikely that any dancer or actor can ever have excelled him in eloquence, variety or poignancy of motion. As for pure motion, even if he had never gone on to make his magnificent feature-length comedies, Chaplin would have made his period in movies a great one single-handed even if he had made nothing except *The Cure,* or *One A.M.* In the latter, barring one immobile taxi driver, Chaplin plays alone, as a drunk trying to get upstairs and into bed. It is a sort of inspired elaboration on a soft-shoe dance, involving an angry stuffed wildcat, small rugs on slippery floors, a Lazy Susan table, exquisite footwork on a flight of stairs, a contretemps with a huge, ferocious pendulum and the funniest and most perverse Murphy bed in movie history—and, always made physically lucid, the delicately weird mental processes of a man ethereally sozzled.

Before Chaplin came to pictures people were content with a couple of gags per comedy; he got some kind of laugh every second. The minute he began to work he set standards—and continually forced them higher. Anyone who saw Chaplin eating a boiled shoe like brook trout in *The Gold Rush,* or embarrassed by a swallowed whistle in *City Lights,* has seen perfection. Most of the time, however, Chaplin got his laughter less from the gags, or from milking them in any ordinary sense, than through his genius for what may be called *inflection*—the perfect, changeful shading of his physical and emotional attitudes toward the gag. Funny as his bout with the Murphy bed is, the glances of awe, expostulation and helpless, almost whimpering desire for vengeance which he darts at this infernal machine are even better.

A painful and frequent error among tyros is breaking the comic line with a too-big laugh, then a letdown; or with a laugh which is out of key or irrelevant. The masters could ornament the main line beautifully; they never addled it. In *A Night Out* Chaplin, passed out, is hauled along the sidewalk by the scruff of his coat by a staggering Ben Turpin. His toes trail; he is as supine as a sled. Turpin himself is so drunk he can hardly drag him. Chaplin comes quietly to, realizes how well he is being served by his struggling pal, and with a royally delicate gesture plucks and savors a flower.

The finest pantomime, the deepest emotion, the richest and most poignant poetry were in Chaplin's work. He could probably pantomime Bryce's *The American Commonwealth* without ever blurring a syllable and make it paralyzingly funny into the bargain. At the end of *City Lights* the blind girl who has regained her sight, thanks to the Tramp, sees him for the first time. She has imagined and anticipated him as princely, to say the least; and it has never seriously occurred to him that he is inadequate. She recognizes who he must be by his shy, confident, shining joy as he comes silently toward her. And he recognizes himself, for the first time, through the terrible changes in her face. The camera just exchanges a few quiet close-ups of the emotions which shift and intensify in each face. It is enough to shrivel the heart to see, and it is the greatest piece of acting and the highest moment in movies.

Harold Lloyd worked only a little while with Sennett. During most of his career he acted for another major comedy producer, Hal Roach. He tried at first to offset Chaplin's influence and establish his own individuality by playing Chaplin's exact opposite, a character named Lonesome Luke who wore clothes much too small for him and whose gestures were likewise as unChaplinesque as possible. But he soon realized that an opposite in itself was a kind of slavishness. He discovered his own comic identity when he saw a movie about a fighting parson: a hero who wore glasses. He began to think about those glasses day and night. He decided on horn rims because they were youthful, ultravisible on the screen and on the verge of becoming fashionable (he was to make them so). Around these large lensless horn rims he began to develop a new character, nothing grotesque or eccentric, but a fresh, believable young man who could fit into a wide variety of stories.

Lloyd depended more on story and situation than any of the other major comedians (he kept the best stable of gagmen in Hollywood, at one time hiring six); but unlike most "story" comedians he was also a very funny man from inside. He had, as he has written, "an unusually large comic vocabulary." More particularly he had an expertly expressive body and even more expressive teeth, and out of his thesaurus of smiles he could at a moment's notice blend prissiness, breeziness and asininity, and still remain tremendously likable. His movies were more extroverted and closer to ordinary life than any others of the best comedies: the vicissitudes or a New York taxi driver; the unaccepted college boy who, by desperate courage and inspired ineptitude, wins the Big Game. He was especially good at putting a very timid, spoiled or brassy young fellow through devastating embarrassments. He went through one of his most uproarious Gethsemanes as a shy country youth courting the nicest girl in town in *Grandma's Boy*. He arrived dressed "strictly up to date for the Spring of 1862," as a subtitle observed, and found that the ancient colored butler wore a similar flowered waistcoat and moldering cutaway. He got one wandering, nervous forefinger dreadfully stuck in a fancy little vase. The girl began cheerfully to try to identify that queer smell which dilated from him; Grandpa's best suit was rife with mothballs. A tenacious litter of kittens feasted off the goose grease on his home-shined shoes.

Lloyd was even better at the comedy of thrills. In *Safety Last*, as a rank amateur, he is forced to substitute for a human fly and to climb a medium-sized skyscraper. Dozens of awful things happen to him. He gets fouled up in a tennis net. Popcorn falls on him from a window above, and the local pigeons treat him like a cross between a lunch wagon and St. Francis of Assisi. A mouse runs up his britches-leg, and the crowd below salutes his desperate dance on the window ledge with wild applause of the daredevil. A good deal of this full-length picture hangs thus by its eyelashes along the face of a building. Each new floor is like a new stanza in a poem; and the higher and more horrifying it gets, the funnier it gets.

In this movie Lloyd demonstrates beautifully his ability to do more than merely milk a gag, but to top it. (In an old, simple example of topping, an incredible number of tall men get, one by one, out of a small closed auto. After as many have clambered out as the

*Harold Lloyd in* Safety Last: *"Each new floor is like a stanza in a poem; and the higher and more horrifying it gets, the funnier it gets."*

joke will bear, one more steps out: a midget. That tops the gag. Then the auto collapses. That tops the topper.) In *Safety Last* Lloyd is driven out to the dirty end of a flagpole by a furious dog; the pole breaks and he falls, just managing to grab the minute hand of a huge clock. His weight promptly pulls the hand down from IX to VI. That would be more than enough for any ordinary comedian, but there is further logic in the situation. Now, hideously, the whole clockface pulls loose and slants from its trembling springs above the street. Getting out of difficulty with the clock, he makes still further use of the instrument by getting one foot caught in one of these obstinate springs.

A proper delaying of the ultrapredictable can of course be just as funny as a properly timed explosion of the unexpected. As Lloyd approaches the end of his horrible hegira up the side of the building in *Safety Last*, it becomes clear to the audience, but not to him, that if he raises his head another couple of inches he is going to get murderously conked by one of the four arms of a revolving wind gauge. He delays the evil moment almost interminably, with one distraction and another, and every delay is a suspense-tightening laugh; he also gets his foot nicely entangled in a rope, so that when he does get hit, the payoff of one gag sends him careening head downward through the abyss into another. Lloyd was outstanding even among the master craftsmen at setting up a gag clearly, culminating and getting out of it deftly, and linking it smoothly to the next. Harsh experience also taught him a deep and fundamental rule: never try to get "above" the audience.

Lloyd tried it in *The Freshman*. He was to wear an unfinished, basted-together tuxedo to a college party, and it would gradually fall apart as he danced. Lloyd decided to skip the pants, a low-comedy cliché, and lose just the coat. His gagmen warned him. A preview proved how right they were. Lloyd had to reshoot the whole expensive sequence, build it around defective pants and climax it with the inevitable. It was one of the funniest things he ever did.

When Lloyd was still a very young man he lost about half his right hand (and nearly lost his sight) when a comedy bomb exploded prematurely. But in spite of his artificially built-out hand he continued to do his own dirty work, like all of the best comedians. The side of the building he climbed in *Safety Last* did not overhang the street, as it appears to. But the nearest landing place was a roof three floors below him, as he approached the top, and he did everything, of course, the hard way, that is, the comic way, keeping his bottom stuck well out, his shoulders hunched, his hands and feet skidding over perdition.

If great comedy must involve something beyond laughter, Lloyd was not a great comedian. If plain laughter is any criterion—and it is a healthy counterbalance to the other—few people have equaled him, and nobody has ever beaten him.

Chaplin and Keaton and Lloyd were all more like each other, in one important way, than Harry Langdon was like any of them. Whatever else the others might be doing, they all used more or less elaborate physical comedy; Langdon showed how little of that one might use and still be a great silent-screen comedian. In his screen character he symbolized something as deeply and centrally human, though by no means as rangily so, as the Tramp. There was, of course, an immense difference in inventiveness and range of virtuosity. It seemed as if Chaplin could do literally anything, on any instrument in the orchestra. Langdon had one queerly toned, unique little reed. But out of it he could get incredible melodies.

Like Chaplin, Langdon wore a coat which buttoned on his wishbone and swung out wide below, but the effect was very different: he seemed like an outsized baby who had begun to outgrow his clothes. The crown of his hat was rounded and the brim was turned up all around, like a little boy's hat, and he looked as if he wore diapers under his pants. His walk was that of a child which has just gotten sure on its feet, and his body and hands fitted that age. His face was kept pale to show off, with the simplicity of a nursery-school drawing, the bright, ignorant, gentle eyes and the little twirling mouth. He had big moon checks, with dimples, and a Napoleonic forelock of mousy hair; the round, docile head seemed large in ratio to the cream-puff body. Twitchings of his face were signals of tiny discomforts too slowly registered by a tinier brain; quick, squirty little smiles showed his almost prehuman pleasures, his incurably premature trustfulness. He was a virtuoso of hesitations and of delicately indecisive motions, and he was particularly fine in a high wind, rounding a corner with a kind of skittering toddle, both hands nursing his hatbrim.

*"The simplicity of a nursery-school drawing": Harry Langdon.*

He was as remarkable a master as Chaplin of subtle emotional and mental process and operated much more at leisure. He once got a good three hundred feet of continuously bigger laughs out of rubbing his chest, in a crowded vehicle, with Limburger cheese, under the misapprehension that it was a cold salve. In another long scene, watching a brazen showgirl change her clothes, he sat motionless, back to the camera, and registered the whole lexicon of lost innocence, shock, disapproval and disgust, with the back of his neck. His scenes with women were nearly always something special. Once a lady spy did everything in her power (under the Hays Office) to seduce him. Harry was polite, willing, even flirtatious in his little way. The only trouble was that he couldn't imagine what in the world she was leering and pawing at him for, and that he was terribly ticklish. The Mata Hari wound up foaming at the mouth.

There was also a sinister flicker of depravity about the Langdon character, all the more disturbing because babies are premoral. He had an instinct for bringing his actual adulthood and figurative babyishness into frictions as crawley as a fingernail on a slate blackboard, and he wandered into areas of strangeness which were beyond the other comedians. In a nightmare in one movie he was forced to fight a large, muscular young man; the girl Harry loved was the prize. The young man was a good boxer; Harry could scarcely lift his gloves. The contest took place in a fiercely lighted prize ring, in a prodigious pitch-dark arena. The only spectator was the girl, and she was rooting against Harry. As the fight went on, her eyes glittered ever more brightly with blood lust and, with glittering teeth, she tore her big straw hat to shreds.

Langdon came to Sennett from a vaudeville act in which he had fought a losing battle with a recalcitrant automobile. The minute Frank Capra saw him he begged Sennett to let him work with him. Langdon was almost as childlike as the character he played. He had only a vague idea of his story or even of each scene as he played it; each time he went before the camera Capra would brief him on the general situation and then, as this finest of intuitive improvisers once tried to explain his work, "I'd go into my routine." The whole tragedy of the coming of dialogue, as far as these comedians were concerned—and one reason for the increasing rigidity of comedy every since—can be epitomized in the mere thought of Harry Langdon confronted with a script.

Langdon's magic was in his innocence, and Capra took beautiful care not to meddle with it. The key to the proper use of Langdon, Capra always knew, was "the principle of the brick." "If there was a rule for writing Langdon material," he explains, "it was this: his only ally was God. Langdon might be saved by the brick falling on the cop, but it was *verboten* that he in any way motivate the brick's fall." Langdon became quickly and fantastically popular with three pictures, *Tramp, Tramp, Tramp, The Strong Man* and *Long Pants*; from then on he went downhill even faster. "The trouble was," Capra says, "that high-brow critics came around to explain his art to him. Also he developed an interest in dames. It was a pretty high life for such a little fellow." Langdon made two more pictures with high-brow writers, one of which (*Three's A Crowd*) had some wonderful passages in it, including the prize-ring nightmare; then First National canceled his contract. He was reduced to mediocre roles and two-reelers which were more rehashes of his old gags; this time around they no longer seemed funny. "He never did really understand what hit him," says Capra. "He died broke [in 1944]. And he died of a broken heart. He was the most tragic figure I ever came across in show business."

Buster Keaton started work at the age of three and one-half with his parents in one of the roughest acts in vaudeville ("The Three Keatons"); Harry Houdini gave the child the name Buster in admiration for a fall he took down a flight of stairs. In his first movies Keaton teamed with Fatty Arbuckle. He went on to become one of Metro's biggest stars and earners; a Keaton feature cost about $200,000 to make and reliably grossed $2,000,000. Very early in his movie career friends asked him why he never smiled on the screen. He didn't realize he didn't. He had got the dead-pan habit in variety; on the screen he had merely been so hard at work it had never occurred to him there was anything to smile about. Now he tried it just once and never again. He was by his whole style and nature so much the most deeply "silent" of the silent comedians that even a smile was as deafeningly out of key as a yell. In a way his pictures are like a transcendent juggling act in which it seems that the whole universe is in exquisite flying motion and the one point of repose is the juggler's effortless, uninterested face.

Keaton's face ranked almost with Lincoln's as an early American archetype; it was haunting, handsome, almost beautiful, yet it was irreducibly funny; he improved matters by topping it off with a deadly horizontal hat, as flat and thin as a phonograph record. One can never forget Keaton wearing it, standing erect at the prow as his little boat is being launched. The boat goes grandly down the skids and, just as grandly, straight on to the bottom. Keaton never budges. The last you see of him, the water lifts the hat off the stoic head and it floats away.

No other comedian could do as much with the dead pan. He used this great, sad, motionless face to suggest various related things: a one-track mind near the track's end of pure insanity; mulish imperturbability under the wildest of circumstances; how dead a human being can get and still be alive; an awe-inspiring sort of patience and power to endure, proper to granite but uncanny in flesh and blood. Everything that he was and did bore out this rigid face and played laughs against it. When he moved his eyes, it was like seeing them move in a statue. His short-legged body was all sudden, machinelike angles, governed by a daft aplomb. When he swept a semaphore-like arm to point, you could almost hear the electrical impulse in the signal block. When he ran from a cop his transitions from accelerating walk to easy jogtrot to brisk canter to headlong gallop to flogged-piston sprint—always floating, above this frenzy, the untroubled, untouchable face—were as distinct and as soberly in order as an automatic gearshift.

Keaton was a wonderfully resourceful inventor of mechanistic gags (he still spends much of his time fooling with Erector sets); as he ran afoul of locomotives, steamships, prefabricated and over-electrified houses, he put himself through some of the hardest and cleverest punishment ever designed for laughs. In *Sherlock Jr.*, boiling along on the handlebars of a motorcycle quite unaware that he has lost his driver, Keaton whips through city traffic, breaks up a tug-of-war, gets a shovelful of dirt in the face from each of a long line of Rockette-timed ditch-diggers, approaches a log at high speed which is hinged open by dynamite precisely soon enough to let him through and, hitting an obstruction, leaves the handlebars like an arrow leaving a bow, whams through the window of a shack in which the heroine is about to be violated, and hits the heavy feet-first, knocking him through the opposite wall. The whole sequence is as clean in motion as the trajectory of a bullet.

Much of the charm and edge of Keaton's comedy, however, lay in the subtle leverages of expression he could work against his nominal dead pan. Trapped in the side-

*"Within hailing distance of Matthew Brady": Buster Keaton with Marion Mack in*
The General.

wheel of a ferryboat, saving himself from drowning only by walking, then desperately running, inside the accelerating wheel like a squirrel in a cage, his only real concern was, obviously, to keep his hat on. Confronted by Love, he was not as dead-pan as he was cracked up to be, either; there was an odd, abrupt motion of his head which suggested a horse nipping after a sugar lump.

Keaton worked strictly for laughs, but his work came from so far inside a curious and original spirit that he achieved a great deal besides, especially in his feature-length comedies. (For plain hard laughter his nineteen short comedies—the negatives of which have been lost—were even better.) He was the only major comedian who kept sentiment almost entirely out of his work and he brought pure physical comedy to its greatest heights. Beneath his lack of emotion he was also uninsistently sardonic; deep below that, giving a disturbing tension and grandeur to the foolishness, for those who sensed it, there was in his comedy a freezing whisper not of pathos but of melancholia. With the humor, the craftsmanship and the action there was often, besides, a fine, still and sometimes dreamlike beauty. Much of his Civil War picture *The General* is within hailing distance of Mathew Brady. And there is a ghostly, unforgettable moment in *The Navigator* when, on a deserted, softly rolling ship, all the pale doors along a deck swing open as one behind Keaton and, as one, slam shut, in a hair-raising illusion of noise.

Perhaps because "dry" comedy is so much more rare and odd than "dry" wit, there are people who never much cared for Keaton. Those who do cannot care mildly.

As soon as the screen began to talk, silent comedy was pretty well finished. The hardy and prolific Mack Sennett made the transfer; he was the first man to put Bing Crosby and W. C. Fields on the screen. But he was essentially a silent-picture man, and by the time the Academy awarded him a special Oscar for his "lasting contribution to the comedy technique of the screen" (in 1938), he was no longer active. As for the comedians we have spoken of in particular, they were as badly off as fine dancers suddenly required to appear in plays.

Harold Lloyd, whose work was most nearly realistic, naturally coped least unhappily with the added realism of speech; he made several talking comedies. But good as the best were, they were not so good as his silent work, and by the late thirties he quit acting. A few years ago he returned to play the lead (and play it beautifully) in Preston Sturges' *The Sin of Harold Diddlebock*, but this exceptional picture—which opened, brilliantly, with the closing reel of Lloyd's *The Freshman*—has not yet been generally released.

Like Chaplin, Lloyd was careful of his money; he is still rich and active. Last June, in the presence of President Truman, he became Imperial Potentate of the A.A.O.N.M.S. (Shriners). Harry Langdon, as we have said, was a broken man when sound came in.

Up to the middle thirties Buster Keaton made several feature-length pictures (with such players as Jimmy Durante, Wallace Beery and Robert Montgomery); he also made a couple of dozen talking shorts. Now and again he managed to get loose into motion, without having to talk, and for a moment or so the screen would start singing again. But his dark, dead voice, though it was in keeping with the visual character, tore his intensely silent style to bits and destroyed the illusion within which he worked. He gallantly and correctly refuses to regard himself as "retired." Besides occasional bits, spots and minor roles in Hollywood pictures, he has worked on summer stages, made talking comedies in France and Mexico and clowned in a French circus. This summer he has played the straw hats in *Three Men on a Horse*. He is planning a television program. He also has a working agreement with Metro. One of his jobs there is to construct comedy sequences for Red Skelton.

The only man who really survived the flood was Chaplin, the only one who was rich, proud and popular enough to afford to stay silent. He brought out two of his greatest nontalking comedies, *City Lights* and *Modern Times*, in the middle of an avalanche of talk, spoke gibberish and, in the closing moments, plain English in *The Great Dictator*, and at last made an all-talking picture, *Monsieur Verdoux*, creating for that purpose an entirely new character who might properly talk a blue streak. *Verdoux* is the greatest of talking comedies though so cold and savage that it had to find its public in grimly experienced Europe.

Good comedy, and some that was better than good, outlived Silence, but there has been less and less of it. The talkies brought one great comedian, the late, majestically lethargic W. C. Fields, who could not possibly have worked as well in silence; he was the toughest and the most warmly human of all screen comedians, and *It's A Gift* and *The Bank Dick*, fiendishly funny and incisive white-collar comedies, rank high among the best comedies (and best movies) ever made. Laurel and Hardy, the only comedians who managed to preserve much of the large, low style of silence and who began to explore the comedy of sound, have made nothing since 1945. Walt Disney, at his best an inspired comic inventor and teller of fairy stories, lost his stride during the war and has since regained it only at moments. Preston Sturges has made brilliant, satirical comedies, but his pictures are smart, nervous comedy-dramas merely italicized with slapstick. The Marx Brothers were side-splitters but they made their best comedies years ago. Jimmy Durante is mainly a nightclub genius; Abbott and Costello are semiskilled laborers, at best; Bob Hope is a good radio comedian with a pleasing presence, but not much more, on the screen.

There is no hope that screen comedy will get much better than it is without new, gifted young comedians who really belong in movies, and without freedom for their experiments. For everyone who may appear we have one last, invidious comparison to offer as a guidepost.

One of the most popular recent comedies is Bob Hope's *The Paleface*. We take no pleasure in blackening *The Paleface*; we single it out, rather, because it is as good as we've got. Anything that is said of it here could be said, with interest, of other comedies of our time. Most of the laughs in *The Paleface* are verbal. Bob Hope is very adroit with his lines and now and then, when the words don't get in the way, he makes a good beginning as a visual comedian. But only the beginning, never the middle or the end. He is funny, for instance, reacting to a shot of violent whisky. But he does not know how to get still funnier (i.e., how to build and milk) or how to be funniest last (i.e., how to top or cap his gag). The camera has to fade out on the same old face he started with.

One sequence is promisingly set up for visual comedy. In it, Hope and a lethal local boy stalk each other all over a cow town through streets which have been emptied in fear of their duel. The gag here is that through accident and stupidity they keep just failing to find each other. Some of it is quite funny. But the fun slackens between laughs like a weak clothesline, and by all the logic of humor (which is ruthlessly logical) the biggest laugh should come at the moment, and through the way, they finally spot each other. The sequence is so weakly thought out that at that crucial moment the camera can't afford to watch them; it switches to Jane Russell.

Now we turn to a masterpiece. In *The Navigator* Buster Keaton works with practically the same gag as Hope's duel. Adrift on a ship which he believes is otherwise empty, he drops a lighted cigarette. A girl finds it. She calls out and he hears her; each then tries to find the other. First each walks purposefully down the long, vacant starboard deck, the girl, then Keaton, turning the corner just in time not to see each other. Next time around each of them is trotting briskly, very much in earnest; going at the same pace, they miss each other just the same. Next time around each of them is going like a bat out of hell. Again they miss. Then the camera withdraws to a point of vantage at the stern, leans its chin in its hand and just watches the whole intricate superstructure of the ship as the protagonists stroll, steal and scuttle from level to level, up, down and sidewise, always managing to miss each other by hair's-breadths, in an enchantingly neat and elaborate piece of timing. There are no subsidiary gags to get laughs in this sequence and there is little loud laughter; merely a quiet and steadily increasing kind of delight. When Keaton has got all he can out of this fine modification of the movie chase he invents a fine device to bring the two together: the girl, thoroughly winded, sits down for a breather, indoors, on a plank which workmen have left across sawhorses. Keaton pauses on an upper deck, equally winded and puzzled. What follows happens in a couple of seconds at most: air suction whips his silk topper backward down a ventilator; grabbing frantically for it, he backs against the lip of the ventilator, jackknifes and falls in backward. Instantly the camera cuts back to the girl. A topper falls through the ceiling and lands tidily, right side up, on the plank beside her. Before she can look more than startled, its owner follows, head between his knees, crushes the topper, breaks the plank with the point of his spine and proceeds to the floor. The breaking of the plank smacks Boy and Girl together.

It is only fair to remember that the silent comedians would have as hard a time playing a talking scene as Hope has playing his visual ones, and that writing and directing are as accountable for the failure as Hope himself. But not even the humblest journeymen of the silent years would have let themselves off so easily. Like the masters, they knew, and sweated to obey, the laws of their craft.

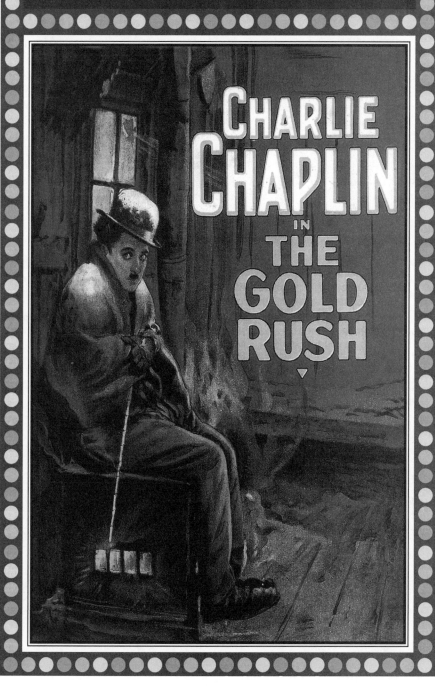

# Comic Play

### Rick Levinson (2001)

In 1965 Buster Keaton was in Canada doing a short film called *The Railrodder* (1965) in which he rides a funny little automated rail car from the Atlantic to the Pacific. That is a long stretch of territory, and the making of the film would have taxed a person half his age. Keaton took to it like it was Cottage Grove, Oregon, 1926—where he'd filmed *The General*—all over again.

The National Film Board of Canada made a one-hour documentary of the making of *The Railrodder*. The documentary is called *Buster Keaton Rides Again* (1965), and it shows Buster handling everything with reticence, dogged good will, and a charming, self-effacing aplomb: the Canadian landscape; the two filming crews, the one working on the short film and the other one working on the documentary; the funny little rail

*Buster Keaton rides again: Canada, 1965.*

30

car; crowds in a Montreal shopping mall; a small town in Manitoba awarding him an honorary plaque and the key to the town; children invited into his combination rail car/dressing room for autographs; the receipt of a freshly killed wild duck for dinner, one of the stipulations in his contract; miles and miles of track and rail cars and whatnot. We see him banter good-naturedly with his wife of twenty-five years, Eleanor; work through the strategic processes of shot placement and direction of the action at a mental pace which leaves both film crews floundering in his wake; get caught up in a play at home plate during a televised baseball game with the passion of a true fan; calmly and gently out-analyze everybody else's hand in a game of bridge; go through fits of coughing spells (the cancer that was to take him was about a year or so away); and talk about and act out, with exuberance and great fondness, a scene in a two-reeler involving Laurel and Hardy, traffic in downtown Los Angeles, and Edgar Kennedy as a traffic cop.

There's a scene in the short film involving Buster going over a single-track railway trestle bridge which spans a gorge; it's a huge bridge in height, like the one that collapsed in *The General*, and three little putt putt railway cars are to come from the opposite side of this single-track trestle; and when they see Buster motoring toward them in his car, they back the hell up and slip back into the little shacks adjacent to and on the opposite side of the bridge where they came from; and Buster glides on through.

Keaton's idea for the scene is: his character opens a huge map just before crossing the trestle; and he gets physically wrapped up in this huge map; and he is completely oblivious to the putt putt cars on the opposite side of the one-track trestle; and the putt putt cars see him coming and back the hell up to get out of the way; and slip back into their little shacks; and Buster glides through, still wrapped in the map, oblivious to the cars during the whole episode. It's very similar to a sequence in one of his silent films, as a matter of fact.

Except the director of the short film has another idea: Buster isn't wrapped up in a map when he reaches the trestle; he's doing laundry. And he has to see and react to the putt putt cars coming to him on this single track.

And they film it that way, with Keaton doing his laundry. But Keaton is not happy with it; he had the gag figured out in his head the night before; he was to be wrapped up in a map and oblivious to the danger of the oncoming cars. The director says the gag's with the bridge, but Keaton says, no, the gag is not with the bridge; the bridge builds suspense; the gag is Keaton's obliviousness to the whole situation. The whole damned thing is to be carried out without his character having a single clue as to what kind of danger he's just gotten himself into and out of.

There's a sequence in the documentary in the aftermath of his disagreement with the director of the short film about the way the bridge sequence should go. Keaton doesn't throw a Hollywood star conniption fit, but instead goes to his railway car/dressing room to stew a bit. He's got this cigarette holder with a black tube and silver tip, and a cigarette plugged into it, and he's puffing away. The cigarette holder would look like a ridiculously ornate affectation on anyone else, but it doesn't look that way on Buster. It looks like something he invented, and it endows him with a quaintness and elegance and a sweet, slightly ornery innocence. His eyes are rheumy and he's got horn-rimmed glasses on. And he's talking to Eleanor about how the scene should play and chiding her for mentioning the danger of his going over the high trestle on the tiny car with the map wrapped around him—"child's play, for the love of Mike"—and that the structuring of a gag sequence usually involves a certain margin for guesswork, but "every now and then—ain't no guess work. This is one of 'em."

And all the while Keaton is ruminating in his railway car/dressing room on the gag sequence—which is eventually filmed his way, with Keaton tangled up in a map—he's playing solitaire. Dealing the cards on the table in neat, orderly rows. His way of stewing and not playing along with anybody else for the moment, but still: playing.

And it would be nice to leave Keaton there, in the railway car/dressing room that is the perfect place for Keaton to be; travelling forward in the railway car across the Canadian border; and backward in his mind to how it was in 1926 in Cottage Grove, Oregon, when he did have to figure out all his magnificent work in *The General*. But he was not playing solitaire in 1926; he was playing baseball with his boys—the crew of cameramen and production guys and gag writers/scenarists—until inspiration struck; and then getting it on film before they lost that day's light.

And then it would be easy to get all mythopoetic and talk of how the men who built the trails and roads and bridges and railways of the American West, having reached the Pacific Coast, with all the work done, and all the liquor drunk and all the whores laid, and all the pay spent, and having nothing else to do, picked up four leftover sacks and stuffed them with dirt, and measured off four even paces to make a diagonal, and placed the bags down at each corner, and sewed up the sack remnants with stitching shaped like the tongue of a wagon, and picked up a railway tie from a waste heap and shaved it smooth and started playing baseball, as if that were a natural extension of how they got there in the first place.

Nothing remotely like that happened. But something like that did happen when actors got to Hollywood in the teens, especially the comedians. Play was a natural extension of what they did for a living. All kinds of play. There's the brief situational pay-off, or gag. Probably the two most celebrated gags in silent comedy: the front of a house falling on Keaton, in *Steamboat Bill, Jr.* (1928), with Keaton situated so that the glassless window frame lands over him, leaving him bewildered but intact; and the face of a gigantic building clock being pulled from its casing by Harold Lloyd in *Safety Last* (1923), leaving him frantic but intact.

But the gag was just one form of play. There were sustained routines as elaborately choreographed as anything performed by Fred Astaire or Gene Kelly: Harold Lloyd in *Girl Shy* (1924) tearing through half of Los Angeles County by car, streetcar, motorcycle and horse to stop a wedding; Keaton in *Sherlock, Jr.* (1924) entering the frame of a film-in-progress and finding himself, via rapid editing cuts, floundering in all the elements; and, later, on a motorcycle, tearing through the other half of Los Angeles County.

And sometimes the choreographed routines were played out on a miniature scale. Think of Chaplin, near starvation in *The Gold Rush* (1925), making an elegant repast out of a boiled shoe, and thereby indulging in the most famous meal ever eaten onscreen; or Harry Langdon, miserable with a cold in *The Strong Man* (1926), making an epic out of his attempts to take cough syrup on a crowded passenger truck.

There was the spontaneous play of making comedy out of the moment: Chaplin, in the course of getting at the innards of a clock in *The Pawn Shop* (1916), turns the clock into a metaphor for just about anything you can imagine. There was the single gag escalating into a series of reciprocated gags until all these neat, proportionate acts ended in utter chaos. This was Laurel and Hardy's specialty: in *Big Business* (1929) they sell Christmas trees in Los Angeles door-to-door and, in the process, get into a tit-for-tat battle with their perennial foil James Finlayson and end up destroying his house.

Billy Wilder, in talking about the casting of Keaton in the card-playing scene in

*Sunset Boulevard* (1950), mentioned that Keaton wasn't just a good or even a better-than-average bridge player; he was a world-class bridge player. And when Keaton's crew was stuck for an idea, they really did stop and play baseball for a while until they worked it out. Watch the scene in *The General* where Keaton works his way to the top of a moving car with his ankle in a chain, and a loaded cannon facing him flush, a good forty to fifty feet or so away. When he picks up a heavy stick of wood and throws it, in utter futility, at the cannon's mouth, damned if he doesn't throw a strike.

Lloyd was also a ferocious player of games; whenever any game like chess or gin rummy was played on the set between breaks, he'd beat every member of his crew at it within a couple of weeks. The thumb and index finger of Lloyd's right hand were blown off by a bomb in 1919—he was shooting a publicity still, of all things, when it happened—and he wore a special prosthetic glove on that hand to conceal the loss.

Keep that in mind when you see him in his post-accident short films and feature films. Try to spot the gloved hand in any of these films. You won't, because he didn't want you to. And even with his maimed right hand, he could beat you at virtually anything to which you could challenge him. He became a champion bowler in the mid-1950s.

Chaplin? Jackie Coogan, reminiscing about *The Kid* (1921) in Brownlow and Gill's television series *Hollywood—The Pioneers* (1979) said that if Chaplin saw someone perform some difficult feat of strength or grace or agility—anything—Chaplin would show up the next day on the set and perform the feat better than anyone alive.

And this sense of play, more than anything else, carried into their work. It's what makes their work a thing of joy and beauty beyond any actual laughter it produces.

Walter Kerr in *The Silent Clowns* mentioned something to the effect that it was really no matter to him whether Keaton was funny or not; his films are so amazing, who cares about laughter? But why limit that to Keaton, or to the silent comedians alone, for that matter? The play of comedians—the situational chaos they work themselves into and out of; the rhythmic nuances of their routines; their actions and reactions—gets to us in a special way, engages us beyond any laughter that it brings. And it doesn't matter who it is, or in what era they performed, or what medium they performed in, or what they were doing: Chaplin or Keaton or Lloyd or Langdon; the Marx Brothers or *Monty Python's Flying Circus*; Phil Silvers or Richard Pryor; Burns and Allen or Gleason and Carney; Bob and Ray or Bob Hope; Bill Cosby or Andy Kaufman; Jack Benny or Lucille Ball; Robin Williams or Ernie Kovacs.

What did John Belushi say once before rushing out onstage in an outdoor concert to perform his Jake Blues character? Belushi said, watch, I make the best onstage entrance since Jimmy Durante. Since Durante. Belushi knew his comedy. They all do, the great ones; they're students of comedy. And then Belushi launched himself onstage, a furious rolling ball of a man, cartwheeling over and over, landing centerstage, ready for action, half cub bear and half Elvis.

Laurel and Hardy? The best rhythm-and-reaction comedians that ever were or ever will be; they'd take a premise of virtually nothing and make twenty minutes of the most beautifully timed physical comedy you'll ever see.

Or take Abbott and Costello and their "Who's On First?" routine. How many times have you heard it? Did you laugh the first time you got it? What made you listen to it from then on and still enjoy it, perhaps more so? The intricacy of their patter, the fluidity and devastating swiftness of their exchanges, the frustration in Costello's voice mounting as Abbott becomes more terse and matter-of-fact; and the flurry of exchanges punctuated by Costello shouting "I don't even know what I'm talking about!"—the frankly beautiful sport they were playing, not the sport they were talking about.

Bruce Campbell is as assured a comic actor as there is working today; his timing is extraordinary. His Autolycus, King of Thieves, in the *Hercules* and *Xena* TV series is an improbable fusion of Douglas Fairbanks, Sr., Groucho Marx and Frank Zappa. Check him out in Sam Raimi's *Army of Darkness* (1993) when he gets Moe Howard eye pokes from graveyard skeletal fingers. Nick Cage? Unbelievably beautiful, idiosyncratic sense of comic timing; his line readings and gentle, almost stoned takes in David Lynch's *Wild at Heart* (1990) are dead perfect parodies of every '60s movie Elvis zombified his way through. Eddie Murphy? Andrea Martin? Michael Keaton? Janeane Garofalo? The Seinfeld group, playing off each other with a sense of precision, a sense of where each left off and where each is going, as fine as anything performed in a jazz ensemble. John Cleese: Basil Fawlty's near tantrums are as brilliant as comedic performance will ever get. The Kids in the Hall? Bill Murray? Murray may be the most original American film comedian since W. C. Fields, taking a despicably self-absorbed bastard, wringing him through a series of gut-wrenching changes, and making you feel the bastard's inner torment, self-realization and budding decency. *Scrooged* (1988) is arguably the wittiest and most faithful film adaptation of *A Christmas Carol* since Alastair Sim's in 1951 (the best one) because Murray, like Sim, had the comedic chops to make the Scrooge redemption scenes palpably real. A great comic, like Fields in his early Paramount films, like Sim, like Murray, knows when to seem negligible with his gifts and knows when to gift his character with unexpected depths of humanity.

David Letterman? The essence of what Letterman does, night after night, is: I'm performing here; it's sheer hell when it doesn't work, and it's sheer hell even when it does work. He's playing off the moment constantly, as if he's standing off to the side and half-thinking: what does this idiot think he's doing before millions of people? Jim Carrey? Chris Farley? Adam Sandler? Don't sneer about dumb and dumber; cerebral gamesmanship has very little to do with it. Comedy hits us viscerally, despite what anyone says. It isn't about satire or scoring ideological points: that's a literary comic tradition, which is a different animal altogether from performed comedy. Sometimes the traditions converge—Mort Sahl is the conventionally cited example, but think of Will Rogers in the past and Dennis Miller in the present—but it's still a type of performed comedy, and timing and delivery and pacing and rhythm are as key as what they're saying. Performed comedy, pared down to its essence, is play.

The comedians want the laughter, of course, and they get it more often than not. Watch a Chaplin or a Keaton or a Lloyd silent film alone on a VCR and chances are you won't smile, much less laugh. "He (or she) never made me laugh"; it's the one statement among comedy fans that will test friendships. It's the line in the sand of personal taste. And it's stated as if it were an objective truth, but it's a subjective point of demarcation, and a silly one at that. If you have a bias in favor of one comedian—and most fans of comedy do have favorites—it is virtually a rule of human behavior that any other comedian working in the same field will not make you laugh. You've got your favorite in mind while you're watching the others, and you're going to be defensive, consciously or not; you're putting yourself out of the mood of suspended engagement that all comedians ask of you. You're not giving "the competition" a chance. You're not playing along.

For all we know, adult laughter may be a social reflex, a communal release—that's a matter best left to psychologists and sociologists. Lloyd, the one major silent comedian besides Oliver Hardy who had never appeared onstage as a professional comic, relied on preview screenings of his films to determine where the laughs were, and where they weren't. MGM production head Irving Thalberg reputedly credited Lloyd with being the first film performer to regularly utilize the preview as part of the post-production process. The process sounds cold-blooded and corporate and makes Lloyd seem unsure of himself as a comedian, but, for comedy at least, the process makes sense; you've got to know where the laughs are, and only an audience can tell you. Oliver Hardy's characteristic of staring balefully, almost mournfully, at the camera came about as a result of audience reaction at screenings. And Keaton's celebrated downhill scamper from an avalanche of seemingly malevolent rocks and boulders in *Seven Chances* (1925) came about because Keaton noticed, during a preview screening of the film, that the audience laughed when he inadvertently tripped over some stones at the top of a hill, sending them flying as if in pursuit of him.

Laughter as a communal reflex: watch a Chaplin or a Keaton or a Lloyd silent film, not alone on a VCR, but in a theatre filled with people; and the laughter will come in ripples and waves and roars, as if the seventy years separating them from us have dissipated,

*"The reason we watch* Duck Soup... *over and over again with anticipation, with delight."*

and all that's left is the immediacy of whatever predicament they're getting into or out of, the astonishing fluency and brilliance of their gestures, nuances, actions, reactions.

But the laughs are a bonus, really; the play of what they are doing defines them, and, for the brief time that we watch and absorb what they do, engages us and brings us joy. Any post hoc rationalization about what the comedian is doing, or what the comedian means or represents in a more profound sense, is a disengagement from that immediate sense of play. It rationalizes something that didn't need rationalizing in the first place. Ranking the profundity of comedians by gauging the level of their understanding of the world around them is a post hoc quasi-philosophical conceit, and a poor one at that when applied to comedic performance of any kind; it may work for a Stoppard play or a Rushdie novel or a Heaney poem, but it isn't the reason we watch *Duck Soup* (1933) or the Hope and Crosby road pictures or *Blazing Saddles* (1974) over and over again with anticipation, with delight. When we stop constructing these post hoc rationalizations about comedic performance, we liberate ourselves and come back to the moment of performance itself, which asks us, above all, to engage ourselves entirely with the comedic moment and temporarily disengage ourselves from our cares and the cares of the world. And during that moment, the rest of the world—which is the place where (we hope) rationalization, post hoc or not, properly belongs, along with sincerity, compassion, fairness, justice, decency, sobriety, civility—the rest of the world, for that moment, doesn't matter.

The play of a comedian is as joyous as any sport or music you can name. Laughter is an echo of that joy.

# After the Gold Rush: Chaplin at One Hundred

**J. Hoberman** (1989)

He sleeps in the gutter and uses a rope to hold up his pants. He is frequently homeless and at best marginally employed. When he does work, his disorderly conduct often wrecks his employer's business, injuring innocent bystanders and bringing the police down. His world is filled with cops, to whom his instinctive response is instant flight—a madly determined, arm-flailing dash.

He is sneaky and sometimes violent. He desecrates public property. A petty thief when need be, he has no respect for authority. He is, of course, Charlie Chaplin's "Little Tramp," and if we stepped over him today on the streets of New York, we might scarcely recognize the prototype for the world's greatest film star, once the most popular man on earth, the icon of the 20th century, Jesus Christ's rival as the best-known person who ever lived.

Charlie Chaplin, born in London a century ago and the subject of a modest fete at the Museum of Modern Art, enjoyed sustained popularity on a scale that is difficult to imagine and may never be duplicated. He was not exactly a plaster saint, although if we judge him by the quality of his enemies (Hedda Hopper, Howard Hughes, HUAC, Hitler), his luster could hardly be greater. Scarcely a corporation man, Chaplin used his power to defy Hollywood mores and go his own way—ignoring the conventions of talking pictures, making highly personal political tracts, reinventing his image in a way no studio would have permitted.

Chaplin wasn't simply the first mass cultural icon, the embodiment of mass man, he *was* mass culture—vulgar, repetitive, shameless, addictive, utopian. In his disdain for language, he personified the universality of silent movies. As Charles Silver points out in his new monograph, Chaplin's two-reelers were immediately apprehendable: "No particular level of sophistication or even literacy was necessary . . . to see that he was special: you only had to *see*." As ancient as these artifacts are, children don't have to be educated to find them funny. His love of play and passion for disorder mirrors their own, although Chaplin's uncanny appeal is perhaps innate. (Is it that toddler walk and those spaniel eyes that, like Mickey Mouse's outsized, infantlike head, push the love button in our brains?)

Although Chaplin has been encrusted with sentimentality (much of it his own doing) and relegated to the realm of the timeless, he is and was a historical being. In the late '60s, when I came of age as a self-conscious moviegoer, Chaplin was being displaced by a revisionist reappreciation of Buster Keaton. Back then, Keaton's formalism and reflexiveness, his stylized cool and absence of sentiment seemed far more interesting than Chaplin's puppy dog, in-your-face humanism and crude theatricality. The icon obscured the artist: Chaplin's well-worn divinity concealed the radical nature of his enterprise, the degree to which his pre-1919 two-reelers thrive on urban chaos and visceral class awareness, the Wobbly esprit de corps that infuses his hatred of work, which he continually subverts and transforms into sport.

The subject and object of mechanical reproduction, Chaplin was the original parody

● ● ● ● ● ● ● ● ● ● ● ● ● ● ● ● ● ● ● ● ● ● ● ● ● ● ● ● ● ● ● ● ● ● ● ● ● ● ● ● ● ● ● ● ● ●

automaton. In a recent issue of *Radical History*, Charles Musser contextualizes him in terms of Henry Ford's newfangled assembly line and the industrial efficiency technique known as "Taylorism." Indeed, reeking of class hostility, the baldly titled *Work* (released in 1915, four months after *The Birth of a Nation*) features Charlie as an assistant paperhanger employed by a bourgeois family called the Fords. *Modern Times* (1936), Chaplin's most elaborate production, is a virtual anthology of such slapstick two-reelers, every skit revolving around the struggle for survival at its most primal level. (Few movies have ever been more obsessed with the act of acquiring food.) "I came away stunned at the thought that such a film had been made and was being distributed," the critic for *New Masses* wrote. "*Modern Times* is not so much a fine motion picture as a historical event."

A historical event but not, relatively speaking, a hit. Today, *Modern Times* (which, among other things, allegorizes the process of studio filmmaking) seems Chaplin's definitive statement. Contrary to the five-year run of IBM commercials that have been spun off it, *Modern Times* criticizes not just industrial capitalism but work itself—as well as authority, the family, and the very nature of adult behavior.

He knew his audience. One thing he never sentimentalized was the rich. "No comedian before or after him has spent more energy depicting people in their working lives," writes Robert Sklar in *Movie Made America* of the star whose first film—a Keystone two-reeler released in February 1914—was aptly called *Making a Living*.

Chaplin exploded out of the Keystone ensemble at a time when the movies had again become rowdy, shaking off the five or six years of defensive gentility that followed the antinickelodeon crusades of 1908. Fittingly, the revolt against the new decorum was led by Mack Sennett, who had apprenticed with order's architect, D. W. Griffith. Although Chaplin perfected his supreme creation several months after leaving Keystone, it was there that he had his first and most extensive contact with the American people, that he mastered his timing and internalized Sennett's grotesque assault on the social order.

Within a year of leaving Sennett, Chaplin was considered the essence of laughter— although not everyone was amused. After *Work* was released, Sime Silverman, the founding editor of *Variety*, complained that "the Censor Board is passing matter in the Chaplin films that could not possibly get by in other pictures. Never anything dirtier was placed on the screen than Chaplin's 'Tramp.'" The association of Chaplin with impurity—sexual, racial, political—was something that would dog him for the next 40 years.

That spring, however, Chaplinitis swept the English-speaking world. By now Chaplin was his own trademark; the tramp was totally industrialized. There were Chaplin songs, Chaplin dances, Chaplin sketches in theatrical revues, Chaplin cocktails, Chaplin dolls, Chaplin shirts, Chaplin ties, Chaplin postcards, Chaplin animated cartoons, and a Chaplin comic strip. It was as if a new religion had been born and everyone wanted a piece of the cross. Placed beneath a marquee, the cardboard image of the little man with the skimpy mustache—his silhouette rendered indelible by bowler hat, baggy pants, and outsized shoes—was sufficient in itself to fill a theater. Demand far outstripped supply. The 26-year-old actor could not produce movies quickly enough to satisfy his fans.

Imitators were legion. "Among the happy youths of the slums, or the dandies of clubdom or college, an imitation of a Chaplin flirt of the coat, or the funny waddle of the comedian, is considered the last word in humor. To be Chaplinesque is to be funny; to waddle a few steps and then look naively at your audience," *Motion Picture Magazine* reported in a 1915 article simply called "Chaplinitis." Soon Chaplin look-alike contests were being held in

*The Tramp in* The Gold Rush. *"Never anything dirtier was placed on the screen
than Chaplin's 'Tramp.'"*

amusement parks all over the U.S. Leslie T. (later Bob) Hope won one such in Cleveland.
So many comedians were impersonating Chaplin on the screen—among them, Stan Jefferson (subsequently Laurel)—that Charlie had to file suit. It was said that for a time costume
balls were ruined, because 90 per cent of the men appeared dressed as the Little Tramp. (In
*The Idle Class,* Chaplin attended one such ball dressed as himself.)

America definitely had Chaplin on the brain. In Cincinnati, a holdup man used a
Charlie Chaplin disguise. In a mysterious occurrence on November 12, 1916, the actor
was simultaneously paged in 800 hotels. Chaplinitis spread to Europe and raged
throughout the Great War. According to the British film historian Kevin Brownlow,
Chaplin cut-outs were kidnapped from the lobbies of British movie theaters and borne
off to the trenches: "These life-sized models were popular with the troops, who would
stand them on the parapet during an attack. The appearance of a crudely painted tramp,

with baggy trousers and a bowler hat, must have bewildered the Germans, who had no idea who he was. To add to the confusion, British officers with a sense of humor would cultivate Chaplin mustaches, and in prison camps, every hut had its Chaplin impersonator." Nor were the French immune. "Charlot was born at the Front," wrote Blaise Cendrars. "The Germans lost the war because they didn't get to know Charlot in time."

Just as the war ended, Chaplin released his own vision of the trenches, the totally apatriotic *Shoulder Arms*, a spiritual precursor of *Catch-22* whose bits include a fantasy of shelling the Germans with Limburger cheese and, an even more visceral evocation of combat, sleeping in a bunk that's virtually under water.

He was taken seriously almost immediately. The author of "Chaplinitis" called him a "genius" and boldly stated that "once in every century, a man is born who is able to color and influence his world . . . . Charles Chaplin is doing it with pantomime and personality." In May 1916, *Harper's Weekly* published "The Art of Charles Chaplin," an appreciation by a well-known stage actress that bracketed "the young English buffoon" with Aristophanes, Shakespeare, and Rabelais.

In France, Charlot was the subject of the first monograph on an individual film artist. In the Soviet Union, archformalist Viktor Shklovsky published a book on Chaplin in 1923. Chaplin was the movies' first *esque*, the only mass culture figure one could bracket with high modernists Eliot and Joyce, a fitting subject for a Cubist collage. (Later, Léger featured him in *Ballet Mécanique*.) It's easy to imagine Chaplin as a character in a Brecht play or Kafka novel, but in America, he was seen as the ultimate Horatio Alger hero. He arrived here a penniless immigrant—bona fide wretched refuse—and, within 24 months, became the highest paid actor in the world. (That Chaplin refused to consummate the myth by becoming an American citizen would be held against him later.)

As an artist, he infused the pathos of the British proletariat—Dickens and the music hall—with the jazz rhythms and streamlined optimism of the newer, American variety, absorbing by osmosis French aestheticism and Jewish soul. (Feckless *Luftmensch* that Chaplin played, he was perceived as Jewish by both Jews and anti-Semites.) In a sense, Chaplin was the mascot of Western democracy. He was mobbed in Paris and London during his 1921 European tour, but ignored in Berlin, where—although some hipster had included his photograph among the Heartfields and Picabias of the 1920 Berlin Dada Fair—his films had not yet been released. Of course, the Germans would soon get their own Little Tramp/Hero of the Trenches/Man of the Century.

In *Modern Times*, Chaplin bid his greatest creation farewell. For the first time, the tramp's voice was heard (singing a nonsense song in a routine that contains in embryo all early Fellini), while the movie's last shot showed the tramp walking off down the road—no longer alone, but hand-in-hand with Paulette Goddard. "It is an ironical thought that the mustached face of Adolf Hitler will be the only living reminder of the little clown," *The New York Times* nostalgically editorialized shortly after the film's release. The thought bothered Chaplin as well. Before Hitler took power, he had been attacked by the Nazi press as "a little Jewish acrobat, as disgusting as he is tedious." (In fact, Chaplin wasn't Jewish, but, as a matter of principle, he never contradicted such accusations.) During Hitler's rule, Chaplin's movies were banned and all mention of his name proscribed. It was inevitable that this pair would go one on one.

Like twin gods in some fertile-crescent myth, the two most compelling personalities of the 20th century were born four days apart, in April 1889. They were both raised in poverty and domestic disorder, both lived as vagabonds, both dreamed of being artists, both captivated the masses, both sought absolute control over their worlds. Many, including Chaplin, believed that Hitler even borrowed his mustache from the Little Tramp. What was the secret of the atom compared to the source of Chaplin's power? Chaplin thought he understood the origin of Hitler's. In *The Great Dictator* he once and for all broke the speech barrier with a full-fledged Hitler rant in gibberish German. Thus did the Little Tramp acknowledge the tyranny of sound.

His reputation has had violent ups and downs. In 1919 *Theatre Magazine* published an article, hopefully entitled "Is the Charlie Chaplin Vogue Passing?" which scored "the appeal of every Chaplin picture to the lowest human instincts." Even when his artistic reputation was at its highest, Chaplin carried intimations of the underclass. "You have to go to squalid streets and disreputable neighborhoods if you want to see Chaplin regularly," Gilbert Seldes advised his readers on the eve of *The Gold Rush*.

No doubt Ronald Reagan would have pieties to mouth on Chaplin's birthday, but there were periods in Chaplin's career when his most passionate defenders were Surrealists or Communists, and not even the mature success of *The Gold Rush* prevented American women's clubs from organizing a boycott of his pictures because Lita Grey divorced him. As movie-phobe H.L. Mencken noted with no small satisfaction, "The very morons who worshipped Charlie Chaplin six weeks ago now prepare to dance around his stake while he is burned." A quarter of a century later, he suffered the most dramatic fall of any star. Small wonder that he would ultimately cast himself as the genteel mass murderer in *Monsieur Verdoux*.

Once a tramp, always a tramp: The subversion of public order, the potential for anarchy, was inextricably bound up in the Chaplin persona. He always found a way up authority's nose. Chaplin was attacked as a draft dodger during World War I, spuriously indicted for violating the Mann Act during World War II, threatened with deportation, and ultimately red-baited out of the United States at the height of the McCarthy period. But all that is forgotten now. On the 100th anniversary of Chaplin's birth, his progeny are everywhere and nowhere—as Garry Wills pointed out, Ronnie and Nancy mimed the last shot of *Modern Times* (embellished with an affectionately Chaplinesque kick in the butt), in *New Morning in America*, the movie shown to the world at the 1984 Republican convention.

Chaplin at 100 has become a free-floating image and an all-purpose *esque*—familiar now because he was familiar then. He is a neutral symbol of the information age, a million dollar trademark licensed to IBM to make their personal computers seem user-friendly. Leasing the Little Tramp's image from his heirs, IBM upgraded his wardrobe and occupational status: a floppy Little Yuppie for the Age of Reagan. (To approximate the full flavor of what in better days we called co-optation, one has to imagine a blue-chip corporation entrusting their $25 million advertising campaign to Richard Pryor in his "Bicentennial Nigger" heyday.)

Welcome to postmodern times: Released from the assembly line, transmuted into the pure being of empty signifier, the Little Tramp has been put back to work; he's making a living once more, earning his keep, sentenced in his afterlife to labor as a flack for the corporate order. But remember that *Modern Times* is set in Brazil and *The Kid* on Lafayette Street; that *City Lights* is a film about Donald Trump and Billie Boggs. Look at the early movies and then look around you. See if you can't find Chaplin—our contemporary—out there on the street.

# The Trickster Kid:
# Harold Lloyd's One-Reel Comedies

**Ken Bowers** (2001)

So much attention has been paid in recent decades to the great silent feature comedies of the 1920s that its easy to forget that as recently as the 1960s, it seemed to many observers that all silent comedy was a jumble of fractured one-reelers with Keaton, Arbuckle, Keystone, Chaplin all part of the same stew, and the features just titles in a few history books. In our day, by contrast, we think of silent comedy in terms of feature films and a few key shorts. Despite the rough hand that time has dealt to silent film, many short comedies survive. They run the gamut in quality and most film buffs are reconciled to chance viewing of such shorts as may happen to turn up with the features.

Harold Lloyd was one of the great filmmakers of the silent era. While his feature films have received wide circulation, his many short comedies have inspired little interest, save perhaps as stepping-stones to the mature Lloyd persona.

The Lloyd short comedies were created in the years 1915 to 1921, and ranged from one-reelers (about ten minutes) to three-reelers. Unlike Keaton, who never worked in the one-reel format, or Chaplin, who moved quickly to two-reelers, Lloyd worked for years, 1915 to 1919, in the ten minute form. The surviving, and available, one-reelers are the subject of my essay, with reference to his later films as needed. These little movies follow the standard set by Mack Sennett's Keystone comedies, with the same emphasis on fast-paced action and silliness.

In sum, they are Punch and Judy shows, with Harold playing a trickster kid who likes to hit others, but will not stand to be hit in return. He's a two-fisted lad, ever ready to count coup on an offender, whether guilty or innocent. This is true both in Lloyd's early incarnation as "Lonesome Luke" and in his revised characterization as a normally dressed individual wearing glasses. The following generalities can be applied, more or less, to all the Harold Lloyd one-reelers:

1. Cops exist, first, to chase and clobber Harold, if they can catch him; secondly, as a convenience whenever Harold needs a rival, father, villain, or unlucky passer-by conked silly. Trickster Harold's method is standard: simply maneuver the victim within striking distance, kick the cop and step aside. The cop will turn and apply his nightstick to the necessary noggin. You may then safely dump the rival in the nearest trashcan.

2. Horseshoes can be found lying about anywhere. Once you spot one you will want to pick it up, spit on both sides, make a wish, and, taking care not to look behind you, throw it as far as you can over your shoulder. The horseshoe will either hit a cop or break a window, next to which a cop will always be standing.

3. To get someone's attention, or just say hello, kick him in the butt. If some perfect stranger doesn't tell you what you want to know, kick or swat him. If the offended party pulls a gun, run for it! Pistols fire bee stings, which invariably miss their target, unless their target is your rump.

4. Don't hesitate to flirt with every woman you see, even if she is twice your age, even if she is standing next to the girl you just flirted with, even if she is standing next to Bebe Daniels, the nominal leading lady of your movie. Feel free to climb on or over, any husband or boyfriend sitting next to the object of your flirtation. If a male, no matter how

*"Bebe Daniels, a versatile teenager," with Harold Lloyd as* The Chef *(1919). Snub Pollard and Bud Jamison look on.*

homely, should happen to drape some article of feminine attire about his person, feel free to flirt with him/her as well.

5.  Playing the female lead is Bebe Daniels, a versatile teenager with a special knack for clearly enunciating words like "I'm hungry" and "Bolsheviks." She plays a variety of roles: sheltered daughters, worldly vamps, defiant ladies in distress, self-reliant country girls. The trickster kid often has to pry her away from throngs of desperate suitors and oily mashers. She is usually attracted to the kid, but seldom offers him the selfless devotion that Harold will enjoy from the leading ladies of the feature films. She is more often a comic type, and not an emotional presence.

6.  Breaking the taboo of picking on a smaller man is a regular source of humor. A bearded little man barely four feet tall named Sammy Brooks fills this role heroically from at least 1917 into the 1920s. In most of their movies, Harold frequently jumps over a strolling Sammy during a chase, while in quieter scenes Harold and other full-size characters knock him down, kick him, trip him, and push him because he is smaller and easier to assault than other game. In *I'm On My Way* (1919) Harold is carrying a towering stack of packages for Bebe. He spots Sammy and stacks the boxes on his head, hoists the seat of Sammy's pants for a rudder, and guides him to Bebe's house in a long traveling shot through the dreamy, gray-tint streets of old Hollywood. In *Ring Up the Curtain* (1919) a snake terrorizes the theater until Harold gets flute player Sammy to charm the snake into a closet. Harold rewards Sammy by kicking him into the closet with the snake.

7.  Despite the legend of early comedy directors grabbing cast and camera and chasing after fire engines, the evidence here finds a higher proportion of scenes taking place indoors than is true for the later silent films. Outdoor scenes usually made use of local city parks and streets. Direction tends to be plain and functional, and at all times is subject to the needs of the gag. In Lloyd's autobiography *An American Comedy*, Lloyd gives himself much of the credit for directing the one-reelers, especially the earliest from 1917 and the last batch from 1919. Other directors include Hal Roach, Alf Goulding and Gilbert Pratt.

Small-time stage actor and sometime extra Harold Lloyd entered silent comedy as a Chaplin imitator in 1915, as much an accident of his friendship with producer Hal Roach as anything else. He achieved minor success with a character named "Lonesome Luke." In *The Cinema Director / Luke's Movie Muddle* (1916), one of four surviving (out of 71) Lonesome Luke films, Luke runs a movie theater with Snub Pollard as the projectionist and Bebe Daniels as one of several female customers with whom Luke flirts. Luke sells a ticket, takes the ticket, ushers people to their fold-up seats very close to a full-size screen, makes sure that men take off their hats, treats men and dowagers rough, and flirts with pretty women—all very Chaplinesque. Un-Chaplinesque is Luke ordering Snub about and extended cameos for bit players such as the piano tuner and an obnoxious fellow in glasses. Lloyd's performance—the back-on-the-heels strut (sans splayed feet), the scrunched shoulders, the posture both diffident and wary, the willingness to fight suggests the startling image of a taller, lankier Charlie. It's a skillful job of mimicry, and suggests, early in Lloyd's unexpected career as a tumbledown clown, a more natural gift than he's been given credit for since.

Lloyd and Roach realized the limited potential of a Chaplin imitation, and looked about for an alternative. Douglas Fairbanks was creating a popular sensation at that time with his original blend of light comedy, acrobatics and youthful abandon, and Lloyd and

Roach adapted the Fairbanks look to Sennett-style slapstick in 1917. Their only conces-sion to traditional clown costuming was adding horn-rim glasses as a comic mask. Lloyd continued to keep an eye on Chaplin though; in *The Nonstop Kid* (1918), Harold crash-es Bebe's party disguised only by his Luke mustache. He immediately turns Chaplin, using intimate gags with just sugar, salt, coffee and a dowager.

The "glass character," as Lloyd preferred to call him, appeared in 81 one-reelers in less than two years, of which 47 survive (my source for these statistics is Tom Dardis' *Harold Lloyd: The Man on the Clock*). The 1917 movies I've seen are incomplete, stunted by lacunae that confuse gags and motivation. Some movies like *The Flirt, Bliss* and *Move On* survive as mere fragments. Nonetheless they are plainly of a piece with the other one-reel-ers. Lloyd, 24 years old in 1917, drops the name "Luke" and becomes simply The Boy, his usual billing through to *Safety Last* (1923). Snub Pollard continues the role of second banana from the *Lonesome Luke* films, and Bebe Daniels continues as The Girl.

The first movie with Harold as the new character with glasses was *Over the Fence*, released on September 9, 1917. Here he plays a tailor who sneaks into a baseball game and is mistaken for a pitcher with a very wet spitball. In the ninth inning, Harold is set to score the winning run when he spots rival Snub in the stands with Bebe. Rather than score, he races into the stands to fight him, and ends up fighting his own irate team. Here in embryo is one of Lloyd's major themes: the protection of the Loved One as a higher calling, overruling the concerns of others. A prime later example is Harold's intense race to save his girl from a bigamist in *Girl Shy* (1924).

In *By the Sad Sea Waves* (1917), Harold pretends to be a lifeguard. A unique moment in the Lloyd canon occurs when Harold disguises himself from a cop by wear-ing his glasses on the tip of his nose. In *Bashful* (1917), Bebe volunteers to play Harold's wife in a story about a bachelor who needs a family to gain an inheritance. Valet Snub completes the illusion by kidnapping a passel of babies. Harold's bashfulness is not made clear in this battered movie. As treasure hunters captured by cannibals in *Rainbow Island* (1917), Snub is fattened-up for a feast while Harold finds favor in the eyes of the chief's fat daughter. This is a weak effort but a serviceable plot, with variations to be found in *Be My King* (1928) with Lupino Lane, and several of the Hope-Crosby *Road* pictures.

In *Somewhere in Turkey* (1918) Bebe is shipwrecked in a desert land, and hauled off as a prize for the Sultan. Archaeologist Harold enters riding a camel with Snub as foot-man. Things happen and Harold rescues Bebe, so much for the plot. Laughter is stymied by "what was that?" gags, for example: Harold is thirsty so Snub collects milky camel spit into a tin can; the Sultan shakes his finger at Harold and he sucks it into his mouth; Harold kicks a stone idol aside, and sits down in its place, right on its jagged looking post; Bebe is famished, so Harold offers her an apple core. All this is not so funny as it may sound. It plays rather like a *Saturday Night Live* skit, enthusiastic but tedious.

Here we find Lloyd struggling to understand the psychology of laughter. He has creat-ed a normal looking boy for whom funny situations happen, but is having trouble invent-ing those situations. With *Somewhere in Turkey* Lloyd experimented with "fringe" humor, stretching his natural rude wit to gags verging on the shocking, or offensive. He may have found that such gagging can give a gleam of craziness to a character designed, in the abstract at least, to be "normal." Lloyd will eventually find laughs more reliably achieved through elaborate constructs of cause and effect: effects that build tension by planting expectations in an audience's mind, then releasing those tensions. The audi-ence expects Harold to lose his pants in *The Freshman* (1925), and their expectations are fulfilled. By 1925 Lloyd was able to thread gags into coherent, motivated story lines. In 1918 Lloyd found himself with a live camel, a fancy Arabian Nights set and a much smaller bag of tricks. He opted for an attempt at "Harold in Wackyland" but for Lloyd that simply meant spears in the rear and repeated hammer blows to the head.

A Coney Island setting was a great source of laughs for Lloyd; witness both *Number Please* (1920) and *Speedy* (1928). In *Why Pick On Me?* (1918) Harold is in full trickster mode: cutting in on Bebe and her wealthy boyfriend; taking funhouse tickets from Sammy; stealing ice cream from Snub and his mannish girlfriend. This last leads to a movielong rhubarb whenever Harold is not being chased by the police. Also featured is one of Lloyd's most acrobatic rallies as he employs handsprings, back-flips, high-bar maneuvers, tumbling, and a race on a circular-spinning floor to escape the police. In the end, however, he is driven from the park without the girl as bullets whiz about him. This movie contains Lloyd's possible first use of one of silent comedy's most universally used gags: the chasee runs through the open door of a car, the chaser follows, the chasee ducks out the other door and slams it shut, the car rolls off with the chaser inside.

*Ask Father* (1919) finds Harold at his most persistent and determined. He spares no effort to ask a father for his daughter's hand in marriage. Most of the movie features a single office set, across which Harold must fight his way. During the course of this amusing movie Harold briefly and confidently climbs the outside of the building. It's interesting to note that Douglas Fairbanks also climbed buildings often (and fearlessly) throughout this period: two examples are *Reaching for the Moon* (1917) and *A Modern Musketeer* (1918).

Chef Harold gets the jump on Buster Keaton with a demonstration of labor saving gadgets for the kitchen in *On the Fire / The Chef* (1919); but unlike similar Keaton gags—where the goal is speed and efficiency—Harold just doesn't like to get out of his chair. Lloyd took great pleasure in playing an arrogant lay-about blessed by a lucky star, as in *Why Worry?* (1923) and *For Heaven's Sake* (1926). But in the longer films Harold is reformed by story's end. No such change occurs here.

It is wedding day for Bebe and Harold in *I'm On My Way* (1919), but Harold is having second thoughts. Neighbor Snub invites him over to "see my happy family," which consists of his muscle-bound wife and seven children ranging from infancy to seven feet tall and 300 pounds. This is a very funny and messy movie with gooey dough and wet things. Harold cleans himself on anything available: tablecloths, other people's clothing. The cheery kids and the jolly amateur jazz band that stops by are full of good feeling, with Harold the only sourpuss. Harold has a vision of himself as a henpecked, scratched and clobbered husband. Awakening, he catches sight of Bebe appareled for wedded bliss and heads for the hills.

These brief early movies often feature impressively large casts, with ensemble horseplay encouraged. In *Next Aisle Over* (1919) the revolving door entry to a department store spins so merrily from the throng of extras that Harold, noticing a window cleaner polishing phantom glass, climbs in through the "plate glass window," a visual pun at the expense of his own set designer. Occasionally Snub or the odd bit player can be found stunting downstage while Harold is trying to perform in the center ring. But Lloyd was always ready to use any available skill: In *Next Aisle Over*, shoe salesman Harold grabs customer Snub's foot and hauls him about the shop, trying to match his selection to Snub's slapshoes. Snub manages so impressively on one free foot that he turns Harold into his straight man.

*Harold Lloyd, "settled in" with Bebe Daniels in* A Sammy in Siberia.

All this is in the style of the time, as can be seen in the comedies of Mack Sennett and Larry Semon, where one must work to pick out the star. Roscoe Arbuckle in particular was in 1919 generously sharing screen time with his sidekicks Buster Keaton and Al St. John. In the classic comedies of the 1920s, stars like Keaton and Langdon often stand alone in an empty landscape, a shift discernible in Lloyd's career as well.

Filmed in a snowbound forest, with gags improvised from found objects in the natural landscape such as a hollow log and a frozen pond, *A Sammy in Siberia* (1919) is a fanciful send-up of a current event: the misfired effort of the victorious Allies to quell the Russian Revolution. Harold, an infantryman from the Lake Shore of Chicago, is first seen relaxing in the cozy Siberian snow while his mates from California and Florida freeze. Introducing Harold in a prone or settled-in position from which he must be "jump-started" to get the action underway is a regular piece of business for Lloyd. It has the advantage of visually giving Harold some instant personality, whether cockiness, confidence, or innocence. Examples abound, including *Captain Kidd's Kids* (1919), *Haunted Spooks* (1920), and *Why Worry?*

Instead of a brash wise-guy whose good deeds, if any, come when they will, the wartime setting pushes Harold—for the first time in the surviving movies—into the unaccustomed role of Hero, able to rescue brave peasant girl Bebe, her father, and two flirtatious sisters from the Reds. Comrade Snub and his cadre of vodka-guzzling Bolsheviks are soundly thrashed by Private Harold. *Sammy* would appear to be a key work forecasting Lloyd's classic character, if upcoming movies didn't contradict this notion.

*Ring Up the Curtain* (1919) was released in April, five months before the Arbuckle-Keaton film *Back Stage*. A comparison of the two comedies reveals some interesting similarities; whether or not the Arbuckle ensemble was inspired by the Lloyd movie one can now only speculate. Both open with theatrical illusions: what seems a bedroom in *Back Stage* is broken down in moments to an empty stage, while Harold's whiskey bar folds up into a portable prop. A rare chance to directly compare Lloyd and Keaton doing the same visual gag occurs when each walks behind a waist-high barricade and drops out of sight, giving the impression of descending stairs where no steps exist. Lloyd shows special panache ascending the "stair," but Keaton's matchless body control cannot be topped. Characteristically, once an annoyed Fatty has removed the prop, Buster continues his movements, demonstrating how the trick was done. Similarly, Harold has just the faintest air of "aren't I grand" as he folds up his barrier.

Fatty and Buster play stagehands called upon to perform when the cast goes out on strike. They have trouble maintaining the illusion of the stage, comically cueing each other while performing. In *Curtain*, Harold, very much a trickster kid, volunteers to take on all back stage chores, but then ruins the show by marching on stage to flirt with Bebe; such gagging at the expense of his profession may irritate more than amuse. Both plots take surprising melodramatic turns: the muscular but winsome assistant to the Strong Man sticks with Fatty during the strike, and the jealous rival, seated in the audience to razz the strike-breakers, pulls a gun and wounds her when she appears on stage. At the end of Lloyd's movie, Bebe walks off with Snub, and Harold commits suicide by wrapping his lips around a gas outlet—a grotesque image. This is the only time he successfully commits suicide in any of his films (although there are sustained routines built around suicide attempts in *Haunted Spooks* and 1921's *Never Weaken*).

Harold often fails to win the girl in his early movies. In *Are Crooks Dishonest?* (1918) Harold and Snub are a real team for once, playing con men rooked by phony medium Bebe. In *Chop Suey and Co.* (1919), Bebe is a snooty actress, whom policemen Harold and Snub rescue from an opium den in Chinatown, only to discover that she was just there to research a role. In *Don't Shove* (1919), one of Bebe's suitors has finally had enough. He pulls a gun and bullets fly as Harold cowers behind Bebe's dress. In the two-reelers and features, Harold always gets the girl, with the singular exception of *Number Please* (1920), which features a comic parody of unhappy endings. As the film opens, lonely men stand silhouetted against tragic horizons as they struggle manfully to forget "the one girl." At the end of the film a rejected Harold has joined their company, as he's carried off by the Coney Island kiddie train.

As playful and lively as these little movies can be, it is equally true that they tend to run together in the memory. One may recall Snub's jolly family but have no idea in what movie they're featured. Generic titles like *I'm On My Way* often leave no clue to what sketchy story line they're connected. The simple but natural premise of *Spring Fever* (1919) seems ideal for a ten minute comedy, and forges an identity for itself: it's a beautiful day and office worker Harold stands pining at a window looking out at the park across the street, absent-mindedly tearing up some papers he is supposed to file. This is possibly the first use of this standard Lloyd gag, i.e. tearing the flowers in *Safety Last*, or the stranger's hat in *Number Please*. Harold finally gives in to the urge and bolts from the office, despite the efforts of his grim coworkers to muscle him back to his stool of labor. Outside at last Harold strikes a pose of Fairbanks-style exultation, before sharing his joy with the loomy denizens of the park. Walter Kerr in *The Silent Clowns* suggested that this is the movie in which Lloyd's later persona first began to replace the Luke-like rascal of his early "glass" movies. While the early office scenes do suggest this, one of Harold's first acts in the park is to dump Sammy Brooks into a trashcan. Harold stirs up a vengeful mob, meets Bebe and gets the mob's wrath redirected onto suitor Snub.

Lloyd's earliest domestic comedy is *Just Neighbors* (1919), with Harold married to Bebe, and best pal Snub and his large wife living next door. This trial run has less success with household humor than *I Do* (1921) or *Hot Water* (1924). Things start off mild with Harold eager to help Snub build a chicken coop, but soon escalate to the level of thrown bricks and vegetables and mutual strangulation. The couples finally make up after an alarming scene of a toddler playing in busy traffic. Gags based on single-minded behaviors—like blindly smashing windows and trampling flower beds in pursuit of chickens—are proven more tedious and annoying than funny.

*Never Touched Me* (1919) is a skit staged on a city sidewalk and two tightly framed interiors. It has a cast of adults set on playing children playing grown-up. But their mood is not carefree, for the cast hotly chases the spirit of fun like kids with ten minutes left before they're called home to baths and homework. Harold and a nurse in both black-face and drag kick a baby carriage back and forth, with Harold then skipping to vamp Bebe's house to join her zoo of sword-fighting mashers. When big, tough Noah Young chases him out Harold talks a washerwoman into beating Noah up for him. Harold then joins the throng at the bistro where he is mistaken for the music director for "he has the droopy eyes common to members of his class." Much foot mashing, trombone shoving, pistol-packing, old lady squashing, man-in-drag fandangoing, bop and bash hilarity ensues. Then the timer reaches ten minutes and the movie stops.

This movie then is as basic as possible, the characters, the locale, the motivation; nothing is explained, it all simply is. Somehow though, *Never Touched Me* is Lloyd's funniest one-reeler. Given the violent context, every action prompts the appropriate reaction, achieving a primeval version of the classic Lloyd gag chain. The gags may be simple, but they breeze by, nothing is prolonged, no one gag is worked to death. By contrast, the lengthy hurly-burly that results when a snake is arbitrarily set loose in the theater in *Ring Up the Curtain* just makes one sorry for the snake. The more inventive labor saving gags of *On The Fire* don't work because Harold expends more energy sitting down than he would have standing up. The inner logic of the gag breaks down, as instead of inducing spontaneous laughter the viewer is driven to ponder potential difficulties confronting a seated cook. But *Never Touched Me* has more than a unified gag scheme, it is the wacky flight of roughhouse whimsy that *Somewhere in Turkey* was meant to be.

"I'm so hungry I could eat prunes, shells and all," says Harold, a penniless trickster kid in *Count Your Change* (1919). He steals a hot dog, then has it stolen from him by a mongrel as a lengthy chase and counter-chase ensues. Chaplin's *A Dog's Life* (1918) may be a big influence here. The chase ends up at a hotel with Harold hiding in Snub's room, and the dog across the hall in Bebe's room. The second part of this eleven-minute speedster begins with Harold sharing a drink with Snub. Snub's bottle is hair tonic and a strange rally of physical agony starts with Snub dashing in a frenzy from room to room and Harold in sympathetic pain following along step for step and jump for jump. They wind up in Bebe's room where they find an insolent thief. "He's a horrid robber, a dishonest one," says Bebe. Harold sics the dog on him then pounces himself, beating up the thief, then the crowd that has gathered outside the room. This burst of Chaplinesque glee, so rare in Lloyd's work, culminates with Harold rushing back to Bebe's room, leaping on the metal bed frame, pulling Bebe to him for a kiss, falling backward to the bed, then leaping up to kiss Bebe again.

While Harold Lloyd's joyous, toothy grin serves as a signal to the audience to "watch my fun," he seldom struts with such playfulness in later films as he does here. It's a moment more common to the exuberance of Chaplin dancing and preening in disregard of the story line, leaving his co-performers to their mundane roles while he embodies the pleasure of his fans in the darkened theater. Lloyd, in his more significant films, never capers more than the story will permit.

The first "glass character" two-reeler, *Bumping into Broadway*, premiered November 2, 1919 and marks a clear change of direction from the one-reelers. The extra time available demands one of two reactions—one can either give the audience twice as much of the same thing, but on a grander scale, as is typified by the films of Lloyd's contemporary, Larry Semon; or one can expand by burrowing from within, fleshing out the boy and girl with jobs, problems and reasons to be concerned with each other. The expanded film becomes more than a romp in the park or a skit or an anecdote, it becomes a real story. Lloyd wisely chose this new direction. In *Bumping into Broadway* Bebe's character is very similar to the put-upon girl of *Count Your Change*, but now we find she's also a rather inept showgirl. The most elemental change of all finds young Harold for the first time with a compelling career goal: he wants to be a playwright. Here Bebe's problems supersede his ambitions but the great success of this film encouraged Lloyd to further develop the theme of striving for success, the driving motive of his most famous roles.

The poor kid of *Count Your Change* is back in *From Hand to Mouth* (1919), but here the kid finds poverty a tougher proposition. This Harold also faces a moral dilemma, which the one-reel tricksters never did. And while Harold is a very thoughtless character in *Get Out and Get Under* (1920), this is dictated by the film's theme: people and their obsessions—cars, gardening, the theater, giving that speedster a ticket. No, the one-reelers are different, slighting story and character, their virtues and intentions best found in an appreciation for comic anarchy. But not in the breakaway messiness of Larry Semon, or the nation-wide anarchy of *Duck Soup* (1933); for Lloyd, the world is a solid, brick-lined place. Lloyd's anarchy lies in the willfulness of the kid's character, and to varying degrees, the willfulness of the characters around him.

Moments throughout the one-reelers do predict the earnest, All-American Harold to come, as for example, the meek honky-tonk piano player mistaken for a tough hombre in the western farce *Two-Gun Gussie*, released in May 1918. It's not a good movie, the gags are mostly poor, with a throwaway romance for Bebe and no story beyond the initial premise. And yet Lloyd's performance has something of Harold wearing his father's badge in *The Kid Brother* (1927). Despite this, one month later, *Somewhere in Turkey* features Harold as the giddiest of marionettes.

This seems odd. With the examples of Fairbanks, Arbuckle and Chaplin before him, the value of creating a more consistently sympathetic character should have been plain. Perhaps he didn't feel ready. But given the evidence of 150 plus roughhouse comedies in four years it's quite possible Lloyd was more at home with slapstick anarchy.

Harold Lloyd has received some tough criticism over the years. The "glass character" has been denounced for yearning after worldly success, yet his cinematic victories are small or local ones, with future success not at all guaranteed. Compare by contrast the endings of *The Gold Rush* (1925) or *Back to the Future* (1984). Lloyd has been decried as the Joke Master, the conformist clown without pathos, rebellion or spirituality. But the real problem for the critics is that they sense, with some justification, Harold Lloyd to be a grinning, back-slapping, don't-mind-me kidder with a natural bent for practical jokes and "gotcha" gags, exactly the sort that sensitive aesthetes prefer to avoid in their daily life. It's a problem for Lloyd too, for as his career took off he felt the need to suppress his instinctive urge to kick you in the pants in deference to an ingratiating character more pleasing to the public, one who sometimes had to take blows without striking back. Lloyd changed from anti-artist to responsible artist, with a creation, no longer quite himself, to be nurtured and developed. His career seemingly became less like off-the-cuff fun and more like hard work, often involving difficult aesthetic problems and decisions. Throughout the 1920s a grand edifice of wholesome comedy was built ever higher as one crowd pleaser after another was released. Then, with a host of new problems and decisions arising from the coming of sound, the lovely facade collapses as the trickster kid returns with a vengeance in *Welcome Danger* (1929), Lloyd's first talkie, a truly career damaging film. Here, at much greater length (12 reels, compared to its silent predecessors' seven or eight), we find a thirty-ish punster with an officious voice just a note short of a whine, still kicking people in the pants, still bopping and bashing, but now with loud sound effects. As a topper, the script calls for the cast to appreciate Harold all the more for being the special person he is. Lloyd's remaining sound films are much better, but under the stress of repeat viewings, finally disappoint in comparison to the classic energy and verve of the silent features.

Still, the lovely facade was always imperfect, the more wholesome blend of slapstick fun clumped with old-fashioned roughhouse knockabout, which supplies the Lloyd paradox: audiences over time have always laughed heartily at the classic films, enjoying the stories, the characters and the spectacular gags and still not felt entirely pleased with Harold. The problem is that Harold can be mean to people, not just deserving villains and pompous asses, but also ordinary working folk. A good example of this is Harold's thievery. All the silent clowns had occasion to "borrow" things in a moment of crisis, but for Lloyd, more than the rest, it was part of the joke for the victim to know about it and come hollering, too late, after the perpetrator. Lloyd never lost the urge to "tweak" others when they weren't looking. That's fine in a ten-minute comedy where madcap marionettes play freer cut loose from story and sympathy; but it's a defect in a longer film set

*Harold Lloyd and Mildred Davis in* Grandma's Boy.

on solving the problem of blending physical comedy with a strong empathy for its boy and girl. Many films have tried and failed. Harold Lloyd mostly succeeded, many times. Most artists, after all, have foibles. Shakespeare couldn't resist punning in the climactic scene of *Hamlet*, Dante took a few lines to complain about backcountry hillbillies in *The Divine Comedy*. Big hearted, regular guy Harold Lloyd preferred that his shadow-self stand free of guilt. After all, no matter what damage he has done he means you no real harm and knows everything will work out for the best. The one exception in Lloyd's work is the scene in *Grandma's Boy* (1922) in which Harold is called upon to join the posse searching for the murderous tramp, but instead runs home to hide in his bed. In the morning he has to confront his guilty conscience. Perhaps this is why Lloyd felt so strongly about this film, his first great feature. He felt it was his best work. For once he studied his material from the point of view of the artist anxious to make a statement, puzzling over issues beyond the pale of his normal way of thought.

## Works Cited

Tom Dardis, *Harold Lloyd: The Man on the Clock* (New York: The Viking Press, 1983).

Walter Kerr, *The Silent Clowns* (New York: Alfred A. Knopf, 1975).

Harold Lloyd and W.W. Stout, *An American Comedy* (New York: Longmans, Green & Co., 1928. Expanded edition, New York: Dover Publications, 1971).

# The Three Stooges and the *Commedia dell' Arte*

## Kathleen Chamberlain (2001)

An elderly, not-too-attractive man leers and grins at a quite attractive young girl. He raises his eyebrows, whispers sweet nothings, keeps trying to stand closer and closer to her. But the young girl rejects him—she loves a younger, handsomer man. The old man persists. Suddenly, in come some servants who try to protect the girl. One servant, who seems to be in charge, pushes the others about and trades insults with the old man, finally bopping him on the head with a stick that makes quite a satisfying bang. Another servant, less sharp than the first, an innocent sort of fool, tries to bop the old man, too. But he trips, falling into the first servant, who falls into the girl, who falls into the old man. In no time, all are involved in a riotous, splendidly noisy chase.

Almost any fan of the Three Stooges will be certain that s/he recognizes this short. Surely it featured Vernon Dent as the old man. And Christine McIntyre as the girl. The innocent fool in the chase scene was Curly, of course. *Three Dumb Clucks* is the title. Or is it *In the Sweet Pie and Pie*?

Actually, the scene comes from the *commedia dell' arte*, the Italian Renaissance form of comedy that represents one of Italy's main contributions to the development of Western drama. Playwrights and comedians from Shakespeare to Molière to Chaplin show the influence of the *commedia's* unique improvisational blend of farce, burlesque, slapstick, mime, acrobatics, and wit. The comedy of the Three Stooges bears strong traces of this powerfully farcical style.

The *commedia dell' arte* flourished in western Europe and England from the mid-1500s through the mid-1700s, although by the eighteenth century, the form had seen many changes. Drama historians often distinguish between two broad categories of Italian Renaissance drama: the *commedia erudita*, or learned court drama; and the *commedia dell' arte*, or popular, improvised theatre that appealed to all social levels, especially the common people.

The term *commedia dell' arte* means "comedy performed by professionals of the art," indicating the high level of physical and verbal skill required of the performers. *Commedia* troupes, some attaining great fame and popularity, toured throughout Europe during the two hundred or so years of the form's life. The *commedia's* performances were distinctly non-literary; the troupes worked not from prepared scripts but from sketchy "scenarios" that were tacked up behind the scenes and that merely described character relationships and the order of entrances. Everything else—movements, dialogue, speeches, plot—was improvised.

Obviously, to make a success of such a form, the actors had to be quick-witted and skilled; their improvisations had to be immediate, smooth, and above all, funny. They would spend years honing particular characters and bits of business; each performer acted only one part for his or her entire career. Plot was of little importance to the *commedia*. The stories usually centered around comic cuckoldings, mistaken identities, and

**53**

young love, but the real focus was on individual characters and on the expected repetitions of comic "business" called *lazzi*—physical tricks, movements, and gestures associated with a given part. Some of the power of the *commedia dell' arte* came from this repetition of *lazzi*. As one critic has noted, "even if the general story were different, the same comic situations came up over and over again. The audience waited to see how the actor would pull off the trick this time" (Kernodle, 401).

Each acting troupe, then, had its own versions of the *commedia* stock characters. Though a given company or performance might contain over a dozen skilled players, the same basic characters were always present. Among those most relevant to the Three Stooges were Pantalone, an elderly man who was often a lecher or cuckold; the equally elderly, pedantic *dottore*, or learned professor; the bragging but cowardly *capitano*; one or more pairs of young lovers; and at least two *zanni*, or servants, one of whom was often presented as sharp and quick-witted, the other as a rustic innocent or fool. These stock characters, with their accompanying identifying comic business and precise movements, form what is probably the most durable contribution of the *commedia dell' arte* to comedy in general.

*Moe, Curly, and Larry in* Healthy, Wealthy, and Dumb: *"As 'low' characters, they are brash, loud and vulgar."*

The character Pantalone, who represents authority, behaves with a pompous dignity that invariably becomes the target of the *zanni's* jokes. The *zanni* are often the most active characters, responsible for innumerable plot complications. As "low" characters, they are brash, loud, and vulgar; they puncture the pretensions of their so-called "betters"; they upend the expected social order. The most famous of the *zanni* roles is the one that developed into Harlequin, a character whose dark mask suggested mystery and deviltry, but whose brightly-colored, patched clothing suggested a poor but cheerful outsider. This character usually carried a flat wooden stick (originally a symbolic phallus) with which he would beat and slap the other characters, hence the term "slapstick." By the eighteenth century, Harlequin had become a gentler, more charming character than he had been earlier. Still, he served as a puncturer of pomposity, a never-absent reminder of human foolishness.

With the exception of the young lovers, all the characters wore stylized masks that covered at least half of their faces. Because the actors could thus not rely on their facial expressions for comedy or emotion, they had to develop gestures and movements as substitutes. The result was an emphasis on mime and acrobatics. Each actor would develop personal trademark gags or actions, those bits of business known as *lazzi*. Although to modern audiences, the masks might seem unnecessarily limiting, they actually helped provide the intensity, directness, and simplicity that farcical comedy requires. The masks not only made each character "type" immediately recognizable to audiences, but they also prevented the development of anything resembling realistic behavior. The result was a rollicking, fast-paced, surreal universe that constantly reminded viewers of the absurdity of what they saw and, by extension, the absurdity of the human foibles portrayed on the stage.

The Three Stooges' humor is typical of the farce associated with the *commedia dell' arte*, as this description of the *commedia* by theatre historian George Kernodle makes clear:

> The wildest kind of physical action was the rule. Some actors specialized in falls on the mouth, the back, the head. Bones were sometimes broken, but many *commedia* actors, among the most agile acrobats of history, kept the pace for years . . . . For other effects, trick doors, trap doors, [and] collapsible furniture added surprise upon surprise . . . . The *commedia* made the fullest use of the technical patterns of farce—quick changes of speed and rhythm; patterned movements with people moving in unison, or imitation; turns and counter-turns; and repetition, with various characters falling over or hitting the same person . . . . When everything clicked and the timing was right, the group gave a whirlwind sequence and climax that kept the audience roaring. (401)

The Three Stooges' comedy parallels this definition almost exactly. Perhaps most obviously, the Stooges demonstrate the physical agility common to *commedia* actors, their many "falls on the mouth, the back, the head" indicating both their abilities and the fine line that farce maintains between surrealism and actual pain. On-screen, no one receives lasting injuries, although the powerful physicality allows the comedy at least to suggest the reality of pain under the fast-paced, consequence-free surface. Off screen, however, the Stooges faced their share of wounds. "Bones were broken," writes Kernodle of the *commedia* players, and the same applies to the Stooges. *Pardon My Scotch* (1935) contains a gag in which Moe stands on a table which Curly inadvertently slices with a power saw. Moe's first movement brings the table crashing down. When the scene was shot, Moe's full-body slide to the floor resulted in broken ribs.

The "wildest kind of physical action" is present in almost every short: pie fights, clay fights, chases through wet cement, madly rolling beer barrels, football field anarchy. The action is never merely unstructured mayhem, however. Each sequence builds, adding to and modifying the basic business so that the scene moves toward a comic climax. The massive clay fight in *Pop Goes the Easel* (1935) provides a typical example. The fight, which takes place in an art studio, begins simply, with one person throwing clay in the face of another. Since a straight back-and-forth throwing contest would become tedious, variations are quickly introduced. One person ducks the clay thrown at him so that it hits another. Curly stands laughing at this sight, and is caught unawares by the glob of clay that hits his own face. The violence escalates. In the next step, a lump of clay hits a plaster bust, sending the bust crashing onto the head of the hapless artist below. Gender and class receive their usual debunking: clay hits a well-dressed woman and a top-hatted man. Finally, the camera pulls back to show the entire art studio engulfed in a melee of clay-throwing.

The structure of the Stooges' physical gags reflects Kernodle's description of "the technical patterns of farce" that were part of the *commedia*: "quick changes of speed and rhythm, patterned movements with people moving in unison or imitation, turns and counterturns, [and] repetition, with various characters falling over or hitting the same person." These patterns allow the comedy to build from the plausible to the surrealistically implausible. Not only is the build-up funny, but the development of the scenes also traces for the audience the direct connection between the real and farcical worlds. In *Calling All Curs* (1939), for example, Curly tries to get soap out of a stubborn dispenser. The "turn" of the gag is that he accidentally shoots soap in Moe's eye, a funny but not impossible scenario. The "counterturn," however, begins to move away from surface realism. Moe returns the initial gesture, sending a stream of soap down Curly's throat. Curly follows this reversal with the build-up: he drinks water, accompanied by hyperbolic "glug-glug" sound effects, which results in his blowing a series of soap bubbles from his mouth. Unlikely? Certainly. But because it has grown from a believable situation, the humor maintains the audience's human link to the characters.

In addition to the structure of individual gags, the Three Stooges are connected to the *commedia dell' arte* through the larger structures of plot. Though plot is not nearly so important as the comic business or *lazzi*, the typical plots of the *commedia*, such as mistaken identity, frequently appear in the shorts. In the Stooges' comedies, mistakes abound in both identity and "soicumstance": in some of the most belief-stretching errors of all time, the boys are mistaken for detectives in *Phony Express* (1943), ace football players in *Three Little Pigskins* (1934), professional escorts in *Termites of 1938*, movie experts in *Movie Maniacs* (1936), sailors (with Curly as the Admiral) in *Three Little Sew and Sews* (1939), psychiatrists in *Three Sappy People* (1939), and even professors at a women's school in *Violent is the Word for Curly* (1938). Plots also often involve the Stooges' elaborate (and usually failed) con schemes, jealous husbands, angry fathers, sweet young lovers, sweet babies, sweet ingenues—all stocks-in-trade of the *commedia dell' arte*.

A great many of the Stooges' gags also depended on the improvisation that was the staple of the *commedia*. Director Edward Bernds, who worked with the Stooges from Curly's final years in the mid-1940s through the Shemp years of the early 1950s, described the genesis of the Stooge shorts on which he worked: "We'd usually have kind of a bull session in which the boys would wander all over the place, ad-libbing, reminiscing, and I would make notes . . . . I would stockpile routines, devise a sort of framework for them to hang on to" (Maltin, 128). Though the complicated gags meant that the Stooges did finally work from a detailed script, they still had room for the impromptu during filming. Bernds explains that "we often let routines run, in the hope of getting unrehearsed, spontaneous ad-lib comedy we could use" (Okuda, 31). Shemp and Curly were particularly adept at ad-libbing. Bernds says, "Shemp was an instinctive actor, a great improviser. Many times when I was directing him, I would actually delay cutting a scene just to see what he would do" (Okuda, 69). Jules White, Columbia Pictures' long-time Stooge director who originally hired the team, said much the same of Curly: "If we wrote a scene and needed a little something extra, I'd say to Curly, 'Look, we've got to fill this in with a "woo-woo" or some other bit of business.' And he never disappointed us" (Okuda, 63).

This improvisational skill goes back to the boys' vaudeville days; in his autobiography, Moe described how Shemp's initial appearance with the Healy act arose spontaneously after Moe, on stage, heard Shemp laughing out in the audience (35). This ability to improvise successfully did for the Stooges what it must also have done for the *commedia dell' arte*: the boys developed an almost instinctive reaction to each other's characters, leading to inspired, precise, and smooth comic business.

The boys' characters suggest another link between the Stooges and the *commedia*. It's unlikely that the *commedia dell' arte* featured zanier *zanni* than Moe, Curly, Larry, and Shemp. As in the *commedia*, the Stooges' basic parts never vary. Curly is Curly, whether he's cast as a sheriff, a plumber, a matador, a Civil War spy, a pawnbroker, a greeting-card salesman, or Madame Cucaracha the opera singer. Moe is clearly the Stooge version of the mentally sharp *zanni*. Though not as devilish as the early Harlequin, Moe is the brainy one (or at least as brainy as the Three Stooges ever get.) He's the leader, the thinker, the purveyor of his own inimitable versions of slapstick beatings. Curly, Larry, and Shemp play variations on the innocent fool whose very foolishness is sometimes smarter than the intellectual's intellect. And all the Stooges qualify as "common men," ones who end up reducing the rich, the snobbish, the smart, and the arty to the lowest common denominator. Just as there are no atheists in foxholes, there are no snobs with a pie in the face.

Though the Three Stooges don't wear actual masks, their typical "look" offers a modern version of the mask that serves the same purposes. Moe's bangs and perpetual sneer, Curly's too-small clothes and billiard-ball head, Larry's wild curls, Shemp's greasy, ever-mobile hair—these trademarks serve immediately to identify the boys as types and to provide the intensity, extremity, and simplicity that is essential to farce. The audience remains distanced, removed from that sort of emotional identification that can destroy the tone of farce. (Other great farcical comics achieve similar effects with their own costumes and business: Buster Keaton's deadpan stare; Harold Lloyd's inescapable spectacles; even the Keystone Kops' uniforms keep the audience emotionally distanced and more receptive to whatever level of satire the comedy may offer.)

As far as bits of business, or *lazzi*, are concerned, many of the Stooges' trademark gestures and responses have become cultural icons. Curly is responsible for the most immediately recognizable ones. Even people who are not fans are usually familiar with Curly's little screams of frustration, his rapid slapping of his face, his habit of jerking his hand before Moe's eyes; his inimitable sounds (usually transcribed as "nyuk-nyuk," "wub-

wub," and "lahni"), and his comic pronunciations, most notably in "victim of soicum-stance" and "soitenly." The others make notable contributions as well: Moe's infamous eye-pokes, Shemp's squeaky screeches, the boys' perfectly-timed double-takes, etc.

The shorts contain what might be called "plot lazzi" as well. For instance, a surpris-ing number of Stooge shorts contain an explosion of some sort. A car blows up in *Violent is the Word for Curly*; a gas-filled cake explodes in *An Ache in Every Stake* (1941); a keg of bootleg liquor goes sky-high in *Pardon My Scotch*. On the one hand, the explosions often serve merely as a convenient way to end a short that has too minimal a plot to be brought to any logical conclusion. On another level, however, these explosion scenes show how the Stooges' comedy suspends the laws of logical cause-and-effect. Because potential catastrophes turn into just one more gag, the Stooges' violence is stylized, stripped of its power and meaning. The result is a surrealism that allows the boys to be both funny and, in their own way, triumphant.

Clearly, the *zanni* element of the Stooges' characterizations can be demonstrated fairly easily. But the shorts did not lack the other characters typical of the *commedia dell' arte*. Vernon Dent and Bud Jamison, one or the other of whom appeared in every Three Stooges short from their Columbia debut in 1934 until their final episode in 1959, often functioned as the perfect Pantalone type, the stuffed-shirt stripped of authority by the anarchic *zanni*. Over the years, Dent and Jamison occupied any number of positions of social responsibility that were invariably diminished: they were policemen who ended up face down in whitewash or mired in wet cement; top-hatted gents who found them-selves on the wrong end of pies and cakes; and hotel detectives who got ink shot into their faces ("I dotted his eye!" chortles Curly about an ink-spattered Jamison in *Healthy, Wealthy, and Dumb*).

Ultimately, the Stooges' comedy, like the farce of the *commedia dell' arte*, depends on incongruity and on breathless, fast-paced movement that builds to a grand climax of total chaos. The incongruity needs little explanation: One needs only envision Moe as Hitler, Larry as a professor, Curly as a participant in a cow-milking contest, or really, any of the boys as anything that has its counterpart in normal life. As the Stooges themselves said in the short *You Nazty Spy* (1940), "Any resemblance between the characters in this pic-ture and any persons, living or dead, is a miracle." The fast-paced, precise movement is the result of years of working together as a team, so that even in the mid-1940s, when Curly's timing is noticeably off, the act still works.

Like that of the *commedia*, the world of the Stooges is simplified. The boys' needs are usually basic—food and shelter in the Depression-era shorts, escape from physical threats, a way (legal or otherwise) to make a living. However wacky, the Stooges, like the *zanni* of the *commedia*, represent the working-class person who so often finds him/herself without social or political power. When they find themselves in social or professional sit-uations that threaten to overwhelm the common man, they respond the only way they can and still survive without losing their identities by being either outcast or assimilat-ed—they give "society" a pie in the eye and a kick in the pants. By simply refusing to accept the standards of the professional or upper classes, they can assert their own power, even if only momentarily.

The surrealism of the Stooges' world adds immeasurably to both their comedy and to their satire. Because the Big Three never pretend to be ruled by the same forces of nature that govern the rest of us, audiences have no trouble accepting anything they do. Thus viewers become receptive to their social satire, which, in keeping with their brand of humor, is rarely profound even at its most overtly political (as in the Nazi spoofs *You Nazty Spy* and *I'll Never Heil Again* [1941]). Like the *commedia*, most of the satire validates the ordinary person's perspective. Through the Stooges, we can see pretension punctured, dignity dumped, and the upper-classes upended. The Three Stooges create a delightfully zany chaos that reminds viewers that total Stooge-like anarchy is never far below the surface of anything we might choose to call "civilization." We may think we're dignified and in control, but like Curly, we're all just "victims of soicumstance" who will triumph nonetheless.

## Works Cited

Moe Howard, *Moe Howard and the Three Stooges* (Secaucus, NJ: Citadel Press, 1977).

George Kernodle, *The Theatre in History* (Fayetteville: University of Arkansas Press, 1989).

Leonard Maltin, *The Great Movie Shorts* (New York: Bonanza, 1972).

Ted Okuda with Edward Watz, *The Columbia Comedy Shorts: Two-Reel Hollywood Film Comedies, 1933-1958* (Jefferson, NC: McFarland, 1986).

## Works Consulted

Maurice Charney, *Comedy High and Low* (New York: Peter Lang, 1987).

Kenneth Richards and Laura Richards, *The* Commedia dell' Arte: *a Documentary History* (London: Basil Blackwell, 1990).

Walter Sorrell, *Facets of Comedy* (New York: Grosset & Dunlap, 1972).

# Laurel and Hardy

## Charles Barr (1968)

Arthur C. Clarke has a short story called *Expedition To Earth* in which beings from Venus discover, on a long-dead Earth, a single can of film. Their scientists devise a machine to project it; historians and psychologists study the film and inaugurate a program of research into this relic of a civilization of which they have hitherto known nothing.

> For the rest of time it would symbolize the human race. . . . Thousands of books would be written about it. Millions of times in the ages to come those last few words would flash across the screen:
>
> A Walt Disney Production

End of story—and one should point out that this was before Disney moved away from cartoons, so it is Donald Duck on screen, not Hayley Mills.

To some, the irony might seem no less if it were a Laurel and Hardy film, yet I am not sure that, in the pleasant game of picking one film suitable to teach aliens about the human race, I would not choose a Laurel and Hardy short. They are the most universal of comics, in range as in appeal, and how can one understand Man without understanding his humor? It is not only that such films as *Scram*, *The Music Box* and *Big Business* actually show laughter as well as arousing it, but that they give us in so clear a form so much of the human condition: pain and joy, authority and subversion, aspiration and disaster, generosity and ill-will, with the directness of allegory. Indeed, all these forces are located in Laurel and Hardy themselves. Hardy never for long ceases to be subservient to authority even when he undermines it, nor to be shocked by violence even when himself exercising it. They are supreme liberators from bourgeois inhibitions, yet essentially they are, or aspire to be, respectable bourgeois citizens. For all the appealing predictability in their films, their feelings and attitudes are not yet hardened to a crust but preserve the fluidity, the "overlapping" quality, the moment-to-moment inconsistencies of childhood. This is why they can play so many different roles, householders and vagrants, criminals and policemen, without undergoing change. Their "Everyman" quality helps to explain the universality of their appeal. It is safe to say that no-one in films has been loved so universally and for so long as Laurel and Hardy. They still seem to be the first comedians to attract children, and the last of whom adults tire; for all the (perhaps merciful) contempt shown for them by many intellectuals, they have never lost their popularity, even while, after 1940, they were turning out inferior films. Their work is still revived successfully on television, and one need only start to project a Laurel and Hardy for an audience, whether of children, film technicians, schoolmasters, anyone, to accumulate as if from nowhere.

Their very "elementality" makes it hard to write of them without being ponderous, trying to reduce to manageable formulae the irreducible. The critic finds himself in the position of the policeman in *Big Business*, who arrives, with notebook, in the middle of a war between James Finlayson on the one hand and Laurel and Hardy on the other. He is

*"The most universal of comics."*

systematically destroying their car while they destroy his house. Through most of the picture, each side acts alternately while the other looks on with cool interest at the destruction, not trying to intervene. What can one report about such a scene, at once monstrously unrealistic and psychologically profound? There is a marvelous discrepancy between the actors' continued activity and the policeman's immobility (to which we return in cut-away shots), and between the inexorable progression of their work and the occasional convulsive notes he is moved to write—as if any one of their acts of destruction were more shocking than the rest. The notebook cannot order the scene, nor can he cope with them when finally he intervenes: as they mime their explanations to him, Laurel and Hardy burst into tears, and these tears infect in succession Finlayson, the policeman, and the spectators. With everyone now committed to a very moral lament for these anti-social happenings, Hardy nudges Laurel and they both laugh. The policeman sees them and gives chase. The cigar which Laurel has given Finlayson as a peace offering explodes in his face. Tears, laughter, anger are given their purest, irreducible form, and the film is as good as a documentary about them, apart from everything else that it is. What better film to preserve for the Venusians ?

# The Gag Man

## Frank Capra (1927)

The gag man is the newest institution of the motion picture studios. So new is he, in fact, that his fame—if such it is to be—has not yet reached the public, and his efforts, which are a large and essential contribution to practically every production, are unrecognized by the millions whom they entertain.

The gag man is the expert in humor—visual humor—who creates laughs where there were no laughs before. He relieves the tension of the sternest drama with a humorous incident; he carries forward the development of a plot with a series of comedy episodes that replace what would otherwise be dull, though essential, sequences. He is the apt story teller, who uses action, rather than words, as his medium.

Gag men, though it is only recently that they have been recognized as such, have been important factors in motion picture productions since the birth of the art. Formerly, every studio worker—the star, supporting players, directors, scenario writers, title writers and others—contributed to the construction of the gags. Within the last few years, a few of these impromptu fun-makers, realizing that their natural aptitude for gagging made them more valuable to producers in this work than in their previous fields, became specialists. And, so, the gag man was born.

The field of the gag man—this newly conceived specialist—was, at first, limited to comedy production. Gag men, rather than writers, or, better, writers who were also gag men, were the scenarists at the Sennett, Roach and Christie studios. Their method of working differs with the varying policies of the several producers. Usually, however, an initial conference is held for the purpose of outlining a simple, skeleton plot, which is essentially humorous in its conception. With this plot as a basis, the gag men work collectively to develop the comedy incidents that work in smoothly with the running narrative of the story. Further conferences between the gag men and the director result in the elimination of many of the gags that are not generally accepted as feasible.

The original story is then adjusted, as may be necessary to fit the selected gags, and these are developed and polished by the combined efforts of the staff. In the production of comedies, to which this immediate discussion is confined, it is usual for one or more gag men to be active on the set throughout the making of the picture. His purpose, obviously, is to co-operate with the director in the staging of the gags and to suggest such new ones as may occur to him as the story is developed.

The recognition of gag men, as such, by comedy producers soon became general with the development of the system that is outlined above. The importance of his work was appreciated is to such an extent that it was not unusual to reverse the general order of story preparation and work out plots to embody series of gags which had been worked out independently. Gag men—still continuing their all-important work of gagging—became comedy scenarists and directors. And, what is more important, the term, "gag man," attained a definite standing in the industry.

Producers of feature productions—dramas or, so-called, comedy-dramas of five reels or more—had been for years making what they now recognize as unreasonable demands

*Gags by Capra: Harry Langdon at the Mack Sennett Studio, circa 1925, where Frank Capra, gag man, helped create his persona.*

on their scenario writers. Every director and every production executive demanded "comedy relief," and this comedy relief, all too often, was not forthcoming. Your comedian, whether he be a clown, a monologist or a gag man, is a specialist, and it is not to be expected that a man who has trained himself in the intricacies of photoplay writing should be able to qualify as equally proficient in gag construction.

The failure, a perfectly natural failure, of the scenario writer in a field outside his own

*"A chance to display your talents": Langdon gets the drop on Vernon Dent in* All Night Long.

opened new precincts to the gag man. His advent in feature production was, at first, in the nature of an experiment. His ready adaptability proved his worth and showed beyond a doubt that he can be a constructive influence in the making of every type of photoplay.

There is a general demand for gag men today. No good gag man is out of work. Unlike almost every other studio worker, he may be busy fifty-two weeks of every year. He has no "vacations" between pictures, because he is needed by every studio for every picture. He does not have to wait until his type of production is being made, because there are very few types of photoplay that do not require his constructive services.

The great need for gag men today has made the field an open one. I do not mean that anyone may become a gag man, but I do know that the qualified man, outside the industry, has a better opportunity of breaking in as a gag man than as a worker in, any other production capacity. If you are confident that you have the ability to create gags, the Mack Sennett studios, the Hal Roach studios and many others will possibly give you a chance to display your talents.

Untrained, inexperienced men who can convince others of some initial comedy ability are accepted regularly by these studios for, perhaps, a four weeks' trial at about one hundred dollars a week. If their first efforts show any promise at all, they will be retained on the studio staffs, advancing in salary and position as rapidly as their aptitude warrants.

There is a limit, of course, to the potential earnings of the gag man, but the limit is high enough to make the goal an end in itself. No gag man earns less than one hundred dollars weekly, and several earn ten times as much, which is, perhaps, the limit. In considering the opportunities of the gag man, or his limits, it is well, however, to bear in mind that he will usually earn his salary, whatever it is, every week of the year.

Many gag men have gained public recognition as directors and scenario writers. These two fields, which may prove more highly remunerative in weekly salaries, are open to established gag men. From gag man to scenario writer or director—I have chosen the latter—is a natural step and, quite often, an advisable one. It seems, however, that it would be decidedly inadvisable under any circumstances for a person to lose his identity as a gag man since—I repeat because it is so important—in no other branch of the profession is the supply of talent so much less than the demand.

No specific training can be suggested to one who aspires to a career as a gag man. The essential qualifications are a matter of natural aptitude or innate talent; they cannot be acquired through any amount of study or practice. Many factors may contribute to the development of your talent, but the talent, itself, cannot be taught.

A general education or, for that matter, any type of technical education, is not essential to a gag man. But the value of education as a broadening influence is beyond estimate in any work, and it is an interesting fact that college graduates predominate among the new-comers in the studios. This, of course, is, to a large degree, a reflection of the fact that the man of education has the first call in every business and profession.

Short story writers, playwrights and newspaper columnists comprise the majority of the gag men. Many of these, attracting attention in their former work, have been sought after by motion picture producers. Their training in these other fields undoubtedly enhanced their value as gag men, just as working as a gag man will make one a better gag man. Their experience, however, did not qualify them as gag men; rather, the abilities that establish them in other fields qualified them, also, for comedy construction.

An obvious question that will be in your mind as you read this is: Is there some minor studio job I can take as a stepping stone to gagging? Definitely, the answer is no. There is no place for untrained workers in motion picture production—no place, that is, except among the gag men, who offer talent instead of experience. Every studio worker is a highly trained specialist, The carpenters and electricians, for example, are specialists within their own trades, attending duties for which average carpenters and electricians would be incompetent.

If there is any short cut to fame and fortune in motion pictures, it is as a gag man. Here you may jump to the top overnight, after the short probationary period, which is long enough to show you whether you have the stuff that makes gag men.

—*Breaking Into the Movies*, edited by Charles Reed Jones (1927)

# The Gag Man: Being a Discourse on Al Boasberg, Professional Jokesmith, his Manner, and Method

**Ben Schwartz** (2001)

*Al Boasberg.*

*Courtesy of the Academy of Motion Pictures Arts and Sciences.*

On June 16, 1937, Jack Benny handed Al Boasberg the Golden Contract. Years later, as its legend grew, writers would marvel that Jack Benny had paid Al Boasberg $1,000 for a single joke.

That wasn't quite true. But then, the truth was even better: It was $1,500. "All he'd have to do was look at what we had written and if he thought it was fine he didn't have to write a word," Benny recalled, "but either way, I paid him."

Benny paid $1,500 a week then—for an *opinion*. And why not? Besides his work on Benny's number-one rated radio show, Boasberg had also written MGM's biggest comedy of the year, the Marx Brothers' *A Day at the Races* (1937). And to Marx insiders, his scripting on A *Night at the Opera* (1935) and *Races* had saved their career. And if you hadn't heard that from them, Boasberg would no doubt tell you himself.

Benny knew Boasberg's talent and wasn't about to lose him. The 1936-37 season that Boasberg supervised had proven to be the pivotal year in the Benny show's history, estab-

**68**

lishing both its ratings dominance and its creative peak. And Benny paid off, handing his gag man as cush a job as anyone ever had in Depression-era America.

For Boasberg, the Benny deal capped fourteen years of work, from 1923-1937, for a writer who altered the shape and substance of American humor more than any other of his generation. Vaudevillians knew Boasberg as the comedy guru who "made" the careers of not only Benny, but also George Burns, Gracie Allen, and Bob Hope. He created the characters they played for decades. Besides his Marx Brothers hits, Boasberg had also co-written Buster Keaton's *Battling Butler* (1926) and Keaton's masterpiece, *The General* (1926), as well as the *guignol* classic *Freaks* (1932) and nearly forty others. By 1932, his annual income neared $75,000. By the time Benny put that contract in front of him it soared to $100,000, or well over $1,000,000 in year 2000 cash.

The comics loved trading stories about him. Physically the laziest man anyone ever knew, he had electric doggie doors built in his house, a glow-in-the-dark clock in the ceiling over his bed, and an ice water spout at his nightstand—all to ensure he never had to get up for the dog, the time, or a glass of water.

A bulky six-footer, Boasberg's penchant for writing in the bathtub (due to a heat sensitive condition) was legendary. Using a custom-made writing board placed over the tub, he'd soak for hours and then call junior writers in to give them notes. "It was like having a conference with a U-boat," recalled Robert Pirosh.

Bob Hope stood in slack-jawed awe of this endless fount of one-liners. "I considered him," said Benny, "perhaps the greatest gag man who ever lived." Groucho Marx thought Boasberg simply the funniest man he ever knew.

But for all this, Al Boasberg remained, if anything, a vague, backstage figure to the public, a fact that ate at him endlessly. After all, unlike playwrights or novelists, gag men are not the writers critics canonize. They write jokes, bits, one-liners—not masterpieces easily recognized. If the gag man does his job well, he remains invisible, tailoring the material to the comic, to the performer's personal style. And this gag man did his job better than anyone.

And as Boasberg looked over his Golden Contract, the deal other jokers drooled over, he also knew it was the final failure in a career full of them. But this, this was the Golden One. The one that proved him a failure once and for all. And so he signed.

That night, at one-thirty a.m., Al Boasberg woke up complaining of chest pains. He took a few steps from his bed and then fell dead of a heart attack. He was forty-five years old.

Albert Isaac Boasberg was born December 5, 1891, in Buffalo, New York, third child of Herman and Hattie Boasberg of 119 Highland Avenue.[1] Although many of Al's famous clients were born to poverty on Manhattan's Lower East Side, the Boasbergs were middle class Dutch Jews, in America since before the Civil War. Herman ran a jewelry store and Al Boasberg's uncle, Emmanuel "Manny" Boasberg, was one of the richest men in town, a millionaire from his Keiser & Boasberg tobacco firm.

Boasberg had two older siblings and an infant sister, Phyllis (his only true friend and confidant in life). He had an unremarkable childhood until 1902, when his mother died. Overnight, family life dissolved. Unable to care for all four children, Herman sent the older kids to school while the baby was raised by cousins. With Herman working late nights, his eleven-year-old was left a lonely, isolated boy. "He was pretty much on his own," says Jim Michaels, Boasberg's nephew, "When your mother dies and your father doesn't pay much attention to you, you don't have a home life. Not being particularly attractive or good in school—he was lazy, never athletic—he was pretty much alone."

What emerged was a boy starved for attention who found that a sense of humor was the way to get it. A class clown, he made prank calls (waking neighbors at four a.m. to ask the time) and played practical jokes. Friends remember him incapable of answering a question with a straight answer. Even when he tried to be serious it had some twist. Like the time his teacher asked a boy next to him how many of his twelve German translations he finished. "One," said the boy, who was spanked. When she came to Boasberg, who had only done one himself, she asked how many he had completed. "All but eleven," he responded. Her laugh saved him and taught him early on that a quick wit had its rewards.

But not everyone found his jokes so funny. One morning, Boasberg's high school principal Frederick Vogt arrived at work to find crowds of men waiting for him, all answering an ad for 500 Italian laborers needed to tear down the school. When Vogt discovered Boasberg as the culprit he expelled him on the spot. The family plied Uncle Manny's political influence at City Hall, but Vogt stood firm. "If Al Boasberg comes back, I go," he told them. A compromise was reached and Boasberg was, as he liked to say, "graduated early."

While cousins went off to expensive schools, Jim Michaels recalls that the family saw Boasberg as "pretty much a nebbish." He took part-time sales jobs, selling everything from Herman's jewels to ties, cars, tires, and sheet music. "He was a hell of a salesman," says Michaels, "but as soon as he got some money together he'd quit and lay off for six months."

A lonely teen with time to kill, he hung out at the vaude houses, the school for fools, soaking up every act he could. The vaudeville of his youth, 1900-1918, shone as the golden age of character and physical comedy. "Character" then meant garishly costumed baggy-pants humor: blackface minstrels, tramps, rubes, Italians, Jews. All were stereotypes easily recognizable to audiences and thus easy targets for jokes, best seen today in the work of Chico Marx. W.C. Fields and Chaplin (on film) played tramps in this period.

Physical acts broke down into their own categories: nuts, bone crunchers, acrobats, knockabouts, pantomimes. Fans saw knockabout child star Buster Keaton hurled at walls by his father Joe. Or the husband and wife "nut act" Hickey and Nelson, who entered in eighteen-inch clam-shaped shoes, handy because at some point Mrs. Nelson kicked a hat off a chair onto her husband's head. Later, Mr. Hickey hung from those shoes off the stage rail as she hauled him up by his pants, leaving him in his longjohns. Though artfully and precisely performed, it was broad, obvious humor at best.

Boasberg devoured it all, memorizing acts and their nuances the way other kids knew Ty Cobb box scores. At twelve he wrote and performed his own minstrel act with a friend (losing their salary when they ruined the family linen with their burnt cork makeup) and when *Variety* ran a "What Is Ideal Vaudeville Bill?" reader contest, Boasberg entered and won. And all the while, he nursed a dream of writing his own musical comedy on Broadway. Love of show business and his own clowning meant he'd find a way to a stage sooner or later, and he made his professional debut in a traveling comedy sketch called "Love in the Suburbs."

The experience of "Love in the Suburbs" stuck with Boasberg all his life. After watching all those acts and just knowing he could do it, too, Boasberg finally wrangled a minor but crucial role in a sketch. His one-line, one-word walk-on came at the comic finale as everyone on stage awaited the arrival of a fearsome visitor. As suspense mounted, they heard a knock at the door. Everyone screamed and hid as Boasberg, playing an ice man, entered, and delivered his line: "Ice!"

And yet, Boasberg was soon out of the show. Reflecting on his one-word part years later, Buffalo's laziest son said acting was too much work. So he quit.

That was the joke version, but after seeing the show Herman offered to double his son's weekly salary not to play Buffalo. And for a young man so close to a dream and as hungry for laughs as Boasberg, it's doubtful he actually quit from exhaustion. If his acting in *Battling Butler* or his other films indicates anything, it's that the zero-range, stone-faced amateur had little talent for it.

After all those years in the house seats, to be told to stay there must have hurt. The incident—a rube's big break turning out to be a punchline to a bad joke—never left him, showing up time and again in his comedy.

And so he returned to Buffalo and Herman's jewelry store, located near the theater district. Actors often stopped in and Boasberg casually ignored locals to crack jokes with them. Some acts asked to use his quips, some offered a five-dollar bill. Unlike today, comics then rarely wrote their own material. At the urging of friends, Boasberg approached accordion-comic Phil Baker backstage at a local theater with three pages of material. He left the meeting with $100 in his pocket, quite a bit for a counter clerk in 1922. If he couldn't make his name acting, writing would do.

By 1923, Boasberg was in Manhattan.

Eulogizing Boasberg, Phil Baker said simply: "He made me."

Although George Burns claims to have discovered Boasberg, his first client was Baker. Between 1919-1922, Phil Baker had put together a serviceable act. Good-looking with a touch of arrogance, he sang and played accordion well but had little talent for humor. As *Variety*'s critics warned, " ... his conception of comedy is faulty and if anything will hinder him."

To remedy his comedy problem, Baker hired Jojo, an audience plant who interrupted the act, begging to sing with him. Plants were old news (Al Jolson started as one). The twist came in that Jojo sang terribly. His Yiddish mangling of popular songs brought laughs, but critics felt Baker weakened it by ridiculing him. Funny, but it wasn't enough to carry Baker to the top Broadway revues in which W.C. Fields and Fanny Brice starred. By the time Boasberg met him, Baker was still working two-a-days in Buffalo.

Boasberg saved Baker's act, but not by saving Baker. Instead of providing the star with a set of punchy comebacks to his pest, Boasberg reconceived Baker's act by expanding the stooge's part, now played by Sid Silvers. Silvers, perched in a balcony box, heckled Baker mercilessly, flummoxing the smooth entertainer with terrible puns. Baker returned fire, struggling to keep his act on track, but was helpless against his nitwit rival.

> Baker:  Oh, how did you get in here?
> Silvers:  On a friend's ticket.
> Baker:  Where's your friend?
> Silvers:  Looking for his ticket.

For 1922 vaudeville, a comic shut down by his own stooge threw fans a wide curve. That it happened to a guy as smug as Baker only made it more funny. Traditionally, comics used stooges as target practice for their wisecracks, as seen in W.C. Fields' *The*

*Golf Specialist* (1930) or in the early film appearances of Ted Healy and his Three Stooges. An impressed Brooks Atkinson of the *Times* noted Baker's concession: "Unlike most jealous and temperamental artistes of the revue stage, Mr. Baker yields most of the laughs to his box heckler .... Mr. Silvers does not have to hang his head for shame like most of the humiliated 'feeders' in comedy teams."

Baker debuted the act at Manhattan's Riverside Theater in June 1922 and killed. *Variety* gave Baker and his Boy-in-the-Box a rave, crowing that the new Baker was "big time all the way." That winter, Irving Berlin cast him in his 1923 *Music Box Revue*, which also presented Robert Benchley's "Treasurer's Report" and George S. Kaufman's "If Men Played Cards as Women Do." Unlike those celebrated wits, Boasberg went uncredited, because Baker's act was meant to look ad-libbed.

Baker and his Boy (he never billed Silvers as a partner) worked the act throughout the '20s. After World War II, Dean Martin and Jerry Lewis revived it in nightclubs, with Dean singing on stage and Jerry, a bumbling waiter, ruining his act from the floor until Dean invites him up. Martin and Lewis later starred in *The Stooge* (1953), based on Baker and Silvers' early days. A bitter Silvers, who quit Baker and became a minor writing rival to Boasberg, provided the film's story. It offers a revisionist history in which Silvers created the act. Settling old scores, he savaged Baker and based the character Al Borden, the world's worst joke writer, on Boasberg.

If Boasberg's comedy opened doors for Baker, Baker opened doors for his gag man, sending him to his ex-partner, violin-comic Ben Bernie, now starting up a dance band. Bernie's act hit bigger than Baker's, and Boasberg, now dubbed "Boasy" by his new Broadway pals, joined the New York comedy scene of the '20s.

They were a young, hungry, tightly knit group of Jazz Age comics, most not yet thirty years old. The group included Baker's boyhood friend Georgie Jessel, both of whom grew up with and performed kid acts with Walter Winchell. Jessel had his own tag-a-long, Nat "George" Burns, who within a year would meet his wife and stage partner, Gracie Allen. Burns' new pal, Ben Benny, a violin-comic from Waukegan, had just moved East after losing a lawsuit that named him a copycat act to Ben Bernie, so now he called himself "Jack." At any time with this crowd you might run into big shots like New York mayor Jimmy Walker, Irving Berlin, or Al Jolson. One night, Boasberg watched Phil Baker blow $4,000 gambling at Cokeley's. Still catching his breath, the recently retired shop clerk then saw Nick the Greek drop $250,000 to underworld mastermind Arnold Rothstein, the rumored fixer behind the 1919 World Series scandal.

In 1923, Boasberg took his first job in the movie business as a publicity man at FBO (later RKO). Selling gags piecemeal was feast or famine income, and FBO offered a steady paycheck. Lee Marcus, FBO sales director and a Buffalo friend, hired Boasberg and became his biggest fan. As Marcus rose in the ranks, becoming president of RKO Pathe by 1933, he brought Boasberg with him and would give him greater creative freedom than any other studio.[2]

Boasberg also went on stage again, now as "The Masked Man From Hollywood." Wearing the mask in question, he did a monologue on movie stars with Nils T. Granlund, the house announcer, heckling and then joining him on stage. It went nowhere, but the fresh material brought new clients. Besides bit parts in his own films, his acting career ended here.

Still, Boasberg craved attention. One joke he liked was standing up in an audience and asking "Is there a Christian Scientist in the house?" When one answered, he'd say "Would you mind switching seats with me? I'm sitting in a draft."

Boasberg's perpetual joking, a personality quirk in his youth, turned to pure profit in New York. But as in Buffalo, he remained an isolated personality. "Al had few friends who could be called intimate," said Baker, "but every one who knew him loved him."

Boasberg had a disease, a humor disorder if you will, that the old guard called "thinking crooked." As veteran comedy writer Bob Schiller described it: "There's people who cannot—it's almost psychotic with some comedy writers—who cannot say anything straight. It's awful because—if you examine it from a psychological standpoint, it's pushing people away, really—you don't let anybody get close to you."

As in his youth, Boasberg's one track mind made comedy his life. If he hid from loneliness in vaudeville houses as a kid, nothing changed as an adult. Radio writer-performer Goodman Ace recalled a Boasberg drawn to comedians. Ace said that when traveling in a strange town, Boasberg instinctively sought out local theaters and caught the comic's act. Then he'd go backstage, introduce himself, and offer free advice—what the big time New Yorkers paid plenty for—making contact through comedy, the only way he knew how.

Boasberg's obsession with comedy made a perfectionist out of him. Instead of simply handing comics a script and taking their money, he went to show after show, watching from the balcony seats (to study both the comic and audience reaction). Deadpan, rarely laughing himself, he evaluated gags and the laughs they drew like a broker studying returns. Notebook in hand, he then went backstage, towering over most of his new clients, to talk about what hit, what missed. Sometimes he rewrote the act, sometimes he shifted the order of jokes. Sometimes a single word saved the whole thing.

The young comics saw Boasberg as an innovator. He wrote a sense of spontaneity into his work. Baker's act looked like a live feud rather than fifteen minutes of scripted jokes (even though it was all scripted). Vaudeville lore credits Boasberg as the first to use Hollywood movie stars and death as monologue material. He created a comedy wire service in which he telegraphed current events gags to comics on tour, insuring fresh material every week, which meant joke thieves couldn't kill the act. And thieving was a problem. In one week he heard his line "You stole my wife, you horse thief!" lifted twenty-two times.

But there was something else about his material. It was fresh. It tweaked old rules. And most important of all in '20s America—it was modern. World War I's aftermath inspired a modernist trend that reached from the *haute couture* salons of Paris to German Bauhaus design to Hemingway's prose, and vaude was no exception.

Of course, words like "modernism" meant little to a drop-out like Boasberg. "I write with my ears," he liked to say, "I get my ideas from what the people around me are laughing at." When pressed on what made Boasberg so unique, the best anyone ever got was Phil Baker's summation, shrugged off in perfect Broadway Runyonese: "His jokes had the distinction of being distinctive."

Whatever that meant, if the modern comics weren't much on theory, then in practice, they were the *avant-garde*. Like the art world, they intentionally broke with the past, stripped down their style to the bare bones, and performed self-consciously as *comedians*—not funny Italians or tramps—but comedians who made their audience very aware of their job and its conventions.

A Jack Benny stood in stark contrast to, say, the Marx Brothers, a wildly costumed and physical pre-war act. Benny simply walked on stage, in street clothes, as "Jack Benny." And then he just stood there and *talked*. No sketch, no giant mustache, no accent—he didn't even fall down. People were amused but puzzled by his flat, no-frills simplicity.

The conventions of vaudeville became their target. Baker no longer played an accordion act, but rather, a comedy sketch about a man *trying* to do an accordion act. In a moment Andy Kaufman might have admired, Benny once torched comedy's oldest opener. "On the way to the theater tonight," he told a 1927 crowd at the Los Angeles Orpheum, "nothing happened." He then paused, wished them good night, and left the stage.

Boasberg's favorite modernist, comedy-about-comedy technique was ridiculing the comic. They entered arrogant and left humble: a comedy of hubris. Baker and Boasberg's "distinctive" act became the model for this generation. Every comic Boasberg worked with soon found himself taken down, either by a stooge or his own hand. Today we call them "fall guys." And over the years, no one became more identified with the modern style than Jack Benny.

"He wrote the first joke I ever used," Benny told reporters at Boasberg's funeral, "way back in vaudeville days."

Benny had played violin in two musical duos before the war, but on his discharge from the Navy, age 25, he returned as a solo musical act: "Ben Benny: Fiddle Funology." The curtains came up as Benny played, back to the crowd. Startled, he spun around and said, "Oh, I guess I'm on." Then he performed popular songs, intentionally hitting bad notes and making faces for laughs. It was no show stopper, but after 18 months of small time Benny jumped to the big time Orpheum Circuit as an opener and found himself on tour with Phil Baker.[3] Enamored of Baker's act, Benny aped him and even introduced himself on stage as "Phil Baker's brother."[4] Benny recalled, "He would always have somebody working with him to get the laughs, like I do on television."

For his part, Baker thought Benny a nice guy and a real snooze, never thinking he'd get anywhere. Still years away from his crisply defined persona, Benny's act came from old jokebooks and what little he created on his own. So Benny watched and Benny learned. An habitual lifter (such charges dogged his entire vaudeville career), he studied Baker, but more so Baker's ex-partner, "the old maestro" Ben Bernie. Like Benny, Bernie worked a violin act. Thus, when Benny jumped to the Eastern Keith circuits that Bernie played, Bernie sent a cease and desist letter (not the first of Benny's career), sued for infringement, and won.[5] Benny denied it, but *Variety's* Sime Silverman decreed him a weak imitator in print. Besides the copycat charges, critics noted his sloppy appearance and suggested tossing the violin. Beaten, branded, forced to change his name (he chose "Jack"), and unable to work much on Bernie's circuit, he retreated West to the Orpheum theaters for the 1921-1922 season.

"Jack Benny was just a 'number two' [an opening act]," recalled one of a group of actors in Bill Smith's oral history, *The Vaudevillians*, "until he bought an act from Al Boasberg." Benny had most likely purchased random gags early on from Boasberg (his rate then up to $25 a piece). But after saving his money for a full act, Benny hired Boasberg in early 1925 for their first major collaboration.

Both men came from middle class backgrounds, grew up Jewish in small cities, and began their careers in comedy with humbling, public failures. Although they never grew particularly close as friends, the "Jack Benny" character they created came the closest to Boasberg's true self. Over the years, he often used Benny's fictional life to mirror his real one.

By the time they set to work, Benny had toured six years as a musical-comedy act. That ended with Boasberg's renovation. The two experimented with new looks, attitudes, and style, all coming to a boil in shows at Wilkes-Barre and Scranton, Pennsylvania in the early spring of 1925.

It was a testing ground. Benny tried going on without the violin, but couldn't bring himself to completely drop it. Still, for all intents and purposes, the violin moved from the center of the act to a mere prop. A crucial shift, because now Benny was simply a talking comic, or to vaudevillians, that rarest of acts, a 100% monologist—no music, juggling, rope tricks, singing, or backflips—just talk. And unlike the old school, he wore no costume: He simply entered in street clothes as "Jack Benny." Finally, he and Boasberg broke the act down to just jokes, what other monologists considered filler between their long stories or recitations of famous works. Benny wasn't the first to do any of this, but rather, the first to combine it all into one act. Thus, it meant the folks in Wilkes-Barre and Scranton got the first ever look at what we now call a modern stand-up comic.[6]

The Pennsylvania experiment completed Boasberg's design. Benny dropped his casual look, often entering in a tux, a statement in itself to working class fans expecting lovable tramps. "How's the show going," he snootily asked the house band leader. "Fine," came the reply. "Well I'll fix that!" snorted Benny.

This Benny *knew* he was on. He billed himself the "aristocrat of humor," but in the act he deconstructed his suave, stuffy image. He told stories of dates, relatives, and his life in show business that revealed him as a self-deluded, puffed-up phony, and yes, a cheap one, at that. Burns recalled a joke Benny liked at the time about one of his dates. "I offered to buy her dinner," Benny said, "She was so excited she dropped her tray!"

Together, Benny and Boasberg crafted the basic character Benny played the rest of his life. Thus, in April 1925, when he opened at Keith's Palace in New York, vaudeville's premier theater, he took out trade ads announcing the show, thanking his agent, and "My Doctor, Al Boasberg." Benny's ad is Boasberg's first known public credit.

As with Baker, Boasberg's material brought Benny to a new level. After catching the Palace show, J.J. Shubert cast him in his revue *The Great Temptations* (1926) as a sketch actor and emcee. Benny soon emceed the Palace regularly, so when MGM decided on a musical presenting vaudeville on film, they cast him as master of ceremonies in *The Hollywood Revue of 1929* (1929).

For the movie, Benny turned to Boasberg, and the two captured their stage act on film. *Hollywood Revue* presents a younger, stiffer Benny than of later years, but one with the Benny character firmly in place. And here we see the first hints of Boasberg using Benny to reflect his own life. Boasberg, as will be discussed, had arrived in Hollywood three years earlier to write movies. Touted as a top New York comedy writer, he soon found that silent comedy and his verbal wit didn't always match, and Hollywood quickly cooled to him.

Thus, Benny acts out Boasberg's comeuppance, as in the scene where a movie star jibes him as a snooty New York stage actor and punctuates his lines by snapping the buttons off Benny's tuxedo and ripping his shirt down the front. Hollywood lets the air out of him, just as it had to Boasberg.

Other bits expose Benny as a show biz phony, a self-styled ladies man claiming he was originally cast in *Revue* as Romeo opposite Norma Shearer. When Benny introduces his co-host as a close, personal friend, he forgets the man's name. Every actress he flirts with slaps him. Benny takes it on the chin from the whole cast—a part he played on radio, television, and for Ernst Lubitsch in *To Be or Not To Be* (1942).

Benny played Boasberg's comedy of hubris brilliantly, and the '20s made a perfect backdrop. Mass media created bigger-than-life legends like Babe Ruth, Charles Lindbergh, and Douglas Fairbanks seemingly every week. Staggering fortunes appeared overnight on Wall Street and a new breed of American, movie stars, lived lives of eye-popping luxury. Yet John and Janey Doe, lucky to make $25 a week, got little of it. Boasberg's fall guy humor, a humor of deflation, fed off the same backlash that drove Walter Winchell's gossipy popularity, the backlash that liked to see these swells brought down to size. "I represent everything that's wrong with anybody," Benny once said, "The minute I come on, even the most henpecked guy in the world feels good."

Thus, Boasberg turned the lifter, the copycat, old cease and desist Benny, into one of the world's most imitated comics. His self-destructing comedian-as-comedian became a standard, informing the '70s stand-up of Steve Martin or Albert Brooks' film *Real Life* (1979). And over the decades, is it possible to count how many thousands of stand-ups followed Benny's lead, going on stage with nothing but jokes, simply as "themselves"?

By the time Burns and Allen hired Boasberg, the team had played vaudeville together for about two years. They had an obvious spark, but remained a middling success with barely steady work.

In *I Love Her, That's Why*, Burns writes that in their debut he assumed *he* was the comic and dressed in baggy pants, a giant red bow tie, and a bent-up floppy hat—all the old school gear. He took the punchlines and soon found the crowd only laughed at Gracie's straight lines. He compromised, splitting the gags with her, and they settled on a so-so "Dumb Dora" routine where he wisecracked and she gave "dumb" punchlines. *Variety* noted their talent, but felt "a smarter and brighter vehicle will have to be secured eventually if they expect to advance."

They were known as a "dissy," a disappointment act, meaning they went on when better acts fell ill and a quick replacement was sought. A sample of their first act, "Dizzy," gives a hint why:

> Burns:  You're dizzy.
> Allen:  I'm glad I'm dizzy. Boys like dizzy girls and I like boys.
> Burns:  Well, I'm glad you're glad you're dizzy.
> Allen:  And I'm glad that you're glad that I'm glad that I'm dizzy.
> Burns:  And I'm glad that you're glad that I'm glad that you're dizzy.
> Allen:  And I'm glad that you're glad ...

Burns considered that the pearl of the act. But now he had another problem: How to treat Gracie? Like Baker with Jojo, if he ridiculed Gracie, he came off a bully. Worse, Gracie's utterly adorable nature meant the crowd hated him for it. Should he get angry? Ignore her? Patronize her?

For two years the team toured the small time until October 1925, when they commissioned an act from Boasberg. Originally titled "Formerly of Ziegfeld Follies' Check Room," it was retitled "Lamb Chops." The act introduced Gracie's "illogical logic" and stories of her loony family. Boasberg cleared up Burns' confusion by making Gracie smarter than Burns—and Burns utterly helpless before her. And from now on, the jokes were all hers.

"Lamb Chops" cast Burns as a wise guy trying to pick Gracie up on a street corner. A big joke at the time was that dating meant buying girls expensive dinners—hence the act's title—so Burns tries his pick-up lines, hoping to avoid that dinner check, but gets nowhere with Gracie, as in this gag:

> Burns:  How many lamb chops can you eat, little girl?
> Allen:  Two.
> Burns:  A little girl like you can eat two big lamb chops alone?
> Allen:  No, but with potatoes I could.

In this one joke, the Burns and Allen team is born. Though goofy, Gracie isn't "dumb," and each gag ends with Burns choking from exasperation trying to keep up with her. Like Baker and his Boy, Burns now saw the act slip out of his control. Crowds liked seeing the over-confident street wolf spun round by this equally confident scatterbrain. Pow-

> AU REVOIR
> **BURNS and ALLEN**
> SAILING MARCH 8 ON BERENGARIA
> OPENING IN LONDON MARCH 18
> IN AL BOASBERG'S
> **"LAMB CHOPS"**
> American Rep.: TOM FITZPATRICK
> European Rep.: JENIE JACOBS and HENRY SHEREK

*Used by permission of Variety.*

ered by Gracie's charm, they broke their "dissy" status and rose to headliners within a year.

*Variety* raved, singling out Boasberg's script as "virtually actor proof." Bob Hope remembered it "setting the trend" for them. As they aged, they modified it, but never past the idea of the rational Burns left speechless before her daft logic. Although he often kidded about riding Gracie's skirts to success, Burns is key to the act, which is always, really, about him. As he struggles with her, we do too, since we're more like him than her.

Once again, Boasberg's modern sensibility created new stars. But it's important to note that no one writer handed talents like these their careers. They had performed for years before ever meeting Boasberg and decades after without him. But Boasberg took their semi-successful acts and zeroed in on what was truly unique about them as individuals. His fall guy model formed the mold, which he filled with their personalities. And despite these successes, he wasn't infallible, as he learned in 1924 when his hipster humor hit a comedy roadblock named Milton Berle.

Boasberg and Berle only worked together once. Despite that, the act gave Berle his main hook, that of comedy's joke thief supreme.

Berle, then 16, needed an act for his debut as a solo comic so his agent hired Boasberg. The act, "Guilty!," had a blackfaced Berle perform imitations of stars Eddie Cantor, Al Jolson, and Ed Wynn, and then ask the crowd to vote on whether or not he stole jokes. Invariably they voted "yes," allowing Berle to do a prison routine after his "conviction."

To Boasberg, blackface was literally kid's stuff. He had written a minstrel act when he was 12, and if he did it now, he wanted to burn down the whole concept. So, a modernist minstrel: Berle entered without makeup, and while he explained the voting bit, blacked up *on* stage. His entrance alone destroyed the illusion of minstrelsy, of white men pretending to be black men. And the act, nothing but imitations of old schoolers, not too subtly pointed up how stale it all was. As in Baker's accordion-act-about-an-accordion-act, Berle didn't play a minstrel, but a man *trying* to play a minstrel. "Guilty!" made you aware of minstrelsy as genre, its conventions, and its limitations.

Boasberg had had enough of minstrels, but audiences hadn't, and the piece flopped. Others saw it as too inside, too dependent on knowing the acts Berle mimicked, something you couldn't expect outside New York. And, quite possibly, the teenage Berle didn't yet have the stage skills to pull it off.

Despite "Guilty!" getting the chair, Boasberg's intuitive understanding of comedians tagged the cloying Berle a joke thief before he really became one. And through Boasberg, Berle began to see himself. "The longer I stuck with 'Guilty!'," Berle wrote later, "The less it worked, but from it I learned what was working for me. It was the brash pushy gags that went over. I began to see me as I thought the audience saw me."

From 1922-1925, Boasberg took himself from salesman to gag man. But he still hadn't written his musical comedy, and although respected by insiders, was still unknown. Whether or not he actually wrote a play during this period is lost to us, but if later years are an indication, he tried and failed. If Broadway wasn't in the cards yet, the movies, and Buster Keaton, were.

"From time to time we brought famous and talented writers from New York," said Keaton, "I don't recall a single one of these novelists, magazine writers, and Broadway playwrights who was able to write the sort of material we needed. An example is Al Boasberg."

At any rate, it began well. In November 1925, at Lee Marcus' suggestion, Boasberg became a title writer on Keaton's boxing comedy *Battling Butler*, writing the cards that appear between scenes in silent films. Keaton even cast him in *Butler* as a marching band leader. With four writers it's difficult to cite anything as definitively Boasberg's, but jokes stand out. In one scene Buster reads a newspaper that kids sportswriter Damon Runyon (it's by-lined "Demon Onion"). In another, Buster asks a boxer's girlfriend about her broken shoe: "How's your heel?" Looking at her brutal boyfriend she replies, "Oh, he's all right."

For *The General*, Keaton promoted Boasberg to full writer and cast him in another role. Typical of Boasberg's luck, the part required a heavy beard and sideburns, making him unrecognizable.[7] But it's here that Boasberg ran into trouble. His verbal artistry did little for the Great Stone Face. "He had a terrible flop when he tried to do sight gags for us," said Keaton. "So were a hundred other writers imported from New York. It is possible, of course, that we kept sending for the wrong ones."

Unlike his other clients, Keaton was a fully formed comedian when Boasberg met him, and Boasberg's impact on Keaton's silent films is hard to delineate. Boasberg, along with fellow vaude scribe Paul Gerard Smith, just didn't fit in with Keaton's company. After a spat with Keaton, Smith quit on location and drove home.[8] Boasberg hung on, but that's all.

Boasberg's major contribution to *The General* may be a story that circulated in Hollywood for years. According to legend, Boasberg and Keaton arrived on set early one chilly day. To keep warm they started a fire, which grew out of control until it burned down the set and much of the Oregon forest surrounding it. The fires were actually ignited by sparks from a train engine, but Boasberg enjoyed any notoriety and the story instantly endeared him to Groucho Marx when they met years later. When Boasberg and Keaton

*Al Boasberg, with drum, at Buster Keaton's wedding in* Battling Butler, *and center-stage with false mustache on location with* The General.

returned home, they remained friendly, but Keaton let him go.[9]

Boasberg settled in Los Angeles and began feeding local columnists quips on California life for the cheap publicity. Noting one harrowing intersection in Hollywood, he wrote "a pedestrian got across the street there the other day and six drivers immediately demanded a rematch."

FBO soon hired Boasberg back, now as a gag man at $450 a week. Owned by Boston financier Joseph P. Kennedy, FBO produced westerns and knock-offs of popular hits. That season the studio favored comedies of the *Abie's Irish Rose* (1925) variety of Irish-Jewish weddings. How an often vocal anti-Semite like Kennedy felt about producing films like *Kosher Kitty Kelly* (1927) and *Clancy's Kosher Wedding* (1927) is unknown, but Boasberg happily cranked them out.

While at FBO, Boasberg met director Sam Wood. They eventually made eight films together, including two for the Marx Brothers. In 1927, Wood jumped to MGM and brought Boasberg along, introducing him to another steady employer, early Hollywood's most profitable producer, Irving Thalberg.

Of the eight features and several shorts Boasberg wrote at FBO, he rarely received solo credit (if any). Although he sold FBO original stories, others worked out the actual scripts and he was forced to share credit, a fact which aggravated him no end.

Boasberg knew funny, brilliantly so, but the man who bragged that he owned but two books, a dictionary and a thesaurus, had never learned the dramatist's skills of act-by-act structure, of developing characters over those acts. Boasberg's limited skills brought him limited work, as most producers simply had no use for his brilliant wisecracks in their silent films.

Like Perelman or Benchley, Boasberg shone brightest in the verbal jab or short piece, a fact becoming more and more apparent to those who worked with him. "I wouldn't have given him ten cents to sit down and write me a script," said Benny, "Even if I told him what I wanted. He just wasn't the man for that." And for his part, Boasberg thought structure and plot the drudge work you could get anybody to do. As he often grumbled, "It's their job to write the script. It's mine to make it funny."

In 1928, Boasberg's movie career slowed to a near halt, and in addition, his private life fell into turmoil. Boasberg married Chicagoan Rosadel Stadecker just as he took the FBO job in L.A. and virtually ignored her (except to fight) while he pursued his career. She left him, as had an earlier wife, Hilda Levy, in 1923. Stadecker sued for divorce. Levy simply deserted him.

To *Variety* Boasberg explained that his hectic schedule on movie locations made a real marriage impossible. In a Chicago court, Stadecker and her friends told tales of "cold indifference," claiming he twice shoved her off his lap onto the ground and ridiculed her mother. From California, he denied it but did not contest the divorce. And, giving an indication of his income, Boasberg agreed to pay her $100 a week, no doubt prompting his oft-quoted line: "There is no amusement tax on alimony."

Three months later he married the petite, pretty, and quiet Rosylind Goldberg, whom he stayed with for the rest of his life. Jim Michaels says: "It was an arrangement. Someone to come home to. There was certainly no warmth in the relationship and he needled her endlessly on her mother and her nogoodnik brother who, I gather, was always into Al for cash .... [He] put up with her because she looked after his comfort."

Except for Boasberg's sister, no one got close to him. The following May, 1928, Herman Boasberg died. At the time, father and son weren't speaking to each other, ending their distant relationship with no real reconciliation.

Boasberg's movie career remained static, but he maintained a serious income from vaude acts using his material, since he now took ten percent or more of their salaries as fee. Burns and Allen alone set him up with a comfortable lifestyle and at one time he collected from half the Loew's circuit—150 acts.

Clearly, vaudeville wasn't enough, but in 1929, a vaudevillian turned his slump around. With talkies in full swing, Benny came West to make *Hollywood Revue*. It played to Boasberg's strength, allowing him to write Benny's stage act on screen. *Revue* hit big, enhancing Boasberg's standing with Thalberg, who put him on two Sam Wood pictures, *So This Is College* (1929), on which he also served as lyricist, and *It's a Great Life* (1929). Overnight, talkies made him a hot property. He adapted *Fifty Million Frenchman* (1930) for Warner Brothers, joined journalist Bugs Baer and cartoonist Milt Gross for the RKO western comedy short *Two-Gun Ginsburg* (1929), and spun out a new act for vaudeville's Block and Sully.

Since 1927, Thalberg had come to appreciate Boasberg. The writer fit easily into his assembly line vision of filmmaking, one who could be dropped into a production to turn a dull scene into comedy and then sent on a new mission the next day. And working several assignments at once was habit to Boasberg. Thalberg once asked him, "Why do you take so many jobs?" "Why did you leave Universal?" shot back his gag man, noting their common trait: ambition.

Thalberg also shared Boasberg's cool, analytical view of comedy. Morrie Ryskind once watched Thalberg soberly read an early outline of *A Night at the Opera* without even a smirk. After silently turning the last page, the producer said only, "That's the funniest thing I've ever read."

One bit of MGM lore about the two began with Boasberg getting a call to catch a New York-bound train that night with Thalberg to work out a new script. He rushed home, packed his bags, received his ticket from the studio, boarded the train, and had just settled in and taken his shoes off when Thalberg summoned him. Finding the producer and his assistants in a private car outfitted as a full office, Thalberg immediately laid out the plot for the script. "Have you got that all clear in your mind, Al?" said Thalberg. "Absolutely, Irving," said Boasberg. "Fine, fine!" said his boss, "When the train stops in San Bernadino in about twenty minutes, you get off, and then tomorrow morning at the studio you can get started on the script." Boasberg soon found himself at the station waiting for the midnight bus home.

Boasberg now made a move whose timing bespoke the ultimate confidence. On October 29, 1929, the day the stock market crashed, plunging America into the Great Depression, he announced that he'd like to go freelance. MGM's spot assignments meant sharing credit (if he got it) and his peculiar skills meant that's all he'd get. With a pick of jobs, he moved on.

One such job came that November. On a trip East, he agreed to take on a kid the new RKO vaudeville circuit was grooming as their new star, a 25-year-old bulldozer out of Cleveland, Bob Hope.

By 1929, Hope had toured vaudeville for four years in a song-and-dance act and then two years as a single comic, one burning to play the Palace. Like Burns', Benny's, and the rest, Hope's early attempts were far from what he became. For his comedy debut, he donned a bright red bow tie, white gloves "like Jolson's," blackface, a bowler hat, and smoked a fat cigar. Hope's instinct was for old school comedy. And he did all right, for Cleveland.

Soon he left Ohio and his burnt cork for Chicago, where he eventually became house emcee at a South Side theater, patching an act together from old jokebooks. He toured the Midwest and South on small time circuits until he got a call to come East. After a masterful audition for the Keith bookers, Hope quickly learned that auditions were one thing, but playing New York another. One Gotham critic harped, "They say that Hope is the sensation of the Midwest. Well why doesn't he go back there?"

Hope needed grooming. Everyone knew Boasberg's skill with comers, so he became the first in the army of Hope writers that followed. Over their four-year collaboration, Boasberg openly took credit for Hope's success, claiming he turned him from a "juggling patterer" into a "smart dress comic." Hope, eleven years younger than Boasberg, marveled at his gag man's wit. In his autobiography, Hope recalls dinners at Lum Fong's, a Chinese restaurant in Manhattan, that lasted until four in the morning. Hope took full advantage of Boasberg's "crooked thinking," even scribbling the writer's dinner conversation down on napkins for possible use. He was "incredibly quick witted," wrote Hope, "he was a great joke mechanic. He could remember jokes, fix jokes, switch jokes around, improvise on jokes," and best of all to a non-writer like Hope, "he could even originate jokes."

Like Benny, Hope bought much more than jokes, as Boasberg revised his whole stage persona. Two gags the comic played with his stooges illustrate the difference in pre- and post- Boasberg material. In earlier days with foil Louise Troxxel, Hope recalls: "... she'd say, 'I just came back from the doctor.' 'Well, what about that?,' I'd ask. And she'd say, 'Well, the doctor said I'd have to go to the mountains for my kidneys.' 'That's too bad,' I said. 'Yes,' she said, 'I didn't even know they were up there.'"

Hope describes Troxxel as "quick and intelligent" but instructed her to hide that and "just be beautiful." Then, when she gave her "dumb" lines, Hope says, "I would look at the audience like a man in pain .... My eyebrows asked, 'What can I do with a dumb broad like this?'" Troxxel, like the early Gracie, went on "dumb" and stayed "dumb."

But with Hope's next tour, 1930-31, Boasberg created *Antics*, a four-act showcase for the comic and the culmination of both their vaudeville careers. *Antics* allowed Hope to work all the Boasberg standards: a stand-up single, a "Dumb Dora" bit with Troxxel, and a battle with box hecklers. It also employed Hope's forgotten talent, song-and-dance man. It's in this tour that Hope's tone began to change. Like Benny, from now on, Hope was the joke. As in this gag depicting a now familiar, boasting Hope:

> Hope:   My brother slapped Al Capone once.
> Louise:  (Really surprised) He did? Why, he's the bravest man I ever heard of.
>          I'd like to shake his hand.
> Hope:   We're not going to dig him up just for that.

Hope the braggart, instantly deflated. Or this exchange, the kind he and Jerry Colonna would engage in for years on radio, done after stooges in boxes on both sides of the stage hammer Hope:

Hope:   Don't you know you can be arrested for annoying an audience?
Stooges:  You ought to know!

Here, the Bob Hope of national fame emerges, one well-versed in the fall guy school. Critics changed their tune, noting how he "razzed himself" and that "he shrewdly gives the gag line to the girl, taking the sock of the repartee upon himself." His conversion to Boasberg's ideas became clear. One critic stated flatly, "Hope has the style of the modern vaude comics." And Robert Benchley, writing in the *New Yorker*, gave roundabout credit to his old *Music Box Revue* cohort, Boasberg, when he noted that "a new quipster of the Baker-Bernie school has been introduced in the person of Bob Hope."

Through gags and nothing but, Boasberg built a character for Hope. The comic played brash, cowardly, grasping, self-centered, yet still likable since he's quickly brought down, always turning to the crowd with that exasperated look—the same one Burns used and the one Benny made an institution. Boasberg only wrote jokes, but as Woody Allen once said: "Jokes become a vehicle for the person to display a personality or attitude. Just like Bob Hope. You're not laughing at the jokes but at a guy who's vain and cowardly .... You're laughing at character all the time. The [comics] that never make it ... no person emerges."

The new Hope pushed hard for the Palace. In late 1930 he announced a date (a false alarm), but after 16 months with Boasberg the Palace booked Hope for February, 1931. With Boasberg-style stooges now a vaude staple, Hope made noise with publicity stunts in which his boys picketed the Palace in sandwich boards that read: "Hope Unfair to Stooges, Local 711!" Meanwhile, Boasberg called in jokes from his California tub for the big show.

But Hope overreached. Nervous, stiff, he sleepwalked through his dream date. Critics tore into him, but the more vaudeville savvy *Variety* recognized him as an inexperienced but obvious talent and reserved its real ire for his mentor: "Al Boasberg is credited with 'special material' but he doesn't deserve it if what Hope used for comedy was Boasberg's stuff."

Boasberg had no one to blame but himself. Literally phoning it in while writing a new Burns and Allen act, two Wheeler and Woolsey movies, and bits for any other joker he happily supplied meant he had spread himself too thin. And Hope suffered for it.

Bloodied but unbowed, Hope toured the Northwest with *Antics* for the rest of 1931. The "Hope" character grew sharper. Like Benny, he entered brashly, following opening acts with "Now that the amateurs are done," mastering his classic flippancy.

That November, Boasberg moved to New York for several reasons (as will be discussed), one of which was overhauling Hope. For the next two months the comic played twelve different theaters in the New York area, perfecting Boasberg's new *Antics of 1932*. With vaudeville as they knew it about to disappear, Boasberg handed Hope gems like this, designed to push the limits of the Palace:

> I was just standing out in front watching the other acts when a lady walked up to me in the lobby and said, "Pardon me young man, could you tell me where I could find the restroom?" and I said, "it's just around the corner." "Don't give me that Hoover talk," she said, "I'm serious."

Boasberg injected some Depression-era reality into Hope, who recalls that gag as one of the biggest laughs he ever got in vaudeville. A groundbreaking joke, it intentionally challenged the Palace's family hour mentality with its mix of politics and off-color humor. Boasberg was chipping at walls that Lenny Bruce, who defined himself with this very mix, demolished a generation later.

By adding political jokes to the set, we see the final piece of the "Hope" character in place. Hope's manic desperation clicked in early '32, a pre-Franklin Roosevelt era when palpable desperation walked the streets. This time, with Boasberg on hand, the retooled Hope rolled off the line into the Palace and killed. On May 30, 1932, *The New York Times* wrote:

> Very properly, the honored "next-to-closing" place is awarded to this Mr. Hope, who arrives with some exceptionally deft material penned by the astute Al Boasberg. That is to say, you may count upon Mr. Boasberg to recognize a good four-a-day gag when he writes it, and upon Mr. Hope to deliver it with respectful skill. It is a consistently amusing and dizzy partnership ...

Boasberg's understanding of Hope shaped the most successful career in comedy history. Together, they staked out the comic's boundaries, discovered what audiences liked about him, and turned him into vaudeville's last true star.

The last, because by 1932 big time vaudeville died its long predicted death as movies and radio stole its audience. Hope's Palace dream was sentimental, but he and Boasberg created *Antics* for one real purpose: showcasing Hope to Broadway producers *à la* Benny and Baker. Boasberg even arranged Hope's first screen test for producer William Perlberg. Hope opened the next season in the legit revue *Ballyhoo* (1932) (using Boasberg's material) and in later musicals like *Roberta* (1935) and Cole Porter's *Red, Hot and Blue!* (1936).

*Antics* created a comic institution in Bob Hope, perhaps the single biggest influence yet on American stand-up comedy. Hope's pace and verve became the gold standard. While comics vary widely in content, few stray from the Hope model: topicality and endless jokes. From Mort Sahl to Johnny Carson to Jay Leno to Bill Maher, it's not what comics do anymore that sets them apart, it's what they say. Hope perfected a simple, high velocity, broadcast-friendly stand-up style that he settled on for good by 1937.

Boasberg's "Hope" played tremendously in movies. Hope modified it, becoming a nicer guy by the end of films like *Caught in the Draft* (1941) and *The Lemon Drop Kid* (1951), but the undiluted Hope appears in his *Road* films with Bing Crosby. The two had worked out the basic relationship on stage at New York's Capitol Theater in 1932, and their films use Boasberg's Boy-in-the-Box formula: Hope the fall guy, Bing the unflappable heckler.

Perhaps the contemporary comic owing the most to Boasberg and Hope is Woody Allen, who said of Hope: "... both of us have the exact same wellspring of humor .... It's everything I can do at times not to imitate him."

To Allen's credit, he explores fall guy humor more extensively than anyone. Since his nightclub days and all through his film career, Allen expands the fall guy concept by giving his cowardly, deluded, wannabe Lothario a sense of self-awareness Hope or Benny never attain. What drives Allen's character is that despite this awareness, he can never change. In *Annie Hall* (1977) he despairs over it. By *Hannah and Her Sisters* (1986) he finds happiness only by resigning himself to it, and in *Decon-*

*structing Harry* (1998) he takes the final fall, his sins landing him in Hell itself.

But no one knew Hope's impact in 1932. For Boasberg, it was just more gag work. And as far as vaudeville dying, well, no love lost. While other vaudevillians waxed nostalgic for the good old days, Boasberg saw the circuits as thankless, unappreciated work, where theater managers allowed acts to steal his best bits and censors hampered his voice.[10] Benny recalled Boasberg saying, "To listen to these guys reigning us in you'd think guys had no dicks and gals had no twats and the stork brought the brats ... by sneezing!" Restraints like these, on his career and art, were why he and his tub preferred the relative freedom of pre-Code Hollywood.

During the Hope period, late 1929-1932, Hope required only a few weeks of rehearsal each season and topical updates by phone. And soon after Boasberg met him, MGM called early in 1930 asking his help in answering a question: What to do with Buster Keaton?

Keaton's career as an independent filmmaker was peaking when they first met, but by 1930 he was an unhappy factory worker at MGM. While Chaplin and Lloyd hesitated with sound, Keaton, characteristically, dove in head first. Boasberg co-wrote Keaton's first two talkies, *Free and Easy* (1930) and *Doughboys* (1930). They were hits, and in large part, Boasberg products.

Boasberg joined *Free and Easy*'s troubled set mid-production[11] to work for Thalberg's brother-in-law, producer Lawrence Weingarten. Here, Boasberg again examines show business. Keaton plays Elmer Butts, a rube's rube trying to help his childhood sweetheart break into movies and finally win her heart. Elmer mucks up everything he possibly can at a movie studio. But his buffoonery turns into an accidental audition and the studio, in the film's final moments, offers Elmer a contract as a comedian. His girl, however, has fallen in love with another. Elmer is left with a show business career and a hollowed-out emotional life, which Keaton expresses in *Free and Easy*'s beautifully understated final shot. As she exits, Buster looks up from the ground to us, directly into the camera, his mournful eyes a revelation of lost love. Career success and emotional failure, show biz triumphs meaning nothing—quandaries both Keaton and Boasberg knew well. And it hit with early Depression audiences.

In *Doughboys*, which Boasberg wrote on from day one, his influence on Keaton truly takes hold.[12] Keaton plays Elmer Stuyvesant, but unlike the rich nitwits Keaton portrays in *The Saphead* (1920), *The Navigator* (1924) or *Battling Butler*, all well meaning *naifs*, Stuyvesant is no innocent. Snooty, insensitive, he mistakenly signs up for the army, haughtily assuming the interview is for a new chauffeur, not for his induction as an infantryman in World War I (that is, for someone to serve him, not for his chance to serve his country). Compare Stuyvesant to Keaton's Johnnie Gray in *The General*, a comedy built on Gray's fervent desire to join the army, and we see Boasberg at work.

For the first time, Keaton plays a modern, self-centered fall guy. Although similar to past Keaton (Stuyvesant must prove himself to get the girl), *Doughboys* rests on an entirely different moral underpinning—Boasberg's. Early Keaton heroes overcame personal flaws via the acrobatic and physical spectacles that Keaton made the centerpieces of his films (boxing matches, train races, cyclones, etc). There, Keaton defeats other men, machines, and Nature itself through sheer force of will.

*Doughboys* works in reverse. Here, Stuyvesant needs a lesson in humility, and what better place than the army? He learns to be one of the boys, to sacrifice, to sublimate his self-centered ego for something bigger—to win the war. Stuyvesant leaves the war humbled, a better man, a Boasberg man, but not a Keaton man.

Ironically, Boasberg's Keaton proved more popular than Keaton's Keaton, meaning MGM ordered more of the same, making the real Keaton miserable. Keaton's alcoholism, divorces, and souring career from this point are well documented. But *Doughboys'* success lifted Boasberg, giving him the single biggest break of his career when RKO signed him as a producer. After five years in Hollywood he now had a chance to make his name as something other than a comic's sideman. And he promptly blew it.

RKO wanted Boasberg to supervise their resident comedy stars, Bert Wheeler and Robert Woolsey. A quirky, shameless pair of jokers (RKO's answer to the Marx Brothers), the team's peak remains *Diplomaniacs* (1933), a surreal satire on American foreign policy. Boasberg made four films with them, beginning with *Cracked Nuts* (1931), *Everything's Rosie* (1931), and later *The Nitwits* (1935), the best of the four, and *Silly Billies* (1936).

Boasberg's four Wheeler and Woolsey films fit easily into the team's series and didn't alter them the way he did other comics. Where his Wheeler and Woolsey work did have

*"RKO treated the public to* Everything's Rosie, *'by Al Boasberg.'" Anita Louise and Bob Woolsey.*

impact, however, was on the Abbott and Costello team years later. When that team's producer, Alex Gottlieb, needed stories, he raked over the Wheeler and Woolsey series for ideas and based their *Who Done It?* (1942) on Boasberg's script for *The Nitwits*. And Abbott and Costello can also tip their hats to Boasberg for the "Map of What and Which" routine from *Cracked Nuts*, an obvious inspiration for their trademark bit, "Who's On First?".

Boasberg received production credit on *Everything's Rosie*, Woolsey's one attempt at a solo feature career. Now a boss, Boasberg announced in *Variety* that his first act as producer was to make himself wait outside his own office for three hours.

And as an RKO producer, the job entitled Boasberg to a prominent credit. As part of a questionable but fortuitous RKO policy of giving writer-producers possessory credit (there were, after all, two other writers and director Clyde Bruckman involved), RKO treated the public to "*Everything's Rosie* by Al Boasberg."

Finally, Boasberg achieved some recognition. Finally, they saw Al Boasberg's *name*. But they saw it on a flop. A so-so facelift of W.C. Fields' *Poppy* (1923), chosen, perhaps, because Woolsey had performed it with Fields on stage, it quickly sent Woolsey back to Wheeler for the rest of his career.

And not long after, due to Boasberg's own arrogance, RKO tossed him. They hired him to bring the studio fresh material: stories, ideas, books, anything they could film, which he did. Of the twelve projects he brought RKO, four were accepted. The other eight Boasberg then sold to rival studios. Figuring they had a man on the payroll twice as productive for the competition, they handed Boasberg his hat.

His producing days over, Boasberg took an MGM rewrite assignment on, of all films, Tod Browning's *Freaks*. Thalberg wanted the ghoulishness of Willis Goldbeck's script tempered with vaudeville-style blackout gags, so he called Boasberg. One gag Thalberg didn't use was Boasberg's suggestion that MGM executives wear studio badges during the film's production—so as not to be confused with the cast.

As a studio mechanic, Boasberg could have spent his days pulling in easy paychecks. Forty years old, making important money, a house in Malibu—most would settle right there. But that life brought him nowhere near his real goal: fame—to be his own man. Thus, he moved to New York for the most ambitious, frustrating year of his life.

Boasberg went East in late 1931 to ready Hope's final tour, and more importantly, for his own first chance at legitimate Broadway, doctoring Vincent Youman's musical *Through the Years* (1932). That died in under three weeks. Meanwhile, the work he shrugged off, Hope's *Antics*, brought him the best notices of his career.

Boasberg's other plays died quickly or remained incomplete. And that meant he needed a job. And in early 1932, so did Jack Benny.

Since *Hollywood Revue*, Benny's movie career sputtered out—not many movies need an emcee—and he had quit the *Vanities* over a pay cut. But when he asked his usual $1,500 a week in vaudeville, his friend Benny Rubin recalls, "The bookers said 'Fifteen hundred—for what? You've been away from vaudeville so long we don't know if you can still do a vaudeville act.' He was advised to show his act [audition] and that broke Jack's heart. He wouldn't show for anybody."

But Rubin knew Canada Dry needed a comic for a radio series Rubin had passed on. Rubin arranged a guest shot for Benny on Ed Sullivan's show as an audition. Thus, a few days later, when Sullivan "bumped into" Benny at Lindy's Deli on Broadway, Benny got the gig. Now Benny needed a hot five minutes. And as he had at each critical juncture in his career, he called Boasberg.

"Hello, folks," Benny said in his radio debut, "This is Jack Benny talking. There will now be a slight pause while you say, 'Who Cares?'" Benny fans cite Boasberg's opener as classic Benny, but that which followed as out of character. They're right, since the rest of the monologue is Boasberg using Benny to vent over Hollywood, as Benny plays the part of a movieland wannabe. "There is quite a lot of money in writing for the pictures," Benny says. "Well there would be, if I could sell one." He then describes his part in a new Garbo film, a body found dead in a bathtub. "It's sort of a mystery show," he said, playing on the old Saturday night bath joke: "I'm found in the bathtub on a *Wednesday* night."

Boasberg, clearly upset with his slump (a public firing, back to MGM spot work, and a Broadway bust out) here harks back to his first embarrassing failure, "Love in the Suburbs." Like Boasberg's big debut, Benny's big chance in a Garbo movie is a flat-out joke. And just like his Buffalo flop, Boasberg got the consolation prize—more work as a no-name gag man. It wouldn't be the last time he used Benny to vent his frustration.

A toss-off to Boasberg, a lifesaver to Benny—the shot got him *The Canada Dry Show* which premiered May 2, 1932. As host, Benny introduced bands, cracked jokes, and read commercials. For material he brought Boasberg. Thus, as Boasberg closed vaudeville with Hope's *Antics* that May, he opened radio with Benny that very same month.

For the six-week Canada Dry run the two men transferred their stage act to radio and little changed. One innovation they did help bring about was ridiculing their corporate sponsor, a tradition carried on today by David Letterman. On one show, Benny claimed to have a telegram from a Canada Dry executive in which the man reported finding eight tourists stranded in the Sahara Desert with no food or water for thirty days. "I came to their rescue," the wire said, "giving each of them a glass of Canada Dry. And not one of them said he didn't like it."

After their six weeks, however, neither man came away thrilled. Boasberg was still just a gag man. And Benny knew instinctively that radio's repetitive nature—listening to the same person each week—meant listeners would soon tire of nothing but a vaudeville stream of non sequitur jokes. He wanted a new format. Boasberg wanted a new job, so they parted amicably.

It's doubtful Boasberg ever took Benny's show that seriously. During its run he placed a full page ad in *Variety*, headlined: "Radio! We Are Here!" Announcing his own independent production company, he offered a "comprehensive plan" to create, write, cast and produce programs. In short, he formed his own studio, hoping to provide a one-stop shopping center for corporate sponsors.

It was bold. After a decade watching the industry work, Boasberg set himself up on the money end of things like Thalberg. Unfortunately, he miscalculated. For if he sought to emulate a West Coast studio system, so did sponsors. They invested in a star system, preferring to sign name performers first, and then let the talent worry about who to hire.

Boasberg easily made the short list for any number of comics seeking writers, but not as producer. As his agency went out of business he became richer than he ever had, earning between $50-75,000 in 1932. He walked out on Burns when Burns tried to nickel and dime him and he received the first ever on-air credit for a writer from Walter O'Keefe on *The Lucky Strike Show*.

As the money poured in, Boasberg shared it. Knowing the fragile nature of entertainment careers and fearing the day he himself might turn has-been, he reached out, helping

*Used by permission of Variety.*

broken-down actors at Christmas, buying them whole new wardrobes and sometimes taking them in. Friends liked recounting the finish to a loud argument he got into with one such actor who threatened him with a swift kick. Boasberg shot back: "With my shoes?"

Boasberg took up residence just off Times Square at the Edison Hotel where he'd hole up for days, cranking out pages of jokes for the bottomless appetite of the radio comedians. He bragged that in one sitting he could fill as many pages as needed for any given time slot.

And that fall, Boasberg finally got a taste of the fame he craved, from no less than America's arbiter of smart humor, *The New Yorker.* The magazine's droll "Talk of the Town" section sent a reporter out for the September 10, 1932 issue. But if Boasberg thought he was now in the company of Algonquin wits, he was mistaken. Titled "Gagster" and co-written by comedy elitist James Thurber, it plays him as a what-will-they-think-of-next curiosity, noting with raised eyebrows that he makes that caboodle of cash from, well, *gags.* To emphasize the absurdity, they quote his most inane work, wryly note his disdain for joke thieves, and write him up—and off—as a dedicated oddball. Boasberg debuted on Broadway in *The Music Box Revue* with Kaufman and Benchley, getting the same laughs they did. But now he was seen as getting above himself.

Fifteen go-nowhere months of theater, radio, backhanded write-ups, and a fortune later, Boasberg still found himself on square one—a gag man. By April 1933, he was back at MGM, working out *schtick* on Jimmy Durante's *Hollywood Party* (1934).

A failed actor, failed screenwriter, failed playwright, failed producer, and failed radio mogul, Boasberg, amazingly, got up off the mat again with new plans. He wanted to direct.

Boasberg's old agent, Sam Baerwitz, now an MGM producer, gave him a shot writing and directing two of the future Three Stooges in a now lost short, *Jailbirds in Paradise* (1933). *Jailbirds* went well and he took a feature assignment directing *Myrt and Marge* (1934), an adaptation of a popular CBS radio soap opera of the same name which presented the backstage trials, romances, and dreams of a mother-daughter vaudeville team.

Boasberg's vaude experience made him a natural for the job, but his lack of an emotional life made a mother-daughter movie a bit of a stretch, which might explain why he filled out a soap opera with comics like Ted Healy and his Three Stooges, Eddie Foy, Jr., Trixie Friganza, and Jimmy Conlin. Add Boasberg's favorite conceits: stage box wise guys, dizzy blondes with dizzy logic, brash comics razzed, and we see him reshaping a radio show into his own vaudeville world. One element he kept from the original show was Clarence (Ray Hedges), an openly gay wardrobe master who freely sasses showgirls and comics in Boasbergian fashion.

Universal released *Myrt and Marge* in early 1934, a year when movie musicals favored Depression-era pep like Shirley Temple in *Stand Up and Cheer* (1934) or James Cagney's let's-put-on-a-show mania in *Footlight Parade* (1933). Boasberg's weary troupe wants to put on a show, too, but only to make enough money to get home to New York and quit the damn thing. Here, entertaining is a job, a grind, except for wide-eyed ingenues, egomaniacs, and those rare talents who can actually move an audience. *Myrt and Marge* is a film tired of show business. The Stooges appear in nearly every scene and only to heckle—their director's geek chorus. Boasberg wrote this in the same acid mood he wrote Berle's "Guilty!" As in the sketch, he deconstructs his movie, revealing the cast as actors in a radio studio at the film's finale. From Jack Benny to *Free and Easy,* Boasberg loved taking shots at the profession. But a whole movie of such sourness? As with "Guilty!", he went too far. He spilled career frustrations out to an audience that didn't care. He was tired of show business. They weren't.

One aspect of *Myrt and Marge* worth noting is Clarence, its gay costumer, who threatens to punch out the show's producer if only it wouldn't ruin his nail polish. Like Gracie or any of the African American characters Boasberg wrote, Clarence plays to the stereotypes 1934 audiences expected. But as with "Guilty!", Boasberg undermines these

*Courtesy of Jim Michaels.*

*Al Boasberg ("Uncle Al") with Myrtle Vail ("Myrt"), Donna Damerel ("Marge") and*
*Ray Hedge ("Clarence") during the filming of* Myrt and Marge.

backward views. His Gracie easily handles Burns. Blacks are as intelligent, if not more so, than the white comedians they play against, and always answer back, never just shuffling off. And Clarence is out of the closet, no apologies. No one remembers Boasberg as any sort of political activist. But anyone with common sense knew the difference between old school stage stereotypes and the women, minorities, and gays you met everyday, and Boasberg tried to show it.

*Myrt and Marge* stands as Boasberg's vaudeville *magnum opus*, and it flopped. "Film was directed by a gag man, Al Boasberg" carped *Variety*, "and the dramatic sequences and general pace of the narrative show it." Today, in an age that's made icons of the Stooges, *Myrt and Marge* comes across a sharp little film, its goofy cynicism no problem for our times. In fact, the Coen Brothers use an extended clip from it in their equally goofy Depression-era comedy, *O Brother, Where Art Thou?* (2000), when escaped convict George Clooney hides out in a movie theater. But *Myrt and Marge*'s initial failure made it the only work Boasberg ever disowned. Although he did cite it as a cinematic first: " ... the only six-reel comedy ever made without a single laugh."

If Boasberg's dark humor hadn't done him any favors on *Myrt and Marge*, it found the perfect home at his old studio, RKO. Lee Marcus signed him to write and direct a six-film series of shorts starring comic Leon Errol. Awkwardly paced, sometimes funny, sometimes not, the series is pure, uncut Boasberg.

Typically, fall guys asked for trouble. But Boasberg's state of mind after *Myrt and Marge* and the string of failures preceding it was such that Errol got it for simply getting up in the morning. More biblical Job than vaudeville Hope, Errol, in *Counselitis* (1934), decides to buy his wife a surprise gift. He is then accused of shoplifting, buying the present for a mistress, brought to trial on civil divorce and multiple criminal charges, found guilty of theft as well as narcotics dealing, murder, and wife beating, and tossed in jail. In the end, when the court realizes its mistake and frees Errol, he's so shell shocked that he refuses to leave the relative safety of his cell.

In short after short, Errol suffers double-talking lawyers, con men, salesmen, bizarre contracts, rules, and regulations, all executed with Boasberg's endless joy in twisting language. And no small coincidence, since from 1930-1937 Boasberg engaged in at least ten lawsuits himself, not to mention his earlier divorces. He hounded acts for his fees, fired eight agents in eight years (including Zeppo Marx, whom he sued for $3,500), sued and was sued over money and plagiarism, and even went to court with a cobbler who sought payment for a pair of shoes Boasberg said pinched his feet. In small claims court, the man making $75,000 a year brought the shoes before a judge and settled for $20.

From 1934 on, Boasberg directed two Errols a year. By their last, *Wholesailing Along* (1936), where Errol decides to save money and install a bathtub himself (which, of course, means he ends up paying tenfold for it), Boasberg's storytelling improved as writer-director and he turned out a truly polished short.

And for once Boasberg wasn't writing about show business. The Errol shorts reflect, bleakly, a man's life, not just his job. As the Depression wore on, Boasberg often waxed philosophical on the increasingly grim nature of his work. "If I can make people laugh at their troubles, if I can make them laugh at death," he told a Buffalo journalist, "I have reached a sort of perfection."

Ambitious as ever, after winning a 1934 Best Short Award at a trade show, Boasberg and Sam Baerwitz announced plans to indie finance a dozen shorts at the Astoria studios and distribute through MGM *à la* Hal Roach. They set up shop at the Essex House in New York to meet investors. Nothing came of it. By fall, Boasberg returned to Hollywood, gagging on another Wheeler and Woolsey, *The Nitwits*.

"The biggest break we ever had was getting him to write for us," said Groucho, "He was the best comedy writer Hollywood ever had."

After his second indie failure, Boasberg continued doctoring scripts and directing shorts, when the ever profitable Irving Thalberg called. He had a perfect project for his favorite gag man: The Marx Brothers.

By 1934, the brothers' gag-a-minute masterpiece *Duck Soup* (1933) had performed well at the box office, but not well enough to justify keeping the expensive and difficult team on the lot, so Paramount let them go. They weren't alone. Radio "nut comics" like Ed Wynn's "Fire Chief," Joe "You wanna buy a duck?" Penner, and Stoopnagle and Budd shot up and then plummeted in the ratings. Eddie Cantor's radio career faded and he often argued with producer Sam Goldwyn, who wanted more story and less gags in Cantor's films. On stage, fifteen minutes of gags from an act you saw once a year was fine. But a half hour every week from the same person? Mass media meant mass expo-

On the set of A Night at the Opera. *From left, Harpo, George S. Kaufman (face in hands), director Sam Wood, Chico, Groucho, and Al Boasberg.*

*Courtesy of the Academy of Motion Pictures Arts and Sciences.*

sure, and vaudeville's joke-joke-joke comedy quickly wore thin. Benny's 1932 instinct hit dead on: Audiences wanted more than gags.

The Marxes were out of style, still playing the pre-war comedy of baggy pants comics running wild. The story-over-gags theory became the essence of Thalberg's offer to bring the team to MGM. As Groucho recalled, Thalberg said, "I can make a picture with you that would have half as many laughs than your Paramount films, but they will be more effective because the audience will be in sympathy with you." Drawing on stereotypes that still hold sway today, Thalberg continued, "Men like your comedy, but women don't ... so we'll give women a romance they can become interested in." Groucho came to agree, commenting to one interviewer, "The plot of the film [*Opera*] revolved around our helping two lovers ... this is exactly what Thalberg wanted."

The other innovation *Opera* offered came in the live tour the studio planned that allowed the brothers to test their material on audiences. Boasberg signed on to rewrite George Kaufman and Morrie Ryskind's "script" (most likely an outline with several completed scenes) and to function as on-the-road comedy doctor. He set to work in early March, 1935.[13]

Thalberg couldn't have found a better man to create sympathy for the Marxes than Boasberg. He got laughs not from obnoxious behavior as they did, but from turning the world in on obnoxious people. From now on, the brothers got as good as they gave.

In the same way that Boasberg humbled Keaton in *Doughboys*, his work on *Opera* reveals a new Groucho: one unable to dominate every scene, one bested by his rival, Sig Rumann, one fast-talked by Chico. Groucho plays Otis Driftwood, a con man out to bilk Mrs. Claypool (Margaret Dumont) of her money, claiming he can break her into society via the New York Opera company. Rumann also wants to bilk Mrs. Claypool, and he just might, since Rumann is as sneaky and underhanded as Groucho. Thus, Rumann beats Groucho in signing the great tenor, Laspari; has Groucho fired; sticks Groucho with that tiny stateroom; and even has Groucho kicked down a flight of stairs. Is this the same Groucho from *Duck Soup* who sent Fredonia to war over being called an "upstart?" Hardly. Groucho, literally, has become a fall guy.

Several scenes in *Opera* work on Boasbergian principles. The contract scene—a masterpiece of legal double-talk written at the height of Boasberg's Errol period—has Groucho and Chico negotiating a contract by ripping out any clause they don't like. It's more or less a Burns and Allen sketch, with Groucho the flustered George, lost in the illogical logic of swindling Chico (now smarter than Kaufman and Ryskind ever wrote him):

> Groucho: That's the usual clause in every contract. . . . That's what they call a
> sanity clause.
> Chico: You can't fool me. There ain't no sanity clause.

Then, of course, they rip the clause out. The sequence universally credited to Boasberg is *Opera's* stateroom scene, and its creation began with one of Groucho's favorite stories about the writer. Facing a deadline, Thalberg kept pestering Boasberg for new pages. Fed up, he told Thalberg and the brothers that if they wanted pages, come get them. By the time they got to Boasberg's office they found it empty: no Boasberg, no furniture, no script, no nothing. Then, Groucho chanced to look up, where, indeed, Boasberg had cut the pages apart and tacked them to the ceiling. After piecing it together, they had in their hands what became the brothers' signature piece, *Opera's* stateroom scene.

The stateroom scene is classic fall guy humor. Rumann sticks Groucho with the tiny room, which then fills up with one visitor after another. Groucho can insult everyone, because, like Hope or Benny, the joke is on him, comic-as-victim. As Thalberg hoped, Boasberg's logic allows Groucho his acid wit and yet still keeps the audience sympathetic. Boasberg also rewrote Kaufman's finale, which called for the opera house to burn down. Arguing that an audience would not laugh watching an on-screen audience in a burning theater, Boasberg won out.

Groucho also admired Boasberg's ear for language, as the writer once tracked a single line of dialogue over 140 tour performances for the comic. Groucho, whose career depended on the fineries of language, came to admire Boasberg more than any of his other writers, with the possible exception of Kaufman.

Over the next two years, Groucho and Boasberg became friends, closer than any comic the writer knew. Groucho picked him up for work each day and took him on family vacations. Two emotionally distant middle-aged men who communicated in ridiculous puns and practical jokes, it's no wonder they bonded. One joke they pulled took place at a party they attended where they presented their hostess with two strips of liver on a napkin, covered in ketchup, and informed her sadly that they were forced to remove her cat's tonsils, and did she still want them?

One night at Zeppo's, Groucho cracked up over a great prank call idea he had heard. Boasberg said he knew just the guy to pull it on and dialed a number, calmly telling the man on the other end that he worked for the Beverly Hills Water Department, and that because of a burst pipe, he should fill every pot and pan in the house with water to last the night. He hung up, with Groucho laughing at the sap now filling the pans. Later that night, Groucho returned home to find every pot and pan in his home filled with water, as Boasberg had called Groucho's number and talked to his house guest, writer Arthur Sheekman.

Not all of Groucho's circle liked Boasberg, especially the comic's writer friends, who tired of his competitive joking. "He seemed to me pressing all the time," said Nat Perrin, "Remembering any little bright thing he thought of or happened to say on the spur of the moment, making sure some columnist got it."

That was nothing compared to the disdain between Boasberg and Ryskind. Most likely, Boasberg knew Thalberg intended to push *Opera* as the product of the famous Pulitzer Prize winning team. Losing credit to Kaufman, whom everyone respected, was one thing. But his assistant was another, and Boasberg bristled, once again the invisible gag man. And the fact that Ryskind didn't even bother to put Boasberg's name on the road tour script (not to mention leaving Kaufman's name off), certainly didn't put him in the good graces of anyone as credit hungry as Al Boasberg.

For Ryskind's part, Groucho felt it irked the Ivy Leaguer that Thalberg equated him with a high school drop-out like Boasberg. The final insult came on tour, when the *Opera* crew happened to stay in the same hotel as the Japanese Olympic tennis team. When Ryskind learned that Boasberg sent anyone who asked for the team captain to the diminutive Ryskind, the two never spoke again.

"I know he resented it very much," says Jim Michaels of his uncle, "That's why he played jokes on guys like Ryskind who got all the credit and were regarded as literary figures. It was his revenge on Ryskind for being a literary snob. And, well, his whole comedy is the little guy's revenge, isn't it?"

The brothers knew of Boasberg's disappointment over the credits, but there was little they could do. They did make their feelings known in Marxian fashion, however, by sending Boasberg a photo of themselves, with the anonymous dedication: "To our pal _____. Sorry, but we couldn't get your name on this picture either."

As Thalberg predicted, *Opera* had half the laughs, made twice the money, and became the biggest hit of the brothers' career. Boasberg's reconfiguration of Groucho paid off. Hector Arce, in his book, *Groucho*, cites *Opera*'s success as the reason we view any Marx picture today. He argues that the Marxes would probably have faded into obscurity with Wheeler and Woolsey had *Opera* not attained classic status, continually renewing their audience. Thalberg had his pay day, the Marxes had a cookie-cutter pattern they stuck to for the rest of their career, and Kaufman and Ryskind took the bows. Boasberg basked in the shadows.

With *Opera* a Christmas hit for 1935, Thalberg gave the follow up to Boasberg and two junior writers, George Seaton and Robert Pirosh, and they set it at a racetrack. Boasberg continued directing shorts and working with Wheeler and Woolsey through late spring of 1936, when he received another distress call from Jack Benny.

Since Benny and Boasberg's split in 1932, Benny had become the number one comic on radio and freely credited his new writer, Harry Conn, with that success. Conn's idea, to expand Boasberg's concept of comedian vs. stooge by surrounding Benny with a cast of stooges (like *Hollywood Revue*), instantly found an audience. Week after week, listeners tuned in to hear what Benny got himself into and his familiar reactions and catch phrases. Conn called his invention "group comedy" (today we call it a "sit-com") and it made Benny, for the first time in his long journeyman's career, a star. Conn's idea has, of course, endured to the present day.

But, according to Benny, as the show's success grew, Conn's ego grew to match it. Benny claims Conn said publicly that Benny was helpless without him and that Benny "couldn't ad-lib a belch after a Hungarian dinner." Benny says he tolerated it, afraid to lose him. But when Conn's salary demands included a jump from five per cent of Benny's income to half the revenues of the show Conn had created, Benny fired him. Conn, who had no legal protection for an intellectual property like a sit-com, faded from the scene. Years later, Benny saw him working as a doorman in New York. Benny eventually sold Conn's creation, *The Jack Benny Show*, to CBS for an estimated $4,000,000.

And so, Benny called Boasberg. Knowing the gag man's writing strengths and weaknesses better than anyone (and never wanting to be dependent on one writer again), Benny also hired two neophyte writers, Ed Beloin and Bill Morrow. Boasberg and the kids galvanized the show, introducing: Phil Harris, a classic Boasberg heckler; Benny's Maxwell Car (vocal phenom Mel Blanc); Boasberg's wildly popular Buck Benny western parodies—later made into a movie, *Buck Benny Rides Again* (1940), and a sandwich, still available today at Canter's deli in Los Angeles; and that winter, the national craze known as the Jack Benny-Fred Allen feud. In short, Boasberg oversaw the creation of much of the Benny mythology, and the show flew higher than ever.

And more good news, as across town, Thalberg approved the script for *Opera's* sequel, *A Day at the Races*, with shooting scheduled for that fall. Things looked great. That summer Boasberg played court jester/script doctor on the *Races* road tour with no Ryskind as competition. And as senior writer, he was sure to get primary credit on *Races*, Pulitzer or no Pulitzer.

But anytime the sun rose on Boasberg's horizon, so too did his bad luck. Two weeks into shooting *Races*, Irving Thalberg died. *Races* halted production. Boasberg and Thalberg had known each other since the writer's first days on the lot, and as the months ahead proved, Boasberg had lost a valuable patron.

With *Races* on hold, Boasberg busied himself with Benny. During Christmas week 1936, ten-year-old violinist Stuart Canin appeared as a guest on comic Fred Allen's show, and Allen used the occasion to casually insult Benny's violin playing. Benny answered the following week, and the two comics eviscerated one another coast-to-coast, Allen in Manhattan and Benny in Hollywood—Benny the fall guy to Allen's unflappable heckling. Their feud became the crescendo of the bickering show business atmosphere that Boasberg himself created with Baker and his Boy so many years ago, but now a comedy standard.

Behind the scenes, a real feud brewed. Lawrence Weingarten, Boasberg's producer on the Keaton talkies (and Thalberg's brother-in-law), took control of *Races*, which recommenced shooting in December. By mid-February 1937, the studio announced the credits: "Original Story and Screenplay by Al Boasberg, Robert Pirosh, and George Seaton."

*"Jack Benny presides at the first reading rehearsal of the script, giving all cast members an interpretation of their lines, including inflections. In the foreground, Kenny Baker. Behind him in the second row, left to right: Blanche Stewart, Mary Livingstone and Ed Beloin. In the back row: Al Boasberg (hat turned down), who has been the gag writer for Benny ever since the comedian's vaudeville days; Phil Harris (standing), Bill Morrow, Harry Baldwin, Hillard Marks, Walter Bunker, Ev Mead and Don Wilson."*
—Los Angeles Times

At long last, Boasberg was named first writer, credited as a major hand in a sure hit. But incredibly, that wasn't enough. Boasberg shot a telegram back that since *Races* was essentially a musical, under Motion Picture Academy guidelines (there was no Writers Guild to arbitrate then) the credits should read: "Original Story and Screenplay by Robert Pirosh and George Seaton. Comedy Scenes and Construction by Al Boasberg."[14]

Since the only reason anyone went to a Marx Brothers movie was for the comedy, MGM felt Boasberg asked too much (privately, so did Groucho) and answered their impudent gag man by demoting him, relisting the names as Pirosh, Seaton, and Boasberg. Boasberg demanded arbitration, requesting *Races'* director Sam Wood (his old FBO pal) as judge. MGM, feeling that something was up if he wanted Wood that badly, refused.

One can only guess at Boasberg's state of mind. But consider fifteen years of no recognition, of watching others rise to fame on his work, of studio politics, of ego (including his own), of failing in every attempt to break free from his phantom world. And now add sharing credit with two nobodies, just like on the Benny show. He reached a breaking point. And he escalated.

The man who took cobblers to court now went up against MGM. Boasberg threatened to sue, and worse, to "go on national radio and tell the whole world the truth about *A Day at the Races*." Only a Hollywood screenwriter thinks the "whole world" cares about proper screen credit, but Boasberg was just that writer. MGM stood firm, now revoking any credit and adding a minor contributor, George Oppenheimer, instead. They allowed Boasberg only a note in the Motion Picture Academy's official files.

Simultaneously, Allen and Benny readied for their on-air showdown with Benny traveling to New York for the broadcast. If Boasberg couldn't get on national radio to vent, he knew a guy who could. He once again used the comic as a stand-in, letting his anger fuel the Benny-Allen face-off.

Both feuds reached their climax on the weekend of March 14th. On the air, the Benny show quickly degenerated into a lengthy exchange of insults. "Why you fugitive from a Ripley cartoon ... I'll knock you flatter than the first eight minutes of this program," sniped Allen. "You ought to do well in pictures, Mr. Allen, now that Boris Karloff is back in England," said Benny. "Why if I was a horse, a pony even, and found out that any part of my tail was used in your violin bow I'd hang my head in my oatbag from then on," said Allen. Eventually, the two went out in the hall for a fist fight as the band played selections from *Hit the Deck*.

Backstage, it got ugly. Academy memos recall Boasberg turning bright red and flying into tirades over any mention of *A Day at the Races*. From New York he instructed his attorney Martin Gang to have his name completely removed from *Races*, including Academy credit. His ego allowed for all or nothing, and the studio complied—he received nothing.

In the end, Benny and Allen laughed it all off. Boasberg, who never laughed much anyway, swore never to work in movies again.

The following day, Benny's crew went home, but Boasberg stopped in Buffalo to visit family and friends. Buffalo was the one place Boasberg was what he always wanted to be—a famous author. He entertained local reporters with gags, insider stories, and posed for pictures in his pajamas, looking miserable on hearing of his mother-in-law's imminent arrival—all of which served to remind the citizenry that the "nebbish" they knew from Herman's shop was long gone.

For the papers, Boasberg covered his anger, coming up with the incredible spin that he *preferred* anonymity. "I have always tried to more or less keep my name off the screen," he said, deadpan as usual, "None of the names mean anything to the customers. Why waste the time and money putting them on the film?"

At his sister's house, things were different. Jim Michaels recalls his uncle on the couch, morose, insecure. "It weighed heavily on him," says Michaels, "He knew he was a talent. He wanted some recognition and resented it. He would lie there and ask, 'What if I wake up tomorrow and I'm not funny? How am I gonna live?'"

All Hollywood knows the roar of studio publicity machines gearing up for summer, and as *Races*' release neared, Boasberg had his nose rubbed daily in Marxist propaganda. To some he cursed MGM. To others he continued his pose of nonchalance, dubbing himself "Hollywood's Ghost Writer," adding "If it helps my pal Sam Wood get a great picture, forget me."

As the Benny season wound down, contract negotiations began. After losing Conn,

Benny took no chances, preparing the sweetest deal he could for his gag man: The Golden Contract. Besides its lucrative bonus, its freedom kept Boasberg and the kids, Beloin and Morrow (who disliked working with other writers as much as he did), apart.

In early June, *A Day at the Races* opened just as everyone knew it would, a smash outgrossing even *Opera*. The Marx blitz hit everywhere: radio, newspapers, personal appearances, even a photo feature in *Life*, but not one word about Al Boasberg. Once opening week tallied up, MGM placed a thirteen-page ad supplement in the June 16th issue of Daily *Variety* thanking everyone. Full pages ran devoted to each Marx, Dumont, Sam Wood, Seaton, Pirosh, even the film's choreographer, but not one word about Al Boasberg.

Besides that, Boasberg had another lawsuit hanging over him. The Graham Brothers, Garret and Carrol, a writing team, claimed that Chico and Groucho had stolen a sketch of theirs and used it on radio. Boasberg was set to testify for the Marxes since he allegedly co-wrote it and OK'd its use. A Federal court found the Marxes guilty, and FBI files published in Simon Louvish's Marx Brothers book, *Monkey Business*, reveal that Boasberg most likely did the not-so-light-fingered lifting himself. The man who hated joke thieves more than anyone had now made it a federal crime.

The same day MGM ran its novel-length ad, Boasberg and Benny met to discuss his new contract. With movies, Broadway, directing, and acting closed off to him, Boasberg resigned himself to his fate—once and for all, a gag man.

After shaking hands on it, Boasberg took home that week's script. The plot had a familiar ring to it: A gloating Benny is cast in a big Hollywood movie, only to find he's been given a one-line, one-word walk on, and worse, he has to speak it from inside a barrel. It was "Love in the Suburbs" all over again, Boasberg's first failure haunting his last. The episode also contains Boasberg's last gift to the world, introducing the most beloved stooge heckler in the Benny show history: the miser's valet, Rochester (Eddie Anderson).

That night, Boasberg collapsed and died from a massive coronary.

"Forty-five years old. What a helluva loss he was," said Benny.

The following Saturday, reporters waited outside Boasberg's memorial service at the B.F. Dayton funeral home in Beverly Hills, more interested in the famous mourners than the mourned. Harpo sighed: "The world has lost another unsung hero in the death of Al Boasberg. Few people knew how much he contributed to the happiness of millions."

The body went home to Buffalo. Rosylind did not make the trip, their cold marriage over. Boasberg provided for her with a complex trust fund, making sure to the last that his in-laws couldn't touch his money. Upon her death during World War II the fund reverted entirely to his niece and two nephews. After returning home from the war, Jim Michaels used his portion to begin a 52-year-career in journalism, eventually editing *Forbes* magazine from 1961-1998.

Cut short as Boasberg was, his body of work still astounds. He created the public personae of Benny, Hope, and the Burns and Allen team. Their collective modern style gave us comedy genres like stand-up and the sit-com. In November 1999, the Library of Congress placed a fourth Boasberg film, *Lamb Chops* (1929), in the National Film Registry, which already includes three others: *The General*, *Freaks*, and *A Night at The Opera*. Add his lasting impact on the Benny show, Berle, Abbott and Costello, Martin and Lewis, and Woody Allen—and Boasberg clearly ranks as one of the most influential satirists of his era, if not the century.

Totaling up the network revenues of Hope and Benny alone, Boasberg's writing racked up hundreds of millions of dollars for the entertainment corporations, billions today, and entertained hundreds of millions of Americans. The modern comics became institutions, and their modern style, the standard which later comics followed or fought.

Boasberg's vision is bleak, coated with disarming silliness, puns, and outrageous situations that lessen the pain, but not the result. Armed with the best comic actors of his generation, he popularized a comedy of failure and frustration to the American people, the comedy of his own life. People responded because within it they saw themselves. He found the cracks and chinks in a dream that doesn't happen for everyone, and then got us to laugh at it.

Boasberg's work stays with us in the way performers play sitcoms, movies, sketches, and stand-up every day. He remains unknown because his legacy isn't a single masterpiece or body of work easily evaluated, but rather, an American comic philosophy. Still, the comics knew. The rarely awed Groucho said simply, "He was a comic genius."

In the end, Al Boasberg's quest for fame is perhaps his best joke. It's so perfect, a call to the Writers Guild of America, founded a year and a day after his death, will tell you they have no record of any Al Boasberg ever writing movies in Hollywood.

## Notes

Due to considerations of space, a complete set of the 210 notes for "The Gag Man" cannot be published here. The following is a source list with selected end notes that represent never before published information on either Boasberg or his clients.

To receive a fully notated copy of "The Gag Man," e-mail your request to: boasberg@freedonia.com.

## Works Consulted

Joe Adamson, *Groucho, Harpo, Chico, and Sometimes Zeppo* (New York: Simon and Schuster, 1974).

Hector Arce, *Groucho* (New York: G.P. Putnam's Sons, 1979).

Jack and Joan Benny, *Sunday Nights at Seven* (New York: Warner Books, 1990).

Mary Livingstone Benny, Hilliard Marks, with Marcia Borie, *Jack Benny* (Garden City, NY: Doubleday, 1978).

Milton Berle and Haskell Frankel, *Milton Berle* (New York: Dell, 1974).

George Burns and David Fisher, *All My Best Friends* (New York: Perigee, 1990).

George Burns, *Gracie: A Love Story* (New York: Penguin, 1989).

George Burns, *Living It Up or, They Still Love Me in Altoona* (New York: Berkeley Medallion Books, 1978).

William Robert Faith, *Bob Hope: A Life in Comedy* (New York: G.P. Putnam, 1982).

Irving Fein, *Jack Benny: An Intimate Biography* (New York: Pocket Books, 1977).

Bob Furmanek and Ron Palumbo, *Abbott and Costello in Hollywood* (New York: Perigee, 1991).

Neal Gabler, *An Empire of Their Own* (New York: Crown, 1988).

Neal Gabler, *Winchell: Gossip, Power, and the Culture of Celebrity* (New York: Knopf, 1994).

Douglas Gilbert, *American Vaudeville* (New York: Whittlesey House/McGraw-Hill, 1940).

Bob Hope, as told to Pete Martin, *Bob Hope's Own Story: Have Tux, Will Travel* (New York: Simon and Schuster, 1954).

Henry Jenkins, *What Made Pistachio Nuts?: Early Sound Comedy and the Vaudeville Aesthetic* (New York: Columbia University Press, 1992).

Milt Josefberg, *The Jack Benny Show* (New Rochelle, NY: Arlington House, 1977).

Buster Keaton with Charles Samuels, *My Wonderful World of Slapstick* (New York: Da Capo, 1982 [1960]).

Betty Lasky, *RKO: The Biggest Little Major of Them All* (Englewood Cliffs, NJ: Prentice Hall, 1984).

Joe Laurie, Jr., *Vaudeville: From the Honky Tonks to the Palace* (New York: Henry Holt, 1953).

Eric Lax, *Woody Allen: On Being Funny* (New York: Charterhouse, 1975).

Shawn Levy, *King of Comedy: The Life and Art of Jerry Lewis* (New York: St. Martin's, 1996).

Simon Louvish, *Monkey Business: The Lives and Legends of the Marx Brothers* (New York: St. Martin's, 1999).

Dennis McDougal, *The Last Mogul* (New York: Crown, 1998).

Leonard Maltin, *The Great Movie Shorts* (New York: Bonanza Books, 1972).

Leonard Maltin, *Movie Comedy Teams* (New York: Signet, 1970).

Arthur Marx, *Life with Groucho* (New York: Simon and Schuster, 1954).

Groucho Marx, *The Grouchophile* (New York: Galahad Books, 1979).

Groucho Marx and Richard J. Anobile, *The Marx Bros. Scrapbook* (New York: Darien House, 1973).

Samuel Marx, *Mayer and Thalberg: The Make-Believe Saints*, (New York: Random House, 1975).

Joe Morella, Edward Z. Epstein, and Eleanor Clark, *The Amazing Careers of Bob Hope, From Gags to Riches* (New Rochelle, NY: 1973).

*Motion Picture News Booking Guide* 13, Oct. 1927, found at the AMPAS Margaret Herrick Library, Los Angles, CA (hereafter referred to as "Herrick Library").

Museum of Television and Radio, *Jack Benny: The Radio and Television Work* (New York: HarperPerennial, 1991).

Lawrence J. Quirk, *Bob Hope: The Road Well-Traveled* (New York: Applause Books, 1998).

Benny Rubin, *Come Backstage With Me* (Bowling Green, OH: Bowling Green University Press). No publication date is given on the copy found at the Herrick Library.

Morrie Ryskind with John H. M. Roberts, *I Shot an Elephant in My Pajamas: The Morrie Ryskind Story* (Lafayette, LA: Huntington House, 1994).

David Skal, *Dark Carnival* (New York: Anchor, 1995).

Bill Smith, *The Vaudevillians* (New York: MacMillan, 1976).

Tony Thomas, "Sam Wood: A Master of His Craft," in Clive Denton, Kingsley Canham, and Tony Thomas, *The Hollywood Professionals, Vol. 2: King, Milestone, Wood* (New York: A. S. Barnes, 1974), 121-188.

Arthur Frank Wertheim, *Radio Comedy* (New York: Oxford University Press, 1979).

Larry Wilde, *The Great Comedians* (Secaucus, NJ: Citadel Press, 1973).

Max Wilk, *The Wit and Wisdom of Hollywood* (New York: Athenaeum, 1971).

Ben Yagoda, *Will Rogers* (New York: Knopf, 1993).

Jordan R. Young, *The Laugh Crafters* (Beverly Hills, CA: Past Times Publishing Co., 1999).

## Interviews

Phil Berle, Irving Brecher, Al Brown, George Burns, Susan Marx (interviewed by Joe Adamson), Jim Michaels, Nat Perrin, Robert Pirosh (interviewed by Joe Adamson and Robert B. Weide), Paul Wesolowski.

## Special Sources

RKO Payroll Cards, University of California, Los Angeles Arts-Special Collections, boxes 149, 196, 212, 219, 260.

Jim Michaels family scrapbook articles, clipped from local newspapers in the days after Boasberg's death. They provide invaluable material on Boasberg's early years in Buffalo.

Al Boasberg clipping files at the Herrick Library and the Billy Rose Theater Collection, New York Public Library, New York, New York (hereafter "BRTC").

## Notable Articles and Periodicals

Hundreds of items relating to Al Boasberg were found in *Variety* magazine, 1919-1938. Also useful were *The New York Times* and several Buffalo newspapers (most now defunct). Of these, several articles were key:

"Being a Discourse in Which the Professional Jokesmith, His Methods and Manners, Are Put on the Spot," Oct. 9, 1932, Al Boasberg clippings file, BRTC.

"Gagster," *The New Yorker*, Sept. 10, 1932.

Arthur Ungar, "Al Boasberg Does an 'Off to Buffalo'; Gagsters Will Miss His Ready Wit," *Variety* (June 23, 1937), 2.

## Notes

1. Although most obituaries give his birthdate as 1892, Al Boasberg's birth certificate, on file in the City Clerk's Office of the City of Buffalo, dates his birth as Dec. 5, 1891. His death certificate, on file with the county of Los Angeles' Registrar-Recorder/County Clerk's Office also lists his year of birth as 1891.

2. Ungar cites Boasberg's 1923 entry into the movie business at FBO as well as a mention about him and Paramount publicity, which leaves it unclear if he worked there. If he did it was short lived.

   Lee Marcus (1893-1969), born in Buffalo, attended the same schools as Boasberg, joined FBO in 1921 and stayed on through the RKO merger until he became president of RKO Pathe by 1933. Besides MGM's Irving Thalberg, Marcus was Boasberg's steadiest studio employer and Boasberg's career at FBO/RKO mirrored Marcus'. When Marcus headed the sales department he hired Boasberg to write publicity. When running the shorts division he hired Boasberg to direct Leon Errol, and when producing features, hired the writer for Wheeler and Woolsey pictures. Biographical information on Marcus found in the Lee Marcus Clippings File at the Herrick Library.

3. *Variety*, March 17, 1919 through Oct. 6, 1919, lists Benny's show dates on small time circuits. These are found in the "Variety Bills" section which listed each week's schedule of vaudeville bills for theaters nationwide, broken down by the theater chains from big time to small time. Benny then joined the Orpheum big time circuits on Oct. 13, 1919 at Chicago's Majestic Theater.

4. *San Francisco Chronicle* (March 29, 1920), 7: "Ben K. Benny says that he is the brother of Phil Baker, who was here last week. And since he is quite as amusing as Baker and has all his tricks of voice and expression, why dispute him?"

5. In *Variety* (Sept. 24, 1920), 34, Benny took out an ad announcing his name change to "Jack Benny," indicating that Bernie's infringement claim had been brought and settled.

   "Variety Bills," *Variety* (Oct. 1, 1920), lists Benny jumping to the Eastern Keith chain (Bernie's chain) on Oct. 4, 1920, at the Hippodrome in Youngstown, Ohio. Given the timing, his jump to Keith appears conditional on the name change.

   Copycat acts like Benny were a specific breed of pest in vaudeville. Whereas joke thieves stole bits whole, a Benny lifted another performer's style of delivery (see note 4) or the idea for an act. That is, if Bernie played funny jazz tunes, Benny played funny ragtime. He copied Baker's delivery too, but Baker had been schooled in comedy by his old partner, Ben Bernie, so it's no wonder Benny appeared to lift Bernie. Copycats were often hired by theater managers who wanted to cash in on a popular style but only pay an imitator's fee (see note 10). This was nothing new to Benny, who had received cease and desist letters from other acts before World War I (Wertheim, 135). After the Bernie suit, Benny hired Ned Miller in 1921 (see note 6), put him in a stage box, and then they lifted Baker's act (Fein, 24).

   Later, critics noted Benny's similarity to Frank Fay (*Variety*, Sept. 9, 1929, 15) and Julius Tannen. One unhappy critic said: "Jack Benny has evidently seen Julius Tannen ... but not often enough" (Fein, 25). When seeking his first radio show, Benny planned to steal Bernie's 1932 radio format by starting a copycat dance band (Wertheim, 139-40).

6. *The New York Times* (Aug. 29, 1926), VII 2:8. Here, Benny recalls the Pennsylvania tests as trial for his 1925 New York Palace debut. Benny revised this story four decades later in his incomplete autobiography, eventually published in his daughter's memoirs (*Sunday Nights at Seven*, 17-8), to

say that the reinvention took place in 1921 right after the Bernie suit. But Benny turned toward music, not comedy, and from 1921-1923 (Fein, 23-4) he toured with pianist Ned Miller and introduced Miller's 1922 hit "Why Should I Cry Over You?" Burns recalls the violin experiment taking place in Wilkes-Barre, and it's doubtful lightning struck there both in 1921 and 1925. Whether faulty memory or self-serving revisionism or two separate experiments, it was after the try-out with Boasberg that it worked.

According to Laurie (170-200), out of 50,000 vaude acts maybe five were true monologists who entered in street clothes and *only* talked to entertain. And no matter what their acts, it was Benny's modern style, and soon after, Bob Hope's, that became standard (see Gilbert, 293-4).

Will Rogers is often cited as an early stand-up comic, as he innovated more than anyone the intimate, conversational style of joke-joke-joke monologues that so many stand-ups use. Still, his act was old school, dominated by rope tricks, song and dance, and even unicycle stunts. See Ben Yagoda, *Will Rogers*, 126-9, 132-3, as well as Yagoda's entire "Vaudeville" section.

7. "Al Boasberg Acting When Not Clowning," *Variety* (June 1, 1926), "Pictures" section. Repeated viewings of *The General* lead one to believe that Boasberg was cut from the film or that he is so made-up as to be unrecognizable.

8. "Paul G. Smith Back; Had Tilt with Keaton," *Variety* (June 30, 1926), "Vaudeville" section, describes Smith driving home to Los Angeles after quitting, although it says Keaton prevailed upon him to stay.

9. "Boasberg Leaves Keaton," *Variety* (Aug. 25, 1926), 9. In the same issue, Boasberg took out an ad thanking Keaton: "Thank you Buster Keaton for your kindness and acceptance of my comedy suggestions during the filming of *Battling Butler* and *The General*."

10. Laurie, 231. Laurie: "When all the acts started stealing from each other, the writer was helpless. The booking office was a lot to blame for booking 'copy acts' because they were cheaper ... The writers became disgusted and luckily walked into other facets of show biz that needed them. They contributed their talents (for much bigger dough) to the new fields of radio and pics ...."

11. Lawrence Weingarten's *Free and Easy* production notes on file at the University of Southern California.

12. "Keaton's War Background," *Variety*, Jan. 15, 1930, reports Boasberg at work on the script for what became *Doughboys*. Keaton scholars Marion Meade and Rudi Blesh differ on the film's source material. Meade says it was a remake of Wallace Beery's *Behind the Front* (1926) with some Keaton ideas added. Blesh says it's a Keaton original. Either way, Boasberg set to work months before its May 13th production start. Marion Meade, *Buster Keaton: Cut to the Chase* (New York: Da Capo, 1997), 196. Rudi Blesh, *Keaton* (New York: Collier Books, 1971 [1966]), 315, views Boasberg as a meddler in what he sees as Keaton's story. Lawrence Weingarten's *Doughboys* production notes on file at USC place Boasberg on set from day one.

13. Marx and Anobile, 204. Ryskind's draft of the road tour script, March 19, 1935, contains an early version of "state room." Since Boasberg initiated this scene (see A. Marx, 193, Arce, 227-8, Ryskind with Roberts, 112) it means he rewrote Kaufman and Ryskind sometime before March 19, 1935. In regards to that Holy Grail of Marx research, the long lost first draft of *Opera* by Kaufman and Ryskind, let's consider this: it doesn't exist. Researchers Joe Adamson, Paul Wesolowski, and Simon Louvish have combed the papers of Kaufman, Ryskind, Groucho and MGM with no such script ever turning up. Then consider Kaufman's own well-documented idiosyncrasies: his time consuming attention to detail, aversion to writing love scenes, writing Marx comedy in "block scenes" separate from the love story, a social life which that month included his tabloid-friendly affair with Mary Astor, and his oft-expressed desire to bolt Hollywood as soon as possible—and it suddenly makes sense that after only five weeks of work that the truncated March 19, 1935 "block scenes" script is all MGM or Boasberg ever got from him. All of which means Boasberg did much more than punch *Opera* up—he co-wrote the script.

14. Boasberg's odd choice of credit—"comedy scenes and construction"—was not idiosyncrasy. The term came from the silent days when comedy writers sought something more impressive than "gag man" as a job description. Boasberg (we can assume) asked journalists to use this phrase when writing of him since items about him or quoting him often do. *Variety* took this about as seriously as

most people do when they hear of garbage men called "sanitation engineers." *Variety*: "More Studio Titles" and "Boasberg F.B.O. Gagger," (Sept. 22, 1926), "Pictures" section; "Coast Notes" column (Nov. 2, 1927); Abel Green, "Among the Talkers," (June 26, 1929), 10. Al Boasberg clipping file, Herrick Library.

## Acknowledgments

Without the help of Jim Michaels, Al Boasberg's nephew, this sketch of Al's life would be a list of film credits, backstage banter, and some good gags. But with Jim's insight, we understand Al Boasberg as a man, what he wanted and never got, and through that, Al's enormous impact as an artist. My thanks to Jim for his time, opening the family books to me, and a great Yankees game.

I would also like to thank the late Betsy Williams (formerly Betsy Boasberg), the Boasberg family as a general rule, Ana Marie Cox, Joe Adamson, Irving Brecher, Nat Perrin, the late George Burns, Irving Fein, Arthur Marx, Todd McCarthy and *Daily Variety*, the late Al Brown (vaudeville's biggest fan), Sam Gill, Janet Lorenz, and the Margaret Herrick Library of the Academy of Motion Picture Arts and Sciences, Francine Della Catena and the *Los Angeles Times*, Anthony Bogucki and the Library of Congress, Joey Anuff for one great idea (not that he hasn't had others), Ed Perry for the leg work, and my friends and family who had no idea who Al Boasberg was, still don't, but listened with great patience to my "exciting" news every time I found a new piece of obscure information.

And finally, I want to thank Al Boasberg, if only for the laughs. Credit where credit is due.

# IV

## MAE WEST

in "SHE DONE HIM WRONG"

with CARY GRANT

*a Paramount Picture*

# Mae West Can Play Anything

**Leo McCarey** (1935)

What did the Queen of Sheba say to King Solomon when she took her first peek at his thousand wives?

In the same spot, Mae West would have said in her husky, languorous drawl, "What you need is one good one."

Can you picture our devastating West playing the Queen of Sheba? I can. Having directed her once, in *Belle of the Nineties*, it is my opinion that she can play anything. I'm serious. As a matter of fact, don't be surprised if Mae actually does appear on the screen some day in her version of the biblical romance.

It has been said that the real artist, an actor or actress of fascinating, dominating personality, can play anything. That's Mae West. She has what it takes. Her interpretation of a character should be scintillating and believable as that of any other outstanding actress. As, say, Helen Hayes, Pauline Lord, Greta Garbo or Ruth Chatterton.

True, she would undoubtedly invest each characterization with her own peculiarly intriguing personality, but what player doesn't? True, she would undoubtedly play for comedy instead of tragedy. But we all know that comedy is the very essence of humanness.

Mae West is essentially a great comedienne. In the art of acting, comedy is regarded as one of the most important requisites.

When I first walked on a Paramount set to direct Mae West, I didn't know whether she was actually an actress, or, simply a woman with an amazing personality. She hadn't finished rehearsing the first scene until I knew the answer to that one.

It was "actress"!

There is none of the poseur in Mae West. She is so genuine in her work that she breathes life into characters that would be flamboyantly artificial in the hands of lesser players. For example: Jeanne Eagels was the only actress who succeeded in making *Sadie Thompson* a believable, sympathetic character.

In her characterizations we know so well in pictures today, Mae West is the soul of rhythm. Neither her seductive walk, her knowing alluring wink, nor her languorous drawl are studied poses. I have seen several clever girls attempt to imitate Mae, but they always fail to even touch the real thing. Their Westian poses are jerky and unconvincing. In other words, the lure is lost.

Like our other few real actress, Mae believes in what she is doing. She understands the necessity of rhythm and relaxation in acting. She reminds me of a "sleeping" leopard, completely relaxed, yet with all her sense fully alert for the big moment. To watch Mae play even an unimportant scene say, strolling nonchalantly across a set, stopping to light a cigarette for a man, is to watch the epitome of grace. But to watch her really turn on the heat and "GIVE"—I'll leave the effect on your system to your own fertile imagination.

I wonder how many people realize that Mae West satirizes sex? She has made our old-fashioned vampires, those mysterious, pallid, emaciated, smoky-eyed females appear as futile as they usually are in real life. Her robust, lusty humor would do much towards humanizing several traditional characters.

Mae has always wanted to do a version of the *Queen of Sheba*. As this glamorous biblical character is almost wholly a legendary woman, the West version, however humorous, is apt to be as truthful as any.

*"A great comedienne" — Leo McCarey on Mae West.*

## Catherine the Great

Observe the billing! I submit Mae West as *Catherine the Great*. Am I mad? Not at all. Read your history. What sort of woman was the amazing Empress of all the Russias? Not the glorified person we have seen in pictures. Not by any stretch of the imagination. Instead, she was a female *Don Juan* or *Casanova*, as well as a remarkably strong, dominating and fascinating woman.

She freely acknowledged taking her fun where she found it.

She was really a woman of great executive ability, and every inch an empress despite the irregularity of her moral life. To the very end, she was a great gal, good-natured and bubbling over with robust humor.

So much for the character that everyone will agree Mae West can play. I'll now go to the other extreme.

Mae could play a *Peg O' My Heart*.

## Mae as Peg

Yes, I know this sounds ridiculous. What, La Belle West in curls and baby-faced innocence? No, that's not the idea. I'm talking about the plot of the play, not the character as played by the unforgettable Laurette Taylor.

If Mae were to play a *Peg O' My Heart* she need only forego the curls. The Irish brogue and mannerisms suit her personality to a T. An Irish-American shopgirl, say, who finds herself suddenly transplanted into stuffy English society because of an inheritance. Can't you picture Mae in these surroundings?

This plot is the same amusing idea, in reverse, as *Ruggles of Red Gap*, which I have just directed. Here we have Charles Laughton and Roland Young, typical Britishers, suddenly transplanted into American Western society as typified by Mary Boland and Charlie Ruggles. It hits the funny-bone.

In *Peg*, everyone frowns upon her American manners. The only one who sees her true value is the English barrister who is administering the estate.

At the climax of the story, there is consternation in the stuffy household when it leaks out that someone has been attending clambakes with the "heavy."

Mae West in the role, realizing that the daughter is the guilty one, would rush to the defense with a crack running something like this:

"Wait a minute. If there is any fun like that going on around here, who do you think would be having it?"

## Tragic Stella

Do you recall the grand performance the late Belle Bennett contributed to silent pictures as *Stella Dallas*?

If Samuel Goldwyn ever makes the picture again, and he probably will, "Stella" would be a sensational success with Mae in the role.

Here is a woman with no culture, no background. A silly butterfly-minded woman who valiantly strives to have her fling out of life, no matter what the cost. Yet she tears your heart out in her vain attempts to be a good mother to the child.

Here is an everyday character much older than *Peg*, much less colorful than *Catherine* and the *Queen of Sheba*.

I should like to see Mae West play the role, if only to demonstrate her latent versatility as an actress.

## Go West

Suppose Mae were to go West? No pun intended, as "West" is a geographical location in this instance. One of the finest roles in all fiction awaits her. A great woman, nurtured in the raw of the man-made Western pioneer world. A stern-fibered give-and-take girl who was much finer than most of her sheltered sisters.

I give you Mae West as *Cherry Malotte* in *The Spoilers*.

In the Rex Beach epic of the Alaskan gold rush days, Mae could go dramatic to the hilt. A touch of rollicking Western humor here and there, but essentially tragic and bitter.

Can you picture, as I can, Mae as the faro dealer taking the boys? Or, playing a losing game for the hero's love with that gay "you can be had" attitude?

What else could she play? Well, how about that swell little person whose kindly, lovable nature captivated *Charles the First* quite as much as her lure as an actress and her sex appeal?

*Nell Gwyn*. I'd give a lot of salary for the opportunity to direct Mae in this gay and romantic, but tragic bit of history. Mae could contribute a characterization as rich and racy, laughable and human as was Charles Laughton's *Henry the Eighth*.

Unlike many of our outstanding screen personalities, Mae West will never be limited. She can play anything, and many surprising things well. She has terrific personal appeal on the screen. Woman like her as well as men. Mae understands the psychology of her own sex.

She never takes a good woman's man away from her.

Never says "Come up and see me sometime" to the wrong guy.

The audiences get a great kick out of Mae. Because they get as many laughs as they do thrills.

I have mentioned a few of the girls Mae West could play if she chose to—*Sheba*, *Catherine*, *Stella*, *Peg*, *Nell*, and *Cherry*. It would not be at all difficult to picture her as *Madame X*, *Salvation Nell*, *Dubarry*, *Salomy Jane*, *Anna Christie*, or even the gal I've reserved for the last.

How about Mae playing opposite, say, John Barrymore, in *The Taming of the Shrew*?

Shades of Shakespeare! This is no jest. After all, you know, the Bard of Avon's women were down-to-earth gals. In my opinion, Mae could play the shrewish Katharina to John's domineering Petrucchio as well as most of our modern actresses.

Why not have a go at some of these girls, Mae?

Why not indeed?

Here are the reasons:

1. . . . *She Done Him Wrong* made picture history.
2. . . . *I'm No Angel* made more money.
3. . . . *Belle of the Nineties* (despite censorship) making new records.
   Sure, Mae West can change her character, but who wants her to?
   I don't.

—*Photoplay*, June 1935

# We Remember Irene

**Richard Schickel** (1991)

He has been bored to tears. His life has been in need of saving. He had begun to wonder, "Don't beautiful women ever travel anymore?" The object of this smoothly practiced seduction—Charles Boyer's delivery is almost languid, hinting at a weariness with the verbal conventions of womanizing that he has yet to admit—eyes him quizzically, an amused yet tolerant light in her eye. She, too, has been here before. "Have you been getting results with a line like that?" she asks.

This shipboard encounter in *Love Affair* is, I think, a quintessential Irene Dunne moment. The mock incredulity of her line reading is impeccably judged. She always knew how to put a man in his place, but at the same time leave him room to maneuver out of it, the best method for which was to join her in good-natured laughter at the all-too transparent stratagems, the all-too-obvious posturings of the male animal. The customary (or real-life) alternatives—sulking, self-pity, indignant reproach—were not options when she was around.

If this image from Leo McCarey's 1939 film is the first to come to mind when her name is mentioned, others, similar in character, tumble quickly upon it. For example, her delicious response to the bumptious presence of Cary Grant, playing her estranged husband Jerry, at her genteel song recital in *The Awful Truth*. Tipping dangerously back in a spindly chair, deliberately trying to catch her attention and break her up, he manages only to break up his chair, eliciting from her a delighted giggle but no loss of pitch or dignity as she completes her aria. Her laughter is only partly at his deserved discomfort; it also acknowledges her continuing appreciation of the prankish spirit that drew her to him. And it promises the reconciliation that is sure (and soon) to come.

Perhaps better still, there is the almost wordless exchange between Dunne and Grant near the beginning of *Penny Serenade*. He has bought a phonograph record from her in the music shop where she works. Now, having walked her home, he asks if he can come in and play it on her Victrola. Puzzlement scuds briefly across her face, then recognition of his ploy: if he doesn't have a machine of his own, there can be only one reason he bought the disc. He smiles shyly; she emits an almost imperceptible chuckle and beckons him into her house, into her life.

These transactions are both an acknowledgment and an invitation. The former, stated without dither or evasion (but without blatancy or cynicism, either), is of her own grown-up sexuality The latter encourages the man to join her on this (to him) new level of self-awareness. It is a test, perhaps, but it is never a tease. Never.

Her playing grounded the conventions of romantic comedy in a sort of idealized reality. Maybe one didn't—doesn't—meet any women like Irene Dunne in life, but because her reactions (and everything we've discussed so far is a reaction) were so unforced, so free of mannerism, one felt—feels —comfortable in her presence as one often does not with a more overtly "screwball" woman like Carole Lombard. To put it another way, Dunne makes you think she is less unusual than she actually is.

Her directness bespoke capability, the capacity to handle any situation—comic, roman-

**110**

*Irene Dunne, Leo McCarey, and a visiting Cary Grant on the set of* Love Affair *(1939)—
remade by McCarey with Grant eighteen years later as* An Affair to Remember.

tic, tragic—life (or a screenplay) presented, in a sensible and simplifying way. That capability, in turn, bespoke experience. And maturity. In her interesting, eccentric recent book on romantic comedy, *The Runaway Bride*, Elizabeth Kendall observes that Dunne came to the movies older than most female stars of her era; she was 32 when she made her screen debut, with a solid career as a working actress in the theater behind her. It is an overlooked, but now that it has been made, obvious point about her.

But that said, there still remains something elusive, mysterious, about the source of the wisdom she wore so charmingly. Her upturned nose suggests a pert sense of fun. Her powerful jaw suggests strength of character. And her eyes enigmatically mediate the conflict we read in her face. As late as 1978, when she granted James Harvey, the expert historian of *Romantic Comedy*, what appears to have been her last extensive interview, he observed in life what he had, of course, observed previously on the screen, "something funny and secretive at the center of her eyes." But he was no more able than anyone else to penetrate to its source.

Most of her movies make no attempt to explain her gently knowing air; they simply accepted it (and trusted the audience to accept it too), as the most salient quality of her screen persona, as defining in its way as Kate Hepburn's hauteur or Davis' imperfectly suppressed hysteria—but more entrancing precisely because it was so subtly stated. Other

*Irene Dunne*

characters responded to it, obviously, but they never commented on it openly and it was never turned into a plot point.

In the Harvey interview, Dunne's attitude toward her work was just what one might have hopefully imagined: she remembered what she chose to remember, and she was in charge of herself and the situation, just as she had been on the screen. She looked back on her past with matronly forbearance—neither living in it nor rejecting it. Decently respectful of her own achievements, discreet and kindly in her recollections of colleagues, her attitude toward her former life is perhaps best described as distantly affectionate.

She sounded only one slightly off-key note. When Harvey asked if she had watched actresses like Jean Arthur and Carole Lombard, she replied rather abruptly (by her standards): "I didn't admire them. . . . I never admired a comedienne." That was, she said, because comedy had come so easily to her, and because she preferred, in any case, "the heavier things."

Preferred *Back Street* to *The Awful Truth*? *Magnificent Obsession* to *Theodora Goes Wild*? *I Remember Mama* over everything? Curious! Perhaps more curious to us than to her, since the conventions of romantic comedy have, if anything, grown yet more appealing with the passage of time, while those of the weeper now require a strenuous imaginative exercise to apprehend appreciatively. Still, looking at examples of the latter, one can see that, as an actress, Dunne made no distinction between comedy and melodrama. Her emotional directness, that straightforwardness that redeems her comedies from implausibility, generally redeems the soap operettas from sentimental excess. Dunne does not deny her emotions—they're right there, entirely visible—but she is always in control of them. She accepts cruel fate with the same steadiness of spirit with which, in other contexts, she accepts masculine posturing.

Take, for example, the first of them, 1932's *Back Street*. When we first meet her Ray

Schmidt in turn-of-the-century Cincinnati she is regarded as "fast." She isn't, of course. She is just a gal who likes to kid around with the traveling salesmen as they pass through town, have a dance or a drink with them in a beer garden, but always knows she can manage these oafs, keep them in line. Indeed, she is so strong in these scenes that she subverts the rest of the film. We just can't believe that this confident woman would abandon her career, however modest, and allow herself to be kept in a "back street" apartment. Not by Walter Saxel (played by the same stuffy and inattentive John Boles who would soon encumber Stanwyck in *Stella Dallas*). And not for her entire life. A couple of years is the most we can imagine our Irene devoting to him before she recovered her senses. Yet, somehow, the picture works. Having subverted it, Dunne then redeems it with something unspoken in her performance—that reserve of wit and intelligence that shines in her eyes. You believe that whatever her outward circumstances, an imaginative and sustaining inner life is being lived as she awaits, with uncharacteristic passivity, her lover's rather perfunctory visits.

Her *Ann Vickers* of 1933 coordinates Dunne's spirit and a fictional situation much more persuasively. In it she plays a prison reformer who falls in love with a casually corrupt judge (Walter Huston), bears his child out of wedlock (he is married when they meet), then bears loss of job and social standing when their liaison is discovered after he is sentenced to prison for his peculations. Theirs is a remarkably adult relationship, more good-humored than passionate, full of respect for the quality of each other's minds. Huston's judge is, indeed, one of the few plausible white-collar criminals in movie history—and also one of the few presented objectively, without resort to moralism. We are encouraged to see him as a confident but not arrogant or cynical man, gracefully carrying a complex understanding of how the social and judicial systems interact, convinced that his manifest intelligence should guarantee his fundamental honesty against any inquiry. How could anyone think a man of his temperament would permit a few stock market tips to cloud his judicial integrity?

The press and public, always eager for the simplified understandings of human motives, refuse to take him on his own terms. And he is too proud—or maybe just too smart—to try to explain himself to them. He contents himself with Ann's perfect understanding. Waiting for him to serve out his prison term, raising their child in severely straitened circumstances, she is serenely at work, earning her living in a new career as a writer. There's no time for self-pity in her life and no room for it in Dunne's playing.

*Ann Vickers*, which is based on a Sinclair Lewis novel, is a movie that, unlike her other Thirties films, permits her the dignity of a serious career and an opportunity to demonstrate how misery can be blunted by getting busy. It prefigures her wartime pictures, *A Guy Named Joe* and *The White Cliffs of Dover*, as well as *Anna and the King of Siam* and *The Mudlark*, in all of which she sustains more permanent and devastating losses (she is a widow in three of them and loses her fiancé in the fourth), but soldiers on, alone and sublimating, improving her own lot and the world's through hard, useful work. Her *Mama* in 1948, though spared widowhood, is the ultimate statement of that ethics. Practical, self-denying, taciturn at first glance, warm and fiercely protective of her numerous family on longer acquaintance, this Norwegian immigrant woman artlessly summarized the values Dunne's generation had been taught to revere and did so in a film the only business of which was to soberly (and lengthily) propagate them.

Her biography—what little we know of it—shows us why she tended to regard this and her other "serious" films more highly than the comedies (she particularly, and correctly, despised the ditsiness of Vinnie Day, *Life with Father's* mother). She had been raised in modestly prosperous circumstances until she was 11. Then her father died, and her family was forced to live with grandparents in what Kendall calls "threadbare gentility" in Madison, Indiana. The way out was—need one say it?—hard work. Dunne was a church soloist, an earnest music student, a failure in an audition at the Met. For nearly a decade thereafter she pursued a theatrical career that was busy and aspiring but only moderately successful, its height being Magnolia in the road company of *Show Boat*— the role she repeated in the 1936 movie version, but first the place where the talent scouts finally found her. Somewhere along the way she married a Chicago dentist, and commuted between that city and Los Angeles during the first years of movie stardom, after which he joined her on the West Coast, where they settled into a comfortable, bourgeois sort of existence. Dunne made her last picture when she was 54, quitting, if not at the top, then when she was still near to it. She did a little television, joined the board of Technicolor, toyed with an autobiography but decided her life was too dull to interest most readers. She lived out the remainder of her days quietly, but not reclusively, and with no apparent regrets about any aspect of her life. To the end she maintained her faith in the twin pillars of her childhood, Republicanism—in the Fifties she did some political errands for Eisenhower—and Catholicism.

In her personal history we can read youthful ambition and realistic, even rather objective, professionalism in her maturity, and what appears to be a grateful sinking back into

Theodora Goes Wild: *Irene Dunne and "womanizing New York artist" Melvyn Douglas, "dying to be tamed by her."*

gentility in her later years. Nothing in it, though, hints at the worldly wit we think we read in her eyes, or at the tolerant shrewdness about the opposite sex that her screen character proposed. In other words, it tends to deepen rather than to elucidate her enigma.

We have, however, left out of this account her curious response to her first comedy and one of her best films, *Theodora Goes Wild* in 1936. When Columbia first proposed it, she rejected it. When the studio persisted, she actually fled to Europe in an attempt to avoid it. Why? Surely she was not that frightened of comedy. Surely she knew that she had gracefully handled funny passages in a number of her early films.

I think it is just possible that the piece cut discomfitingly close to the bone. Theodora is a small-town girl living demurely with her aunts. Her life is not unlike that which Dunne knew as a child. Under a pseudonym, she writes a wicked bestseller exposing the hypocrisies of small-town life. Her anonymity is then threatened by the pursuit of the womanizing New York artist (Melvyn Douglas) who drew the book's jacket. Dunne's character can, of course, handle him. Indeed, he's a man just dying to be tamed by her. What Dunne couldn't handle—or didn't want to handle—was a character who betrayed one of her deepest values. No, not Republicanism. And not Catholicism— not directly, anyway. What she didn't want to betray overtly was basic old-fashioned middle-class decorum. That was just not her way.

She was, after all, brought up in a period when funny girls were not encouraged, and intelligent ones were taught to suppress that quality—especially in small Indiana towns. Theodora flouts those rules both in her work and in her behavior, thereby criticizing the society that promulgates them.

I have the feeling that despite her success in this film (it brought Dunne her second Oscar nomination and the beginnings of a new career path just as the fad for weepers faded), she was determined never to break the rules so rudely again. I'm convinced that the secret her eyes could never entirely veil, her spirit never entirely suppress, was an intelligence of a rebellious or at any rate a very independent kind. Writing about her, thinking back on the women of her time and class, the women who were the mothers of my generation, I recall seeing that light shine briefly in other eyes, eyes which never faced any camera bigger than a box Brownie. It was as quickly dimmed because the knowledge it bespoke was a private knowledge, a knowledge that if fully vented tended to subvert the right order of things. This order was not dependent on specific political belief or religious conviction, but it was founded on the sense that conventions of middle-class morality must be publicly upheld, whatever one's private knowledge of their failures and hypocrisies.

Now, of course, everyone is free to criticize that morality as shrilly as they like. But the world is not appreciably better for that freedom. And the art of screen acting is appreciably poorer because on the whole it lacks the kind of tact, delicacy and, yes, shyness with which Irene Dunne let undermining truth slip forth—between the lines convention insisted on drawing.

# Edgar Kennedy:
# The Bull of the Woods

**Donald Phelps** (1998)

Among my hopes for the hereafter is the establishment of my ideal film studio for the perpetuation of joy and light not available elsewhere. I don't have in mind any very high-flown film concepts—*The Divine Comedy*, say, in actual locations, or once-and-for-all-time refutation of the evolutionists, with introduction and voiceover by Alistair Cooke. Rather, my idea is to unite or in some cases reunite creative film personalities that I feel belong together, working with their own material. The truncated career of that richly expressive talent John Candy might be resumed at the hands of the droll and keen-eyed Gregory La Cava. Lee Tracy might find himself at last happily enfolded in Preston Sturges' repertory company, as would that flavorsome and generally forgotten comedian George Gobel (whose movie *The Birds and the Bees*, indeed, was a hopelessly mismounted and misfired attempt to remake *The Lady Eve*). Among such fantasies, however subject to reconsideration and recommendations from fellow enthusiasts, one is paramount and unchangeable.

I mean the reunion of Leo McCarey and Edgar Kennedy. The reunion, that is, of a comedic maestro whose style mingles filigree-like sophistication with the wide-gaited leisureliness and breezy physicality of that Northwest that he commemorated in *Ruggles of Red Gap* or the persona of Ralph Bellamy in *The Awful Truth*, and one of his first musicians: a roaring buffoon whose façade seems as uncomplicated as boilerplate and as finely tuned as a boiler factory; yet who, in a nearly twenty-year cavalcade of two-reel comedies, plus innumerable supporting, featured, and at length cameo roles, discloses sidelights of humanity that engage our sympathies where we never expected to spend them. Kennedy should rightly have joined the likes of Charles Ruggles, Victor Moore, and Dean

*Edgar Kennedy*

**116**

Jagger in McCarey's portrait gallery of perplexed middle-aged family men fighting the daily skirmishes of family life on darkling plains.

They were brought together during the Twenties by their common participation in the careers of Laurel and Hardy, whose directors then included McCarey, George Stevens, and James Parrott (brother of Charley Chase). They helped nurture the joint style—distanced deliberation and explosive slapstick—of those genial, plaintive, and gallant gentlemen-in-waiting. And it is highly possible that L&H's inherent style in its pomp and wistfulness and whimsical mischief delivered some messages to Kennedy. He also directed them under the elegant nomenclature E. Livingston Kennedy in *You're Darn Tootin'* and *From Soup to Nuts*.

## Who Started All This?

Kennedy's recurrent role in Laurel and Hardy's adventures was almost always that of a policeman: a character and a countenance to which the cop persona and uniform seemed as though wedded. He was a burly man with a chest like a kiln, atop two strikingly long and slender legs. His arched bald head, fringed with hair, sets off a face that in repose recalls Thomas Nast's caricatures of Irish immigrants. It was at rest, however, only for momentary interludes in a procession of writhing grimaces, anguished contractions, with eyes, mouth, and nose squeezed as in a fist; popeyed horror; and, much less often, sunbursts of beaming joviality, nearly always at some likely-seeming prospect of wealth which, invariably, sooner or later collapsed. He might have passed for a bilious Friar Tuck, or a Humpty Dumpty who had attempted to repair himself, aided by a home-carpentry guidebook. What a slapstick Job he might have made! He had a fine tenor voice, which he used in the Forties with startling eloquence in *Hitler's Madman*; when first recorded in 1929 for Laurel and Hardy's *Unaccustomed as We Are*, it registered too high and dismayed Hal Roach, who found it effeminate. Kennedy thus adopted the bearish gruffness that spared him the fate of John Gilbert in a similar situation.

In the Laurel and Hardy movies (see esp. *Leave 'em Laughing* and *The Finishing Touch*), he would show up in the last throes of some unimaginable traffic pileup. His hands are planted on his hips; his face a pudding of suspended responses: incredulity, stolid determination, and gloomy challenge, all bothered, like a hair in the pudding, by the hideous suspicion that he is entering the Augean stables with a dustpan and whiskbroom. Such an expression Fortinbras might have worn when walking in on the fifth-act carnage of *Hamlet*. Actually, in nontheatrical life, Fortinbras' question—directed as much to the universe as to the mess before him—might have been Edgar's: "Who started all this?"

In such moments, and throughout his career, he was that ever-present and invaluable emblem of vaudeville and, until a few decades ago, movies: the Foil. He was the guardian of the status quo: the jaunty, mellow, and sardonic George Burns; the patient Bertie McCullough. They were straightmen in the sense of upright presences, stanchions against the frothy zaniness of Gracie Allen and Bobby Clark.

Laurel and Hardy intermittently played foil to each other, though basically, of course, theirs was a joint operation. Their recurrent foils were often opponents—Billy Gilbert, James Finlayson, Cliff Hall. There were occasional menaces, like Dick Cramer's gunman in *Saps at Sea* or George Marshall's vengeful mess sergeant in *Pack Up Your Troubles*; but they were antagonists and threats, rather than stooges. The strictly comic opponents of L&H were present mainly to react, including those deliberative duels in

The Finishing Touch *and* Duck Soup: *Kennedy and friends.*

*Big Business, Tit for Tat,* and *Battle of the Century.* However, as true blue foils, they embodied reality, albeit with a twist. In their flinty meanness (Finlayson), pomposity (Gilbert), and ferrety distrust (Hall), these foils represented the underside of a middle-class style to which Stan and Ollie usually aspired. And they were very special catalysts, igniting the injured gallantry and, underneath, destructive mischief that Stan and Ollie held in reserve. Kennedy, by contrast, was a classic foil in both his brief and prolonged appearances, but especially in the walk-ons described he was essentially a square peg stoically but uneasily seeking a square hole. That unease, that suggestion of a wormlike suspicion that he was in the wrongest possible place at the wrongest possible time, would complicate and enrich Kennedy's screen character in appearances for decades to come.

For his part, director Leo McCarey imprinted with his deft, gracious, and impish style one of comedy's immemorial pillars: the milking of a comic situation or line. In his 1937 masterpiece *The Awful Truth,* the sequences of Cary Grant trying on a suspiciously ill-fitting homburg, or of Grant and Irene Dunne bidding for the affection of "Mr. Smith" (a pet terrier), are made to dance like kite tails, without obvious embroidery or forced complications. McCarey's best films have a pervading rhythmic sensitivity, expressed through those dawdling, sparring dialogue bouts between Grant and Dunne. They generate an affection laced with eroticism between thirtyish married folks that may be found even in the earliest scenes between Helen Hayes and Dean Jagger in McCarey's overvehement yet powerful *My Son John.*

## Edgar, Leo, Harpo

McCarey—and, unseen but manifest, Laurel and Hardy—were on hand in the 1933 Paramount feature *Duck Soup.* McCarey reportedly complained that the Marx Brothers overleaped his directorial influence. To a degree, perhaps, they may have. But in at least one portion of that film—I mean, the pantomime suite that comprises the scenes involving Harpo, Chico, and Edgar, plus the Paul Revere sequence with Harpo and Edgar—McCarey's influence prevailed and triumphed. One might mention also the impersonation sequence, more widely cited, of three Grouchos in nightcaps and nightgowns before a nonexistent mirror. The latter sequence, and probably the earlier sequences in their slapstick patterns, are almost certainly of far-reaching vaudeville and, surely, *commedia dell'arte* ancestry. However, the dallying, teasing rhythms of the mirror sequence—the true Groucho and bogus Grouchos trying to entrap each other with abrupt turnarounds, side glances, and buck-and-wings—are, to me, unmistakable and precious McCarey.

Together, the pantomime segments probably add up to the longest pantomime sequence in any Marx film. They surround the brothers with the airy liberty of silent films, delivering them from their pattered monotony. Moreover, they lend a sense of structure and fluidity to the sometimes shapeless and desultory funmaking. Converted, rather than transplanted, vaudeville.

In the scenes with Kennedy, Chico and Harpo are working a peanut stand in between gigs as espionage agents for two imminently warring countries. Kennedy runs a neighboring but not neighborly lemonade stand. He asks Chico to reduce the volume of his expostulations to Harpo, on the somewhat improbable grounds that they are driving away his customers (none of whom are to be seen). Chico apologizes with a further battery of expostulation; while Harpo, possibly suspecting that they are ganging up on him, joins in the roiling non sequiturs by snatching Edgar's derby. Kennedy's accouterments, in addition to the bowler, include rather tight-fitting black pants that emphasize his slender legs, a striped shirt, and a short black vest. Attire familiar in prints of 19th century Hell's Kitchen, and also the costume worn by Eric Campbell as the Bully in Chaplin's *Easy Street*.

There follows a reprise of the old schoolyard game Piggy-Keepaway. Edgar's frenzy escalates into semiarticulate bellowing. One's laughter is slightly soured by the gratu-itousness of the brothers' sport; and by the thread of genuine anguish in Edgar's bellicose act. One feels that the eruption of rage is unwelcome and even oppressive to him.

Presently, however, like a musical segue, the hat-snatching becomes an adagio dance: Edgar seizes Chico's Tyrolean bonnet, while Chico grabs Harpo's conspicuously used topper. From a dubious exercise in bear-baiting, the action becomes a lyrical caper of men and hats that suggests a Magritte painting. Beyond that, it strikes a note of charm that evokes Leo McCarey's aptitude (a) for prolonging and attenuating a comic mood and (b) for leavening slapstick with antic agility and even beauty. The hat motif repre-sents another vaudeville-derived toccata. The vaudeville hat, of course, was an immemo-rial prop for cane-flourishing dancers; a handy visual tag for the comedian (see Ed Wynn with his imperial headgear); and, to be sure, a target for many imaginable missiles. This last function, by the way, recognizes the hat as the symbol of everyday gentility; and, as such, was adopted by McCarey with a typical injection of whimsical inventiveness. Beside Grant's changeable homburg, one recalls the mingling of Charles Laughton's British bowler with all those Stetsons (*Ruggles of Red Gap*); and as a tiny grace note to *The Bells of St. Mary's*, the kitten that commandeers Father Bing O'Malley's straw boater with poltergeist-like effects (an exorcism at this point, for the hat and for the film as a whole, might have proved both entertaining and otherwise beneficial). Some sweet pantomime with ousted father Victor Moore's old hat in *Make Way for Tomorrow* reminds us of McCarey's tenderness toward gentility with the gloss worn off.

The second segment does not follow immediately, but only after a few reels' interlude of Groucho, Margaret Dumont, and Louis Calhern. I readily confess that after some years' viewing of *Duck Soup*, I thought of the Harpo-Edgar sequence as a seamless whole. One's first thoughtless response might be that the two segments properly belong together. Such a response, however, misunderstands McCarey's craft in the contrapuntal interweaving of two sequences.

When we return to curbside, Harpo is standing beside his peanut wagon as Edgar appears. There is a certain purpose in Edgar's bearing, his unmistakable swagger. Harpo, too, appears to sense the change, for he responds with an unaccustomed uneasiness, per-haps heightened by Chico's absence. He greets Edgar with an affable smile and nod, plus a complimentary salute to the straw boater that has replaced the beleaguered derby. Indeed, his behavior is much closer to the amiable first-person Harpo of the autobiogra-phy than in any of his previous films.

It soon becomes obvious, however, that the amenities occur too late. Edgar, too, is straying slightly from his familiar persona. His fuse is down to the nub; he is ready to fulfill his bullyboy costume. In continued silence, he picks up a bag of peanuts; and, when Harpo gently pantomimes a payment request, smears his open hand with a spatula bear-ing what appears to be mustard. Harpo, his affability only slightly frayed, wipes his hand on Edgar's apron. At this point, one may become aware of watching two discrete silences: Harpo's formal mime silence vs. Edgar's menacing dramatic silence with its fleeting shadow of film noir. Both seem encompassed by an amphitheater of silence as recollected from silent films. The solemnized violences of Laurel and Hardy are with us again.

Yet the full significance of this scene and the sequence in which it occurs may not dawn on the viewer until much later. It ends, of course, with Harpo, having defended his peanut wagon against Edgar's assault, retaliating with a barefoot tarantella in Edgar's lemonade vat. The slapstick is so familiarly enjoyable that only, perhaps, after a third or fourth viewing might one realize its hidden edge as a miniature counterpoint to the movie's main theme: the hysterical futility of war. It should also be clear at this point that despite his disclaimers, Leo McCarey's craft has achieved a comic unity and depth unknown to the Marx Brothers in their previous films.

But if one's awareness requires an additional shake, the coda arrives in the bathtub scene two-thirds through the film. Harpo, as an al fresco Paul Revere, is bearing the news—we never find out exactly how—of Freedonia's going to war. He pauses for a house call on an attractive blonde. Harpo's recruitment is interrupted by the approaching wagon wheels of her husband: none other than the lemonade vendor. "Fredonia is going to war!" cries the updated Barbara Frietchie. "I'm going to take a bath!" is Edgar's nitty-gritty response. However, as he settles himself for this consolation, a mysterious honk sounds from the tub's lower depths. Edgar is apparently trying to decide whether to question the bathroom's plumbing or his body's, when—shades of Aphrodite!—a Regency cock hat emerges from the water followed by Harpo; who—as a parting cordiality—beckons Edgar, as mute as he, to join the troops. The audience is left to savor the memory of a compact satirical depiction: War visits the homefront, as portrayed by René Clair in collaboration with Georg Grosz, with a liberal hand from Leo McCarey. Possibly the most cohesive and poignant work ever to emerge from the wandering Brothers.

## Who Did You Say Started All This?

One might suppose that Kennedy's 17-year lace-curtain saga began at Hal Roach Studios; a likely greenhouse for gritty, offhandedly realistic comedy. In fact, however, apart from the Laurel and Hardy shorts, Roach included Kennedy in a few Our Gang comedies in which his capacity for near-apoplectic impatience received frontline training. Prior to Roach, and after childhood and early youth in Monterey, he did songs and comic turns on stage, and, as an aspiring boxer, reportedly fought 18 rounds with Jack Dempsey. In 1914 he signed with Mack Sennett, under whom he did bits in *Tillie's Punctured Romance*, *Caught in a Cabaret*, and others. Here, no doubt, he perfected the art of making as vivid an impression as possible within a small compass. Joining with Roach in the Twenties, he rounded out four years before engaging with RKO, and launching the two-reeler sequence that would extend from *Rough House Rhythm* (1931) to *Contest Crazy* (1948). During the ensuing Thirties, he can be seen as a cheerful factotum, bringing the same humorous fervor to roles of drastically varying size. His jovial confidence fills and distends every one; making palatable and amusing, by a sort of reverse English, the kind of trapped uncertainty that he was called on to display again and again. In 1931, in that era of venturesome casting, he turns up as Daddy Warbucks to Mitzi Green's *Little Orphan Annie*. 1934 finds him wearing a handlebar mustache as a small-town judge and fielding the repartee of W.C. Fields in *Tillie and Gus*. In 1939 we espy him in floundering pursuit of elfin Claudette Colbert and bemused but dogged James Stewart as a much-hoodwinked police lieutenant (*It's a Wonderful World*). Somewhere among those stints, he found time to impersonate a dishcloth magnate, who spars with rival washrag tycoon Gregory Ratoff in covetous pursuit (for business purposes only) of Ginger Rogers (*America's Sweetheart*).

During the Thirties, Kennedy was part of a gray mainstream: a throng of balding, usually burly, predominantly Irish character actors, among whom one readily identifies William Demarest, William Frawley, Guy Kibbee, James Gleason, et al. The lot of them could plausibly fill out the attendance of any union hall, East Side saloon, or St. Patrick's Day Parade. Yet each is distinct from his fellows, retaining the voltage of a peculiar history and individuality. For example, mark the distinction between the tempers of Kennedy and Demarest, whose fury, as against Kennedy's harried desperation, is downright jubilant; he cannot wait for an excuse to pounce, whether on Eddie Bracken or an unoffending ship's purser. And, unlike either of them, Bill Frawley is an amiable bluff, whether complaining or gladhanding. Kennedy, who retained more of the clown in his persona than many of the others, embodies the transition from the liberty and fantasy of silent comedy to the white-collar frustration and impotence of the Depression humorists.

As the silent clown tradition shriveled (though never expired), the Kennedys, Demarests, and their varied ranks became the trustees of another august tradition: character comedy. The Chaplins and Keatons had marketed comic personality; personality, i.e., a mechanism combining one's self-image with various habits and skills of self-projection; the function of which is to imprint oneself upon one's world. Character was involved with sheer autonomy; quirky, gratuitous, mysterious. Personality might be said to involve design, rhythm, and composition; character, texture and color, rather like a fabric. Kennedy, like W.C. Fields, combined the hyperbole of clown imagery with the shimmering complexity of character comedy.

## The Bull Who Owned a China Closet

During the Thirties, which Kennedy's two-reel series covered and exceeded, the two-reel comedy had become a natural vehicle for the eccentrics, flotsam, and everyday pedestrians who helped patent character humor. James and Lucille Gleason, Grady Sutton, Sterling Holloway, and numerous others peddled their various brands of not-quite-ordinariness in a multitude of situations; yet, by the end of the Thirties, only a few survived, like Leon Errol: a snappish, agile edition of Mr. Punch for adults only, who was, in certain important ways, along with W.C. Fields, Kennedy's counterpart.

Kennedy's own character was originally designated "The Average Man." He had very little in common, however, either with the gentle, dawdling self-deprecation of Robert Benchley's lecturer, nor the wry, breezy journalism of George O'Hanlon's Joe McDoakes in O'Hanlon's later series "Behind the Eight Ball." Kennedy's series was cemented in one of the most popular and tirelessly paraded myths of middle-class married life: the underdog husband besieged by a censorious, extravagant, and monolithically unreasonable wife. Occasionally flanked by in-laws, the wife would almost inevitably prevail, either through shrewish harassment, iron will, or brute force. Cartoonists like Thomas Aloysius Dorgan, T.E. Powers, and George McManus (whose Maggie in *Bringing Up Father* was probably the Dragon Queen of them all) offered their fellow males a daily feast of self-commiseration in papers like Hearst's *Evening Journal*.

Edgar's white-collar hellhole, however, offered an interesting variation or two on the abject stereotypes of his class. For one thing, he could no more be described as henpecked than Jiggs could be a first cousin of Harry Hershfield's Abe Kabibble. Not that his hide was necessarily immune to pecking; but his wife, Florence, far less resembled a hen than a twittering, anxious mother wren. She was played by Florence Lake, a slender,

*"Edgar's white collar hellhole": Kennedy and wife, here played by Sally Payne, in* I'll Fix It *(1941).*

attractive blonde, who invested her character's occasional bouts of nonstop babbling with a plaintive mixture of affection and distress—both obviously grounded in the warmest feeling for her husband. Edgar, on the other hand, had a well-stocked battery of vocal resources to call on; not against Florence alone, but against Florence attended by two dark, overly familiar spirits: Mother-in-Law (played with the zest of a hanging judge by white-maned Dot Farney) and Wife's Brother (initially played with effete nastiness by William Eugene; subsequently, with a nimble mischievousness that was more engaging, by Jack Price). The density of their ungloved malice both enriched the complexity of the situation and provided a rationale for Edgar's explosive jeremiads. The setup was lent an additional emotional curve; since the complaints and petitions of the trio were by no means always unreasonable; although the joint manner of the two in-laws could snatch unreason from the jaws of reason at any given point. The result, probably more often recognized than identified, was very like a slapstick counterpart of classical tragedy: catharsis, through both engaging one's laughter and also widening one's perspective.

To underscore this analogy, Edgar himself demonstrated in boldface the same bedeviling perplexity that his face and bearing had proclaimed as a cop in the Laurel and Hardy films. Like two Swedish wrestlers encased in a phone booth, two kinds of pressure eternally bore upon Edgar. They were the demands of being both manly and reasonable, in terms of civilization's not always crystalline guidelines. From this quandary, he produced his immemorial gesture: drawing his hand slowly down over his face, as though gentling a potentially savage dog; or, perhaps, drawing a hood over his darkest feelings; or, trying to squeeze the last drops of black bile from his uneasy system. This gesture came to be known universally, though not entirely accurately, as "the slow burn." Not always accurate, because Edgar often resorted to it when his rage was already at full furnace blast. It's partly a semaphore to the audience from stage tradition, like the beseeching stares, audienceward, of Oliver Hardy and Jack Benny. In Edgar's case, it's evidently a gesture of both self-reassurance and of girding his loins for the vengeance that may yet fall ("I know not what they will be as yet, but they will be the terrors of the earth"). And, in the inevitable denouement, came the cinching of slapstick/tragic irony: the blow of retribution always fell on the wrong head, at the worst possible time. When Edgar decides to build a wing on his house (*I'll Build It Myself*), the visitor whom he topples into a trough of paint is not the expected and unwanted contractor, but the awaited building inspector (who winds up the film by duplicating Edgar's gesture over his paint-smeared face). In the 1937 *Tramp Trouble*, after banishing the convention of tramps who have followed in the wake of his ill-selected protégé, Billy Benedict, Edgar arms himself with a kettle of hot soup, in grim readiness for the next caller—forgetting the dinner invitation he extended to his boss and wife.

What sustained the series, I suspect, for seventeen years was not merely Edgar's ever-flowing adrenaline supply, but also a kind of blowzy good nature that injected a frolicking note, distinguishing the series from the tight-lipped dourness of, say, W.C. Fields' domestic Dry Tortugas. Intermingled with this was an unflagging alertness to opportunities for varying the mood and enlarging the milieu as much as possible. Jack Price played the brother-in-law as a lively if no-account young jackanapes whose theatrical bent, although never taking him anywhere near Broadway, involved him in endless disguises, usually with Edgar's ruin in view. Florence Lake's plaintive wife was spelled on occasion by a much hardier matron, Vivien Oakland, an able and engaging comedienne, who, however, was too hardy a match for Edgar. She never quite supplanted Lake's poignant counterpoint. The household was occasionally transported on cross-country vacations; and, in at least one instance, took over a roadside filling station.

Edgar also occasionally showed another side to that choleric red sun. The 1937 *Hillbilly Goat* shows him, conveyed by a mule-drawn van, high-pressuring a line of electrical appliances to a backwoods community. Edgar's orotund sales pitch somewhat suggests the engaging unction of his old playmate Oliver Hardy; not to mention the jovial mock grandiosity of the man who signed his directorial stints E. Livingston Kennedy. This side was to be rediscovered years later by none other than Preston Sturges. And at least one film in the series—*Vocalizing* (1937)—offers a glint of sheer charm. At the very end, after a disaster-mottled night of chauffeuring his wife's friend and the friend's housesitter hither and yon, Edgar, ambling down a moonlit path, is overcome by the situation in an unaccustomed way: neither roars nor tears, but a few rueful chuckles. He tears off a few bars, in his pleasing tenor, of the old hoedown song "I'll Be Seeing Nellie Home" (this provided the title for a remake by Leon Errol; here, you can see the two men almost as twins). Sherwood Anderson with a touch of softshoe.

The prototype for Kennedy's persona in the two-reelers always seemed to me a certain comic strip character. Not Daddy Warbucks, but rather a recurrent figure in a series of daily single-panel cartoons drawn during the Twenties and Thirties by a fine American artist: the as-yet-to-be-rediscovered J.R. Williams. Williams' continuing title for this character's appearances was "The Bull of the Woods." He was a supervisor in an unidentified factory: a man promoted from the ranks, who obviously had never made his peace either with his new position or with much else in his world. As he intruded his advice, furious rhetorical questions, and free-flying jeremiads into the ongoing work of his former fellow laborers, his overalls would buckle around his knees as though disclaiming any further association. Hollywood being, as always, long on opportunity instinct and short on imagination, Williams's series of vignettes was never filmed. Should this writer ever achieve heaven, however, it will provide a hot property for Hereafter Studios. Adaptation and direction by Leo McCarey, of course.

Hitler's Madman: *Victor Kilian, Kennedy, Jimmy Conlin. "Character humor visible with the dirt of reality on its boots."*

## Edgar at Large

The Forties brought Kennedy at least three opportunities—of which he made zestful use—for something like full-scale humorous portraiture. Indeed, the dual onslaught of Hollywood World War II films, with their often hamfisted yet earnest attention to panoramas of ordinary humanity among GIs, defense workers, etc., and the swiftly evolving film noir's unsweetened tabloid approach to urban life offered numerous character actors a respite from the yellowing pastures of Laffmovie programs, as well as a chance at enlarged perspective in the eyes of audiences. Watching Percy Kilbride in *Fallen Angel*, or Jack Oakie deepening his oafish role in *Thieves' Highway* with dramatic grace notes, is like the rediscovery of elderly relatives whom one recalls only from single-dimensional perspectives from childhood as clowns or heavies; returning in later life to reveal other facets, startling and chastening.

Edgar Kennedy's first breakthrough in this respect came in Douglas Sirk's *Hitler's Madman*, produced by Seymour Nebenzal for MGM in 1943. The film's confining budget restriction, as deployed by Sirk's skill and sensibility, gives it—the story of Nazi governor Heydrich's assassination, followed by Himmler's attempt to lobotomize history by wiping out the male population of the Czech village Lidice—a nightmarish dispatch. The film belongs to a largely forgotten and in too many instances self-dishonored Hollywood genre, the European homefront melodrama. Factors like the deplorable title and, at first glance, the casting of John Carradine as Heydrich (actually, possibly Carradine's best performance since Casey in *The Grapes of Wrath*) may offer difficulty in quarrying its virtues from the surrounding rubble. But only if one relies on first glances. Douglas

Sirk, dealing with European terrain, here validates the sensibility that I confess to finding starchy and oppressively theatrical in his much-garlanded U-I Sirk operas of the Fifties. *Hitler's Madman* is informed not only with the hatred to which Hollywood could pander all too easily but with a sense of grief mixed with reverence for a loving and vigorous style of life which Sirk sees as being shockingly pulverized. The only reminder of those haute couture touches that resonated like lead shoes in *Imitation of Life* or *All That Heaven Allows* is the voiceover that recites Edna St. Vincent Millay's "The Ballad of Lidice" at the film's beginning and end. The recollection, I hasten to add, is solely by contrast: as delivered with a dry, heartsick fury, the ballad is a more than apt supplement to the remarkable representations of Czech settings, interiors, and costumes (the uncredited contribution, according to an interview with Peter Bogdanovich, of Edgar G. Ulmer).

Kennedy's role in the film is of a jovial rogue, a poacher of suspect loyalty (which he more than redeems by the film's end). The role is not one of those quick-change reversals suggested by the old phrase about the clown playing Hamlet. Rather, Sirk has provided Kennedy with a new and valid terrain, a context in which his character humor is visible with the dirt of reality on its boots. Sirk has used Kennedy, I believe, partly as a memento of the great European clown tradition, which, in fact, was a signpost of European culture, and as such, an inevitable casualty of the mechanized barbarism. I may be overperceiving in what I noticed as a possible sly aside: arising in his forest hut, Edgar completes his morning wash with the slow burn gesture. And yet, Sirk by no means wants us to forget Edgar's history; nor those of affable, frog-faced Al Sheehan, who plays the village priest; or that skittish Woody Woodpecker lookalike Jimmy Conlin, long of Sturges' repertory. Sirk clearly envisioned these players as good-natured trolls, safeguarding civilization in their own way. His use of them is both as shrewd and as sensitive as his use of Edward Everett Horton, remembered as the dissolute count in *Summer Storm*. Kennedy even gave play to his rarely heard fine tenor voice in a defiant paean cut off by Nazi gunfire.

The next two major innings of his career—perhaps the last two of his life—offered him scope and context, though neither as abundantly as might have been supposed or wished, given that both were the films of Preston Sturges. Indeed, both were somewhat elegies of Sturges's volcanically fecund career as screenwriter and screenwriter-director. Perhaps the more painful of the two is the 1947 *The Sin of Harold Diddlebock*, which, indeed, advance reports led one to expect as the herald of a full-blooded comic renaissance. Alas, the heraldry—the expertly used footage from Harold Lloyd's *The Freshman*, along with Lloyd's interview by Raymond Walburn—gave way to a footsore-shambling circus parade. The saddest and most alarming aspect is the distance one senses between Sturges and his past material: like Harold Lloyd's Diddlebock, it seems the work of a man entering retirement and packing his bags. The situation is Capra, and second-gear Capra at that: Lloyd, a retired office drudge, stokes up his once-blazing expectations by investing his retirement money along with racetrack winnings in a circus with which he invites various bankers to change their unpopular image. Sturges' formerly jaunty and gallant grip on reality has given way here like a ruptured tendon. Even the rhythm has suffered. The former shimmering, cat's-cradle fluency of crisscrossing figures, dialogue, and actions is supplanted her by an oratorio-like pace. The familiar and treasured faces of Jimmy Conlin, Al Bridge, Franklin Pangborn, and (in a delightful cameo as Lloyd's twin sister) Margaret Hamilton succeed each other in huge closeups, like people delivering testimonials to the honored dead. Some of the old steam is recalled by a barbershop staff responding to a radio broadcast horse race, and Harold's winning. Later, however, all promise is dissolved in a shapeless welter erupting around Lloyd and the decrepit lion he is using for his sales pitch to the bankers.

Yet in the processional of Sturges actors described above, space was reserved, thanks be, for Edgar Kennedy. He plays the bartender and, one suspects, manager of a downstairs cocktail joint to which Jimmy Conlin escorts the downsized Harold. Kennedy's performance—a marvelous fugue of jovial sagacity—comes probably as close to putting wheels under the film's tired feet as human agency could. His catechism of lifelong teetotaler Lloyd as he prepares his celebrational Diddlebock cocktail is a miniature ode to bartending skills and philosophy. Kennedy demonstrates here as well as anyplace else in his career, I suggest, how suasive a role control and timing play in his most overflowing performances. One must wonder that Sturges never found room for him before; possibly he felt that the choler quotient supplied by William Demarest was sufficient for any given film. At that point, according to James Curtis' biography *Between Flops*, the filmmaker was at odds with Demarest over a contract quarrel. It can only be guessed at, otherwise, whether Kennedy's role might have gone to Demarest. But, even if possible, it is not imaginable while watching Kennedy: the measure of a man making a role his own.

The 1948 *Unfaithfully Yours* leaves less to be said about itself, and, in fact, says nothing very new about Sturges, other than a further shriveling of his skills and his overview. The thin-lipped, distinctly snide double view it presents of high culture is like a mean-spirited dilution of *Sullivan's Travels*, with the latter's message of humility. *Unfaithfully Yours* by contrast proposes a view of classical art seen from deep inside an upper-class milieu and the ego of its singularly disagreeable protagonist, symphony orchestra conductor Rex Harrison. The film is as sealed off from the reality Sturges once explored and paraded, as, in fact, was *Diddlebock*. Also, as in the previous film, Sturges at the climax resorts to slapstick administered with a hand both heavy and unsteady; reminding us, sadly, of the stylish contrapuntal skill with which he treated slapstick in his earlier films.

Kennedy's role is that of a private investigator, Mr. Sweeny, who bears mistaken witness to Harrison about the disloyalty of his wife (the virtually invisible Linda Darnell). Once more, Kennedy can be seen as a sole spokesman for a younger Sturges, of freer-flowing sympathies. The private eye, it seems, enjoys a private ear as a lover of classical music. In an interlude that recalls Sturges's onetime rough and ready kinship with Dickens, Kennedy protests his cultural brotherhood with Harrison: "Nobody handles Handel like you handle Handel!" He gives flesh to the line, and buttresses it with a touching personal recollection of his own about the discovery of disloyalty, which beautifully sidesteps sentimentality. The mixture of delicacy and comic perception involved is a first-class collaboration of performer and director. Unfortunately, this glowing scene only underscores the mean ineptitude of a later scene, in which Kennedy and his friend Julius Tannen (who provided a hilarious moment earlier) are shown in an opera audience as the victims of popping celluloid collars: the bursting seams of Sturges' erstwhile talent.

The Kennedy persona reached its natural terminus in Norman Lear's *All in the Family*'s Archie Bunker and Carroll O'Connor's richly nuanced supplement to Kennedy's original characterization. But the aggregate of Kennedy's performances testifies to a comic range beyond the limits of prototype or stereotype. His own niche, which he carved long ago, still holds its low-burning, slow-burning flame.

# Cary Grant: Comedy and Male Desire

**Andrew Britton** (1984)

*It should be said at the outset, in explanation of the method of this essay, that I wish to be concerned with the functions and thematic content of the Cary Grant persona; what follows is neither an account of Grant as a performer, nor a biography or history of his career.*

*Obviously, much might be written on the subjects I have chosen to ignore. A theoretical interest in modes and traditions of performance could find no more complex and rewarding theme than comic acting in the popular American cinema; and in Cary Grant we have a striking, and highly specific, conjunction of diverse European and American comic conventions — British music-hall, American vaudeville and variety, and the line of sophisticated comedy initiated by Lubitsch. For an historian of the star system and its evolution, the details of Grant's career would have their significance. Grant was the first major star to go "independent": after his contract with Paramount expired in 1937, he was never again under exclusive contract to any studio, and was centrally involved in the selection of his material and collaborating personnel.*

*The first of these subjects seemed to raise issues too large to be dealt with profitably in a short monograph on a single actor: the responsible discussion of performance (discussion, that is, radically unlike the familiar kind) would have demanded an attention to its contexts and lineage, and a range of comparative reference, which lie beyond the scope of this essay. The second, on the contrary, threatened either to narrow or to blur the focus: it acquired a secondary importance beside the things which it seemed to me most necessary to say about Grant.*

*These things concern definitions of masculinity, the use of comedy to criticize and transform traditional gender roles, and the extent to which characteristics assigned by those roles to women can be presented as being desirable and attractive in a man; and I have chosen, accordingly, to concentrate on specific films and on Grant's meaning as the hero of them.*

*I would like to thank Robin Wood and Richard Lippe, who provided me with hospitality while I was writing this essay, and who read the first draft and made a number of very helpful suggestions. I dedicate the essay to them. —A.B.*

There is a tendency to assume that the great stars are a known quantity. In an attempt to account for the appeal of Cary Grant, David Shipman writes:

It is his elegance, his casualness, his unaccented charm; he is, as Tom Wolfe put it, "consummately romantic and consummately genteel" — "the old leathery charmer," in Alexander Walker's words (regretting his earlier, more interesting existence as a "hard-eyed cad"). It certainly isn't from acting ability: his range must be the most limited of all the great matinee idols. His gift for light comedy has been much touted, but it's been a mite heavy at times and one can think of half a dozen names who were sometimes better. (Shipman, 254)

That is probably representative. The "limited range" needn't detain us: the assumption involved is so clearly that which inspires Pauline Kael to remark that "one does not necessarily admire an icon, as one admires, say, Laurence Olivier, but it can be a wonderful object of contemplation," and to suggest that Grant "might have become a great actor" if he had "taken more risks like *None But the Lonely Heart*" (Kael, 25–6). But the "charm" and the "romantic" obviously call for comment, and it may be useful to begin by emphasizing an aspect of them which is habitually ignored. Consider the dialogue of the love scene on the train in *North by Northwest*.

> Eve: This is ridiculous. You know that, don't you?
> Thornhill: Yes.
> Eve: I mean, we've hardly met.
> Thornhill: That's right.
> Eve: How do I know you aren't a murderer?
> Thornhill: You don't.
> Eve: Maybe you're planning to murder me, right here, tonight.

*Monkey Business: Cary Grant and Marilyn Monroe.*

> Thornhill: Shall I?
> Eve: Please do. (They kiss)
> Thornhill: Beats flying, doesn't it?
> Eve: We should stop.
> Thornhill: Immediately.
> Eve: I ought to know more about you.
> Thornhill: Oh, what more could you know?
> Eve: You're an advertising man, that's all I know.
> Thornhill: That's right. Oh, the train's a little unsteady.
> Eve: Who isn't?
> Thornhill: What else do you know?
> Eve: You've got taste in clothes, taste in food—
> Thornhill: Taste in women. I like your flavor.
> Eve: And you're very clever with words. You can probably make them do anything for you . . . sell people things they don't need . . . make women who don't know you fall in love with you . . .
> Thornhill: I'm beginning to think I'm underpaid.

The sense of an ironic lack, or refusal, of intimacy which this communicates is an inflection of something which is, in fact, characteristic of Grant's love scenes, and of his playing of them. Hitchcock, characteristically, takes the exchange of sophisticated wit to the verge of the unpleasant: Thornhill's self-regarding self-possession is assimilated, on the one hand, to the economic values of Madison Avenue, and on the other to an irresponsible male sexual consumerism. In retrospect, of course, the irony is complicated by our discovery of who Eve is, but the revelation that Thornhill's feeling of urbane mastery in the love scene is illusory doesn't alter the fact that it is there to be cultivated. Indeed, it is the crux of the irony that prior to Eve's deception of him (which, unlike his own sexual confidence, isn't inspired by egotism) Thornhill has told her that "honest women frighten (him)."

The use to which Hitchcock puts Grant here isn't unprecedented. In his fifth film, *Blonde Venus* (Sternberg, 1932), Grant plays a wealthy businessman who uses Helen Faraday/Dietrich's need for money to make her become his mistress. Two films later, he was cast as Pinkerton in a version (nonmusical!) of *Madame Butterfly* (Gering, 1933). In *Sylvia Scarlett* (Cukor, 1935), he plays a confidence trickster who appears, at the outset, to embody for Sylvia/Katharine Hepburn the promise of liberating adventure, but who is gradually revealed to be cynically exploitative. In *Indiscreet* (Donen, 1958), Philip Adams pretends to Anna Kalman/Ingrid Bergman that he is married and unable to obtain a divorce so as to keep her as his lover while avoiding a substantial commitment to her. *Suspicion* (1941) and *Notorious* (1946), the first two of Grant's four films with Hitchcock, fully elaborate this aspect of the persona, subordinating it entirely to the director's thematic concern with the male need to possess and subjugate female sexuality. In the Devlin of *Notorious*, sexual egotism becomes an extraordinarily convoluted misogyny—Devlin seeks to turn Alicia/Ingrid Bergman into a whore so that he can then despise her for being one—and imagery and narrative movement link the romantic hero directly to his antagonist, Sebastian/Claude Rains: the film begins with Alicia's relapse into alcoholism in response to Devlin's refusal to trust her, and ends with Sebastian's attempt to poison her. Like his counterpart, Mark Rutland/Sean Connery in *Marnie*,

Devlin can only accept the heroine when she has been reduced to a state of complete emotional and physical prostration. The long-take kissing sequence, with its disturbingly impersonal sensuality (it anticipates the train sequence in *North by Northwest*), is usefully emblematic of these things. Asked by Devlin to explain her remark that "this a very strange love affair," Alicia replies—"Perhaps because you don't love me."

It is not merely perverse to preface an account of Grant by noting a use of him which no one will argue to be fully characteristic. What these roles have in common is an urbane amoralism and irresponsibility, issuing in the exploitation of women; but "irresponsibility"—which turns out to be a key word in discussing Grant—can be defined in more than one way, and Grant is not only a lover-figure, but also a comedian. In *Notorious* and *Suspicion*, irresponsibility appears entirely negatively, as sexual opportunism, and Alicia and Lina/Joan Fontaine are subtly complicit with their exploitation. Significantly, both women initially see the Grant character as a means of detaching themselves from, and rebelling against, fathers they hate, only to discover that they have become subject to another form of patriarchal oppression, to which they then succumb out of masochistic fascination (Lina) or a self-contempt which the man relentlessly exacerbates (Alicia). The Hitchcock films are distinguished from, say, *Indiscreet*, by the absence of the comedy of male chastisement: Donen's film really takes off, after its turgid exposition, when Anna discovers that she has been deceived and sets about exacting retribution. And it is in general true that when, in comedy, the Grant character is closest to the cynical emotional detachment and exploitativeness of Devlin, he is partnered by an active heroine who contests the terms of the relationship between them and undertakes his "spiritual education."

"The comedy of male chastisement"—Grant's movies are full of scenes in which he is subjected to the most extreme discomfiture, humiliation and loss of face by women. *Bringing Up Baby* (1938) and *I Was A Male War Bride* (1949) are obviously the most excessive cases—Hawks takes the persona as far in this direction as Hitchcock does in the other—but examples could be multiplied. Consider the magnificent sequence in *The Awful Truth* (McCarey, 1937) in which Lucy Warriner/Irene Dunne, masquerading as her husband's sister, discredits him in front of his new fiancée and her upper-class family; or the sequence in *Mr. Lucky* (Potter, 1943) in which Dorothy Bryant/Laraine Day compels Joe Adams/Grant to join a group of women war-relief workers and learn to knit while male passers-by gradually gather, astounded, at the window; or the moment in *Houseboat* (Shavelson, 1958) in which Tom Tinston/Grant, immaculately attired for work, finds the gang-plank of the houseboat slowly subsiding beneath him, to the delight of Cinzia/Sophia Loren and his children.

Given that the comedy of moments such as these is so often bound up with the undermining of masculinity, or at the least, of male prestige and dignity, it is remarkable that the comedy is never hostile, and that since the Grant character is not ridiculed, the sense in which he appears ridiculous is a complex one. It is partly a matter of the loss of dignity being continuous with the loss of qualities which have no positive value whatever: the social world of the Vances in *The Awful Truth*, and the diplomatic milieu of *Houseboat*, are rejected by the films. At the same time, Grant's acting characteristically conveys an ironic distance from, or pleasurable complicity with, his degradation: at first appalled and embarrassed by Lucy's eruption into his fiancée's home, Jerry is more and more delighted by it, and *Bringing Up Baby* ends with David Huxley/Grant's admission that the day he spent with Susan/Katharine Hepburn was the most wonderful of his life.

Here, loss of dignity involves the acquisition of a kind of irresponsibility which is very different from the kind Grant embodies in *Suspicion*.

Discussion can be focused by referring in greater detail to the great comedies of the late '30s: the first of them, *The Awful Truth*, clinched Grant's status as a major star. McCarey's film begins with Jerry Warriner stretched out under a sun-lamp at his club, trying hastily to cultivate the tan which his wife will naturally expect him to have acquired during a supposed visit to Florida. Jerry's deceit of her is accompanied by the conviction (quite unfounded) that Lucy has been unfaithful to him, and in the ensuing recriminations the two agree to divorce. If Jerry's combination of possessive jealousy and duplicity is viewed negatively, his ebullience appears in a more favorable light in comparison with Lucy's new suitor, Daniel Leeson/ Ralph Bellamy, who may be described with every propriety as "straight." Daniel offers Lucy a conventional respectability and probity, and a conventional sexual role: he treats her with deeply-felt but labored gallantry and deference, which will be her reward for uncomplaining acquiescence in the duties of a wife. But while Jerry and Daniel are sharply distinguished from each other, they have in common a refusal to trust Lucy which is rooted in two opposite but complementary forms of masculine complacency. Jerry takes for granted his own right to a life independent of his marriage, and to lie to Lucy about it, but swells with proprietory indignation when Lucy claims the same right for herself. Daniel, in turn, assumes that Lucy can have no desire which life with him cannot satisfy. His sentimental chivalry is the counterpart of Jerry's insincerity, and each conceals a possessiveness which denies any freedom or autonomy to Lucy herself and is all too ready to conclude that she has "broken her trust."

The action of the film consists in the comic correction of Jerry's insincerity and the comic confirmation of his energy: the function of the comedy, that is, is to distinguish between, and evaluate, two forms of "irresponsibility." The insincerity, and the associated proprietoriness, express a conviction of male sexual right, and correction takes the form of loss of face. Consider the sequence in which Jerry, convinced yet again that Lucy is having an affair with her singing teacher, Armand Duvalle/Alexander D'Arcy, bursts into Duvalle's apartment only to discover that Lucy is singing, to Duvalle's accompaniment, before a large audience. Jerry attempts to save the situation by taking a seat at the back of the room, but is further confounded when the chair collapses; and Lucy, delighted by his humiliation, converts the closing phrase of her song into a gentle laugh of triumph.

If *The Awful Truth* chastises male presumption and opportunism, the energies it affirms are energies which Jerry shares with Lucy. Masculinity, as Ralph Bellamy invaluably embodies it, is presented, in that unadulterated form, as stolid, lumpish and boring, and his peculiar relationship to energy is given us in his performance on the dance floor and his rendering of "Home on the Range." The tone of the reference to the Western is crucial, both to an understanding of screwball comedy and to the significance of its supreme male practitioner. The West, where definitions of masculinity are concerned, traditionally provides the norm of potency, and derives its meaning from its opposition to "settlement" and "civilization"—the domesticity which, in American culture, is synonymous with the oppressive power of women and which threatens the male with emasculation. *The Awful Truth* retains one part of this opposition and reverses the other. Civilization is still associated with femininity, but it appropriates from the West the free play of anarchic energy, and the Western hero appears as the spokesman of repression, propriety and constraint.

To say no more would be, of course, to simplify. "Civilization" in *The Awful Truth* is also the Vances, just as, in *Holiday* (Cukor, 1938), it is the Setons and in *Bringing Up Baby* the dinosaur, and it is an essential characteristic of the couples created at the end of these films that they cannot exist in established bourgeois society: *The Awful Truth* ends in a snowbound ski-lodge in the mountains, *Holiday* on a liner between America and Europe, and *Bringing Up Baby*, most drastically of all, on a rickety scaffolding with the dinosaur, the film's central image of bourgeois patriarchy, lying in ruins beneath it. If *The Awful Truth* recognizes the enabling possibilities of civilization, it also perceives that what is enabled is incompatible with civilization as it is, and indeed, expresses itself in defiance of it: Lucy's disruption of the Vances' dinner-party, Linda/Katharine Hepburn's departure from her father's house (*Holiday*) and Susan's destruction of the skeleton (*Bringing Up Baby*) have obvious points in common.

"The enabled" is, in each case, a revision of bourgeois gender roles: it is the Grant character's commitment to, and acquisition of, a subversive "femininity," and the consequent redistribution of power within the couple, which makes the couple socially impossible. In each case, too, femininity partakes both of civilization and of the drives which civilization alienates. Femininity in *Bringing Up Baby* is not only the leopard but also Miss Katharine Hepburn, New England heiress, Bryn Mawr graduate and notorious representative of high-toned culture. The anarchic energies released in these films do not subserve a fantasy of regression to a pre-cultural stage, and have nothing in common with that model of the return of the repressed enacted by the Gothic, shared by Freud, and leading both, finally, to stalemate. We may feel that a return of the repressed is involved, but it doesn't have the suggestion of "dark primal forces" which so often accrues to the monster in the horror film, and which allows the genre to rationalize the reinstatement of repression. If the "femininity" which erupts in *The Awful Truth*, *Holiday* and *Bringing Up Baby* is inimical to the society it disturbs, it is also associated, as is usual in the American tradition, with sophistication and refinement; and this dual character makes the repressed that returns not the monstrous inhabitant of the "seething cauldron of excitements" (Freud's own phrase) which precedes social life, and on whose containment social life depends, but the harbinger of a more free and pleasurable culture.

I have noted that, as regards Jerry, the comedy of *The Awful Truth* has two distinct functions, and it will be obvious that, throughout the film, he and Lucy visit humiliation on each other. Jerry's insincerity and negative irresponsibility are very much a part of the world of the Vances in which he figures as urbane and eligible male, and in which the aspects of sophistication to which the film is opposed are concentrated, and the scenes of which he is the butt serve to chasten his presumptuous possessiveness of Lucy (the concert) and to expose, and detach Jerry from, the ethos in which insincerity is a constituent of urbane form (Lucy's masquerade). Yet it is what Jerry and Lucy have in common that allows Jerry to function as he does in Lucy's relationship with Daniel Leeson, and that makes the hilarious sequence in which, concealed from his rival behind a door, Jerry repeatedly makes Lucy laugh at Daniel's heart-felt recitation of his doggerel love-poem by tickling her under the arm, so unlike an exercise of power over her. It is always apparent that Daniel is Lucy's drastic overcompensation for what is at fault in Jerry, and that she recognizes, and resists, from the outset the staid sexual decorum that Daniel brings with him. Jerry, in the scene just mentioned, evokes Lucy's own sense of absurdity: the scene would be distasteful rather than funny if we felt that anything more than politeness was involved in not laughing at Daniel's poem.

The substance of this point can be demonstrated by comparing *The Awful Truth* and *His Girl Friday* (Hawks, 1940), the thematic parallels being so close: Hawks' film is another comedy of re-marriage in which, again, the marriage has broken up because of the Grant character's irresponsibility, and in which the alternative man is played once more by Ralph Bellamy. The astonishing brilliance of *His Girl Friday* is legendary, but merely to place it beside the McCarey (or *Bringing Up Baby*) is enough to reveal the drastic limitations summed up neatly by Robin Wood: "Given the alternatives the film offers, the only morally acceptable ending would be to have Hildy walk out on *both* men; or to present her capitulation to Walter as tragic" (Wood, 1981, 77). Walter Burns, of all Grant's comic characters, is the closest to Devlin, but while in *Notorious* the loathsomeness of the character is clearly and consistently the issue, in *His Girl Friday* it isn't, and by the time we get to "Stick Hitler on the funny pages!" the confusion of attitude could hardly be greater. The confusion is generated by the transportation of the asocial male group of the Hawksian adventure film into the bourgeois world of the comedies, and by Hawks' inability to decide whether the group is implicated in that world or an answer to it. The indecision is reflected in the treatment of Hildy/Rosalind Russell. She is hardly a representative Hawks comic heroine: Bruce Baldwin would have to be played by Cary Grant rather than Ralph Bellamy to make that of her. At the same time, because Hawks does not really know what he thinks of the values of the group, he is unable fully to endorse the theme of the heroine's assimilation to it characteristic of the adventure films. Hildy's withering "Gentlemen of the Press!", in the aftermath of the journalists' brutal harassment of Mollie Malloy/Helen Mack, implies a definitive judgment on the group to which the film gives great weight, but from which it is entirely unable to follow through.

The particular material of *His Girl Friday* deprives the male group of its value as a positive alternative to bourgeois society while also demanding a reconceptualization of the comic function of the Hawks heroine which Hawks is unwilling, or unable, to undertake. For if Walter Burns scarcely needs to have alienated energy liberated, he is very much a candidate for the correction of male arrogance and complacency. Walter is obviously exploiting Hildy, and *His Girl Friday* demands, uniquely in Hawks' comedies, an *explicitly* political, and *explicitly* feminist, development of the theme of the woman's education of the hero. Such a development is hardly conceivable, and Hawks responds by producing a Hawks comedy in reverse: the film traces the process by which Hildy is worn down into submission, and ends, astonishingly, after she has been reduced to tears, with her following Walter out of the press-room weighed down by baggage which he refuses to help her carry.

The process by which Lucy is detached from Daniel Leeson in *The Awful Truth* is, for all the structural similarity, very different. In effect, Lucy and Jerry function as the return of the repressed for each other: each intrudes in turn to prevent the other's entry into a world of family in the company of partners who respectively embody, in parodic form, the accumulated associations of "West" and "East." That much of the film's comedy consists in the dramatization of repression is particularly clear in McCarey's use of Mr. Smith, the Warriners' pet terrier. Mr. Smith, standing in for a child, clearly represents the marriage. The divorce hearing ends with a dispute over custody, and Mr. Smith is unable, when invited, to choose between the partners, though Lucy finally wins his preference by the underhanded stratagem of producing, surreptitiously, his favorite toy. In one of the film's most sustained comic set-pieces, Lucy finds herself having to conceal from Jerry the fact that Armand is in the apartment, and then, surprised by a visit from Daniel, to conceal the presence of both men from him. Having hidden the men themselves, Lucy notices the compromising presence of their bowler hats, and throughout the sequence Mr. Smith, with pertinacious insistence, and to Lucy's increasing discomfiture, repeatedly retrieves the hats from their hiding-place, to return with them, and the threat of scandal, to the parlor. The sequence ends with the eruption of Jerry and Armand from concealment, and the besmirching of Lucy's reputation which puts an end to her relationship with Daniel. The comedy is beautifully succinct: Mr. Smith, as emblem of the marriage, acts through the submerged logic of Lucy's "forgetting" of the hats and realizes her desire to check the onset of domesticity.

The use of Mr. Smith both as symbol of the Warriners' union and as focus of the comedy of repression is crucial to the significance of *The Awful Truth*. In not being a child, but replacing one, Mr. Smith dissociates the marriage from reproduction, or the prospect of it—a function fulfilled even more strikingly in Asta's next incarnation, as George in *Bringing Up Baby*, where he actually deprives David of the phallus by burying his "old bone" in the garden, thus fulfilling David's unexpressed desire to stay at Susan's farm and to fail to complete the skeleton of the dinosaur (I will return to the sexual symbolism of Hawks' film in greater detail later). Indeed, far from *representing* a child, Mr. Smith (again, like George) seems at once to express and to provide an occasion for a kind of childlikeness in the couple. Consider the sequence in which Jerry and Daniel first meet at Lucy's apartment. As Daniel and Lucy talk about the divorce, Jerry romps boisterously on the floor with Mr. Smith, and Lucy responds to Daniel's evident surprise at such behavior by remarking merely, with a marvelously off-handed drop of the wrist, that *that* is her husband. *Bringing Up Baby* gives us an exactly analogous moment. Susan's aunt, believing David to be a big-game hunter, discovers him chasing after George through the shrubbery in a desperate search for the missing bone, and on asking Susan, in astonishment, if that is what David understands by big-game hunting, receives the reply that "David is playing with George." Both incidents turn on a discrepancy between the behavior of the Grant character and a conventional paradigm of masculinity ("the West" and Hemingway machismo respectively), and in both cases the fact that the discrepancy also involves an opposition between the liberation of energy and its constraint gives to "playing with the dog" a strong positive connotation. Masculinity appears here as a code learned from the book of myth, and we are invited to laugh at the decorous inhibitedness of the student.

Juxtaposing the central couples of *The Awful Truth*, *Bringing Up Baby* and *Holiday*, we see that ideas of "play" and the "childlike" are fundamental to all of them, and that in each case play is directly linked to a rebellion against patriarchal sexuality. I have analyzed *Holiday* at length in my book on Katharine Hepburn (Britton, 1983), and will do no more here than point to the significance of the play-room, and its association, through Linda's mother (who died, Ned/Lew Ayres tells us, trying to be a good wife), with oppressed and liberating nonphallic sexual energy. The principle of all three films is to identify "play" in the sense of recovered infantile polymorphousness (which is, effectively, the meaning of "screwball") with "sophistication," the apogee of cultivated adulthood. The sophisticated couple is the couple whose sexuality is no longer organized by the phallus. The characteristic co-presence in these works of the two apparently distinct comic modes of farce and wit is the expression of this thematic principle. The partners engage in rough-house and in epigram and repartee; the anarchic consorts with

*Comic play: Grant with Katherine Hepburn in* Holiday *(top) and in* Bringing Up Baby.

the urbane; the infantile drives which precede maturity and civilization are suddenly definitive of them.[1]

The Grant characters in these films can be distinguished by virtue of their precise relation to these drives. In *Holiday*, they unite Linda and Johnny from the start: Linda's commitment to the playroom and Johnny's to his holiday represent two parallel forms of "irresponsibility," the alignment of which, as the film progresses, gradually defines play equally as nonphallic desire and as the refusal of alienated labor. In *Bringing Up Baby*, Susan is David's liberator: the hero's polymorphous energies have been entirely repressed, and the male ego must be destroyed in order to release them. *The Awful Truth* embodies a kind of middle term, in that the hero's education involves the correction rather than the liberation of energy. The films are united, remarkably, by their affirmation of a feminized hero, and of a couple whose validity and vitality is continuous with his feminization. Hawks' film, as the most extreme of the three, demands closer consideration here: the way in which it redefines a process which we might be tempted to describe as "emasculation" is fundamental to our sense of the value of the Grant persona.

*Bringing Up Baby* begins with Professor David Huxley on the verge of final and complete assimilation to a world of "order" which is defined in terms of three interdependent characteristics.

(1) A particular concept of reason, logic and rational inquiry, the sterility and obsolescence of which are already implied by its being dedicated to the reconstruction of the skeleton of a brontosaurus: as Susan later remarks of the intercostal clavicle, "it's only an old bone." As the film progresses, this model of reason is increasingly generalized so as to refer to a whole organization of the ego. David's consciousness and sense of self are entirely bound up with his status as a scientist.

(2) Bourgeois marriage. David's imminent marriage to Alice Swallow/Virginia Walker is immediately linked to the dinosaur through David's remark, on receiving the telegram announcing the discovery of the missing bone, that it's so marvelous that "two such important things should happen on the same day." Alice tells David that their marriage will have "no domestic entanglements of any kind"; and while he goes on to mention having children, it is sufficiently clear, even if one doesn't know either Hawks' work or the genre, that what is at issue is not reproduction but sexual pleasure. The marriage will be "purely dedicated to your work"—that is, to the repression and alienation of sexual energy.

(3) Capitalism. David's rational inquiry is to be funded by a million dollar grant which he must devote himself to extracting from the legal representative of Mrs. Carlton-Random/May Robson, the benefactor.

The brontosaurus is the film's inclusive image for this world. Later, casting round desperately for an incognito for David, Susan settles, with perfect accuracy, for "Mr. Bone." He is about to enter patriarchy, and his destiny will be to perpetuate it.

The whole meaning of *Bringing Up Baby* turns on the evidence, in the opening sequences, of David's resistance to this destiny. The resistance is, at this stage, unconscious, and manifests itself in a series of Freudian slips. David has forgotten who Peabody is ("Peabody? What Peabody?"), and also has to be reminded of Mrs. Carlton-Random and the prospective endowment. In the next sequence, on the golf course, he has again forgotten that Peabody is only Mrs. Carlton-Random's lawyer, and does not actually have the money in his gift. When he arrives at the night club, David is unable to make up his mind whether to keep or to check his top hat, an item of the formal uniform he has put on to impress Peabody: a few moments later, his second meeting with Susan is marked by his slipping up and squashing the hat ("*You* throw an olive and *I* sit on my hat—it's all perfectly logical").

Thereafter, the meaning of these "errors" is clarified: they cease merely to express an antagonism to what David thinks he wants, and become explicitly the means of fulfilling a wish for what he thinks he *doesn't* want. After Susan has torn his coat, David tells her that he is going to count to ten with his eyes closed, and wants her to have disappeared when he opens them. She promptly walks away, and it is revealed that David has been standing on the hem of her dress, so causing the "accident" that forces them together again. Two sequences later, David watches appalled as Susan tries to wake Peabody by hurling pebbles at his bedroom window, and, having virtually confessed his complicity ("I think we ought to go now, but somehow I can't move"), sees her fell the man on whom his future depends with an enormous rock.

One aspect of David's slips is especially important, given the film's thematic, and that is the forgetting or confusion of names and identities—and more generally, the breakdown of rational discourse: much of the comedy of *Bringing Up Baby* is a matter of the disintegration, simultaneously, of the apparently stable male ego and its language. As David leaves the museum for the golf-course, he is already saying "Good-bye Alice—I mean, professor": even at this stage, his slips are being connected with the mistaking of gender. Subsequently, Hawks uses this motif to link David and the film's other representative patriarchal figures—the agent of law, Constable Slocum/Walter Catlett; the adventurer, Major Applegate/Charles Ruggles; and the psychiatrist, Dr. Lehmann/ Fritz Feld. Susan tells her aunt that David's name is Mr. Bone, without forewarning David himself. Aunt Elizabeth proceeds, in all innocence, to introduce David to Major Applegate as Mr. Bone, and David, attributing the unfamiliar name to the Major, says "Hello, Mr. Bone" at the same moment that the Major does; the scene ends with the Major calling out, "Good-bye, Major Applegate," as David leaves. Throughout the jail sequence, Constable Slocum persists in believing that the characters cannot be who they say they are and adheres tenaciously to Susan's fantastic misrepresentation of them. Having explained to Susan that psychiatrists do not believe that everyone who behaves strangely should be described as "crazy," Dr. Lehmann, the film's professional adjudicator of the rational, produces a massive, unconscious facial convulsion. In each case, the patriarch's assurance of competence and self-possession is shown to be illusory: the harmonious male ego is jangled by the slightest vibration.

The themes of language and repression are again interconnected during the amazingly dense expository sequence in the museum. When finally reminded of who Peabody is, David becomes wildly vivacious and enthusiastic, and tells Alice that "I'll knock him for a loop," only to receive the stern admonition: "No slang, David! Remember who and what you are!" It is clearly important, given Susan's masquerade as Swinging-Door Susie in the jail sequence, that David's failure to remember who and what he is should express itself here in the use of slang.

Thus Susan's sudden appearance on the golf course isn't arbitrary. She is both, as David's future lover, a character in her own right, and the embodiment of repressed impulses in David himself—impulses which he fears but to which he's sufficiently drawn to conjure them up so as to prevent his induction into patriarchy. Susan's value is defined through a series of reversals of the values of David's world. Consider, for example, Susan's language, which impedes rational discourse as strikingly as David's errors, but in an entirely different way. Both constitute a return of the repressed, but whereas in David's case the repressed appears merely as an interruption of language, in Susan's it has itself been organized as a language. One incident must suffice for demonstration. Susan tricks David into coming to her apartment by pretending that she is being mauled by her leopard (which, at this stage, David has never seen). Arriving breathless to find Susan in perfect health, David refuses to believe that the leopard exists, but when he discovers it in the bathroom he panics at once, and cries desperately to Susan that "you've got to get out of this apartment." Unperturbed but bewildered, Susan replies, "But David, I have a lease."

In terms of rational discourse, Susan's reply is nonsense; but "there is sense behind joking nonsense such as this, and it is this sense that makes the nonsense into a joke" (Freud, 94). The joke consists in the cryptic dramatization of two attitudes to the repressed: David's injunction makes no sense to Susan because she cannot conceive of the leopard's being an object of fear, though from David's point of view the fear is rational, and the comedy is produced by the collision between the two orders of logic. The source of Susan's power in the film is that while David's slips disturb his speech incoherently, Susan disturbs it coherently: her logic is the articulate expression of the forces internal to David's which his seeks, nevertheless, to disown. Elsewhere, of course, Susan's language is characterized by the kind of verbal play which Freud sees as being essential to the pleasure of jokes, and which Susan indulges most freely as Swinging-Door Susie. The different use of language has its corollary in a different model of identity. David's rational discourse and rational ego, depending on repression, are constantly vulnerable to disturbance, but Susan is both stable and Protean. Her constant metamorphoses embody a real consistency which instantly exposes the factitious wholeness of patriarchal order.

Susan is the antagonist not only of the linguistic order of the bourgeois world, but also of its organization of property. On her first appearance she walks off with David's golf ball, and responds to his attempt to establish the distinction between "mine" and "thine" by remarking that she's "not too particular about things like that." She proceeds at once to take his car, and fails completely to understand a lengthy conversation in which David tries to tell her that the car *is* his. Later in the film she appropriates another car, in the course of evading a conviction for having parked in front of a fire hydrant, and agrees to return it not because of moral qualms but because "I don't like it anyway." The significance of Susan's lack of concern for private property is crystallized in her exasperated question to David in the parking lot: "*Your* ball? *Your* car? Does everything in the world belong to you?" Capitalist property is organized by men; and the second car that Susan takes belongs not just to anyone but to Dr. Lehmann, from whose table, in the nightclub sequence, Susan has already removed a bowl of olives before creating the confusion in which David is accused of stealing Mrs. Lehmann's purse. The fact that the main violation of property rights in the film—the appropriation of David's bone—is performed by George, the third (with Susan and Baby), of the agents of the return of the repressed, makes the significance fully explicit. The undermining of property is also the undermining of phallic power, and the phallus ("It's rare! It's precious!") the quintessential commodity. To describe Susan as a thief would be inaccurate, in that it would imply that she knows what private property is. It is the case, rather, that she thinks of things in terms of their use-value only, and is unable to conceive of their belonging to anybody:

having come to the golf course in a car, she will naturally leave in one. When, in the jail sequence, Susan pretends to be a notorious thief, she is not identifying with crimes against property (which can't have a meaning if property doesn't) but improvising a solution to the problem of the moment—the virtue of crime, from Susan's point of view, is that it will capture the imagination of Constable Slocum. Her own imagination is fired by the idea of playing with the linguistic idiom of the *film* gangster (David tries in vain to convince the Constable that Susan is "making it all up out of movies that she's seen"), and Hawks extends the play, through an in-joke about Grant's previous role as "Jerry the Nipper" in *The Awful Truth*, to the conventions of his own film.

The appropriation of the phallus—it might be thought that what Susan does to David can be summed up as "castration." It is, in fact, the distinction of *Bringing Up Baby* to have dissociated the theme of a man's discovery of his "femininity" from the idea of loss—loss of dignity, loss of status, loss, ultimately, of the balls. What Hawks emphasizes is the gain: the losses are themselves felt to be positive. Indeed, it is the *acquisition* of the phallus which is associated with deprivation: *Bringing Up Baby* would be a completely different film if it were not so emphatically established that Susan enables the resurgence of a "femininity" which David already possesses and which, despite himself, he is unwilling to renounce. This premise makes of an action which might be rendered as "castration" an experience of release and pleasure, and the moment when David is at last prepared to admit that it was pleasure is the moment that the dinosaur collapses. Having hunted for the bone with desperate fervor, David refuses it when Susan brings it to him, and his refusal is the admission that the hunt had less to do than he thought it did with its ostensible object. For him, as for George and Susan, it was play, and in noting this we make a fundamental point about the Grant persona. If "castration" in *Bringing Up Baby* becomes something else, it is because Grant's acting conveys the enjoyment of incidents which are theoretically demeaning.

The extraordinary nature of the kind of hero embodied by Grant in his comedies of the late '30s has hardly been recognized, but in what other male star, classical or modern, is the realization of a man's "femininity" endorsed so specifically and explicitly? And what other male star is both romantic hero and *farceur*? There is clearly a relationship between the two propositions. Consider the moment in *Bringing Up Baby* when David, harassed, beleaguered and attired in ill-fitting hunting pink (Susan having stolen his clothes), tries to get Susan to grasp how vital it is that her aunt should not find out that David is in fact the eminent Professor Huxley. Susan listens dutifully, with an expression of entranced abstraction, but when David has finished she betrays her real preoccupation by telling him that "you look so handsome without your glasses." David's comic indignity, which has been, by this time, very clearly equated with feminization (his previous costume was Susan's negligée), doesn't make him the less attractive; and the fact that it doesn't has a corresponding effect on the idea of "indignity"—David's glasses are part of the constraining uniform of Professor Huxley. Characteristically, we are asked to find Grant romantically attractive because, rather than in spite of, his being made to look "ridiculous," and it is significant that in order to transform Grant, in *Notorious*, into the most detestable leading man in the American popular cinema, Hitchcock has entirely to subdue the comedian. The point made by Hitchcock's casting, here and in *Suspicion*, is that being the romantic lover—self-consciously tall, dark and handsome—is in itself to be in power: the situation in these films, and in the "persecuted wife" melodrama generally (think of the practice of casting famous lover-figures—

Charles Boyer in *Gaslight*, Robert Taylor in *Undercurrent*—as the oppressive husband), is the reverse of that in film noir. It is because the heroines of *Suspicion* and *Notorious* desire the Grant character that they become vulnerable to him.

To say no more than that Grant's being, generally, both romantic and comic removes the sexual threat won't quite do: though that is importantly part of it, the formula is too negative in suggestion. What we have in *The Awful Truth, Holiday* and *Bringing Up Baby* is something like an image of a positive bisexuality—something with which we are familiar in the personae of many of the great female stars, but which it is difficult to parallel amongst the men. All three films are concerned with the elimination of the differential of social/sexual power within the heterosexual couple, and use Grant to formulate a type of masculinity which is valuable and attractive by virtue of the sharing of gender characteristics with women. The particular beauty of Grant's collaboration with Katharine Hepburn consists (questions of acting apart) in the complementary bisexuality of the Hepburn persona: I have made the case for the radical bearing of the partnership elsewhere (Britton, *op. cit.*).

Given the thematic content of the early Grant persona it is, perhaps, hardly surprising, that Cary Grant the person sometimes became the object of anti-gay animus and innuendo. Kenneth Anger's book *Hollywood Babylon* reprints a cartoon of Grant which bills him as the star of a film called *"Who's a Fairy?"* (Anger, 177). In her biography of Grant, Lee Guthrie suggests that studio executives were at one time so worried about Grant's image, particularly after he began to share a house with Randolph Scott, that they set out expressly to manufacture publicity which would build up Grant's "virility," and quotes from a contemporary interview with Scott which appeared beneath the caption, "Randy says the guy's regular" (Guthrie, 104–5). For all their gratuitousness, such things have a marginal critical interest as evidence of a felt discrepancy between the Grant persona and the dominant social norms of "masculinity."

The screwball comedies, and in particular *The Awful Truth*, invite comparison with the romantic comedies of Grant's maturity—*An Affair to Remember* (McCarey, 1957), *Indiscreet, Houseboat* and *North by Northwest*. The Grant characters in these later works have obvious points in common. Each is defined, at the outset, in terms of spiritual emptiness and aimlessness. Nickie's grandmother/Cathleen Nesbitt tells Terry/Deborah Kerr in *An Affair to Remember* that Nickie has abandoned his painting because "he has been too busy—'living,' as they call it," and adds that "everything came too easily to him." In *Houseboat*, Tom tells Cinzia that he is "one of the undomesticated animals," and that while adults admire him for being "suave and debonair," children "look right through me as if there was nothing there. Maybe there isn't." In *North by Northwest*, Thornhill tells Eve/Eva Marie Saint that the middle initial of his monogram (R.O.T.) stands for "nothing." In each case, the emotional shallowness is associated with the Grant character's being sexually "unattached." Nickie is a playboy; Philip Adams in *Indiscreet* lies to Anna so as to avoid marrying her; Tom is a widower whose dedication to his profession has alienated him from his children; and when Thornhill, in response to Eve's charge that he "doesn't believe in marriage," tells her that he's been married twice, she replies, "See what I mean?" Shallowness is answered and corrected, in each case, by falling in love.

The schema is, of course, reductive: the limits of the present purpose should not be allowed to suggest that masterpieces (which I take the McCarey and the Hitchcock to be) can be exhausted in a formula. *An Affair to Remember* is one of the cinema's most poignant inquisitions of romanticism and the conditions of its realization. Terry's remark to Nickie's grandmother as the couple leaves her house ("It's a perfect world. Thank you for letting me trespass") establishes McCarey's theme. The "perfect world" is a walled flower-garden, and the film is preoccupied with the way in which the impulse to return to it creates the conditions in which it is lost. It is while she is "looking up" to "the nearest thing to heaven" that Terry has her accident, and her obsession (we may compare her to Ophuls' Lisa) with refusing to contact Nickie until she is actually well enough to go to him in person almost succeeds in destroying the relationship. Terry's redemption of Nickie, then, has its irony, and the play between the demeaning idealization of women characteristic of Nickie's bachelorhood ("Every woman I meet I put up there") and Terry's romantic idealism has a greater complexity than might at first appear.[2]

*North by Northwest* is virtually unique in Hitchcock's work in that here male sexuality does not remain, at the end, unregenerate: it might be compared in this respect with *Notorious*, in which Devlin's "change of heart" is ironically undercut. Roger Thornhill, exemplary capitalist male, successful, urbane and cynically confident of his secure possession of himself and his world, finds himself, "by chance," the pawn of the ruling class of that world. For the Professor/Leo G. Carroll, the film's supreme patriarch, and the guardian of democratic law, Thornhill's fate is a matter of pure contingency, and in being reduced to a mere agent for the preservation of the structure of power which the Professor represents, Thornhill is placed in a position like Eve's: each is being used to "get Vandamm," the patriarchal challenger. On Vandamm/James Mason's first appearance, he and Thornhill are paralleled to each other, Hitchcock's intercut panning shots as the two men circle each other establishing the one as the other's mirror image (and the casting of James Mason, whose persona shares with Grant's a suave urbanity which has often been identified with calculating sexual oppressiveness, is clearly relevant here).[3] The Professor, Thornhill and Vandamm have in common the exploitation of Eve: the Professor uses her to seduce Vandamm, who uses her in turn to seduce Thornhill, and Thornhill, as the dialogue I began by quoting indicates ("I'm beginning to think I'm underpaid") sees her as an occasion for the demonstration of his sexual charisma. The action can be defined in terms of Thornhill's gradual identification with and commitment to Eve, through an experience of powerlessness—of the woman's function in patriarchy—and an accompanying disengagement from the Professor and Vandamm, who, though political antagonists, are equally patriarchs. *North by Northwest* ends, famously, with one of Hitchcock's most brilliant images of patriarchal power, the presidential monoliths of Mount Rushmore, which impede the couple's escape; and we note that while the statues embody, of course, a bombastic myth of the bourgeois-democratic state, it is Vandamm's house which is concealed behind them. The final images—the cut from Thornhill lifting Eve to safety on the mountain to his lifting her into his berth on the train—are deeply ambiguous in suggestion, and the content of the ambiguity is enacted in the last shot of the train's disappearance into a tunnel. The phallic symbol ("But don't tell anyone") completes the partial reinstatement of male authority—Eve has been passive to Thornhill's rescue, and to his renaming of her ("Come on, Mrs. Thornhill")—but it is also clear that the concluding image dramatizes a withdrawal from the world of patriarchal struggle in which the action has been set. The dissonance isn't resolved, but I think we feel it to be different in kind from the bleak, ironic dissonance on which *Notorious* ends: Devlin hasn't been separated from Sebastian as Thornhill has from Vandamm and the Professor (who end up

*The romantic comedies of Grant's maturity. "A perfect world": Grant, Terry (Deborah Kerr) and her grandmother in* An Affair to Remember *(1957); Grant with Leo G. Carroll, "the supreme patriarch," and Eva Marie Saint in* North by Northwest *(1959).*

side by side on another peak of the mountain), and it is, indeed, of the essence of Devlin's "conversion" that it allows him, in taking over Sebastian's role, to assume power over Sebastian and Alicia at the same time.

*Indiscreet* and *Houseboat*, for all their charm, are very much simpler propositions. The Grant character's attractiveness and desirability consist in his being "one of the undomesticated animals," and the films seek to reconcile the contradiction between the allure characteristic of the sexual wanderer and domesticity. Grant hardly ever plays action heroes (he has never made, and is unimaginable in, a Western), and when he does we are primarily aware of how unlike an action hero he is. The unlikeness is brilliantly exploited by Hawks in *Only Angels Have Wings* (1939), in which Jeff's toughness, the insistently signaled "masculinity" of the leader of men, is analyzed as the camouflage of vulnerability, and it is significant, given the persona established by the screwball comedies, that the homoerotic component of Hawksian male friendship is more clearly focused in the relationship between Jeff and Kid/Thomas Mitchell than in the equivalent relationships in *To Have and Have Not* and *Rio Bravo*. Yet as my description will have implied, the use to which Grant is put in *Houseboat*, and elsewhere, can be discussed in terms of the opposition between settling and wandering so fundamental to the action hero.

The inflection, however, is unique. Wandering, as Grant embodies it, is urban (Ernie Mott in *None But the Lonely Heart* described himself as "a citizen of the Great Smoke—and I don't stay put!") and, whether Cockney or sophisticated, is associated not with male achievement in the adventurer's sense, but with the pursuit of "idle pleasure"—a hedonistic commitment to ease and comfort which may survive on chicanery (*Sylvia Scarlett*, *Mr. Lucky*), and which is almost always at one with the bachelor's desire to "play the field." Ernie Mott calls his rags "the uniform of my independence," and Roger Thornhill might have said the same of his executive's suit. Even as a wanderer, Grant does not inhabit the world of male action, and we cannot conceive of the adventurer's wandering, whatever else it may come to mean (in, for example, James Stewart's work for Mann and Hitchcock), being equated with emotional shallowness. The project of *Houseboat* is to extricate from the shallow "the suave and the debonair," growth of the same soil, and transplant them into the home.

The strength of *Houseboat* and *Indiscreet* is clearly the comic education of male presumption, the comedy issuing in recognition and change, but it could hardly be maintained that the couples formed at the end of these films have anything like the radical suggestiveness of those produced by the screwball comedies. The difference consists in quite distinct conceptions of what "falling in love" means; or rather, in the absence, in the screwball comedies, of anything approximating to what "falling in love" conventionally denotes. The phrase hardly covers the experience of David and Susan in *Bringing Up Baby*, despite Susan's plangent cry, as she realizes that she is going to have to steal David's clothes again to prevent his getting away, that he is "the only man I've ever loved." As for the Warriners, long-married and in the throes of divorce, the romantic belongs to the past: even when they return, at the end of *The Awful Truth*, to the mountain chalet they knew in happier days, it is not for the re-enactment of a nostalgic yesterday, but for the last act in the comedy of the reorganization of gender roles—comedy organized by one of the cinema's most delightful erotic metaphors (the large black cat which valiantly holds shut the door of Lucy's bedroom with its paw, frustrating, Jerry's attempts at entry until Lucy herself permits it). Linda and Johnny, in *Holiday*, *do* "fall in love" in something more like the familiar sense, and their doing so produces two of the film's most beautiful moments—the solitary waltz to the tune of the musical box on New Year's Eve, and Linda's confession of her love to Ned. Yet here again, the film's very premise—Johnny has already fallen in love with, and become engaged to, Julia/Doris Nolan with exemplary romantic dispatch—makes something different of the Johnny/Linda relationship, which grows out of a mutual allegiance to the complex oppositional values embodied in "play."

It may be said that the screwball couples don't fall in love because they learn to "have fun" instead, and that the beginning of "fun" is the end of "romance." To put the same thing in a different way, they don't fall in love because they dispense with the phallus, and with it the phallic organization of desire—the organization which may be sublimated as "love," and which entails an opposition between being in love and being "one of the undomesticated animals." In *Houseboat*, the hero's education is tied in with the theme of the domestication of the wanderer, the containment of male sexuality within the couple and the home. In *Bringing Up Baby* David becomes "undomesticated," but not in any sense that can be easily grasped by the settling/wandering antinomy. Male sexuality is not "contained" but transformed; the screwball comedies are thinking towards a concept of sexual relations in which sexual energy is not of the kind which is either contained (in the interests of social reproduction) or dissipated. The films produce, in fact, a utopian resolution of the romantic and the polymorphous—a stable, monogamous couple in which bourgeois gender identities, and their normative social function, no longer obtain.

The resolution is a difficult one, and the difficulty appears strikingly in the fact that Grant can be cast not only in films which seek to reconcile the charm of the bachelor and man-about-town with domesticity, but also in comedies of the male's domestic repression. Compare *Houseboat* and *Room for One More* (Taurog, 1951), the subject of which is the impossibility, for "Poppy" Rose (the theme of the father's emasculation is sufficiently blatant), of having sex with his wife because of her obsessive impulse to adopt into the Rose home, swelling the ranks of the couple's own children, a succession of deserving orphans. It is characteristic of the Grant persona that the experience of domestic constraint should be as little a matter of the yearning for adventure as wandering was the pursuit of it: there is no hint in *Room for One More* of George Bailey/James Stewart's desire, in *It's a Wonderful Life*, to "lassoo the moon." Consider the sequence in which "Poppy" undertakes to give Jimmy-John/Clifford Tatum, Jr. a sex education lesson, illustrating his lecture by drawing the outline of a male and female figure in the sand with a stick. Anna/Betsy Drake, his wife, remarks on how badly the female figure is sketched, and "Poppy" replies cryptically that he has had to "draw from memory." In its commitment to the inestimable value, for the orphans, of a "good home," the film is also committed to the value of the hero's celibacy, and his patient, self-abnegating fulfillment of a father's responsibilities is rewarded in the final shot, but the comedy depends throughout (as it does, though with a very different emphasis, in *Houseboat*) on the contradiction between the Grant persona and domesticity. A similar theme is implicit in *Mr. Blandings Builds his Dream House* (Potter, 1948), in which the hero's dissatisfaction with settlement expresses itself, ironically, in the compulsiveness with which he pursues his ambition of constructing the perfect family home. That, at least, is potentially the theme. The film in fact submerges it, and is left hesitating between the opinion that the "dream house" represents a valid democratic aspiration; that it is "irresponsible," because Bland-

*The return of the repressed:* Monkey Business *(1952), with Ginger Rogers, Charles Coburn and Grant.*

ings' obsession with it threatens to disrupt the family; and that Blandings is neurotic (see, for instance, his paranoid jealousy of Bill Cole/Melvyn Douglas).

The themes from which Mr. Blandings withdraws are fully dramatized in Grant's last film for Howard Hawks, *Monkey Business* (1952), whose radical dissimilarity to *Bringing Up Baby,* magnified by the superficial resemblances is eloquent of the completeness with which the synthesis of screwball comedy has disintegrated. There is nothing here of the reconciliation of alienated sexual energy and "refinement." The return of the repressed in *Monkey Business* is much closer to that characteristic of the Gothic: there is, that is to say, no equivalent for Susan. The energies liberated by B-4 are no longer capable of transforming the ego which denies them, but are instead refracted through it: they have the character at once of being "primal" and of having been generated by "necessary" *social* constraints that we associate with the horror film, and with its difficult impasse. The completeness of Hawks' hostility to bourgeois society keeps *Monkey Business* a comedy, but it is clearly significant that it is the last of his comedies (if we set aside the attempt to remake *Bringing Up Baby* as *Man's Favorite Sport?*). The ability, in the period which produced Sirk's melodramas, to conceive of any creative energies surviving the middle classes is already strained to the limit. Consider the extent of the distance between the discomfiture the Warriners inflict on each other in *The Awful Truth,* or the kind of play involved in the hunt for the bone in *Bringing Up Baby*, with the sequence in *Monkey Business* in which Barnaby/Grant and Edwina/Ginger Rogers bedaub each other with paint, or that astonishing climactic scene where Barbary and the children, dressed as Indians, prepare to scalp Hank Entwhistle/Hugh Marlowe. Oppositional "play" has become retributive violence, and "having fun" has taken on a Hobbesian complexion. *Monkey Business* is an extraordinary work, but by 1952 the exhilaration of release in screwball comedy has lost, irretrievably, its utopian dimension.

Is pleasure democratic?

The word I first proposed for Grant was "irresponsibility," but it will have been apparent that the transition is an easy one. "Pleasure," in fact, in bourgeois language is a profoundly dubious quantity. Bourgeois rhetoric promises "life, liberty and the pursuit of happiness," but it turns out, when we read the representative documents, that "liberty" is the liberty of the free market, and that these felicities are for the industrious. Pleasure involves a venal moral relaxation, and a willingness, where the necessities of life are concerned, to have something for nothing. Moral relaxation expresses itself in, and conduces to, social parasitism, and pleasure is an addiction of all classes except the bourgeoisie.

The interplay between ideas of pleasure and irresponsibility in the Grant persona explain its peculiar class character. Grant can play, on the one hand, the working-class man as feckless Cockney, indigent, carefree and work-shy: Ernie Mott in *None But the Lonely Heart* (Odets, 1944) is representative ("You know me, ducky—tramp of the universe!"). He can also play the idle rich, executives and professionals of that level of attainment at which the notion of labor tends to acquire a theoretic air and we are primarily conscious of its rewards. The Grant persona is profoundly incompatible with industry, and this, of course, an essential aspect of its attractiveness. Yet it also raises ideology problems, which appear in the fact that each class type can merge into the confidence trickster. Thus we have Jimmy Monkley in *Sylvia Scarlett*, the proletarian adventurer as charlatan and glib opportunist, or, in *Mr. Lucky*, Joe Adams, illegal gambler and draft-dodger (and, though American underworld, still Cockney). Conversely, Johnny Aysgarth in *Suspicion* is an upper-class English playboy, who until the arbitrary happy ending, is living off and conspiring to murder his wife, and the Grant characters in *Indiscreet*, *Houseboat* and *North by Northwest* all share a duplicity which is clearly correlated with class privilege.

The kind of issues raised by the conflict between a commitment to pleasure and a democratic fife of moral probity and honest toil emerges very clearly in *Holiday*, which seeks to solve the problem by introducing a distinction, classically left-populist, between the spirit of "democracy" and its actual operations. Johnny embodies the ideals of the first insurgent bourgeoisie (the holiday is his "Declaration of Independence") and Mr. Seton a contemporary capitalism which is felt to have lost touch with those ideals through an obsession with accumulation: for Mr. Seton, Johnny's lack of interest in making money is "un-American." This hiving off of democratic principle from capitalist reality, as a thing distinct and superior in kind, allows *Holiday* to reclaim energies which express themselves in an aversion to profitable labor, and it does so in such a way as to restate the problem: as I noted earlier, the film is compelled to conclude that the American spirit cannot survive in America.

The representation of Grant as a viable democratic figure, then, depends upon the holding together of a standard of bourgeois-democratic responsibility and qualities which, by that same standard, can be construed as *irresponsible*. *Holiday* succeeds, insofar as it does, by arguing that bourgeois rhetoric, embodied by the aspirations of the Founding Fathers, and bourgeois practice have no connection with each other, and *People Will Talk* (Mankiewicz, 1951) enacts a variant of the same strategy: the moral values and allegiances of Dr. Praetorius, while they incite the wrath of the hide-bound petit-bourgeois community, express a real, normative democratic feeling.

The case appears at its most fascinating, as we might expect, in Grant's appearances in the "commitment" film—that transgeneric cycle of the '40s in which the action turns on the winning for the democratic cause of a previously uncommitted, and thus irresponsible, figure. It is of the essence of the Grant persona that he can be cast both as the spokesman of democracy—*The Talk of the Town* (Stevens, 1942), *Once Upon a Honeymoon* (McCarey, 1942—and as the commitment figure—*Mr. Lucky*, *None But the Lonely Heart*: Grant's penultimate film, *Father Goose* (Nelson, 1964), is still able to exploit this motif.

The peculiar success of *Once Upon a Honeymoon* (to which Robin Wood [Wood, 1976] has devoted a splendid article) lies in its closeness to the screwball tradition—a tradition which is still, at this point, artistically viable, and from which the film derives a normative concept of the democratic couple in which the idea of "irresponsible" plea-

*"The recovery of sexuality and pleasure": Cary Grant and Ginger Rogers in*
Once Upon a Honeymoon *(1941).*

sure has great positive value. It is against this norm that the kind of irresponsibility represented by Katharine Butte-Smith/Ginger Rogers is measured. She aspires, essentially, to the World of the Vances and the Setons, which means, here, not the American haute bourgeoisie but European fascism (though the possibility of the link was always there: see, for example, Capra, or the emphasis in *Holiday* on the fact that the Seton Crams/Henry Daniell and Binnie Barnes are sympathetic to Hitler). The persistence of this tradition allows the director of *The Awful Truth* to associate, in *Once Upon a Honeymoon*, Katie's progress towards commitment with the recovery of sexuality and pleasure: the couple can be politically responsible while continuing to occupy the outskirts of the realm of play. What is lost in the fusion is the sexual progressiveness of screwball comedy. The propaganda theme necessitates a conservative dramatization of gender—the couple must be, however "heightened," the *normal* American couple, associated in the film's imagery with reproduction, and "play" in *Once Upon a Honeymoon* (Grant's tape-measure and saxophone) is phallic.

Yet the inner tensions of the Grant persona create an occasion for the most fascinating inflections of the "commitment" thematic. The persistent gender ambiguity of the persona manifests itself, in *The Talk of the Town*, in the way in which the Rogers part from *Honeymoon* comes to be played by a man. Nora Shelley/Jean Arthur, while being obviously necessary for appearance's sake, is no less conspicuously irrelevant to the relationship between Leopold Dilg/Grant and Michael Lightcap/Ronald Colman, and her redundancy is nowhere more apparent than in the penultimate scene in which Lightcap renounces her to his "rival"—at the very point at which, were Lightcap a woman, he would be united with Dilg himself. Indeed, the terms in which Lightcap describes Dilg, and Dilg's love, to Nora, suggest unmistakably his own declaration of love, and the stolidity of *The Talk of the Town* is very much a matter, not merely of George Stevens, but of the necessary impossibility of realizing the film's latent content.

In *Notorious*, Hitchcock continues to use Grant as the spokesman for democracy, but deprives it of all positive significance by dissolving the absolute distinction between democracy and fascism on which the commitment film depends. This inflection, or more precisely, negation of the genre is, of course, characteristic. Three years before *Notorious*, in *Lifeboat*, Hitchcock had argued that fascism rises to power with the connivance, and on the basis of the deadlocked class antagonisms, of bourgeois democracy, and as we have seen, the relationship between Devlin and Sebastian is taken up again, though with crucial new developments, in *North by Northwest*. The dominant popular reading of the Grant persona—"consummately romantic and consummately genteel"—is essential to Hitchcock's purpose in *Notorious*, and it is powerfully evoked in the sequence built round Alicia's party and the ensuing intoxicated car ride. The revelation that Devlin is an American agent and the first manifestation of brutality to Alicia (here, physical brutality—Devlin knocks her out) come together, though Hitchcock's imagery has already prepared us for it: from his first appearance, Devlin has been associated with the predatory oppressiveness of the male look at women which the film's opening shot has established as a crucial motif. It is a motif which links Devlin with Sebastian, and it is developed with astonishing power and complexity in the film's great central sequence at Sebastian's reception—the sequence that ends with Devlin's staging, for Sebastian's gaze, of the embrace which leads to the discovery that Alicia has been working for the Americans, and the attempt to murder her. The suave fascist male acts through the sexual impulses of the suave democratic male—it having always been clear that both

● ● ● ● ● ● ● ● ● ● ● ● ● ● ● ● ● ● ● ● ● ● ● ● ● ● ● ● ● ● ● ● ● ● ● ● ● ● ● ● ● ● ● ● ●

Devlin and Sebastian see Alicia primarily as a means of consolidating their sense of their own potency. *Notorious* takes up the connection between the heroine's democratization and male tutelage from *Once Upon a Honeymoon*, but inverts its meaning.

In *Mr. Lucky*, we have *Once Upon a Honeymoon* in reverse, with Grant in the Rogers part. Katie O'Hara, the Brooklyn burlesque queen, becomes Joe Adams, the Cockney/Brooklyn con-man, and the film sets out to infuse the "democratic" with the trickster's acumen and ebullience while submitting its anti-social character to democratic correction. The mix produced a clear class character. In *The Talk of the Town*, where Grant plays the representative of democracy, Dilg's plebeian origins carry no suggestion of the shady or the shiftless (though the film demonstrates its awareness that such a connotation is latent in Grant's working-class characters by making of Dilg an obstreperous worker who has been *falsely* accused of burning down a factory). In *Mr. Lucky*, where Grant plays the commitment figure, the link between the plebeian and dishonesty is fully realized, and must be dissolved in the course of the action. At the same time, Joe Adams, though the commitment figure, is also a man, and "education" is reciprocal in *Mr. Lucky* in a way that it isn't in *Once Upon a Honeymoon*: Dorothy Bryant/Laraine Day must be democratized too, not in the sense of learning commitment, but in that of surrendering, through her experience of Joe, the complacency of a daughter of the upper middle-classes.[4]

It is clearly crucial, in the light of the persona developed by the screwball comedies, in which the tone and content of the comedy of education is so very different, that the anarchic energy associated so strikingly in the earlier films with femininity should appear increasingly as "boyishness." The hero's phallic status is partially restored, and Grant's sexual charisma becomes that of the lover who is also a scapegrace son. It is often brought against the screwball comedy, from a "left" position which it is certainly proper to call "vulgar," that the genre is a celebration of wealth and of the wealthy. Nothing could be further from the truth: the hostility to wealth and the social/class privilege endowed by its accumulation could hardly be clearer than it is in *The Awful Truth* and *Holiday*. The wealth of the screwball couple, like its childlessness, is a means of detaching the partners from any social function: it is a precondition for the destruction of the gender roles which are defined by their social function. Wealth in its capitalist meaning becomes valueless. Its purpose is to eliminate the "realm of necessity" and permit the leap into the "realm of freedom"—or at the least, of "post-scarcity anarchism"—whose values, as I've indicated, are categorically non-bourgeois. In the nature of things, such a project is impossible in the commitment film, though the passage into the realm of bourgeois democracy may drive from it something of its élan.

In a sense many of Grant's films are commitment films—comedies of the commitment of the errant male to marriage and settlement, which celebrate the reconciliation of the pursuit of pleasure with social forms which may not at first appear to conduce to it. Of the later films, *North by Northwest* is, perhaps, the closest to the tendency and suggestion of the masterpieces of the late '30s. It is the value of Cary Grant to have embodied a male heterosexuality which is so different in tone from that of the action hero, and which is arrived at through a different kind of relationship with women—a relationship in which the woman appears so often as the educator of the male, and of his pleasure. But it is in the screwball comedies, where that process takes on so radical a character and is distinguished most drastically from a concept of patriarchal "domesticity" and "domestication," that the value is completely realized. Here, uniquely in the popular cinema, Grant's acting *creates* the attractiveness of male femininity and of the relationships enabled by it.

If I have failed to take up the question I raised at the beginning—the question of Grant's imputed "limitations" as an actor—that is not only because I take the answer to the question to be obvious, and see little point in addressing a failure to perceive it; the reasons which make the proposition that "Cary Grant is a great actor" the reverse of a commonplace require diagnosis, but not refutation. The more important fact is that the felicities of comic acting are more difficult to describe and discuss than acting usually is, and I have preferred to avoid the laboriousness involved in demonstrating that performance is "productive of meaning." How does one describe Grant's reaction, in *Bringing Up Baby*, to the news that his marriage is to have "no domestic entanglements of any kind"?—the slight hesitation, the movement of the head (both brilliantly judged), the shift from incomprehension to startled inference, all of which contribute so much to the comic force of the pay-off line, "I mean 'of *any* kind,' David." Yet if the screwball comedies are the essence of the persona, they also provide the basis for an evaluation of the performer's skills. Here, surely, are imaginative and technical resources comparable to those of Laurel and Hardy and Keaton.

## Notes

1. Farce and wit co-exist in other sophisticated comedies, but it is not, of course, the case that the sophisticated couple always acquires the meaning that it does in *The Awful Truth*, *Bringing Up Baby* and *Holiday*. In *It Happened One Night* (Capra, 1934) and *My Man Godfrey* (La Cava, 1936), the hero presides over the heroine's democratic education, as does the Grant character in *Once Upon a Honeymoon* (McCarey, 1942). In *Holiday* and its two predecessors, we have a mutually enabling encounter between stars, director and genre, in which the radical possibilities of each are realized.

2. *An Affair to Remember* is a close remake of McCarey's own *Love Affair* (1939), in which Nickie had been played by Charles Boyer, and there are evident affinities between the Grant characters in *Gaslight* and *Notorious* and the Boyer characters in *Gaslight* (Cukor, 1944), *A Woman's Vengeance* (Korda, 1947) and *The Thirteenth Letter* (Preminger, 1951) or between Grant in *Indiscreet* and Boyer in *Back Street* (Stevenson, 1941). In Boyer, too, the charisma of the romantic lover has often been continuous with the vicious, the corrupt and the cynical; yet the difference between the two personae appears in the fact that while RKO compelled Hitchcock to tack on a happy ending to *Suspicion* to protect Grant's image, no such scruple was allowed to impair the dramatic logic of *Gaslight*, in which Boyer, playing a variant of the same melodramatic type, remains unambiguously the villain.

    In accounting for the difference we may note, to begin with, that if Grant rarely plays action heroes, and Boyer doesn't play them at all, Grant appears even less frequently in woman's pictures (*An Affair to Remember* and *Penny Serenade* [Stevens, 1941] are the major exceptions) and Boyer appears in them all the time. Given the thematic of the woman's film, and the privilege accorded by the genre to the exhaustive intensity of the heroine's passion—an intensity that comes to be synonymous with emotional integrity and disinterestedness—the withholding of intimacy and of full reciprocal engagement which Boyer shares with Grant are inflected in another direction. In, say, *The Garden of Allah* (Boleslawski, 1935) or *All This and Heaven Too* (Litvak, 1940), where the Boyer characters refusal to commit himself to "love" is associated with a tragic moral dilemma, and the claims of passion are contested not by those of egotistic self-assertion but by those of self-abnegating duty (to religious vocation and family respectively), Boyer is presented sympathetically. In *Back Street* and, supremely, *Conquest* (Brown, 1937), Boyer embodies a ruthless male ambition which withdraws from love to achieve power and position in a public world from which the heroine is excluded: in both cases, the heroine is reduced to the ignominious role of "mistress," and finds herself in an indeterminate hinterland between public and domestic life, without a secure and recognized position in either. The theme of a woman's exploitation by a love to which her "destiny" as a woman commits her but which the man, though he has appeared to share it, does not return, is taken to an extreme in *Gaslight*, in which the lover's charisma and allure are, from the outset, weapons in a confidence trick. Significantly, while Grant can still be cast as a desirable romantic male until virtually the end of his career, a number of Boyer's later performances, such as those for Minnelli in *The Cobweb* (1955) and *The Four Horsemen of the Apocalypse* (1961), emphasize the desiccation of aging charm, and associate the strained, insinuating facility which are all that remain of it with the character's moral bankruptcy. Here, the feeling that the Boyer character's ambitions are worthless (already clear enough in *Conquest*) is compounded by the evident meretriciousness of the manner which once made him plausible.

It is crucial here that the suggestion of Boyer's "Europeanness" is very different from Grant's. As the French lover, Boyer inherits the bad connotations of Europe along with its glamour, and in that he does so he can be used to dramatize with particular cogency the suspicion, implicit in the woman's film, that a woman's destiny can very easily become her oppression. Grant's "Europeanness," by contrast, is hardly an issue at all. Even when he plays British characters, the emphasis falls on their class position rather than their national origins, and in American settings we am invited to read him as American. In this, he can be distinguished not only from Boyer but from, say, Ronald Colman, whose romantic attractiveness is inseparable from his being an *English* gentleman, and whose persona has no suggestion either of insincerity or of sexual manipulativeness.

3. During the lull in his career in the early '50s, Grant was in fact offered the part of the fading movie star Norman Maine, eventually played by Mason, in Cukor's re-make of *A Star is Born* (1954), but turned it down because he thought it might harm his image.

4. Compare *Mr. Lucky* with *The Philadelphia Story* (1940) in this respect. The animus against Tracy Lord/Katharine Hepburn in Cukor's film (or Barry's play—it might be argued that Cukor qualities it) is so intense, and the commitment to transform her into "a first-class human being" so relentless, that we can be asked to write off the moral weakness of Dexter Haven/Cary Grant as a mere by-product of his ex-wife's intransigence. At the same time, Haven's unfitness to be the hero is tacitly acknowledged in the presence of Mike/James Stewart, who undertakes Tracy's democratization in his stead before returning her to her husband. *The Philadelphia Story* manages to give the Grant persona an entirely negative content (his femininity becomes castration, and his "irresponsibility" dissoluteness) while also requiring us to see it, in the light of Tracy's aberrations, sympathetically. In this, and as a reactionary comedy of re-marriage, the film also invites comparison with *The Awful Truth* and *His Girl Friday* (the second of which is also disturbed by an uncertainty as to what our attitude to the Grant figure is to be).

## Works Cited

Page references are to the first editions listed.

Kenneth Anger, *Hollywood Babylon* (San Francisco: Straight Arrow Books, 1975; New York: Dell, 1981 [reprint]).

Andrew Britton, *Katharine Hepburn* (London: Tyneside Cinema, 1983).

Donald Deschner, *The Films of Cary Grant* (New York: Citadel Press, 1979).

Sigmund Freud, *Jokes and their Relation to the Unconscious* (New York: Penguin, 1978).

Lee Guthrie, *The Life and Loves of Cary Grant* (New York: Drake, 1977).

Pauline Kael, *When the Lights Go Down* (New York: Holt, Rinehart & Winston, 1980).

Ernest Lehman, *North by Northwest* (New York: Viking, 1973).

David Shipman, *The Great Movie Stars: the Golden Years* (New York: Crown, 1970; London: Angus & Robertson, 1979 [revised]).

Robin Wood, *Howard Hawks* (London: British Film Institute, 1981).

Wood, "Democracy and Shpontanuity: Leo McCarey and the Hollywood Tradition," *Film Comment* (January-February 1976), 6–15.

CARY
GRANT
ROSALIND
RUSSELL

in HOWARD HAWKS'
*HIS GIRL FRIDAY*
WITH
RALPH BELLAMY
GENE LOCKHART

Based on a play by
BEN HECHT
CHARLES MacARTHUR

Screen play by
CHARLES LEDERER
Directed by
HOWARD HAWKS

A COLUMBIA PICTURE

# Ernst Lubitsch:
# The Actor vs. the Character

Dan Sallitt (2001)

Even on brief acquaintance with Ernst Lubitsch's films, one observes that his actors characteristically come to a dead stop after every line, and that a beat of silence separates each bit of dialogue from the next. The actors further emphasize the artifice by using a rise-and-fall delivery that makes every line a set-up or a summation, stylizing any hints of psychology into elements of rhythm. By contrast, directors like McCarey, La Cava or Capra try to preserve psychology, and create rhythm more between lines than within them. Compare, say, the scene in La Cava's *Bed of Roses* (1933) in which Constance Bennett impersonates a journalist in order to seduce wealthy John Halliday, with the scene in Lubitsch's *Trouble in Paradise* (1932) in which Miriam Hopkins impersonates a secretary to gain access to the house of wealthy Kay Francis. In addition to the startling resemblance of Bennett and Hopkins in their mousy working-girl disguises—was La Cava "quoting" the Lubitsch film?—the dialogue in both scenes snaps back and forth in similar ping-pong style. But the scenes play quite differently: Bennett embroiders her charade with little bits of characterization that take her speech patterns in many directions, whereas Hopkins' moments of concealment and unwitting revelation are confined within a narrow tonal range that emphasizes the musical aspect of the repartee.

This acting style, which occurs throughout Lubitsch's sound films (and, in spirit at least, in the silent films as well, where actions and gestures are similarly discrete), reminds us that Lubitsch had his start in the theater. Though Lubitsch the actor eventually ascended to Max Reinhardt's theater company, the acting in his films evokes "lower" forms of comic theater: operetta of course, but also farce and vaudeville skit humor. The resemblance between the measured, often exaggerated acting style found in these comic traditions and in Lubitsch's films points to a more interesting correspondence: Lubitsch's actors, like their theatrical counterparts, tend to establish a direct relationship with the audience, an understanding based on a shared knowing perspective on the fiction. In the most pronounced instances (such as Maurice Chevalier's characters in the '30s musicals), Lubitsch characters feel free to address the audience directly, and walk through the plot with the smiling detachment of vaudeville entertainers; they are as much narrators of as participants in the drama. One can see the same tendency, in a more restrained form, in other Lubitsch characters—like Herbert Marshall in *Trouble in Paradise* or Charles Boyer in *Cluny Brown* (1946)—who remain more or less within the boundaries of the fiction but express the same amused overview on the action that Lubitsch encourages in the audience.

Not all characters in Lubitsch films enjoy the license of these unofficial masters of ceremonies, of course. But Lubitsch so desires direct communion with the audience that he devises acting strategies to produce it even when the character is not a stand-in for the audience's perspective. To illustrate one of these strategies: in a scene from *The Smiling Lieutenant* (1931), Chevalier, asked to educate sheltered princess Miriam Hopkins in

**154**

worldly matters, tries to explain what a wink means. After a moment of uncertainty, Chevalier finds an explanation: a wink conveys not only affection, but also the desire to do something about it. Hopkins, realizing that the conversation has moved into a dangerous area, composes herself suddenly and says, "That's enough for today."

The joke in this characteristically Lubitschian exchange lies in the character's attempt to end the conversation casually when the audience knows that she is alarmed. There are two common ways to treat this kind of material:

a) The character can make an effort to conceal her anxiety and end the conversation naturally by delivering the last line matter-of-factly and using diversionary tactics. The audience would then be in the superior position of seeing through the character, who is unaware how much she is revealing.

b) The character can use looks, knowing smiles, etc. to convey to the other character that she is ending the conversation because of the escalation of intimacy, her words to the contrary. The character would then exhibit a self-awareness that makes the joke hers instead of the film's.

Lubitsch creates a third possibility: he makes the actor aware of the joke while keeping the character in the dark. It is not simply exaggeration that creates this separation of the actor from his or her character: it is that the actor's mannerisms put emphasis on things that the character isn't aware of. Because the acting contains deliberate strategies that are not conscious strategies of the character, a gap opens up between actor and character. In the example given, Hopkins' stylized delivery conveys a full awareness of the situation. Clearly her character is not trying to let her primness show, either humorously or seriously; the context forbids such a conscious attempt on her part. But the acting deliberately brings her motivations out in the open, annihilating all naturalistic semblance of a coverup. Her face goes blank with exaggerated suddenness, and her line is delivered with the emphatic finality of her maidenly conviction, not modulated to appear natural. These are the actor's ways of letting the audience know that she is conscious of her character's visible loss of composure, of which the character is unconscious.

In this example, just as with the more openly knowing Chevalier characters, Lubitsch establishes an understanding between the actor and the audience. In one case, the character participates in this understanding, and in the other she does not; but the direct connection between actor and audience is in both cases the goal of Lubitsch's direction of actors.

Another example, from a later period of Lubitsch's career: in *Heaven Can Wait* (1943), Gene Tierney breaks down crying over her imminent marriage to Allyn Joslyn, and tells Don Ameche the story of her engagement. Though she goes out of her way to express her affection for her parents and her home state in the course of this story, she lets slip one phrase after another that shows her true dislike of each.

> Tierney: Well, you see, I always wanted to live in New York. I don't want to say anything against Kansas, but—life on my father's estate . . . Don't misunderstand me, we have all the modern conveniences and luxuries, but . . . oh, and you don't know Father and Mother.
> Ameche: Well, I've only just met them.
> Tierney: Don't you think they're sweet?
> Ameche: Well, yes, very sweet.
> Tierney: Yes, they are. But it's not very easy to live with them. You see, most of

> the time they don't talk to one another. And whenever a young
> man—and there were some very nice ones . . .
>
> Ameche:  Oh, I'm sure of it.
>
> Tierney:  . . . if one of them asked for my hand, and my mother said yes, my
> father said no. And when my father said yes, my mother said no. But
> Albert came at one of those rare moments when they were both on
> speaking terms. And if I hadn't said yes, who knows when my parents
> might have been talking to each other again. I might have spent the
> rest of my life in Kansas. Don't misunderstand me—I love Kansas. It's
> just that I don't feel like living there. Besides, I don't want to be an
> old maid. Not in Kansas!

As with the scene from *The Smiling Lieutenant*, there are two usual approaches to such material: Tierney's hostile feelings toward family and home could slip out without her meaning to reveal them; or she could show an awareness of her emotional contradictions by acknowledging them. Instead of either approach, Tierney delivers both positive and negative feelings in identical tones of tearful confiding; she is completely untroubled at moving from one extreme to the other without transition. Tierney the actor realizes the contradictions of which Tierney's character is plainly unaware, demonstrating this by leveling her affect to heighten the contrast between content and delivery.

If we look at the scenes discussed above and the three alternative acting approaches that I've suggested—the poles of unawareness and awareness, and Lubitsch's actor-aware/character-unaware strategy—it's interesting to note that, in the context of the scriptwriting, only Lubitsch's approach is obviously comic. Both the other approaches tend to illuminate the character's psychology; if we try to apply them to the scenes in question, the tone moves a notch toward drama, mitigating against big laughs. This is not to say that psychologically oriented acting can't be funny—there are almost as many counterexamples as there are comic directors—but it does suggest that Lubitsch's comic style is built into his material, and that his acting strategies work only because they are set up at the writing stage.

(The Chevalier-Jeanette MacDonald musical *One Hour with You* [1932] is a Lubitsch project begun by George Cukor but eventually completed by Lubitsch. Intriguingly, there are acting moments in the film in which Chevalier partly abdicates his usual winking position outside the narrative and drifts toward naturalism. The most memorable example is the "That's What I Did Too" number, in which Chevalier's defensive and anxious self-justifications are for once motivated by the plight of the character; he displays less knowledge of himself than does the audience. Typically, one would expect Chevalier to grin and nod at the audience during a Lubitsch musical number no matter what his character's emotional state might be. Hardly an open-and-shut case, but one wonders if one detects in Chevalier's performance the influence of Cukor—also a man of the theater, but far more inclined toward immersion in the story's emotions.)

What Lubitsch loses in immediacy by showing himself behind the curtain, he gains in reflexivity and perspective. A few examples show that Lubitsch's seemingly playful strategies could be the means to unusual and subtle ends. Consider the last shot of *Angel* (1937), in which Herbert Marshall, having bid farewell to his unfaithful wife Marlene Dietrich, leaves her with her lover and walks toward the door, the camera tracking behind him. Dietrich unexpectedly overtakes the camera (having taken leave of her

*Collaborative styles: Jeanette MacDonald and Maurice Chevalier in* One Hour with You, *by Lubitsch and Cukor.*

lover off-screen), enters the frame and walks to Marshall's side; without breaking his stride, and barely looking at her, Marshall gives Dietrich his arm, and the two walk out of the house together with the composure of actors returning for a curtain call. A more naturalistic ending would give the audience a chance to observe Marshall's surprise and Dietrich's contrition; Lubitsch, preferring not to provide us such an advantage over the actors, abandons psychology and allows the characters the grace and composure that they would like to present to the world. A related example occurs at the beginning of the grand waltz scene in *The Merry Widow* (1934). Chevalier and MacDonald are quarreling bitterly, with no hint of affection or play beneath their anger; but when they hear the first chords of the "Merry Widow Waltz," they pause for a moment, then fall into each other's arms with choreographed grace, whirling off onto the dance floor as the camera recedes to lose them amid the other dancers. Here Lubitsch is playing with the conventions of the musical comedy, according to which the characters must reconcile; the actors therefore abandon psychology and comply with genre. In a different mood, one can imagine Lubitsch carrying this scene off with a wink, but the tone here is more serious, as if the too-abrupt triumph of musical convention has suggested to the filmmaker by contrast the precariousness of real love: the echoes of the rather harsh quarrel remain in our ears, and the lovers do not smile as they spin away. We can see in their faces either the compliance of actors moving to the director's instructions, or the resignation of the lovers to the troubled but compelling bond between them.

Perhaps Lubitsch's only reason for drawing on the conventions of theater is the opportunity they provide him to insert his overseeing viewpoint into the fiction. His actors acquire an all-knowing aura which is nonetheless curiously life-sized: they sit in the privileged seat of the film spectator.

# "Don't Ask Me": Indeterminacy and *5th Ave Girl*

## Chris Fujiwara (2001)

Gregory La Cava made anti-masterpieces: films intended not to offer a seamless design, but to pose problems. Even *My Man Godfrey* (1936), his most enduringly popular and most frequently revived film, feels unresolved, its ending uncomfortable, as if to remind us that it isn't the film's job to reconcile the contradictions it has dealt with, to suggest that to go on dealing with them is our job. Any of his films could be called *Unfinished Business*. La Cava films address the viewer specifically and unmistakably: they leave spaces that the viewer must fill imaginatively, and they refer to problems that are assumed to be those of the viewer's everyday private and public lives.

La Cava's *5th Ave Girl* (1939) is a comedy about a middle-aged millionaire, Timothy Borden (Walter Connolly), whose wife and children treat him with familiarity-bred contempt. Alone on his birthday, he meets the jobless Mary Grey (Ginger Rogers) in Central Park and hires her to pose as his mistress in order to win back his family's respect. The film's telling of this story hinges on a crucial ambiguity: it's not until late in the film that we realize that Miss Grey (as she is most often called by most of the characters, including Borden) has been merely *posing* as Borden's mistress. This ambiguity is part of a more general indeterminacy by which La Cava gets us to confront the issues raised in *5th Ave Girl* as problems, rather than merely accept them as conventional, generic elements.

Already, with the opening titles of *5th Ave Girl*, there is no way to be quite sure about the experience the film proposes, no way of knowing, above all, why the film's title is spelled as it is: "5TH AVE GIRL," with the number 5 and the abbreviation "Ave," and furthermore with no period after the "Ave." A secondary problem is posed by the main titles, which ingeniously and elaborately layer the title cards—in the form of street signs—over shots of New York streetscapes. Each title is superimposed over a shot of a street, whereupon there is a dissolve to a shot that tracks forward so that the street sign/title and the street are both brought closer to the camera and, simultaneously, slightly change in relation to each other. The track-in verifies that the two components of the image are not merely in an optical relation, but in a spatial relation.

Let's propose a third problem. Maybe it's not a problem. Or if it is, the sense in which it is a problem is not, perhaps, immediately clear. But here it is: after Ginger Rogers, who has her own title card, several other actors are listed: Walter Connolly, Verree Teasdale, James Ellison, Tim Holt, Kathryn Adams, Franklin Pangborn. The problem is twofold. First, a male co-star for Rogers appears to be absent. Walter Connolly is a major character actor, but he is too old to be a romantic lead. Ellison and Holt might be plausible as romantic leads but are not stars. This is a problem that, as we shall see, relates to a difficulty in the narrative of the movie. The second expression of the problem with the cast is that it's a little unclear what order the actors are supposed to be listed in, because the names are in two columns, and there's no obvious way to tell whether we're meant to read the names row-wise (i.e., starting at top-left, then moving to the right, then down

**159**

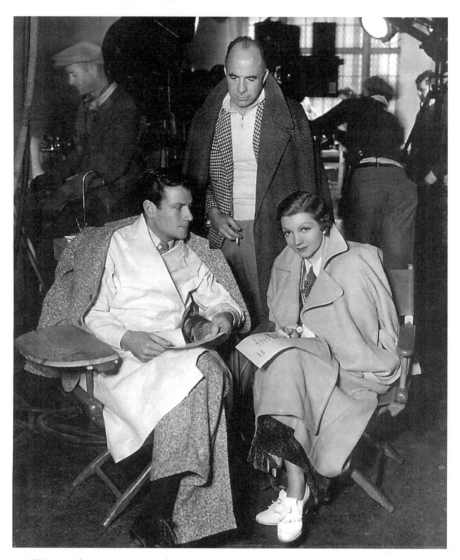

*"We sense that it is a La Cava film." Gregory La Cava, on the set of* Private Worlds *with Joel McCrea and Claudette Colbert.*

diagonally, etc.) or column-wise (i.e., first the whole first column from top down, then the second column).

So let's say we're a little thrown off, a little disoriented by this presentation of the cast of the film. Just as we're already disoriented by the title of the film, not so much by what it means, although this too may become a problem for us if we wish, but by the way it's spelled. And just as we're disoriented by the images of the title sequence, their way of bringing together surfaces, in layers, one on top of the other, of turning the street scenes into surfaces.

But we have no way of resolving these problems as yet. We can only suspend them. We can only agree to ignore them provisionally, to pass over them to get to the next thing. We may simply forget all three problems altogether, but we will probably at least carry with us into the experience of the rest of the film, if nothing else, a sense that the title sequence is strange.

The first shot of the narrative resumes the theme of the title sequence, the visual motif of one surface on another, but it adds depth—the depth of the narrative, dialogue, the social world, in particular, the depth of a movement from foreground to background, enacted by the female secretary and by the camera. The shot is of a door. The secretary, on our side of the door, opens the door, revealing a large office in which a group of men are sitting around a table talking. Then the secretary walks into the office, the camera dollying with her, and she interacts, within the limits of her professional role, with her boss, Borden.

The sound is also important, because before the door opens, we hear the discussion taking place behind it. This detail alerts us already to the importance sound will have in the film, an importance we may already be on the lookout for, if we've seen *Private Worlds* (1935) and *Stage Door* (1937) and taken note of their extraordinary sound work.

In other words, we sense that it is a La Cava film. And this sense is confirmed by the camera movement that follows the secretary, giving her an importance that belies her inferior social role, reminding us of the constant critique of social distinctions in La Cava. It is confirmed also by the men's dialogue, with its explicit airing of ideological differences: labor vs. management, the mindset of the owners vs. that of the workers. Note how the references to government and taxes play into this conflict and give us the sense, as often in La Cava, that he is a right-wing anarchist who, like Leo McCarey but unlike Frank Capra, would be amiably unembarrassed to turn up at a meeting of the radical left; and who, unlike both McCarey and Capra, would be able to participate in the discussion articulately and on its own terms.

We note the harried detachment of Borden; at a certain point he can't follow the discussion anymore, it's too fast and there are too many acronyms being thrown around (how modern is this reference to the alienating function of acronyms in professional discourse!): he's the boss, the owner, but after a certain point he doesn't understand what's going on and he doesn't care. This is very sharply and economically shown by the film; at the same time, we are unsure how the film means us to respond to Borden. Certainly we can feel sympathetic to him, but we may also feel that the film is criticizing him, that it's saying, "Well, this is what business is, if it's too much for you, you'd better get out." That it's pointing out a character flaw. The film absolutely does not allow us to applaud the character, as we might in a Capra film, as a lovable eccentric who embodies "freedom," whose ignorance and craziness are liberating. (Let alone react to him in the way we might to one of the Marx Brothers in Borden's situation.) If anything he appears inadequate to a reality that is also, to be sure, criticized and certainly not held up as some kind of ideal arrangement of society, but which has the status of reality and in other words must be dealt with.

The film shows Borden inadequate to his world and his social role. This inadequacy is next revealed as a refusal to express an opinion, in the incident that follows his termination of the meeting: his secretary gives him a tie, which, his reaction suggests when he opens the box and sees it, is somewhat loud; she expresses a doubt; he assures her that it is in fact "conservative." And then we see him alone in his car, holding up the tie against his shirt. It's consonant with the way the film has been going so far that we can't judge the loudness or quietness of the tie either from visual evidence—the film is in black and white; the tie looks like it could be a very nice patterned tie—or from the other characters' reactions, since no one else sees the tie. The secretary is biased, blinded: she chose the tie. Only Borden can give us a clue as to what the tie is like, and his opinion is ambiguous.

We proceed to the world of Borden's mansion: a huge hall, a vast staircase, evidently a sizable landing on top of the staircase, then, off the downstairs hall, openings to other areas, one of which, following Borden, we penetrate, and it is also spacious. The camera gives us a medium long shot to take all this in; and its movement heightens our feeling of the set's largeness and reality. The set is excessive. We feel there is no need for the set to be this large, that Borden's wealth (and, as this is also undoubtedly one of the scene's meanings, his lostness within the world of his wealth; as he says later, he never wanted all this) could have been established adequately, for purposes of the narrative, with a more modest set.

The set inspires awe. Why does the film want this awe? What is it able to do with it? One answer is quite simple: this awe puts us in the position of Miss Grey, who, later, having been picked up out of Central Park, out of her life of a week's rent paid up and uncertainty after that, is introduced into this waxworks world that until that moment she has seen only from the outside. The awe ensures that we remain somewhat outside the world of the rich characters for the time being, so that we can share in the movement of progressive understanding and sympathy that takes place in Miss Grey, who by the middle of the film can concede magnanimously, "I guess rich people are just poor people with money."

Our outsideness causes us to identify with the estrangement of the old man, Borden, small and alone in this vast monument to his fortune, a strangeness that shows how much he has sacrificed (why? This is a question that, perhaps, we don't yet ask) to what the film insistently refers to, through the mouth of Michael (James Ellison), the Bordens' Marxist chauffeur, as "the capitalistic system."

An exchange between Borden and his butler, Higgins (Franklin Pangborn), follows. It shows us, for the second time in the film, Borden engaged, awkwardly, in conversation with an inferior. (The film can be read partly as concerned with the difficulty of having conversations.) In the interim, and in the butler's dialogue, the absence of Borden's wife, son, and daughter is strongly marked, with a pathos that we may call understated (it's Borden's birthday) in the sense that the film states, simply and repetitively, a situation that is undeniably sad, and through the simplicity and repetitiveness of the statement allows us not to become the oppressed victims of maudlinity, since it is clear that Borden is also able to overcome it. The dialogue with the butler is La Cavian: we don't quite identify with either character, although we understand their attitudes and enter into a certain empathy with each. Each character's attitude tacitly criticizes the attitude of the other: the millionaire wants the butler to be human, to be his equal, and this humanizing, liberal desire criticizes the stuffy reticence of the butler; on the other hand, the butler wants to maintain the social division because of the psychological advantages it provides (as he puts it, "We servants enjoy the luxuries of the rich and have none of the responsibilities") and doubtless also because of a certain austere realism (you are my employer, I am dependent on you, therefore our equality is an illusion, which I refuse to indulge), and this attitude criticizes the sentimentality of the millionaire. (Later in the film, in the scene of the morning after Borden and Miss Grey's wild night at the Flamingo Club, the film will assert that Borden and Higgins are, in fact, brothers, with their complementary black eyes: Borden's right eye, Higgins' left.)

The next scene is pivotal: the meeting of Borden and Miss Grey in the park. The film sets up right away, and continues to dwell on, the park's status as a separate place, a place in which something about everyday life is suspended. The possibility of paying attention to something for a prolonged period is the first sign of this suspension: Borden has come to look at one of the maple trees Higgins so admires, and pauses to stare at it. Soon other people, seeing him, stare up at the tree too, without knowing what they are staring at. Borden walks on into the park. At the end of the sequence, we return to this site as Borden and Miss Grey leave the park: a small crowd has gathered under the tree, placidly and curiously staring upward, reduced to helpless idiocy.

When Borden looked at the tree, he had an object; he was looking at something. What he saw, no one else can see. The others merely look, in an aimless, imitative looking that is like a mass trance. This looking is a metaphor for watching a movie: an engagement that is engaged with nothing, that submits to being engaged with nothing, the passive activity of a benumbed, becalmed group, a following after a look that is no longer there and whose object is no longer there, a searching among traces, among tangled patterns of light and shadow. The first person to look—Borden—is, precisely, a "director," someone who directs the gaze of those who come after.

It's also significant that everyone looks up. In a Buñuel version of the same situation, perhaps everyone would be looking down. For La Cava, what is to be seen is up there, above us. The verticality of La Cava's cinema is again stressed: compare the slope of the hill where the forgotten men live in *My Man Godfrey*, descended upon by the scavenging rich, and the significant staircases in *Private Worlds*, *Stage Door*, and several other La Cava films. But what is to be seen, importantly, doesn't exist for those who try to see; it only existed before, for someone who already left. This is the role of the cinema, for La Cava: to divert, distract, delude, seduce, to spread a pall of nonexistence. And he uses this film to analyze and criticize this role.

It's important, however, that the cinema is innocent. The first person who looked had no intention of causing others to imitate him; he was just looking. The others want to be seduced and diverted. They have nothing to do with their lives; that's why they're in the park: to see things. To see what? To see "life," "the world," "nature"—these entities that are outside them, that they are not part of, that are other than they.

The next person Borden encounters in the park is a man looking at a seal. Borden interposes himself between this man and Miss Grey and joins them in looking at the seal. The man's discourse makes clear he is an expert on seals. Miss Grey's desultory remarks criticize this expertise and its uselessness. She gives voice, for the first time in the film, to a protest against distraction and irrelevance. But the film also criticizes Miss Grey: she herself has no aim, no program, nothing to put in the place of the discourse on the seal, which she can only try to undermine with her blasé wisecracks.

Who is Miss Grey? We don't know who she is; she could be anyone; the only positive thing about her is that she is Ginger Rogers. We know, therefore, that the film is going to be concerned with her. Miss Grey is introduced in the film as someone otherwise (other than in being Ginger Rogers) completely negative, negativity itself. She criticizes the seal expert, she criticizes the "Fifth Avenue cadavers" she knows, at this point, only from the outside. At the end of the sequence, we still don't know her name. And several more scenes will go by before the film inconspicuously pronounces her Christian name, Mary. Her namelessness makes us see her as a cipher, standing in place of something (initially, perhaps, the ranks of the unemployed—the female equivalent of the "forgotten men" of *Godfrey*), an algebraic sign that could stand for anything, someone who is not yet anything in particular, who has yet to make the choice that will determine her as something. Perhaps her surname is a sign of this indecision, this indifference: she's neither black nor white.

She and Borden form, provisionally, for purposes of celebrating his birthday, a couple (the park, as the film more forcefully reminds us in the later scene when she returns there accompanied by Borden's son, is a place of couples): the bond between them, the symbol of their couplehood, is the very item that divides them socially—money (he gives a wad of it for her to hold, to prove that it, and he, are real). They go to the Flamingo Club, where she soon starts criticizing the people at the next table (where a man is holding forth pompously on government interference in business and business interference in government). The Flamingo Club is the setting for a simulacrum of harmony: the headwaiter, who at first keeps them waiting, suddenly finds a table for them after Miss Grey tips him ten bucks; the other patrons are all tolerantly willing to sing "Happy Birthday" to the old man who has bought every table a bottle of champagne. The world La Cava shows us here is a machine that functions beautifully if only enough money is put into it.

The film dissolves from the patrons singing in the club to a grandfather clock in the second-floor landing of Borden's house; it, too, appears to be singing, in a sickly metallic voice. It is the morning after. This shot dissolves to one in front of a door that opens: Borden emerges through it, his right eye black. The ensuing scene, in which Borden encounters first his wife, Martha (Verree Teasdale), emerging from her own door on the same level, and then Miss Grey, unexpectedly descending an upper staircase from the guest room, is the first of several key scenes in the film that take place on the staircase and on the second-floor landing. The staircase is, always, a central dramatic fixture in the world of La Cava: it has a social meaning, emphasizing his constant critique of the vertical structure of society; it also has a purely dramatic meaning: it's where things happen, where he likes to stage things, because movement up and down is emotion, conflict, contrast—it's interesting.

In *5th Ave Girl* the staircase is a site of surprise, questioning, and surrender. The narrative ellipsis has created mystery: neither we, nor, apparently, Borden and Miss Grey, know what happened last night: how Borden got his black eye, how Miss Grey came to spend the night, and whether the two of them had sex. The ellipsis is justified subjectively by the effect of alcohol, and it is, so to speak, prolonged visually by the mise-en-scène of the architecture, in particular La Cava's elegant crane shot downstairs in front of Borden and Miss Grey, framing them in two-shot as they descend, still not knowing what has happened to them but struggling to waken to a reality that awaits them at ground level. (The building of an alcoholic blackout into the narrative structure is a device that La Cava will use again, even more disorientingly, in 1941's *Unfinished Business*.)

Over breakfast with Mary, Borden tries to vindicate himself: "Now I know you don't like the rich. But I'm not a capitalist, I'm a victim of the capitalistic system." But La Cava makes sure that our pity for him is tempered by Michael's diatribe, later in the sequence, when Borden's daughter, Katherine (Kathryn Adams), visits the kitchen to request two bottles of champagne as "medicine" for a friend who has swallowed some goldfish: "Do

*"Who is Miss Grey?" Borden (Walter Connolly) and Miss Grey (Ginger Rogers)*
*in* 5th Ave Girl.

you realize there are 40 million people in these United States—this land of opportunity—whose annual income is less than 12 cases of that? Seventy-eight percent of the population have less than 25 cases. And 67 percent of the 78 percent cannot afford medicine
without depriving themselves of the necessities of life!" To be sure, Michael is undercut,
both by the unconscious humor in the champagne-case metaphor and, especially, by his
histrionic attitude (which, throughout the film, suggests that he takes himself too seriously and prepares us for his final switch from proletarian to capitalist). But Borden is undercut, too: as in the first sequence, at the office, our willingness to see him the way he sees
himself is mitigated by the awareness of the benefits he derives from his wealth.

Our first impressions of the members of Borden's family are all negative. The mounting impression of negativity—during the sequence that introduces us to them—acts on
Miss Grey at the same time, and rate, as on us, prompting her decision to accept
Borden's offer of a job. It's important, by the way, that money is not presented as a primary motive for this decision (although neither is it discounted). It thus appears to us as
highly ambiguous, indeed, La Cavian. Perhaps the decision is purely ethical—she will
teach the family a lesson for ignoring the good Borden—and motivated by a desire for
social justice: Borden may be rich but "rich people are just poor people with money,"

she eventually decides, and in standing up for Borden she is taking a stand for all the ignored poor. Or perhaps her decision is purely, as we might say, aesthetic: a dramatic experiment, a disinterested seeing-what-will-happen to certain human subjects, among them herself, in a certain situation.

We perceive Miss Grey primarily as an outsider, an observer, and so does she. Her first intuition tells her to leave: "My advice to me" (Borden has just asked her for advice) "is to get out of here while I'm still in one piece." She doesn't belong, and her not belonging causes her melancholy and puts her in danger of being torn apart. Miss Grey's detachment and suspendedness imply an availability for experience that also bars her from experience. It's important that we know nothing about her previous life, or about any contacts or activities she has away from the Bordens. She's like Celestine in Renoir's *Diary of a Chambermaid*; and just as Renoir sees Celestine as a symbol of the ideals of the French revolution, La Cava sees Miss Grey as a symbol of American adaptability. In Higgins' account of the pair's return home from the Flamingo Club, Borden refers to her as "Miss America"—a reference echoed by Katherine's saying later that her mother looks like the Statue of Liberty.

Ginger Rogers' performance is a remarkable balancing act: she seems constantly to be both holding herself back and to have nothing to hold back. It's worth remembering that Rogers' claim to be considered a major screen personality rests largely on her performances for La Cava—in *Stage Door*, *5th Ave Girl*, and 1940's *Primrose Path*—and in a few roughly contemporary La Cava-esque films to which she brings much of the same spirit, if not the same maturity: Garson Kanin's *Bachelor Mother*, Leo McCarey's *Once Upon a Honeymoon*. In her films with Fred Astaire, she is a beautiful, charming, irreproachable ideal rather than an expressive individual—and the films, however beautiful and charming they are, are limited to about the same extent as Rogers' ability, in them, to manifest a complete, complex character. Howard Hawks' *Monkey Business*—probably, along with *Stage Door*, the most significant film in which Rogers appeared—is marred slightly by Rogers' coldness and straining for effect.

In her scenes with Martha and with Timothy, Jr., called Tim (Tim Holt), Miss Grey is deadpan, low-key, neutral, indifferent. By refusing to betray emotion—exceptionally for a star performance in a classic Hollywood film—Rogers makes of the character a blank on which the other characters can read whatever they are predisposed, by appearances, to read. Yet occasionally she also participates in this construction of her persona, encouraging them to think her a gold digger. "I've got my claws in plush and I like the feel of it," she tells Tim. When Martha generously credits her with being in love with her husband and not merely interested in his money, Miss Grey replies so as to make herself appear cynically mercenary: "But he has quite a lot of it, hasn't he? There should be enough for both of us. After all, you deserve something for living with him all these years."

We're insistently led to ask: is Miss Grey playing a role, and what role is she playing? And for whose purposes, her own or Borden's? "Just what is your racket?" Tim asks her as they walk downstairs in a later scene. "I haven't made up my mind yet." And, even more pointedly, Michael later tries to discuss her existence in terms of a relation to "class" and "position," fixed categories whose applicability she rejects: "Aren't you stepping out of your class?" he asks. She replies: "Me? I haven't any class." "Just what is your position in this household?" "Don't ask me."

The narrative makes it impossible to answer these questions—makes them into questions to begin with—by not specifying the nature of the job Miss Grey accepts at the

Borden house. Because of this crucial indeterminacy, we are free to see her as having neither racket, class, nor position, free to read the film as about her search for them and for an answer to the question of what they mean to her, and about, more generally, racket, class, and position in America and what they mean for the individual. The indeterminacy has a sexual significance; it's positioned in the film in sexual terms, and it encourages us, and the other characters, to read the relationship between Borden and Miss Grey as sexual. Perhaps more importantly, however, we are led to question the importance of this question of whether a physical sexual intimacy occurs, to ask whether it isn't more important for the two of them to have each other's companionship. It's remarkable that this kind of questioning can take place at all within the context of the Production Code, reminding us once again of the sophistication that not infrequently characterized Hollywood film's discussion with its audience about sexual matters during the late '30s and '40s.

Partly because of our uncertainty about Miss Grey, we become drawn more closely to the other members of the Borden family. As repellent as they all are when we first see them, we want to like them, and we come to like them. In every La Cava film, the people improve over the course of the film, become more ethical. This goes not only for the shallow, selfish people in *My Man Godfrey* and *5th Ave Girl*, but for seemingly beyond-redemption figures like the car-obsessed playboy and the grotesque, mercenary father in *The Age of Consent* (1932). The people in La Cava films never merely fit into predetermined patterns; they have the chance to be unprogrammed and spontaneous, to change. An important sign of La Cava's attitude toward the people in *5th Ave Girl*, and of how he wants us to react toward them, is the scene in which Borden's family meets with Terwilliger (Theodore von Eltz), the company's lawyer, and Kessler (Louis Calhern), a psychiatrist, to discuss Borden's behavior. These slick, dark-suited professional men at first seem cousins of the people who try to put Deeds away in *Mr. Deeds Goes to Town*, and Borden's behavior is Deeds-like: he and Miss Grey have acquired a colony of pigeons which they maintain on the roof. But over the course of the scene, it becomes clear that these men, who represent society and the world of professions, are on Borden's side; Kessler thinks that flying pigeons "looks like fun" and joins Borden and Miss Grey.

To Kessler, Martha is the neurotic, not Borden. When he recommends that she get "professional counseling," he implies a diagnosis that will resonate throughout the rest of the film. When Katherine jokingly calls her "old enough to be my mother," Martha nearly faints and must be helped upstairs. "Mother's in a pretty nervous condition," Tim warns his father. Later, Miss Grey, adducing reasons to call off the masquerade, assures Borden that Martha is "cured," and at the end, Borden refers to her as having been "on the verge on a nervous breakdown." Of all the characters, Martha is the one for whom the stakes in the film are put in the most serious terms: at one point, Katherine remarks, "We're sort of welcoming Mother back from the grave," echoing Miss Grey's jibe (in the park) against "Fifth Avenue cadavers." Her eventual cure takes two decisive forms: first, her temporary usurpation of the role of cook, when she cooks beef stew for her husband; second, her acceptance of motherhood and aging, in the scene in which the two look at the family album.

Tim matures over the course of the film from shallow polo-playing snob to responsible executive. Was this the film that made Orson Welles decide to cast Tim Holt in *The Magnificent Ambersons*? As Tim, Holt has much the same unselfconsciousness at projecting selfconsciousness, the same juxtaposition of youthful stiffness, pamperedness, and peremptory disdain that he would give George Amberson Minafer. The two characters parallel each other to some extent: both were born rich, have strong mothers and weak fathers, and are forced by necessity to take jobs. Tim's rebuke to his father and Miss Grey—"Are you two fastened together with wires or something?"—has the same overtones of amazement and petulance that would come through in George's stunned complaints about everyone else's willingness to countenance his mother's remarriage.

Strangely, the characters in the film who (apart from Borden and Miss Grey) start out seeming the most likable eventually become the least likable: Katherine and Michael. This undoubtedly has to do with the special relationship these two characters have to sincerity. All the other characters in the film know they are play-acting when they are play-acting, but only Katherine and Michael believe that they always really are what they pretend to be. Thus, they become obnoxious and even dangerous. In the crucial scene in which Miss Grey goes to the kitchen to try to argue Michael into realizing that he loves Katherine, Miss Grey's criticism of him—"You try to drag everybody down to where you are"—has a bitterness that she reserves only for him, among the members of the household, and Katherine's repudiation of Miss Grey is so vicious ("Why you little blonde hussy, I'll tear every hair out") that it deserves the unexpected rejoinder it gets, Miss Grey's grabbing a huge knife and chasing her around a table.

Miss Grey's presence continues to pose a problem in the film, which the film articulates sharply in terms of faking and sincerity. Out riding with Borden, Miss Grey says: "I'm not a very good faker. When I do things I want to mean them. Don't you think I'd better be getting on my way?" However, as Borden notes, "Whatever you're doing, it seems to work." The point is that Miss Grey really is a good faker, since her act, or perhaps her mere presence, produces strong effects on the intended audience of Martha, Tim, and Katherine. "I understand perfectly about you and my father," Katherine tells her; then, later, conceives the bizarre idea that "You only go out with him every night so you can be near Michael." Tim says to his father: "Mother doesn't know what this is all about and neither do I. Are you going to marry the girl or—?" Martha announces that she is "stepping aside" in favor of Miss Grey.

Miss Grey's not being a good faker has to do with the consequences of her performance for her own psyche. She has no place to go where she can be herself, or even merely "by herself"; when she tries to take a walk in the park alone, Tim follows her; when she goes to her room, someone is always waiting for her. Only at stray, odd moments do we see her by herself—and these moments, which all occur in the last third of the film, accentuating the brooding calm, the combination of serenity and anticipation, that gather as the film nears its end, are key to the film, they give us clues to the concealed nature of this person we are so interested in.

In three successive sequences, it becomes clear that the perpetual need to wear a mask is taking a toll on Miss Grey. First, after Borden sends her away for the evening so that he can talk with his wife, Miss Grey feels the urge to return to the park, perhaps in search of her essential solitude. Just before her excursion, she finds herself in front of the house with Tim as if she had been sleepwalking and says, "I feel a little peculiar all of a sudden." Significantly, her search for solitude is not only frustrated by Tim, who insists on going with her to the park, but criticized by the bewildering profusion of couples there. La Cava emphasizes the otherness of these couples. Sailor-suited Jack Carson, serenading a girlfriend on a ukelele, is positioned in the scene as someone we can comfortably reject—why? Because he has a sailor suit and a ukelele—but at the same time, we feel that he is in the right and Tim in the wrong in the argument that develops when

Tim asks him to be quiet. The next couple to come along is Asian. Their presence allows La Cava to underline the discomfort of Tim and Miss Grey in a subtle way: since the couple speaks Chinese in an English-language film set in New York, they are the marked term in the duality English-speaking/non-English-speaking; but since they are affectionate and familiar with each other in a site that has been strongly portrayed as a site for heterosexual couples, they are the unmarked term and the two principal characters are the marked term in the duality romantic couple/non-romantic couple. La Cava tracks in from a wide shot of the four, as the Chinese man puts his arm around the woman, to a close shot of Tim and Miss Grey: he turns and kisses her. She jumps up and goes; he follows.

The next sequence in which Miss Grey appears to unravel takes place in her room, where, rushing to escape from everyone else after returning from the park, she finds the maddened, sobbing Katherine lying in wait for her. Katherine accuses her of deliberately trying to alienate her from Michael and complains: "He doesn't love me. Someday it'll happen to you, and then you'll know." As if to herself, Miss Grey murmurs, "So that's what it does to you." The two women sit on the edge of the bed in two-shot, both facing forward. Miss Grey is in the right side of the frame staring past—to screen left of—the camera. Previously in the film, La Cava has framed her like this in two-shots and had her gaze in the same direction: first in her first scene, as Borden stands beside her at the fence before the seal pond, and then as they sit on the bench. More appositely to our present purposes, she is also so framed in the scene in which she and Borden drive through the park. She asks Borden, "You're still in love with your wife, aren't you?" and then stares into the space beyond the camera while listening to his answer: "Well, no, but, you see, after a certain time when love goes away, something else is left in its place which is even more important."

As she listens to this explanation, her look is peculiar. She seems almost afraid, as if she were unwilling to face the possibility of an end to romantic love. And we're reminded that we know so little about her that we don't even know whether she has ever been in love. So the space into which she looks is a space of complete indeterminacy: it could be a past, against which she tests Borden's wisdom, or it could be the might-have-been future of some past that now has no future, or it could be a merely undetermined future into which she projects the possibility, for her, of love going away and something else being left. And when, in the scene with Katherine, she says "So that's what it does to you," while gazing past us into that same space, we hear the line as meaning, at least, that she hasn't known unrequited love. Perhaps it should be understood as meaning that she has no experience of love of any kind. But the film doesn't tell us how to read this statement: it fixes no particular vision, or even a temporal direction, to Miss Grey's look.

After Katherine leaves, Miss Grey remains on the bed, seemingly shocked by Katherine's outburst, wondering at it, and resenting it. Then she looks down, emotionally exhausted, brings her right hand up along her left arm to her face, and buries her face in her hand with a whimper, shaking her head.

The third sequence of Miss Grey's unraveling allows her, once again in the film, to play a role. She enters the kitchen to rebuke Michael for hurting Katherine. Then, aware that Katherine is eavesdropping, Miss Grey slaps him and insults him. When Katherine rushes to his defense, Miss Grey grabs a knife and chases her around the table, only to stop suddenly and exclaim: "What's come over me? What's happened to me? What am I doing?" With a histrionic hand to her forehead, she exits left. In the very next shot, her self-possession and mildness in talking to Higgins in the hall shows that her rage in the kitchen was an act. But the extremity of the role she chooses—that of a madwoman—suggests that it's an outlet for a Hamlet-like inner perturbation.

What Miss Grey's apparent unraveling signifies, and what has caused it, are not entirely clear from the film, just as the film hasn't made very much clear at all about her, her position, her motives and intentions. Perhaps it's impossible to interpret these matters except in light of the end of the film. Every La Cava film is concerned with the constitution of the couple—an event delayed, avoided, turned away for so long (as in *My Man Godfrey*) that the director almost manages to make us not feel it as not inevitable when it finally occurs in the last moment of the film. LaCava was the master of the art of making the inevitable feel accidental. At the end of *5th Ave Girl*, three couples are constituted: Borden and Martha, Michael and Katherine, and Tim and Miss Grey. The coupling of Michael and Katherine poses no particular problem and occasions no special joy: it's merely expected, inevitable. The other two couplings are weightier and more problematic, and whether the film "works" or not for us (for me it does, precisely as a problem film) depends on how we feel about them.

The remarriage of Borden and Martha is the logical conclusion toward which the film is moving. (The term "remarriage" comes from Stanley Cavell's study of '30s comedy, *Pursuits of Happiness*, to which my reading of *5th Ave Girl* is indebted. Although he doesn't discuss *5th Ave Girl*, La Cava's film clearly belongs to Cavell's genre of the comedy of remarriage.) It has three stages. The first is their forgiving each other—an act that must take place before anything else can happen between them, and which can be seen as having all the more symbolic significance in that the film leaves it a little unclear what they are forgiving each other for. *5th Ave Girl* is "obviously" a film "about" adultery, but as we watch the film it becomes clear that whether either Martha or Borden have actually committed adultery is both a central ambiguity of the film and an irrelevance. It's made irrelevant by their forgiveness.

The second stage is the touching scene in which the two of them, at Martha's initiative, pore over the family album. As I noted above, this scene marks Martha's acceptance of her motherhood and of aging. In a film so filled with dialogue, the brief silences of Martha and Borden as they look at the album have considerable force: perhaps their silence indicates the "something else" that Borden said is left in place of love when love goes away, something inexpressible in words (thus, love can be talked about, perhaps can *only* be talked about—the person in the film who talks the most about it, Katherine, is the one we feel has the least capacity for it).

The third stage in their remarriage is the renewal of their sexual relationship, elegantly conveyed by La Cava in a single shot on the second-floor landing: Borden, abashed by the exposure of his plot, is about to slink into his room when his wife's voice off, calling his name, stops him: he turns and walks toward the place of the voice, the camera tracking alongside him to reveal the open door to Martha's room, her shadow, projected from inside, disappearing from the face of the door; Borden stands for a moment looking into the room before his face breaks into a smile and he goes in, shutting the door behind him.

The reuniting of Borden and Martha is a happy ending, but we are made painfully aware that something is sacrificed to clear the way for it. This cost is made evident in Borden's mock repudiation of Miss Grey: "You're a wicked, conniving woman. You're a gold digger, a vampire, a siren. You've hypnotized me. You've disrupted my household." Even though Borden's exaggerated wink shows us that his tirade is for his family's bene-

*"The film has completely failed, or indeed not even attempted, to make us believe that Tim and Miss Grey are in love." Tim Holt and Ginger Rogers,* 5th Ave Girl.

fit, part of the act (and we saw it rehearsed in Borden's study, when he called her ironically and affectionately, "you homewrecker, you siren, you vampire") the emphasis on Miss Grey's desolate reaction (the last part of the speech is played over a medium close-up of her) proves that, for her, the stakes of the game have become too great. "I can't play any longer," she replies, bitterly and near tears. "I wasn't doing anything to anybody. I was just sitting on a park bench, minding my own business. I didn't ask you for this job, you forced it on me. I'm sorry I ever saw you. I'm sorry I've ever been in this place. I can't take it any longer." She runs upstairs, leaving Martha and Tim—who didn't miss the telltale "job"—converging menacingly on Borden.

In the final scene of the film, the loss of Miss Grey is brutally recuperated, when Tim intercepts her as she is leaving the house, hoists her over his shoulder, and carries her back inside. Although she holds on to her dignity by protesting angrily, her consent to this procedure is marked by her retort to a passing cop who wants to know what's going on here: "Why don't you mind your own business?" It's easy to feel dissatisfied with this ending. The film has completely failed, or indeed not even attempted, to make us believe that Tim and Miss Grey are in love, and has only lightly indicated that she even finds him attractive. In relative star power, Tim Holt is utterly unsuited for Ginger Rogers. Yet that the ending is not completely unsatisfying (for me at least) suggests that the closure the film reaches here is more than merely formal, that there is a sense in which it answers the deeper questions raised by the film.

It's entirely possible to read the film as saying that Miss Grey has really been in love with Borden (as both Martha and Katherine were willing to believe), perhaps without realizing it. In this reading, their moments together—flying pigeons on the roof, driving through the park with his head on her shoulder, she tying his tie in the study—are understated epiphanies, stages of a love story, in which their contentment, affection, and mutual understanding compensate for an apparent lack of physical passion and in which, nevertheless, their casual physical intimacy suggests that physical passion might previously have occurred or might yet be possible. Her momentary confusion on the front porch ("I feel a little peculiar all of a sudden") could manifest an (unacknowledged?) sadness at being sent away by Borden so that he can spend the evening alone with Martha, after which she begins to unravel under the pressure of emotion. Finally, her emotional dropping of the mask ("I can't play any longer") could be read as an acknowledgment of the truth of Borden's accusation that she has come between him and his family (an ironical truth, since her "job" was to do just that, for the ultimate benefit of him and the family)—that is, an acknowledgment of the truth that she (unconsciously?) wanted to separate Borden from his family and have him to herself.

In forming a couple with Timothy, Jr., Mary Grey couples with the reborn Timothy Borden. Tim's assumption of his father's place at the head of Amalgamated Pump has been presented as his becoming what his father once was—a self-confident young man with courage and innovative ideas. So the film's conclusion could be seen as positing an ideal couple in two different forms (which could also be two different life-stages of the same couple): Martha and Borden, and Miss Grey and Tim. And in leading to this point, the film seems to have tested a third form—Miss Grey and Borden—and found it inadequate. The inadequacy is not strictly, or primarily, a matter of the difference in age between them (which Miss Grey, Katherine, and Martha all explicitly discount as a disqualification in a case of true love). What the film seems to be saying, through Miss Grey's climactic protest at the foot of the stairs, is that Borden and Miss Grey can be a couple only in "play," and that since the full seriousness of emotion requires that love be played at sincerely, they must drop their pretense.

In abandoning the mask, Miss Grey returns to the position of freedom in which we found her at the beginning of the film, but it's no longer an abstract freedom: her love has given it a definite content. Thus the film has progressed from the abstract to the concrete, from our not knowing anything about Miss Grey to our knowing quite a lot about her capacity for love and her attitude toward life. This progression is just as essential to the film as its positing of the ideal couple (and of the couple as necessary to complete, to crown individuation). But in the film's way of securing its closure—the displacement of Miss Grey's love interest from father to son—the mystery of *5th Ave Girl* lingers. It's fitting, then, that the last moment of the film ("Why don't you mind your own business?") draws the curtain of privacy over the entire affair.

# Slap-Happiness: The Erotic Contract of *His Girl Friday*

Marty Roth (1989)

Howard Hawks' 1940 film is a crisp and rollicking sequence of movement and speech; it is all great fun, and it ends in a conventional register of success. If some of us feel that the reconciliation of Hildy Johnson (Rosalind Russell) and Walter Burns (Cary Grant) is unseemly, the film is not aware of this and treats the ending as just the right thing. Only, while all this fun was going on, a prostitute named Mollie Molloy (Helen Mack) threw herself out of a second-story window. She didn't die, but there is no report on her condition; no attempt is made to recuperate her into the happy ending. If this were a detective story, a smart move would be to assume that the purpose of the crisp speech and movement was to create a cover for the bumping off (or bumping up and down) of Mollie Molloy.

The film dances over broken bones. At its mid-point, it dramatizes a need to get rid of Mollie in the sense of both crushing her and forgetting about her. This sequence takes place just before Walter first enters the press-room, and he waves aside Hildy's hushed report—possibly the only real news in the film, as Mollie had declared just before she jumped: "I'll give you a story, I'll give you a wonderful story, only this time it'll be true."

The crippling of Mollie Molloy spells out a garbled message, and, since the audience has traditionally been instructed in how to read this film by Walter/Cary Grant/Howard Hawks, it is ignored. Certainly the film is constructed to make us understand, in a general way, that in marrying Bruce Baldwin (Ralph Bellamy), Hildy would be throwing her life away, but just as certainly the freight of Mollie's image is not supposed to be attached to that understanding. Mollie is a version of Hildy, but a version that belongs to another story that is thrown out of the window and forgotten. Mollie is also a career woman who yearns to be private and domestic. Unlike Hildy, Mollie is the image of the devoted woman who will sacrifice all for love and the promise of private happiness. This other story had already been told five years earlier in a pretty and false way, in another film directed by Hawks, *Barbary Coast*.[1] There, the opposition between professionalism and domesticity is resolved in the other direction and in another register—that of sentiment rather than cynicism. To the credit of *His Girl Friday*, it is the other story—the woman throwing up her work to fulfill herself in love—that is most often told; for example, in *She Married Her Boss* (directed by Gregory La Cava, 1935), *Lady in the Dark* (directed by Mitchell Leisen, 1944), or *Hired Wife* (directed by William A. Seiter), another film made in 1940 with Rosalind Russell.

Against its own interests, the film is suggesting that Hildy's circuit back to Walter, however much it may be celebrated, is also crippling and suicidal. Hildy, like Mollie, jumps out of a window to get away from a newspaperman: holding his hand to his heart, Walter tells her "There's been a lamp burning in the window for you honey, here," and Hildy snaps back, "Oh, I jumped out of that window a long time ago." The last image in the film is of a crushed and battered Hildy: she is loaded down like a beast of burden and off-balance as she hurries to keep up with Walter, and at the same time, transfer a suitcase from her chest to her hand, as Walter had ordered.

This article follows two previous readings of *His Girl Friday*.[2] They need to be written over for one obvious reason: they are both written within the ideology out of which the film was produced and they are put in place to protect that ideology. Because the film performs and celebrates the pairing (and hence, by inference, the love) of Walter and Hildy, they justify this connection, primarily by valorizing Walter, by making him sufficient to a legitimate mastery and by reducing Hildy to an insufficiency. I want to protest this intuitively. The great trap or hoax of the film is the attraction of Cary Grant/Walter Burns marked by the knowledge that he is despicable—the problem of the darling. Hildy states the problem: Walter is "wonderful in a loathsome sort of way," but the obverse points it more clearly—he is loathsome in a wonderful sort of way. No one should want to be in his company, much less connected to him, for any period of time. It is as if the film accepted a perverse challenge, blindly to celebrate a damaging relationship as a happy union; and Hildy has already packed this understanding into a pun: "he should make some girl real happy—slap happy."

*The problem of the darling. Rosalind Russell and Cary Grant, "wonderful in a loathsome sort of way."*

The film begins presenting the relationship between Hildy and Walter as a painful one: Hildy has divorced Walter and wants to stay free of him. At the end, the film proposes a resumption of their relationship. It does so quite thoughtlessly and callously. There is no suggestion that anything has changed during the period of their separation, and, as a result, it must assert that what is different now, and terminal, is Hildy's need for victimization. Narrative assurance masks the utter rupture of the ending. It is so brazen, so out in the open: it just happens. (The condition of Hollywood endings is staged in a Grant film of 1939, *In Name Only*, directed by John Cromwell. Believing that his love for the character played by Carole Lombard is hopelessly blocked by his wife, he has lost the will to recover from pneumonia. The doctor tells Lombard the prescription for fixing patients and films, and his assured tone of voice leaves us in no doubt that it will not fail: "Tell him whatever you think he wants to hear. You must tell him that there is hope, in fact, tell him that there is certainty. If you think he wants you to say that you love him, then say that you love him, if you think he wants to hear that an obstacle in that love has been removed, then tell him so.") And, as if to mark the absurdity of it, we are forced to witness the transformation of a sparkling, active character into a "woman" or "infant"— a crying, whimpering, pleading Hildy Johnson. As part of its gaiety, the film even calls off the honeymoon for the second time—one of Hildy's specific complaints when she was trying to make Walter see that the marriage was impossible.

The major question raised by *His Girl Friday*, then, is why Hildy chooses to return to Walter for the last time. Going away and coming back are connected and involved, not simple and separate. The film opens by going out of the city room in order to come back in. Hildy, who has been away, comes back to Walter to tell him that she is going away. There is no clear answer to this major question, simply the neurotic complications of narrative and an historical set of anxieties about sexual difference. I propose, first, a close reading of the gender logic of the film[3] as this is suspended by the overriding value of the *darling*—the narcissistic and exhibitionistic male performer. The affective bond that cannot be asserted at the level of gender can be written self-reflexively: Hildy stays connected to Walter for the same reason we do—a reason that is figured by hypnosis (a figure that has severe implications for criticism) and countered by the more theatrical trope of the *double cross*.

However obvious the outside reason for Hildy's return, it must always be stated: the story is the one we expect from Hollywood cinema and the one we always read. Cary Grant is the leading man, Ralph Bellamy is only a supporting actor. The audience has been taught to demand this resolution. The film was set up to work this way. Hildy's return to Walter is a frame-up, a double-cross, the crime that the apparatus was designed to perform. The power that watches over *The Morning Post* is the power that wills Hildy and Walter back together, the power of dominant narrative. Given its history, we can say that it was set in place to do what it does repeatedly, to enact the subjugation of women in the name of fulfillment and happiness.

One of the strategies used to fix Hildy's decision is to naturalize it: she is a "born" "newspaperman"; reporting is in her "blood." Rival journalist Sanders gives the marriage six months, then three months, and offers three to one against it. We see Hildy responding immediately to the ringing of a fire bell, which locates reporting at the level of a reflex (or an addiction). Hildy is, also naturally, a superb reporter, although this is fantastically represented: she is the only reporter of six who knows what and where the story is—better yet, the only reporter capable of making the story happen. Hildy confirms all

"A *born newspaperman*": Hildy Johnson and the gentlemen of the press.

of this in her parting speech to Bruce: "If you want me, Bruce, you've got to take me as I am instead of trying to change me into something else. . . . I'm a newspaper man." Along the line of theme, then, we are merely watching Hildy discover the truth about herself.

Both Stanley Cavell and Gerald Mast balance their readings of the film on these "natural" truths: Hildy belongs to the newspaper game, and Hildy and Walter belong together. The way this is expressed by the title, however, suggests that Hildy belongs to Walter. The natural for Mast is present through a resonance which he calls "exuberant teamwork" (209), which is a curious knot, since acting more naturally signifies falsity or hoaxing; for Cavell, it is the quality of the two being "at home with one another" (167). As additional evidence, Mast cites the scene where Hildy and Walter are handcuffed together, "a linking that even the corrupt mayor . . . believes makes them 'look natural'" (236); and the unused script ending for the film, a shotgun wedding, with the barrel of the gun "trained on a still recalcitrant Hildy" (241). Leaving aside the authority of a corrupt mayor, the images are hardly natural, or even neutral; they express a violent conjunction, a fascistic fantasy of nature, which has always played a large part in the dream work of Hollywood.

For both Cavell and Mast, Walter is the more natural of this natural pair: he is aware of his nature, while Hildy is not. Once again the woman is guilty of deficiency, of lack, and once again the man is simply in the position of teaching the woman her nature. In the film, Walter claims that he created Hildy, and Mast reproduces that fiction outside the film: Walter is allowing Hildy to become a "real and full 'woman'" (239), forcing her to realize and repudiate her "spiritual, moral, emotional, and psychological errors" (239). Cavell also sees Walter as educating Hildy, sending Hildy on the Williams story so that she may acquire a piece of saving knowledge; he is too "good a therapist" (165) not to know her desires for her and prescribe for them. Given all this paternal affection, it is not only understandable, but right and natural, that the film should administer a loving punishment to Hildy at the end.

When Sanders predicts the doom of the marriage, he means two incompatible things. He means that Hildy will never leave the paper for marriage because it would be unnatural for her to do so and that she will never leave because Walter won't let her. However incompatible, both will be affirmed, scripted throughout. The second meaning is both offensive and absurd: you can't restrain people in that way, on the job or as a wife; what you get, if you could do it, isn't worth the having. But this is exactly what the film shows. If we attend only to the behavior of Walter and Hildy, we could conclude that Hildy is beaten down, brainwashed, manipulated into subjection by an arrogant bully.

One way of putting Hildy's dilemma is that she must decide whether she is a man or a woman. This is a necessarily confused way of putting it, since man and woman here refer only to the gender constructions of popular culture. The gender equation at the heart of the film—the line along which we read with most delight—is that Hildy Johnson is a man.[4] She is functionally male, performing a man's job in competition with other men and doing it much better than they can. She is also a man in the history of the text, slotted into a character space which is almost always designated as male—into a specific lineage occupied before and after her by a line of Hildebrand Johnsons: Lee Tracy, Pat O'Brien and Jack Lemmon.

In *The Front Page* directed by Lewis Milestone (1931), for some unknown reason Hildy yells after Peggy, "If you want me you'll have to take me as I am, instead of trying to make a floozy out of me"—which is roughly what *His Girl Friday* does. Gender transformation is written into it and continues to haunt Hawks' projects, perhaps because it is the underlying secret of character in Hollywood comedy. Mollie Molloy calls the reporters "tramps," and since she is a prostitute, she must restore to this bisexual term its feminine component. Hildy describes Bruce to Walter and he says: "sounds like a guy I ought to marry." As if in compensation, in *I Was A Male War Bride* (1949), the sex-change (now transvestism) works the other way and is specifically fastened upon Cary Grant. Grant is also momentarily in drag in *Bringing Up Baby* (1938), in a dressing gown with puff sleeves, a scene which is repeated in *Gentlemen Prefer Blondes* (1953) and fastened upon Malone (Elliott Reid). Like Grant, he gets water spilled on his pants, but, unlike Grant, he is not in control of the ploy: he is humiliated and debagged by two suffocating females. *Bringing Up Baby* is also *His Girl Friday* writ backwards, and it is interesting that the opposition of male and female clothing corresponds to a manic-depressive opposition between Grant in *Friday*, on the one hand, and *War Bride* on the other. It is no longer a premise about character but a humiliating and victimizing disguise, a function of plot and situation: it's wonderful for a woman to be a man (under certain conditions), humiliating for a man to be a woman. In *Rio Bravo* (1959), someone as "manly" as Sheriff John T. Chance/John Wayne gets teased. Carlos/Pedro Gonzalez-Gonzalez holds the bloomers he has bought for his wife up to his waist as Feathers/Angie Dickinson passes the bedroom. She approves of the fitting, and calls after the retreating Wayne: "Hey sheriff, you forgot your pants."

Stanley Cavell has suggested that Hawks' title does not derive unilaterally from Defoe's novel but is mediated by the soap opera, *Our Gal Sunday*.[5] Let me offer another candidate: *My Man Godfrey* directed by Gregory La Cava (1936). Most of Hildy's relationships and exchanges in the film are with men, with Hildy talking to men as a man. Her presence in the press room —entrance to which is barred to women—is accepted. Hildy is just one of the boys. In passing the cigarette to Earl Williams (John Qualen), she notices and apologizes for the lipstick traces, a random and embarrassing sign of her femininity. She had refused the assignment at first, claiming it was the kind of poetic sob-sister stuff she couldn't write. In her farewell speech, her contempt for the profession rests on a deeper layer of contempt for the newspaper readers whose frustrated desires make the whole circus move, and those readers are identified as private domestic women—"A million hired girls and motormen's wives"—precisely the class to which Hildy also claims she wants to transfer her allegiance.

Hildy's presence, then, does not promise or generate sexual energy. The film is remarkably devoid of any person or exchange that we can directly feel to be sexual. The easy intimacy of voice and body that Walter has with Hildy is not erotic. The figure given to Walter is that of castration, and it is vaguely pointed at several times in the film: when Hildy, told that Walter is in a bad humor, cracks that "somebody must have stolen the crown jewels"; when Walter deliberately spills water in his lap in the restaurant; when Walter tells Bruce a story against himself which cuts at least three ways—during his marriage to Hildy, she unexpectedly brought the Governor back to the hotel, not knowing he was there, and he "came walking out of the bathroom without—mmmp." The most overtly sexually-constructed presence in the film, Diamond Louie's blonde, Evangeline, is seen twice briefly, in a stationary pose, and the only sexual plot in the film is a fraud—Bruce is arrested for "mashing." That the place of sexuality is outside the film is the message performed by reporter McCue, who locates it just outside the press room. He is nicknamed "Stairway Sam" by fellow reporter Sanders because he regularly stations himself at the door or window, following the progress of women up the stairs of the Criminal Court building by twisting his neck and body as they move up and around in a futile attempt to see up their skirts. He tells us in another way that Hildy is not a "skirt," and, in a remarkable cheesecake scene, the film reinforces this, as, facing the camera in a middle shot, she hikes her skirt up almost to her crutch so that she can run after Coaley.[6]

The light Hollywood rapture between Hildy and Bruce at the entrance to the city room proclaims that the sign of eroticism belongs to their relationship. But this quickly evaporates: Hildy's attitude to Bruce becomes one of an instructor toward a rather dim-witted child who can't get anything right. And in the scene where Hildy presumably makes her choice not to go to Albany, Bruce is given the woman's lines in the exchange. Sexuality in this film has been packed into adventure and delinquency—the absurd images of newspaper reporting at its "best" that *His Girl Friday* celebrates. Hildy phones in the first Williams story in a love-choked voice—her most erotic performance in the film. The opening opposition is presented as love and marriage to Bruce on the one hand, or success and excitement with Walter on the other—a phony semantic (a double-cross) because excitement is here the site of the erotic, and Hildy is "married" to the paper. The film fuses them with only one side showing, and leaves, on the other, some vague dream of fussy domestic contentment, the "death" we return to when the film ends. (Russell had earlier starred in the first film version of the play that most deeply inscribed domesticity as death in North American culture. In an uncanny move at the opening of *Craig's Wife* [1936], Harriet is away from home, in Albany [the site of domesticity in *Friday*] at the hospital bedside of her dying sister. Russell has two film voices, her competitive wise-cracking voice and a soft whispery one that she uses in *Friday* only in the opening scene with Bruce and the prison scene with Earl Williams. There is a series of roles that belong to the second voice, versions of the devoted domestic woman—in, for example, *China Seas* [1935] or *The Citadel* [1938]. The culminating role here would be her version of the totally understanding and nurturing woman/wife/mother in *Roughly Speaking* [1945] contrasted with *Auntie Mame* [1958], where she undermines and explodes domesticity from within.) The domestic ideal, we are told elsewhere in the film, is also a lie; Mollie angrily accuses the group of reporters: "Yuh made that up. And about my bein' his soul-mate and havin' a love-nest with him."

Though femininity is marked by contempt, we are told that the tension which the film produces comes about because Hildy desires, in some way, to become a woman. Whether woman here is the private and domestic creature that she describes tauntingly to Walter and the reporters or whether it is the sexually desired creature that the early scene with Bruce evokes is not clear. Hildy's deepest dream is to have Bruce grafted on to Walter, to have Walter recognize her as a woman, have him fuss over her, pet her, coo to her and yet be her partner in exciting adventures and hoaxes. She will never get this, because the man she has chosen to load with these desires possesses, as one of his traits, an extremely misogynistic attitude.

Walter shows extreme anger only twice, both times towards a woman: once to Butch's girl, a "ten-cent glamor girl," whom he threatens to kick in the teeth, and once to Mrs. Baldwin, "a grey-haired old weasel." On the other hand, the three men who are nice to women, Bruce, Williams and Pettibone, are all locked up in "jails." We might take seriously Mollie's cry to the reporters (who are all tin-plate replicas of Walter): "you're persecutin' me, because Earl Williams treated me so decent and not like an animal." A private and feminine Hildy is given a one-time appearance in the early interlude with Bruce in the waiting room. This is a soft, dreaming Hildy, who allows herself to be lost in the spaces of imagined love—a Hildy with depth, at least to the extent that there is dissolution of the surface. When Hildy and Walter get together at the end, her voice will not be like this, but infantile and whiney. Hildy's passage through the *Morning Post* office is marked by a repudiation of femininity. While everyone stops work to greet her, there are only two moments of extended communication: the first a warm, girlish chat with two telephone operators and the second an aborted conversation with Beatrice, the advice-to-the-lovelorn columnist. Hildy accepts the first, but repudiates the second exchange. Beatrice wants to talk domestically, intimately, but Hildy keeps walking so that Beatrice has to deliver her lines to her moving back. Hildy tosses a wisecrack back over her shoulder. Beatrice is trying to talk about giving birth, and we could probably read the end of the narrative out of that episode.

One name for the private woman that Hildy yearns to be is "mother," although the reporters picture it as a big laugh: "Can you picture Hildy singing lullabies, and hanging out diapers?" A mother, Mrs. Baldwin, figures prominently in the film. She doubles Hildy in several ways, most obviously as a woman who makes her way into the forbidden space of the press room; and she is also the accidental possessor of key secrets, of stories. But Hildy is opposed to Mrs. Baldwin; for one thing, Hildy is the reporter who always gets the stories, while "mother" is the person who always blows them, leaks them. Mrs. Baldwin is the "original source," the informant whose testimony led to the capture of Earl Williams, but as we track past the reporters at their individual phones after his capture, she is denied, dissembled, rewritten as an "anonymous note" and a "mysterious telephone call." A black child is born as the special rifle squad races across town after Williams. His mother goes into labor on the street, and they deliver the child, who is named after Sheriff Hartwell. But that birth is also criminal, and the deputies examine the child carefully to see if he is Earl Williams who, they believe, is hiding somewhere in the vicinity.

When Beatrice tells Hildy that her cat just had kittens, Hildy snaps, "it's her own fault." As the last in this series of gender identifications for Hildy, let me call her male-identified, because she is a second Walter. She is his errand boy, flunky, stooge and straight man. She imitates him (although that is often no more than saying she is a good "newspaperman," since the virtues of reporting in this film are also a profile of Walter): when Gus asks her what she will have for lunch, she says, "Oh, I'll have the same [as Walter], I guess"; and one of the verbal figures performed by Hildy in the film is literal imitation, or copy-catting. Hildy has most of Walter's traits, and, through her performance, they are reproduced in yet another register of charm. She rattles off her own set spiels; she is verbally and physically manipulative—she tackles and sits on Coaley; she is rude and dismissive; she cons Bruce and Coaley. She uses Mollie and Earl Williams ruthlessly. Mrs. Baldwin accuses her of being a double-crosser. Her featured interview of Williams (framed in a flamboyant expressionistic manner) is a hypnotic session, and it is set up in tandem with another hypnotic session, Dr. Egelhoffer's interview with Williams. Hildy's interview is set at a low auto-suggestive level and she feeds Williams the script that she will later write up as her scoop.

Hypnosis is a major trope in the film, but it is Walter who is the master hypnotist. Hildy scornfully calls him "Svengali," and Bruce tells him: "she wanted to get away from you and everything you stand for, but you were too smart, you caught her and changed her mind." Hildy's staying is patterned as a "hooking in" to lures and a subjection to hypnotism—her decision to stay is made in a trance. Hildy is continually pulling free and then falling again under some spell or other, yet she is not the passive subject of hypnosis; she is a sharp, critical presence, countering Walter, devoting herself to his exposure. But the business of the film is to demonstrate Walter's power, and the place of the critic (of Hildy, of Dr. Egelhoffer, of Cavell, of Mast) is identified as the most treacherous place to be.

Hildy's alternation between criticism and a hypnotic acquiescence is also located as a split in herself. She alternates between a determination to leave, to achieve distance, and a falling prey to the snares of Walter and "story" (often literally Walter's; always equitable with Walter). The film is all about what Hildy wants. She says she wants a home and respectability: the absence of narrative, of story; but the film goes on despite her protestations. Walter assigns no meaning to her statements of desire; he assumes that they are nonsense. Bruce also raises the question of whether that is what Hildy really wants. We are invited to wonder too and, according to the laws of narrative, to wonder is to know that that is not what she wants.

At the heart of the hoax of *His Girl Friday* is the paradox of the *darling*, the double bind of the contract to adore despicable behavior. The darling and the star are always structurally synonymous, often characteristically so—nakedly in the narrative careers of actors like Erich Von Stroheim, Mickey Rooney, or Gene Kelly. As filmgoers, we are also the victims of hypnosis, and casting Cary Grant as a spell-binder or hypnotist writes into the role the power that constitutes it in the first place. It is, however (always) a terrible charm, charm within the context of an affectless nightmare; in the case of this film, charm as an autonomous mechanism.

Walter is an extravagant image of primary narcissism. Our first sight of Walter is of him looking at himself in a mirror and wearing a bib under his chin. Walter feels himself to be omnipotent and inhabits an unlimited subjectivity that is proof against otherness; he is, as Hildy calls him, the "Lord of the Universe." One of the strongest features of Grant's performance is that he acts as if he were alone and unimpeded on the set, talking to himself, peopling that space with effigies created out of his own shifting and inconsistent ideas. Walter notices the presence of other people with mild surprise: this mannerism, like most of his others, is poised on the edge of a put-on, but, even if it is a put-on, it is still narcissistic. Walter is upset by the mobility or density of others—he is furious that the Governor is not there when he wants him. Walter registers other people with difficulty; if they manage to infiltrate the mirrored surface of his narcissism he may respond to them with annoyance—Bruce in the press room—or, in the case of Butch's girl and Mrs. Baldwin, he may shift into a frighteningly pathological key and respond to their obstructive presence with rage.

Walter's anarchic energy enters the line of the action as manipulation and appropriation, and this is centered in the hiding of Earl Williams in Bensinger's desk and Walter's subsequent hare-brained scheme to move the desk out of the courthouse and back to his own office. Walter appropriates other people's lives—he puts Bruce in jail twice, and the whole film is devoted to his manipulation and appropriation of Hildy—and their space: in the restaurant scene, Walter plays musical chairs with Bruce; he refuses to count off chairs, and, when Bruce lowers himself into his appropriate social space, he finds himself sitting on Walter's lap; Walter then literally moves him with both hands down the line to the third chair. Throughout the scene that follows, Bruce is metaphorically sitting in Walter's lap, like a ventriloquist's dummy; earlier, Walter had patted his lap and beckoned Hildy to it, but she had refused.

Walter's impromptu finesse in moving people into the wrong place and putting people in their place is the subject of a wonderful piece of office theater at the beginning of the film. Entering the reception room of the newspaper to greet Hildy's new fiancé, Walter walks by Bruce and warmly greets an old bald man instead, forcing Bruce to "knock" at his arm—placing him in the role of a crude opportunist. Walter gratuitously exchanges the identities of the two men, while they sputter, fore and aft, in an attempt to correct his mistake. When he decides that the take has gone on long enough, Walter turns the scene, inverting the areas of warmth and chill that he established, now treating the old man as a cunning impersonator. He no longer shuts Bruce out, but, instead, he turns him into an object, first, by shaking the handle of his umbrella, and, secondly, by shifting his address to Hildy (who stands by, both sardonic and admiring), so that Bruce becomes the "he" that they are talking about.

In the restaurant scene that follows, Walter controls the space and the talk. With the exception of two reaction shots of Hildy, every shot in the sequence goes through Walter. This dominance is encapsulated at the end of the scene: as Walter finishes his telephone conversation and moves to leave the booth, we see, in the background of the space he is just vacating, a small image of Hildy and Bruce at the table. In visual, emotional and theatrical terms, he is blocking and obscuring their relationship. As I mentioned earlier, both Mast and Cavell have an investment in defending Walter against charges of criminal abuse. Mast, who praises Walter for being a transcendental actor with Hildy—a performer so consummate that his acting is "natural"—also acquits Walter on the basis of bad acting: "that Walter is that unscrupulous and selfish [is] . . . never really very convincingly established" (210). Cavell also reproduces a transcendental Walter: "his transcendence of consequences makes him the embodiment of the idea of life as improvisation" (179). He asks us to see Walter's manipulation as a program of Socratic "illumination" designed to bring Hildy to the light. Cavell faces the problem of Walter and Mollie Molloy, sets up a sequence of possible readings that spin dizzingly in a full circle, until he can conclude that Walter's indifference to her suicide is the nod of one consummate performer for another: "Walter might even assume Molly [sic] knew what she was doing, even admire it as a successful piece of improvisation" (180).

Above all, Walter is a con-artist, a fabricator of ploys—a manipulator of events and people through pose and speech, through performance. He possesses an easy ability to shift shape verbally—to modulate through a variety of vocal roles and poses. This unhinged exhibitionism that may be said to belong to narcissism is the essence and the practice of the actor. What is instinctive in the infantile monster/darling/brat is social and professional in the actor. Cary Grant is a great actor, and Walter Burns is a great actor, and what Grant signifies through Burns is the actor and acting. Walter evokes the styles of Cagney and Robinson: machine-gun speech and control through energy. He takes his powerful mutter from W.C. Fields. The performer-as-performer he most resembles is Groucho Marx, who exists to appropriate space and speech, to browbeat, and to bully and abuse. Walter also functions as a director, as the director; he resembles the Hollywood director generally, and Howard Hawks in particular, in his single-minded pursuit of the story, at any cost, even that of human life.[7] So it is no surprise that there is collaboration between the film and Walter, particularly in the matter of effacing Mollie Molloy and hooking in Hildy Johnson.

One of the things that *His Girl Friday* is about is what it so stunningly performs: sharp speech patterns, overbearing interchanges, stichomachia; it is a film about the disease of speech. The centrality of the telephone in this film has been noted: telephones ringing, interrupting, lunged for, or walked around and cradled like infants. The motif appears in the opening as we travel left and then return to two telephone operators at the threshold of the city room; they are bonded to Hildy but connected to Walter. The first functional use of the telephone, however is phone-y. Walter tells Gus to come to the table and tell him that there is a phone call for him. Later in the film, Hildy's story is torn up over the phone, and, a little later, the telephone connection between Hildy and Walter is itself torn out.

The rapid-fire staccato dialogue is primarily Walter's. He is pre-eminently associated with a controlling flood of male speech that he shares with his two most immediate models, Petruchio in *Taming of the Shrew* and Shrike in *Miss Lonelyhearts*. Walter talks in order to leave no gaps through which other voices might enter. Walter never hears other people or their dialogue. In the opening scene with Hildy she can't get him to hear what she has come to say: "Are you going to listen to what I have to say," and Walter responds, "Look, look, what's the use of fighting, Hildy? I tell you what you do, you come back to work on the paper." Walter can't hear because he is constantly talking. Once he starts talking, he hypnotizes himself. He can't be stopped or deflected by other

*Walter the con-artist, fabricator of ploys. Gene Lockhart, Rosalind Russell, Cary Grant, Billy Gilbert and the Mayor, Clarence Kolb.*

people; it is not talk to an end, it will never come to a social or semantic close. He holds dialogues with himself, answers himself. The image of reporting that is so attractive and so paradoxical involves not listening to sources, but writing and attributing to them lines out of one's own brain track. When other people are talking, Walter has a habit of muttering or humming to himself, keeping alive the only voice that registers. In *Bringing Up Baby* (1938) and *Arsenic and Old Lace* (directed by Frank Capra, 1944), Grant also talks and mutters to himself throughout, but for the opposite reason—because the others in his frame are shutting *him* out, refusing to acknowledge *his* anxiety.

Grant's voice, as it is used in most of his films in the 1930s and early 1940s, is a bizarre instrument—very metallic, highly theatrical, vaudevillian in its lilts and takes. Like the voice of the stand-up comic or blues singer, it is syncopated, often anticipating or dragging behind the beat. It is a powerful voice, always overcharged, both bursting with potentially aggressive energy and repressing that energy. This is the film where the role is written for the instrumentality of his voice. The voice cannot exhaust the energy of its source, and it is regularly inflected with muttering, popping, rumbling, a very peculiar percolator effect, vocal explosions and the like.

Grant's voice is a master of public rhythms—the voice of the high-pressure salesman, of the huckster and the barker; it is the voice of hawking, and the speech unit is the spiel. At one moment of pure vocal identification, Hildy, who has been trying to get Walter to listen, has been cut off, drowned out, shouted down, and so she echoes and parodies Walter's prattle through the tobacco auctioneer's chant of merged and mangled words and sounds, keeping pace with Walter, finally bringing his speech to a halt, and capping it with "Sold American." Walter's speech is business, theatrically and economically; it is also "the business." Like the announcer, Walter comments on everything, repeating it again for an audience. Walter controls speech and keeps it diseased. Even when Walter says something as possible as "Sorry to see her go," Hildy answers, "I'd like to believe you meant that," because she knows that all of his verbal acts are gambits, situational punctuation, all lies. Hildy runs out of speech; Walter never does. Hildy defers, knowing that speech belongs to him. Not content with her acknowledgment of his power, Walter tries to tear down her writing too, dismissing her journalism in a scene that should strain credulity, considering that the movie has both announced and demonstrated that she is his star reporter.

Walter is the actor, the ham—the reincarnation of John Barrymore in *Twentieth Century* (directed by Howard Hawks, 1934), or, like Harry Greener, the broken-down vaudevillian in Nathaniel West's *Day of the Locust*, a sequence of old takes with no center. The mayor is Walter's double in this, always quoting from a campaign speech in syrupy prose, himself a master at shifting positions without a break for human response: "Probably insane, drunk or something, why, if this unfortunate man Williams has really been reprieved, I'm personally tickled to death, aren't you Pete?" Like Walter, the mayor is misogynist and antifamily: he'd "hang his grandmother" to get elected. And he is the only power figure in the film, apart from Walter. He is also the character who almost gets Walter, almost stops his charge—almost silences him.

A series of male figures is ranged in opposition to Walter. They are all versions of one another, or all versions of Bruce, the man who is to be rejected: the series consists of Bruce, Williams, Bensiger, Sheriff Hartwell and Pettibone. They are all exposed as pathetic or ridiculous, all inadequate men. Most of them are put away, put on hold, sequestered: Bruce, in jail twice; Williams, in jail, in an interview cell, in a desk; Pettibone in a safe house. (Hildy, at one point, snaps at Walter: "I see. I'll keep. I'm like something in the icebox, aren't I?", and Walter says, "Yeah.") All of them are identified as victims, specifically as the butt of hoaxes or jokes. Several of them are connected by the image of the umbrella—Bruce and Pettibone carry one and Hildy harshly fancies that the Sheriff lent Williams an umbrella for his getaway—and by a characteristic drawl or whine in their voice. Bruce, Bensiger, the sheriff and Pettibone are all associated as family men: the first travels with his mother, the second writes "mother" poems, the third has all of his relatives on the payroll, and the fourth cannot make a move without consulting his wife. Bruce and Williams are both in the numbers game, an insurance salesman and a bookkeeper (as such, he "belongs" in a desk). Bruce and Pettibone both come from small towns; more importantly, they both represent the nemesis of story, early closure.

The performance figure most centrally associated with Walter is, of course, the double-cross. He performs it casually, gleefully; it is an obsession masking itself as spontaneity. Walter double-crosses inconsistently, against his own interests: certainly his repeated attempts to renege on his promise to Hildy to exchange a life insurance premium for the story on Earl Williams should be fatal to his larger scheme, whether it be to get the Williams story or to get Hildy to stay. Walter double-crosses Bruce, Earl Williams and Bensiger. During Walter's first performance in the film, Hildy gibes, "Well Walter, I see you're still at it." Walter turns to her and says, "first time I ever double-crossed a governor, what can I do for you?" and proceeds to institute a feature-length double-cross of Hildy.

The entire film is performed under the sign of the double cross, but its history is also written under that sign. The original ancestor, Ben Hecht and Charles MacArthur's *The Front Page*, is dedicated to an intersection: to Madison and Clark Streets.[8] The dedication or preface to *His Girl Friday* is also a double cross (or cross). The visual record starts in the depths of the city room, and we track back through the heart of that busy office. We are tracking a woman whom we leave at Duffy's cubicle. The camera continues to move left (through a dissolve just before the switchboard and an invisible cut at the boundary between newspaper and public space), and stops to pick up the figures of Hildy and Bruce who have just come out of the elevator. After a short scene over the low gate that separates the public waiting room from the professional offices, Hildy retraces the movement of the woman, through the city room, to the narrative excitement that waits on the other side in Walter Burns' executive office. Although Hildy exposes the contents of the city room, since everyone raises their body or their face to greet her (to say hello and good-bye), she and her story do not belong there, she is passing through. The work of putting a newspaper together is not the story that we are tracking. The opening sequence is a documentary which theoretically would go another (perhaps the opposite) way from the narrative we have contracted for.

On the level of comic technique, the double cross is a double take (or take—also a unit of filming and a unit of performing): it is a sudden shift of physical and emotional/cognitive direction that catches us by surprise, that disrupts our investment in continuity, but seduces us by its brevity and economy. Walter performs double takes from time to time, but, from this perspective, the center of the film is the actor Billy Gilbert (as Pettibone), who takes the film to a movement as a vaudeville mode to which it doesn't belong. His performance is a series of double takes; he seems to be present in the film only to perform the double take.

Hoax, hypnotism, double-cross, double-take, the fictions pile up and they are all alternate figures for the story. The front page is a surface and a cover for stories, and this equates it with the classical narrative film.[9] The two stories are opposed, however, in that the front page story claims to be historically or socially central, of overwhelming relevance to the audience. But that is also a story. Like all newspaper movies, this story is about a story, getting a story, and that phrase covers both its production and its consumption. The legendary preface alerted us to this: "In the 'Dark Ages' of the newspaper game—when to a reporter 'getting that story' justified anything short of murder." Mollie Molloy pleads with the reporters to get her story straight, but the film demonstrates that no story is or can be got straight; there is no straight story to get. As Earl Williams is finally led away along the line of reporters, each whispers a different story into the phone to cover the pathetic arrest we have just witnessed. Pettibone stands out because he can't understand the stories that are told to him, but Walter, who as usual has the last word, jiggles with frustration in the presence of stories: everybody takes too long, no one can tell it directly enough for him.

## Notes

1. *Barbary Coast* is also, in a small way, about a newspaper editor who takes on a crooked city machine, but, there, "bursting the machine" is initially literal and is inflicted by Edward G. Robinson's bully boys on the newspaper itself.
2. Stanley Cavell, "Counterfeiting Happiness," in *Pursuits of Happiness* (Cambridge, Mass.: Harvard

University Press, 1981), 163–187; and Gerald Mast, *Howard Hawks, Storyteller* (New York: Oxford University Press, 1982), 208–242.

3. Tom Powers devotes his pioneering article "Screwball Liberation," *Jump Cut* no. 17–19, (April–December 1978) to this topic, but, as with Cavell and Mast, the equations he finds are patriarchally dictated.

4. See Gretchen Bisplinghoff, "Hildy Johnson—A Question of Gender," *Film Reader* no. 5, 227–231.

5. Cavell, 168.

6. An enigmatic character—Joseph McBride, in *Hawks on Hawks* (Berkeley: University of California Press, 1982), lists him as Coaley; Mast as Jacobi; and Cavell as Dooley.

7. According to Captain Samuel Triffy, the technical advisor on *Air Force* (1943), "Hawks and the film company 'were ruthless! Absolutely ruthless! If they could have damaged [an] airplane in flight so I would have had an accident, they would have done it. Really! I couldn't trust them. I mean it.'" Quoted in Lawrence Howard Suid, ed., *Air Force* (Madison, Wisconsin: University of Wisconsin Press, 1979), 21.

8. *The Front Page* (New York: Covici/Friede, 1928).

9. Milestone's *Front Page* and *Friday* both open upon images of the newspaper: in the latter it is a newspaper one cannot read, the film happens on top of it; in the former, one must read the newspaper, submit oneself to the turning pages as the only way to get into the story.

# The Old Dark House
## James McCaffery (2001)

It could be argued that horror, as a genre, is closer to comedy than it is to tragedy. Black magic is always lurking behind a magic show. Horror stars and directors often talk about what is scary in the same way that comedians talk about what is funny. The Grand Guignol, the nineteenth-century French theatrical ancestor to the spook shows and splatter movies that later made the reputation of American drive-ins, regularly alternated their horror shows with bedroom farces. Film pioneer Georges Méliès mixed fantasy and trickery to produce effects both delightful and grotesque. The experiments of Dr. Pretorius in James Whale's *The Bride of Frankenstein* (1935) hark back to Méliès, and the more naturalistic special effects of *The Invisible Man* (1933), also by Whale, recall the trick films of the Brighton school, Méliès' British followers. A severed head is horrific, but a severed head that talks (as in *The Brain That Wouldn't Die* [1959] and *Re-animator* [1985]) is funny.

The site on which comedy and tragedy meet is the haunted house, Elsinore with crazy mirrors, where once noble minds now o'erthrown continue their parody of the tragic struggle from beyond the grave. The "old dark house," a decaying manse in the middle of nowhere, in the dead of night, inhabited by a decaying aristocracy if by anyone at all, has always been one of the more venerable and versatile settings for comic horror films. The one undeniable masterpiece of this genre is *The Old Dark House* (1932), the least well-known of the four great horror films James Whale made for Universal between 1931 and 1935, beginning with *Frankenstein* (1931), and concluding with the aforementioned *The Invisible Man* and *The Bride of Frankenstein*. *Frankenstein* has moments of surreal levity (the drowning of the little girl can be seen as a sick joke that creates the same uneasy feeling in the viewer as the murder of the gardener's son in Buñuel's *L'Age d'Or* [1930]), but it was with *The Old Dark House* that Whale perfected his sense of humor, allowing it to arise naturally out of his sympathy with the outcast and the grotesque.

A bickering young married couple, Philip and Margaret Waverton (Raymond Massey and Gloria Stuart), and their cynical bachelor friend, Roger Penderel (Melvyn Douglas), later to be joined by a businessman and his mistress, take refuge in the eponymous house on a dark and stormy night. They are met at the door by a grunting, hirsute servant, Morgan (Boris Karloff), and greeted by the Femms: Horace, apparently a once epicene youth now grown into nervous middle age, by turns petulant and panicky; and his religious fanatic sister, Rebecca (Eva Moore). Unlike most decaying mansions, there is nothing the least bit charming about the sparsely furnished, box like house. "No beds! You can't have beds!" the half-deaf Rebecca yells with the force of moral imperative. "As my sister hints, there are, I'm afraid, no beds," Horace repeats apologetically, revealing immediately the balance of power and the philosophical differences between the siblings.

Over a spartan dinner of potatoes, vinegar and gin, fissures also appear among the guests, as for example between Sir William Porterhouse (Charles Laughton, husband of Elsa Lanchester, who would become the Frankenstein monster's bride), a self-made,

*"A quiet, restful night": Morgan (Boris Karloff) with Gloria Stuart and Lilian Bond, and wrestling with Melvyn Douglas and friends in* The Old Dark House.

self-loathing boaster, and his traveling companion Gladys DuCane (Lilian Bond), a chorus girl who stays with Porterhouse because she believes that she does not deserve any better. After dinner, Morgan gets hideously drunk in his kitchen. Penderel and Gladys go out to the garage for a drink. The lights go out, and as Horace and Phillip go to fetch a lamp from the top of the stairs, Porterhouse accompanies Rebecca to her room to shut an open window. Left alone in the dark, Margaret Waverton is attacked by the drunken butler; her husband Philip intervenes and succeeds in knocking Morgan down the stairs. In an upstairs bedroom the Wavertons discover centenarian Sir Roderick Femm (Elspeth Dudgeon, billed as "John Dudgeon"), who explains to them the tragic history of his family and warns them about the pyromaniac brother Saul (Brember Wills), locked up in uppermost room in the house, guarded and tended to by Morgan.

Morgan regains consciousness and goes berserk. He releases Saul, who turns out to be a surprisingly meek little man (in J. B. Priestley's novel *Benighted*, on which the film is based, he's huge and brutal—the comic contrast to Morgan is Whale's invention, and a stroke of genius it is). He pleads with Penderel for help, then knocks him out. When Roger comes to, Saul is on the second-floor landing igniting a tapestry with a torch. Roger attempts to subdue him and they both tumble over the railing. A weeping Morgan carries an unconscious Saul back up to his room.[1] As Roger regains consciousness again, Gladys exclaims, in an hommage to *Frankenstein*, "He's alive! Alive!"

The next morning, the sun is shining as Roger proposes to Gladys, now free of Porterhouse, who doesn't seem at all offended. Morgan politely hands the Wavertons their luggage, and the Femms see off their guests as if they had all spent nothing more than a restful, pleasant night together.

In Whale's dark comedy, humor conveys atmosphere, develops characterization, and drives the plot to a greater degree than in any other "old dark house" movie before or since. In the silent *The Cat and the Canary* (Paul Leni, 1927), Creighton Hale's silly antics are an unnecessary distraction from the film's expressionist depths. By contrast, in Roland West's *The Bat Whispers* (1930), the action is kept moving at such a breakneck pace, and the characters are all such outrageous parodies, that despite all the gothic trappings, true dread never penetrates the spectator's consciousness; *The Bat Whispers* easily exceeds *The Old Dark House* in camp value. Each of these films in its own way has more in common with Bob Hope's later horror comedies, *The Cat and the Canary* (Elliot Nugent, 1939, a remake of Leni's silent film) and *The Ghost Breakers* (George Marshall, 1940), than with *The Old Dark House*.

Unlike Hope's snappy one-liners, which tend to distance the actor from the character he plays and the plot he takes part in, the wittiness of Horace and the unintentional humor of Rebecca contribute to the sense of horror rather than distract from it. When the lights in the Femm mansion flicker, Horace explains, "We make our own electric light here and we're not very good at it." Later we learn that Rebecca is completely opposed to electric light, and won't have it in her part of the house. The simmering antagonism between Horace and Rebecca is one of the film's most successful running jokes. This antagonism is established at the very beginning when Horace takes some flowers out of a bowl and says wistfully, "My sister was on the point of arranging these flowers," then tosses them onto the fire. Thesiger somehow managed to establish a manner for Horace that is at the same time simpering and haughty. Offering drinks to his guests, he says apologetically, "It's only gin, you know, only gin." Then a pause before he smugly adds, "I like gin," as Whale cuts to a scowling Rebecca. The fact that these sibling rivals are somewhere in their sixties makes their bickering extremely funny and at the same time all the more unsettling.

Thanks to Christopher Bram's novel of James Whale's last days, *Father of Frankenstein*, and its subsequent adaptation to film as *Gods and Monsters* (Bill Condon, 1998), James Whale's reputation has lately undergone a marked revival. The title of Condon's film comes from a speech delivered by Dr. Pretorius (Thesiger) to Dr. Frankenstein (Colin Clive) in *The Bride of Frankenstein*, referring to the new race that the two mad scientists may bring about through their collaboration. In *Gods and Monsters*, Condon examines the dangers that beset the creative mind that can no longer distinguish between the aesthetic and the social worlds. Focusing on *The Bride of Frankenstein*, Condon's film attempts to show how Whale's homosexuality and his experiences in the trenches of World War I contributed to his art. Following a series of strokes, Whale (Ian McKellen) begins to experience flashbacks, including memories of a fellow soldier with whom he had fallen in love. The soldier was killed while on a night patrol in no-man's land and remained entangled in barbed wire for days in plain sight of the battalion. Whale spends the rest of his life trying to reconstruct this decimated body, first through art in the form of Karloff's monster, then in life in the form of his gardener, Clayton Boone (Brendan Fraser).

Just how much Whale's personality and art were actually affected by his experiences in the war is an open question.[2] Though Whale fought in the disastrous Flanders campaign, his actual time at the front was brief, probably less than a month, before he was captured and spent the last fifteen months of the war at the German POW camp at Holzminden, where he won his fortune at cards and found his calling directing theatrical evenings for the other prisoners. Two of Whale's films, *Journey's End* (1929) and *The Road Back* (1937) are set during the war, the former serving to establish his reputation, the latter to destroy it. A scene in *The Bride of Frankenstein* in which villagers chase the monster through a desolate wood resembles troops charging across no-man's land. The central activity of the Frankenstein films, the stitching together of a creature from the corpses of human beings, can be seen as an exaggeration of the practice of plastic surgery, an art that saw its first successes, as well as its most spectacular failures, in the endless supply of cannon fodder being returned alive but broken from the front.

*The Old Dark House* can also be interpreted as a reaction to the war, albeit a more complicated one than that depicted in *Gods and Monsters*. Priestley originally intended *Benighted* to be a serious psychological study of the aftereffects of war, with Roger Penderel its tragic hero.[3] Although Whale and Levy considerably lightened the tone of the story, some of these elements remain. The travelers seek shelter from a sea of muck (they even narrowly escape a landslide, which was a constant threat during trench warfare) in a box-like house resembling the dugout setting for *Journey's End*. When Horace inquires, "I presume you are one of the gentlemen slightly, shall we say, battered by the war?" Penderel answers, "Correct, Mr. Femm, war generation, slightly soiled, a study in the bittersweet, the man with the twisted smile—and this, Mr. Femm, is exceedingly good gin." Penderel treats the war as a sick joke, and uses a very curious word in connection with it—"bittersweet." If Whale felt more comfortable sublimating the horrors of war in ironic humor than in direct protest, perhaps that is because there was something more contradictory in his reaction to the war than is generally acknowledged.

As dreadful an experience as it was, the war freed James Whale from his working-class background and gave him his vocation. Jimmy Whale, destined to become the sort of common laborer he sometimes identified with Karloff, was transformed into James Whale, artist and aristocrat.[4] Whale's memories of the war, meanwhile, turned Frankenstein's monster from the organic feral creature that Bela Lugosi depicted in early make-up tests for original *Frankenstein* director Robert Florey into the heavy, angular, tank-like Karloff. In *The Bride of Frankenstein*, Dr. Pretorius contrasts his own method of growing normally proportioned but miniature human specimens "from seeds" with Frankenstein's industrial assemblies. The Great War was, or at least appeared to be, the Götterdämmerung of the Industrial Revolution, as the gods of Industry and Progress, futilely barricading themselves in obsolete fortresses, destroyed each other while creating a new race of monsters out of the fusion of flesh and metal in the trenches. Dudley Castle, overlooking the factories of Whale's youth, combined with Pommern Castle, the headquarters from which his commanding officer ordered the Passhendaele assault, formed Frankenstein's castle. After the castle's self-destruction, all that was left was an old dark house with a neurotically childish aging family. The mad scientist was reduced to a meek pyromaniac locked in the attic ("I know things about flames nobody in the world knows—sharp and cold—they burn like knives!"). *The Old Dark House* is situated in a diminished world, a world of guilty and enfeebled survivors, Ezra Pound's "old bitch gone in the teeth,/...a botched civilization."

Penderel's bittersweet remark about the man with the twisted smile, it may be remembered, is followed by a compliment to the gin. This serves to emphasize the glibness of Penderel's self-characterization and the sardonic irony that reflects the moral contradictions of Whale's own background. It also allies Penderel with Horace against Rebecca and reveals his willingness to enter into the spirit of Horace's rusty attempts at gentility. Horace and Penderel are further identified with each other by their behavior at dinner. Just as Horace can put any number of subtexts into the invitation to "Have a potato" (note the lower-class associations of that food, especially when simply baked whole, as here, contributing to the humor), so Penderel responds to one of Rebecca's moralistic diatribes with the friendly offer of a condiment: "Vinegar, Miss Femm?"

*The Old Dark House* is similar to other effective horror films of the '20s and '30s, such as *The Golem* (Paul Wegener, Germany, 1920) and *King Kong* (Cooper and Schoedsack, 1933), in that the horror arises not out of the forces of pure evil but out of the unnatural acts that a being excluded from the natural order is driven to commit. When the humanity of the outsider was rendered more ironically than pathetically, as it was in Whale's horror quartet, the result was invariably more comic than melodramatic. This does not serve to make Whale's approach colder, more distant, or even more intellectual than that of other directors. On the contrary, the transition from pathos to irony allows us to feel more deeply about the characters as it elevates our response from sympathy to understanding.

Stanley Kubrick's strangely affecting depiction of the HAL 9000 computer in *2001: A Space Odyssey* presents a later illustration of this principle. HAL's performance of the song "A Bicycle Built For Two" near the end of that film recalls Morgan crying over Saul at the end of *The Old Dark House*. What saves both of these scenes from sentimentality is the use of irony and ambiguity to open up the narrative precisely at that point where some sort of resolution is expected. Does HAL genuinely experience emotion, or only mimic it? At the base of HAL's catharsis is the metaphysical question of whether emotion is not simply a product of rational processes after all. Consciousness, the ordering and storage in memory of electrical impulses, is everything, no matter whether it is produced biologically or mechanically. This monism would appear to be supported, at least aesthetically, by the effect of the scene on the viewer, where the emotional impact is actually deepened by the universal intellectual themes of Being and Consciousness. Likewise, Morgan's tears in Whale's film are completely unexpected, considering his earlier drunken brutality toward Mrs. Waverton and the coldness and sarcasm with which all members of the Femm household treat each other. Whether this uncharacteristic tenderness indicates genuine compassion toward the man who has been in his care all these years, or points toward some undisclosed secret regarding Morgan's paternity, or is simply the effect of Morgan's drunken stupor, it still serves to divide the audience's sympathies between the "normal" and "outsider" characters, rather than directing the audience to identify with one particular character, as melodrama usually does.

Harry Benshoff in *Monsters in the Closet* argues that Whale used campy black humor in his horror films, *The Old Dark House* in particular, to comment on the status of the homosexual with respect to the dominant culture. The Femm household, as the family name implies, is at the very least androgynous, a characteristic emphasized by Whale's casting of a woman (Elspeth/"John" Dudgeon) in the part of the centenarian patriarch. The house itself stands as a repository of all manner of outsider sexuality: "Incest, necrophilia, male and female homosexuality, androgyny, sadomasochism, and orgiastic behavior are all hinted at to greater or lesser degree and used to characterize the house and its denizens as queer."[5] Rebecca's religious fanaticism represents the repressive hegemony of "normal" morality, from both outside and within the individual (the scene in which Mrs. Waverton changes clothes in Rebecca's bedroom while Rebecca herself, her face reflected grotesquely from several different angles in a broken mirror, recounts the sad fate of her sister and scolds Mrs. Waverton and all young women for their immorality, has marked lesbian overtones). Benshoff sees the eventual "heterosexualization" of the couples, particularly Roger Penderel and Gladys, as Whale's concession to the "generic imperative." This convention goes back at least as far as Shakespeare's *A Midsummer Night's Dream* (in which mismatched couples spend an eventful night beyond the reach of civilization and pair off happily by morning, just as in *The Old Dark House* ), and should not be simply dismissed as a sop to official morality. Penderel, out of all the travelers, has been most at ease in the Femm mansion and most closely allied with Horace against the repressive moralism of Rebecca. To interpret his character as he is literally portrayed, as a tolerant and enlightened heterosexual, need not compromise the film's gay sensibility. Most rewarding of all may be a double reading that acknowledges the ambiguity and openness of the ending; Penderel after all addresses Gladys by her real last name, Perkins, as one might a male friend, leaving open the possibility that their impending marriage may be one of platonic companionship, like that of the real-life Laughtons.

Robin Wood takes a similar tack in his comments on horror cinema in *The American Nightmare* (1976), *Hollywood From Vietnam to Reagan* (1986), and essays like "The American Family Comedy: from *Meet Me in St. Louis* to *The Texas Chainsaw Massacre*" (1979). Discussing the Halloween sequence of Minnelli's film, Wood describes how the scene "draws lavishly on the iconography of the Horror film."

It is introduced by a shot of the Smith home that turns it (with the aid of darkness and thunder) into the Old Dark House of the Horror film—or the Bates house of *Psycho* —a figure that, recurring in American fiction, both prose and film, from *The Fall of the House of*

*Usher* to *Mandingo* and *The Texas Chainsaw Massacre*, seems primarily to signify the terrible weight of the past, the legacy of repression.[6]

In other words, the old dark house has become decadent. The old morality has become outdated and a little bit insane; it is tyrannical parental authority refusing to loosen its grip on the younger generations, with the result that they become overgrown children. Wood draws upon motifs of the claustrophobic family and the overgrown child, staples of camp humor. In many of these families, the mother is absent, exerting her iron grip on the family from beyond the grave, as it were. Rebecca Femm is Horace's sister, not his mother, and though childless herself, she fills the role of the matriarch with excessive zeal. The father, portrayed by an actress, is too decrepit to have any real influence.

The role of matriarch by proxy is filled in Alfred Hitchcock's *Psycho* (1960). Norman, with his bag of candy and his Oedipal double entendres, is both overgrown child and undead mother. Norman's "mother" screeches and moralizes just like Rebecca Femm. Like Horace, Norman uses wit to express subtly what he can't say directly; "Mother's not herself today." *Psycho*, however, requires more violence than *The Old Dark House* in order for the horror and the humor to balance out. By 1960, the Victorian gloom of the Bates residence must have seemed eccentrically old-fashioned for someone of Norman's mother's generation, and temperance society morality no longer held even the rearguard position in the public conscience that it had in the '20s.

By the '80s and '90s, the dread of Victorian-style moralism had completely dissolved, and the old dark house had become a funhouse attraction. The old moral order has been completely reversed in today's horror comedies. In films such as *Beetlejuice* (1988), *The Addams Family* (1991) and *Casper* (1994), it is the older inhabitants who represent freedom and individualism, while the contemporary characters represent conformity and repression. The aristocratic charm and eccentricity of the old houses shaped the personalities of their inhabitants in the same way that the gloom and puritanism of virtually identical houses shaped the personalities of their gothic forebears. The context in which the satire operates has changed—our fears are different now. We are no longer oppressed by the past—we are more likely to be alarmed at the increasing speed with which it is disappearing. James Whale's modern heir Tim Burton makes the connection clear with the ghostly nostalgia which permeates *Beetlejuice*, *Edward Scissorhands*, and *Sleepy Hollow* .

## Notes

1. Most accounts of *The Old Dark House* assume that Saul is killed in the fall from the balcony, as he was in Priestley's novel. (See for example Nollen, 66; Buehner, 100; and Jensen, 25.) However, Roger also dies in the novel, which is much more serious in tone than the film. I believe that in Whale's film, Saul, like Morgan and Roger, suffers a nasty fall but survives. Even a family as psychologically unsound as the Femms must be affected in some way by the death of one of its sons. After all, it was their sister Rachel's death, supposedly by a fall from a horse, that unhinged them in the first place. In order for the ending to be psychologically true, nothing must have changed for them. Life will go on interminably as they wait for the next group of stray travelers.

2. Whale undoubtedly saw some horrendous action, as did his friend Ernest Thesiger, who in his autobiography told of the time his battalion was hiding out in a French barn eating breakfast when a German shell crashed through the roof. All that remained of a man with whom he had been eating

chocolate not thirty seconds before was a pair of boots, each one filled with a few inches of leg.
3. For example, Nollen, 66; Buehner, 100; and Jensen, 25.
4. Thesiger, 118-119, quoted in Skal, 185-186.
5. For a comprehensive comparison of the film to the novel, see Jensen, 23-31.
6. "A truck driver," Whale would point out contemptuously, referring to one of the odd jobs Karloff took to supplement his acting career before the Monster made him famous. Of course, it was Karloff, the son of a British diplomat in India, who had the more distinguished pedigree. Taylor, 103-108.
7. Benshoff, 45
8. Wood (1979), 10.

## Works Cited

Harry M. Benshoff, *Monsters in the Closet: Homosexuality and the Horror Film* (Manchester: Manchester University Press, 1997).

Christopher Bram, *Father of Frankenstein* (New York: Plume, 1996).

Mark Bronski, "Gods and Monsters: The Search for the Right Whale," *Cineaste* 24:4 (1999).

Beverley Bare Buehrer, *Boris Karloff: A Bio-bibliography* (Westport, CT: Greenwood Press, 1993).

James Curtis, *James Whale: A New World of Gods and Monsters* (London: Faber and Faber, 1998).

Paul M. Jensen, *The Men Who Made the Monsters* (New York: Twayne, 1996).

Scott Allen Nollen, *Boris Karloff: A Critical Account of His Screen, Stage, Radio, Television, and Recording Work* (Jefferson, NC: McFarland, 1991).

David J. Skal, *The Monster Show* (New York: Penguin, 1994).

John Russell Taylor, *Strangers in Paradise: the Hollywood Emigres, 1933-1950* (New York: Holt, Rinehart and Winston, 1983).

Ernest Thesiger, *Practically True* (London: William Heinemann, 1927).

Robin Wood, "The American Family Comedy: from *Meet Me in St. Louis* to *The Texas Chainsaw Massacre*," *Wide Angle* 3:2 (1979).

Wood, *Hollywood From Vietnam to Reagan* (New York: Columbia University Press, 1986).

# The Fraidy-Cat: Seeing is Believing

Bob Stephens (2001)

For seventeen years, from the appearance of Tod Browning's *Dracula* (1931) until the release of Charles T. Barton's *Abbott and Costello Meet Frankenstein* (1948), comedy and horror were forced into an uneasy and usually unnecessary relationship in Universal horror films. Today, moviemakers such as Joe Dante, Frank Henenlotter and Peter Jackson routinely merge the genres in the conviction they can be used in a way that each intensifies the other. And it is true that when horror and comedy reach their most feverish pitch, they both become forms of hysteria. Furthermore, the cruelty of comedy often coincides with the bleak pessimism of horror: In a universe full of slippery banana peels and concussions, the physical world may be reasonably considered hostile toward mankind.

My feeling is that in the past, comedy was included in American horror films out of a mistrust of the viewer's ability to deal with manifestations of the inexplicable and the irrational. Studio heads and producers seemed to fear that many moviegoers weren't interested in, or were afraid of, supernatural subjects. So it might have occurred to them that members of the audience who resisted unfamiliar material could be entertained, helped to get through these films, by means of extraneous humor. But artistic difficulties arose when the comedy became an aggravating distraction for those who were drawn to the mysterious, who especially wanted to watch a horror movie.

In European films of roughly the same period, the idea of the infiltration of our daily lives by otherworldly evil was treated far more seriously. If there's any humor at all in vampire movies such as Carl Theodor Dreyer's *Vampyr* (1931) or F.W. Murnau's *Nosferatu* (1922), it is incidental or an ironic consequence of despair.

Fortunately, a few American directors found a way to deal with the problem of the genre's divergent tendencies: They began to exploit the kind of black comedy that grew out of Renfield's entomological epicureanism in *Dracula*. As portrayed by Dwight Frye, the infamous bug-eater with the maniacal laugh is unnerving and funny. (Renfield's ghastly guffaw is no doubt provoked by visions of absurdity and the dreadful emptiness of death.)

This kind of warped humor derives from the same source as morbidity in horror and, in spite of the dominance of a more naive comedy, gruesome gags did resurface from time to time. Another successful, daring mixture of horror and pathological comedy appears in Roland V. Lee's *Son of Frankenstein* (1939). Sick jokes about amputation abound in Lionel Atwill's performance as Inspector Krogh, a police officer who was mutilated by Dr. Frankenstein's monster as a child. For example, in an exquisite display of manners, Krogh grimly but energetically snaps his artificial arm into position with his intact hand and delivers a noisy, mechanical salute to all. In addition, a hunchback named Ygor (Bela Lugosi) gleefully pounds on the jutting vertebrae of his broken neck as if he were knocking on wood.

However, most horror films continued to rely on parochial humor, excruciating demonstrations of the "ordinary" man's self-congratulatory incomprehension of extraordinary events. Devotees of supernatural cinema were made to suffer through a series of irritatingly sarcastic, stupid asylum guards; policemen full of adolescent fear; foolish, bumbling fathers; drunken, nosey old women and numerous other buffoons.

These secondary figures revealed nothing about the essence of horror or a credible response to it, but made clear, as I mentioned before, the timidity of unimaginative studio executives. The real terror evidently resided in the hearts of men confronted by a new, emerging force in cinema, one that reflected the subversion of a secure empiricism by superstition in a series of incarnations known as the horror film.

James Whale's perverse, multi-faceted wit, so wonderfully expressed in *Bride of Frankenstein* (1935), seemed to be another alternative, but his humor is idiosyncratic and it never had much of an influence. (It may, however, have given birth to a later artistic generalization, the idea of camp.) Despite Whale's sophisticated outlook, he also suffered from lapses into conventional comedy, particularly in his acceptance of Una O'Connor's silly, shrieking interpretation of the role of a maid. But, for the most part, Whale's humor is unprecedented. It's a prim, pursed-lips kind of satire embodied by Ernest Thesiger as the frighteningly fastidious Dr. Pretorius. Uniquely, this self-aware form of humor even mocks itself.

Still, the question remained: Was there a way, beyond the use of potentially offensive black humor, to blend comedy with horror in the movies? Roland West's silent, *The Bat* (1926), and his early sound era remake, *The Bat Whispers* (1930), could be cited as early examples of the fusion of comedy and horror, but their expressionist visual designs are so overwhelming that the horror fans I know are transfixed by the lyrical nightworld on the screen and nobody pays any attention to the jokes.

Independents, poverty row studios and majors that had no tradition of supernatural filmmaking took an experimental leap into the subgenre of comic chillers with such pictures as the Ritz Brothers and Allan Dwan's *The Gorilla* (1939), Bob Hope and Elliott Nugent's remake of *The Cat and the Canary* (1939), Hope and George Marshall's *The Ghost Breakers* (1940) and Phil Rosen's *Spooks Run Wild*, with Bela Lugosi and the East Side Kids (1941).

Haunted house comedies in particular became more common, but it was only after Gordon Douglas' adept merging of horror and conventional humor in *Zombies On Broadway* (1946), an RKO movie, that Universal decided to combine two of their most popular subgenres, the multi-monster cavalcade and Abbott and Costello theme comedies—movies that played off a specific setting or social group. *Zombies* featured the great horror actor Bela Lugosi and a pair of counterfeits of the Universal funny men, Alan Carney and Wally Brown. This must have encouraged the executives at Universal because they had the authentic duo under contract. The studio had already taken a tentative, yet profitable, step toward horrific comedy in 1927 with Paul Leni's silent, original version of *The Cat and the Canary* and in 1941 with Arthur Lubin's *Hold That Ghost*, a fake supernatural film starring their boys.

And rather than being the expected artistic compromise of either genre, the hybrid *Abbott and Costello Meet Frankenstein* reinforces their individual strengths. First of all, A&C makes it possible for us to recognize the fear, often our own, that hides behind a superficial bravado. The film also questions whether or not we can offer convincing proof of an encounter with the uncanny whenever we return to the daylight world. In an attempt to accomplish the latter, A&C provides its own variations on the maxim "Seeing is believing."

Lou Costello portrays Wilbur Gray, a "fraidy-cat," who must persuade his cynical co-worker Chick Young (Bud Abbott) that they are threatened by a supernatural being and a man-made creature—Count Dracula and the patch-work dead man known as the Frankenstein Monster. (The Wolf Man is on the scene too, but he's Wilbur and Chick's ally.)

In its presentation of the story, A&C relies on images of eyes that attempt to discern the meaning of unfolding events, hypnotic stares that control human behavior, eyes that inadvertently reveal imminent danger, and a resort to the averted glance as a hopeful means of escape from a supernatural presence. (This last, evasive use of the eyes is symptomatic of magical thinking in which a frightened man pretends that unacknowledged horrors, things he looks away from, will cease to exist.)

In his own inarticulate way, Wilbur tries to communicate the immediacy of the threat by insisting "I saw what I saw when I saw it." Chick repeats that assertion when he finally believes in the reality of the monsters. The comedy and suspense of A&C revolve around moments when Wilbur sees what others do not, or will not see, because they're afraid to set aside the delusive protection of rationality. It's obvious that action cannot be taken against evil creatures, supernatural or scientific, until their existence is accepted.

Eye imagery, or acts of trying to see, appear right from the beginning of the film: Lon Chaney Jr., as Lawrence Talbot/the Wolf Man, peers through Venetian blinds into a foggy London evening, aware that night in another part of the world (Florida) will bring with it the release of old monsters who are now disguised as exhibits bound for a wax museum. Talbot places a phone call to warn Wilbur, a clerk in the shipping company that's holding the boxes. But Talbot changes into a werewolf before he can finish the conversation and his urgent message is lost in feral growling.

Wilbur discovers the creatures after he starts unpacking the crates in the showroom of McDougal's House of Horrors. The little guy is afraid he'll let the monsters out if he opens the boxes. He's terrified because he read the exhibit cards that describe the activities of Dracula and the Frankenstein Monster. Wilbur already has a case of the shivers from the eerie surroundings—a room full of hooded executioners, hanging skeletons, murderers and a mummy's sarcophagus. He doesn't want to finish unpacking because he's already seen too much.

Chick, who's impatient to get the job done, says "Come on, you fraidy-cat. These things can't harm you, they're made out of wax." Wilbur is then left alone and has to confront the very things he doesn't want to see. When he opens up the Monster's crate, he lets out a whoop of fear and stuffs the packing material right back over the hideous face. Wilbur tries to cover the creature up in the futile hope that what he can't see won't hurt him.

Shortly thereafter, Wilbur is hypnotized by Dracula (Bela Lugosi), who has risen from his coffin. The count revives the Monster (Glenn Strange) with an electrical discharge from his ring. When the grotesque giant tears himself free from the box, the violent sounds of cracking wood break the spell Wilbur is under and the little guy whimpers helplessly. Then he catches himself and looks away, pretending he's still hypnotized. Wilbur prays that his impassive, unknowing stare will make him safe, in the superstitious wish, once again, that what he can't see won't hurt him.

How did Wilbur get into this mess? Because the creepy conspirators want his brain for a transplant into the Monster's body. Dracula's surgeon, Sandra Mornay (Lenore Aubert), intends to reanimate the dormant Monster with large jolts of electricity, but the count doesn't want the creature to have an unruly, independent mind. The ancient vampire insists "This time the Monster must have no will of his own, no fiendish intellect to oppose his master."

*Courtesy of Ronald V. Borst/Hollywood Movie Posters.*

*Dracula tries to reassure the Frankenstein monster after he's frightened by Wilbur's face.*
Abbott and Costello Meet Frankenstein.

Sandra, who flirts with Wilbur and pretends she's attracted to him in order to lure him to her laboratory, promises Dracula that "The new brain I've chosen for the Monster is so simple, so pliable, it will obey you like a trained dog."

When Wilbur visits a nearby island to pick Sandra up for a date, he unintentionally enters the subterranean world of his adversaries: Inside the castle, there are long stairways that descend to dark waters, extensive, gloomy caverns and hidden doors that spin around in stone walls, revealing and concealing, by turns, the creatures he wants Chick to see.

Later, at a masquerade ball, Wilbur and Chick are joined by Sandra, Dr. Stevens (Charles Bradstreet), her lab assistant, Joan Raymond (Jane Randolph), a female insurance agent who's trying to retrieve the House of Horrors' lost exhibits, Lawrence Talbot, and, daringly "costumed" in a cape as himself, Count Dracula.

Sandra takes Wilbur on a walk in the garden, then gives him the vampiric stare in an effort to seize control of him. He sees bats flying in her irises and skedaddles. Eventually, everybody ends up back at the castle and a complicated chase sequence begins. This stretch has the giddy quality of a children's game in which kids provoke "monstrous" adults into pursuing them.

Wilbur and Chick scream and holler exuberantly as the Wolf Man hunts Dracula and the Monster comes after them with his odd, robotic goose step. Running through a series of rooms, Wilbur and Chick are forced to keep on the go as the Monster rams his fist through a panel in one door and knocks another off its hinges. Wilbur grabs the table cloth on a cabinet and with a quick yank, pulls it free, leaving a candelabra and other articles standing intact. He foolishly pauses to enjoy the results of his magician's dexterity, then scrams. After that, he emerges from his hiding place and covers his face with the table cloth, simulating Dracula's cape, and utters commands to the Monster. Seeing him in the master's garb, the creature backs off. Wilbur, however, starts laughing at his own trick and the Monster goes after him again.

Eventually, the Wolf Man leaps off a balcony, catches Dracula in the form of a bat, and both die in a fall to the sea. The Monster tosses Sandra out of a high window, killing her as well. And Frankenstein's creation is finally consumed by the roaring flames of a gasoline fire.

Wilbur and Chick, in a rowboat, feel tremendous relief over the destruction of their enemies. The little guy, suddenly cocky from victory, says "The next time I tell you that I saw something when I saw it, you believe me that I saw it!" Chick responds in irritation, "Oh, relax. Now that we've *seen* (my emphasis) the last of Dracula, the Wolf Man and the Monster, there's no one to frighten us anymore."

Then a cigarette suddenly appears, floating in thin air. An unctuous, disembodied voice (that of Vincent Price) contradicts Chick's declaration: "Oh, that's too bad. I was hoping to get in on the excitement. Allow me to introduce myself, I'm the Invisible Man."

The confidence Wilbur and Chick had in the value of sight as a method of proof and a means of defense evaporates. The emergence of this visually elusive antagonist not only complicates their problem, but, from a historical point of view, makes the boys' future in horror farce open-ended. For the rest of their careers, they would rarely be free of monsters of one kind or another.

In subsequent years, the comedy team met the *Killer* (Boris Karloff/1949), *The Invisible Man* (Arthur Franz instead of Price/1951), *Dr. Jekyll and Mr. Hyde* (Karloff again/1953), *the Mummy* (1955), and, on television's *Colgate Comedy Hour* (1954), they faced the Creature from the Black Lagoon and had an unwelcome reunion with the Frankenstein Monster.

Except for a memorable moment or two, these encounters do not equal the humorous or horrific elements of the comedy team's best movie, *Abbott and Costello Meet Frankenstein.*

At the opening of Barton's film, comedy and horror are brilliantly combined through the use of animation. The credits begin with a "funnybone" sequence: A cartoon version of the Monster knocks loudly on two coffins, and the frightened skeletons of Abbott and Costello leap out. In a state of panic, they accidentally run into each other and their bones scatter from the impact, forming the words of the title. After that, animated silhouettes of the growling Wolf Man, Dracula with his batwinged cape, the biceps-flexing Monster and a sloe-eyed, curvaceous Sandra march across a cartoon Gothic landscape as the cast is announced.

Animation has always been a source of humor, and its fundamental process, the impelling of a cartoon character into movement line by line, parallels the stage-by-stage transformations of a man into monster in horror movies. In such marvelous images, the comic and horrific are organic extensions of the same method. (Much like the characters in A&C, moviegoers demand to see the cinematic formation of a monster or a display of its remarkable talents in order to suspend their disbelief.)

Few dramatizations of a vampire's animal phase are as impressive as A&C's animated bat. When the flying mammal turns into Dracula, the human figure magically unfurls from its scalloped wings, and when Dracula wishes to fly, the extended shape of a man rolls quickly up—like a shade drawn tight, then let go—into a fluttering black thing. A hand-made model is then utilized for extended flights.

The bat's face has an appropriately ambiguous quality that conforms to the movie's duality: Its expression is both ferocious and comic-book funny. Moreover, the matte illustration of Dracula's castle has plenty of atmosphere and a cartoon-like vivacity.

In an homage horror pays to hilarity, the Monster gets to participate in a good joke. When the creature is first led away from his crate by Dracula, he's startled and jerks back in fear from Wilbur's hilarious face. Figures of horror and comedy obviously find the strangeness of each other's visages shocking. It's useful to remember that distortions of the human face can make an audience laugh or tremble.

But a lot of the humor in *A&C* is verbal as well as visual. The vaudeville/burlesque show patter that made Abbott and Costello famous is an ever-present source of film comedy.

Chick, trying to get the spooked Wilbur to settle down on their visit to the House of Horrors, reads an exhibit card called "The Legend of Dracula" with a sneer. In a sing-song voice that suggests ridicule, he says "Count Dracula must return to his coffin before sunrise where he lies helpless during the day. That's the bunk!" Wilbur quickly agrees with this homonym: "That's what I'm trying to tell you. That's his *bunk*."

And there's an inevitable joke that links werewolfery with the 1940s metaphor of the

*The monster, Costello, Bud Abbott and the Wolfman: "Letting their hair down."*

wolf as a flirtatious male. Talbot tries to alert the boys to his homicidal metamorphosis, saying "In half an hour the moon will rise and I'll turn into a wolf." In response, Wilbur blurts out "You and twenty million others guys!"

There's also humor in Dracula's avuncular pretense of normality. When the count meets Wilbur and Chick, he's operating under an alias and acts as if he were just plain folks. He makes soothing small talk like an amiable Rotarian, but his statements are full of malicious irony. Stroking Wilbur's skull approvingly, Dracula says "What we need today is young blood . . . and brains." And, when the visitors indicate they're about to leave for the party, the count sighs paternally and says, "Ah, you young people, making the most of life . . . while it lasts."

In several of his films, Lugosi makes macabre jokes by leading off with an apparently innocent statement, letting his listeners linger momentarily over his words, then concluding with a murderous afterthought.

Lugosi was no stranger to comedy, of course, even if his was sometimes unintentional. He had a second career in which he labored mostly in low-budget horror movies. But if Lugosi was very good in well-executed films, he was terrific in a different way in tawdry ones. The exaggerated theatricality he brought to hopeless roles achieved such delirious effects, that a hallucinatory quality lifted bargain-basement chillers to the level of not only the supremely laughable, but the bizarrely unforgettable. Consequently, there were two great Bela Lugosis in the history of cinema, and each is remembered on his own peculiar terms.

As in perhaps no other figure of dark fantasy, humor and horror were united in Lugosi's melodramatic declamations, from *Son of Frankenstein* in 1939 until the actor's death in 1956. Such titles as *The Devil Bat* (1940), *The Corpse Vanishes* (1942), *The Ape Man* (1943), *Voodoo Man* (1943) and *Return of the Ape Man* (1944) demonstrate that Universal's loss was definitely PRC and Monogram's gain. These cheap gems are confirmation of the distinctive, dime-store nature of the American imagination. Pulp poetry didn't just survive in poverty row cinema—it prevailed.

The monsters in *A&C* clearly enjoy letting their hair down, like more conventional Hollywood celebrities who appear in skits that spoof the basis of their renown. Under these circumstances, the legendary figures sacrifice some of their impact, but they manage to retain their integrity by refusing to shed additional aspects of horror. For example, the sense of mystery that surrounds them and the ominous notions of weirdness they evoke makes the monsters seem as much themselves as ever.

Throughout *A&C*, the supernatural transformations of the Wolf Man and Dracula, the powers of mesmerism, the castle's eerie architecture and the somber, primordial beauty of the swamp (however briefly presented) are marvelously rendered on celluloid.

The gloom of night does threaten to erase the luster of comedy, so there's a certain amount of tension, even if we are sure, from past experience, that everything will turn out all right. And, while the film doesn't deal with an objective reality, it's internally consistent and readily submits to the proof of Lou Costello's seeing, his bearing evidence of nocturnal wonders as Wilbur. If the Invisible Man presents Costello with problems of visual substantiation, we know there are plenty of other monsters that he *can* see. And, quite reliably, he will always remain a genuine fraidy-cat.

Most important of all, the little guy serves as a proxy for our own mortal ambivalence—our fear of the inescapable destiny that horror implies and our gratitude for the philosophical fatalism of humor.

# VII

SPENCER TRACY  JOAN BENNETT  ELIZABETH TAYLOR

The Bride gets the THRILLS! Father gets the BILLS!

M-G-M Announces the Event of the Season!

**Father of the Bride**

Father of the Bride

DON TAYLOR · BILLIE BURKE
SCREEN PLAY BY FRANCES GOODRICH and ALBERT HACKETT
BASED ON THE NOVEL BY EDWARD STREETER
Directed by VINCENTE MINNELLI
Produced by PANDRO S. BERMAN
A METRO-GOLDWYN-MAYER PICTURE

# Preston Sturges:
# Success in the Movies
## Manny Farber with W.S. Poster (1954)

By all odds, the most outstanding example of a successful director with a flamboyant unkillable personality to emerge in Hollywood during the last two decades has been that of Preston Sturges, who flashed into the cinema capital in 1939, wrote, produced, and directed an unprecedented series of hits and now seems to be leaping into relative obscurity. Hollywood destiny has caught up with Sturges in a left-handed fashion; most whiz-bang directors of the Sturges type remain successes while their individuality wanes. Sturges seems to have been so riddled by the complexities, conflicts, and opposed ambitions that came together to enrich his early work that he could not be forced into a mold. Instead of succumbing to successful conformity, Sturges has all but ceased to operate in the high-powered, smash-hit manner expected of him.

It is a peculiarly ironic fate, because Sturges is the last person in the world it is possible to think of as a failure. Skeptical and cynical, Sturges, whose hobbies include running restaurants and marketing profitable Rube Goldberg inventions, has never publicly acknowledged any other goal but success. He believes it is as easily and quickly achieved in America, particularly by persons of his own demoniac energy, mercurial brain, and gimmick-a-minute intensiveness. During the time it takes the average American to figure out how to save $3 on his income tax, Sturges is liable to have invented "a vibrationless Diesel engine," a "home exerciser," the "first nonsmear lipstick," opened up a new-style eatery, written a Broadway musical, given one of his discouraged actors his special lecture on happiness, and figured out a new way to increase his own superhuman productiveness and efficiency.

In fact, Sturges can best be understood as an extreme embodiment of the American success dream, an expression of it as a pure idea in his person, an instance of it in his career, and its generalizer in his films. In Sturges, the concept of success operates with purity, clogging the ideology of ambition so that it becomes an esthetic credo, backfiring on itself, baffling critics, and creeping in as a point of view in pictures which are supposed to have none. The image of success stalks every Sturges movie like an unlaid ghost, coloring the plots and supplying the fillip to his funniest scenes. His madly confused lovers, idealists, and outraged fathers appear to neglect it, but it invariably turns up dumping pots of money on their unsuspecting heads or snatching away million-dollar prizes. Even in a picture like *The Miracle of Morgan's Creek*, which deals with small-town, humble people, it is inevitable that bouncing Betty Hutton should end up with sextuplets and become a national institution. The very names of Sturges' best-known movies seem to evoke a hashish-eater's vision of beatific American splendor: *The Great McGinty, The Power and the Glory, The Miracle of Morgan's Creek, Hail the Conquering Hero, The Great Moment, Christmas in July* reveal the facets of a single preoccupation.

Nearly everyone who has written about Sturges expresses great admiration for his intelligence and talent, total confusion about his pictures, and an absolute certainty that Sturges should be almost anything but what he nakedly and palpably is—an inventive

American who believes that good picture-making consists in grinding out ten thousand feet of undiluted, chaos-producing energy. It is not too difficult to perceive that even Sturges' most appreciative critics were fundamentally unsympathetic toward him. Throughout his career, in one way or another, Sturges has been pilloried for refusing to conform to the fixed prescriptions for artists. Thus, according to René Clair, "Preston is like a man from the Italian Renaissance: he wants to do everything at once. If he could slow down, he would be great; he has an enormous gift, and he should be one of our leading creators. I wish he would be a little more selfish and worry about his reputation."

What Clair is suggesting is that Sturges would be considerably improved if he annihilated himself. Similarly, Siegfried Kracauer has scolded him for not being the consistent, socially-minded satirist of the rich, defender of the poor, and portrayer of the evils of modern life which he regards as the qualifying characteristics of all moviemakers admissible to his private pantheon. The more popular critics have condemned Sturges for not liking America enough; the advanced critics for liking it too much. He has also been accused of espousing a snob point of view and sentimentally favoring the common man.

*"The most spectacular manipulator of sheer humor since Mark Twain": Preston Sturges.*

Essentially Sturges, probably the most spectacular manipulator of sheer humor since Mark Twain, is a very modern artist or entertainer, difficult to classify because of the intense effort he has made to keep his work outside conventional categories. The high-muzzle velocity of his films is due to the anarchic energy generated as they constantly shake themselves free of attitudes that threaten to slow them down. Sturges' pictures maintain this freedom from ideology through his sophisticated assumption of the role of the ruthless showman deliberately rejecting all notions of esthetic weight and responsibility. It is most easy to explain Sturges' highly self-conscious philosophy of the hack as a kind of cynical morality functioning in reverse. Since there is so much self-inflation, false piety, and artiness in the arts, it was, he probably felt, less morally confusing to jumble slapstick and genuine humor, the original and the derivative together, and express oneself through the audacity and skill by which they are combined. It is also probable that he found the consistency of serious art, its demand that everything be resolved in terms of a logic of a single mood, repugnant to his temperament and false to life.

"There is nothing like a deep-dish movie to drive you out in the open," a Sturges character remarks, and, besides being a typical Sturges line, the sentence tells you a great deal about his moviemaking. His resourcefulness, intelligence, Barnum-and-Bailey showmanship and dislike of fixed purposes often make the typical Sturges movie seem like a uniquely irritating pastiche. A story that opens with what appears to be a bitingly satirical exposition of American life is apt to end in a jelly of cheap sentiment. In *Hail the Conquering Hero*, for example, Eddie Bracken plays an earnest, small-town boy trying to follow in the footsteps of his dead father, a World War I hero. Discharged because of hay fever, Bracken is picked up by six Marines who talk him into posing as a Guadalcanal veteran and returning home as a hero to please his mother. The pretense snowballs, the town goes wild, and Bracken's antics become more complicated and tormenting with every scene. After he has been pushed into running for Mayor, he breaks down and confesses the hoax. Instead of tarring and feathering him, the townspeople melt with admiration for his candor and courage.

This ending has been attacked by critics who claim that it reveals Sturges compromising his beliefs and dulling the edge of his satire. "At his beginning," Mr. Kracauer writes, referring to *The Great McGinty*, "Sturges insisted that honesty does not pay. Now he wants us to believe that the world yields to candor." Such criticism is about as relevant as it would be to say that Cubists were primarily interested in showing all sides of a bottle at once. To begin with, it should be obvious to anyone who has seen two Sturges pictures that he does not give a tinker's dam whether the world does or does not yield to candor. Indeed his pictures at no time evince the slightest interest on his part as to the truth or falsity of his direct representation of society. His neat, contrived plots are unimportant per se and developed chiefly to provide him with the kind of movements and appearances he wants, with crowds of queer, animated individuals, with juxtapositions of unusual actions and faces. These are then organized, as items are in any art which does not boil down to mere sociology, to evoke *feelings* about society and life which cannot be reduced to doctrine or judged by flea-hopping from the work of art to society in the manner of someone checking a portrait against the features of the original.

What little satire there is in a film is as likely to be directed at satire as it is at society. The supposedly sentimental ending of *The Conquering Hero*, for example, starts off as a tongue-in-cheek affair as much designed to bamboozle the critic as anything else. It goes out of hand and develops into a series of oddly placed shots of the six Marines, shots which are indeed so free of any kind of attitude as to create an effect of pained ambiguous humanity, frozen in a moment of time, so grimly at one with life that they seem to be utterly beyond any one human emotion, let alone sentiment. The entire picture is, indeed remarkable for the manner in which sequences are directed away from the surface mood to create a sustained, powerful, and lifelike pattern of dissonance. The most moving scene in it—Pangborn's monumentally heartfelt reactions to Bracken's confession—is the product of straight comic pantomime. The Marine with an exaggerated mother-complex sets up a hulking, ominous image as the camera prolongs a view of his casual walk down the aisle of the election hall. The Gargantuan mugging and gesturing of the conscience-stricken Bracken provokes not only laughter but the sense that he is suffering from some mysterious muscular ailment.

Such sequences, however, though integral to Sturges' best work, do not set its tone. The delightfulness, the exhilarating quality that usually prevails is due to the fact that the relation to life of most of the characters is deliberately kept weak and weightless. The foibles of a millionaire, the ugliness of a frump are all projected by similar devices and exploited in a like manner. They exist in themselves only for a moment and function chiefly as bits in the tumultuous design of the whole. Yet this design offers a truer equivalent of American society than can be supplied by any realism or satire that cannot cope with the tongue-in-cheek self-consciousness and irreverence toward its own fluctuating institutions that is the very hallmark of American society—that befuddles foreign observers and makes American mores well-nigh impervious to any kind of satire.

Satire requires a stationary society, one that seriously believes in the enduring value of the features providing its identity. But what is there to satirize in a country so much at the mercy of time and commerce as to be profoundly aware that all its traits—its beauties, blemishes, wealth, poverty, prejudices, and aspirations—are equally the merchandise of the moment, easily manufactured and trembling on the verge of destruction from the moment of production? The only American quality that can conceivably offer a focus for satire, as the early moviemakers and Sturges, alone among the contemporaries, have realized, is speed. Some of the great early comic films, those of Buster Keaton, for example, were scarcely comic at all but pure and very bitter satires, exhausting in endless combinations of all possible tortures produced as a consequence of the naif belief in speed. Mack Sennett was less the satirist of American speed-mania than its Diaghilev. Strip away the comic webbing, and your eye comes upon the preternatural poetic world created by an instinctive impresario of graceful accelerations. Keystone cops and bathing beauties mingle and separate in a buoyant, immensely varied ballet, conceived at the speed of mind but with camera velocity rather than the human body as its limit. Sturges was the only legitimate heir of the early American film, combining its various methods, adding new perspectives and developing the whole in a form suitable to a talking picture.

Since Sturges thought more synoptically than his predecessors, he presented a speed-ridden society through a multiple focus rather than the single, stationary lens of the pioneers. While achieving a more intense identification of the audience with the actors than in the earlier films (but less than the current talking pictures, which strive for complete audience identification with the hero), Sturges fragmented action, so that each scene blends into the next before it comes to rest, and created an illusion of relative motions. Basically, a Sturges film is executed to give one the delighted sensation of a person moving on a smoothly traveling vehicle going at high speed through fields, towns, homes, and even through other vehicles. The vehicle in which the spectator is traveling never stops but seems to be moving in a circle, making its journey again and again in an ascending, narrowing spiral until it diminishes into nothingness. One of his characters calls society a "cockeyed caravan," and Sturges, himself, is less a settled, bona fide resident of America than a hurried, Argus-eyed traveler through its shifting scenes, a nomad in space observing a society nomadic in time and projecting his sensations in uniquely computed terms.

This modern cinematic perspective of mobility seen by a mobile observer comes easily to Sturges because of his strange family background and broken-up youth. He was the son of a normal, sports-loving, successful father and a fantastic culture-bug mother who wanted him to be a genius and kept him in Paris from the age of eight to about fifteen. "She dragged me through every goddam museum on the continent," he has rancorously remarked. Glutted at an early age, by an overrich diet of esthetic dancing, high-hatted opera audiences, and impressionist painting, Sturges still shows the marks of his youthful trauma. The most obvious result of his experience has been a violent reaction against all estheticism. He has also expressed fervent admiration for his father's business ability and a desire to emulate him. The fact that he did not, however, indicates that his early training provoked more than a merely negative reaction in him and made him a logical candidate for Hollywood, whose entire importance in the history of culture resides in its unprecedented effort to merge art and big business.

As a moviemaker, the businessman side of Sturges was superficially dominant. He seems to have begun his career with the intention of giving Hollywood a lesson in turning out quick, cheap, popular pictures. He whipped together his scripts in record-breaking time, cast his pictures with unknowns, and shot them faster than anyone dreamed possible. He was enabled to do this through a native aptitude for finding brilliant technical shortcuts. Sturges tore Hollywood comedy loose from the slick gentility of pictures like It Happened One Night by shattering the realistic mold and the logical build-up and taking the quickest, least plausible route to the nerves of the audience. There are no preparations for the fantastic situations on which his pictures are based and no transitions between their numberless pratfalls, orgies of noise, and furniture-smashing. A Capra, Wilder, or Wellman takes half a movie to get a plot to the point where the audience accepts it and it comes to cinematic life. Sturges often accomplishes as much in the first two minutes, throwing an audience immediately into what is generally the most climactic and revelatory moment of other films.

The beginning of Sullivan's Travels is characteristic for its easy handling of multiple cinematic meanings. The picture opens abruptly on a struggle between a bum and a railroad employee on top of a hurtling train. After a few feet of a fight that is at once a sterling bit of action movie and a subtle commentary on action movies, it develops that you are in a projection studio, watching a film made by Sullivan, a famous director, and that the struggle symbolizes the conflict of capital and labor. As Sullivan and the moguls discuss the film's values and box-office possibilities, Sturges makes them all sound delightfully foolish by pointing up the naive humanity of everyone involved. "Who wants to see that stuff? It gives me the creeps!" is the producer's reaction to the film. When Sullivan mentions a five-week run at the Music Hall, the producer explodes with magnificent improbability: "Who goes to the Music Hall? Communists!" Thus in five minutes of quick-moving cinema and surprise-packed dialogue, a complex situation has been set forth and Sullivan is catapulted on his journey to learn about the moods of America in the depression.

The witty economy of his movies is maintained by his gifted exploitation of the non sequitur and the perversely unexpected. In nearly every case, he manages to bring out some hidden appropriateness from what seems like willful irrelevance. In *The Miracle of Morgan's Creek*, a plug-ugly sergeant mouths heavy psychiatric phrases in an unbelievable way that ends by sinking him doubly deep into the realm of the psychotic. With nihilistic sophistication, Sturges makes a Hollywood director keep wondering "Who is Lubitsch?" till you are not sure if it is simply fun or a weird way of expressing pretentiousness and ignorance. Similarly, in *The Conquering Hero*, the small-town citizens are given a happy ending and a hero to worship, but they are paraded through the streets and photographed in such a way that they resemble a lynch mob—a device which flattens out success and failure with more gruesome immediacy than Babbitt-like satires.

What made Sturges a viciously alive artist capable of discovering new means of expressiveness in a convention-ridden medium was the frenetic, split sensibility that kept him reacting to and away from the opposite sides of his heredity. These two sides are, in fact, the magnetic poles of American society. Accepting, in exaggerated fashion, the businessman approach to films, he nevertheless brought to his work intelligence, taste, and a careful study of the more estimable movies of the past. He also took care to disappoint rigid-minded esthetes and reviewers. Although it, has been axiomatic among advanced movie students that the modern film talks too much and moves too little, Sturges perversely thought up a new type of dialogue by which the audience is fairly showered with words. The result was paradoxically to speed up his movies rather than to slow them down, because he concocted a special, jerky, spluttering form of talk that is the analogue of the old, silent-picture firecracker tempo. Partly this was accomplished by a wholesale use of "hooks"—spoken lines cast as questions, absurd statements, or explosive criticisms, which yank immediate responses from the listener.

Sturges' free-wheeling dialogue is his most original contribution to films and accomplishes, among other things, the destruction of the common image of Americans as tight-lipped Hemingwayan creatures who converse in grating monosyllables and chopped sentences. Sturges tries to create the equally American image of a wrangle of conflicting, overemotional citizens who talk as though they were forever arguing or testifying before a small-town jury. They speak as if to a vast, intent audience rather than to each other, but the main thing is that they unburden themselves passionately and without difficulty—even during siesta moments on the front porch: "I'm perfectly calm. I'm as—as cool as ice, then I start to figure maybe they won't take me and some cold sweat runs down the middle of my back and my head begins to buzz and everything in the middle of the room begins to swim—and I get black spots in front of my eyes and they say I've got high blood pressure . . . ."

As the words sluice out of the actors' mouths, the impression is that they teeter on the edge of a social, economic, or psychological cliff and that they are under some wild compulsion to set the record straight before plunging out of the picture. Their speech is common in language and phrasing, but Sturges makes it effervesce with trick words ("whackos" for "whack"), by pumping it full of outraged energy or inserting a daft idea like the Music Hall gag. All of this liberated talk turns a picture into a kind of open forum where everyone down to the cross-eyed bit player gets a chance to try out his oratorical ability. A nice word-festival, very democratic, totally unlike the tight, gagged-up speech that movies inherited from vaudeville, radio, and the hard-boiled novel.

Paradoxically, too, his showman's approach enabled Sturges to be the only Hollywood talking-picture director to apply to films the key principles of the "modern" revolutions in poetry, painting, and music: namely, beginning a work of art at the climax and continuing from there. Just as the modern painter eschews narrative and representational elements to make his canvas a continuum of the keenest excitement natural to painting, or the poet minimizes whatever takes his poem out of the realm of purely verbal values, so Sturges eliminated from his movies the sedulous realism that has kept talking pictures essentially anchored to a rotting nineteenth-century esthetic. In this and other ways, Sturges revealed that his youth spent "caroming around in High-Bohemian Europe" had not been without a positive effect on his work. Its basic textures, forms, and methods ultimately derive from post-impressionist painting, Russian ballet, and the early scores of Stravinsky, Hindemith, et al. The presence of Dada and Surrealism is continuously alive in its subsurface attitudes or obvious in the handling of specific scenes. Sturges' fat Moon Mullins-type female, playing a hot tail-gate trombone at a village dance, is the exact equivalent in distortion of one of Picasso's lymphatic women posed as Greek statues.

Sturges' cinematic transpositions of American life reveal the outsider's ability to seize salient aspects of our national existence plus the insider's knowledge of their real meaning. But the two are erratically fused by the sensibility of the nostalgic, dislocated semiexile that Sturges essentially remains. The first impression one gets from a Sturges movie is that of the inside of a Ford assembly line smashed together and operating during a total war crisis. The characters, all exuding jaundice, cynicism, and anxiety, work feverishly as every moment brings them the fear that their lives are going to pieces, that they are going to be fired, murdered, emasculated, or trapped in such ridiculous situations that headlines will scream about them to a hooting nation for the rest of their lives. They seem to be haunted by the specters of such nationally famous boneheads as Wrong-Way Corrigan, Roy Riegels, who ran backward in a Rose Bowl game, or Fred Merkle, who forgot to touch second base in a crucial play-off game, living incarnations of the great American nightmare that some monstrous error can drive individuals clean out of society into a forlorn no man's land, to be the lonely objects of an eternity of scorn, derision, and self-humiliation. This nightmare is of course the reverse side of the uncontrolled American success impulse, which would set individuals apart in an apparently different but really similar and equally frightening manner.

Nearly all the Sturges comedies were centered with a sure instinct on this basic drive with all its complex concomitants. Using a stock company of players (all of a queer, unstandard, and almost aboriginal Americanism), Sturges managed to give his harrowing fables of success-failure an intimate, small-town setting that captured both the moony desire of every American to return to the small world of his youth and that innocent world itself as it is ravaged by a rampant, high-speed industrialism. The resultant events are used to obtain the comic release that is, indeed, almost the only kind possible in American life: the savage humor of absolute failure or success. Sturges' funniest scenes result from exploding booby traps that set free bonanzas of unsuspected wealth. In one episode, for example, two automat employees fight and trip open all the levers behind the windows; the spouts pour, the windows open, and a fantastic, illicit treasure trove of food spills out, upon a rioting, delightfully greedy mob of bums, dowagers, and clerks. In *The Palm Beach Story*, members of the "Ale and Quail" club—a drunken, good-humored bunch of eccentric millionaires—shoot up a train and lead yapping hounds through Pullmans in a privileged orgy of destruction. This would seem the deeply desired, much fantasized reward of a people that endures the unbelievably tormented existence Sturges depicts elsewhere—a people whose semicomic suffering arises from the disparity between the wild lusts generated by American society and the severity of its repressions.

*"Cinematic transpositions of American life": Al Bridge, Betty Hutton, Diana Lynn in*
The Miracle of Morgan's Creek *(1944).*

Sturges' faults are legion and have been pretty well gone over during his most success-ful period. Masterful with noisy crowds, he is liable to let a quiet spot in the script pro-voke him to burden the screen with "slapstick the size of a whale bone." A good businessman believes that any article can be sold if presented with eardrum-smashing loudness and brain-numbing certitude. From a similar approach, Sturges will represent hilarity by activating a crew of convicts as though he were trying to get Siberia to witness their gleeful shrieks. To communicate the bawdy wit of a fast blonde, he will show the tough owner of a lunch wagon doubled up like a suburban teenager hearing his first dirty joke. The comic chaos of a small-town reception must be evoked by the use of no less than four discordant bands. Sturges has been accused of writing down to his audi-ence, but it is more probable that there is too much of the businessman actually in his make-up to expect him to function in any other way. The best of his humor must come in a brash flurry of effects, all more or less oversold because there is nothing in his back-ground that points to a more quiet, reasonable approach to life.

But even these vices are mitigated somewhat by the fact that they provide an escape from the plight of many intelligent, sensibility-ridden artists or entertainers of his period whose very intelligence and taste have turned against them, choking off their vitality and driving them into silence or reduced productivity. The result is that artistic ebullience and spontaneity have all but drained down to the very lowest levels of American entertainment. Even in the movies these days, one is confronted by slow-moving, premeditated affairs—not so much works of art or entertainments aimed by the intelligence at the glands, blood, and viscera of the audience as exercises in mutual criticism and good taste. The nervous tantrums of slapstick in a Sturges movie, the thoughtless, attention-getting antics combined with their genuine cleverness give them an improvised, blatant immediacy that is preferable to excesses of calculation and is, in the long run, healthier for the artists themselves.

As a maker of pictures in the primary sense of the term, Sturges shows little of the daring and variety that characterize him as a writer and, on the whole, as a director. He runs to middle shots, symmetrical groupings, and an evenly lit screen either of the bright modern variety or with a deliberately aged, grey period-finish. His composition rarely takes on definite form because he is constantly shooting a scene for ambivalent effects. The love scenes in The Lady Eve, for example, are shot, grouped, and lit in such a way as to throw a moderate infusion of sex and sentiment into a fast-moving, brittle comedy without slowing it down. The average director is compelled to use more dramatic composition because the moods are episodic, a completely comic sequence alternating with a completely sentimental scene. Sturges' treatment is fundamentally more cinematic, but he has not found a technique equal to it. Fluent as a whole, his pictures are often clumsy and static in detail, and he has not learned how to get people to use their bodies so that there is excitement merely in watching them move. In a picture like Howard Hawks' *His Girl Friday*, Cary Grant uses legs, arms, trick hat, and facial muscles to create a pixyish ballet that would do credit to a Massine. But, when Sturges selects an equally gifted exponent of stylized movement, Henry Fonda, he is unable to extract comparable values from a series of falls, chases, listings to portside, and shuddering comas. Stray items— Demarest's spikey hair, Stanwyck's quasi-Roman nose—clutter up his foreground like blocks of wood. Even dogs, horses, and lions seem to turn into stuffed props when the Sturges camera focuses on them.

The discrepancies in Sturges' films are due largely to the peculiar discontinuities that afflict his sensibility, although such affliction is also a general phenomenon in a country where whole eras and cultures in different stages of development exist side by side, where history along one route seems to skip over decades only to fly backward over another route and begin over again in still a different period. What Sturges presents with nervous simultaneity is the skyrocketing modern world of high-speed pleasures and actions (money-making, vote-getting, barroom sex, and deluxe transportation) in conflict with a whole Victorian world of sentiment, glamour, baroque appearance, and static individuality in a state of advanced decay. In all probability, his years spent abroad prevented his finding a bridge between the two worlds or even a slim principle of relating them in any other way than through dissonance. A whole era of American life with its accompaniment of visual styles is skimped in his work, the essential problems thus created being neatly bypassed rather than solved.

But his very deficiencies enabled Sturges to present, as no one else has, the final decay of the bloated Victorian world, which, though seemingly attached to nothing modern and destined to vanish with scarcely a trace, has nevertheless its place in the human heart if only for its visual splendors, its luxurious, impractical graces, and all too human excesses. From McGinty to Harold Diddlebock, Sturges gives us a crowded parade of courtly, pompous, speechifying, queerly dressed personages caught as they slowly dissolve with an era. His young millionaires—Hickenlooper III (Rudy Vallee), Pike (Henry Fonda), and rich movie director Sullivan (Joel McCrea)—a similar type of being—are like heavily ornamented bugs, born out of an Oliver Twist world into a sad-faced, senile youth as moldy with leisure and tradition as an old cheese. Incapable of action, his obsolete multimillionaires gaze out into a world that has passed them by but to which they are firmly anchored by their wealth.

A pathetic creature in the last stages of futility, Vallee's sole occupation consists of recording, in a little black book, minute expenditures which are never totaled—as though be were the gently demented statistician of an era that has fallen to pieces for no special reason and has therefore escaped attention. Fonda as Pike, the heir of a brewery fortune ("The Ale That Won for Yale"), is the last word in marooned uselessness. A wistful, vague, young, scholarly ophiologist nicknamed Hoppsey, Pike's sole business in life consists of feeding four flies, a glass of milk, and one piece of white bread to a rare, pampered snake. In between, be can be seen glumly staring at a horde of predatory females, uncooperative-ly being seduced, getting in and out of suits too modern for him, sadly doing the oldest card trick in the world, and pathetically apologizing for not liking beer or ale. Oddly enough, his supposed opposite, a fast, upper-class cardsharp (Barbara Stanwyck) is no less Victorian, issuing as she does from a group of obsolete card Houdinis with an old-fash-ioned code of honor among thieves and courtly old-world manners and titles.

If Sturges has accomplished nothing else, he has brought to consciousness the fact that we are still living among the last convulsions of the Victorian world, that, indeed, our entire emotional life is still heavily involved in its death. These final agonies (though they have gone on so long as to make them almost painless), which only Sturges has recorded, can be glimpsed daily, in the strange, gentle expiration of figures like Shaw, Hearst, Jolson, Ford; the somewhat sad explosion of fervor over MacArthur's return (a Sturges picture by itself, with, if the fading hero had been made baseball czar, a pat Sturges ending); and the Old World pomp, unctuousness, and rural religiosity of the American political scene.

Nowhere did Sturges reveal his Victorian affinities more than by his belief in, use, and love of a horde of broken, warped, walked-over, rejected, seamy, old character actors. Some of these crafty bit players, like Walburn, Bridge, Tannen, made up his stock company, while others like Coburn, Pangborn, Kennedy, and Blore appear only in single pictures. They were never questioned by critics, although they seemed as out of place in a film about modern times as a bevy of Floradora girls. They appear as mon-strously funny people who have gone through a period of maniacal adjustment to capi-talist society by exaggerating a single feature of their character: meekness, excessive guile, splenetic aggressiveness, bureaucratic windiness, or venal pessimism. They seem inordi-nately toughened by experience, but they are, one is aware, not really tough at all, because they are complete fakers—life made it inevitable. They are very much part of the world of Micawber and Scrooge but later developments—weaker, more perfect, bloated, and subtle caricatures—giving off a fantastic odor of rotten purity and the embalmed cheerfulness of puppets.

They all appear to be too perfectly adjusted to life to require minds, and, in place of hearts, they seem to contain an old scratch sheet, a glob of tobacco juice, or a brown banana. The reason their faces—each of which is a succulent worm's festival, bulbous with sheer living—seem to have nothing in common with the rest of the human race is precisely because they are so eternally, agelessly human, oversocialized to the point where any normal animal component has vanished. They seem to be made up not of features but a *collage* of spare parts, most of them as useless as the vermiform appendix.

Merely gazing at them gives the audience a tremendous lift, as if it were witnessing all the drudgery of daily life undergoing a reckless transmutation. It is as if human nature, beaten to the ground by necessity, out of sheer defiance had decided to produce utterly useless extravaganzas like Pangborn's bobbling cheeks, Bridge's scrounging, scraping voice, or Walburn's evil beetle eyes and mustache like a Fuller brush that has decided to live an independent life. It is all one can do to repress a maniac shriek at the mere sight of Harold Lloyd's companion in *Mad Wednesday* [aka *The Sin of Harold Diddlebock*]. His body looks like that of a desiccated 200-year-old locust weighed down by an enormous copper hat. Or Pat Moran's wrecked jeep of a face, and his voice that sounds as if its owner had just been smashed in the Adam's apple by Joe Louis. These aged, senile rejects from the human race are put through a routine that has, in one minute, the effect of a long, sad tone poem and, after an hour, gives a movie a peculiar, hallucinatory quality, as if reality had been slightly tilted and robbed of significant pieces.

No one has delineated sheer indolence as Sturges has with these characters. When one appears on the screen, it looks as if he had wandered into the film by mistake and, once there, had been abandoned by the makers. When a second one of these lumpen shows up, the audience begins to sit on the edge of its seat and to feel that the picture is going to pieces, that the director has stopped working or the producer is making a monkey out of it. After a few minutes of lacerated nothingness, it becomes obvious that the two creatures are fated to meet; considerable tension is generated, as the audience wonders what build-up will be used to enable them to make each other's acquaintance. To everybody's horror, there is no build-up at all; the creatures link arms as the result of some gruesome asocial understanding and simply walk off. In *Mad Wednesday*, this technique yields a kind of ultimate in grisly, dilapidated humor, particularly in the long episode which begins with Harold Lloyd meeting the locust-like creature on the greasiest looking sidewalk ever photographed. The two repair to a bar presided over by Edgar Kennedy, who slowly and insanely mixes for Lloyd his first alcoholic potion. This entire, elaborate ritual is a weirder, cinematic version of the kind of "study in decrepit life" for which e. e. cummings is famed; certainly it is at least comparable in merit and effectiveness.

Sturges may not be the greatest director of the last two decades; in fact, it can be argued that a certain thinness in his work—his lack of a fully formed, solid, orthodox moviemaker's technique—prevents him from being included among the first few. He is, however, the most original movie talent produced in recent years: the most complex and puzzling. The emotional and intellectual structure of his work has so little in common with the work of other artists of our time that it seems to be the result of a unique development. Yet it is sufficiently logical and coherent to give it a special relevance to the contemporary American psyche—of precisely the kind that is found in some modern American poetry and painting, and almost nowhere else. Nothing is more indicative of the ineptitude of present-day Hollywood than its failure to keep Sturges producing at his former clip.

# The Comedy Without, The Gravity Within: Father of the Bride

**Blake Lucas** (2001)

With *Father of the Bride* (1950), director Vincente Minnelli commenced a cycle of comedies centered on courtship and marriage, seen in a different though related perspective in each case. There is nothing original about the subjects; they are the same ones that most American comedies treat, with more or less the same cultural values pervading through the '30s, '40s and '50s and into the early '60s. But like other masters of the form (George Cukor, Leo McCarey, Frank Capra, Howard Hawks, Mitchell Leisen, Billy Wilder), Minnelli revitalizes these familiar subjects through personal inflection and stylistic refinement. The cycle includes *Father's Little Dividend* (1951), *The Long, Long Trailer* (1954), *Designing Woman* (1957), *The Reluctant Debutante* (1958), and *The Courtship of Eddie's Father* (1963), and displays interesting evolution on every level.

As the initiating work, *Father of the Bride* provides a model for the cycle—in stylistic essentials, emotional dynamics, and characteristic mood. It is also a model in affirming the deeper social paradigm of traditional marriage—not always untroubled but always finally validated, and explicitly identified here as being part of its own cycle, with children growing up, marrying, and creating their own families. All of Minnelli's comedies cooperate with the paradigm, and if his oeuvre as a whole shows some tension between his sensibility and the warming validation which this film especially requires, he does give himself to it with ease and, one feels, genuine sincerity.

The simplicity of this modestly scaled black-and-white work is deceptive. A compact story of a conventional, reasonably balanced man's experience of his daughter's engagement and wedding set in upper middle-class suburbia may seem like a limited subject for this director. It's also a subject which seems to lean heavily on MGM's traditional stake in the received wisdom and values that Louis B. Mayer perceived to be the bedrock of Americana, even at a time when Dore Schary was beginning to displace Mayer as the studio's guiding force. Yet the film's prosaic essence, creatively treated by Minnelli and his collaborators, is ultimately an artistic strength, placed by and enhancing in turn sophisticated formal and psychological dynamics which encourage us to penetrate the commonplace sentiments on display and find within them unexpectedly affecting insights. Often, surface limitations are the stuff of which freedom is born. So it is with *Father of the Bride* .

The eponymous celebrant, Stanley Banks (Spencer Tracy), is, according to Minnelli, a casually fictionalized version of the source novel's author, Edward Streeter. The film preserves Banks' point of view; he narrates, choosing the moments presented and unifying them with his perspective. This first person narration and the subtle distancing it helps to create are essential features of the film, helping determine its emotional content as well as its form. The initial mood is rueful while also setting a humorous tone—Stan-

**215**

ley begins his reflections in the aftermath of the reception, addressing us directly. We safely assume everything is now happily resolved and that he himself has emerged emotionally intact from the experiences he will evoke for us. As the flashbacks begin to mingle with his words, a pleasing aesthetic strategy is revealed—that of counterpoint, with the spontaneity of the action as we perceive it contrasted to the immutability of events which Stanley emphasizes with caustic insistence. The privileged position he enjoys as commentator/protagonist also has an effect on the story material, basically a series of little episodes seamlessly linked because Stanley never digresses from his one subject—the wedding and related events that precede it.

Most vitally, the structure—presented as if it were Stanley's own creation—quickly identifies him as the character who will claim our empathy. As our self-elected guide into the film's world, he presents situations and characters, including himself, in a highly subjective light, but his point of view does not seem to be a distortion of what we see. The film's greater perspective may not be identical to his, but the difference is unlikely to give comfort either to those who would like to see the film's world ridiculed or those who would like to perceive it as a model of mainstream American life. The Stanley Banks who emerges in the course of the story is a limited man, representative in every way of the narrow world he describes. Even so, it is part of the film's chosen task to affirm him, to reveal an innate dignity that is preserved through every hazard and to celebrate an essential nature that is strong, resilient, and even imaginative.

All but a few minutes at the beginning and end of the film are contained within the narrated flashback, but those few minutes are crucially important. They are a frame which provides Minnelli an opportunity to inflect his sensibility through a purely omniscient *mise-en-scéne* . The film begins with the camera descending from a photograph of the newly wedded couple to the floor, where it sweeps through the debris of the reception in a slow, beautiful tracking shot until it comes to rest at Stanley's feet. An equally lovely boom shot that reverses the camera's direction—though it now moves through the air out onto the patio, away from Stanley and his wife Ellie (Joan Bennett) as they dance romantically inside—provides the complementary final image. Such shots had been characteristic of Minnelli from the beginning of his career, but their importance here—beyond any ineffable effect we might want to consider—is that they are untypical of the body of the film. When the camera does move, it does so functionally—even a virtuoso glide through the house and out onto the patio during the crowded reception corresponds to how Stanley himself describes the occasion. So the opening and closing shots are privileged, instilling feelings independent of those expressed in Stanley's autonomous narrative. Intriguingly, the difference is almost indiscernible, as Minnelli displays a becomingly subtle directorial empathy at one with his character's emotions.

Minnelli's style and vision had evolved through his early musicals and, just before *Father of the Bride*, in the darker *Madame Bovary* (1949)—here he extends himself further, not in the direction of more aggressive stylization but toward a contrasting aesthetic moderation. The decor is quietly perfect and no less expressive than in the best and most spectacular color films Minnelli made before, especially in the principal setting—the Banks family home. At the same time, an imaginative stylistic leap in the realm of mood is made—surprising for a Metro picture in this genre—in the cinematography of John Alton, who had made his reputation in classy film noir at Eagle-Lion with Anthony Mann and moved on to MGM with that director. Minnelli and Alton give *Father of the*

*Bride* a dark, low-key look, in striking contrast to what formerly had been the look of the studio's comedies. The resulting mood supports the quality of nightmare Stanley wants to imbue in his story, and becomes one of the stylistic principles which define the whole.

Stylishness, of course, is the least we would expect from Minnelli, so the film should not be commended too strongly just because it looks so good. I would never want to be too complacent, though, about my impulse to respond with affection to the visual texture of any Minnelli film. It leads one into that film's world as an eager and attentive viewer, and it is definitely a quality that keeps drawing one back to his films to discover more about them. So the film's physical world and its presentation in terms of composition, framing, lighting and decor is an apt starting point for our impressions.

Turning our attention first to decor—always vitally important to Minnelli—we receive an immediate, very powerful sense of how the Banks family experiences day-to-day living (the set decorator was Keogh Gleason, who would become, after this initial collaboration, one of Minnelli's most valued and frequently used associates). The Banks' suburban home, though not very expansive, is comfortable and tasteful; Stanley and Ellie appear to have put in a lot of cooperation in making it both attractive and harmonious with their lifestyle. There is a mirror just inside the doorway and an adjacent staircase that neatly links the upstairs with both the living room and the front door. French windows open onto a patio surrounded by a garden. Pictures, flowers, cameos and a piano adorn the downstairs, and, without cluttering the space, there seems to be a cozy chair of some sort in just about every corner of every room, so that a family member can fall into a relaxed attitude either alone or in a conversation. In an early scene, Stanley, Ellie and daughter Kay (Elizabeth Taylor) are shown eating by candlelight, and as it is not a special occasion, we assume such a soft atmosphere is constantly enjoyed. One truly feels that Stanley and Ellie have created the ambiance of the house together and are both at ease in it, which explains the understated but quite tangible sense that they are basically attuned to each other in a caring and loving way, despite the considerable tension between them that the storyline promotes.

Within their shared image of a family home, Stanley and Ellie grant freedom. So Kay's room is her own—a youthful femininity informs its every detail, as mementos of childhood coexist charmingly with manifestations of developing maturity. Consistent with Minnelli's previous portraits of young women, it is the room of a dreaming girl with a spirit of her own aching to express itself—although Kay is in most respects not as individualized as her predecessors in, for example, *Meet Me in St. Louis* (1944), *The Clock* (1945), or (no less instructive a comparison) *Madame Bovary*, where the adolescent Emma of the early scenes seems so like her Minnellian sisters. One touch that Flaubert's heroine as interpreted by Minnelli would have loved is daringly imaginative in the overall context of the Banks home. On the morning of the wedding, Stanley walks into Kay's room and, for the first time, we see a large three-paneled mirror in which Kay—who stands at the right in the composition in her wedding dress—stares at her multiple reflections. The effect is visually breathtaking and almost surreal—the mirror had not been revealed in previous scenes set in the room—yet we are so convinced by now of the reality of this family's life that this momentary heightening of that reality registers convincingly.

Kay's two younger brothers, Ben (Tom Irish) and Tommy (Rusty Tamblyn) have minimal significance in the film, so Minnelli never even shows us their rooms. On the other hand, Stanley and Ellie's room is more important than Kay's. In contrast to the profuse decor downstairs, this bedroom is distinguished most by space and a relaxed feeling. Regrettably, the Production Code makes it impossible to know if they would, at this point in their lives, have the separate beds shown, but the room still suggests warmth and intimacy.

On the whole, the Banks house contrasts to other significant domestic settings in Minnelli. In comparison to the Reynolds house in *Tea and Sympathy* (1956), for example, it reflects an accord between husband and wife that is disturbingly absent in the relationship between Bill and Laura (Leif Erickson and Deborah Kerr), even though one feels that Laura has knocked herself out to create the decor for a home she and Bill could both be happy in. The Hunnicutt house in *Home from the Hill* (1960) offers a different but related comparison; again, it possesses a more startling beauty in many of its details than the Banks house, but cross purposes between family members are everywhere evident, so much so that each room seems to have its own psychological purpose in helping to maintain conflicts and neuroses. And yet, Minnelli never seems to be trying to promote the decor of *Father of the Bride*, or the kind of world it suggests, as emblematic of fulfillment. Without evoking the sadness and sense of failed relationships that the cited decors of *Tea and Sympathy* and *Home from the Hill* do, the *Father of the Bride* interiors do suggest considerable emotional limitations in both the characters and their world. It is not so much embrace of conventionality and attachment to stolid routine that inhibits them, but complacency and self-imposed repressions which are too comfortably worn. Comparison with one other contrasting Minnelli decor—this time a more positive example—will illuminate further how the real virtues of this world are undermined by its stuntedness.

The Smith house in *Meet Me in St. Louis* is also fixed in decor, stable in ambiance, made warm and comfortable by a husband and wife and other family members who enjoy sharing it. But unlike the Banks home, this turn-of-the-century home that dominates the earlier film seems to encourage fluency of emotion. Here husband and wife can drift to the piano while grandfather and children happily gather in the background to silently participate in a moment that is both intimate for the couple and communal for the family, and here the little internal dramas of the characters may be freely played out. The Smith house is, simply, more stimulating than the Banks house, even if both seem designed to affirm a certain style of family life. Partly because *Meet Me in St. Louis* is set in the past, and also because both the period and use of color encourage a certain kind of rich detail and atmospheric vibrancy that a comparable contemporary setting could only achieve if it were false to its time and place, the Smith house is a dream house; and we, too, yearn to live there.

Even more crucially, in the six years that separated the making of the earlier film and *Father of the Bride*, Minnelli evolved in his interests. Perfect material reality—even that of an idealized past—no longer has a claim on him. The point is worth stressing because the two films are often thought of as being more similar than they are. Even the purpose behind idealization of characters, present in both works—*Father of the Bride* actively asserts this idealization only in images of the wedding itself, though very pointedly, while *Meet Me in St. Louis* engages in it constantly but very subtly—is no longer the same.

Still the Banks home is basically a happy one. But if Stanley always remains essentially at ease within it, he nevertheless becomes increasingly alienated and helpless as it is transformed by casually malevolent forces. Not only does he have to struggle to maintain authority in the face of the sometimes complementary and sometimes diverging intensities of wife and daughter, but he is also subject to petty humiliations inflicted by friends, relatives, and strangers alike. These pressures—and corresponding psychological ones—

*One man's family:* Father of the Bride.

are the key to understanding why a benign decor is subject to the darkening mood imparted not only by lighting but also by staging and framing.

The camera is sympathetic to Stanley's presentation of the narrative, as is Minnelli's handling of dynamic action within the frame. Master shots dominate, and Stanley usually appears thrown into the middle of a scene, powerless to affect its flow. Although he establishes himself at the outset in a long-held close-up, during which he carefully solicits our sympathy for his point of view prior to the flashback, he rarely receives a close-up as the subsequent narrative unfolds (the close-ups of him that do come to mind most quickly are in the "idealizing" wedding sequence). When a figure is singled out for intimate treatment by the camera, it is usually someone else, as with Kay—lingered on in entranced close-up as she sits dreamy-eyed, slowly eating her ice cream—during the early dinner table scene that introduces her. At other times, a character may dominate simply through force of personality, like the imperious caterer (Leo G. Carroll), even when the compositional principle for the scene is an interplay of characters in master shots.

Characteristic scenes of *Father of the Bride* display three persistent visual attributes, each with its own purpose. The imaginative contrasts in the lighting, which call attention to black or shadowy areas of the compositions, are a steady reminder that all events are filtered through Stanley's highly subjective point of view. Even when his perceptions seem bemused or dispassionate, the mood creates a constant empathy with his deeper emotions and aligns our response to the comic spectacle with his experience of it. On the other hand, the camera's role in illustrating events may seem humble by comparison. As noted, except for the opening and closing shots, movements of the camera are both purely functional and kept to a minimum. Static frames do not, of course, preclude considerable animation within the frame—people bustle here as always in Minnelli. Often, the longer takes are those involving an elaborate orchestration of people, as one would expect from him. Still, a typical scene is broken into shots in a way that will most fluently propel the narrative; Minnelli's long-take tendencies are here contained within an approach at one with classical models. Intriguingly, though, this simple manner also corresponds to Stanley's articulation of the narrative; he is, after all, a straightforward no-nonsense kind of guy—or at least likes to present himself as one.

The third pervasive visual strategy—a distinction of this particular Minnelli film—provides counterpoint. A perspective outside of Stanley's is subtly inflected through moderately high camera angles, just a little above eye level but enough to suggest an omniscient view in tension with the dominant subjective tone. These angles frame scenes filmed in deep focus with different planes of action and are especially noticeable in scenes that best convey both the subject and the flavor of the film, like the dismantling and refashioning of the house for the overcrowded reception. Here, Stanley is locked helplessly to a phone in the foreground while Minnelli stages the background action—with his usual exhilarating verve—as an ever wilder whirl of people and objects; but the camera is perched up and away from Stanley so that he seems a helpless, undynamic figure frozen in the middle plane of an extremely long-held shot. Such scenes convey the sense that the impending wedding is being guided by its own acclerating momentum, which Stanley can never quite catch up to and control. To Stanley, such a situation may appear to have a steadily intensifying nightmarishness about it, but the more distanced and objective eye of the camera tempers that view by seeing all the action and everyone's behavior—including Stanley's—as natural and inevitable. The film's calmer perspective through the remembered events preserves in Stanley the equilibrium he fears losing.

Imperiled equilibrium, a leading motif of Minnelli films of all kinds, is especially conspicuous in his comedies. Much of the manic energy and contrasting melancholy which distinguishes them is attributable to its presence in the characters. While comic types can be very effective in Minnelli's hands—commonly as aggravating forces in the action—they are often not as funny as the "normal" characters, who, ruffled by matter-of-fact malevolence and disingenuous outrageousness, are pushed into spontaneous responses and behavior which are typically hilarious. *Father of the Bride* is most representative in this respect, so much that it impresses me as relatively less sophisticated than *The Long, Long Trailer* or *The Reluctant Debutante*, where the primary aggravating forces—the respective heroines—are also among the "normal" characters struggling against the spectre of disequilibrium. Here, Stanley stands alone as the voice of reason. Without exaggerating any other character, however peripheral, into a grotesque, or portraying himself as aloof, he sees virtually everyone and everything outside of himself as, at one point or another, the manifestation of unleashed furies in a world gone temporarily insensate.

And yet, in retrospect, he is willing to be indulgent of such a world, for as the opening shot stabilizes—with Stanley fully lit against a nearly black background—he massages one of his feet and smiles sheepishly before gazing candidly at us to state, simply, "I would like to say a few words about weddings." Already the disarray that has preceded his appearance, his sore feet, and the dark atmosphere in which he is addressing us are enough, juxtaposed to his directness and laid-back authority, to raise a chuckle. The method of the film is exposed; at every turn, laughter is induced because Stanley, so in earnest, does not invite it.

As the flashback begins, we are now in an expectant mood, so ready to laugh at the punch line to this introduction that we might not notice that humor is at first subordinated to a detailed observation of the interaction of Stanley, Ellie and Kay at the dinner table and the establishing of a wonderfully palpable, immediate reality. It is characteristic of Minnelli to observe such things, for it is out of atmosphere and behavioral nuance that comedy, when it surfaces, flows most comfortably and convincingly. Minnelli here appreciates the balance between intimacy and hesitancy among the three characters made possible by Frances Goodrich and Albert Hackett's careful writing. His direction plays up pregnant pauses, retreats into introversion and outbursts of emotion as, with sudden casualness, Kay informs her parents that she is going to marry Buckley Dunstan.

While always remaining a discreet study of father, mother and daughter that intimates much about their subsequent behavior, this fairly lengthy sequence is laced with some delightful moments which benefit from Minnelli's refusal to strain for a laugh. An awkward lull in the conversation allows Stanley to recall, in a series of concise images, Kay's various suitors, whom he describes for our benefit in his accompanying narration while trying to remember which one of them Buckley is. Minnelli clearly enjoyed creating these vignettes because they underscore his ideas about personal perception, and he understands no exaggeration is necessary to provoke an amused response because all of the humor is in Stanley's sarcastic simplifications. Each of the suitors looks affable enough—even Carleton Carpenter as a jitterbug enthusiast, dancing manically into the foreground of his shot, looks like he would be fun to be around. Intriguingly, a handsome and relaxed Buckley (Don Taylor), casually introduced in the midst of the other vignettes, seems like the most logical boyfriend for Kay even though Stanley reacts to the thought of him with especially acute distaste; we suspect that Stanley intuitively knows he is the fiancé. How gracefully and charmingly the film has introduced the central dramatic issue underlying the story—Stanley's difficult adjustment to being displaced as the man in his daughter's life.

A second source of humor is directly related to the first, for the vignettes set off in Stanley uncontrollable emotions that he tries to cloak in reasonableness as he undermines his daughter's intention to marry by treating it as a caprice to which she has given no serious thought. Sensitive to her father, Kay reacts to the projection of his own fears and displays the emotionalism that *he* is repressing. Like the vignettes of the boyfriends, her sudden hysteria may have been Minnelli's idea or may reflect his general influence on the script, but whatever the inspiration, the precise handling of the idea is an especially good demonstration of how the director perceives behavior to be, in such moments, the result of an interplay between outwardly expressed emotion and imaginative heightening of that emotion through abruptly unbridled inner anxiety. Here, Kay forcibly reminds us of Margaret O'Brien's Tootie in *Meet Me in St. Louis*, as she becomes suddenly childlike and defends her choice of man with irrelevant assertions that become more ridiculous as her intensity escalates. "I wouldn't care if we had to live in the gutter!" she finally exclaims, in a line that charmingly evokes some of Tootie's dramatic declarations.

The film's first big laugh derives directly from the moments already touched upon and what they have suggested about the psychological dynamics between father and daughter—and mother, too, for Ellie has already stepped into the role of mediator. Buckley comes to pick up Kay, while Stanley surreptitiously watches his arrival from the window and winces in recognition. A few idle pleasantries are exchanged among the four characters near the doorway, but then, as Buckley and Kay are about to leave, Stanley suggests she take a coat. She says that she doesn't need it and he makes the same suggestion more vigorously. Her assertion that she will not take the coat also becomes more intense. Suddenly, Buckley quietly says, "I think you should take it," and, her voice softening, she turns toward him and responds, adoringly, "You do?" There is real magic in the humor of this moment because, with perfect unexpectedness, the psychological issues that were amusingly repressed earlier have suddenly flown into the open in a moment of innocent unguardedness. The way in which Minnelli gives the moment maximum effectiveness is a superb example of his skill. The exchange is filmed in a long take of the group, with Buckley and Kay in the background facing the camera and Ellie and Stanley in the foreground but partly turned away from us (although this simplifies the action—not one of the four is completely still). Already, this is sound directorial style for not making any element of the scene too emphatic, but the most brilliant touch is in an extra moment's wait after Kay's "You do?" before the inevitable reverse shot that will reveal Stanley's reaction. Anticipating his expression before we see it, we are already laughing when the cut is finally made; and Stanley's voiceover acknowledgement that in this moment he knew he had been displaced by another man becomes amusingly redundant.

Classical editing demands the reaction shot of Stanley as surely as does Spencer Tracy's ability to register with marvelous effectiveness the character's response; but the preparatory long take and offbeat placing of the cut are personal touches, while the reaction shot is also richer and funnier than it might be in other hands because Minnelli includes Ellie in it. Of course, it all happens quickly and without discernible effort, but that should not obscure how familiar cinematic language can be revitalized by distinctive treatment. The lighthanded precision of this particular effect, wedded to the leisurely buildup of the dinner table sequence, also neatly establishes the kind of comedy this will be—a comedy of human behavior propelled by credible emotional and psychological pressures. Neither clever lines nor broad gags are absent, but both are secondary to the steadily captivating flow of humor generated by interplay among the characters.

This first evening of Kay's still unofficial, if inescapably real, engagement ends with another amusing scene. As Stanley and Ellie prepare to sleep, he is still understandably under intense emotional pressure, while Ellie, cool and at ease about the prospect of her daughter's marriage, has been of no help; on the contrary, her attitude has made him even more alone in his feelings. So Stanley takes it out on his wife in the imagined portrait of Buckley he shares with her, ever more harrowing in its details as he begins to savor his powers of invention ("Those are the ones . . . those soft-spoken fellows who look you right in the eye and would put a bullet in the back of her neck and never turn a hair . . . "). This release of anxiety has exactly the desired effect: he goes right to sleep, while Ellie lies awake, suddenly in terror that his speculations might all be true.

I enjoy this scene. It so aptly reflects the rising inner fears that Stanley has held in check throughout a challenging evening, while intimating that he prefers to cope with his unsettled feelings by behaving foolishly rather than by hurting or undermining Kay or openly trying to humiliate Buckley. Because he can betray, in whatever convoluted ways, his anxieties, his adjustment has already begun. Even so, I find the next few sequences more excruciating than funny for all their cleverness of observation: Stanley's planned meeting with Buckley to discuss the other's financial prospects, and Stanley and Ellie's visit to his parents, Herbert (Moroni Olsen) and Doris (Billie Burke)—with Stanley alone taking advantage of the relaxing of formality to overindulge in alcohol. These scenes contribute to Stanley's painful psychological evolution prior to the engagement party—in which he is further frustrated by being trapped in the kitchen making drinks—but they also create a sense of what is most oppressive in the middle-class world the characters share. All the talk of money and standards of material security and of etiquette and acceptable lifestyles uncomfortably highlights narrower attitudes than we are accustomed to seeing in a Minnelli film, which might not be a defect of the film itself except that the director seems surprisingly indulgent and uncritical of these attitudes.

Much more endearing are all the ensuing sequences, in which plans take shape for the ever more elaborate and expensive wedding and reception, and the climactic day becomes an appealing blend of comic frenzy reaching apotheosis (the transformation of the house and the reception) and delicate sentiment (the wedding itself). There is the rushed rainy day rehearsal, with Melville Cooper as a church functionary who manically puts everyone through their paces with the confusing cheerfulness of some obscure Cordova*; the pre-nuptial stress of Kay and Buckley which erupts in an inevitable rift, followed by the just as inevitable reconciliation, in which Stanley, who has attempted to act as sober mediator, finds himself suddenly forgotten and walks up the staircase behind the emotionally reunited couple with a memorable air of bemused resignation; the devastating encounters with the caterer—Leo G. Carroll has never been at once so haughty and patronizing, yet so impeccably, chillingly courteous, as in this role; the sight of Stanley uncomfortably corseted into his old cutaway for several scenes—one of the most hilarious things in the movie as played by Tracy, and with a great payoff when the coat finally rips under the caterer's gaze as Stanley tries to yank open the door to the patio; the contrasting gravity of the mid-film nocturnal colloquy between Stanley and Ellie—solemn, reflective, moodily lit and composed before those same patio doors; and, also in counterpoint, the wedding itself—noticeably attenuated in relation to other sequences though this is one of the qualities which makes it so satisfying a resolution of all the earlier tensions—with its dignity, calm, and lovely, lingering compositions. And there is the reception, with Stanley once more a frustrated bit player—when he goes to check on how the champagne is holding out, a surly waiter, in one of those wonderful moments Minnelli handles with such flair because of his liking for extras, reduces him to mute humility with a scornful "OK, OK, mister . . . don't worry, you'll get yours."

There is also, famously, a dream sequence. It is the night before the wedding, and the dream begins with a close-up of Stanley's frightened open eyes over a church scene. Stanley dreams he is is late, and as he tries to hurry down the aisle, his shoes stick to a gelatinous floor that begins to alternately bounce and sink. Desperately, he flails at air as the bridal couple, Ellie, and the entire gathering watch in horror. Finally, lurching helplessly forward in Kay's direction, he loses his pants. There is a close-up of Ellie, her face a mask of fury, and a shot of Kay screaming and burying her face on Buckley's chest beneath the eerie light of the church window. Stanley wakes up, startled and momentarily unsettled.

---

\* See the Minnelli musical *The Band Wagon* (1953).

*The Wedding Party: Joan Bennett, Elizabeth Taylor, Spencer Tracy, with Melville Cooper
(left) as "some obscure Cordova."*

Though it runs less than a minute, Stanley's literal nightmare is invariably singled out
as an inspiration directly attributable to Minnelli's directorial presence. Maybe so, but
whether or not he introduced it into the film is less important than the extent of its actual
artistic merit. For me, the dream is funny but facile. Apart from its economical treatment
and Alton's subtly eerie lighting, it boasts a freshness that one would not expect in such a
sequence—distortions of human figures are not too pronounced, space is just weird
enough, and the floor retains the black-and-white checkerboard design of the one in the
actual church. The dream can claim a pleasing unpretentiousness because of its coupling
of psychological acuity with bracing physical comedy, making the more elaborate and
solemn dream sequences of many films seem heavy-handed by comparison. However,
against its inventiveness, there is its relative obviousness, as opposed to all of the sequences
that truly distinguish the film—scenes in which the interplay of characters is orchestrated
within realistic settings and may deceptively seem prosaic. In those more subtle scenes, a
surehanded approach projects the shifting emotions of a number of characters, often
within a single shot, so that nuances of character overlap and float quickly and almost
imperceptibly into the texture of the whole. Such a style is a good foundation for wonderfully rich sequences that are brisk and funny without being shallow. That's directing.

None of Minnelli's comedies after *Father of the Bride* has a dream sequence, nor, for that matter, do any of his other subsequent films. Instead, the experiences of his characters may resemble dream states and serve similar purposes to dreams, but their reality is more complex. They are not dreams but daydreams, hallucinations, reveries and visions—given special potency because the director makes such a point of the open-eyed gazes that bring them into immediate waking experience. The "prosaic" comedies become, in fact, especially good examples of Minnelli's gift for creating fanciful atmosphere with an increasingly supple inventiveness. So this dream sequence is, in the larger scheme of things, hardly one of his major artistic triumphs.

And yet, one can understand the reason for it. The dream is the single overt manifestation of Stanley's sexual feelings about Kay. But so essentially innocent are these feelings that Stanley can perceive them only in his unconscious, and only when events leading to the wedding have pushed them near the surface—for by the next day, his adjustment must, and will, be complete. Just as he is honest and open as far as his understanding allows elsewhere, he is here, too. He courageously and unselfconsciously shares the dream with us and tacitly allows our interpretation of it, and this is the only time he becomes a buffoon. Stanley has imagination, but he is less free within it than other Minnelli characters, so for us to understand him fully, he must have this dream.

It should also be noted that this scene is stylistically balanced by the one that immediately follows, in which Stanley and Kay meet in the kitchen and talk over a glass of milk in a simple two-shot. She also is unable to sleep and has her own anxieties; Stanley calms himself by reassuring her. It's a nice little scene, but the fact that it is less interesting than the parallel father–daughter milk-drinking conversation in *The Reluctant Debutante* which is modeled on it illuminates further relative limitations in *Father of the Bride* .

For Kay—like everyone else apart from Stanley—is not a fully fleshed–out character. She is customarily a poised and lovely young lady while at other times girlishly overemotional in her behavior—Kay has a personality, but it is not explored. Ellie is necessarily developed with only a hint of dimension so that she can function reasonably sympathetically; her obsessive drive in planning the wedding is, after all, one of the antagonistic elements which undermines Stanley's equilibrium, though mother—like daughter and father—will finally be thrown into an idealizing light. Other characters invite even less scrutiny, for they tend to be expertly realized types (even so crucial a figure as Buckley readily fits this description) who contribute gracefully to the action while bringing nothing very significant to the work's emotional resonances. The heart and soul of *Father of the Bride* is Stanley—his feelings, his experiences and his perceptions.

Spencer Tracy's performance is, fortunately, the film's single greatest asset. He gets laughs and registers nuances even beyond those in the script or those encouraged by Minnelli's direction, but it should be emphasized that this was always anticipated by Minnelli and producer Pandro S. Berman; contrary to Schary, who planned to cast Jack Benny, they believed the film would only be effective with an actor skilled in drama, and Tracy was their first choice. Tracy's earnest, down-to-earth playing is what makes all of the humor work, and, too, what brings to the often giddy action the overriding sense of a compassionate appreciation of a man's emotions. And he is best when simple, never more than in the moment at the wedding when he stands quietly watching, as his voiceover begins "Who giveth this woman . . . this woman . . ." and ends " . . . something inside me began to hurt." The truth of the character is always at his command, and his performance contributes to Minnelli's rapid evolution during this phase of his career by making the director comfortable, for the first time, with a subject revolving solely around a male protagonist; after this film, increasingly diverse types, both male and female, will be the emotional centers of Minnelli's expanding world. And in his conviction that an essentially real personality is ideal for comedy, Minnelli is suggesting one of the defining attitudes of his later work: nightmarish experience induced by imperiled equilibrium may be a good theme on which to compose a comic/dramatic universe, but behavioral believability must be the keynote.

The theme of imperiled equilibrium does recur in each of Minnelli's comedies, and commonly, the obsession of at least one character is a driving force. Characters generally become more whimsical and unpredictable after the earliest two films, but the culminating work, *The Courtship of Eddie's Father*, while not reversing this tendency, is even more down-to-earth in its emotional content than *Father of the Bride*. From film to film, the promotion of empathy through a subjective point of view is enriched by steadily more complex approaches: in the sequel *Father's Little Dividend*, Stanley again narrates, though to different effect; in *The Long, Long Trailer*, about a honeymooning couple (Desi Arnaz and Lucille Ball), the husband once more tells the story, but this time his obsessive wife is the true protagonist and elicits sympathy in counterpoint to his "voice of reason" perspective without undermining the empathy he also claims; in *Designing Woman*, again about newlyweds (Gregory Peck and Lauren Bacall), there is a multiple perspective, with husband, wife and three other characters taking turns in the narration, each hilariously contradicting the subjectivity of each of the others; in *The Reluctant Debutante*, narration is dropped yet the subtly projected emotional content that floats beneath the surface is at times more piercing than ever; and in *The Courtship of Eddie's Father*, which again has no narrator, the child Eddie (Ronny Howard) brings a more intense subjectivity into the film than any of the earlier narrators, while not reserving an exclusive claim on our empathy—other characters have an equal emotional resonance, and Eddie is not even present in a number of key dramatic moments.

Stylistically, all of the comedies tend to follow *Father of the Bride* in their relative simplicity. Camerawork tends to be functional, decor and costumes are expressive without being ostentatious, and the emphasis is on efficiently staged character interplay—though *The Reluctant Debutante* is one of the most thorough instances of Minnelli's "choreographic" staging. Unlike the two *Father* films, the others have bright surfaces and demonstrate Minnelli's mastery of color, while *Father of the Bride*'s distinctive deep focus cinematography and moderately high angle framing are generally displaced by other visual strategies.

Love, sex, marriage and family were, of course, familiar elements in Minnelli's work before the cycle of comedies—and are strongly treated in other of his films throughout his career.* But *Meet Me in St. Louis* and *The Clock*, which might be thought of as anticipating the cycle, are both different kinds of films—and not just because the first is a musical and the second, exclusively *about* courtship and marriage, is graver in tone and more deli-

---

* Despite stylistic and thematic affinities, *Goodbye, Charlie* (1964) lies outside the cycle, for Minnelli is here treating (with characteristic sympathy) an essentially different subject— repressed homosexual attraction in a male friendship. George (Tony Curtis) is only able to come to terms with the relationship and make peace with it when Charlie (Henry Madden) temporarily comes back from the dead—as a woman (Debbie Reynolds).

*Ellie and Stanley:* Father of the Bride.

cately articulated than the comedies. In these two works, Minnelli projects an idealization of love, sex, marriage and family which, however sophisticated, is a world away from the challenging, even disturbing realities which propel the comedies with such hilarious force. For the comedies as much as the melodramas are wrestling with the difficulty of making domestic realities—heterosexual love, relationships between husbands and wives and with children—correspond to our dream of what we want them to be. Whether in preparation for a wedding, on a honeymoon, even during a season of debutante balls, people—even those who love each other—exert profound pressures on each other; the heterosexual ideal is easy to hold but hard to live out. Minnelli will finally be able to assert, without any idealizing at all and so with especially poignant effect, that it *is* possible.

This happens in *The Courtship of Eddie's Father*, and it is fascinating to see how the domestic bliss that is at last intimated is notably hard-won, for the couple (Glenn Ford and Shirley Jones) must transcend an unusual problem and are only able to do so thanks to a child's influence. The woman was the best friend of the man's late wife, and the possibility that they were always attracted to each other (very likely, given our immediate sense of the chemistry between them) makes them antagonistic in the face of their natural impulses. They must learn to see clearly and bring to rest their understandable guilt before they can find the best and truest expressions of themselves within the present. The film is further enriched by a little subplot about insecurity, with Stella Stevens as a lovely and talented young woman amusingly bereft of even a semblance of confidence. Her story is integrated with the most artful casualness but completes with a maximum of feeling Minnelli's vision of the positive sense of self that must be nurtured for individuals to succeed in relationships, for insecurity, too, had always been a major undermining force in the courtship and marriage rituals described by his films. With the artistic affirmation of domestic fulfillment—always at least hoped for and given a sense of value in the earlier comedies—the cycle ends.

The special qualities that mark Minnelli's musicals and melodramas and give them their intensity are, as noted, scaled down in the comedies, and they may seem humbler and less passionate. And yet, Minnelli's evolution is most palpable in them. Exploring the relationship between his particular obsessions about personal reality and essential life events like marrying and creating a family and an ordered life, he deepens. So while other of his films made in between these comedies jump out vigorously to claim our first attention, these are the films that move his body of work toward a grace note—in *The Courtship of Eddie's Father* —which affirms both emotional health and the humanistic maturity that Minnelli attains.

So in the prosaic sentiments of *Father of the Bride*, a profound artistic impulse is born. It may be argued that from *The Long, Long Trailer* to *The Courtship of Eddie's Father*, the later comedies get progressively richer and more interesting. Yet in a consistently popular group of films, *Father of the Bride* remains to this day the most popular. Understanding its enduring appeal cannot help but attune us to the deeper feelings that are so gently evoked. That appeal lies in the film's recognition of the complex and contradictory emotions generated by any wedding, and its perceptiveness is not diluted by dated specifics of time and place and prevailing cultural values.

My own marriage helped me to see how well the film captures pre-marital stress. And although my perspective was that of the bridegroom—a very marginal one in the film—it suggested to me that all participants in a wedding who have a meaningful relationship to either the bride or groom or both may be experiencing a wrenching, though perhaps subtle, emotional change. It certainly takes no exceptional understanding to imagine how the long held, deeply charged relationship of a father and daughter would be affected by the daughter's marriage. My wife's father had died many years before we ever met, yet on our wedding day, her feelings of closeness to him were never stronger; as much as Stanley here, he was present, because the reality of father-daughter interplay was present. Later, when we watched *Father of the Bride* together, my wife was amused to inform me that when he was alive, her father told her that when she was ready to be married, he would give her money to elope. Perhaps he got this idea from the film, for Stanley, once the wedding plans start to escalate, makes exactly that proposition to Kay. There is little doubt that the film impressed fathers as much as daughters, that it offered role models to each for the moment of the daughter's marriage, and that it presented—in the idealized beauty of the ceremony—a vision of marriage equal to that of the happiest daydreams.

Perhaps the reality in 1950 was more complex in every way; the film even suggests, in its discerning treatment of the repressions and stifling conformity that are a part of the characters' lives, that it was. There has surely been more divorce between couples wed at that time than fulfillment. No doubt some viewers might like to condemn the film for encouraging unreal expectations. But is their consciousness any more evolved than that of the characters, let alone the filmmakers? For good reason, our later perspectives cannot dispel the sense that the film is validating something genuine—not only the hopefulness with which marriage deserves to be regarded, but also the leap of consciousness the event makes possible for the parent who is at once truly responsible and truly aware of his or her most challenging feelings.

So adept at projecting the pretty illusion, Minnelli also sees and cares for the truth within it. And the truth of being an ideal father to a daughter is to manifest total love and appreciation for the daughter's own spirit, her beauty, her sexuality, her selfhood. It is, ironically, this love and appreciation that will enable her to properly choose her mate and so leave the father to the heartbreak of his loss, for he can never ask for the same kind of love and appreciation in return. *Father of the Bride* is a model for understanding this. Perhaps that is why it is warm and generous in its inflections, rather than a bleak portrait of a naively malevolent culture. Stanley may in many moments look foolish as he goes through his wrenching but necessary adjustment, but he comes through it with commendable grace. Above all, this is because Minnelli personally appreciates his emotions and makes certain they are respected. The man we see at the end may be sad and subdued but he is also manifesting hard-won self-knowledge and the strength and wisdom to let life evolve.

That brings us back to Ellie—who has been somewhat mysterious to us—and that moonlit dance that so touchingly concludes the film. For if the father must suffer and heal himself privately so that his daughter can enter upon her marriage freely and happily, then surely this creates in the mother a corresponding pressure, for she must witness in silence this giving up of the other woman in his life at the same time that her own changing role as a woman is presenting her with a personal challenge—at the brink of marriage, her daughter now projects her own image of her youthful self and has innocently stolen her youthful dreams. Surely these related challenges explain the obsessiveness with which she is driven to magnify the event, so that it overwhelms the more difficult private feelings of the participants; in Ellie's case, I am certain they explain her behavior much more than her ruefulness over not having had a church wedding of her own when she and Stanley were married. In her way, she, too, is graceful under pressure. The dance is an extraordinarily tender acknowledgement by both Stanley and Ellie of the melancholy passages of each through an emotionally challenging period, and a gesture of renewed harmony between them. It is as much a moment of consolation as of romance. And there is nothing wrong with that. Consoling of one's partner, no matter what the nature of the sorrow, is also part of marriage. In the intimacy of this consolation, shadows lift and sweetness returns.

# Film Favorites:
# *Bells Are Ringing*

## Raymond Durgnat (1973)

Alongside the generally accepted trio of classic post-war musicals—*On the Town*, *Singin' in the Rain*, *The Band Wagon* —I've long wanted to range a fourth: *Give a Girl a Break*. Between these and honorable third-line material like *The Pirate*, *Summer Holiday*, *Funny Face* and *Kiss Me Kate* I'd place some which grapple, more or less ruefully, with some post-war disillusionments: *It's Always Fair Weather*, maybe *The Girl Most Likely*, *Three for the Show* and *The Girl Can't Help It*, and certainly *Bells Are Ringing* (if one classes it as a musical rather than as a comedy with musical numbers).

My record-sleeve summarizes the plot thus: "Ella Peterson (Judy Holliday) has never met Jeff Moss (Dean Martin) but has fallen in love with him while handling his calls at Susanswerphone, a telephone answering service which she runs with her cousin, Sue." The partners personify the alternative attitudes which are positive and negative poles of the film's morality. Ella is always sympathizing with the unseen clients for whom she takes and leaves messages. Sometimes, not content with worrying, she quits her switchboard to do what she can to help. Sue, older and more wearied, reproaches her for worrying, for getting involved.

Ella has come more recently from a stifling small town, and despite her need to escape its stifling pretension (she worked for "The Bonjour Tristesse Brassiere Company"), she has brought the small-town, neighborly, busybody spirit with her into the big impersonal city, where every contact with other people is in the style of a quick telephone message. The contrast is pointed in the scene where Ella and Jeff, standing on the edge of the sidewalk waiting for the crossing signal, turn to a big scowling stranger beside them and say: "Hello." "Whaddya say?" he bellows, and when they repeat "Hello" he breaks into a smile: "No one's said hello to me for fifteen years—Hello!" A chain-reaction of "Hellos" commences.

Another type of communication between strangers underlies Ella's blind date, at an expensive restaurant, where her gaucherie nips romance in the bud. The antithesis of impersonality and (hopeful) intimacy implicit in the idea of a blind date underlies the film's title (telephone bells, wedding bells)—even the name of the answering service. For Susanswerphone recalls sousaphone, and a sousaphone recalls the old-fangled solidarity of brass bands, union chapters and workingman ethnic groups. The brass band as symbol of unity is the theme of *Stars and Stripes Forever* and *The Music Man*—the "76 trombones" being close relatives, acoustically, of the sousaphone. In Dick Lester's *Petulia* it is either (I can't remember) a sousaphone or a tuba—musically similar instruments—which Julie Christie brings back from one of her democratic forays. And it's a tuba which Gary Cooper's Mr. Deeds plays on the train taking him from his small town to New York.

These variations on the theme of sound and solidarity lead into innumerable aspects of the communications comedy. At first the cops seem to be crooks setting up a protection racket (notably the assistant who's a classic pug-ugly type, a sort of pudgy Jack

**230**

*Telephony suggests telepathy: Judy Holliday, with Jean Stapledon, behind the switchboard in*
Bells Are Ringing, *directed by Vincente Minnelli.*

Palance). Mistaken identities. But when they turn out to be law and order that's just as
bad. For they whip out a tape recorder and play back Ella's half of a telephone conversation, making the answerphone service sound like a call-girl agency. Thus the cops set up
two sets of ambiguity: of clothes, and of words. The former is taken up in the Method
actor's impersonation of a top-hat-and-coat-tails-type swell. The latter is a constant
theme, climaxing when Jeff, the writer with the emotional block, settles for the crudest
and most desperately random type of communication there is. Standing in the middle of
streets chosen at random, he bawls "Melisande Scott," which he thinks is the name of
the girl he loves, although it isn't, because she gave him the wrong name out of panic or
out of shyness—these emotions being the hang-ups which snag any conceivable communications system.

    Telephony suggests telepathy. When Ella goes to visit Jeff for the first time, it just so
happens that he wants coffee and a sandwich to help him kick his alcohol habit, and it
just so happens that she's got both in her bag. A nice piece of womanly white-magic, and
all rationally explained because it's her own lunch, which she daren't admit, partly

because she's pretending to be chic Melisande. Communication by feeding—the mother, the housewife—in a placidly unpointed antithesis to the swish blind-date dinner. To explain how she can anticipate Jeff's wishes, Ella has to pretend to be telepathic and psychic, which is the ideal type of communication (indeed, frighteningly so). And telepathy finds its converse in—is it a duet, is it a pair of synchronized solos, and what's the difference?—"Better Than A Dream," dreaming and telepathy being a natural pair of intrapsychic opposites.

A conspicuous form of communication is art, and the film abounds in creative artists of one kind or another. Jeff can't write for drinking. In fact he drinks so deep that he can't even communicate with himself—he has to leave rude notes to himself via Susan-swerphone. Another client, Otto, pretends to be selling classical music to the masses—Titanic Records—but in fact he's an illegal off-track bookie, using classical music titles as a code ("Humperdinck is Hollywood"). Another artist is the dentist who daydreams about making the hit parade and composes little melodies to himself on his airhose. And the embittered Method actor breaks into the big time when he finally consents to stop starving for his art and instead uses his art to get some food (he pretends to be a Fred Astaire type). Matching the cops' impersonation—only this is repersonalization.

All these artists are on their inspirational uppers, and it's Ella who brings them new inspiration, simply by putting them in touch with one another. She describes the dentist to the playwright, who puts him in his play, where he'll be played by the Method actor. The intrigue builds up into an intriguing meeting—face-to-face—between the actor, the author and the living original—such a meeting might well be awkward. Remember Old Joshua, in Prévert's *Les Enfants du Paradis*, savagely reviling Baptiste for "stealing his identity" by putting him in his play? And certainly any playwright will recall all the legal dangers involved in unintentionally describing someone. The dentist might well feel edgy at being studied by the actor. But their sensible symbiosis—and commensalism, over a meal or a drink—occurs in a setting offering further reflections on the theme of art/entertainment encountering reality. They're in a bunny club where chorus girls come down off the stage and start drawing mustaches on our heroes' faces—the three faces of one character. But our friends take no notice of all these fake intimacies, this pseudo-happening; they just carry on talking as if the bunnies weren't there. The name of the number the bunnies are singing is "The Midas Touch"—Midas being the patron saint of the profit motive, and no friend of natural togetherness.

Themes of art and acting interweave with themes of mistaken identity and misdirected communication. Cops and actors are only two groups of impersonators. First Jeff assumes that Ella is a white-haired old lady. Then she pretends to be Melisande Scott, the sophisticate, not realizing that he isn't fooled and likes her as she is. Sue thinks Otto is a missionary of cultural sweetness-and-light-musical communion for the masses. And Ella plays as many parts as the Method actor. Mistaken identity begins to shade into something like confused identity, and finally she reproaches herself: "Other people's lives became more real to me than my own. . . . I didn't even know who I was. . . ." Good-neighborliness also has its traps.

To be someone one isn't is a special form of being only a nobody, a face in the crowd. And Ella gets to the theatrical party where she knows nobody, feels a nobody, and everybody else does the Name Dropping number (the film's director being one of the names). Its un-smart, democratic converse is established by the crossing-the-road number, where suddenly every nobody gets to know everybody, so that everybody's somebody. Another

*Mistaken identities: Jeff unmasks Ella.*

kind of togetherness for the lonely crowd is to be found when Otto briefs his agents in the furnace-room. "It's a Simple Little System" links the highbrow intricacies of classical music with the lowbrow intricacies of illegal gambling. The musical number, which he conducts with the umbrella of his false respectability, becomes an amiable series of visual puns. One shot picks out a group of middle-aged matrons warbling away as if singing an oratorio. And at that point the bookies' agency merges with the church-based social activities that are the pride and joy of Middle West society. A few shots later, and all involved are waving their hands as if they were a Negro Baptist congregation. By way of grand finale they scale the heights of pop religiosity, and sing to the tune of the Hallelujah Chorus. Of course it hasn't the cheerfully blasphemous charge of the singing trial scene in *Duck Soup*—it's about the co-existence of social worlds—the middle-class church in-group, and the big-city betting in-group. (Wasn't it Pascal who based his religion on a bet?)

*Bells Are Ringing* is highly ingenious and inventive, for not only every situation, and therefore (given Hollywood's discipline, in the interests of directness, clarity and strength) every line of dialogue, but every conspicuous visual detail or configuration opens up intriguing aspects of the basic theme. There are two scenes at railroad stations—railroads being another form of communication line, and railroad stations being switchboards for people rather than voices. Jeff, going off to the country to work undisturbed (so that communication becomes separation!), says good-bye to Melisande, and pushes his way through a suddenly-busy swirl of crowds; the world is full of people, a bustling but human world. Later, alone and forlorn in search of her, he stands in a telephone booth, centrally placed in the left-hand side of the Cinemascope screen. The empty right-hand side is filled by the long length of a train, which slows to a halt. The doors open automatically, directly opposite the telephone cabin. It occurs to us that maybe, by Hollywood magic, or by the magic of l'amour fou, or by the magic of prayer-by-telephone, Ella may step off the train. But no. The carriage remains empty. The doors slide close. The steel train slides out. Jeff hangs up. Communication-by-separation went with crowds, people like corpuscles of blood, circulating, pulsating. But this desert of empty steel and plate-glass is an eclipse (as Kim Novak was an orchidaceous icon of alienation before *L'Avventura*. And isn't Judy Holliday an ebullient, unfrozen semi-double of Kim Novak? a converse, in sympathetic energy, to the affectations of Monroe? halfway between Novak and Monroe, and devoid of a neurosis which can reasonably be regarded as not merely personal things, but as having social determinants or reinforcements also?).

If the simple little system becomes the Hallelujah Chorus, it's to urge a peaceful coexistence between respectable morality and its opposite. The small town has its affectations, splendidly symbolized by the name "Bonjour Tristesse Brassiere Company," i.e., innocence yearning for disillusionment. (And surely those brassieres are, in some way, gay deceivers!) So Ella herself suffers from inverted snobbery and the villain of the piece isn't just Jeff's drinking but, equally, her inferiority complex, her inverted snobbery. Jeff almost jokes her through it, and, before taking her into the party (where a great deal of communication by notes goes on), raises her spirits by parodying some vaudeville routines—vaudeville being a characteristic expression of the rags-to-riches, egalitarian theme. But society is a structure of separations as well as of communications, and the hidden weakness of small-town neighborliness is the fear born of snobbery, inverted or otherwise.

As part of the whole communications theme the film affably satirizes its own conventions. To judge from audience reaction, the moment when an audience of Royal College of Art students finally decided, after some hesitation, that this was a bad film—to be laughed at rather than laughed with—occurred when Ella, in Jeff's apartment, takes a step or two away from him and begins her musical soliloquy: "Better Than A Dream." Jeff, fired by the new inspiration she has brought, continues typing, not noticing her having burst into song (again: communication-as-separation). But the audience, oddly literalistic about plausibility, even in a musical, laughed incredulously at what is, of course, the moment of friendly self-mockery through which the film reminds us that "this is a film." Communication (as semiologists will remind us) extensively depends on conventions—without which all the unconventionalities of originality would have no purchase, no grip, no community. The convention is doubled up, and simultaneously convulsed and re-established, when Jeff sings to himself simultaneously. And this "separate togetherness" is an inversion of the scene when Jeff, peering morosely into the mirror, fails to con himself into a mood of massive confidence (one man doubled and talking to himself is quite different from two people talking to themselves because they've really met). Often enough the film seems theatrical, in the sense that the musical numbers leave us with a general feeling of being done in long-shot, as on a stage. And though the real reason may have been a budget-minded studio's insistence on general shots (sparing all the expense involved in multiple set-ups and more dynamic editing, *Singin' in the Rain*-style), the effect harmonizes with the film's theme well enough (though possibly precluding it from classic status?). At the end, also, the characters are brought in, in quick succession, as one might bring them on to take their bows at the end of a stage performance. The effect (of a device paralleled in *La Dolce Vita*) is of the director's wistful joke about this film being adapted from a Broadway musical. He leaves some of the stage quality inside the film, yielding a tender irony which isn't quite sad, for even though the flesh-and-blood uniqueness of stage presence has been replaced by celluloid facsimiles, enough of the spirit gets there just the same.

The shots behind the opening credits stress the demolition of old brownstone houses in New York. Then a commentator-type voice gives us a bright and breezy explanation and jet-age "image" of answering services. Finally we see that this particular one is run from the one remaining house in this tatty old street. The difference between the mental image produced by the commentary, and the physical reality, is another case of mistaken identity. The houses, too, recall something which isn't exactly the small-town spirit, and isn't exactly the immigrant ethnic-group spirit, but splits the difference between the two. It recalls old-fashioned, pre-skyscraper New York, *neighborhood* New York, and implies, very covertly, that maybe the small town never had a monopoly of good-neighborliness either. The inhabitants of such brownstone houses perhaps appear as the crowd at the road-crossing. That crowd's physiognomic-ethnic-diversity is rare in Hollywood movies, and surpassed, to my knowledge, which isn't encyclopedic, in the Sixties, only by *Fitzwilly*, where it was played off against the exotic WASPery of a dear old rich lady and her devoted butler—and where the casting director got an especially enormous screen-credit. Doubtless picturesquerie à la Damon Runyon provides both films with a convenient accepted convention. But *Bells Are Ringing* remains one of the few Hollywood movies to concede that New York is a cosmopolitan place. *On the Town* didn't, quite, although the longshoreman's aubade had its pastoral beauty.

It may or may not be pushing discursively atmospheric detail too rigidly into the thematic line to be reminded, when one of the answerphone girls stands over a fan to cool herself in sweaty summer, of Marilyn's skirts wafted on high in *The Seven Year Itch*—and thus of that erotic dream turning into this exasperated reality. But the film certainly makes use of show-business parody. Jeff, pretending to believe Ella is the 63-year-old lady as which she's ineptly posing ("false personalization"), drops onto one knee before her and sings "Mammy," like Al Jolson. The hoofers-from-the-stockyard-district vaudeville-routine links such parodies with the name-dropping routine and the stageplay-within-the-film effects.

There's little need to comment on the way the style and glitter of the players and décor shift everything into a key which is so much Hollywood wish-fulfillment that the real sting and throb of everyday loneliness is mellowed and softened and modulated into the sentimentality implicit in the Ella-Jeff relationship. Doubtless musical comedy, like comedy, has its minor leagues, and the period's profound films on city life and miscommunications remain *Two for the Seesaw*, *The Apartment*, and so on—those which continue where *The Crowd* and *Lonesome* left off. The bitter musical which I would dearly love to see remains unmade, although *Pal Joey*, *It's Always Fair Weather* and *Porgy and Bess* and *West Side Story* all made gestures towards it. Like *The Man in the Gray Flannel Suit* and *The Ladies' Man*, *Bells Are Ringing* might be described as Riesmanesque—its ideas and images criss-cross with those of *The Lonely Crowd*, as does its tone, of serious, concerned, yet optimistic liberalism, which will turn conservative as the riots and sit-ins begin. Perhaps it's a tribute to Riesman's analysis, but his book might have been the bible of Hollywood after McCarthyism, as Freud was its bible just before it.

*Bells Are Ringing* certainly doesn't feel like the product of book-learning. Its clear and economical structure betrays the play of sensitive and agile intelligences, of a director perfectly attuned to the theme underlying the diversity of the writers' situations, scenes and terms. The composer (Jule Styne) certainly gets the point—after Ella has sung, *"I'm in love with a man—Plaza oh, double-four, double three, What a perfect relationship—I can't see him—he can't see me"*— the music switches to a passionate tango to *"And yet I can't help wondering—What does he look like?"*—the tango implying the archaic absurdity of expectation, of daydreaming. The communications network is also a labyrinth, offering so many options that one easily becomes the slave, not of the lamp, but of the switchboard. Certainly the film has too much common sense to subscribe to McLuhan's idiotic myth of the global village. The woman who slaves over a hot switchboard has to cool her skirts over an electric fan.

That the film's thematic unity is likely to "communicate before it is understood" indicates the absurdity also of Truffaut's erstwhile, and much admired, disdain of the well-constructed script. Probably most spectators find *Bells Are Ringing* a relaxed, even sprawling film, compared with, for example, *Singin' in the Rain*, although that Comden-Green story is thematically the more diffuse. It answers to the underlying theme of friendship vs. show-business. The latter's illusions are represented by things as diverse as the apparent vista which turns out to be a painted scene when Donald O'Connor runs up it, the image of Cyd Charisse who switches from gangster's moll to bridal white-and back again—and the film studio's machinations and manipulations of sound. The dance-within-the-story might have been more pointedly apposite if Cyd Charisse had played—not a gangster's moll, responding as if hypnotized to his archaically-tossed gold coin, but—the actress whom Gene Kelly loves, and who prefers to him the money of the studio's chief executive producer, and to whom he must, perforce, prefer Debbie Reynolds' girl-next-door friendliness (which survives Hollywood as Judy Holliday survives New York). But Louis B. Mayer wouldn't have liked that. And maybe American audiences, in 1952, would have been startled at the sudden assertion, in a musical of all places, that corruption and immorality weren't a monopoly of gangster milieu. Oh, those Hollywood gangsters, answering for so many respectable sins!

I'm not arguing that moral realism and/or tight structures are sine qua non of good movies—although I do suspect that *The Band Wagon* would be even better if the Jack Buchanan part were played by Orson Welles, whose style in screen megalomania is more dynamic, more *American*, and altogether better adjusted to the terms of the rest of the film. For an actor's personality is as much part of the structure as the scriptwriter's situation. It often happens that a film working with the grain of comfortable myths and ambiguities can work up a greater animal energy and emotional subtlety than a film which, without resorting to the counter-energy of scandal, as Wilder so brilliantly does, works against the grain, and so may jolt and fumble and, by trying to be tactful, seem awkward. In defending *Bells Are Ringing* I am in effect defending another category of film—the film which, accepting all that is true in the conformist myth, nonetheless does so with an intelligence and sensitivity which reveal at least the outlines of those parts of reality against which the myth is braced. It may thus *involve* one—emotionally as well as intellectually—in a way which musicals have too rarely explored, and which critics have too often resented.

# Some Like It Hot
## Gregg Rickman (2001)

**I.**

"You sure make with the words."
—Lorraine Minosa, *Ace in the Hole*.

Billy Wilder's characters are frequently trapped in language, creatures of words. As characters they not only originate in words on a page (Billy Wilder's screenplays), but they are also characters who time and time again become trapped in words, imprisoned in the prison house of language in a fashion not unlike the POW anti-heroes of his *Stalag 17*.

Wilder's characters more often than not are con artists, manipulators of other people's emotions, usually through their skilled use of language. Many work with words for a living: the writers (or in two cases songwriters and a film producer) of *The Lost Weekend*, *Sunset Boulevard*, *Ace in the Hole*, *Kiss Me, Stupid*, *The Front Page* and *Fedora* all struggle to complete just one more project. Others "make with the words" (as Jan Sterling's character puts it in *Ace in the Hole*) as the conmen and hustlers of Wilder's universe: salesmen in *Double Indemnity*, *The Emperor Waltz*, and *The Fortune Cookie*; corrupt army officers in *A Foreign Affair* and *Stalag 17*; the capitalist boss of *One, Two, Three*, and so on. Again, words are these characters' tools, long precisely nuanced speeches Wilder directed his actors to deliver just so, and word for word.

When Wilder's protagonists employ non-verbal means of getting ahead, they tend to employ costumes and false hair, visual means of adopting a false name (which they frequently also employ). Ginger Rogers in *The Major and the Minor*, Marlene Dietrich in *Witness for the Prosecution*, Curtis and Lemmon in *Some Like It Hot*, Lemmon in *Irma la Douce*, Genevieve Page in *The Private Life of Sherlock Holmes* are all examples of this type. Throughout his long career Wilder employed blocks of words as cinema and costumes as words. They're an essentially word-bound filmmaker's idea of something visually interesting.

This is not necessarily to criticize Wilder, who in his career as a film director was never less than competent as a *metteur-en-scene*, and at times inspired. He merely treated the visual aspects of cinema as a means to film the screenplays he and his collaborators had worked over so long and so hard. As he told Cameron Crowe, he was "just a writing director—a writer who was also directing." The words always came first—"The last thing I do is to figure out, where do I put the camera? First you have to have it on paper . . . . The words must come to life" (Crowe, 128, 130). He continually searched for the right word even as an Alfred Hitchcock thought and rethought his screenplays in search of the right image. Wilder's images were there, primarily, to serve the script.

Wilder's command of the language was learned. A German-speaking Jew, Wilder had had to learn English almost from scratch when he emigrated to the United States in 1934. He'd thrived in Germany as a screenwriter, but in Hollywood he encountered

**237**

many setbacks trying to master his new tongue. According to biographer Ed Sikov, his new boss at his first Hollywood job "was visibly shaken when he realized that the studio's newest screenwriter barely spoke English. He angrily dispatched the embarrassed immigrant to the writers' building in short order" (Sikov, 103). Years later Wilder commented "when you are a writer, when you are deprived of your language, you know, more or less, you are dead" (Sikov, 106-7).

Wilder's scripts often trace a resurrection through words, as with the way the demoralized writer Don Birnam (Ray Milland) regenerates himself at the typewriter in *The Lost Weekend*. His early screenplays, filmed by other directors, often deal with a character's sudden immersion in a new idiom—that of Ninotchka (Greta Garbo) in Paris in Ernst Lubitsch's 1939 film, the thickly accented Georges Iscovescu (Charles Boyer) trying to scheme himself into the United States in *Hold Back the Dawn* (Mitchell Leisen, 1941), or Professor Bertram Potts (Gary Cooper) discovering the realm of slang in *Ball of Fire* (Howard Hawks, 1942).

Once Wilder became a director, though, he moved swiftly to filming stories less often about innocents like Ninotchka and Potts, and more often about hustlers like Iscovescu who take control of their environment with the aid of verbal and other forms of mastery. His American directorial debut, *The Major and the Minor* (1942), is a transitional work, Ginger Rogers using disguise to pass herself off as a helpless young girl, camouflaged for safety in the alien environment of a boys' military school. Later Wilder protagonists take command in harsher environments yet.

The typical Billy Wilder protagonist is male, and unlike Ginger Rogers' Susan/Susu Applegate more aggressive in their con games. He is often paired with an innocent he takes advantage of. Joe, the Tony Curtis character in *Some Like It Hot*, hustles his buddy Jerry (Jack Lemmon), while also hustling the naive singer Sugar Kane (Marilyn Monroe). Joe is ultimately redeemed by the hustler's confession so common as an escape device in Wilder's work: "No man is worth it," he tells Sugar. Because the film is a farce, he gets away with it.

Wilder hustlers operate by storytelling. They tell lies, they build a fantasy world of lies, and they sometimes come a cropper by buying into someone else's delusional fantasy, or by starting to believe their own. Thus *Sunset Boulevard*, or *Kiss Me, Stupid*, where a jealous husband hires a prostitute to impersonate his wife in order to win over (by sleeping with) a possible client. He then throws out the client in a fit of jealousy.

This self-destructive madness relates to Wilder's penchant for masquerade and disguise, adapted for survival (*Some Like It Hot*) or for gain. The alcoholic Don Birnam is a master at hiding his bottles of booze in *The Lost Weekend*. These masquerades lead to madness or insanity, as with Don's hallucinations, Norma Desmond's fate in *Sunset Boulevard*, and so on. The comic version of all this—our concern in the rest of this piece—is Jerry's certainty that "I'm a girl" in *Some Like It Hot*; he *becomes* his disguise.

## II.

"Tell the other girls to watch their language."
—Sweet Sue to Joe and Jerry, *Some Like It Hot*.

*Some Like It Hot* (1959) is commonly considered Wilder's greatest film; some even list it as the greatest comedy of all time. The writer Poul Anderson has suggested that authors should appeal to more than one of the senses when creating their fictions. Billy

*Marilyn Monroe as Sugar Kane in* Some Like It Hot. *Behind her, Tony Curtis and Jack Lemmon offer musical support.*

Wilder and his screenwriting collaborator I.A.L. Diamond make that appeal in *Some Like It Hot*, which helps to explain the film's enduring popularity.

In *Some Like It Hot* body language and sheer physicality is more prominently on display than in Wilder's other films. Marilyn Monroe, a star whose appeal relied more than most on an overpowering physical presence, was written as being so tactile in Wilder's previous film with her, *The Seven Year Itch*, that her character kept her underwear in the refrigerator. *Some Like It Hot* continues to trade on the visceral appeal of her photographed image (something she as a performer had worked very consciously to develop, as the sensitive studies of her acting by Graham McCann and Carl E. Rollyson Jr. make clear). When first glimpsed by the film's heroes, musicians Joe (Curtis) and Jerry

(Lemmon), Jerry likens her to "Jello on springs," the first in a series of metaphors appealing to the sense of taste that the film associates with her. Her character's name, "Sugar Kane," calls up that sense as does Jerry's gleeful dream, after spotting her, of being "locked up in a pastry shop." His initially censorious pal Joe tells him, "No pastry no butter and no sugar," but himself uses food in his successful campaign to seduce Sugar in his guise as an impotent millionaire. "Mint sauce or cranberries? . . . What good is food?," he wonders, nibbling on a quail leg. His metaphoric description of his supposed impotence continues throughout the seduction, always in terms of sensory experience: "It's like taking someone to a concert when they're tone deaf" and "It's like smoking without inhaling." Ultimately Sugar's skill at kissing—she used to "sell kisses for the milk fund"—moves Joe physically, as his glasses steam up and his feet rise in the air.

Sugar herself responds erotically to such non-linguistic cues as Joe's kisses and, throughout the film, music: "Eight bars of 'Melancholy Baby' and my spine turns to custard." It's no wonder that she's drawn to musicians. The period tune which becomes her theme, "Sugar Blues," plays under the film's opening credits. Conversely, she herself

*Tony Curtis, Billy Wilder and Marilyn Monroe during the filming of* Some Like it Hot.

seeks a millionaire boyfriend, who she envisions lacking unaided command of the printed word: he'll wear glasses, as he has "weak eyes from reading long columns in the *Wall Street Journal*."

To complete his disguise as a millionaire, the impoverished Joe swipes the glasses of the figurehead manager—a dithering, impotent figure—of the all-female orchestra in which he and Jerry are hiding out. That character represents a failed masculine authority even as the film's gangsters, who pursue Joe and Jerry, embody the most brutal of masculine stereotypes. They don't command language, they command fear. The violence of their machine-gunning of rival criminals and innocent garageman alike at the Saint Valentine's Day Massacre is markedly unsoftened. The gangster boss Spats' kicking a toothpick out of the mouth of the dead Toothpick Charley is the blunt gesture, at once horrible and mock-polite, that ends the massacre.

Echoing in their way the film's theme of disguise, throughout the film the thugs consistently offer up a series of physical objects hidden in plain sight as something else. In the film's opening scene they transport liquor hidden in a coffin. When pursuing police machine-gun their hearse, the coffin squirts alcohol instead of blood, a macabre image worthy of *Sunset Boulevard*. Later, police officer Mulligan (Pat O'Brien) grimaces at the "coffee"/scotch offered up at Spats' speakeasy, and when Spats' birthday cake is opened it turns out to contain his gun-firing assassin.

Disguise is of course the mainspring of *Some Like It Hot*'s narrative, as Joe and Jerry transform into "Josephine" and "Daphne." Joe is nonplussed when Jerry suddenly takes "Daphne" as his monicker after first being introduced as "Geraldine," and the substitution is never explained. This is in fact a clever reference on Wilder and Diamond's part to the Greek myth of Daphne, who resists Apollo's advances by transforming herself into a laurel tree. "When Jerry says, 'Hi! I'm Daphne,' he effectively says farewell to his masculine self," says Graham McCann (107). "Jerry's adoption of Daphne is a permanent pose," McCann adds, leading inexorably to the patient deflection by the lecherous millionaire Osgood Fielding (Joe E. Brown) of all of Jerry's objections to union with him in the film's final scene: "Nobody's perfect." Joe, meanwhile, takes on the vocal inflections of Cary Grant in his disguise as a millionaire, an imitation of a real star to further his seduction of the film's star. At one point Curtis appears in three guises at once, rising from a bathtub with "Josephine's wig and makeup, the millionaire's blazer and white pants, and Joe's formidable anger as he . . . dumps his yacht cap full of water on Jerry's head" (Rollyson, 155).

It follows that Wilder's comedy of the senses extends to Joe and Jerry's gender change. The steady association of Sugar Kane with food imagery quite obviously suggests a feminist analysis, with Sugar being "consumed" by men. The film's point, however, may instead be that it is the men who are ultimately "consumed" by Sugar, as Joe gives up his con (wo)man ways for her even as Jerry's male identity slips away: "'How *do* they walk in these things?' asks Jerry/Daphne, carefully observing Sugar's movements in the high heels he can barely master. 'I tell you, it's a whole different sex,' he exclaims, swinging his shoulders in imitation of her mobility" (Rollyson, 150). By the film's midpoint he's very confused: "I'm a boy," he keeps telling himself. "I wish I was dead." And in his happiness after Osgood Fielding proposes, Jerry rises above and beyond verbal language, punctuating each of his sentences with a shake of his maraccas. His joy communicates musically.

Carl E. Rollyson Jr. has noted how well Wilder uses both the human voice and music in the film: "Lemmon modulates his voice between high and low pitches so that it often cracks somewhere between male and female registers. Similarly, Curtis drops his voice an octave on the word 'really' when he learns Sugar goes for male saxophone players, and Sugar roughs up her voice to say 'some like it hot' when she describes the jazz the female band plays" (Rollyson, 153-4). As Sugar tries to "seduce" him, Joe protests his impotence, as noted, by claiming "It's like smoking without inhaling." "So inhale!" she tells him. "The utter relaxation of her voice and the ease with which she commands him to let go of all inhibitions are inimitable" (158). More so than in most Wilder films, the meaning of words in *Some Like It Hot* is less important than the way that they are said, their sound; and those sounds in turn are less important than physical gesture and the pure sound of music. Wilder cuts away from Joe and Sugar to show "Daphne and Osgood dancing, the lead switching between them, in perfect matchup with Joe and Sugar who have also alternated in their pursuit of each other . . . (S)exuality in this film is portrayed as an endlessly variable dance" (156).

For all its stature as a beloved screen comedy, the making of *Some Like It Hot* was, infamously, the site of much conflict between Wilder and his star. Wilder's language-bound insistence on having every word of his screenplays meticulously delivered as written marks him more often than not as a filmmaker of word, not image. The very physical actor James Cagney retired from the screen for two decades after undergoing Wilder's direction in *One, Two, Three* in 1961, two films after *Some Like It Hot*. Wilder insisted on Cagney's including the word "morning" in a long speech which took 52 takes to achieve. Similarly, in *Some Like It Hot*, Monroe was forced into 47 takes to deliver the line "Where is that bourbon? Oh, here it is." Improvisation—an actor's freedom—was anathema to Wilder ("He was overwhelmingly the dictator-director. Every little jot and tittle had to be done in his way"—Cagney, quoted by McCabe, 323.) Thus, perhaps, Monroe's body panic while making *Some Like It Hot*, which contributed to her frequent absences from the set: "Before each take, Marilyn would close her eyes and enter a deep trance. She would pull down on her creeping-up bathing suit, style 1927, then suddenly start to flail her hands violently, up and down, as if she were desperately intent on separating her hands from her wrists" (McCann, 105, quoting Lloyd Shearer in *Parade*, Dec. 7, 1958). All sensitive commentators on Monroe note the physicality of her performances, and it is really the brilliant body language of the film's performances (the men's as well as Monroe's) that make the film the classic it is. Given Wilder's relative indifference to physicality in his other films—epitomized perhaps by Cagney's boredom as his secretary-mistress (Lilo Pulver) vigorously dances on a table to bewitch some Russian emissaries in *One, Two, Three*—the success of *Some Like It Hot* may be credited perhaps as much to the convergence of three highly physical actors as to Wilder and Diamond's brilliant screenplay and Wilder's fine direction.

## Works Cited

Cameron Crowe, *Conversations with Wilder* (New York: Knopf, 1999).

John McCabe, *Cagney* (New York: Knopf, 1997).

Graham McCann, *Marilyn Monroe* (Cambridge, UK: Polity Press, 1988).

Carl E. Rollyson Jr., *Marilyn Monroe: A Life of the Actress* (Ann Arbor, MI: UMI Research Press, 1986).

Ed Sikov, *On Sunset Boulevard* (New York: Hyperion, 1998).

# VIII

☞ **Please do not reveal the middle of this picture!** *Jerry's a mouse chemistry prof who invents the greatest drink since Dracula discovered bloody marys.*

PARAMOUNT PICTURES presents **JERRY LEWIS** as

**"THE NUTTY PROFESSOR"**

(A Jerry Lewis Production)

☞ ☞ **What does he become? What kind of monster?** ⚞ ⚞

*Well, any scientist who makes a girl like this can't be all mad.*

TECHNICOLOR

CO-STARRING **STELLA STEVENS** · DEL MOORE · KATHLEEN FREEMAN · PRODUCED BY ERNEST D. GLUCKSMAN

WRITTEN BY JERRY LEWIS and BILL RICHMOND · DIRECTED BY JERRY LEWIS · A Paramount Release

# Tashlin's Method: An Hypothesis

Paul Willemen (1973)

In the late '50s and early '60s Frank Tashlin emerged as one of the major American directors: his influence was evident in the films of the New Wave, particularly those of Godard, and interest in his work by film critics in both England and France constituted part of a wider movement aimed at challenging prevailing critical assumptions about the cinema. Tashlin's seminal influence on both the emerging cinema and critical ideas, however, was short-lived. The Dziga Vertov group (Godard and Gorin) are the only film-makers who still acknowledge their enormous debt to Tashlin. In the field of film criticism, the only major critic who has continued a defence of Tashlin is Robert Benayoun, who, significantly, is better known as an expert on Jerry Lewis. Tashlin's pivotal film, *The Disorderly Orderly*, which was made after interest in him had fallen away, has largely been viewed as part of the Jerryo Lewis *oeuvre*. In the meantime, Tashlin has died, almost unnoticed, in Hollywood.

What, then, does the cinema of Tashlin have to offer audiences today? In the sense that his cinema is compounded of the epherma of show business and appears so firmly intertwined with a complex variety of other texts making up the visual discourse of his age, it might appear to thematically-oriented critics, that his cinema is now out-moded. If there were no more to Tashlin than his topical satirization of the America of the '50s, it would seem extraordinary and incongruous that revolutionary filmmakers like Godard and Gorin should find his films so important. In fact, it is only now that the avant-garde nature of Tashlin's practice of filmic writing can begin to be appreciated. Recent studies of the *nouveau roman*, and in particular the literary practice of Claude Simon, cast quite a different light on Tashlin's work. In the words of Stephen Heath: "What can it really mean to speak of the author as the source of the discourse? Far from being the unique creation of the author as originating source, every text is always (an)other text(s) that it remakes, comments, displaces, prolongs, reassumes. A text opens in and from that complex formation of modes of articulation that gives, as it were, the theater of its activity, a series of settings always already there as its very possibility."

Tashlin's modernity, then, rests not so much with his subject matter, but with his radical break with the notion of an author communicating his personal "vision" or "truth" about his "world" view. In Tashlin's films reality is deconstructed, re-activated and re-produced. "In the space of the text in the practice of writing, there is no longer a movement forward to the fixing of some final Sense or Truth, but on the contrary, an attention to a plurality, to a dialogue of texts, founding and founded in an intertextuality to be read in, precisely, a *practice* of writing" (Stephen Health, *The Nouveau Roman*, 1972).

A thorough analysis of Tashlin's work, of any single film, or indeed, of any single aspect of any single film, still has to be undertaken. (Roger Garcia's anthology *Frank Tashlin* [BFI, 1994] has changed this situation.—Author's note, 2001.) The sheer density of Tashlin's film texts demands the time and facilities for extremely detailed analysis

**244**

which I was unable to take for this book: however, I would like suggest what admittedly must be no more than a working hypothesis, a way of approaching Tashlin's work which might prove fruitful if elaborated further, or, indeed, even disproved after a more detailed and rigorous study of the films concerned.

The essential features of a Tashlin film are two-fold:

(1) A Tashlin film does not profess to be a single, unique work, entirely closed in upon itself, standing as a completely self-sufficient and "organic" whole. Rather, his films present themselves as comprising part of a network of visual texts produced in a particular society at a particular time (i.e. in the USA in the late 1950s/early '60s). Obviously, all texts, whether visual or otherwise, form part of such a network: there is not one single work of any kind in existence which does not form part of a larger "text" which comprehends it: nevertheless, there are few films or indeed auteurs, who make this fact into an active, productive principle in their own system. Tashlin is one of these few exceptions. The forms this artistic procedure takes are varied:

(a)  References to other Tashlin films (e.g. the reference to *The Girl Can't Help It* in *Will Success Spoil Rock Hunter?*).

(b)  Indirect references to other Tashlin films. There are few Tashlin films which do not contain allusions to, or quotes from, his other films (e.g. the repetition of a gag from

*"A network of visual texts": Jayne Mansfield with Joan Blondell and reading matter in*
Will Success Spoil Rock Hunter? .

*The Lemon Drop Kid* in *The Man From the Diners' Club*, in which Bob
Hope/Danny Kaye is flung along the floor, face downwards, and comes to a stop
with his head against a flower pot, whereupon, the [obviously plastic] leaves fall off,
leaving a naked stem).

(c) References to film genres (e.g. the first shots of *It's Only Money* making reference to
the gangster genre, and the figure of the private eye in the same film).

(d) References to (and often collages with) other types of visual discourse, such as television and film advertisements, TV programs (e.g. the shrinking of the Cinemascope screen to TV size in *Will Success Spoil Rock Hunter?*), comic books, animated
films etc.

(e) Specific quotes from films by other directors or from classic anthology pieces (e.g.
the Laurel and Hardy quote in *Rock-A-Bye Baby* —the use of a finger as a
candle/lighter; the quote from Sirk's *Written on the Wind* in the same film, in the
scene by the lake, substituting Dorothy Malone and the voice of Rock Hudson as a
child, with Jerry Lewis and Connie Stevens, and including the heart carved on the
tree and the flashback to childhood).

(f) Direct statements to the effect that a film is not an autonomous product, but that a
film has been manufactured by many people. Moreover, apart from demystifying
the production process, Tashlin incorporates into his films various examples of film
consumption, thus inscribing into his films the entire itinerary of the art product,
from the first idea and/or basic constraints, up to the viewing of the finished product
(e.g. the sequence in *Susan Slept Here* where Dick Powell reads the credits of a
film; in *Caprice*, Doris Day goes to a cinema showing . . . *Caprice*; in the prologue
to *The Girl Can't Help It*, Tom Ewell specifies that we are about to see a film in

The Girl Can't Help It... *in Cinemascope and "glorious color by Deluxe." Tom Ewell,
Edmond O'Brien, Jayne Mansfield and Henry Jones.*

Cinemascope and "glorious color by DeLuxe", no doubt to differentiate it from a television program). Undoubtedly Tashlin's most eloquent attack on the myth of spontaneous creativity is the prologue-suspense sequence in *The Disorderly Orderly*: i.e. three possible heroes are presented to the audience; the particular hero for the purpose of the film is selected in a fairly arbitrary manner—it transpires that it is to be the one who falls down first! Implicit in this presentation is the fact that the two "heroes" who succeeded in remaining standing could have served the purpose equally well; the result would have been a different film, or maybe even an identical film structure, but with different occupants—characters/objects/plot functions—of the nodal points of that structure.

(2) The second essential feature of a Tashlin film, which relates closely to the first one, is its combinatory nature (i.e. a structure where the meaning is produced strictly through the relations between separate elements, the elements themselves being largely arbitrary). In fact, it would appear that elements are chosen with a view to their combinatory potential, or, to put it the other way round, the fact that the basic procedure of a Tashlin film involves combination (e.g. addition, subtraction, multiplication, juxtaposition, condensation etc.) determines the nature of the elements which can function in such a context. This determines, for one thing, the nature of the gags in Tashlin films.

A few examples of what this involves may clarify the issue and perhaps stimulate further research. The intricate network of quotes, parodies, pastiches, satires serves to embed one text into another and constitutes one level of combination. Another consists of the exploitation of the standard and given forms of combination in all film texts, such as sound and image (noise, music and speech plus image). There are a great many instances in Tashlin's work where gags are generated through the logical but incongruous use of sound effects (e.g. Dick Powell mouthing, i.e. speaking) the lines of both male and female characters in the TV film in *Susan Slept Here*; the microphone in the sugar cube, simultaneously magnifying noises and obliterating speech in *Caprice*.) A variation of this type of procedure is the exploitation of optional combinations of these elements, such as speech and subtitles (cf. *The Disorderly Orderly*), varying screen sizes (cf. *The Girl Can't Help It* and *Will Success Spoil Rock Hunter?*) and distorting lenses/objects (cf. *Artists and Models* and *The Man From the Diners' Club*). Gags are also produced through the combination of various filmic, non-cinematic codes, to use Metz's terminology (i.e. codes which occur in films but are not specifically cinematic), such as the combination of the lower half of Robert Morley's face with the upper half of Tony Randall's and vice versa, in *The Alphabet Murders*; or, the parallelism between Jerry Lewis and a plaster dummy in *Hollywood or Bust* (incidentally, the verbalization of this gag reveals a double parallelism—a verbal one as well as a visual one). Another type of combination is that of multiplication: Jerry Lewis' mouth dispensing an endless supply of clothes pegs in *Rock-A-Bye Baby*; Jayne Mansfield's seven, herculean brothers (again, on the verbal level, there is also a reference to *Seven Brides for Seven Brothers*) in *The Girl Can't Help It*; and lastly, there is the example of the final escape sequence in *The Man From the Diners' Club* where a dozen secretaries in identical dresses, a dozen delivery boys on bicycles carrying flowers and a dozen taxi cabs invade the streets.

Finally there are a great number of gags based on variations of the basic forms of combination. If we accept that the basic forms of combination consist of the bringing together of two or more items to produce a new structure, then a variation is constituted

*The mechanical aspects of gag construction: Assembly and disassembly in*
The Man from the Diners' Club.

by such gags as the baby getting lost in the powder in *Rock-A-Bye Baby* or the man in a plaster cast disappearing in *The Disorderly Orderly*. The plaster cast gag is not merely a form of subtraction, because the viewer is not supposed to consider the unfortunate invalid as a composite of parts of equal value—plaster cast plus man. In the same way, neither is a powdered baby regarded as a combination of two elements of equal value, either of which can be withdrawn from the equation—the baby without the powder/the powder without the baby. In this way, Tashlin's gags of this kind literally deconstruct, disassemble visual/semantic units.

From the examples given above, it appears that there are a great many types of combinations at work in Tashlin's films, classifiable according to the nature of the elements combined (the various codes) or to the type of combinations used (rhetorical/mathematical procedures). A classification according to the type of combination is perhaps more fruitful in the case of Tashlin, because these procedures are dominant, and the combination of different codes is always secondary in this type of comedy. As far as this type of comedy goes, it is not of primary importance to note that speech, effects, music and image are being combined; these kinds of combinations appear in almost all types of film. Comedy is generated primarily by the type of combination used—illogical, incongruous, breaking the laws of verisimilitude etc.

Unfortunately, this enumeration of examples is far from systematic; a rigorous classification could only be achieved after systematic study and analysis of the rhetorical procedures he employs, which is beyond the scope of this essay. It would seem, however, that an approach along the lines I have outlined would facilitate coming to grips with the fairly widespread idea concerning his work: critics who have taken the trouble to examine his work have remarked on the "mechanical" aspects of his gag constructions. If the hypothesis above is correct, this impression of a mechanical quality would be produced because the Tashlin film in its entirety stands under the sign of "bricolage," of assembly and disassembly (dismantling). This may stem from Tashlin's background as a cartoonist—when drawing cartoons/comic strips etc. the artists has total control over every line, shape or figure in his frame (for the sake of simplicity, we identify the artist with the "subject" of the discourse he produces). In the cinema, Tashlin extended this control over the codes on the soundtrack and on movement, which, in his films, is often divorced from the laws of gravity and inertia. The overwhelming impression created by this kind of "bricolage" is that of almost mathematical systematicity: given a number of codes to play with, Tashlin proceeds to exhaust all the possible ways of combining them into original constructions. None of the codes, however, is unique to Tashlin; all are available to all film-makers and all have been used before Tashlin's intervention. The obvious analogy to draw in this context, is that of the meccano set — everyone has an identical number of pieces and blueprints at his disposal, but Tashlin winds up with magnificent, strange and outlandish constructions, not quite like anyone else's.

It would appear that Tashlin did, in fact, succeed in realizing Mr. LaSalle Junior's dream in *Will Success Spoil Rock Hunter?*: to grow a new species of rose. Through meticulous calculation trial and error, and endless cross-breeding, Tashlin did finally create/manufacture his entirely new rose: the Tashlin work. Some critics (cf. Raymond Durgnat in *The Crazy Mirror*) have described what they believe to be the central themes in Tashlin's films, which center round a satire of the American consumer-oriented society. This is not as straightforward as it might appear. If the hypothesis advanced in this essay is correct, then such notions as "artificiality" and "stereotyping" of many aspects of American society, is the result of a method of constructing social reality homologous to Tashlin's method of structuring his films. In other words, Tashlin's films are isomorphous with the ideology of American consumerism: Tashlin "makes" his films in exactly the same way that Carla Naples/Marilyn Maxwell in *Rock-A-Bye Baby* is made into a film star—her body, plus a wig, plus caps on her teeth, plus padding etc. The construction of an attractive female form is an elaborate process, and proceeds along the same principles which underlie Tashlin's films. As the ideology of consumerism is a vital and necessary part of the American economy and cannot be understood apart from the economic base, so Tashlin's films form part of the movie business, and cannot be understood when abstracted either from its economic base, or from the complex network of film texts produced within the context of the Hollywood movie industry.

Author's Note: Parts of this essay were co-written with Claire Johnston.

# Jerry Lewis:
# The Deformation of the Comic
## Frank Krutnik (1994)

> There's not much in this world left to horrify [William] Burroughs, but being told that he, [David] Cronenberg, and Jerry Lewis have each been elected members of the French Order of Arts and Letters is nearly enough to send him on another heroin jag. "We need to vote him out, then," shouts Burroughs.[1]

This comment, made during the publicity junket undertaken by Burroughs and Cronenberg to publicize the film of *Naked Lunch*, says much about the peculiar reputation of Jerry Lewis. Burroughs deems it appropriate that the French Order of Arts and Letters should include a wife-murdering ex-addict novelist and a maker of visceral horrorfests, but Lewis—comedian, filmmaker, and Telethon-host—cannot be tolerated within such exalted company. Rarely has a public media figure been so deeply loved, and so intensively and so easily vilified. If art is in the eye of the beholder, what is that art that can frame the fearful dissymmetries of Jerry Lewis—his "spastic" physical contortions, his pretensions to godhead? The extremism that marks Lewis' public reputation—as man or myth, genius or embarrassment—began in the 1960s, when, following hot on the heels of the heretical *politique des auteurs*, French film critics launched their most devastating broadside yet against the fortress of traditional evaluative criteria. In 1967, for example, Jean-Luc Godard had the nerve to proclaim that "Jerry Lewis . . . [is] the only one in Hollywood doing something different, the only one who isn't falling in with the established categories, the norms, the principles. . . . Lewis is the only one today who's making courageous films. And I think he's perfectly well aware of it. He's been able to do it because of his personal genius."[2]

Like many other French film critics of the 1960s, Godard was perfectly well aware of the "scandal" of celebrating Lewis' "personal genius." Faced with such heady European validation of the comedian-director, even Andrew Sarris, the most ardent American auteurist, felt obliged to restore some "sanity" to the proceedings. In his 1968 book *The American Cinema*, Sarris fired off a 12-pronged salvo against Lewis' value-as-an-artist, and against the French critics' fundamental error of taste and judgment.[3] But Lewis had himself fanned the flames of the controversy by canonizing himself as a "total film-maker" and declaring that:

> When you make a film yourself, write it, produce it, direct it, perhaps star in it; a piece of your heart enters the emulsion. It stays there the rest of your life, good film or bad. . . . [A]s a total film-maker, I'm convinced that there is a greater chance of inconsistency when the four separate minds of writer, producer, director and actor collaborate.[4]

In his earlier, phenomenally successful cabaret, film, and TV work with Dean Martin, Lewis had developed a particularly extreme version of the comic misfit,

**250**

described by its creator as "The Idiot" or "The Kid." The early Lewis-figure was a glaring inversion of acceptable standards governing the body, maturity, and masculinity, and the grotesquery of Lewis' onscreen performance could not comfortably be accommodated within established paradigms of aesthetic value. Lewis' performance style transforms his body into a battleground upon which a range of competing "aberrances" assault the protocols of 1950s American masculinity. The deviances of the Lewis-figure—his verbal and physical uncoordination, sexual confusion, and fragmented or uncentered sense of self—amount to a hysterical "voicing" of dysfunctional masculinity. But Lewis' excesses are measured against Dean Martin's idealized and self-assured masculine presence. Playing the straight "handsome man" to the disordered antics of Lewis' "monkey,"

*"The Idiot" or "the Kid": Early Jerry Lewis.*

Martin was essential to the dynamic of the team's performance; he served as a pretext, a balance, a cover for Lewis' extremism. When the team split after a ten-year partnership, the contextualizing function of Dean Martin as register for and container of the Lewis-figure's aberrance was gradually appropriated by Lewis himself. Through the early 1950s, the comedian demanded an increasing say in the production of the Martin-Lewis film vehicles, but the most telling proof of his ambitions came in 1960, with *The Bellboy*—the first of 11 films Lewis starred in, directed, and often co-wrote. Whereas the onscreen Lewis-figure lacked coordination and control—in even greater measure than before—the post-Martin, behind-the-scenes Lewis was an accomplished and ambitious achiever. This paradox irked Lewis critics no end.

Lewis' self-directed films not only subject his familiar comic persona to some highly accented transmutations but they also display an idiosyncratic cinematic and narrative style that marked a significant departure both from Lewis' earlier work and from the generic norms of the comedian-comedy. In their cultivation of a personal style and a personal voice, the self-directed films reveal a self-conscious auteurist project. They assert the victory of the Creative Presence "Jerry Lewis" over the regimentation of the Hollywood "entertainment machine," and in the process they also open up a multifaceted discourse of their subject.

## Deformation and the Creative Presence

With the widening gulf between the spasticity of the Idiot-Kid and Lewis' flamboyant aspirations, Lewis was attacked by established reviewers for his "betrayal" of comic innocence—especially for films like *The Errand Boy* (1961) and *The Patsy* (1964), which addressed the processes of stardom and comedy and the values of entertainment. In 1978, Leonard Maltin echoed the sentiments of the 1960s American reviewers when he berated Lewis for overextending himself:

> Then Jerry Lewis decided that he wanted to write and direct his own films, to become "the total film maker." The difference in his films was obvious: they were ponderous where once they had been light and airy, pretentious where once they had been so unassuming. Although Lewis was concerned with his characterization, he no longer supported it with a strong story line, preferring black-out gags instead. Worst of all, especially to a young and nonanalytical viewer, his films were simply not as funny as those that others had written and directed for him.[5]

In such accounts, Lewis is persistently castigated for self-indulgence, for his refusal to be "simply funny." Moreover, his aspirations to totalizing authorship are attributed to an ego run riot. "There was no longer anyone to veto an idea," Maltin accuses, "so Jerry indulged his every whim, allowed Jerry the comedian to milk gags far beyond endurance, and discarded conventional notions of good taste, modesty, continuity, and—oddly enough—humor."[6]

American critics like Maltin seem affronted by the way that the self-directed films upset the *balance* between creative individualism and conformity that normally exists in the comedian-comedy.[7] By disrupting structural conventions of continuity and humor, and by offending standards of tasteful self-effacement, Lewis could no longer be so easily contained within the acceptable province of the comedian-as-jester. But the "problem" with Lewis pre-exists his directorial work: in many ways the extremism of his auteurist films is an extension of the excesses of his performance style. In a review of the comedian's first screen appearance in the 1949 film *My Friend Irma*, Bosley Crowther wrote that:

> The swift eccentricity of his movements, the harrowing features of his face and the squeak of his vocal protestations, which are many and varied, have flair. *His idiocy constitutes a burlesque of an idiot*, which is something else again.[8] [italics added]

Crowther identifies here a key feature of Lewis' style: the complex relations he establishes with both the conventional figure of the comic misfit and the conventions of comic performance. "Idiocy" is "burlesqued," it is not presented directly or innocently; and Lewis is perceived to be moving beyond the basic requirements of the comic spectacle.

Lewis amplified such comic hyperbole in his later work as a performer—as is highlighted by the *Newsweek* review of *The Geisha Boy* in 1958, where Lewis' performance meets the same kind of criticism that later greeted his directorial work:

As in all Lewis movies, the trouble with this one is that its star seems not to know where to stop. Instead of building a bit of funny dialogue to a climax and then leaving it there to simmer, too often he messily lets the pot boil over. He does not allow himself a simple, artful double take; he has to make it a triple or even quadruple take.[9]

Underlying this complaint is the idea that comic effectiveness depends upon *restraint*. Lewis quite clearly commits gross offenses against the desired decorum of comic delivery—his performance ensures that gags and comic reactions are far from clean, precise, and contained.

Restraint and precisioned delivery play a crucial role in enabling the spectator to escape from potentially disconcerting ramifications of the comic spectacle. In an integrated film narrative, gags operate as moments of potential *rupture*. They halt, and throw into comparative disarray, procedures of logic, communication, and bodily function. But the rupturous effect tends to be trammeled: like narrative in general, gags have their own familiar conventions of ordering—of elaboration and containment. What is important to the process of the gag is not the disruptive event in itself, but how it is made over as a *controlled* and *contained* moment of "disorder"—so it can "cleanly" generate laughter. But if the film lingers upon the victim of the pratfall and his or her injuries, then pain or embarrassment can intrude. The gag allows potentially serious events to be transformed through disavowal—it simultaneously displays yet pulls away from the serious consequences of the action. But if the *balance* is upset, and the "machinery" of comic disavowal is thrown out of alignment, then the carefully hidden "other face" of the gag may be revealed. This is always a possibility in forms of "low comedy" like slapstick, in which the human body is the prime channel for comic disruption.

Lewis' performance articulates a particularly contorted and unruly language-of-the-body. This becomes clear when he's compared with Harpo Marx, another comedian whose body is a vital expressive tool. In the 1933 Marx Brothers film *Duck Soup*, there's a scene where Harpo is quizzed by Groucho; when asked where he lives, Harpo opens his shirt to reveal a picture of a dog-kennel tattooed on his chest. As Groucho looks at it, a "real" dog's head comes out of the kennel and barks. This characteristic Harpo Marx gag illustrates his liberation from the real-life constraints bearing upon the human body. Rejecting the regime of conventional speech, the Harpo-figure communicates his presence through the signifying surface of his body—by actively exhibiting the picture of the kennel and "knowing" that, against the dictates of possibility, the dog lies within. Harpo takes a childlike delight in shocking with the magical body, over which he has the power of a *metteur-en-scène*.

The extent to which Lewis' performance constructs a far different relationship between subject and body can be gauged from a scene in the 1951 Martin-Lewis vehicle *Sailor Beware*. As in the other Martin-Lewis service-comedies, *At War with the Army* (1950) and *Jumping Jacks* (1952), many of this film's comic sequences are generated by the conflict between the Lewis-figure's unruly body and the masculine regimentation required by the military. Seeking to enlist in the Navy, Lewis' hypochondriac weakling, Melvyn Jones, has to provide a blood sample for a medical test. Although he's already donated a pint to the blood bank, the Navy medics insist on taking their own share. But when they shove a syringe into Melvyn's arm, they draw *water* from it. The medics repeatedly puncture his body with their needles, with the same result. The sequence ends with two gags: Melvyn drinks a glass of water after his ordeal, and the liquid spurts out through the holes in his arms; and then a sailor carrying a power drill walks into the room, and Melvyn faints dead away. Where the first gag reemphasizes the deformation of Melvyn's body, the second plays on a problematic relationship between self and body (with Melvyn believing, "seriously," that the drill may be used on him). Where Harpo's controlling performance of his magical body surprises and overpowers his audience (Groucho), the characteristic Lewis-gag makes it plain that the Lewis-figure lacks any such control over his bodily deformations.

This is taken to extremes in the self-directed films, where, as a performer, Lewis' reactions are often so overextended that they outstrip the motivating context of the gag. These films are especially interesting for the way that Lewis' bodily and linguistic deformations are accompanied by a pervasive deformation of familiar principles of gag structure and articulation. As director-performer, Lewis repeatedly diverts the gag from its ostensibly-signaled direction: many of his gags refuse to build to conclusions—they frequently lack a conventional pay-off climax or finish with an expressly weak one. Jean-Pierre Coursodon suggests that Lewis specializes in the "eluded" or "eliminated" gag, the gag that provides, instead of the expected mechanism of disruption and reordering, a process of deformation through which, paradoxically, the "gagness" of the gag is itself frustrated, dissipated, or gagged.[10]

While American critics like Leonard Maltin tend to regard Lewis as *failing* to provide the conventional pleasure in gag-comedy, Coursodon implies that Lewis' comedy operates as a "second order" process of "gagging." The raw material of many Lewisian gags consists of already familiar gags, or of recognizable gag-situations. They are, in essence, "metagags." Where comic play is generally set in motion by the disruption of rules, procedures, and discursive registers—if only to reinstate them—Lewis' films themselves play with the conventional forms and procedures of comic play. As Coursodon remarks, ". . . these fascinating films are not always very funny. but their originality lies precisely in the fact that, while nominally slapstick routines, they so transcend categories that laughter in their case ceases to be the test of success or failure."[11]

The process of gag-deformation finds its most symptomatic articulation when, as comic performer, Lewis himself serves as its vehicle. A characteristic example occurs near the beginning of *The Patsy*. The entourage of recently deceased comedian Wally Brandford hit upon the idea of training "some nobody" to take his place. The Lewis-figure, bellboy Stanley Belt, bursts into their hotel room bearing a tray of drinks. Under intensive scrutiny from the Brandford group, Stanley is seized by a fit of stuttering inarticulacy: "The bellboy . . . I . . .um . . . er-er. The-we-ye-say. Who? Ahm. I mean . . . see, when I-er . . . I had it-m-all my clothes . . . were wet. So I changed my clothes because when I . . . I that's why I was *long*. Should I pu-pu . . . or not? Just stand? I'll close the door. I'll . . . I'll-er." Squirming with the pain of embarrassment, Stanley then drops the tray and crouches down to clear up the mess. The ostensible point is that the incompetent Stanley is the inverse of the slick Wally Brandford. But this is established as soon as he appears. The sequence stretches so far beyond this that it ceases to operate as a polished gag structure. It produces, instead, a fixation upon the spectacle of maladjustment presented through Stanley Belt.

Such moments of elaborated embarrassment are common in Lewis' films. They pinpoint his difference from a well-oiled gag-comedian like Bob Hope, whose verbal resilience is the ammunition which allows him to master whatever misfortune his character suffers. Hope's controlled wisecracks serve to wrap up and seal off the threat to the ego, but when the Lewis-figure is faced with an intimidating situation he offers not verbal mastery but linguistic *breakdown*. Stuttering, stammering, physically contorting,

Lewis' misfits lose control over both body and language. Whereas Hope's characters can overcome the threatening situation quickly and efficiently, the Lewis-figure seems *branded* by it. In his performance, the mouth becomes disconnected from the mind—in order to turn the speech act into an expressive vehicle for the unruly body. And this is made all the more excruciating for the spectator when, as in *The Patsy*, the situation is not inherently threatening. This kind of deforming strategy permits the film to make an exhibition of the Lewis-figure's inability to deal at all adequately with the external world.

The extent to which Lewis' self-directed work applies to the "body" of the film the "performing" techniques he developed for his corporeal, performative body is highlighted by Scott Bukatman. Bukatman observes that these films foreground *structural* "inarticulacy"—in the form of hesitancy, fragmentation, and obsessive repetition:

> [T]he carefully delineated narrative situations and conflicts which constitute the logic of the syntagmatic chain inevitably fall victim to a degeneration into a series of isolated sketches unrelated to the main narrative. The discursive operations of these films are dominated by digression and repetition, rather than by causal logic and narrative closure.[12]

Just as Lewis' gags and performative routines slide away from their signaled and anticipated trajectory, the self-directed films persistently deform conventions of narrative structure. The insistence of such structural deformations—of narrative, of the gag, of the body, of language—may invite the temptation to enthrone Lewis as some kind of (post)modernist *roi du crazy*. But the motivation behind Lewis' drive to assert himself as "total filmmaker" merits closer attention.

Once more, the opening sequence of *The Patsy* provides a useful starting point. After Stanley makes a spectacle of himself in the doorway, he is approached by Brandford's staff. He backs away as they advance, spluttering and squirming, until he finds himself against an open window—and falls out. When his "persecutors" begin to peer out of the window, the film cuts to a view of the hotel's exterior. Stanley, facing the camera, starts to descend through the center of the image. But this is a still-photographic image of Stanley—his figure is frozen in movement, suspended in mid-air. This still-image is then pushed over to one side by the appearance of large blue letters announcing the name "Jerry Lewis"—the beginning of the film's credits. Stanley Belt, the fictional Lewis-figure, is halted in his descent by the intrusion, from outside the diegesis, of the name of the Creative Presence, the name of the performer turned Author.

The ending of the film rhymes with this sequence. After a triumphant appearance on "The Ed Sullivan Show" boosts Stanley to immediate stardom, he makes a brash proposal of marriage to Ellen Betts (Ina Balin) in his hotel room. Ellen then advances towards him, and Stanley retreats from her nervously, backing out onto the patio. He reaches the balcony wall—and topples over it. Hands covering her face in sorrow, Ellen turns around to face the camera. But Lewis then reenters from the side. He addresses Ina Balin by her real name, rather than "Ellen," and announces that they're standing on a studio set, and not a "real" hotel patio. Lewis steps out of the fictional guise of Stanley Belt to present himself as "Jerry Lewis," director—and he commands the film crew to break for lunch.

*The Patsy* first presents the ascendancy of the Lewis-figure as a comic performer, and then moves rapidly beyond this—to provide Lewis' apotheosis to a more elevated status. Out of the "death" of Stanley Belt—the conventional Lewis-misfit turned showbiz success—comes the "birth" of the "total filmmaker." The end of this film provides a telling gesture—when, as *Jerry Lewis*, Lewis orders the end of *The Patsy*, he signals that the film obeys his dictates rather than those of Hollywood convention. A self-willed metaphor for Lewis' career, this film presents Lewis' advertisement-for-himself as a totalizing presence who exceeds both his familiar space as star-comedian and the "entertainment machinery" of Hollywood. *The Patsy* demonstrates how Lewis' deformations of structure, performance, and comedy are motivated by the desire to assert and to validate his own differentiated space within the Hollywood system, and to flaunt his newfound enunciative power. But this amounts to more than a simple case of self-promotion, for the auteurist films produce a series of contradictory representations of "Jerry Lewis." Although Michael Stern sees Lewis seeking within these films to come to terms with "the conflicting concepts of Jerry the ordinary guy—or extraordinary genius,"[13] the Lewis-problem exceeds such a simple dualism. Coinciding with their fervent self-promotion, the self-directed films open up a complex series of schisms within the subjective and discursive presence "Jerry Lewis."

By contrast, the solo films Lewis made with Frank Tashlin[14] in this period—*Rockabye Baby* (1958), *The Geisha Boy* (1958), *Cinderfella* (1960), *It's Only Money* (1962), *Who's Minding the Store?* (1963), and *The Disorderly Orderly* (1964)—invest in an Oedipal narrative paradigm. Although subjected to parodic treatment, this nonetheless serves as a means of defining and localizing the deviance of the Lewis-figure. The Tashlin comedies operate, that is, within the familiar dialectical process that marks classical, formalized Hollywood comedian-comedy—the conflict between the comic performer and an ordered narrative process which has as its goal the consolidation of normative masculine identity and sexuality.[15] The Tashlin-Lewis films show, as Michael Stern puts it, a "linear and socially-oriented approach," where the Lewis-figure is cast as an "innocent" in order to satirize the "plastic culture" of the U.S."[16] The films directed by Lewis, however, reveal a more complex investment in the Lewis-figure.

The narrative dislocations of the self-directed films persistently free or divert the Lewis-figures from the conventional pathway of social and sexual identity. These films are especially fascinating—or, to some tastes, infuriating—for the degree to which Lewis defines himself not by means of the conventional cultural machinery of Oedipal narrative but in relation to different facets of "Jerry Lewis"—as famous star, as comedian, as enunciator. He flamboyantly hijacks the Hollywood comedian-film and reroutes it in the process, transforming it into an insistently nontraditional vehicle for "self-expression," for the construction and presentation of a discourse of the self. Although—as *The Patsy* shows—the concept of control is crucial to this discourse, the films themselves offer a more radical splitting of Lewis—not simply into performer and auteur, but into multiple personae.

At the same time that Lewis increased the roles he performed *behind* the camera he began, to an obsessive degree, to multiply himself *within* the films.[17] He plays dual roles in *The Bellboy, The Ladies' Man* (1961), *The Errand Boy* (1961), and *The Nutty Professor* (1963). *The Patsy*, besides offering both Stanley Belt and Lewis-the-director, also features Lewis' impersonation of a female singing trio. He plays a total of seven parts in *The Family Jewels* (1965), five in *Three on a Couch* (1966), and three in *The Big Mouth* (1967). The more evident Lewis' totalizing presence as auteur, the more this presence is subjected not only to a noticeable multiplication but also to insistent fragmentation. And this process mushroomed beyond the films themselves; various media forms of the 1960s witnessed a proliferation of Lewisian personae:

(a)   the Idiot-Kid, the familiar Lewis-figure;
(b)   Las Vegas Jerry, the slick showbiz professional, increasingly evident in nightclubs and on television (as in Lewis' work as guest-host for NBC's "Tonight" show in 1962 and his own live ABC show in 1963);
(c)   Jerry Lewis, Hollywood director, another "successful" persona;
(d)   Telethon Jerry, the persona that ascended with the decline of Lewis' film career, but prefigured in the sentimental didacticisms of films like *The Errand Boy* and *The Nutty Professor*.

In the self-directed films, these personae jostle against one another. In *The Nutty Professor*, for example, the Lewisian misfit Julius Kelp transforms himself into his desired alter ego, cool and handsome nightclub entertainer Buddy Love. Love evokes Dean Martin's presence in Lewis' earlier films, but he has even greater resonance. The manipulative and self-obsessed Buddy Love is also a monstrous incarnation of "Las Vegas Jerry" [18]—implying that Lewis has "consumed" his former partner! *The Nutty Professor* explicitly pinpoints how Lewis' self-directed work is engaged in a process of rewriting its subject's "history." It is *The Patsy*, however, that provides Lewis' most sustained and polemical discourse on his "art" and career.

## A Big Night in Hollywood

Like *The Errand Boy*, which is set in a Hollywood studio, *The Patsy* propagandizes for entertainment that comes from the heart—more specifically, from Lewis' heart. The uncoordinated misfit Stanley Belt is taken in hand by Brandford's executive committee, who seek remorselessly to shape him into an all-round entertainer, a showbiz machine. Out of the unpromising raw material presented by Stanley, the Brandford team seek to manufacture a star who is a puppet to their collective dictates. In their view, individual talent can be shaped, and even created. Just as *The Nutty Professor* uses the familiar narrative framework of the Jekyll and Hyde story, *The Patsy* invokes the Frankenstein myth.[19] In this case, though, the role of the overachiever is taken by a committee that is well versed in the business of stardom. At the start of their corporate adventure, Chic Wyman (Everett Sloane), the leader of Brandford's retinue, declares that "This kid can and will be whatever we want him to be." What they demand is "some nobody," a will-less automaton who can be programmed and controlled.

Within this paradigm, that star is nothing but a designed personality whose distinguishing traits are the well-worn tricks of showbiz experts. From the start, the slick entertainment routines designed by the Brandford team are sabotaged by the eruptions of Stanley's unruly body. The committee relentlessly drills him for a stand-up comedy act, but at his debut at the Copa Cafe Stanley is overwhelmed with stage fright. He stumbles onstage, knocking the microphone over, and instead of delivering a barrage of prepackaged verbal gags, he offers a characteristically Lewisian—yet uncommonly discomfiting—spectacle of maladjustment. Stanley presents his jokes in the wrong order, turning them inside-out, and fails to accommodate himself to conventions of pacing. The extent to which this scene cannibalizes and deforms a familiar comic performance mode qualifies it as the most emphatic and extended "second-order" gagging sequence in Lewis' films. It offers simultaneously the "gagging" of a conventional process of gag-delivery and a persuasive representation of the character's *pain*: as with the opening scenes of the

*Processes of stardom:* The Errand Boy and The Patsy.

film, the spectator is made acutely aware of Stanley's suffering. The ambivalent feelings raised here make it difficult for both the club-audience and the film-spectator to accept this as "funny" in anything like a conventional sense.

This calamitous outing contrasts with Stanley's solo performance after the Brandford team have deserted their misbegotten star. Determined to show his would-be puppet-masters what he can offer on his own, Stanley replaces the stand-up routine with a sketch entitled "A Big Night in Hollywood." He casts himself as a movie-struck kid—similar to the Lewis-figures in *Hollywood or Bust* (1956) and *The Errand Boy*—who gazes on in fascination at the movie stars attending a swank Hollywood premiere. Rescuing two discarded $100 tickets, the kid sees a path into the star-packed playground of his fantasy. Out of his humble street clothes—with the aid of a knife, a can of black paint and some fast-motion cinematography—the kid improvises a top-hat, cane, black tie, and dress suit. Now that he looks the part, he strolls jauntily off to the theater, and is allowed to enter—and the sketch ends.

As in *The Errand Boy*, Lewis/Stanley plays the eternal fan who, through his innate talent, realizes his ambition to become part of the magical (Hollywood) world of entertainment. Although outwardly he must conform, inside he retains the integrity of the kid. For Stanley, the sketch is the articulation of his own *ideal* of stardom—and, indeed, he becomes an immediate success as a result of it. But the sketch also functions as an allegory of Lewis' own rise to power. When the kid struts into the movie theater at the end of "A Big Night in Hollywood," it is simultaneously the walk that Stanley makes into the big-time of showbiz success. Yet it is also a journey that Lewis has already made himself. Everything in the sketch—and ultimately within the film itself—is defined blatantly in terms of the pervasive textual and intertextual presence "Jerry Lewis." In the circuit of subjective overdetermination revealed through "A Big Night in Hollywood," Jerry Lewis (director) uses Jerry Lewis (performer) to play Stanley Belt (the Lewis-character), whose *impersonation* of the familiar Lewis-figure brings him fame. Furthermore, "A Big Night in Hollywood" is itself an extended version of a sketch Lewis had performed on one of his TV specials in 1957, when he was attempting to consolidate a solo career after the trauma of the "divorce" from Dean Martin.[20]

After the Ed Sullivan show, Stanley's elevated status enables him to take control, and out of Wally Brandford's old crew he fashions his own team. Although Stanley directly turns the tables on Brandford's men, a different tactic is required for Ellen Betts. The only two people in the film who, from early on, recognize and encourage Stanley's natural talent are women: Ellen, and gossip-columnist Hedda Hopper. At a promotional party, Stanley takes one look at a ludicrous umbrella hat worn by Hopper and is unable to restrain his desire to collapse into hysterical laughter. But instead of feeling affronted, Hopper says to Stanley's PR agent: "You've come across someone who hasn't learned to be phony. He thought something, and he said it—which was real and honest. And now if you apply that to his performance, you've got a great success." Ellen also recognizes Stanley's worth; she is guided by an idealistic and familial agenda that contrasts with the mercenary motives of the men in the Brandford team. She beseeches: "Let's have an understanding as to why we're going to do this—if it's at all feasible. Are we going to do this because we're spoiled—and used to a comfortable, well-oiled machine? Or is it simply because we've been happy working as a family, and we hate the thought of breaking up?" It is revealing, though, that Stanley is not merely *incorporated into* the "family" at the end of *The Patsy*, but he secures the *central* position of power. This suggests that the driving motive behind Stanley's success is not really the finding of a place *among* others—a sense of belonging—so much as the achieving of dominance over them. This receives a somewhat ambivalent representation.

Stanley's humanizing of the machinery of professional entertainment coincides with his total control, but in the process Stanley is himself transformed. As he fires off instructions to his newly appointed staff, the business-suited Stanley Belt acts with the polished self-assurance (and implicit self-regard) of Buddy Love. However, once the danger of corruptive egomania is introduced as a possible consequence of stardom, Stanley is immediately killed off. This is not the only foreclosure involved here, for Stanley's brisk "demise" serves also to block the consummation of his relationship with Ellen soon after he has brusquely commanded her to marry him. Lewis kills off the fictional obligations that constrain him, to create himself as totalizing presence, as the film's director. Within the discourse of self-creation—of vital importance to the films Lewis directed—heterosexual procreation cannot easily find a place. The process of creating "Jerry Lewis" out of the Lewisian misfit Stanley Belt directly substitutes for "normal" sex—the "Jerry Lewis" who appears at the end of *The Patsy* is not "of woman born."

The most acutely self-mythologizing of Lewis' films, *The Patsy* postulates that the self can be destroyed and reformulated at will, and that the creation of the self is precisely the responsibility of the "creative self." Throughout most of the film, Ellen's principal function is to serve as a maternal presence: she provides emotional and psychological support, nurturing Stanley's fragile ego in his moments of dejection. When Stanley proves that he can make it on his own, his need for such external support is eliminated. His forced exit from the film is swiftly followed by Ellen's own eradication. But where Stanley *disappears* from the screen for his miraculous rebirth as "Jerry Lewis," the mask of "Ellen" is stripped from Ina Balin onscreen—and at the command of her director. As Lewis leads her out through the studio in the final scene, Ina Balin becomes merely one of the personnel over whom he exerts control. Within this particularly accentuated and male-centered discourse of the self, woman occupy, of necessity, a secondary place. So when the *story* moves towards an inevitably more active role for the woman—as sexual partner, as procreator—it is jettisoned. Ellen Betts is exposed as a controlled part of the filmic masquerade that is very firmly in Lewis' own hands.

The ending of *The Patsy* suggests how Lewis' self-directed project necessitates an insistent reformulation of difference. The divisions of sexual difference are, along with more general distinctions between self and other, subjugated to differences existing within the self. Lewis simultaneously exploits and reorders the Hollywood cinema's capacity for heightened illusionism, for fantasy-making. For Lewis, film is expressly a vehicle for magic—it makes possible a reformulation of the world, of the self, and of the traditional relations that exist between the two. More pointedly, Lewis' comedies celebrate the nonconformist desires of the "child" who, through fantasy, can reshape the adult world in accordance with his own desires. By giving expression to the "kid" within him, for example, Stanley Belt proves his superiority to the group of manipulative adults who had tried to make him conform to their wishes. Lewis' films repeatedly enact such childlike fantasies of revolt against the demands of the adult world, the sexual world, the world of differences. But what distinguishes Lewis from most film comedians—who frequently show a proclivity toward child-like play and fantasy—is the protection and privilege granted to the radically deforming performer by the director.

*The Patsy* also exemplifies the problems which began to develop within this project.

Lewis continued to invest value in the figure of the "kid," the unspoiled, unknowing exponent of a pre-adult regime equated with honesty, simplicity, and caring. But the "Jerry Lewis" who takes the film in hand at the end of *The Patsy* is himself a shrewd and knowing professional who displays his mastery of the cinematic machine. And in between these two is the brief eruption of Las Vegas Jerry, elided through blatant prestidigitation. The extreme gear–shifts at the end of the film present, in rapid succession, *opposed*, as well as *distinct*, Lewisian personae. Although the joking "assassination" of Stanley Belt appears to be his punishment for deserting the values of the "kid," the slick director "Jerry Lewis" is at a similar extreme from such simplicity. Even though the film ends as an unmistakable celebration of the magical artificiality of film, the controlling presence of "Jerry Lewis" is inscribed as its fundamental premise. In Lewis' films, the seductive fantasy of eternal childhood is overtly established in resistance to the adult regime. "Jerry Lewis," however, is a very *adult* manipulator, and his towering presence makes it difficult to specify what form of wish-fulfillment is ultimately offered by the film. Does *The Patsy* celebrate the child triumphing over the adult world, or is it concerned more with the adult *seeking* the eternal fantasy of childhood? Or is it, perhaps, the Lewis-film in which the latter most obviously overwhelms the former? The self-directed films offered Jerry-the-Kid the opportunity to take charge of the filmic process of fantasy-making, and to reorder the world in his own image. But to what extent has the idealism of Lewis' Big-Night-in-Hollywood become tarnished by his consolidation as a flamboyantly successful and long familiar component of the Hollywood entertainment machine?

## Coming from the Gut?

In the mid-1960s, Lewis' long run as a major cinematic attraction drew to a close. From 1951 to 1963 his films had figures repeatedly among the annual top ten box-office grossers,[21] but his subsequent ventures as star and/or director fared less well, especially after he terminated his 17-year relationship with Paramount Pictures in 1965. After *The Patsy*, Lewis completed only four more films as a director-star before disappearing from the screen for a decade, making a modest return as a total filmmaker in the 1980s, with *Hardly Working* (1981) and *Cracking Up* (aka *Smorgasbord*, 1983). The most significant recent addition to Lewis' film canon, though, remains *The King of Comedy* (1983), Martin Scorsese's cult movie which is itself a twisted reworking of *The Patsy*. While famous comedian Jerry Lewis is cast in a straight dramatic role—as Jerry Langford, a comic who has become an institution as a slick talk-show host—serious actor Robert De Niro plays Rupert Pupkin, a would-be comedian-celebrity who kidnaps his idol Langford in a desperate bid to achieve television stardom. A disconcerting black comedy that probes the obsessions of fandom, *The King of Comedy* turns on its head the discourse of stardom in *The Patsy*.

With the decline of his film career in the mid-1960s, Lewis invested his energies increasingly in his role as the presenter and driving force of "The Jerry Lewis MDA Telethon." This annual television event provides a further twist to the dynamics of Lewis' rise to power as it is represented in *The Patsy*. In that film, the professional entertainment machine is ultimately tempered not through the idealistic familial agenda proposed by Ellen but through the strongly self-centered regimes consolidated by, respectively, Stanley Belt and Lewis-the-director. The Telethon, although it is so firmly dominated by its star presenter, nonetheless espouses a rhetoric of "family" that is remi-

*Processes of stardom:* The King of Comedy, *"a twisted reworking of* The Patsy."

niscent of Ellen's ideal. Lewis and his aides refer continually to the supportive "family" of presenters, performers, and sponsors who donate their time, talent, and money to the cause of the Muscular Dystrophy Association. Lewis' extended surrogate family, however, comprises not simply the "abled" who present the show and the disabled who form its pretext ("Jerry's Kids"), but also the Telethon viewers—who are bonded to Lewis and to the MDA by the "Love Network" (the name Lewis gives to the combination of local stations who contribute to and relay the show). The Telethon's family discourse gains special force from its regular annual presence within the domestic spaces of the United States. Throughout the U.S., Labor Day is Telethon Day—and Jerry Lewis Day—networked for a guaranteed 22 hours into potentially every home in the country. Given that his "family" now encompasses more or less the whole of northern America, it is difficult not to see the Telethon as the apotheosis of Lewis' self-willed celebrity. ( . . . )

## The Strange Career of Jerry Lewis

Lewis has certainly come a long way since he began nervously treading the boards in his teens, performing exaggerated mimes to accompany popular and operatic records. When Dean Martin took over the role of the "voice," the security of his sheltering presence left Lewis free to play out his masque of the dysfunctional masculine body. But after the split with Martin, Lewis had only himself—or, rather, a profusion of selves, spun out from a center which seemed increasingly incapable of holding together such an atomic dispersal of personality. The Telethon celebrates simultaneously Lewis' multiplicity and his limitations. It makes a fascinating culmination to his career, but it is difficult not to perceive Lewis' role within it as an exercise both in awesome self-aggrandizement and grotesquely unaware self-parody.

Above all else, the annual MDA extravaganza brings into sharp focus a problem Lewis has faced throughout his career—the problem of how the performer can be reconciled with the extremity of that which is performed. In the Martin-Lewis period, the "straight" man sketched in an idealized profile of masculine identity and sexuality as a backdrop against which Lewis could perform his deformations. As a director, his project was far more ambitious, not only furthering his celebrity as a solo performer but also establishing his stylistic signature as a "total filmmaker" through calculated deformations of the conventions of genre, narrative, and comic delivery. But where these distinctive achievements as a comic star and filmmaker are premised upon *distancing* himself from familiar rules, norms, and conventions, the persona of Telethon Jerry invites and requires proximity. However, Lewis' sentimental embrace of the cause of the disabled is filtered through the distancing conventions of professionalized televisual/Las Vegas entertainment, where the demands of the "show" are inevitably a second-order substitute for and simulation of "feeling."

Through forceful manipulation of his "personality" and his history, the Lewis of the Telethon holds together a grandiose mixture of in-your-face pathos, variety spectacle, fundraising campaign, and corporate self-promotion. Telethon Jerry is at a far remove from the Idiot-Kid: his body no longer functions as a signifying simulation of disability and disadvantage, and he presents himself as an extraordinarily able vehicle for expressing the plight and the hopes of the disabled. While the Lewis who prowls in front of the Telethon cameras is manifestly a slick professional, a grand old man of the media entertainment machine, the backgrounds are dominated by an affectionate caricature sketch of the young, unkempt, uncoordinated Lewis. And his earlier performative strategies of comic deformation still erupt repeatedly through the staid professionalism of the Telethon host—although in a far more restrained and controlled manner. Lewis will interrupt the rehearsed performances of others, or will draw attention to and mimic the cue cards held in front of him, or he will rush up to the camera and push his face into it—a technique Lewis was known for in his 1950s TV work. These moments of familiar "spontaneity" are important evocations of the young, pre-Telethon Lewis. They serve to reaffirm Lewis' history as a comedian, but, at the same time, they make plain the difference between Lewis-the-comic and the crusading man-with-a-mission.

As Telethon Jerry is bombarded by continual onscreen eulogies from both sufferers of dystrophic disease and familiar showbiz personalities, the "Love Network" carries a forceful message of love for "Jerry Lewis"—man, messiah, institution. The evocations of Lewis' earlier comic style serve both to "humanize" and to deify the man. They are a reminder of the self-contained past that the man-god "Jerry Lewis" has grown out of but not abandoned. Telethon Jerry, the humanitarian, has ascended from the ranks of mere mortal celebrity. As in his auteurist films of the early 1960s, the Lewis of the Telethon deforms the norms of his past, "simple" celebrity. He has reassembled the elements of his earlier personae to create a startlingly new, yet equally contradictory, vision of "Jerry

Lewis." Thirty years ago, when Lewis reinvented himself as a "total filmmaker," the adventurous deformation of structured self-containment—of narrative, gag, and mood—was accompanied, inevitably, by a studied reformulation of "Jerry Lewis." The same principle holds for Telethon Jerry, although what is remarkable about this particular incarnation is that Lewis' vehicle is no longer a deformation of the operating principles of comedy, but a deformation of the figure and the clearly self-centered rationale of Jerry Lewis, comic.

## Notes

1. Lynn Snowden, "Fifty ways to kill an insect by an exjunkie exterminator," *Esquire*, February 1992.
2. "Struggling on Two Fronts" [Godard in interview with Jacques Bontemps, Jean-Louis Comolli, Michel Delahaye, and Jean Narboni], in Jim Hillier, ed., *Cahiers du Cinéma: 1960–1968: New Wave, New Cinema, Re-evaluating Hollywood* (Cambridge, MA: Harvard University Press, 1986), 295.
3. Andrew Sarris, *The American Cinema: Directors and Directions: 1929–1968* (New York: E. P. Dutton, 1968), 243.
4. Jerry Lewis, *The Total Film-Maker* (New York: Warner Paperback Library, 1973), 32–33.
5. Leonard Maltin, *The Great Movie Comedians* (New York: Crown, 1978), 217–18.
6. Ibid., 218.
7. For a general consideration of the comedian-comedy, see Steve Seidman, *Comedian Comedy: A Tradition in Hollywood Film* (Ann Arbor, MI: UMI Research Press, 1981).
8. Bosley Crowther, "*My Friend Irma*," *The New York Times* (September 29, 1949).
9. "*The Geisha Boy*," *Newsweek* (December 24, 1958).
10. Jean-Pierre Coursodon, "Jerry Lewis," in Coursodon and Pierre Sauvage, *American Directors*, volume II (New York: McGraw Hill, 1983), 197.
11. Ibid., 190.
12. Scott Bukatman, "Paralysis in Motion: Jerry Lewis' Life as a Man," *Camera Obscura* 17 (Fall 1988), 197.
13. Michael Stern, "Jerry Lewis b. Joseph Levitch, Newark, New Jersey, 1926 res. Hollywood," *Bright Lights* 1:3 (Summer 1975), 6.
14. In his work as gagman, writer, and director, Frank Tashlin was one of the distinctive creative forces in American screen comedy from the late 1940s to the early 1960s. His brash, flash comic style—nurtured in the animated short—was perfectly suited to the context of 1950s consumerism, as is shown by his satirical swipes at Hollywood artifice (*Hollywood or Bust*, 1956), rock'n'roll (*The Girl Can't Help It*, 1956), and the advertising business (*Will Success Spoil Rock Hunter?*, 1957). In Lewis, Tashlin stumbled upon the nearest possible human approximation to a cartoon figure—a point made explicitly at the end of *The Geisha Boy*, where Lewis impersonates Bugs Bunny (a former Tashlin protégé). The relationship was highly productive: Lewis worked with Tashlin on two of the final Martin-Lewis vehicles and on six of the solo films made between 1957 and 1964. On numerous occasions, Lewis has claimed that his own style as a gagman and director owed a substantial debt to his experiences with Tashlin.
15. Frank Krutnik, "A Spanner in the Works? Genre, Narrative and the Hollywood Comedian," Henry Jenkins and Kristine Karnick, eds., *Classical Hollywood Comedy* (New York: AFI/Routledge, 1994), 17–38.
16. Stern, "Jerry Lewis," 5.
17. Ibid., 4 ff.
18. Ibid., 10.
19. The horror-story associations persist in discourses on Lewis and his career. Leslie Bennetts concluded her recent profile of Lewis by suggesting that within the "monstrous" machine "Jerry

Lewis," a fragile and pained Joseph Levitch (Lewis' real name) is seeking refuge, or perhaps escape: "The voice on the other end of the phone is the powerful one of the 67-year-old man, but inside it I hear something else, something faint but as persistent as an echo that follows you wherever you go. It is the pain of the angry little boy, and I suddenly realize that the message delivered by the protesters is the one he has heard in his nightmares all his life: They don't love you. No matter how much you try to do for them, they don't love you." "Jerry vs. The Kids," *Vanity Fair* (September 1993), 37.

20. "The Jerry Lewis Show," NBC, December 27, 1957. This sketch was recently included in "Jerry . . . Alone at the Top," the third part of "Martin and Lewis: Their Golden Age of Comedy," shown on the Disney cable channel in 1992.

21. Corbett Steinman, *Reel Facts: The Movie Book of Records* (New York: Vintage Books, 1978), 405.

# "I Can Take a Hint": Social Ineptitude, Embarrassment, and *The King of Comedy*

## William Ian Miller (1996)

The phrase "I can take a hint," when said seriously, contains its own denial. It reveals that the speaker has not been very adept at recognizing the hints already given, nor very graceful about not making a scene once he has recognized them. Its very utterance has the effect of punishing the hint-giver by making her hint fail as a hint. The truly successful hint works by gaining its end with no extra awkwardness added to the social encounter. The good hint should be barely perceived by the person toward whom it is directed. We could even say that it should not really become a part of his active consciousness. It should simply trigger a sense that it's time to go or that the line he is pursuing needs to be terminated. The good hint achieves the invisibility of the natural.[1]

People vary in their sensitivity to hints. The vast majority of us, in most settings, seem to pick up on them with reasonable facility. But we shouldn't be picking up on too many of them. That would be a sign of paranoia or self-loathing, if we are being hypersensitive, or a sign of how little we are in fact esteemed, if we are only middlingly sensitive. Yet we should worry if we are picking up on no hints. Few of us are so delightful all the time that we could never be the object of a distancing hint. It might be that our competence in reading signals is so habitual, so much a matter of second nature, that we are not conscious of the hints we discern and act upon properly. But it might also mean that we are being somewhat dense.

We are hint-givers as well as hint-receivers. And this fact should help us hone our skills as hint-receivers. But not necessarily. Hints can be given with focused intention, or hints can just be read (rightly) into rather unfocused unconscious distancing signals. There is no reason that the unconscious hint-giver need have any special aptitude for discerning when she is the object of someone else's hint. The person skilled in giving intended hints, however, should also be proficient in discerning when she is the object of someone else's hint. That skill is often what we think of as the very substance of good manners and tact, of refined social sensitivity. I am assuming, of course, that these hints are successful ones, that is, those that do their work anonymously.

The situation needs to be complicated a little more by noting that hints whose failure has the capacity to produce scenes come in two varieties: those that are distancing, that reveal the hinter as wishing to be free of the other, and those that seek greater closeness, as in hints of sexual attraction, of continued social relations, of desires to give or receive gifts. Each type involves somewhat different social and psychological risks. The risk of making distancing hints is of giving offense and the attendant awkwardnesses that accompany giving offense: embarrassment, regret, maybe even guilt and remorse. The risks of making hints of desired contact are the risks of rejection and its attendant pains:

as before, embarrassment, but more seriously and centrally, humiliation, shame, chagrin, indignation and resentment. Both hints of distance and closeness tend to establish a moral and social hierarchy in which the distancer or the desired one has a higher status. There is a certain moral economy here. The two types of hint often appear in tandem: the hint of closeness, not unusually, provokes hints to keep away, while the distancing hint often prompts desperate and pathetic hints of closeness and reassurance from the rejected party. It is clear that a certain right inheres in the distancing position, a right to be free of relations not consented to.[2] The person seeking closeness is always cast in the role of a seeker of favors, or more accurately, of the other's consent to have her social spaces intruded upon.

The structure of this moral economy means that, somewhat perversely, we are inclined to find the seeker of closeness to be more off-putting than we are to find the distancer off-putting. Social obtuseness in the former produces in others contempt, disgust, annoyance, emotions that motivate removal and distancing; social ineptness in the distancer produces hatred, indignation, resentment, emotions that, though hostile, impel us to get closer even if only to wreak havoc or take vengeance. The seeker of closeness is thus a nudnick, a nerd, a creep, a dork, a schnorrer (Yiddish seems to make a myriad of refined distinctions in this social type), and more recently, a harasser or a stalker; the distancer is rude, boorish, a cold fish, or more charitably, shy or reserved. Ineptness in the distancer is not, however, simply a matter of giving offense. There is another kind of ineptness: failing to keep others off, being too accessible. Thus the patsy, pushover, chump, on the one hand, or the gracious, sweet, long-suffering soul on the other. Gender figures in this also. We usually envisage men as more likely to violate the norms of distance than women: it is men who are usually treated to epithets like nerd and creep. A woman who doesn't pick up on distancing signals might be pushy, or aggressive, whiny or dependent, but not a dork or a nudnick. Men, on the other hand, are cut more slack for being rude as distancers than woman are, even though women are caught in the double bind of being condemned both for not being circumspect enough about men approaching them and for not being generally more welcoming when approached.

"I can take a hint," as I indicated above, is already a sign that a hint has not succeeded in doing its work without social disruption, that is, without giving offense and without that offense becoming the basis for "making a scene," for "I can take a hint" makes a scene. It is the indignant response of someone who feels that he hasn't been treated to the respect he feels himself entitled to. But if indignation is the emotion of the nudnick who finally gets the message, embarrassment and mortification, or a more generalized sensation of awkwardness, are likely to characterize the emotional position of the hinter and observers of the scene. Embarrassment figures more insistently in the world of hints than just as a response to making a scene. The inept reader of distancing signals embarrasses us even before he must be disciplined by being forced to "get the hint" or "get the message." It is his denseness that makes the situation awkward for others long before it degenerates into a "scene."

This is a long prologue to a tale which I must make a bit longer still, for the failure of hints and the embarrassment generated by inept hint takers are the central motifs of *The King of Comedy*, which is my subject in this essay. Let me sketch briefly some salient features of embarrassment. It has been observed that embarrassment and certain closely related sensations of awkwardness and social discomfort can be experienced vicariously. We can feel embarrassed on someone's behalf even though that person does not feel

*"Embarrassment is also contagious." Robert De Niro embarrasses Diahnne Abbott in* The King of Comedy.

embarrassed but, as our own sensations judge, should feel so. This allows us to experience a doubling of the embarrassment. Not only do we feel the embarrassment we would feel if we were in Rupert Pupkin's predicament, but we also sympathize with the embarrassment that Rupert's ineptitude has caused the other party. In fact, it is this latter embarrassment that triggers the former. Because Rupert embarrasses others, we imagine to our own embarrassment what it would be like to be so embarrassing and so dim as not to have perceived we were.

Embarrassment is also contagious; that is, we can catch it from another who does feel it. In these instances it is not the case that we are feeling embarrassed by what the other is feeling embarrassed by—that would simply be another example of vicarious embarrassment. The contagion of embarrassment is a function of the fact that the display of embarrassment can itself be embarrassing. Embarrassment can thus feed on itself, producing more embarrassment in the embarrassed person who now can add the embarrassment of a loss of poise to whatever failings gave rise to the initial embarrassment. The manifest embarrassment of another also embarrasses others who witness it. Blushes produce blushes because embarrassment makes demands on our tact which we are not always up to. Do we pretend not to notice? Do we notice and say something to defuse the situation? Or does our embarrassment at their embarrassment do just the right thing by making us a community of equals again? Embarrassment, it has been observed, is not only disruptive of a smooth social order; it is called upon in many situations to do the remedial work of restoring smoothness to a disturbed social setting.[3] Embarrassment works, as we all well know, to effect apology, to make amends for our gaffes and awkwardnesses. In fact, if we are not embarrassed or embarrassable we are unlikely also to be very adept at picking up on the distancing signals that others give us.

There lurks here an issue which may be of special interest to film theorists: the process by which the viewer develops identifications with characters, themes, or the camera's eye might vary with the particular emotion at stake. Certain depicted emotions, like embarrassment, because contagious and vicariously experienceable, prompt the reproduction of themselves in the viewer; other emotions cannot reproduce themselves. Compare, for instance, jealousy: one does not feel jealous on someone else's behalf. We can sympathize with their jealousy or understand it, but we do not feel it. In this regard, it is unlike embarrassment. Any theory of the identificatory process in film will remain forever oversimplified without a more detailed consideration of how spectator sympathy works in conjunction with different kinds of emotions.

Embarrassment is an emotion that has a strangely insistent connection with laughter and comedy. We might think of embarrassment as occupying the middle ground between humiliation on its dark side and amusement on its light side. Embarrassing incidents are the same things that provide mirth to observers and even to the poor embarrassed soul within hours or days of the event. Embarrassing events are thus distinguishable from humiliating ones. We will regale others to our own and their delight with our embarrassments, but we will guard our humiliations and reveal them to no one unless we are engaged in certain ritualized degradations like confession or psychoanalysis.[4] Yet humiliation too partakes of the comic world, for our humiliations often occur to the delight of others, producing in them Hobbes' "sudden glory"[5] and the gray mirth of Schadenfreude.

The emotion we name amusement,[6] and by this I mean the feeling that we have in response to things deemed humorous rather than the sense of amusement as when we say we amuse ourselves by playing basketball, seems to find in the embarrassing much of the occasion for its elicitation. Not only is it that the same events that are embarrassing can with a slight shift of perspective also appear amusing, but also that embarrassment itself provides amusement, if not to the embarrassed person then surely to others. But this is tricky, for we think of embarrassment as an unpleasant emotion; indeed it is sufficiently painful to provide much of the discipline and threat that keeps us functioning as mannerly and sociably presentable people. Embarrassing situations are embarrassing for all concerned, the one who embarrasses, the one who is embarrassed by the one who embarrasses, and those that witness the spectacle. At some level watching others make fools of themselves is painful. We do not want our humanity so utterly vulnerable, our bases for self-respect so fragile. Yet it is precisely the fragile basis of our respectability that produces the comic: what is a clown, what are the grotesque, slapstick, black humor, burlesque, if not the spectacle of our ineffable foolishness? We are dealing here, rather obviously, with some pretty deep-seated ironies of the social and psychological.[7]

Here I note as an aside that it has been a commonplace of literary theory since Aristotle that certain emotional experiences in the observer may be as constitutive of a particular artistic genre as its other formal generic structures. Aristotle was clearly onto something when he made the elicitation of certain emotions the signature of tragedy. We have even come to the point where we categorize films by the emotions we expect them to elicit: horror film is named after a type of fear, revenge films engage the passion of vengefulness and its close associates: indignation, resentment, and the satisfaction of justice done. Tear jerkers often elicit a range of emotions from wistfulness to pity. Action films exhilarate and partake of aspects of apprehension, revenge and horror. We would need to distinguish more precisely the differences between the emotion we experience as an observer of a fictional representation from the one we give the same name when the representation is not fictional or to the one we say we feel when we are one of the principal actors. We would also want to recognize that our precise emotional responses depend to some extent on what we figure the emotional situation of the observed party to be. Thus the apprehension we experience in horror films may well have a different structure depending, say, on whether the character in the film is also experiencing fear and terror or whether she is blithely oblivious to the danger that lurks behind the closet door.

Embarrassment and amusement also share some of the same somatic features. Laughter, central to the bodily presentation of amusement, is no stranger to embarrassment either, although distinctly less central than blushing. Laughter, as we all know, can mark a variety of psychic, social, and somatic states: embarrassment, malice, contempt, joy, anxiety, awkwardness, getting tickled, being amused, or simply supplying the necessary signs of engagement in amiable conversation. It may be that these states share nothing more than the fact that they all can trigger laughter. Is there anything really similar between the awkward laughter of embarrassment, and the laughter of genuine amusement? It is never too difficult to tell one from the other. Yet they are both laughters; they are not different genera, but species within a genus and they share a certain common relation with the ridiculous, the ludicrous, the humiliating, and the embarrassing, and the comic universe in which they thrive.

Like laughter, comedy cuts across a number of emotional domains. Comic laughter is not only the laughter of amiability. Most any laugh provoked by the comic (we may thus except the laugh of being tickled) is over-determined: part nervous, part "sudden glory," part just joining with others who are laughing, part amusement and mirth and part relief in the style of "oh please be funny enough, so that I don't have to feel embarrassed by your not being funny." This last item is surely some of what motivates laughter at the performances of that most vulnerable of souls, the standup comedian, the modern clown. Is it possible to separate our fear of his embarrassing us by his being embarrassing from the total experience of the comedy? Consider the emotions elicited by observing an unfunny comedian, something we will take up again shortly when we meet Rupert Pupkin. If humiliation lies in pretending to bigger shoes than you can fill, then the unfunny comedian humiliates himself and one of the sure indications that you are watching someone humiliate himself is that you will be embarrassed by the display.

Embarrassment, comedy, stand-up comedians, and the norms of respectable and competent social behavior, especially as these have to do with the practices surrounding leave taking, conversation and interaction closure all come together in Martin Scorsese's underappreciated classic, *The King of Comedy*.[8] The movie, according to press critics and Scorsese in interviews, is about the American obsession with celebrity. The film presents the story of Rupert Pupkin's obsessive drive to get his break on network television as a stand-up comedian. Rupert (Robert De Niro) is a pathetic 34-year-old messenger boy who enjoys an active fantasy life imagining himself the host of his own talk show which he stages in a room of the house he shares with his mother amidst life-size cardboard cutouts of Liza Minnelli and Jerry Lewis.[9] Jerry Lewis plays Jerry Langford, the popular host of a late night talk show and the object of Rupert's emulation and fixation. One night Rupert insinuates

*"Rupert Pupkin, ladies and gentlemen, let's hear it for Rupert Pupkin."*

himself into Jerry's car after having helped him brave a throng of autograph hounds and groupies like himself; he confesses his ambitions to Jerry, asks Jerry if he would listen to his act, and extracts from him an unfelt concession to contact his office. The film then treats us to the painful experience of Rupert's numerous attempts to see Jerry as he remains oblivious to the rebuffs and brush-offs from Jerry's staff people. Interspersed with scenes of Rupert cooling his heels in the reception area of Jerry's office are Rupert's fantasies: Jerry begging Rupert to take over his show, Jerry declaring Rupert a comic genius, Rupert getting married on the Langford show to Rita, a bartender who was once the object of Rupert's fantasies from afar when they were in high school. Pursuant to Jerry's invitation in one of these fantasies to visit Jerry's summer home, Rupert actually shows up with Rita and is rudely sent packing. In the next scene, Rupert, with the assistance of another psychotic Langford fan, Masha (Sandra Bernhard), kidnaps Jerry and the end of it all is that Rupert uses Jerry as a hostage to secure his own appearance on Jerry's show after which he blithely goes off to jail, but not before he, we, and Rita view his monologue on network TV in Rita's bar. The movie closes with various voice-overs in the style of the evening news in which we find that Rupert Pupkin's name has become a household word, that his performance was viewed by 87 million households, that he was sentenced to six years in the white collar minimum security facility in Allenwood, PA, that Rupert's memoirs have been purchased by a New York publishing house for more than a million dollars, that Rupert was released after serving two years and nine months of his sentence, that his best-selling autobiography will be appearing as a major motion picture. And in the final scene the resonant voice of an announcer introduces the one and only King of Comedy Rupert Pupkin who now has his own network show. "Rupert Pupkin, ladies and gentlemen, let's hear it for Rupert Pupkin. Wonderful. Rupert Pupkin, ladies and gentlemen. Rupert Pupkin, ladies and gentlemen. Let's hear it for Rupert Pupkin. Wonderful. Rupert Pupkin, ladies and gentlemen."

Let me touch on a few small items before taking up the issues of misreading social cues and the emotional responses such misreadings provoke that are so central to the movie's feel. Rupert loves his name; thus his first words to Jerry in the car: " . . . my name is Rupert Pupkin and I know the name doesn't mean very much to you but it means an awful lot to me. Believe me." At some level he seems to know it may be his best joke. He leads with it when he gives his comedy routine, even after it has been given by the announcer. Names, some think, dictate our destiny. Rupert's surely dictates his. It takes a very special person to overcome a name. Nerdy names go a long way to making their bearers nerds. In any event, the movie industry operates on such an assumption, for if names can't quite make a star, they surely can prevent one from being born. We thus have Clark Gable and Rock Hudson, names which have a style every bit as parodiable as the names we give residential subdivisions. Could Rupert possibly be a skilled social actor with such a name? He does not disappoint our expectations.

The movie ends by obsessing on Rupert's name and getting it right, something no one but Rupert in the movie does. To others he is Mr. Pumpkin, Mr. Puffer, Mr. Pipkin, Mr. Pubnik, Mr. Krupkin, Mr. Potkin, etc. Together with the improbable number of households (the entire U.S.) viewing Rupert's night on the Langford show, this repetition of his correct name by someone other than himself, presented somewhat slower than it would be in reality, is a very insistent indication that the extravagant news items and voice-overs at the end of the film are just another one of Rupert's fantasies. Critics have taken it straight, some going so far as to chastise Scorsese's irresponsibility in depicting the rewards obtainable by criminal devotion to celebrity.[10] In the beginning of the film Rupert's fantasies are clearly marked as such. When Jerry finally extricates himself from Rupert after their first encounter, Rupert falls into reverie and the scene breaks to Jerry and Rupert having lunch. Here it is Jerry who is importuning a reluctant Rupert to take over his show for six weeks which a self-satisfied Rupert deigns to do. Scorsese makes sure we do not mistake the reverie for reality by breaking to Rupert in his room acting the part of Rupert in the fantasy. Rupert must even suffer the indignity of his mother's off-screen interruptions ("What are you doing down there so late?"). It is striking that the Rupert of the fantasy speaks with more reserve (but still it is a reserve with many indicia of "showbiz" vulgar) and less volume than he is actually uttering the lines in his room. We thus see explicitly the metamorphosis Rupert's self-conception effects on the raw reality of Rupert's self that others see. Rupert does not hear himself as others hear him, nor does he see himself as others see him. Maybe. There is more than an occasional indication that Rupert is not without some strange access to insightful self-knowledge, of which more anon.

If the reality of the final scene is less obviously the stuff of fantasy, that is only because Rupert and the movie have insistently moved to make his fantasy and his reality converge into a kind of "fan-reality" in which fans become the performers. Earlier fantasies were clearly signaled as such, but now we, like Rupert, are not sure anymore where fantasy ends and reality begins. This is a film that delights in all kinds of ambiguities that arise when the boundaries between reality and fantasy, play-acting and playing at acting, television and life, good jokes and bad jokes, are not clearly demarcated. Was Rupert's monologue supposed to be funny or supposed to be bad? The critics split on this question, as have people I have polled; even Scorsese and De Niro split, the former thinking it weak, the latter thinking it great.[11] Ambiguities and ambivalences figure in the casting. We thus have dramatic actors such as De Niro trying to do comedy just as Rupert Pupkin is trying to do comedy and as De Niro as Jake LaMotta did comedy at the conclusion of *Raging Bull*, Scorsese's film before *The King of Comedy*. Sandra Bernhard, a standup comic, gets her acting debut as a dramatic actress. Tony Randall, Victor Borge, Joyce Brothers play themselves, but they are not just being themselves, but playing themselves, self-enacting. And if De Niro is remarkable because he seems to come less determined by his prior roles than most big stars, less encumbered with the sludge of his public person, the opposite is the case with Jerry Lewis, about whom no one does not have an opinion, and, unless French, usually a negative one. Lewis is a comedian playing a dramatic role, but playing a comic in that role. Lewis figures greatly in what I take to be one of the central implicit issues raised by the film: the unfunny comedian, the generally inept social actor, and the embarrassed discomfort he creates in his auditors. For every occasion someone might have actually laughed at Lewis one has cringed in

Rupert's fantasy: Rupert and Jerry

embarrassment at least three times. The real Lewis, in other words, has caused us almost as much discomfort as Rupert will cause us.

Rupert's fantasies are wonderful stuff. They are pure wish-fulfillment, but they are not ends in themselves; rather they motivate Rupert to actualize them. The strength of his fantasies seems to overwhelm the embattled reality of others. When Jerry, in a desperate attempt to bring closure to Rupert's verbal barrage in the car, tells Rupert to call his office and ask for his secretary, Rupert replies: "You know how many times I had this conversation in my head? This is beautiful." Jerry responds with cool patronizing contempt: "And did it always turn out this way?" Rupert: "Yeah, it did." Later, he goes to Jerry's summer home with Rita because Jerry, in a fantasy, invited him. In these fantasies Rupert, more successfully than he can in real life, adopts Jerry's cool competence, while Jerry is reduced to acting like Rupert (or the real Jerry Lewis) as he fawns, importunes, and tells lame jokes. Yet Rupert's visions are indelibly Rupert's, still manifesting tastelessness and bad social judgment. In one he imagines his high school principal as a special guest on the Langford show, called there to pay homage to Rupert and marry him to Rita on national television. The taste mimics the tackiness of Tiny Tim but reproduces it as something to aspire to rather than to parody (as even Tim was able to do). And the irredeemability of his smallness of character manifests itself in the apology his vision extracts from the principal on behalf of all those who made Rupert's high school life miserable. Rupert thus constructs humiliation rituals (pathetic ones in the form of fantasized apology and deference) for others as a source of his pleasure. At dinner with Rita, Rupert links himself with one well-attested Christian tradition which makes the joys of heaven the delight of watching the pains of the damned in hell. He paints Rita a future of bliss in which they will be able to "look down on everybody and yell, 'Hey, tough luck, suckers. Better luck next time.'"

Triumph is the contempt of losers for losers, Nietzschean *ressentiment* writ small. Rupert thus consistently manifests contempt not only for Masha but for the other autograph seekers outside Jerry's studio. But there is something about Rupert's sheer obliviousness that makes him an object of a kind of reluctant awe. Don't we root for him because his triumph will come at Langford/ Lewis's expense? Our willingness to discover appealing characteristics in this psychotic nebbish is not quite separable from the fact that he annoys Jerry Langford, someone for whom we have as little love as we do for the actor who plays him. Thus do we participate in Rupert's Schadenfreude.

Rupert is so inept that his ineptitude produces perverse consequences, that is, ones that cannot readily be distinguished from aptitude. De Niro's Rupert is a wonderfully subtle portrait of someone who lacks subtlety, who gets all the little things wrong and misreads everyone else's hints and cues. His hair, his dress, his body posture, his facial posture, his verbal and tonal tics all capture precisely someone who just doesn't quite get it. The remarkable thing about human sociability is how subtle we are in discerning the slightest deviation in these matters. But Rupert lacks key components of this competence: he is largely clueless. We need, however, to distinguish between at least two kinds of clueless person: the one who is simply oblivious and the one who at some level of consciousness uses his ineptitude strategically.[12] We all know cases of each. The difficult matter is what kind of consciousness to attribute to the latter. They are not sufficiently clued in to have the ability to become properly socialized, yet they are not without some awareness that the offenses they give others get results. Others back off, others don't want to make scenes, others are too well socialized to be so rude as to call them on their rude-

*"Triumph is the contempt of losers for losers." Robert DeNiro and Sandra Bernhard in* The King of Comedy.

ness, their intrusiveness, their boringness, boorishness, etc. These are the people who prey off the general sociability of the majority. Yet it would be hard to attribute to them the classic mentality of the predator: that preternatural hyperawareness of each move of its would-be victim. The Ruperts of the world are not subtle hunters, nor are they generally cruel in a focused way. Such persons don't pretend, convincingly that is, not to want what they want; in this they are unlike the predator who studies how not to tip off danger alarms in his prey.[13] Yet at some level of consciousness they are not displeased with the consequences of their behavior. In straight economic terms the cost of their nerdiness, the cost of their violating all these myriad of social norms, does not outweigh the benefits they obtain by violating them.

Rupert is at different times both kinds of clueless. He really does think the excruciatingly awful jokes he tells are funny. He thinks the picture of his Pride and Joy, a card picturing the household products of the same names is witty. Yet at the same time he is not without awareness that the way to get where he wants to go is to make it very uncomfortable for others not to let him get there. But only some of the time, for his fantasies do not make him the best of cold rational actors. He does, after all, overplay his hand by showing up at Jerry's summer home for the weekend with Rita in tow. That blunder finally provokes Jerry into making a scene of his own, the one in which Rupert finally acknowledges that he can take a hint. And when the violation of little norms won't get Rupert where he wants to go, he shows little reluctance at violating big ones, such as kidnapping laws. It is not without interest that the movie cuts from Rupert's finally admitting he can take a hint at Jerry's place to him and Masha in the car with the toy gun waiting to abduct Jerry.

There is in this another clue as to what constitutes so much of the offensiveness of the socially clueless person, whether instrumentally so or not: clueless people are not forgiving of other people's similar lack of competence. Masha embarrasses Rupert as he does her; Rita embarrasses Rupert when she makes herself a little too at ease at Jerry's before Jerry arrives, putting on the record player ("You really shouldn't put that on, you know; it's not polite.") or when she takes herself on a sightseeing expedition upstairs ("No, Rita, I . . . No, Rita, I wouldn't go up there. Rita. Rita, Rita. I don't think it's a good idea . . . . Rita, I don't think you have the right to go upstairs. Rita, please, don't go up . . . Rita."). Rupert's incompetence is not a general incapacity to feel embarrassment, or even a lack of knowledge of broad ranges of appropriate behavior. It is just that he can only feel embarrassed by another and only recognizes inappropriate behavior when it is someone else's. Thus it is that Rupert will brazenly maintain to Masha that he didn't get thrown out of the building in which Jerry's office is located even though she saw him get unceremoniously chucked out by two security guards. To Rupert's mind the grossest violations of the norms of appropriate social interaction are Jerry's, not his.[14] Jerry's tact fails him and thus is Rupert forced to have to take a hint:

> Jerry:    You understand English? Take your things and go.
> Rupert:   All right, all right. I can take a hint, Jerry. I just want to ask you if you'll listen to my stuff for fifteen minutes, that's all. Is that asking too much?
> Jerry:    Yes, it is. I have a life, okay?
> Rupert:   Well, I have a life too.
> Jerry:    That's not my responsibility.
> Rupert:   Well, it is when you tell me to call you and then you don't . . . .
> Jerry:    I told you to call to get rid of you.
> Rupert:   To get rid of me?
> Jerry:    That's right.
> Rupert:   Okay. All right, I can take a hint.
> Jerry:    If I didn't tell you that, we'd still be standing on the steps of my apartment.

Rupert will not suffer such rude treatment and he now feels justified in taking revenge.

An actor of less genius would have made this movie into the satire on celebrity that at one level it is and nothing more.[15] But with De Niro doing Pupkin we have a serious piece of social psychology, the kind of insightful comedy of manners we rarely find except in the best novels. His Rupert is a master of using the form of apology as a conversational wedge: "Jerry, I'm sorry. I don't mean to disturb you. I just want to talk to you for a minute." His "I'm sorrys" are frequent and they are always of the preemptive variety, never designed to remedy a wrong done, but to introduce and defuse an offense about to be given. Other instances in this genre are the "I don't mean to bother you but . . . " or his "Really, I don't mind" to Jerry's vexed administrative assistant which skillfully traverses any suggestion that he shouldn't wait around any longer. With the passive aggression of his use of the apology, there is the excessive thank-youing of desperate, but not to be denied, obsequiousness; hands are shaken too often and held too long. First names are used excessively and De Niro gets the style of intrusive familiarity exactly right: he drops Jerry's name to others while in Jerry's presence it becomes a mantra, a magic charm intended to counteract Jerry's desperate efforts at closing their encounter: "Thanks Jerry, thanks. Thanks a lot. It's a pleasure meeting you Jerry . . . . Jerry, Jerry, let me show you a picture of my Pride and Joy . . . . Jerry, seriously, if you ever want lunch, my treat." De Niro gets the accompanying body movements, smiles, tones, and rhythms exactly right in their wrongness.

More than thirty minutes of the film are taken up watching Rupert trying to get by Jerry's staff to Jerry. He is subjected to every kind of distancing move imaginable and we feel awkward suffering—not only vicarious embarrassment and vicarious pain of rejection, but embarrassment for the staff people whom his cluelessness puts in awkward situations. His phone calls are not returned. There is no record of his appointment. Receptionists don't recall talking to him and as mentioned, no one gets his name right. And Rupert, true to form, does not get the message or take the hint. Instead he waits until they and we can't bear it. He is willing to endure the awkwardness of waiting in a reception area that he and we are told is not a waiting room. Even Rupert, we should note, experiences the minor awkwardnesses of trying to maintain "normal appearances," trying to enact oneself acting normal. So Rupert doesn't quite know where to rest his eyes or which way to cross his feet or what expression he should wear on his face as he waits.[16] He tries various postures, never holding any of them long enough to do the work of enacting one's normal self very successfully. He cranes his neck back and looks at the ceiling with a quizzical air: "Is that cork?" he says after what to us and the poor receptionist seems like an eternity. She: "I don't know what it is. Is it dripping on you?" He: "No. I was looking at the patterns. You know cork is good for sound . . . It's very quiet in here." Rupert's ineptness is complex. It is not that he does not feel awkward, it is not that he does not know about trying to act normal, it is not that silence doesn't bother him, or that he feels out of place in some settings, it is that he totally botches how to remedy the awkwardnesses he feels so as to help others avoid feeling awkward for his incompetence.

Missing cues and not taking hints without making scenes: I would say I was riding my own hobby horse and not the movie's if it weren't for one scene that seems to make the matter of missed cues the organizing metaphor for the film. Rupert has made up cue cards containing the message that Jerry, fake gun to his head, is to read over the phone to his producer. Rupert bungles the card turning: one card is blank, he turns two at once and has to go back, another is upside down. The broad comedy of this scene actually goes on longer than the burlesque-type joke warrants, but that too is emblematic of missing cues. No one has their timing right. Cues are missed, bungled, not read right and as a result people stay longer than they should, try things they have no business trying, etc. Not even the woman at the studio who is to turn the cards Rupert penned for his intro times it right. Tony Randall, subbing for Jerry, has to call attention to the audience that his bad timing is her fault not his: "Turn it over please." Miscues and missed cues, Rupert's behavior in a nutshell.

Let me return to Rupert's monologue and take up again the matters I raised in the prologue of this essay: the relation of comedy to embarrassment and other emotions. If we laughed at the monologue (and I did), I suspect that no small motivator of that laughter was relief, particularly relief at being saved the embarrassment of witnessing Rupert's humiliation if his routine turned out to be utterly awful. Whatever the case, his routine seems no worse than most stand-up comic fare but that is beside the point. More crucial is that Rupert's routine, by any measure, was nowhere near as bad as he had led us to believe it would be. We, after all, had cringed along with Jerry at the Pride and Joy card, the feeble attempts at wit at Jerry's (J: "You're a moron." R: "Ordinarily I wouldn't allow anybody to speak that way about Rita . . . "), even the lame attempts in his fantasies ("Delores? That's my father's name."). Rupert has been the cause of making us feel uncomfortable and embarrassed both by and for him throughout the film. And in the end he spares us any further discomfort. Could it be that the King was simply softening us up so that with our low expectations he could only succeed on national TV? And what effect does casting Jerry Lewis as the successful comedian Jerry Langford have ultimately on our expectations and standards of competence when it comes to comedians?

There is an enormous literature on comedy, laughter, and humor. I do not want to get into its intricacies or its failure to develop interesting intricacies. I wish to set forth, by way of assertion and hypothesis, stated more strongly than may be justifiable, a few thoughts on the social psychology of stand-up comedy and Rupert. Rupert reveals that *relief* figures in our laughter at the comic more than we are likely to concede as a preliminary matter. Not relief from our own pent-up frustrations as in Freud's theory of jokes, but the emotion relief, the experience of having escaped a fate which we feared might materialize.[17] Consider all those things that make us laugh at a comedian that have nothing to do with whether the routine is funny. We laugh because others are laughing, for, like embarrassment, laughter is contagious; we also laugh to connect with other laughers, some of whom might be together with us, some of whom are just sharing space with us, but a space defined as one in which laughing is supposed to take place: a comedy club, a movie, a lecture. And we laugh because we have precommitted ourselves to it: we have gone to the video store to rent a comedy because we want to laugh; we have paid for tickets to enter the comedy club; we are invested in laughing. That the comic is supposed to produce laughter makes it easier to laugh. The very label "comedy" cues us to think laughter is expected and thus lowers our critical threshold for what is funny. Comedians have an even better thing going for them than these helpful precommitments and expectations. Much laughter is motivated by social norms that tell us it is inappropriate not to. The comedian, after all, is asking us to laugh and we usually oblige him because it is easier to do that than not to, easier for us to let him maintain his self-respect than embarrass everyone with the truth. The comedian, in short, benefits from our tactfulness, our decency, our capacity for saving someone else's face when that other has jeopardized it by incompetence. That tact is motivated by an uneven mixture of fellow-feeling and the desire to save ourselves the embarrassment of witnessing and participating in another's failures. Sympathy for the poor devil up there partly motivates our concern to save him from himself, save him from the humiliation he will suffer if he could see himself as we see him, because we can only imagine too well what we would feel like if we were being judged at that moment by the likes of us. By saving him we hope to save ourselves.

So the unfunny comedian gets his laughs and the moderately funny one, like Rupert, gets heartier laughs than, strictly speaking, the material deserves because of the added emotional input relief, in its strange dance with embarrassment and amusement, gives to laughter. But if the social rules that make us save another's face, that make us honor his claim to respectful treatment, give the comedian one big assist in gaining laughter without regard to any special merits of the material that is fair compensation for the impossible situation stand-up comics put themselves in. We usually think that the funniest of things, the things that make us laugh the hardest, are spontaneous, unpredictable, and most often, not contrived, but "real." The bore who prefaces a joke with "I'm going to tell you a joke—it will really make you laugh" has killed the joke before its birth and will only get the laughter that tact, sympathy, and normal politeness can muster. But that is what the comedian does too. The very performance is one big announcement that reproduces the bore's exactly, except with one big difference: the bore bores us without our consent; we have consented to endure the jokes of the comedian and even invested in them. The remarkable thing is that an occasional genius does genuinely make us laugh and the ones who do usually do so by teaching us something about social norms, the same thing I have been trying to do here.

I consider my account too sweet, too filled with empathetic and sympathetic mechanisms or benign ones like embarrassment and relief. We also laugh out of contempt, Hobbes' sudden glory again. This is sticky stuff. Many comedians try to coopt contempt and make themselves the indulgent object of theirs and yours: Woody Allen, Rodney Dangerfield, Rupert Pupkin. Their style is to preempt a kind of cold and malicious contempt, the contempt that borders on disgust and revulsion, the contempt that we would feel for your pretense of thinking you are funny when you are not, with a benign contempt, the contempt that often accompanies amusement at the antics of animals and kids.[18] Some comedians adopt another strategy for dealing with contempt, not being funny on purpose. This is a very self-reflexive style which discovers the comic by thwarting its conventional expectations: the jokes are meant to be bad, the timing is meant to be off, the atmosphere meant to be something less than convivial. The skill here is in signaling conventional competence only to undo the expectations arising from it, the violation of those expectations constituting the basis for humor. This style can also indulge a kind of self-loathing, a contempt for the stock-in-trade of being a comedian in the conventional mode. And this self-contempt has a way of becoming a malign contempt for you. You become the contemptible fool, the butt of his jokes, the sucker. But loathing the audience is not unique to this style. One suspects it also motivates types like Woody Allen. They might pose as sad-sacks, but they let you know that their knowledge and especially their self-knowledge is superior to yours and that that is the respect in which they differ from you.

I know. I know. I can take a hint. My account misses so much of the experience of laughing at Rupert's monologue or any other comedian for that matter. Can it only be a race to see who can hold whom in contempt first? We may indeed have to admit that some gentle contempt figures in our laughing at Rupert's monologue, but then mostly because Rupert gave us permission to have those feelings. We are laughing *with* those who are laughing at Rupert, one of whom is also Rupert. There is a community formed, a community of laughers, and it produces and is produced by amusement and *relief* that he and we survived the threat of our embarrassment at his humiliation. Surely my account is partial: what about the simple fun, the exhilaration, the feeling of freedom and escape that often accompanies the laughter that comedy provokes? And isn't that sense of freedom and escape a liberation from the constraints imposed upon us by the myriad of social norms that keep us civilized if not exactly content, even as those same norms are constraining us, in part, to laugh so as to transcend them?[19]

Let me make one final observation. The discomforts of failed attempts to elicit our laughter seem to be remarkably resistant to variations among visual representational media. Rupert Pupkin can make us just as uncomfortable as any real comedian we see fail on television or live before us in a comedy club. But if we read bad jokes or read cartoons in the newspaper that are not funny we are not embarrassed for their author who remains, for us, a disembodied name. Instead we have contempt for the people who would find such stuff funny. We cannot imagine ourselves as them at all. Thus does our imagination limit the objects of our sympathy. We can sympathize with someone being laughed at, whatever the reason they may be the objects of laughter, but we cannot sympathize with the laughers unless we accept the beliefs and the perceptions which underpin their laughing. It is thus very hard, if not impossible, to sympathize with senses of humor that are not also ours. And nothing elicits our contempt quite so easily as laughter we cannot participate in. Ultimately the whole array of emotional experiences involving the intersection of laughter, the comic, social ineptitude and the emotions it evokes depends on a capacity for imagining ourselves in the other's shoes while we at the same time remain in ours; in effect, we achieve a kind of double consciousness, one part feeling vicariously what we judge the other should feel, the other part feeling as we do when we judge the other. And if we are good enough at that double vision we should never have to say, "I can take a hint."

## Notes

1. Let me stake out some definitional limits here. I mean to discuss those hints that are subsumed in the category that gives the phrase "I can take a hint" its sense, that is, hints that are distancing and can thus be perceived by the other as somewhat hostile. Although we may give other people hints of encouragement, that is not the type of hint I will be dealing with here. In fact, one could conceive of almost any kind of social indirection as a hint. But little of analytical value would be gained by doing so. Nonetheless, I will have to make some references to a slightly broader class of hints in the discussion that follows than that entertained by the notion of the hostile hint.

2. The strength of the distancer's right to keep another at bay varies with the moral status and the urgency of the seeker's claim. If the seeker is a child, handicapped, sick, the distancer maintains his distance at the cost of being thought callous, selfish, cruel.

3. See Erving Goffman, "Embarrassment and Social Organization," *Interaction Ritual: Essays on Face-to-Face Behavior* (New York: Pantheon, 1967), 97–112.

4. See William Ian Miller, *Humiliation* (Cornell University Press, 1993), 159.

5. "Sudden glory, the passion which maketh those grimaces called laughter and is caused . . . by the apprehension of some deformed thing in another, by comparison whereof they suddenly applaud themselves." *Leviathan* I, vi.

6. Both philosophical and psychological literatures generally consider amusement an emotion; see Ronald de Sousa, *The Rationality of Emotion* (Cambridge: MIT Press, 1990); Robert Sharpe, "Several Reasons Why Amusement is an Emotion," John Morreall, ed., *The Philosophy of Laughter and Humor* (Albany: SUNY Press, 1987).

7. The issue of finding discomfort pleasurable or the witnessing of others' discomfort as pleasurable engaged Aristotle and was much discussed by literary theorists of the eighteenth century; see Aristotle, *The Poetics*, and Steele, *Tatler* No. 82 and Addison, *Spectator* No. 39. Why, for instance, is tragedy pleasurable? Some may find the explanation in a kind of commitment to masochism as the chief motivator of human psychic life; others may prefer a more complex account of aesthetic emotions.

8. The film was also a box office failure. It exceeded its $14 million production budget by almost $5 million. Its American box office take was less than one-sixth that amount. See Les Keyser, *Martin Scorsese* (New York: Twayne, 1992).

9. The coding of Rupert's ethnicity is complex and I relegate some brief observations to this note. De Niro's Rupert is not so clearly Jewish as his surname, his nagging mother, and his pushy nerdiness would indicate. His Jewishness fades into a kind of lower-middle class east-coast ethnic, an amal-

gam of vulgar Jewish, Italian, and Irish styles that itself is the ethnic base of the vulgar showbiz style pilloried in the movie. The Jewish predominates in this mix, as one would expect, but it is not the pure thing. Nor is this style the fashionable way to self-present Jewishly in a film. Brash and pushy confidence, not very self-reflective, as perhaps exemplified in the Marx Brothers has given way to the self-involved, obsessively self-doubting, wimpy, intellectualized neuroticism of Woody Allen. Rupert's filmic Jewishness is the old Hollywood; he is manifestly dated.

10. See Gary Arnold, "Unroyal 'King': Wrong Tone, Wrong Time in Scorsese & De Niro Film," *Washington Post* (April 15, 1983), C1, and Marilyn Beck, "The King of Comedy," *New York Daily News* (Feb. 2, 1983), 37. These writers seem to hint that Scorsese should take special care given that he must bear some responsibility for the production of John Hinckley, Jr., Reagan's failed assassin whose obsession with Jodie Foster dated from her appearance in Scorsese's *Taxi Driver*. See, however, Krin Gabbard and Glen Gabbard, *Psychiatry and the Cinema* (Chicago: University of Chicago Press, 1987), who suggest that the film's closure may be fantasy. But we should never underestimate the American media culture's ability to make such fantasies not quite implausible. Consider the fame of the likes of Oliver North, Amy Fisher, the Bobbitts, etc.

11. See Keyser, 134–35. Note John Simon's befuddlement:

This is where things become particularly muddled. The monologue strikes me as only slightly less funny than most such monologues, which I don't find very funny either. Are the filmmakers saying that Pupkin's comedy is junk, but that on the Langford Show, introduced by Tony Randall, it enchants an audience of Pavlovian fools? Or are they saying that Pupkin does have that minimal talent needed to make anybody's success in this abysmal business? Is the film about weirdos cannibalizing their betters, or are there, no betters, and are large numbers of—if not, indeed, all—Americans a breed of imbeciles? Is the satire specific or all-inclusive? (*National Review*, May 13, 1983, 574.)

12. I owe this distinction to a student, Spencer Gusick.

13. See Erving Goffman, *Relations in Public* (New York: Basic Books, 1971), 238–47.

14. Grand social theory tends to ignore the crucial but homely questions that the social theory of Goffman took as central. Some of these are, do bores get bored by bores, boors offended by boors; do nerds have contempt for other nerds? Do we have the self-knowledge to know these things? Can they be answered? Since I have been from time to time both a bore and a boor I draw on my own experience to suggest that evidence warrants answering Yes. About nerds I plead agnosticism, but I suspect yes, for the key to all these character types is not the failure to recognize others for what they are, but to fail to recognize the content of others' recognition of ourselves.

15. This is not to say it doesn't work well as such a satire. De Niro's genius is given more than an able assist by Paul Zimmerman's psychologically and socially rich script. Another theme the movie deals with is the failure of any characters to connect with any others. All are obsessively self-referential and unwilling to admit the claims of others. Thus it is that Masha can never get a letter delivered to Jerry. When she gets Jerry's unlisted number, he hangs up (and presumably gets a new number). In the end she can only get to him by mummifying him in duct tape and treating him to a one-way conversation. Rupert can never get to Jerry; even Jerry can't get through to his own people when he calls them with the toy gun to his head, for he is indistinguishable from a would-be comedian who does a Langford impression and who also plagues Jerry's office. The opening credits roll against Masha's hands splayed out against Jerry's car window desperately clawing at the glass shield that, like the television screen, separates her TV-idol from her. No one connects. True, Rupert and Masha find each other, but as indicated in the text each is contemptuous of the other; they are only united by the strange convergence of their psychoses.

16. It is no wonder that he must struggle to find some place to rest his eyes. Places designated as waiting rooms are marked as waiting rooms by having old magazines available to ease the awkwardnesses that attend eye-parking. And, as Rupert has been told, he is waiting in a reception area, not a waiting room. But again, it is not that Rupert is utterly without some inkling of propriety. When he calls Burt Thomas, Jerry's producer, after kidnapping Jerry, he shows some awareness that he might not have a right as yet to first-name Burt: "No, Burt, if I could call you Bu . . . ."

17. Jon Elster notes astutely that "although we have different feelings when a disaster just misses us,

when a probable disaster fails to materialize and when an unpleasant state of affairs ceases to obtain, the single word *relief* covers them all. By contrast, the corresponding emotions defined with respect to positive core emotions are verbally distinguished as regret, disappointment and grief." *Nuts and Bolts for the Social Sciences* (Cambridge: Cambridge University Press, 1989).

18. This kind of benign contempt has a dark side to it also. It goes hand in hand with some pretty unsavory manifestations of power and hierarchy. It is thus also the contempt of the master for the servant, the white for black, the Christian for the Jew. But this kind of contempt also has its own reciprocity. The lower-status person might as well find the higher-status contemner a worthy object of her own contempt. Few of us have either not been the object or the agent of the blistering contempt of the black for the white, the Jew for the Christian, women for men, and teenagers for adults. The contempt of the high for the low differs in some respects from that of the low for the high. The former might involve disgust, but more often is characterized by a kind of indifference, a refusal even to see the other. If, as Hume theorizes, contempt is a mixture of hatred and pride, then the contempt of the high for the low is made more of pride than hatred, whereas in the contempt of the low for the high hatred would surpass pride; see David Hume, A *Treatise of Human Nature* Bk. II, Pt. ii, Sect. x.

19. It is a commonplace that comics elicit laughter by breaking various norms of appropriate decorum. Thus Rupert tells about his mom and dad puking, makes jokes about his mother's death, and confesses to having kidnapped Jerry to get on the show. The mirth generated by watching someone break such norms is complexly motivated. There is contempt for the lack of decorum of the comedian vs. admiration for his nerve and insight, nervousness at the breach of deeply held rules vs. delight at the feast of misrule aspects of breaking them, relief over not being punished for breaking them vs. anxiety that we still might be, etc.

# IX

JOSEPH E. LEVINE
PRESENTS

A
MIKE NICHOLS
LAWRENCE TURMAN
PRODUCTION

This
is
Benjamin.

He's
a little
worried
about
his
future.

## THE GRADUATE

STARRING
**ANNE BANCROFT** AND **DUSTIN HOFFMAN · KATHARINE ROSS**
SCREENPLAY BY                                           SONGS BY
**CALDER WILLINGHAM** AND **BUCK HENRY** **PAUL SIMON**
PERFORMED BY                  PRODUCED BY
**SIMON** AND **GARFUNKEL** **LAWRENCE TURMAN**
DIRECTED BY
**MIKE NICHOLS** TECHNICOLOR® PANAVISION®

United Artists
Entertainment from
Transamerica Corporation

# Blake Edwards: "Weather's fine. Having a little party. Wish you were here"

**Richard Combs** (2001)

W as it inevitable or redundant that Blake Edwards should eventually make a film called *The Party* (1968), in which parting—after a pre-credits plot set-up—occupies the whole movie? Both, probably, and a culmination none the less, a wonderful compendium of almost-silent slapstick and gags that drift inexorably—with a slow, stunned, trying-to-keep-a-grip gait—towards utter social collapse. This was the film-as-party as it could only exist in the '60s: bubble gum-ish credit titles, trippy sitar music, wistful theme song ("We're not expecting rainbow-colored skies"), and two social misfits whose romance is left to take place beyond the movie because nothing so fragile (or perfunctory) could survive within the movie.

By the time, of course, Edwards had already done parties in all shapes and sizes. *Breakfast at Tiffany's* (1961) contained one of his finest set-pieces, the Holly Golightly thrash that ends in a police raid and includes an emblematic moment of abandon: one guest laughing at herself in a mirror and then dissolving, along with her mascara, into tears. That vulnerability is extended, only two years later, into a serious case of post-party blues in *Days of Wine and Roses*. *What Did You Do in the War, Daddy?* (1966) imports the film-as-party into the least likely genre, the war movie—a strategic coup that might make it Edwards' best film. *The Great Race* (1965) is a genre-busting, custard pie-throwing epic, a mood that is picked up, post-*Party* by *Darling Lili* (1969), a thrash to end the '60s and the war to end all wars.

To be quite accurate, these last two aren't really party films but blockbusters that contain party pieces. *Darling Lili* has singalongs, a band of gypsy violinists who can be unpacked for romantic picnics, and a closing burst of actual partying—a messy montage of streamers, merrymaking and newsreel footage to toast the Armistice. Compared to this ramshackle tipsiness, *The Party* is a model of formal sobriety, with its unity of time and place, its level observation of behavior, and its careful development of a one-joke structure. There's another distinction that might be allied to this: that where *The Party* is a self-sufficient, self-generating comedy of behavior, *The Great Race* and *Darling Lili* are comedies of movie behavior, genre send-ups.

In practice, though, the distinctions hardly matter. One reason for *The Party*'s prominence, in whatever variation, is that it allows things to run together. It initiates a chaos, a precarious equilibrium, say, between gleeful and anxious abandon, between the pratfall as a comedy mainstay and its repetition as an opening (a matter of character, fate or Feudian slip?) to real pain. Physical pain features regularly in Edwards' comedies, particularly the Panthers.

Similarly, he may pile on the sentimental cliches to a point beyond send-up where they acquite the same kind of (charmed? benumbed? inevitable?) reality. No wonder critics find it so hard to agree on whether an epic statement like *Darling Lili* is his masterpiece or his biggest disaster. Unexpectedly, though most characteristically, the repetition of pain and embarrassment doesn't add up to a comedy of Schadenfreude but to a blurring and blending of sympathies (a matter of acquiescence, alienation or stupor?). Peter Sellers' hapless Indian extra suffers an accumulation of humiliations and set-backs whose sum total is—zero, his pratfalls being gathered up in social indifference, a universal unwinding, as *The Party* goes on.

It's the formal rectitude, of course, the dead-level gaze, which makes the unwinding funny. It makes the onset of chaos seem not like a crushing disaster, more a slow, implacable trickle; like the rising tide of foam in the bathing-the-elephant sequence, it's the implacable invasion of human silliness or ineptitude, which is the most common disaster after all. *The Party* may be unique in that one steadily mounting joke, the holding-together act, the imposture of dignity ignoring its own glassy-eyed collapse, structures the whole film. But it is echoed in the party-piece films by the acts replicating within them, by the performances onstage and off, for instance, in *Darling Lili*. And *The Party* shares with *The Great Race* the fact that it is, in its own way, a movie *hommage*—to the slapstick of Laurel and Hardy.

Imposture, performance, grateful absorption and painful insecurity—they all come together at the party. And Edwards has staked this out as his territory; it's as particular a terrain as Ford's Monument Valley, a source of comedy and pathos, metaphor and meaning. But still it is not easy to say what his own act is. It does touch on other Hollywood acts: George Cukor's fables of show-biz life and the showbiz quality of everyday life (the drag of *Sylvia Scarlett* and the drag of *Victor/Victoria*); Douglas Sirk's romances of social sadness and madness (Holly Golightly's imitation of life finally provokes a fit of destructive rage); Billy Wilder in general, but particularly on death and the Hollywood mask (*Sunset Boulevard*, *Fedora* and *S.O.B.*). Edwards seems both more brittle and more detached than any of them, perhaps because he is, in Andrew Sarris' phrase, "a new breed . . . post-Freud, post-sick joke," or perhaps because he is, as his detractors would claim, just a slick, glossy entertainer.

But the truth is that there is an instability to Edwards, a messiness of form, that belies the sense of both detachment and slick manipulation. It's the messiness that partly makes him hard to define, and that allows the controlled party film to seem just a stage on the way to the sprawling party-piece film, and vice versa. It's the messiness evident in the way so resilient an entertainer—he began as an actor and writer and has directed since 1955—has talked of a less containable personal side to his film-making, in relation to *Days of Wine and Roses* ("I'm a kind of obsessive-compulsive type myself") or *10* and *S.O.B.* ("both films have the theme of death and the recognition of one's own mortality"). And it's the messiness of a forty-year (and apparently still running) career which has contained so many periods—and so many peaks and troughs which can't be easily matched to what is most or least personal in the films.

David Thomson, one of the detractors, deplored the 1993 decision of the Directors' and Writers' Guilds to give the Preston Sturges Award to Edwards ("somehow the decline of Hollywood had been encapsulated"). But Sturges' own directorial career only lasted one film longer than a decade, and Thomson (along with almost everyone) numbers his best films as the first five. In the fine mess that Edwards has left us, it might be hard to sort out a comparable period, although there are distinguishing features. The late '50s produced some witty service comedies, the '70s belonged mostly to the Pink Panther (only an obsessive-compulsive would have the nerve and the lack of taste or discretion to drive them beyond the point of their star's death), and the '80s turn querulous with personal grievances (*S.O.B.*, *That's Life*). It is the '60s that were his glory years, the period when Mr. Slick also produced his most rewarding, comically inventive and thematically consistent work. And it has the greatest parties.

In order to justify the slickness, or to get around it, many of Edwards' champions have tried to find a place for it outside the films, to connect it to the real world. Thus, George Morris writing in *Film Comment*: "Edwards' movies are slick and glossy, but their shiny surfaces reflect all too accurately the disposable values of contemporary life." And Andrew Sarris: "The world he celebrates is cold, heartless and inhuman, but the people in it manage to preserve a marginal integrity and individuality." This is the film auteurist's version of the pathetic fallacy: identifying a stylistic or temperamental feature in a filmmaker with some supposed quality in the human condition.

But the sense of slickness, of sentimental, facile Hollywoodness, in Edwards is a symptom of what he does best—to create fantasies, and to create fantasies about people creating fantasies. His best films do this the most, which can leave a certain undischarged excess—an excess of phoniness (or call it "fictiveness")—in the air. One of his best, *Breakfast at Tiffany's*, ends with the *de trop* scene of the two stars standing bedraggled in the rain, having found each other, and the heroine's rashly abandoned cat, in a studio alleyway. The cat is called just "Cat" because he is part of a flux of people and things who don't have specific identities, a world of transients like Holly (Audrey Hepburn) looking for a place where "me and things go together."

It's at this point, in order to shore up the fragile romanticism of the notion of fragility, that critics start reaching for metaphors about a cruel and uncertain world. But it isn't necessary. The film is its own tight and coherent metaphorical structure, Cat being the key—to names borrowed, adopted, imposed, interchanged. The hero, novelist Paul Varjac (George Peppard), is immediately dubbed Fred by Holly after her beloved brother, is called "Lucille" over the phone by his wealthy "patronness" (Patricia Neal) when her husband is inconveniently nearby, and his fragile writing career to date consists of one book, called *Nine Lives*.

"It could happen to anyone," says Holly to Paul at the beginning, when he misplaces his key and has to ring her bell to get into the apartment building (it happens to her all the time). The answering line to this is Paul's at the end, when he says, "I'm not everybody—or am I?," as Holly seems about to treat him as one of her disposable admirers and take off for a better offer in Brazil. More than nine lives are in circulation here, and money is a major factor in making them go round. In fact, for a romantic comedy, *Breakfast at Tiffany's* is still quite risqué for basing its meeting-cute on the hero and heroine's recognition of their mutual prostitution.

"Is she or isn't she?" is the question posed about Holly by her agent, O.J. Berman (Martin Balsam). The question is allowed to hang in the air long enough to suggest the possibility, is she or isn't she a hooker?, before he clarifies: "Is she or isn't she a phoney?" O.J. decides she is, but "a real phoney." It's a question that could be asked of other Edwards heroines, with permutations that range across the world of commerce, the theatre of self, and show-biz proper. "Is she or isn't she a man?," for instance, of Julie Andrews in *Victor/Victoria* (1982), or "is she or isn't she a spy?" in *Darling Lili*. This is the broadest permutation, allowing her to be unequivocally—unrepentant and unpunished—a German spy while still boosting our boys' morale with gusto on stage.

Edwards' unstable form and his comedy of instability also intertwine in the most consistently interesting, shifting pattern through the '60s: a shifting of weights and balances, of theme and variation. Edwards' own intertwining with other writers is obviously a major factor. *Breakfast at Tiffany's*, with a solo script by George Axelrod, is delicately connected, a skein of makeshiftness, pushing insecurities on to the surface in the witty play with names. When Edwards teams up in the late '60s with the pre-*Exorcist* William Peter Blatty—who wrote *What Did You Do in the War, Daddy?* and co-wrote *Darling Lili* with Edwards—the permutations indeed become broader, the makeshiftness becomes escalating imposture, and the insecurities become wilder comic convolutions.

*What Did You Do in the War, Daddy?* is a defining moment, a film that even Edwards' detractors tend to like, but a film that both admirers and detractors get wrong by describing it as a send-up of war movie heroics. For one thing, when it does get around to tying up its war movie plot, it goes casually for type, allowing its ragtag group of displaced GIs to mop up a German company, or division, or army, with the elan of the Dirty Dozen. Secondly, send-up has never been the aim of even Edwards' most extravagant burlesques, merely an opening on to a chaos that will impose its own—a natural oxymoron—logic: reversal and interchange, confusion and conversion. And finally, the form of *Daddy* is more than unstable; it's a piece of sleight of hand, a trick.

It seems to be as sprawling a burlesque as *The Great Race*, beginning with the invasion of Sicily in 1943 and including a cameo of Hitler himself taking charge of the situation. But actually, it is as neat and contained as *The Party*, an extended one joke and a compacted universe. There's a lengthy pre-credit sequence, as in *The Party*, which maps the world at large: the invasion; General Bolt (Carroll O'Connor) ordering the uptight, inexperienced Captain Cash (Dick Shawn) to seize the vital town of Valerno; Cash taking insecure command of the battle-worn C Company and its senior officer, Lieutenant Jody Christian (James Coburn). The credits end as the company reaches Valerno—like Sellers arriving at the party—and thereafter the action is confined to the town. Or rather, all the world, Hitler included, focuses on Valerno.

There's an exemplary piece of war movie staging as C Company enters the apparently deserted town, with the men infiltrating from different directions and a single panning and tracking camera movement picking them up. Edwards frequently combines long, fluid takes with a certain distance of viewpoint, a placidly uninvolved camera—a comedy technique (used, with rather less movement, by Jacques Tati) which heightens the humor by deliberately not underlining it. It may be an illusion, but the takes seem to be longest in films like *Daddy* and *The Party*, where there is least room to move, where the shrinking of the world to this one place and time is the essential conceit.

When C Company eventually encounters the enemy—the town's garrison and its entire populace are at a football match—they prove cheerfully willing to surrender. (The happy-go-lucky or battle-shy Italian is another war movie cliche that is happily accepted). But what their commander, Captain Oppo (Sergio Fantoni), is less agreeable to is their evacuating the town until they are allowed to hold a planned fiesta. What this is actually meant to celebrate is never specified—the point is, simply, the party. And after Captain Cash overcomes his horror at having to communicate this situation to General Bolt—"Weather's fine. Having a little party. Wish you were here"—the party becomes the film.

Or rather, it becomes a centripetal force, drawing in everyone who approaches the town and luring them to self-abandonment. The GIs swap uniforms with the Italians, and later, to effect an escape, don German uniforms; an intelligence officer (Harry

*"The party becomes the film": Dick Shawn, Sergio Fantoni, Aldo Ray in*
What Did You Do in the War, Daddy?

Morgan) who threatens to restore order is driven insane. And as it winds on, the saturnalia transforms itself, from innocent merrymaking to masque of war, from blissful forgetfulness to self-conscious stratagem. This is one party Edwards pushes right through the looking glass, to arrive at a wonderful paroxysm, a Pirandellian core. To protect themselves from the reconnaissance planes of both the American and German armies, the GIs and the Italians stage a furious but mock battle in the town square, directed by a whistle-blowing Lt. Christian ("Cecil B. Christian," remarks a sarcastic Cash).

As a joke about movie-making, or a crazy mirror reflection of war's insanity, it's a much better jest than the kind of parody the film is usually taken for. But the reason it plays so well is that it's basically an extension of the partying mood: soldiers drunkenly imitating the enemy (when they're en masse, the Italians are inclined to break into a rendition of "The Eyes of Texas"), the film imitating itself. Along with these dissolutions, there are blendings and overturnings of a less seriously Pirandellian kind. Like the "trippiness" of *The Party, Daddy* picks up on the mood of the times for dissolution—for turning on and dropping out, for making love not war.

The morning after the first night of partying, there is a long silent sequence as the camera tracks through the town square, a landscape now transformed by mountains of streamers and confetti. Crouched, huddled or sprawled in this simulated snow are the passed-out GIs, still in uniform, so that a scene which has the peacefulness of sleep also has the strange, slightly surreal peacefulness of simulated death. The camera finally tracks up to a machine gun, with a white pigeon—or a dove?—perched on top and a flower sticking out of its barrel. Later, as the GIs and the Italian soldiers mow each other down with playacted fury, the villagers sit stuffing empty cartridge cases with pretty pieces of cloth for blank ammunition.

There is also a spread of sympathies in Edwards' best films, a generosity towards all the characters, that constitutes another kind of blending and dissolution. It is facilitated by—and probably partly inspired by—that liking for long takes, the all-inclusive sequence shot. Its most characteristic dramatic form is a certain confusion between—a trading-off between—the roles of hero and sidekick. Coburn is the nominal star of *What Did You Do in the War, Daddy?*, and he plays with an energy, that rather wolfish amiability (a unique combination of laid-back Westerner and edgy city boy), that gave him such a rarely tapped gift for comedy. But the focus keeps slipping away to the less sympathetic Dick Shawn, a by-the-book soldier and a rather cartoonish figure who can only be transformed with some bending and twisting.

*Darling Lili* has an interesting variation on this pattern. The romantic hero (Rock Hudson) has a comic sidekick (Lance Percival) who keeps his conventional place. But the heroine, traitorous Lili (Julie Andrews), has her spymaster and vague romantic "uncle," the "good German" von Ruger (Jeremy Kemp). He becomes the film's moral litmus, the key to its comedy of heroic derring-do: the patriotic singalongs invariably end with the camera finding von Ruger in the crowd, joining in with the ditty of the moment ("La Marseillaise," "It's a long way to Tipperary").

*Darling Lili* is chaos without the concision of *The Party* or *What Did You Do in the War, Daddy?* Or perhaps its chaos is centrifugal rather than centripetal: in place of that circling in to the "performed" battle of *Daddy*, it throws off permutations on performance. As Edwards' first film with Julie Andrews, it introduces show business itself as metaphor and medium for all manner of insecurities and trade-offs, role switches and drag acts.

It may not be Edwards' masterpiece, but it contains one of his finest coups in this area. Suspecting that Major Larrabee (Hudson) is involved with a dancer called Crepe Suzette, Lili goes to catch her act. Appalled and fascinated, she is confronted with a brazen strip show. At that moment, trapped behind enemy lines, Larrabee escapes by making off with the plane of his own arch rival, the Red Baron (stage name for Manfred von Richthofen). The film then cuts to Lili beginning another sweetness-and-light stage show, which she literally rips apart to go into a Crepe Suzette number. Something borrowed, something renewed: the two pieces of action are a double coup, one operating alongside, or inside, the other.

The best evocation of the mood of a Blake Edwards party is not contained in anything written on his films, but was penned by F. Scott Fitzgerald:

> . . . The lights grow brighter as the earth lurches away from the sun and now the orchestra is playing yellow cocktail music and the opera of voices pitches a key higher. Laughter is easier, minute by minute, spilled with prodigality, tipped out at a cheerful word. The groups change more swiftly, swell with new arrivals, dissolve and form in the same breath— already there are wanderers, confident girls who weave here and there among the stouter

and more stable, become for a sharp, joyous moment the center of a group and then excited with triumph glide on through the sea change of faces and voices and color under the constantly changing light.

Isn't "yellow cocktail music" exactly what Henry Mancini has contributed all these years to Blake Edwards' films? And wouldn't *The Great Gatsby* have made an interesting Edwards subject? Surely Jay Gatsby, mystery man, poseur, little boy lost, is an ideal Edwards protagonist, a sort of male Holly Golightly. His constant reinvention of himself in pursuit of success, of a romantic chimera, again plays around the anyone/everybody perplexity. And if not "the" Gatsby, didn't Edwards somewhere miss making his *Great Gatsby*, in which the perplexity could be light, bright and show-biz wispy ("whistling in the dark" as Lili's theme tune has it) and still impose itself as a substantial subject? In a way, Edwards' signature, and his dramatic problem, is not unlike Fitzgerald's.

Of course, apart from *Breakfast at Tiffany's*—and, less memorably, *The Carey Treatment* and *The Tamarind Seed*—Edwards has not gone in for literary adaptation. To an unusual degree, his films have been originals, devised alone or in collaboration with other writers. This might have given him a different kind of substance as a personal filmmaker, one who has fought for independence as a writer-director, who has had scarring battles with the Hollywood establishment, and who has worked through his own production companies, named after his children or, with a larger sense of fiefdom, Blake Edwards Entertainment (sometimes just BEE).

*"Yellow cocktail music"*: The Party.

The latter also has the ring of some of the personal production set-ups of Hollywood's auteur-moguls, the erstwhile Movie Brats. Edwards might have led them, the proto Brat: he grew up in the movies, with both a father and a grandfather in the business, and has paid his own hommages, from the exact (*The Party*) to the galumphing (*The Great Race*) and the misconceived (*A Fine Mess*). Yet his films seem to discourage a personal reading, or rather what operates as a substantial personal theme—the obsessive-compulsive problem, for instance—seems to run counter to his true strengths as a filmmaker. *Days of Wine and Roses* has met the same objection from both an Edwards supporter and detractor: "the removal of the director's rose-colored glasses reveals an unpleasant vision of the plastic forms of urban life" (Andrew Sarris); "its pessimism got out of artistic control and showed a dark side that Edwards has otherwise concealed" (David Thomson). It sounds as if, in being too true to himself, Edwards had also betrayed himself.

Which rather leaves him in the position of being damned if he doesn't remove the rose-colored glasses and damned if he does. Perhaps it also raises a more general problem about what is often too glibly assumed, or construed, as "personal" about a filmmaker, particularly a Hollywood filmmaker. There may be at least two personal filmmakers in Edwards: the one who achieved such detached, deadpan mastery of a rose-colored cinema of romantic-comedy-drama, and the one who overidentified with the emotional content of *Days of Wine and Roses*. This would have something to do with that messiness of creative personality, the instability of forms, that affects all his career, not just one film. Arguably, more problematic than *Days of Wine and Roses* are such later films as *S.O.B.* (1981) and *That's Life* (1986), in which the form becomes a rather inert showcase for some personal grievances—with the movie business, with chimeras of success and happiness—and some personal locations (the Edwards family home).

That obsessive-compulsive streak may even tickle a critical fancy in one context where it proves a turn-off in another. Andrew Sarris, for instance, has explained his belonging to "a handful of hardcore Edwardians among the critical corps" in the early '70s as in large part due to "my appreciation of Edwards' devotion to [Julie] Andrews *a la folie*." Edwards' cinematic devotion to his actress-singer–wife has been unswerving since then, to the extent that he abandoned the cinema in the mid '90s to showcase her Broadway comeback in the musical version of *Victor/Victoria*. Can his dedication to her career be compared to his unflagging support of Inspector Clouseau?

The Andrews persona has been a further problem about her husband's films for many critics. Their sticking point is the deadening wholesomeness of her Mary Poppins past, a problem that Edwards has obviously perceived since he has organised a couple of breakouts: the Crepe Suzette number in *Darling Lili* and the breastbaring in *S.O.B.* They had little effect, presumably because it takes more than a little striptease to unclothe a persona. But then this is only a subsidiary problem anyway. The real obstacle is the perfection of Andrews' own act, that crystalline enunciation and singing voice, which predates Edwards and actually forestalls what it should facilitate: the dangers of performance, the uncertainty of roles. This is particularly striking in *Victor/Victoria* which, with its multiple slipsiding of roles and gender, looks an ideal Edwards project in theory. A meticulous chanteuse in any role or gender, Andrews simply overrides them all.

In his best films, of course, the two personal filmmakers in Edwards—and any of the variations on them—will be working at their best. And then the messiness, the instability of forms, may be a more creative tension, a pointed interruption or reversal of emphasis, even the stab of a psychological (or medical) problem other than the obsessive-compul-

• • • • • • • • • • • • • • • • • • • • • • • • • • • • • • • • • • • • • • • • • • • •

sive. If Edwards' most noticeable stylistic trait is the long take—to establish a comic community—equally significant is the sudden high angle, and occasional overhead, for moments of individual uncertainty, vulnerability, loss of equilibrium. Some overheads combine vulnerability with self–abandonment, a helplessness before fate: the morning-after soldier in *What Did You Do in the War, Daddy?*, unconscious and asprawl in the town fountain; the griefstricken Holly Golightly prone on her bed amid the wreckage of her apartment, feathers drifting down like the "snow" of forgetfulness in *Daddy*. And of course Jack Lemmon, straitjacketed, thrashing about in the throes of the DTs in *Days of Wine and Roses*.

There's a scene in *Darling Lili* where romantic foreplay between Lili and Major Larrabee finally leads to the moment when she asks him to carry her into the bedroom. As he stoops to lift her, the camera cuts to a high shot behind the Rock's back, a movement which signals that this is not going to be as easy as it sounds and that it will lead not to consummation but to romantic misunderstanding and coitus forestalled. Edwards' own testimony suggests that the moment is as medically accurate as it is cinematically expressive: "I have had a high degree of hypochondria in my life, where bad backs and things like that would show up in lieu of having to perform either artistically or sexually or whatever. So, obviously, the best way to be able to overcome that, the best way to be able to live with it and not make it too painful was to laugh at it."

In the midst of so much instability, so much switching and interchanging, it would probably be perverse to expect a single definitive work—even in the '60s, Edwards' most "together" decade. Even so, there may be a holding form behind the shifting forms, a rationale to the movement. Along with Cat, an incidental detail that is a key to *Breakfast at Tiffany's* is Holly's tormented Japanese neighbor, Mr. Yunioshi, whose bell she always rings when she has forgotten her key. Mickey Rooney plays him as all-out caricature: jabbering, bespectacled, buck-toothed. He's one of the many cartoons among Edwards' characters—a slippage (or *hommage*) which, like Peter Sellers' Indian, has a tricky, very non-PC look today.

But the point about Mr. Yunioshi is that he's a professional photographer, and as he angrily protests to Holly after being woken in the early hours of the morning, "I got to get my rest. I'm an artist." Which makes this particular apartment building something of a house of art—Varjac has his writing and Holly is her own work-in-progress—which in turn is why it can also seem like a house of prostitution. There is a teasing congruence between the two, like Larrabee escaping as the Red Baron while Lili "comes out" as Crepe Suzette. This is not so much a theme as an ambience that does hold the '60s together—through the delight in artifice that overtakes *What Did You Do in the War, Daddy?* and that is built into *Darling Lilli*.

This could be another link between Edwards and the Movie Brat generation, with the self-consciousness and movie-referencing that is now part of any filmmaker's equipment. Except that in Edwards it is neither as precious nor as limited as that. For self-consciousness, it is all quite overt and straightforward, part of the emotional content and what makes his characters most touching. The art-making fuses with the playacting and the partying. Even *What Did You Do in the War, Daddy?*—where we see the cameras turning in the battleground become amateur film shoot—only uses the movie joke to deliver a more generous message. It's a message that invokes the spirit of the times even while rephrasing it: make movies not war.

# Bridge Over Troubled Water: *The Graduate*

**Jonathan Rosenbaum** (1997)

> If I feel myself as the producer of my life, then I am unhappy. So I would rather be a spectator of my life. I would rather change my life this way since I cannot change it in society. So at night I see films that are different from my experiences during the day. Thus there is a strict separation between experience and the cinema. That is the obstacle for our films. For we are people of the '60s, and we do not believe in the opposition between experience and fiction.
> —Alexander Kluge, 1988

*The Graduate* opened in December 1967, the same month the first successful human heart transplant was performed. It was a few weeks after the premiere of *Bonnie and Clyde* and about three months before the launching of *2001: A Space Odyssey*. Among the albums that came out the same year were the Beatles' *Sgt. Pepper's Lonely Hearts Club Band*, the Rolling Stones' *Their Satanic Majesties Request*, and the Mothers of Invention's *Absolutely Free*. Simon and Garfunkel's *Sounds of Silence* and *Parsley, Sage, Rosemary and Thyme* had both come out in '66, and *The Graduate* appropriated tracks from both of them on its sound track. (The "Mrs. Robinson" lyrics were added for the sound track album.)

For many fans, including myself, of Mike Nichols and Elaine May who had seen them perform live or heard their ferociously funny records, Nichols' early career as a director seemed tame, considering both his comic gifts and the political cast of the '60s. *The Graduate*, his second feature (his first was *Who's Afraid of Virginia Woolf?* in '66) was entertaining, but hardly the rallying cry of a rebellious youth explosion that some claimed it to be once it took off at the box office (it was the second highest grossing movie of the '60s, after *The Sound of Music*). Even now, when new prints of the movie struck from the original internegative are being released, the only "revolutionary aspect" of *The Graduate* described in the press book is the use and impact of the Simon and Garfunkel songs—not the songs themselves but the new marketing possibilities derived from transplanting "found" material into a Hollywood hit, which clearly set a lot of wheels spinning.

"She was always brave," Nichols said of May during their partnership as a comedy team. "But I became more and more afraid." This certainly appears to be the case if one compares their subsequent careers as directors. (For a candid look at the complex dynamics of their relationship during the height of their fame as a team, see Edmund Wilson's posthumously published journals, *The Sixties*.) On the other hand, according to Janet Coleman in her book *The Compass*—a fascinating study of the mid-'50s Chicago improvisational comedy workshop from which Nichols and May sprang—they both, along with comedian Shelley Berman, lost some of their edge when they became famous:

"On becoming stars, each member of the trio once referred to as 'Two Cocksuckers and Elaine' had unwittingly pulled some plugs from the main currents of ordinary life that had charged their improvisations with humanity. They had been almost instantly

**293**

isolated from the ensemble work of their peers, the extraordinary improvisational foot soldiers. Thus, their passage into celebrity did not return to the political comedy of the improvisational theater any insights into the issues of status and money, or hard looks into the workings of power in the arts and society, or revelations about the entertainment industry. Without the focus and urgency of the improvisational theater, they were atomized from their most integrated and revealing work. Substituting for commonality and spontaneity the narcissism and obsessions of show business, they grew silent in the society they once had satirized."

As a passionate fan of the four features May directed—A *New Leaf, The Heartbreak Kid, Mikey and Nicky,* and *Ishtar*—who finds plenty of "insights into the issues of status and money," "hard looks into the workings of power in the arts and society," and even a few "revelations about the entertainment industry" in these dark, vibrant movies, I feel that Coleman's basically sound observation applies differently to the careers of May and Nichols. In many ways, May, unlike Nichols, is too large and unwieldy a talent to accommodate herself to the entertainment industry in a manner that can easily translate into fame and success, and given the complex and tortuous skirmishes she had with studios on all four of her features, it is hardly surprising that she has worked in Hollywood chiefly as an anonymous script doctor. More recently, she has teamed up with Nichols again as a writer on *The Birdcage* and, as reported in a lengthy article in the March 3 *New York Observer,* on an adaptation of *Primary Colors* budgeted at $65 million and starring John Travolta and Emma Thompson as the Clintons—a project that seems highly political. It will be interesting to discover to what degree May's dangerous satirical gifts

The Graduate: *Elaine (Katharine Ross) and Benjamin (Dustin Hoffman).*

and Nichols' commercial savvy can work in tandem. *The Graduate*, Nichols' main ticket to mainstream success, replays various aspects of the Nichols-May partnership in telling ways—as does *The Heartbreak Kid* (1972), May's own second feature, which can be read in many ways as a response to *The Graduate*. Both movies chart the hero's ditching of a dark, overpowering woman for an inaccessible WASP princess (each monomaniacally pursuing her to the university she's attending, where he hangs out on the campus), echoing Nichols' abandonment of the dangerous side of his routines with May. Furthermore, Charles Grodin, who plays the lead in *The Heartbreak Kid*, was originally cast by Nichols to play the lead in *The Graduate*, and Jeannie Berlin, who plays the ditched woman in *The Heartbreak Kid*, is May's daughter. The two movies take notably different approaches toward ethnicity: Nichols pretends it isn't there and May flaunts it. Though Nichols and May are both Jewish, May grew up in the Yiddish theater, and the anomaly of a Jewish New York actor playing Waspy Los Angeleno Benjamin Braddock in *The Graduate* has to be weighed against the explicitly Jewish New York wedding at the beginning of *The Heartbreak Kid* and the explicitly WASP Minneapolis wedding that closes it. In other words, May accentuates ethnic difference whereas Nichols muddles it. *The Graduate* ends with a Christian wedding of its own, but in this case, significantly, the hero isn't the groom; and the fact that Benjamin winds up using a cross both as a battering ram and as a tool for escape can be read allegorically as Nichols' own determined flight from his roots in courting mainstream success. Even the uses of pop songs as anthems of their hero's aspirations have ethnic implications: in contrast to the euphoric Jewish assimilation (and mainstreaming of folk music) of Simon and Garfunkel in *The Graduate*, *The Heartbreak Kid* offers multiple versions of a pop single associated with the Carpenters, "Close to You," and each successive version registers as more bitterly ironic.

"Don't trust anyone over 30" is the only '60s counterculture motto honored in *The Graduate*, though the picture has only two under-30 characters of any importance, neither of them especially well defined apart from their southern California affluence, and the innate corruption of all the over-30 characters is more felt than analyzed. Dustin Hoffman wears a jacket and tie throughout the picture, and his rebellion relates exclusively to personal rather than social or political issues—his determination to marry the daughter, Elaine (Katharine Ross), of his father's law partner after having an adulterous affair with her mother, Mrs. Robinson (Anne Bancroft, whose style and authority make her a clear stand-in for May). Indeed, one of the film's running gags is the erroneous impression of a suspicious rooming-house landlord in Berkeley that the straitlaced Benjamin is some sort of campus radical.

In fact, Benjamin has no convictions, no politics, no ambitions, no ideas, no friends, no professional interests, and, apart from sex and romance, no nonprofessional interests of any kind. He doesn't take pot or acid, his exemption from fighting in Vietnam is assumed rather than spelled out, and apart from the conspicuous affluence of his background, his remoteness from the world around him, Berkeley included, is defined iconographically rather than ideologically: it's a movie-star pose. Yet somehow he's perceived as a social rebel, and Nichols' transplant of the "heart" of counterculture, not to mention the "heart" of his satiric routines with May, into the Hollywood mainstream clearly struck some kind of elemental paydirt. To borrow the title of a subsequent Simon and Garfunkel album, his movie provided a bridge over troubled water that millions were happy to take.

To understand this alchemy, it's helpful to consider what the other top moneymaking pictures of the '60s were that had some relationship with "rebellious" youth culture: *Splendor in the Grass* (1961, set mainly in the late 1920s), *Bye Bye Birdie* (1963, an adaptation of a stage musical about the impact of a rock-and-roll singer on a small town), *A Hard Day's Night* (1964, a film about and starring the Beatles), *The Wild Angels* (1966, an exploitation feature about a motorcycle gang), *Blowup* (1966, Michelangelo Antonioni's art film about "swinging London"), *2001*, and *Easy Rider* (1969). None of these pictures with the possible exception of the last can be described as an expression or even an accurate representation of '60s counterculture apart from a few passing elements.

When Antonioni dealt directly with American counterculture in *Zabriskie Point* (1970), the film was a resounding flop with audiences and critics alike, and the same could be said of Otto Preminger's grotesque if fascinating *Skidoo* the previous year; perhaps only *Woodstock* (1970) succeeded both in dealing directly with the counterculture and in reaching a wide mainstream audience.

No doubt the sense of "newness" projected by *The Graduate* came less from the film's subject matter than from the offscreen Simon and Garfunkel songs, from the comic dialogue (the obvious legacy of Nichols' satiric routines with May, adroitly adapted by screenwriters Buck Henry and Calder Willingham from Charles Webb's source novel), and, above all, from the eclectic, free-wheeling, and attention-grabbing visual style. Much of that style had clear antecedents in some of the better-known art films of the early '60s work by such filmmakers as Truffaut, Godard, Antonioni, Fellini, and even Cassavetes.

The film's first extended sequence is a party given for Benjamin by his well-to-do parents (William Daniels and Elizabeth Wilson), attended exclusively by the parents' friends, filmed almost entirely in claustrophobic closeups and hand-held camera movements. The style has a great deal in common with the style of party sequences in Cassavetes' *Shadows* (1959) as well as in his subsequent Hollywood feature *Too Late Blues* (1962), although Andrew Sarris, in his contemporary review of *The Graduate*, noted that these "bobbing, tracking, lurching heads in nightmarishly mobile closeups looks like an 'hommage' to Fellini's *8 1/2*," which indeed may be a likelier source. Either way, it looks nothing like standard Hollywood filmmaking of the early '60s. (Pointedly, in his same review of *The Graduate*, Sarris noted that "A rain-drenched Anne Bancroft splattered against a starkly white wall evokes images in [Antonioni's] *La notte*.")

An even more striking example of this mainstreaming of New Wave techniques comes at the end of the protracted comic seduction of Benjamin by Mrs. Robinson (the only name he or the dialogue ever assigns her), who orders him to drive her home from the party and issues a series of commands to him when they are alone in her house—to have a drink, to accompany her upstairs, and so on—as she proceeds to remove her clothing. This climaxes when Benjamin, alone in Mrs. Robinson's daughter's room, sees reflected in a framed portrait of Elaine the nude figure of Mrs. Robinson entering the room and closing the door behind her. When Benjamin spins around to face her, this single gesture is broken up into four separate dovetailing shots, each filmed from a different angle, all but the last of which is so brief that the effect is mainly subliminal. (The successive lengths of the four shots—at least in my unrestored video copy—are 15 frames, 13 frames, one single frame, and then, as Benjamin says "Oh, God!," 70 frames.) Insofar as the early features of Godard and Truffaut can be said to have visual tropes, this is clearly one of them, though the use of it here is more pointedly tied to the viewer's identification with the subjectivity of a single character than it would have been in the French originals.

This is followed by other shots of Benjamin's frantic responses to Mrs. Robinson, punctuated by other near-subliminal shots of her nude body—ten frames of her midriff, four frames of one of her breasts, and five frames of her navel—which effectively suggest the sources of his panic without spelling them out. In this case, it is more difficult to point to precise New Wave counterparts and more likely that the pressures of studio censorship led to some of the subliminal abridgements of shots. (*The Graduate* came out after the far-ranging revision of the Production Code in 1966 and prior to the launching of the rating system in 1968—a transitional period in more ways than one.) But the titillating effect of these brief inserts and their stylistic eclecticism point to the inroads made by New Wave films on Hollywood thinking and practices.

And the same could be said for many of the movie's other stylistic flourishes, ranging from sound overlaps (such as the beginning of a scene's dialogue over the end of the previous sequence) to fancy camera setups (e.g., Mrs. Robinson appearing at a hotel bar rendezvous with Benjamin as a reflection on a glass table) to extended uses of first-person camera (such as the sequence featuring Benjamin inside a deep-sea diving suit, nearly all of it seen and heard from his vantage point).

The differences between the uses of such techniques in New Wave pictures and their uses in Hollywood usually have to do with the mechanics of storytelling and the identification of the viewer. The stylistic play of *Breathless* and *Shoot the Piano Player* generally had the effect of making the viewer identify with the filmmakers, while the stylistic play of *The Graduate* made the viewer identify with Benjamin—even if a greater awareness of the director's role ensued from the process.

Seeing *The Graduate* again recently, I enjoyed pretty much the same things that I enjoyed 30 years ago: Bancroft's robust, superlative performance (until the script turns her into a one-dimensional monster she's the only real character in the movie); the smoothness and assurance of the sketch humor, most of it having to do with Los Angeles affluence and sexual embarrassment; the graceful, dreamlike transition between Benjamin emerging from his swimming pool at home and entering a hotel room with Mrs. Robinson for another bout of lovemaking; the foregrounding of the ebullient and wistful Simon and Garfunkel music (recently appropriated and parodied in Albert Brooks' *Mother*, and so integral throughout *The Graduate* that when Benjamin's car runs out of gas at a climactic juncture, the guitar vamps slow down).

What I don't enjoy is the cruelty, the glib mindlessness, and the insulated, pampered narcissism that makes the whole thing possible. (If Benjamin had run off with Mrs. Robinson, the movie would have been genuinely rebellious.) By studiously avoiding everything about the '60s that is worth remembering today, apart from some of its energy, Nichols can flatter the audience for its knowingness only by assuming the audience knows nothing at all. "The small triumph of *The Graduate*," Pauline Kael wrote in 1969, "was to have domesticated alienation and the difficulty of communication, by making what Benjamin is alienated from a middle-class comic strip and making it absurdly evident that he has nothing to communicate—which is just what makes him an acceptable hero for the large movie audience. If he said anything or had any ideas, the audience would probably hate him . . . . Mike Nichols' 'gift' is that he lets the audience direct him; this is demagoguery in the arts." As a bridge over troubled water and a clever piece of merchandise, *The Graduate* is at best only following the same escapist principles followed today by *Independence Day*—or *The English Patient*, for that matter.

# The Producers

## Gregg Rickman (2001)

Faulkner is supposed to have said that the dead past isn't dead—it's not even past. One filmmaker who appears to have taken Faulkner's words to heart is Mel Brooks. Brooks is usually thought of these days as a talented comic writer whose films gave way sometime after his *annus mirabilis* of 1974 (the year of *Blazing Saddles* and *Young Frankenstein*) to a series of increasingly slack parodies of ever more irrelevant genres. (Or he was before the success of the Broadway production of *The Producers* in the spring of 2001. See Daniel Mendelsohn's essay for a reappraisal of Brooks based on this success.)

Why is Brooks so interested in revisiting these old forms? What secrets do their decayed formulae contain? Do Brooks' films merely lazily take on one genre after another? An alternate reading is possible. A review of the films suggests that Brooks appears to be genuinely interested in history—specifically, in how it exists in modern memory, in how people and events are remembered. His view is at once optimistic, as it posits a cultural memory shared by all, and pessimistic, in that the events remembered are so painfully bleak.

*History of the World Part I* (1980) demonstrates this. Its reworked histories of the Stone Age, the Old Testament, Rome (including the Last Supper), the Inquisition, and the French Revolution all insist, in their strongest passages, on the miseries inflicted on the poor and the helpless by the powerful. This is most painfully evident in the film's best sequence, the Spanish Inquisition, which, after prolonged scenes of mordant Hasidic Jews being tortured by Spanish monks, suddenly turns into a Busby Berkeley-style production number, with an Esther Williams-style water ballet thrown in for good measure. Brooks insists on the horrors of history, but is willing to playfully tweak the record by imagining victims and villains of history alike dancing and singing.

This is a radical variant on Richard Dyer's notion of the utopian nature of the musical, posited in his 1977 essay "Entertainment and Utopia." Dyer suggested that entertainment in general, and musicals in particular, offered "the image of 'something better' to escape into . . . . Alternatives, hopes, wishes . . . what utopia would feel like rather than how it would be organized" (177). Brooks suggests by contrast that a singing-dancing *dystopia* can not only be imagined but realized—that hell and entertainment go together very well.

And he does this in his very first feature film, *The Producers* (1968). In that film, two evidently Jewish producers (Max Bialystock and Leo Bloom, played by Zero Mostel and Gene Wilder) decide to guarantee their failure on Broadway (and subsequent financial windfall) by putting on a play by an author (Franz Liebkind/Kenneth Mars) so deluded he has rewritten World War II with Hitler as its hero. Bialystock and Bloom accept that World War II was indeed won by the right side, and also assume that their Broadway opening night audience will reject Liebkind's vision in horror. Instead the audience, rather than being appalled, stay to laugh and cheer, and our producers are caught with a hit they don't need or want.

Franz Liebkind is Brooks' notion of a revisionist historian, or perhaps even a counterfactual one, pace *Virtual History* (1997), Niall Ferguson's collection of essays reflecting the

**298**

*Revisionist history: Kenneth Mars, Gene Wilder and Zero Mostel in* The Producers.

new popularity of "alternative history" among professional historians. "Hitler was a terrific dancer," Liebkind informs his producers, and he promises to give them "The Hitler you loved, the Hitler you knew, the Hitler with a song in his heart." Brooks inoculates himself against the charge of endorsing Liebkind's vision by having Bialystock and Bloom tear off the Nazi armbands he's given them and throw them away. (Bloom spits on his.) The producers' failure comes not from misreading Liebkind or his play, but from misreading their audience, which sees Liebkind's play "Springtime for Hitler" as a hoot, not a horror.

This passively amnesic audience can be read as Brooks' stand-in for an American elite willing to ignore the stark realities of history in the name of a good laugh. As such, Brooks' film might be read as a conservative critique of the bad taste black comedy of the 1960s rather than as a famous example of same. Unfortunately, and characteristically, Brooks undermines this argument by having Liebkind's play put on the boards by a stage director who's a flamboyant gay stereotype ("The whole third act has got to go," he declaims as he reviews Liebkind's script. "They're losing!") and also by having his Hitler acted out by Dick Shawn's mock hippie, who wins the part with his delirious ode to "Love Power." Given that homosexuals were a target of the Nazis and that the hippies Brooks satirizes were anti-fascist by definition, these digressions work against the film's coherence in a way, say, that the Nazi inflections of Peter Sellers' Dr. Strangelove do not in Kubrick's film.

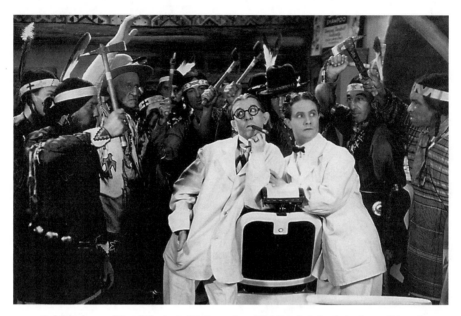

*Bob Woolsey and Bert Wheeler in* Diplomaniacs. *Mel Brooks is firmly in the tradition of these vaudevillians, down to the ethnic humor.*

To be sure, coherence is not a particular goal of the subgenre of film comedy Henry Jenkins has described as "anarchic" in his discussions of the vaudeville-influenced, performance-oriented comedies of the early 1930s. Certainly *The Producers* (and several of Brooks' other films, in particular their musical numbers) can be seen as a modern variant of such spoofs as *Million Dollar Legs, Duck Soup*, and *Diplomaniacs* (all 1932-33). The "Springtime for Hitler" production number in particular might seem in this reading a new version of the Marx Brothers' "We're Going to War" number in *Duck Soup*, or Wheeler and Woolsey's reduction of a peace conference to shambles in *Diplomaniacs*. Jenkins has written of such scenes as mere platforms for comedians' performance skills ("the podium becomes a stage and the delegates . . . an appreciative audience for their elaborate show," he wrote of *Diplomaniacs* in 1990), dismissing the films as political satire per se. In a similar fashion, "Springtime for Hitler" showcases the performance skills of Dick Shawn and ensemble. One problem with this argument is that in parts of *The Producers* (the aforementioned armband scene) and his later films as well Brooks does indeed seem to be aware of the political meanings of his work, as with the satire directed against racism in *Blazing Saddles*, or against the cruelties of the powerful in *History of the World Part I* ("It's good to be the king," says Brooks' Louis XVI, who employs peasants for target practice). Brooks' many returns to the persecution of the Jews in his films about history indicates he is indeed interested in the historical memory of the Holocaust, and the persecution of his people generally: thus the relevant scenes of *The Producers, History of the World*, and also the remake of Ernst Lubitsch's 1942 film *To Be or Not to Be* that Brooks starred in and produced in 1983. The many lame jokes of these films seem in consequence more damaging than they might in an unalloyed farce, such as *Silent Movie* (1976) or *High Anxiety* (1978); less anarchic and liberating than instead a millstone of a dead comic past. But then Brooks' whole career can be thought of as an act of historical revisionism, in his reworking of genres past in *Blazing Saddles*, *Young Frankenstein* and other films. They summon a counterfactual world where burlesque never died.

Mel Brooks' great failure as a comic film artist is his compulsive literalization, his protracted, rebus-like illustrated puns and the reflexive genre parodies of genres that are so worn out they can't withstand comic reexamination, as if the naming itself of a spoof target is enough to render the spoof funny. Puns and incongruous juxtapositions alone are not enough to compensate for unimaginative premises: thus, to single out a particularly glaring example of comic bankruptcy, the disaster of Dom DeLuise's tedious parody of Marlon Brando's Godfather that turns up in the middle of *Robin Hood: Men in Tights*.

But all this is characteristic of an artist like Brooks, who at root does not think visually, but instead in terms of words. *Silent Movie* is the great test case—stripped of vocalizing, the film's funniest gags are still essentially verbal: the fly in Henny Youngman's soup, the mime Marcel Marceau's spoken "no." Thus the move of Brooks' characters in his films from inarticulateness to mastery, expressed in particular through their mastery of musical performance, and more generally through their new command of the language. In *The Producers* Leo Bloom is reborn, thanks to the scam he conceives, from being an honest drone who clutches a security blanket and is barely able to speak, to an individual who's an articulate courtroom advocate, loyal to his partner, and capable of mounting a musical show in prison at film's end. The Ron Moody character in *The Twelve Chairs* (1970)

*"Springtime for Hitler."*

undergoes a similar transformation and puts on his show (of epileptic seizure) in the final scene of that film. In *Young Frankenstein* the monster (Peter Boyle) moves from inarticulate grunting to reading the *Wall Street Journal*, via his masterful performance of "Putting on the Ritz." In *High Anxiety* psychoanalyst Richard H. Thorndyke (Brooks) signals his move away from paralyzing vertigo via his successful lounge act. Brooks' heroes, be they two conmen in search of a lost fortune (*The Twelve Chairs*), a drunken Hollywood director (*Silent Movie*), or an arrogant billionaire (*Life Stinks*), are all reborn, frequently through a symbolic death or humiliation, in film after film: Ron Moody's rolling on the ground at the end of *The Twelve Chairs*, or—to list three films starring Brooks—Mel Funn's drunken debauch in *Silent Movie*; Goddard Bolt's loss of his fortune, his identity, and his mind in *Life Stinks*; or the bird crap that spatters Thorndyke in *High Anxiety*.

A seeming exception to this pattern is the ever smooth Bart (Cleavon Little) of *Blazing Saddles*, in command of every situation. Unlike the Frankenstein monster, who must painfully learn Brooks' beloved Broadway melodies, and Thorndyke, who reveals an unexpected musical flair once he's met the right woman, Bart knows his Cole Porter (and can summon the Lionel Hampton Orchestra at will) from his first screen appearance. For all that, however, he too must be rescued from death by hanging, rescue in his case coming at the hands of his later archenemy Hedley Lamarr (Harvey Korman), a villain so inept he can't even control his own name. Bart, also, is willing to fake his own humiliation—taking himself hostage, dressing up as a telegram delivery man—to win ultimate victory.

Brooks' last interesting movie, his only film since *Silent Movie* not dismissible as a genre parody and nothing more, is *Life Stinks* (1991). Goddard Bolt's climb from riches to poverty (and back to riches) is presented as a spiritual progress, its turning point a dance number with his true love (Lesley Ann Warren's exuberant bag-lady). Control of language, of naming, is again at issue, as Bolt is driven to pure fury by a fellow bum's insistence on naming himself "J. Paul Getty," an insistence which seems to mock Bolt's own claims that despite his disheveled looks he is indeed a dispossessed billionaire. It's significant that the one film beside *The Producers* in which Brooks directly addressed Hitler's attempt to erase Jewishness from the earth is *To Be or Not to Be*, a farce built around mistaken identity. Characteristically for Brooks, however, and very unlike Lubitsch, irrelevant gags intervene to muddy the film's thrust.

But, as in *The Producers*, a show is ultimately put on. Bialystock and Bloom, like others of Brooks' characters, despite their failure by success, still have lived up to their claims: they *are* producers. "Putting on a show" has been sufficient plot justification for many a great musical comedy and it may perhaps be in this particular subgenre (rather than as a satirist or performer) Brooks may ultimately best be remembered. He's not a Lubitsch, or a Leo McCarey, director of *Duck Soup*, or even a William A. Seiter, director of *Diplomaniacs*; but rather instead is a Busby Berkeley of comedy—not a great dramaturge but rather a showman capable of amazing spectacle.

## Works Cited

Richard Dyer, "Entertainment and Utopia," in Rick Altman, ed., *Genre: The Musical* (London: Routledge & Kegan Paul, 1981), 175-89.

Henry Jenkins III, "'Fifi Was My Mother's Name!': Anarchistic Comedy, the Vaudeville Aesthetic, and Diplomaniacs," *The Velvet Light Trap* 26 (Fall 1990), 3-27.

Daniel Mendelsohn, "Double Take," *New York Review of Books* (June 21, 2001), 12–15.

# Let Life Begin: Harold and Maude

**Aneta Chapman** (2001)

> The child from whom for any reason parental affection is withdrawn is likely to become timid and unadventurous, filled with fears and self-pity, and no longer able to meet the world in a mood of gay exploration. —Bertrand Russell[1]

Hal Ashby's *Harold and Maude* (1971), a satiric black comedy written by Colin Higgins about a young man attempting suicide, is also an adult American fairy tale. Ashby presents a melancholic death-obsessed young protagonist who by the end of this film is transformed into a free-spirited, life-affirming man.

Although classic fairy tales developed in Europe, before the industrial age and long before the modern mechanized world of Harold Chasen (Bud Cort), their themes are universal and timeless. These stories generally center around individuals struggling with their place in society. While there are no witches or goblins, there is a character trying to steal the soul of Harold Chasen. Like a modern Snow White or Cinderella forced to deal with problematic parents or guardians, Harold must face his mother, the oppressive authority figure in his life.

> There are certain elements common in most fairy tales of European and Celtic traditions. The classic fairy tale is about one person, or one family, having to cope with a supernatural occurrence or supernatural protagonist during a period of stress. The hero is almost invariably a young person, usually the youngest member of a family, and if not deformed or already orphaned, is probably in the process of being disowned or abandoned. The characters in the stories are, nevertheless, stock figures. They are either altogether good or altogether bad, and there is no evolution of character.[2]

Ashby's protagonist struggles with isolation and alienation. Harold is not truly an orphan, for his mother is alive, but her inability to provide him with emotional security makes him a probable candidate for abandonment. Harold's use of magic to fight his alienation by staging dramatic attempted suicides comes close to a supernatural phenomenon. During the course of the film, Harold constantly feigns bodily torment. Ashby pays homage to Alfred Hitchcock when he shows Harold, covered with fake blood, lying in a tub. While the viewer knows that Harold is not harmed—he smiles after his mother finds and leaves him—his several staged suicides clearly demonstrate the dysfunctional status of the Chasen family.

In the second of these feigned suicides, the pool drowning, Mrs. Chasen (Vivian Pickles) enters the pool like Esther Williams performing a water ballet. She swims past Harold who is floating face down in the pool like Joe Gillis in *Sunset Boulevard*. Ashby's juxtaposition of Harold's film noir-style staged death and Mrs. Chasen's Esther Williams-style performance shows how both people function within a fantasy world. Without dialogue and with wicked humor, Ashby conveys how both mother and son engage in theatrical behavior but fail to communicate. Harold's mother has abandoned him on an emotional level.

Maternal mothers are rare in Ashby's films. In this film and in *The Landlord* (1970) the protagonists' mothers are sexy, stylish upper-class women who hold provincial bourgeois views. They are more concerned about social norms and appearances than their own sons' well-being. In *The Landlord*, the mother warns her son against dating a black woman, adding that if he does, then a light-skinned black is preferable. In *Harold and Maude*, the mother's acceptable criteria for the dating service's applicants is that they are neither fat nor ugly. Both mothers are good at warning their sons but not helpful in providing practical advice or solutions for their sons' problems. In Harold's case, the mother suggests military service and marriage.

Harold is emotionally but not physically repressed. He demonstrates that he has an incredible imagination as well as physical agility. He successfully attempts the most dangerous antics. To hang oneself without actually killing oneself is not an easy feat. Harold manages to do it complete with sound effects. His choking sounds are ghastly but also funny. His tongue sticks out and he drools. He swings in the air like a pathetic creature, regressed to an infantile state. He is a perfect clown, a white-faced Pierrot. One critic, indeed, has compared him to Harry Langdon, pasty-faced and impish. He is mostly mute until he meets and befriends Maude. Each staged suicide is executed with brilliant timing and little dialogue. Ashby's editing is concise and clean. For example, Harold aims his revolver at his mother but fails to shoot her. Instead, he turns the weapon on himself. Shooting his mother would be pointless; it would not release Harold from his misery as killing himself would.

"What activity gives you a different sense of enjoyment from the others?" asks his therapist. Harold, who dresses just like his therapist, withholds his answer, then delivers a clear concise unemotional response: "I go to funerals." Harold does not articulate his real reasons for attending funerals: a preoccupation with death, a theatrical interest in high drama and ceremony.

The first response of the audience is laughter at such weird macabre behavior. But as Ashby shows Harold at these funerals, we begin to see an individual seeking community. The funerals offer a safe, formal environment. Ashby finds humor in the weary emotionless clergymen delivering uninspiring eulogies, the absurdity of a dead man buried in a "Permaseal" casket. Who wants the dead? Even as this coffin is being loaded into the hearse, a school marching band files by the funeral scene. The simple message is that life continues.

Harold's mother devises two schemes to stop his antics and pranks, aimed at encouraging him to assume responsibility. First, she suggests that he join the military. One of the best sight gags in the film is the introduction of Harold's Uncle Victor (Charles Tyner). Harold is told that he is going to meet the right-hand man of General Douglas MacArthur. When we see Uncle Victor, he is missing his entire right arm. In a device perhaps borrowed from Kubrick's *Dr. Strangelove*, he has rigged a device to lift his arm sleeve to salute. Uncle Victor is a poster-boy for why one should shun military service.

"There is action, adventure, advising. And you get a chance to see the war firsthand. And there will be slant-eyed girls," says Uncle Victor to Harold. Racist notions of Manifest Destiny and repulsive exoticized ideas about Asian women negate any honorable

intentions or endeavors. Uncle Victor is delusional and does not recognize the destruction that the military lifestyle has caused him. This role model must be and is rejected by Harold. For the man has no soul, only bitterness and disappointment.

"Harold, I think I can see a little Nathan Hale in you," bellows Uncle Victor. Nathan Hale, the dead Revolutionary War hero, is an apt reminder about how tragic life can be. Ashby cuts to an infantile-looking Harold on the sofa who does not physically or in spirit resemble the war hero. It is ironic that Hale should be chosen as a proper war hero, for he was in his day a rebel and an independent actor. "I regret that I have but one life to give for my country," said Nathan Hale. Ashby uses the sound of gunfire on the soundtrack as a reality check. Nathan Hale was shot by the British.

As Harold tours the military facility, old soldiers fall dead on the ground as he passes. The scene is funny and pathetic. This is not the type of ending for soldiers that General MacArthur had in mind when he stated before Congress that "old soldiers never die, they just fade away." These soldiers' bodies are broken and their spirits are destroyed. The uncle cannot see the deleterious impact of fighting on the psyche and body. The military environment is not the proper milieu for either healing thyself or escaping from oneself. There is no honor here.

Military service seems like a preposterous career undertaking for Harold. Here is a man playing at committing suicide, not at all interested in killing other people. His mother's second scheme to try and marry off Harold is equally ludicrous. When one thinks about someone contemplating marriage, we envision a mature person seeking a loving and caring partner. One does not envision an arranged marriage with someone who has suicidal interests. In a poignant scene, Harold's mother fills out his question-naire for the dating service. One question asks, "do you often get the feeling that perhaps life is not worth living?" Mrs. Chasen checks, "not sure."

The scene is amusing because Harold is staging another suicide while his mother is trying to arrange a match for him, mingling in one scene the mother's blinkered opti-mism and Harold's pessimism about life. The viewer realizes that the dating candidates will reflect his mother's interests and passions, not Harold's choices. Here again, the mother presumes to know what is best for her son who, although a grown man, is treated like a child. Until Harold forms a relationship, the characters all function in a vacuum. Emotional blindness and deafness permeate the film.

*Ruth Gordon as fairy godmother.*

Harold's mother arranges three dates for him from a reputable dating agency. Her criterion is that the service screens out the "fat and ugly." Unfortunately, the three women who Harold meets are all fat and/or ugly, like the step-sisters in the story of "Cinderella." In that story, the step-mother and the two step-sisters are stock characters with no evolution in their character. They begin evil and they remain evil. In *Harold and Maude*, Mrs. Chasen and Uncle Victor are stock characters as well—their thinking and actions do not change throughout the film.

To Harold's rescue from the evil plotting of his mother and his uncle comes Maude (Ruth Gordon). Maude is the fairy godmother of this fable. She's an unconventional fairy godmother but this is an unconventional film. Unlike the dates his mother provides him, Harold meets Maude at an unlikely place—a funeral. As in old Hollywood films, Ashby arranges a classic "meet-cute" for the couple. We first see a small woman darting in and out of pews trying to get closer to Harold. She makes "psst" sounds trying to get his attention during the ceremonies. Unlike Harold, Maude pays little attention to the service. She finds funerals fun. She shuns the traditional drab clothing worn at funerals for lighter shades. Later in the film, at another funeral, she carries a yellow umbrella. All the other mourners have dark umbrellas. Maude's disposition is sunny compared with Harold's gloom.

The *Oxford American Dictionary* defines a fairy godmother as "a benefactress who provides a sudden unexpected gift." Maude's unexpected gift to Harold is her spirit. As in many fairy tales, the fairy godmother protects the protagonist from evil and also acts as a conductor in showing the protagonist the right path in life.

> They [fairies] hate miserliness above all things, and love an open cheerful character. Perhaps because of their interest in fertility, they are rather free and wanton in their own conduct, and are friendly towards lovers.[3]

"I'm acting as a gentle reminder, here today, gone tomorrow, so don't get attached to things," says Maude to Harold. Her words are a prescription for living a meaningful life. Together they embark on adventures that will pit them against institutions and authority figures like his Uncle Victor. Maude's words to Harold are also a caveat regarding the future of their relationship.

As *Harold and Maude* was being made, many young Americans were protesting the war in Vietnam, fighting for civil rights, or establishing their own identities independent of their families and communities. They demonstrated their own style of clothing with bold colors and bold patterns. They had their own language which was more reflective of their feelings than standard usage. The youth in America questioned the authority of government and challenged the status quo. This was reflected in the cinema of the time in films about disaffected and rebellious youth, including such comedies as *Alice's Restaurant* and *Brewster McCloud* (which also starred Bud Cort).

*Harold and Maude* reflects its time in its anti-war sentiments. Together the pair devise a plan to keep Harold from being drafted into the Vietnam War by his uncle. Harold brings a shrunken head to a meeting with him. During the course of their meeting, Maude, posing as an anti-war demonstrator, grabs Harold's shrunken head. Harold freaks out and chases Maude, upsetting the uncle. The shrunken head at once symbolizes Harold's withered manchild status, his morbidity, and how the Establishment has tried to brainwash him.

"I'm always looking for the new experience," says Maude to Harold. When they meet, she is seventy-nine years old and he is twenty. She will soon be celebrating her eightieth birthday. Maude introduces Harold to new experiences by reawakening his senses: taste, smell, sound, touch and hearing. She offers him organic foods and wines. She introduces him to an Odorific machine that simulates smells. She sings and dances and encourages him to play instruments to bring out his joyous and creative side. Maude gently encourages him to experience his sensual nature through art and lovemaking.

Of course, it was the sexual relationship between Harold and Maude that initially caused the film to be dismissed. According to the producer, Charles Mulvehill, "the idea of a twenty-year-old boy with an eighty-year-old woman just made people want to vomit."[4] However, the detractors failed to realize that Maude never assumed a grandmotherly role with Harold. When she invites him to her railroad car, she treats him like an equal and like a man. When one reviews the aftermath of lovemaking between them, we see an ebullient Harold but a sleeping Maude. It is her last gift to him.

Traditionally, fairy godmothers do not remain in the lives of the people they help. After the protagonist is rescued or healed, the godmother exits. Maude commemorates her birthday by committing suicide. This day becomes Harold's rite of passage into full adulthood. He recognizes the difference between playing at suicide and committing suicide. He finds his full voice by making his first loud exclamation of the entire film. He screams.

By the end of the film, Harold has learned a lesson about the art of living and the art of dying. He realizes that he is responsible for his own happiness. Thanks to Maude, Harold finds himself restored. He is capable of giving love and receiving love. He has learned to treasure his life and the lives of other creatures. When we see him walking away playing a banjo, we recognize a free and independent spirit.

## Notes

1. Bertrand Russell, *The Conquest Of Happiness* (New York: Liveright, 1971), 139.
2. Iona Opie and Peter Opie, *The Classic Fairy Tales* (London: Oxford University Press, 1974), 15.
3. K.M. Briggs, "Fairies," in Richard Cavendish, ed., *Man, Myth & Magic: The Illustrated Encyclopedia of Mythology, Religion and the Unknown* (New York: Marshall Cavendish, 1995), 830.
4. Peter Biskind, *Easy Riders, Raging Bulls: How the Sex-Drugs-and-Rock-Roll-Generation Saved Hollywood* (New York: Simon & Schuster, 1998), 174.

# Romantic Comedy Today: Semi-Tough or Impossible?

**Brian Henderson** (1979)

## 1.

It is a scandal of culture that there has never been a widely accepted theory of comedy, to organize the general sense of the subject and to orient particular studies within it. Since Aristotle there has been a theory of tragedy, more or less the same one. (Hegel's and Bradley's theories have different emphases but are compatible with it and relate to their object in a similar way.) But each theorist of comedy has worked in a vacuum. Nevertheless each has set out boldly to do the whole job—as though Aristotle had merely omitted to do it.

As bad as the state of affairs itself is that we do not know why it is so. Determining its causes may be equal to solving the theoretical problem itself, and as difficult. A speculation: each theory of why comedy faces a double task—to account for comic forms, i.e., the laws of comic discourse, literary/ dramatic/(filmic), and to account for the phenomenon of laughter, and of course to relate the two. Perhaps, in different ways, each theory of comedy has shattered or distended itself on this double task. The more successful theories, notably Freud's, tend to concentrate on one of the tasks and to ignore the other, though this entails incompleteness.

No theory can deal with both questions successfully; yet each must try to do so because the questions are linked. Producing laughter is a fundamental effect of comic discourse,* hence it is a part of the art of comedy writing, directing, acting, which no treatise can leave out. The two phenomena are linked but they seem to lie along different axes.

Henri Bergson's theory of comedy as the mechanical encrusted on the organic is exposed as simplistic by the case that it seems to fit best: Buster Keaton. The latter's creative misadaptation of objects to various survival needs is a positive evolutionary force. So is his turning his body into machines of various sorts to surmount various perils, such as becoming a pendulum to rescue his fiancée from a waterfall in *Our Hospitality*.

Freud's *Jokes and Their Relation to the Unconscious*[1] (1905) may well be the best book on the subject, but it limits itself to the simplest of comic discourses, the minimal unit of humor the joke, epigram, or humorous remark. Hence it is of more limited value to our inquiry than might appear. A comic film such as *Bringing Up Baby* (1938) contains many jokes and instances of humor in Freud's sense but is not reducible to them. Its construction, effects, humor operate on several levels at once. No single element may be understood by itself either discursively or in regard to spectator relation, only in relation to the multi-tiered whole. Although the book is one of his most brilliant, Freud was

---

* Dare one call laughter a rhetorical effect? No, because the figure may be written and no one laugh. In comedy we identify the figure with the effect—as though metaphor were dependent on audience effect to be that.

**310**

no more satisfied than the reader seeking a full treatment of comedy. James Strachey reports that Freud's other books of the period (*Interpretation of Dreams, Psychopathology of Everyday Life, Three Essays*) were expanded and modified almost out of recognition in their later editions. Half a dozen small additions were made to *Jokes* in 1912 but no further changes were ever made in it. References to it are rare in the other works, but in the *Introductory Lectures* he speaks of it having temporarily led him aside from his path; in the *Autobiographical Study* there is an apparent deprecatory reference to it. Twenty years later he returned to the problem with a short paper on "Humor" (1927), which recasts the subject by the metapsychological scheme id-ego-superego.

In the cases of practitioners Ben Jonson and Lope de Vega the *absence* of a theory of comedy became the foundation for their thinking on the subject. In Jonson's *Every Man Out of His Humor* (1600) there occurs the following remarkable speech by Cordatus.

> No, I assure you, signor. If those laws you speak of had been delivered us *ab initio*, and in their present virtue and perfection, there had been some reason of obeying their powers: but 'tis extant that that which we call *Comoedia* was at first nothing but a simple and continued song sung by only one person, til Susario invented a second; after him, Epicharmus a third; Phormus and Chionides devised to have four actors, with a prologue and chorus: to which Cratinus, long after, added a fifth and sixth: Euppolis, more: Aristophanes, more than they: every man in the dignity of his spirit and judgment supplied something. And though that in him this kind of poem appeared absolute and fully perfected, yet how is the face of it changed since! in Menander, Philemon, Cecilius, Plautus, and the rest, who have utterly excluded the chorus, altered the property of the persons, their names, and natures, and augmented it with all liberty, according to the elegancy and disposition of those times wherein they wrote, I see not then, but we should enjoy the same license or free power to illustrate and heighten our invention as they did: and not be tied to those strict and regular forms which the niceness of a few, who are nothing but form, would thrust upon us.[2]

In his poem "The New Art of Making Comedies" (1609), Lope de Vega argued that popular comedy ignores rules.

> The true play like every kind of poetic composition has its proposed goal, and that has been to imitate the actions of men and to paint the customs of their age. Any poetic imitation is made up of three things: speech, rhythm, harmony or music. . . .
> For a subject tragedy has history and comedy has feigning: for this reason comedy was called flat-footed, of humble plot.[3]

## 2. Fifteen Kinds of Snow

The Eskimos have special names for many different kinds of snow (fifteen, if I remember rightly) because variations in the quality of snow greatly affect their living . . . A different name for snow implies a different kind of hunt. Some names for snow imply that one should not hunt at all.

—KENNETH BURKE, "LITERATURE AS EQUIPMENT FOR LIVING."[4]

Romantic comedy: a genre, a family of genres (marriage, manners, screwball), a category of production and marketing, a category of analysis, a realm of specialties (Ernst

Lubitsch, Gregory La Cava), a notion. Definition, even delimitation, is difficult or impossible because all Hollywood films (except some war films) have romance and all have comedy. We might specify "comic *about* the romance" but nearly always at least some of the comedy concerns some of the romance. A workable subset "romantic comedy" might refer to those films in which romance and comedy are the primary components or to those without other such components as crime, detection of crime, Western adventure, war, etc. But what is "primary" in a given case is difficult to determine where romance and comedy are pervasive. Moreover, even if crime, westerns, war, etc. films are eliminated, the remainder is vast and its modes of conjoining romance and comedy myriad.

## 3. Special Names

It may be that subdividing romantic comedy into its component types or genres will further analysis of it. The definition that is elusive might be easier to accomplish at a level of greater particularity. Let us take "screwball comedy," a term one finds in critical contexts of all sorts. Beneath the common term, however, there is no agreement, neither from critic to critic nor within the work of a single critic. The weekly critics use the term again and again without definition, implicit or explicit, or even an approximate sense. In the hands of its users, "screwball" seems to refer to a general impression of zaniness received by the critic.

A working definition is provided by Howard Hawks, in speaking of *Bringing Up Baby*.

> I think the picture had a great fault and I learned an awful lot from it. There are no normal people in it. Everyone you met was a screwball. Since that time I have learned my lesson and I don't intend ever again to make everybody crazy. If the gardener had been normal, if the sheriff had been just a perplexed man from the country—but as it was, they were all way off center.[5]

Hawks defines screwball comedy as a film in which everyone is a screwball. He seems to limit the category to one instance and claims to regret that as a mistake, but Hawks' definition does have to do with structural factors, not with impressions of craziness. Its import is clarified by these observations on ancient comedy.

> The representation of manners always supposes some philosophy of conduct, some standard by which we judge, and some method of discovering it. Aristotle had only put it into form when he laid down his doctrine of the Mean. This doctrine is at the root of Theophrastus' *Characters*, and is everywhere implied by such comedies as Menander's. Virtue once admitted to be the mean, it became necessary to define all the extremes, the too little and too much of the social appearances of man.[6]

Against this backdrop screwball comedy is that which omits (or departs from) the philosophy of conduct traditional to comedy. In a comedy of characters who are all crazy, there can be no mean or standard. Even to say that all are in excess implies an external standard since there is no inner one.

But in what is called screwball comedy there often is comparative judgment of behavior and therefore at least an inchoate "philosophy of conduct." It is certainly not abstract like Aristotle's *Ethics*, it may be closer to Lévi-Straussian "savage thought," a thinking with empirical entities. In *The Awful Truth* and *His Girl Friday*, the Ralph Bellamy character is exemplar and exaggeration of conventional morality—both a character norm, against which to contrast the eccentricities of the leads, and a social norm, against which the film directs its satire. (These functions are not always embodied in a single character.) The main characters are screwballs in relation to him, but this is not mere madness, for it exemplifies the value of spontaneity, which reigns supreme in thirties romantic comedy, where it stands in for and includes wit, intelligence, genuine feeling vs. conventional response, adaptable moral response, vitality, life. In films without a Bellamy type, less prominent background figures such as policemen, judges, storekeepers, relatives perform one or both functions. In both films mentioned, the heroines plan to marry Bellamy at one point, which indicates that they waver between the two moralities.

*Holiday* would not be called a screwball comedy by most. The action is carefully plotted, emerges logically from consistent, well-motivated characters, etc. It is a well-made film of a well-made play. Yet the main characters Linda and Casey (and the Potters) are celebrated as some kind of screwballs in contrast to the convention-bound, predictable other characters. Its philosophy of conduct is clear-cut, but it champions a pair of (semi) screwballs. Is it a screwball comedy?

A different instance is Preston Sturges, in whose films all characters speak a heady, epigrammatic prose, improbable in all but a few cases. Probability is violated in this respect and in some outrageous plot twists (usually at the end), but there are few if any screwball characters if screwball means to *act* spontaneously and crazily. The dialogue is the main, usually the only crazy element. The actions, events, plots sometimes are rather

*Exemplar and exaggeration of conventional morality: Ralph Bellamy with umbrella and Rosalind Russell in* His Girl Friday.

conventional, predictable. The characters played by Joel McCrea, Henry Fonda, Eddie Bracken, even William Demarest are not "spontaneous." They perform no "flips" like Johnny Case in *Holiday* and hardly, if ever, run as the characters in *Baby* do constantly. They rarely laugh, sigh, sing, or do slapstick like McCarey's characters. Mainly they exchange words—it is the words which flip, sigh, run, get out of breath. But at this level—the lines themselves are screwball. They may come out of any figure in the frame and very often express surprising sentiments. Character consistency is often sacrificed for a good speech—another screwball element (or is it?).

We have chased the notion of screwball around the clock of filmic elements. We went in one door and came out another—without encountering an iota of certainty or consistency, not even a vector between two points that pointed in a definite direction.

**4.**

If we cannot define romantic comedy, can we talk about it at all? Aristotle says no. Wittgenstein says yes.

> Instead of producing something common to all that we call language, I am saying that these phenomena have no one thing in common which makes us use the same word for all,—but that they are related to one another in many different ways. . . .
> Consider for example the proceedings that we call "games." I mean board-games, card-games, ball-games, Olympic-games, and so on. What is common to them all?—Don't say "There *must* be something, or they would not be called 'games'"—but *look* and *see* whether there is anything common to all.—For if you look at them you will not see something that is common to *all*, but similarities, relationships, and a whole series of them at that . . . we see a complicated network of similarities overlapping and crisscrossing: sometimes overall similarities, sometimes similarities of detail . . . I can think of no better expression to characterize these similarities than "family resemblances. . ."[7]

**5.**

Romantic comedy is a family of resemblances. Filmic romantic comedy is one branch of that family but also, as we have seen, a family in itself with diverse sub-branches. Since the branches of romantic comedy include entire art forms and their traditions—ballet, drama, painting, novel, opera, poem, symphony—it is necessarily true that the differences among them, which are material, are greater than the similarities, which are semantic, abstract, thematic. (As is the heading "romantic comedy" itself.) This is why transformations of subjects or themes from one medium to another are never automatic and never equal and why they offer an excellent perspective on the signifying processes of both, especially on the second or receiving system, on which the burden of transformation falls.

Consider the oft-told story of Ben Hecht's adaptation of Noel Coward's *Design for Living*—what is its point? Hecht is said to have boasted that he had kept only one line of the original (or was it a line from *Hay Fever?*), but critics agree that the film is far inferior to the play, even those virtually uncritical of Lubitsch's work. This story, like all Hollywood stories, emphasizes personalities, but far more important is the work process. Under the prevailing censorship, a woman could not live sexually with a man if they were not married, let alone two. The suggestion that Leo and Otto had been or were lovers was also inadmissible. The play (or its title, though even that no longer made sense) had to be turned toward an acceptable category, in this case competition between two men for a girl, with the twists that it remains cheerful to the end and that there is no final choice. For Hecht or any Hollywood writer the project was the same—to turn *Design for Living* into a romantic comedy.

## 6.

*Semi-Tough* (1972) is a non-romantic comedy,[*] a football/sex/Texas-boy novel (by Dan Jenkins) that is transformed into a romantic comedy of the same name (1977—written by Walter Bernstein, directed by Michael Ritchie) at a time when the concept of romantic comedy itself seems vaguely problematic, extinct, or transformed. Thus in considering this problem, we are defining and pursuing an equation with two unknowns. What is romantic comedy now? How is this particular non-romantic comedy transformed into one? There are also two (more or less) knowns that we may use—what romantic comedy used to be and what this non-romantic comedy was before transformation.

The novel *Semi-Tough* (1972) belongs to a tradition of vernacular fiction that goes back (at least) to Mark Twain's *Adventures of Huckleberry Finn* (1885). The tradition is a popular one—at its beginnings opposed to high literature—and has often been a profitable one. Twain himself was a best-selling author and the Huck Finn formula—colorful (rural) characters recounting colorful adventures in a colorful idiom—has been the basis for countless books (and later films) including *True Grit, No Time for Sergeants, To Kill a Mockingbird, Little Big Man. Semi-Tough* too is narrated by its central character, Billy Clyde Puckett. His diction is far less distinct, region-specific, and consistent than Huck's because it is a composite of Texas-, New York-, and football-ese and because it developed in an age of media saturation of virtually all regions. Even so it is the vernacular narration of Billy Clyde and its interaction with the events recounted which organize the *enunciation* of the book and the reader's pleasure in reading it. Word choice, distinctive local constructions, dialects are far less important here than certain rhythms of spoken speech (more or less Texan) which strongly imply a listener and indeed, though not too forcibly, specific listener reactions. The reader is worked into these rhythms and laughs or whatever in the right places. When the words are themselves funny, the effect is doubled. Like all good comic timing, it is the effect.

## 7.

The book's plot recalls Twain also. Three childhood friends from Texas now live in New York—football pros and roommates Billy Clyde and Shake Tiller and ad woman Barbara Jane Bookman. Shake and Barbara Jane have been romantically involved since high school. The three are roughly equivalent to Huck, Tom and Becky Thatcher in *Tom Sawyer* and *Huckleberry Finn*. Barbara Jane is from the highest class in the region just as Becky is the daughter of a Judge. Tom is a middle-class boy, Huck a semi-orphan and outcast, a member of the lowest white class. So Shake's father owns a paint store while Billy Clyde is an orphan/outcast. "My daddy ran off before I ever knew him . . . My mamma was a waitress and

---

[*] Of course the book has its own comedy and its own romance. These are transformed entirely in making it into a romantic comedy.

maybe a couple of other things, and she ran off, too. Which left me with Uncle Kenneth, who was not much more than a golf hustler, a pool shark and a pretty good gin rummy stud."

We ask the question that is fundamental to literary semiotics, New Criticism, and various old criticisms: how does the first-person narration and vernacular idiom interact with the story? (On this point alone *Huck Finn* leaves the others far behind.) Billy Clyde's perspective and diction are used mainly to add salt to the games, orgies, New York and Texas types that he describes. (Similarly his outcast status is a childhood note that has virtually no effect on the rest of the book.) There is a possible exception. The book builds to a double climax of pre-game orgy and Super Bowl. But there is a third climax concerning the dawning of love between Billy Clyde and Barbara Jane. This "new hermeneutic" is introduced before the telling of the game and finished later. Billy Clyde tells of Shake's not appearing after the game and of Barbara Jane's suggestions after a while that they get together. He also narrates his own refusals, continued even when Shake writes them to get together, without comment. She guesses what he might be thinking, occasionally he says what he is thinking in dialogue, but he never speaks it directly as narrator. This device is familiar from Hemingway and others. The first-person narration creates tension and defines character (and sometimes an ethics or a metaphysical position) by what it does not say, by its avoidance of areas or topics to which it has access. At the end of his account—during which he is presumably working through the taboos inhibiting him, Billy Clyde describes their finally hitting the right mood and beginning to make love, then stops.

## 8.

The film drops nearly all of the book's football and casual sex and all of its material about the characters' shared childhood. It makes the three friends roommates. It eliminates the love relationship between Shake and Barbara Jane—none of the three has apparently had sex with another when the film opens. This has been called the film's *Design for Living* premise, but it is not that. In the play the three try each of three possible pairings before they go off to live as three at the final curtain. The initial arrangement of *Semi-Tough* is merely a set-up for romantic comedy of a more usual sort—a competition of two men for a woman that will favor first one then the other.*

* PLOT SUMMARY: Barbara Jane returns from a several-month absence. During this time Shake has gotten heavily into BEAT—"it changed my life." This change precipitates changes in the other characters and their relationships and leads to the events of the plot. Barbara Jane admires Shake's new self-mastery, they become closer, by the next road game they are sleeping together. Billy Clyde's distress is expressed in various ways (to the audience only), though the exact cause is unclear. He counter-attacks by proposing to write a book but he blows this bid for her esteem by making a joke of it. At the next game week, Shake saves a life through BEAT. Barbara Jane's anxiety at the event becomes hysterical admiration for Shake, and they decide to marry. At this Billy Clyde drops the book and carries the battle to the enemy's territory by faking his way through a BEAT weekend and pretending to have IT, just as Barbara Jane suffers through to please Shake and does not get IT. During the wedding preparations Billy Clyde plays off Shake's anxieties that a "mixed marriage" will not work: Shake says "I don't" at the altar, the ceremony becomes a brawl, Billy Clyde and Barbara Jane escape. He says they should go to Hawaii, they walk together down the beach.

*Two men, one woman:* Design for Living *(Fredric March, Miriam Hopkins, Gary Cooper) and* Semi-Tough *(Jill Clayburgh, Burt Reynolds, Kris Kristofferson).*

The film has no narrator, no voice-over, it presents the action objectively. Billy Clyde's book project is retained as a narrative episode—a few scenes show him writing and taping. This has only to do with the enounced (the told) whereas the taping is the enunciation principle of the entire book as well as sometimes part of the enounced, as when Billy Clyde describes himself speaking to the recorder, etc. The film plays Gene Autry songs almost constantly, sometimes diegetically when the characters play them, listen to them and react, sometimes non-diegetically over a football game, etc. Perhaps the ubiquitous voice of Autry, with its recurring "I" and "I'm," stands in for the absent narrational voice of Billy Clyde as a displaced principle of enunciation.

## 9.

He (Philip Barry) was a subtle writer, but nothing muddy about him. A clarity at the back of it all. I don't like muddiness. I like clarity. It has nothing to do with being literal, and it doesn't cut out mystery—of course, there are times when you don't want to say everything—but I like to know that I can look into the pool of water when I want to and find it clear at the bottom.

—GEORGE CUKOR[8]

Would sophisticated characters walk into this drama-machine so naively or be so surprised by pitfall No. 1, sexual jealousy? The book's characters might discuss the proposal amusingly but each would vote no at the end. The film begins with three friendships and moves to one love match then to another. What is the nature and strength of the friendships, of the loves, how and why do they arise or fall apart when they do? On these points the film is unclear.

When do Billy Clyde's feelings for Barbara Jane change—before she returns from Africa? An early line "love me or leave me alone" suggests yes but if so how far back do they go and why hasn't he acted on them? When the Shake-Barbara Jane romance starts Billy Clyde is evidently unhappy but why—exclusion by friends, jealousy of Barbara Jane, sex rivalry with Shake or slow-ripening love for Barbara Jane quickened by the pressure of events? These are confused or insufficiently differentiated—Billy Clyde's quest remains ambiguous.

Friendship is partway established between Shake and Barbara Jane and between Billy Clyde and Barbara Jane but not between the two men. Though they are said to be old and close friends, what we see is Billy Clyde competing with Shake ruthlessly for Barbara Jane. "Nobody ever said it wasn't going to be semi-tough." The book's line and title refer to the Super Bowl. In the film Billy Clyde speaks the line to himself about breaking up the wedding and winning Barbara Jane. Thus the film's displacement of competition from sport to love and its elimination of friendship and teamwork.

## 10.

Basic to romantic comedy is the dyad old love/ new love. Nearly all romantic comedies may be divided according to it. *Bringing Up Baby, Holiday*, etc., treat new love; *The Awful Truth, His Girl Friday, Twentieth Century*, etc., treat old love. *The Philadelphia*

*Story* treats both, though the new is only a flash, as do most films by Lubitsch.

*Semi-Tough* is a story of new love and of new rivalries for it, wherein ruthlessness, stunts and dissembling are traditional. But when a story of new love is laid over a story of old friendship the results are unsavory and unattractive. Were Cary Grant the close friend and work partner of Ralph Bellamy, his taunts and ruses would not be so funny. A work that faced squarely this disturbing mixture and its consequences might well be interesting. But if it insists on the new love quest and sweeps the residues under the rug, as this film does, then the viewer will be confused and disturbed at the end, perhaps without knowing why. This happens here when the hero is shown triumphant in love, but his friend lies slain by him just off screen.

# 11.

Friendship must be established and built, not just posited, even if (especially if) the friends later fall out over a love object. This is proven by the films of Hawks and Ford, among others, as it is by Coward's *Design for Living*.

In *Semi-Tough* both friendship and love are posited abstractly. We must infer Billy Clyde's love for Barbara Jane from his writing and disrupting the wedding, not from the way the two relate to each other onscreen. Their confrontations, in brief, tangential scenes, are awkward. Another "obligatory" scene that is missing is one between Shake and Billy Clyde confronting the issue of Barbara Jane. As BEAT follower Shake might propose the talk, though follow through glibly. Billy Clyde might become tense or refuse to take it seriously or actually speak his feelings. How it was done would not matter, their usual banter would suffice, so long as it were banter under pressure.

Another posit: Billy Clyde is said to like only fucking and football but neither liking is shown. He has two meager sexual encounters—why only this for an alleged stud? Because even a semi-intense scene between Billy Clyde and a woman might throw off his alleged passion for Barbara Jane and the campaign he is mounting to fulfill it. (In very skillful hands such a scene could be used to clarify his feelings for Barbara Jane.) In all these respects the film lives a life of denial to protect its house of cards premise. It might have been better to accept the weakness of the premise and go after some old-fashioned character interaction. In this way the premise might have been abandoned or rediscovered or changed or developed.

It is true that some classic films present love indirectly—to be consistent with hardbitten heroes and/or the conflict of strong egos too proud to submit to love. This is the case in scripts by Jules Furthman, especially those directed by von Sternberg and Hawks (*Morocco, Shanghai Express, Only Angels Have Wings, To Have and Have Not, Rio Bravo*, etc.). Each of these films presents the love attraction early and with great vividness, often in great set pieces, so that later when we see the characters choking on the attraction as it slowly turns to love, we know what they are choking on. Furthman's law is that the hero cannot say "I love you"—hence the messages on mirrors, carvings on tables, two-headed coins, threatened handbills, tickets for the morning stage, bus, plane and boat. But the attraction has to be felt viscerally first if the later doubts, hesitations, betrayals, the goings back and forth, and the complex movement toward resolution are to make sense, have dramatic impact and emotional force. Otherwise one creates a set of logical complications that have no referent, the plot gets more and more abstract as it doubles over, achieves new levels of tangles in relation to its basic love premise—it refers to nothing in the viewer's emotional memory of the film. Of course this is a fine strategy for modernist films which proceed systematically, like Marguerite Duras' *Woman of the Ganges* and Yvonne Rainer's films, but we are not speaking of that here.

## 12. Heroine

At the start of the film, film and book Barbara Jane seem close—the changes do not seem to matter, but if we compare them at the end of the film, the difference is enormous. At the end, Barbara Jane has just come close to a third marriage, been spurned by Shake, and hustled away by Billy Clyde. It dawns on her slowly that she has been a fool about Shake (going against her nature to learn BEAT), and that Billy Clyde has contrived to break up the wedding, therefore he must love her. She asks him "Do you want to marry me?" When he says no and suggests a trip to Hawaii, she asks like a child, "What will we do there?" The last-minute rescue from a bad wedding is a fixture of romantic comedy, but the pathetic dependence of the heroine on the rescuer is not. In thirties comedies the heroine might turn on her benefactor at rescue point and strip him of his pretensions. In *Morgan!* (1966), Vanessa Redgrave laughs at the disorder caused by her psychotic rescuer, and is thereby complicit in it. Even *The Graduate* (1967) does a better wedding breakup by playing it as drama rather than comedy and by having the heroine come to the hero. (When will we see a film in which the woman does the rescuing?) In *Semi-Tough* the heroine does nothing after the rescue except to be catatonic. We do not notice this on first viewing because the wedding brawl creates a slight sense of

*The "catatonic" bride: "There can be no romantic comedy without strong heroines."*

breathlessness that almost lasts through the final scene. The latter is very short anyway but is made to seem longer through a trick. The new couple takes a long slow walk down the beach as the camera watches them, a shot that continues as the credits come up. This fills out a sense of time while providing no new information or emotion. The hollowness of the film's romantic comedy premise surfaces here.

Billy Clyde's break-up and refusal may be meant to cure Barbara Jane of her marriage compulsion. He may sense that she marries knowing it will not work, therefore he will live with her to make their relationship last. This is a kindly guess as the script supplies few clues. Nor are there enough to evaluate such a supposition on Billy Clyde's part. In any case it implies a psychiatrist-patient or parent-child relation, not a romantic comedy one.

The final scene marks the collapse of the filmic Barbara Jane—it reveals that there never was a character at all. With her collapse, the film collapses. There can be no romantic comedy without strong heroines.

## 13.

He'd [Jules Furthman] been writing a thing for Bacall for an introduction—really good scene, where she'd had her purse stolen. He said, "What do you think of it?" and I said, "Well, Jules, if anything makes me sexually excited it's a girl who's lost her purse." And he looked bemused and began to stare at me. "You son of a bitch." he said, and he walked out. And he came in and he wrote a story about how the girl stole a purse. Made a lot better picture.

—Howard Hawks[9]

We need not review Hegel on the master-slave dialectic or Simone de Beauvoir on the man-woman dialectic to observe that a fictive mode that debases the heroine thereby debases the hero also and thereby subverts itself. We note also that the novel's Barbara Jane is strong, independent, and virtually equal to her two friends. It is she who pursues Billy Clyde at the end, as the mate she believes best for her. The long last chapter concerns the overcoming of Billy Clyde's reservations. This makes the film's transformations especially alarming. As an answer to the question "What is romantic comedy now?" it is even more alarming.

Romantic comedy posited men and women willing to meet on a common ground and to engage all their faculties and capacities in sexual dialectic. Later work such as the Kanin-Gordon-Cukor films brought work, political dispute, and psychological complications to this engaged ground and extended the age range of its participants. What we begin to see now in films is a withdrawal of men and women from this ground (or of it from them). Or we see—in effect the same thing—false presences in the sexual dialectic or divided ones (one realizes at the end that one did not want to play the game at all) or commitments for trivial stakes only. It seems that when the new self pulls itself together, it is away from the ground of full sexual dialectic. To argue this is to argue the death of romantic comedy.

## 14. King Sun

One need not subscribe to any theory of art as mimesis to recognize that social and political changes have transformed the making and reception of romantic comedy since the classical period. These changes are vast, complex, interwoven, and not yet sufficiently understood in themselves to permit application to subtopics like our own. This is true even if we limit ourselves to changes in the family and in sexual life: the doubling of the divorce rate in the last decade, the rise of the single parent, the political and social impact of feminist movements and gay rights movements, etc. One factor, the rise of working women, has been called "a revolution in the roles of women that . . . is a worldwide phenomenon, an integral part of a changing society. Its secondary and tertiary consequences are really unchartable."[10] The striking fact is how little these changes have made their way into films of any kind, comedies, dramas, or documentaries.

We will discuss another factor, perhaps a simpler one, the sharply increased movement of the American population from (Eastern) cities to the Sunbelt in the last ten years. Since 1970 the nation's eight largest metropolitan areas have declined in population growth. This development stands in contrast with practically all preceding periods since 1790. The more rapid growths of large urban concentrations as compared to nonmetropolitan territory has been one of the most persistent of American demographic trends. Five of the eight areas had a net loss of population during this period.

During the next 15 years there will be a pronounced shift of income away from the Northeast and North Central regions of the country to the Southern and Western regions. "The question is not so much one of decline but one of: Can the Northeast age gracefully?"[11]

The romantic comedy has always been urban and urban-oriented, aggressively, smugly assuming the superiority of city over country. This pattern of thought and response is old and deep in US culture and European too. It characterizes the great age of industrialism and capitalist expansion, which is now beginning to be over.

In sophisticated films and plays, the sticks were always ridiculed, especially the visitor from the sticks, and the immigrant to the city from the country. The full fury of urban scorn was vented on those who retained any narcissistic pride in the provinces. The immigrant had to adapt to capitalism and its life ways in a hurry. *The Awful Truth*: "What's wrong with Oklahoma City?" "Nothing, Bruce, nothing." Jokes based on urban superiority had an unquestioned sense for audiences for 180 years and more that they are beginning not to have. What sense does Walter Burns's put-down of Albany make (in *His Girl Friday*) now that New York City is dependent on Albany for survival?

What a cinema of the Sunbelt will be we do not know. (Perhaps *Badlands* [1974] and *Three Women* [1977] are versions of this. "The silence of those infinite spaces terrifies me."—Pascal. )

## 15. Enunciation

Enunciation signifies the act of uttering a message. It is opposed to *enoncé* which signifies what is uttered. The system of enunciation which governs particular acts of enunciation is in turn governed by the semiotic system involved—which creates a limited number of enunciation possibilities—and by historical, social and other contextual factors. French linguist Emile Benveniste distinguishes two distinct and complementary, systems of enunciation, that of story (*l'histoire*) and that of discourse (*discours*). In language these systems divide up all verb tenses between them—what does not belong to discourse (only the aorist) belongs to history.

The historical utterance . . . characterizes the narration of past events. These three terms—
"narration," "event," and "past," are of equal importance. Events that took place at a certain
moment of time are presented without any intervention of the speaker in the narration. In
order for them to be recorded as having occurred, these events must belong to the past.[12]

Discourse must be understood in its widest sense: every utterance assuming a speaker
and a hearer, and in the speaker, the intention of influencing the other in some way. It is
primarily every variety of oral discourse of even nature and even level . . . But it is also the
mass of writing that reproduces oral discourse or that borrows its manner of expression and
its purposes: correspondence, memoirs, plays, didactic works, in short, all the genres in
which someone addresses himself to someone, proclaims himself as the speaker, and organizes what he says in the category of person.[13]

*Histoire* suppresses or hides all traces of its telling, it refers neither to speaker or listener but only to the events it relates. The effects of different modes of enunciation on the
receiver is a complex, largely uncharted area, but it is clear that *histoire* in general is used
to make the events related seem more real, vivid, present, whereas *discours* modes continually break such illusions, or at least may do so.

Applying these concepts in film analysis creates several problems, the first of which is
that films are apparently perceived as told in the present. That in any case is its most transparent mode, and in this it resembles *histoire*. Romantic comedies of all decades belong to
this mode. They are dramatic—they present what is happening now, without mediation.
Pace and timing are important and a sense that the characters are under pressure and must
react quickly. Lines of dialogue are delivered fast, often unexpectedly, and must be countered fast. Of course this is carefully engineered illusion, but it is the impression which
romantic comedy must create if it is to achieve the effects which define it.

Related to this enunciative mode is a thematic constant of romantic comedy (at least
in the thirties)—an ethos of spontaneity. Not only are lines of dialogue rendered spontaneously, so are physical actions. We see Johnny Case's excited face and rising inflections
in *Holiday* and suddenly he does a "flip," lands on his feet, utters a few more lines and
goes out the door. Any evidence of enunciation in this passage would ruin the effect of
the scene. Imagine a film noir (like *Raw Deal* [1949]) with ghostly voice-over, eerie
music, expressionist fighting, webbed, tangled mise-en-scène: "I did a flip on my way out
the door. As I stood there looking at my friends it seemed to me that everything was
upside down. The room was going round and round . . . I knew that I had to get to Helen,
who was waiting in the car, but I could not move." The example is ridiculous, I beg your
indulgence, but it should make clear the difference between enunciation that is heavily
marked and enunciation that is transparent and—very roughly—the kinds of subjects traditionally appropriate to each. (Film noir is especially interesting because its plethora of
signifier chains, its multichanneled redundancy, works as often to pull the viewer in—i.e.,
the film naturalizes itself as a "complex world"—as to distance the viewer.)

Works of *histoire* suppress signs of enunciation, but no work can do this completely.
The analyst must look more carefully in such cases but all works betray signs of their
telling. *Baby*'s first close-up, about a third of the way through, shows us Susan's distress at
hearing that David is to be married. This shot betrays a previously transparent discourse—someone is showing us this detail, is marking it as important (so that we will
understand Susan's behavior later). In *The Awful Truth* there is a gap after Bellamy
departs—an affair for Jerry is needed in a hurry so that Lucy may play disrupter and the

film continue. The film presents a rather typical montage of society column excerpts, shots of the couple at racetrack, watching polo, motorboating, etc., before the music dies down and the next funny scene starts. Here it is the banality of the presentation, the simplicity and obviousness of the message, the tediousness of its "process" that call attention to the enunciation, as well as its marked difference from the rest of the film and its odd placement in its late middle. Perhaps also the switching from dramatic/ improvisational to narrational mode and from a constant use of scenes to a bracket syntagm. Thus a passage's difference from a film's principal mode of enunciation can mark one mode of transparent enunciation from its fellows.

Romantic comedy's banishment of enunciation marks is reflected in *Semi-Tough* too. The book has an interesting enunciation structure: not only a first person but a second person too. Billy Clyde narrates the book to Jim Tom, a reporter friend who will edit it. Every so often he asks Jim Tom if he's listening and tells him what to disregard if he wishes etc. At times he speculates alone or in imaginary colloquy with Jim Tom what the publisher's editor is likely to think. Billy Clyde sometimes describes himself taping, the presence of others while he's taping; he also has to account for all his comings and goings which relate to the taping—why he can tape now, etc. And of course he cannot both play football and narrate what is happening on the field. This requires continual maneuver. The film eliminates these complexities in one stroke, opting for the dramatic mode of entirely present action and dialogue rather than narration. In doing so it maximizes the values of spontaneity and vividness and diminishes those of perspective, layering, temporal and presentational complexity. In short it adopts the enunciative mode that has always been obligatory for romantic comedy. This dictates in part the transformation pattern that romantic comedy imposes on its diverse materials—which is to say that it is part of the definition of romantic comedy.

## 16.

At one point in *Semi-Tough* the heroine says to the hero, "How come we never fucked?" It is arguable that romantic comedy depends upon the suppression of this question and that with its surfacing romantic comedy becomes impossible.

The sexual question always circulates in romantic comedy, it is its utterance that is forbidden. On this prohibition romantic comedy stands. Indeed one can see the entire spectrum of romantic comedy as so many variations on this unuttered question. In comedies of old love, the unspoken question is "Why did we stop fucking?" In comedies of new love, it is "Why don't we fuck now?" There is a virtual Freudian declension system operating here, the terms of which define the principal modes of romantic comedy.*

It seems, then, that the various modes of romantic comedy posit a condition of nonfucking. In comedies of new love this is the initial situation; the plot extends it by prolonging aversion or indifference, by mistaken identity, and/or by a repetition of frustrating encounters, etc. Old love comedies posit a cessation of fucking, due to suspected infidelity (*The Awful Truth*), to "leaving the newspaper business to settle down" (*His Girl Friday*), or whatever. In comedies of both kinds it is the entire film, but no line

---

* From his analyses of Schreber's memoirs, Freud concluded that the principal forms of paranoia can all be represented as contradictions of the single proposition: "I (a man) love him (a man)," and that they exhaust all the possible ways in which such contradictions can be formulated.

in it, that poses and explores the question "Why are we not fucking?" and "How can we get (back) to fucking?" Romantic comedy lives on the problem of nonfucking and is over when, and only when, it is resolved, when fucking (re)starts. This is explicit in *The Awful Truth*, when the boy and girl figures on the clock finally go through the same door, just before "The End"; and in *It Happened One Night*, when the "Walls of Jericho" come down at the same moment. These films end just as the characters begin to fuck. In *Holiday* and other films, the film ends as the characters "go off" together, marking the same occasion less literally. *Semi-Tough* concludes this way, but the overall film is muddied because the characters are childhood friends—it is the story both of new love complications and of exploring an old bar, "Why haven't we ever fucked?" In fact the second question is not explored—beyond a throwaway from Billy Clyde about how they had meant too much to each other for "fun" sex along the way.

An exception: Lubitsch's *One Hour with You* (a remake of *The Marriage Circle*) is a romantic comedy about a happy couple. Of course the plot turns on a slow-building threat to the marriage, but it breaks them up for only a short time (one night) before they get back together.

Note that in romantic comedy resolution of the problem of non-fucking involves both a theoretic question and a pragmatic one (as in psychoanalysis). Determining why we are not fucking and overcoming the barrier by actually fucking are quite different things, though romantic comedies and their characters consistently confuse them. The theoretic answer to the question does not necessarily lead to the desired result and achievement of the desired result does not necessarily imply that the theoretic question has been answered. Perhaps it is anxiety over the problem and the desire for its pragmatic overcoming, both overdetermined, that are the mainspring of the genre. Seeking theoretic knowledge is one solution among others that are tried, with no very strict housekeeping as to which one actually works. For one thing, there is not the time, patience or mental calm necessary to try one solution at a time—the notion itself is comic (though not romantic)—all are tried at once. This is a realm in which "savage thought" and *bricolage* dominate, despite a surface appearance of rationality.

Although romantic comedy is about fucking and its absence, this can never be said nor referred to directly. This is perhaps the fascination of romantic comedy. It implies a process of perpetual displacement, of euphemism and indirection at all levels, a latticework of dissembling and hiding laid over what is constantly present but denied, unspoken, unshown. We perceive the sublimation system and the thing itself at every point, a system of repression suffused with a libidinal glow. In "Humor" (1927) Freud defined humor (as opposed to jokes) as proceeding from the super-ego, in reward for a survival-enhancing act or attitude.

Language in romantic comedy has a special status. What stands between sexual desire and its fulfillment is language. In romantic comedy language is the medium in which all things occur, arise and are discharged or not. Visual metaphors like figures on a clock and walls trumpeted down, and actions such as "going off" are resorted to for the absolutely unsayable. In romantic comedy it is the past sex lives of the characters and present sexual problems that constitute a referent that cannot be named directly. *Angel* and *The Awful Truth*, both concerned with the possible infidelity of a marriage partner, cleverly make the enunciative conditions of romantic comedy the predicament of the inquiring characters—they have only indirect, oblique signs to interpret. Also in both the question is never resolved, for the character or for us. The enunciation system is inscribed by displacement in the plot. Lubitsch's dollies into and static shots of closing bedroom doors do the same thing at a different level.

The effective prohibitions of romantic comedy are prohibitions within language. It is this that makes speaking the question "Why haven't we ever fucked?" destructive of romantic comedy. It wrecks the language-game on which it rests. In that game you can refer to anything but cannot speak of it. (See again the works of Lubitsch.)

The first reason that *Semi-Tough* says "How come we never fucked?" is that it can say it. In the thirties such language and such linguistic reference were prohibited—you could not say "Why haven't we ever made love?" either. That you can say something does not mean that you must do so. But has any realm of art invented for itself a system of censorship not imposed upon it? On this ground alone, it may be that romantic comedy is not an art that can flourish in this period.

### Notes

1. Sigmund Freud, tr. James Strachey, *Jokes and their Relation to the Unconscious* (New York, 1900).
2. Ben Jonson, reprinted in *Literary Criticism: Plato to Dryden* ( Detroit, 1962), 534, 537–38.
3. Lope de Vega, reprinted in ibid., 540, 542–3.
4. Kenneth Burke, *The Philosophy of Literary Form* (New York, 1957), 253–254.
5. Interview with Howard Hawks by Peter Bogdanovich, *Movie* No. 5, 11.
6. G.S. Gordon, "Theophrastus and His Imitators," in G.S. Gordon, ed., *English Literature and the Classics* (New York, 1969), 53.
7. Ludwig Wittgenstein, *Philosophical Investigations* (New York, 1958), 3le–32e.
8. Gavin Lambert, *On Cukor* (New York, 1972), 123.
9. Interview with Howard Hawks by Peter Lehman et al., *Wide Angle* 1:2 (Summer 1976), 57.
10. "Vast Changes in Society Traced to the Rise of Working Women," *New York Times* (November 29, 1977), 1 ff.
11. "Influx of Population Down in Urban Areas," *New York Times* (June 16, 1975), 1 ff.
12. Emile Benveniste, tr. Mary Elizabeth Meek, *Problems in General Linguistics* (Coral Gables, 1971), 206.
13. Ibid., 208–9.

# Runaway Brides

**Gregg Rickman** (2001)

Few film critics have been paid the singular honor offered up to Elizabeth Kendall with the appearance in 1999 of Garry Marshall's film *Runaway Bride*, an attempt at a modern-day screwball comedy modeled in part after the premier screwball comedy of the 1930s, Frank Capra's *It Happened One Night* (1934). Kendall's 1990 study of the screwball comedy cycle took its title from the memorable scene at the end of that film when bride-to-be Ellie Andrews (Claudette Colbert) ran away from her own wedding to social climber King Westley in favor of an elopement with her true love, Peter Warne (Clark Gable). Peter had met Ellie while she was on the road from Florida to New York, trying to rejoin Westley after escaping from her millionaire father, who opposed the union. An unemployed reporter, Peter joins her in hopes of selling her story, but instead forms a couple with her, which is sundered and then rejoined.

In Marshall's film, Julia Roberts plays Maggie Carpenter, a plumber in the small town of Hale, Maryland (joke). She achieves national notoriety when New York columnist Ike Graham (Richard Gere) writes up her habit of running away from her scheduled weddings. Ike's misreporting of the details of her non-marriages costs him his job, and he travels to Hale in hopes of confirming the broader truth of his story about her. Ike's involvement in her life leads Maggie to break off with her current fiancé, attempt to marry Ike instead, and run away from him as well. Ultimately Ike and Maggie are reconciled, and do marry.

*It Happened One Night* is one of the more celebrated films of the 1930s, variously analyzed as a key document of the social history of the Great Depression, a film about women's liberation, a film about women's oppression, a "comedy of remarriage" (in Stanley Cavell's memorable term), a landmark in the careers its director and stars, and of course as a classic screwball comedy. No such literature is likely to accrue around *Runaway Bride*—not that it won't have its place in film history, as a turn-of-the-millennium star vehicle built on the framework of a vanished but still revered film cycle.

Virtually any comparison between the two films is all to the older work's advantage. The filmmakers are aware of this—the image of the "runaway bride" itself aside, Marshall also quotes from *It Happened One Night* by giving Maggie and Ike a rustic walk by a farmyard that recalls Peter and Ellie's nocturnal love scene near a barn. The new film never comes close to the original's luminous beauty of Joseph Walker's cinematography in this and similar scenes, and despite a game effort by Roberts fails to capture *It Happened One Night*'s seemingly effortless feel in its playing. Thus Kendall on the latter film: "the two actors seem to be soaring on inventiveness." It's almost cruel to point out the shift between the lightness of Gable and Colbert to the lack of chemistry between a straining Roberts and the sleepwalking Gere.

During his long career Frank Capra prided himself in making his character actors and day-players the stars of any scene they were in. Witness the rightness, in *It Happened One Night*, of not only the showy supporting parts played by Roscoe Karns and Alan Hale but also those of the bit actors who so believably handle the roles of the various

**327**

*"Soaring on inventiveness" (Clark Gable and Claudette Colbert in* It Happened One Night*);
"lack of chemistry" (Julia Roberts and Richard Gere in* Runaway Bride*).*

night camp managers, down to the old couple discussing the couple's purchase of a trumpet in the film's final scene. In *Runaway Bride*, by contrast, the character actors (even a normally charming player like Joan Cusack) overract for effect.

Gere's somnolent performance may perhaps be excused as underplaying, but he does little to animate his role, that of a misogynist newspaper columnist. Like so many other of today's contemporary, "post-feminist" Hollywood comedies, *Runaway Bride* is built around its characters' learning empowering life lessons, usually of a narcissistic nature ("You complete me," as Tom Cruise tells Renee Zellweger in *Jerry Maguire*). This stricture applies to other mainstream films as well, in films as disparate as *Rain Man* and *Pulp Fiction*, or to the seemingly endless stream of Robin Williams dramedies cluttering the new millennium's multiplexes. "What's my arc?" the junior mobster and would-be screenwriter Christopher bewailed in a memorable episode of *The Sopranos*. In this case, however, Ike's generalized dislike of women—the reason given for his bile-filled column about Maggie in the first place—is never really undone. (He does, however, learn enough about his emotional blocks to apologize to his ex-wife for the failure of that marriage, which counts for something in modern Hollywood. Love means always having to say you're sorry.)

What the film is really about, though, is reeducating Maggie, described by Roberts in the *Runaway Bride* press notes as "unconsciously psychotic in her behavior" as she breaks off marriage after marriage. The classic screwball comedy has been criticized for rendering its women's rebellion a short-term thing. But even the cycle's detractors, such as Diane Carson in her feminist critique of screwball, admit to the greater space they allow their female stars than did most other Hollywood films of that era or since. ("Although we may read the films as presenting animated women only to denigrate their defiance, the vitality of their joyful rebellion resists facile dismissal"; Carson, 214.) As both Stanley Cavell and Kathleen Rowe point out in their essays on the film, the trumpet at the end of *It Happened One Night* that represents the consummation of the couple's marriage is hers, not his. It may well be true, as Carson argues, that female acts of resistance in *It Happened One Night* and the other major screwball comedies "engender extreme retaliatory strategies intended to reduce their power." She cites the physical violence threatened or in some cases acted out by Peter Warne and the other screwball comedy heroes. It might be said that while a critic like Ray Carney is listening to the film's music ("the pregnant pauses and silences between the two of them communicate the opposite of their toughness, independence, and self-sufficiency"; Carney, 242), a feminist like Carson is listening to its words, quoting Peter's declaration to Ellie's father, "What she needs is a guy that'll take a sock at her once a day whether she has it coming to her or not" (Carson, 216-17). *Night* lacks the male-female punch-ups of *Nothing Sacred* or *The Philadelphia Story*, but the ideology of domestic abuse is there, even if it seems unlikely that the gruff Peter would actually embark on such a program. By the standards of 1934, he's demonstrating his true maleness, through his words, to the woman's father, proving to him he's his worthy heir.

Even more than *It Happened One Night*, *Runaway Bride*, however, is built around a scenario that insists on putting the woman in her place. In this case it's Maggie's women friends who turn against her: "You spaz out with excess flirtatious energy," her best friend (Cusack) tells her. We are further meant to agree with Ike that the "SS Maggie leaves quite a wake" and that she "shows no remorse" for her numerous jilted ex-boyfriends, all of whom are now in sad shape: a clueless Deadhead, a drunken entomologist, a priest we're meant to infer she's driven to celibacy. The film instructs her, moreover, that she does not have a mind of her own, a claim symbolized by her changing taste in eggs, a fertile food symbolic of motherhood that she likes fried, or poached, or egg white only, depending on the taste of her boyfriend *du jour*. Ellie Andrews most decidedly has a mind of her own, down to her final act of running away from one marriage and toward another.

Whereas *Runaway Bride* and other contemporary romantic comedies are all dutifully "post-feminist" in giving lip service to the freedom of their female characters, their major drive is, finally, nothing more or less than completing a couple; while *It Happened One Night*, by contrast, seems to be about a dozen different things at any one moment, so mercurial is its handling. Both Claudette Colbert and Julia Roberts were 31 years old at the time these films appeared. But Colbert in 1934 seems infinitely more mature than Roberts in 1999. More so than with the classic screwball comedies of the 1930s, with performers like Colbert, Irene Dunne, Carole Lombard and Jean Arthur, their contemporary equivalents—in the performances of Sandra Bullock, Meg Ryan or, as here, Julia Roberts—seem built around the moues of their female leads. In *Runaway Bride* Roberts falls flat on her back with her feet in the air, imitates a duckbilled platypus, and otherwise carries on like an indulged child, giving this film (and the equivalent Bullock and Ryan films) the air of a daycare center, with their swains along as grumpy grown-ups. When a star like Irene Dunne cuts up, in *Theodora Goes Wild* or *The Awful Truth*, it's an act knowingly put on by an adult woman. When Roberts, Bullock or Ryan go on a face-pulling spree we seem to be learning who the character really is. (An exception to this trend is the other Roberts vehicle of 1999, *Notting Hill*, with Roberts playing the disengaged grown-up to Hugh Grant's indulged and pampered child, the actor encouraged in his own set of tics and mannerisms, as rococo in their way as Rodney Dangerfield's twitchy tie-tugs.)

Frank Capra's films comprise a continuum of different portrayals of male sexuality, from Harry Langdon on one end of the scale to such virile characters as General Yen (Nils Asther, in *The Bitter Tea of General Yen*) or *Night*'s Clark Gable, on the other. It's interesting, though, that while Clark Gable's persona is generally considered an archetype of male prowess, Elizabeth Kendall's reading emphasizes the film's shifting gender roles (with "Colbert still in bed and Gable at the stove" in the sequence where he fixes her breakfast). "Gable's Peter Warne . . . has no pretenses to social power," she writes. "He's broke, he's out of a job; he can't even run fast enough to catch the guy who stole Ellie's suitcase. He's a surprisingly frank embodiment of the ineffectuality of the American male in the face of the Depression" (45). Kendall's Gable anticipates Susan Faludi's diagnosis of the contemporary disabled male in her 1999 book *Stiffed*. Raymond Carney, meanwhile, in his book about Capra, *American Vision*, puts Gable in line with Capra's other lost and lonely dreamers, emphasizing how both Peter and Ellie "are zanily gifted, if quite clumsy, self-centered, and headstrong improvisers" (232). He adds that "(a)s in so many of Capra's other films, from *Platinum Blonde* on, the reporter character is a representation of postmodern man in all his glory and despair . . . an ideal deconstructionist of all of the texts of his own society." Peter's free circulation among society's different groups has allowed him recognition of their arbitrary codes, at the cost of "moral and social involvement and belief . . . intimacy, commitment, or love of another human being" (237-8). The cynical Ike seems cut from this same cloth. Such contemporary work as *Michael* (Nora Ephron, 1996) and *Runaway Bride* recirculate these images about reporters, images that have been by now worn down into cliché .

*Class struggle. Matthew Broderick and Reece Witherspoon in* Election.

Reporters are key figures in many a film precisely for the way they move through different levels of society, like a detective in a film noir. Both *It Happened One Night* and *Runaway Bride* sketch in but don't dwell upon the mass media of their respective times, a mass media which is at once exposed to view and hidden, its effects on peoples' lives taken for granted. Ike reads the small town of Hale, Maryland through the scrim of *The Andy Griffith Show* ("Shazam, I think I'm in Mayberry"); he whistles its theme song and calls a minor character "Aunt Bea." The film audience is encouraged to make the same recognition, as Hale is full of lovable eccentrics just as that TV show was. (Compare the sharp edges on the bit players of Capra's film! Or, for that matter, the darker view given small-town life in the late '90s fantasies *Pleasantville* and *The Truman Show*.) But the lives of these loonies are also cued by more contemporary media: a wedding photographer says he takes Scorsese as the model for his handheld cinematography, while the clerk at Ike's hotel lives behind his VR goggles. Most egregiously, the journalist Ike's right to invade Maggie's privacy is never seriously challenged by her friends and family, who even welcome him to a crab dinner at her home. (Peter Warne does insinuate himself into Ellie's life on their bus trip, but is reasonably circumspect when crashing her wedding, paying his respects to her father, not to her.) While like *Runaway Bride*, Ellie's flights in *It Happened One Night* are mediated through the mass media of the day—banner headlines, the newsreel camera at the Andrews-Wesley wedding, and of course Peter's plans for an exclusive story, Ellie's earlier life isn't on videotape for Peter to view. All of Maggie's previous failed weddings are, however, available for Ike to see and critique, and the mass media is out in force at the film's climax to catch the new couple's latest humiliation.

It *Happened One Night* takes place largely on the road, *Runaway Bride* in a small town with a few cutaways to big city life in New York. A distinguishing characteristic of many of the better comedies of the late 1990s/early 2000s has been their new interest in class: sometimes literally, as in the schoolroom uproars of *Election* and *Rushmore*. The talent shows of Christopher Guest's *Waiting for Guffman* and *Best in Show*, the beauty pageants of *Drop Dead Gorgeous, Happy, Texas,* and *Miss Congeniality* all provide the occasion for some easy laughs at the expense of the locals, but even this is a sea change: in earlier American films it was the small town community which was normal and the city slickers or the carnies who travel through town the ones who were "different," the outsiders.

*Runaway Bride* is something of a throwback to this older approach, given its emphasis on the likability of Hale and its rural virtues set against Ike Graham's shiftiness. *It Happened One Night*, by contrast, is a road picture, with good people and bad at every step of the way (in the city, King Westley; on the road, two thieves). Class enters into the picture in the film's contrast between the "spoiled" heiress Ellie Andrews and man of the people Peter Warne. Class wars between men of the people and rich bratty women were staples of 1930s comedy, as has often been commented; Gregory La Cava's *My Man Godfrey* (1936) and Capra's own *Platinum Blonde* of 1931 are two well-known examples.

Kendall argues that while *Platinum Blonde* fixed its "coy class war" in favor of the reporter, *It Happened One Night* distributes power more evenly among its duo (42). Kathleen Rowe writes interestingly on *It Happened One Night*'s portrayal of class in her comments on the film in her book *The Unruly Woman* (1995), arguing that the film's structure shifts the "slippery" issue of class back onto "the more readily managed ones of gender and generation" as the film follows a New Comedy structure "ending with the victory of the son over the father and the constitution of a heterosexual couple" (125). My reading of the film is rather different: Peter Warne proceeds to win Ellie in the film's final scenes with the crucial permission and encouragement of Ellie's father (Andrews/Walter Connolly). It's not a victory of the "son" over the father at all: Peter has won Andrews' full support by the modesty of his financial demands (as opposed to the gold-digging of King Westley), by his aforementioned masculinist breast-beating, and also by the declaration of his love for Ellie the old man forces out of him. Rather than an royal overthrow, it's a changing of the guard as the old king gives way to the new—indeed, a drunken Peter is introduced at film's beginning with the cry of "make way for the king" from his fellow reporters. At film's end Peter is revealed as the rightful "king" for Ellie, in place of the false king, King Westley.

By contrast, Maggie's father Walter (Paul Dooley) is something of Hale's town drunk, and presented as another burden for Maggie to bear. Some of Maggie's troubles with men can be ascribed to this lack on the part of the men she's involved with—her jilted lovers are all a batch of King Westleys, leaving a gap in her life which only the more than adequate Ike is able to fill. He does this, however, by allowing Ellie to find herself, in the fashionable mode of a late 1990s rhetoric of empowerment and selfhood.

But that rhetoric is hardly new: *It Happened One Night* can also be seen as participating in it. Ellie learns to be her own person through Peter's tutelage. As Stanley Cavell notes, father-daughter relationships are crucial to the "comedies of remarriage" he writes about (particularly *The Lady Eve* and *The Philadelphia Story*), and Peter takes over a paternal role here for the runaway Ellie.

(T)hroughout her escapades with Clark Gable, Claudette Colbert is treated by him as a child, his child, whose money he confiscates and then doles back on allowance, who he mostly calls "Brat," and to whom he is forever delivering lectures on the proper way to do things, like piggyback or hitchhike . . . . In the genre of remarriage the man's lecturing indicates that an essential goal of the narrative is the education of the woman, where her education turns out to be her acknowledgment of her desire, and this in turn will be conceived of as her creation, her emergence, at any rate, as an autonomous human being. ("Somebody that's real," the man will say, half out of a dream-state, at the climax of the film, "somebody that's alive. They don't come that way anymore.") (84)

Ellie learns to become real, an act the film signals by her becoming a runaway bride. Given this act's importance, however, it's quite interesting how this, the film's climax, is relatively unstressed. Ellie's flight silences both the film's stars. As Raymond Carney comments, "(w)hen the time comes in the wedding ceremony for her 'I do,' Ellie does not give an angry or impassioned speech; she significantly does not say anything at all. She merely gives a strange shrug of her shoulders, a kind of shudder ripples through her body, and she turns away from the camera to run away across the lawn" (260). We don't hear from either Ellie or Peter again, for the rest of the film. The lovers fall "out of the narrative world of the film and out of all social expression and into some inscrutable, unphotographable, unscriptable other form of existence and relationship" (261).

By contrast, the reasons for Maggie's flights from the altar form the rationale for the entirety of the new film; they're talked to death. One of Maggie's escapes, on horseback, takes place under that film's opening credits, and we return to that image again and again.

It might be suggested that a profound ambivalence toward marriage and its ceremonies may be expressed by the film's use of this recurring image. Only in the most reluctant manner is Maggie finally brought to the altar. But then again the delayed wedding may be only a plot device, one the film's screenwriters have used repeatedly. *Runaway Bride* was written by the team of Josann McGibbon and Sara Pariott, who appear to specialize in contrived scenarios built around wedding ceremonies, such as *Worth Winning* (1989), in which to win a bet a man has to secure proposals from three women picked out for him by his friends; their sequel to the popular *3 Men and a Baby*, *3 Men and a Little Lady* (1990), wherein the three bachelors try to break off the marriage of the mother of the child they care for; and a forthcoming project scheduled as of this writing for Sandra Bullock, *Exactly 3:30*, where the star, worried about getting to her wedding on time, hires a psychiatrist to make sure she does, only to fall in love with him.

This reduction of a privileged moment in film history to a plot device, a gimmick, is just another reason *It Happened One Night* will still be debated a hundred years from now, while *Runaway Bride* will be little more than a footnote to its star's career.

## Works Cited

Raymond Carney, *American Vision: The Films of Frank Capra* (Cambridge: Cambridge University Press, 1986).

Diane Carson, "To Be Seen but Not Heard: *The Awful Truth*," in Carson, Linda Dittmar, and Janice Welsch, eds., *Multiple Voices in Feminist Film Criticism* (Minneapolis: Univesity of Minnesota Press, 1994), 213-25.

Stanley Cavell, *Pursuits of Happiness* (Cambridge: Cambridge University Press, 1981).

Elizabeth Kendall, *The Runaway Bride* (New York: Knopf, 1990).

Kathleen Rowe, *The Unruly Woman: Gender and the Genres of Laughter* (Austin: University of Texas Press, 1995).

# "My goal was to make him Cary Grant": Eddie Murphy and *Boomerang*

Aneta Chapman (2001)

Eddie Murphy said it to me ten years ago.
He said, "cool and funny," don't mix.
—Will Smith (quoted by Zeman, 135).

The 1992 film *Boomerang* was a contemporary romantic comedy showcasing Eddie Murphy's talent as a cool and funny romantic leading man. Murphy's previous films such as *48 HRS, Trading Places,* and *Beverly Hills Cop* were primarily action-adventures that focused on his quick wit and his mischievous nature in defying authority. *Boomerang*, written by Barry W. Blaustein and David Sheffield and directed by Reginald Hudlin, was not however a major box office success like those other films. At the time some said the film was not a good vehicle for Murphy and had nothing new to say about romantic relationships. These arguments make some valid points about Murphy's toned-down characterization, but the role required a different, more cosmopolitan approach which Murphy successfully negotiated. Criticism about the story line not being new ignores an important element about American romantic comedies and those whose lives have typically been presented on screen in them.

*New York Times* film critic Janet Maslin found *Boomerang* to be an old-style romantic comedy. "The presence of the dapper, dressed-for-success Mr. Murphy . . . locates *Boomerang* in a strangely retrograde Fantasyland." Kenneth Turan, of the *Los Angeles Times*, noted that the most interesting aspect of *Boomerang* was "its racial composition, for this film takes pains to create a reverse world from which white people are invisible except when comic relief is called for" (quoted in Langdell, 75). These comments are problematic in their failure to recognize that the working relationships of an educated black bourgeois were not and still are not common film stories. *Boomerang*'s cast is primarily African American with two brief scenes with white characters. This "reverse world" is based in fact: Chantress and Lady Eloise, the two cosmetic companies in the film, have real counterparts such as Fashion Fair Cosmetics, a black-owned and-operated corporation based in Chicago.

Although the representations in *Boomerang* are not new in romantic comedies, they are indisputably underrepresented in Hollywood films. Professional black life is rarely a major subject even in so-called black films. There is a tendency to focus on the urban inner-city experience or the Southern experience. Middle-class and upper-class blacks usually serve as foils for lower-class blacks who are presented as being more "authentic" in their ethnic mores and ways. Characteristic here is Matty Rich's comedy *The Inkwell* (1994), which presents two male adults: the conservative upper-class uncle who mocks

**334**

black identity and mimics white manners, and the father, a former Black Panther, who is socially and politically astute about the struggles in the black community. *Boomerang's* professional black men and women do not question the validity of their presence in corporate America. Their main issue is a universal drive for "having it all" in romance.

According to Janet Maslin, "the person who disrupted the status quo in an Eddie Murphy movie used to be Eddie Murphy. But in this new role Mr. Murphy enthusiastically becomes part of the establishment he once made fun of." Many screen artists have been put into a box whether they like it or not. For example, John Wayne became an American icon representing American strength and determination because of the many Hollywood westerns he acted in. If the artist is comfortable with the box and the studios are comfortable with the actor, then the actor may have a long career playing similar roles in Hollywood films. An issue arises when a particular actor is dissatisfied or uncomfortable with his box. Perhaps he wants to expand his acting horizons. If such an actor has clout in Hollywood, he may get an opportunity to do so. This artistic freedom can be a blessing or a curse, depending on the judgment of critics and audience as to whether the actor made the right decision in leaving the comfort of his box.

Did the movie audience accept this new version of Eddie Murphy? Some critics found Murphy's role in *Boomerang* somewhat reminiscent of Cary Grant's roles in romantic comedies from the 1930s until the 1960s. According to Hudlin, "my goal was to make him Cary Grant" (Guerrero, 195). Although associated mostly with light comedy, Grant did successfully essay broad farce (*Arsenic and Old Lace*) and character-based drama (*None But the Lonely Heart, Notorious*). Comedic actors today who have easily and successfully moved between film genres include Robin Williams and Whoopi Goldberg. Williams gives fatherly and uplifting performances in serious dramas like *Dead Poets Society* and *Good Will Hunting*. Audiences accept such serious performances as well as his outrageous and gross female impersonation in a film like *Mrs. Doubtfire*. Likewise, Goldberg is accepted playing serious roles in such melodramas as *The Color Purple* and *Clara's Heart*, while her performances in comedies like *Jumpin' Jack Flash* and *Sister Act* are also bankable in Hollywood.

However, movie studios and audiences have had problems with Goldberg playing romantic leads. Goldberg's fuzzy, warm film *Corrina, Corrina*, co-starring white actor Ray Liotta, did not do nearly as well at the box office as *Sister Act*. *Sister Act* is a straight farce, with Goldberg allowed one screen kiss with Harvey Keitel, who shortly thereafter tries to have Goldberg killed. The film does everything to desexualize her character. Social commentator bell hooks sums up the limited range of roles and portrayals for black actors in Hollywood films that audiences readily accept.

> Better to give them what they are used to, stereotypical representations of black males as always and only lying, cheating dogs (that is, when they are involved with black women) and professional black women as wild, irrational castrating bitch goddesses (hooks, 57).

Unlike Cary Grant or Tom Hanks, white actors who have played romantic leads without any problems, Murphy in *Boomerang* entered territory that few black actors have had an opportunity to penetrate. In its successes and failures *Boomerang* deserves careful consideration.

*Boomerang* is basically a simple tale about a marketing executive playboy named Marcus Graham who is bested by a female counterpart named Jacqueline Broyer (Robin

Givens). The film explores the downfall of the playboy as he receives his comeuppance for being a cad to women. As with many romantic comedies, it is after the character's downfall that he finds his true love.

Some film critics felt *Boomerang* employed a formulaic story line from the 1950s. The film did satisfy old-style romantic comedy conventions. According to Steve Neale, there are certain conventions present in all romantic comedies prior to the 1980s: "meet cute," "wrong partner," "eccentricities," "having fun," and sometimes a "neurotic sidekick." In *An Affair to Remember* (1957), the potential couple "meet cute" when Nickie Ferrante (Cary Grant), looking for his cigarette case aboard ship, sees Terry McKay (Deborah Kerr) with his case. She kiddingly "confesses" to him that she is a jewel thief and they have a lighthearted discussion about the inscription in the case. In *Boomerang*, Marcus approaches Jacqueline after seeing her at a newsstand and tries to pick her up for a date. He thinks she is a model trying out for a commercial spot but learns in the elevator that she is actually his new boss.

Another romantic comedy convention is the "wrong partner." "The wrong partner is nearly always a source—and a butt—of jokes, gags and humor, of local comic effects" (Neale, 290). Neale cites Ralph Bellamy's character in *His Girl Friday* (1940) being all wrong for Rosalind Russell. Another example would be Rosalind Russell's character as Auntie Mame (in the 1958 comedy) who tries to save her nephew from marrying an anti-Semite. She selects a bright unbigoted woman for him. In *Boomerang* Marcus' neighbor, Yvonne (Tisha Campbell), was a partner so wrong he has to get a restraining order to keep her away from his property. Physically, Yvonne seems all wrong for Marcus—she appears disshelved with rollers in her hair, and she carries signs warning Marcus' dates about his playboy ways.

A third convention is eccentricity, which "serves, in particular, nearly always to bestow signs of uniqueness and individuality—of 'specialness'—both on the couple and its members, and on their romance." (Neale, 291.) In *It Happened One Night*, Clark Gable and Claudette Colbert teach each other how to hitchhike. In *Boomerang*, Marcus and Jacqueline are competitive business people, primarily self-absorbed but not eccentrics. However, Marcus' insistence that the women he seriously dates have feet without blemishes qualifies as an eccentric mannerism. After he consummates his relationship with Jacqueline, he crosses his fingers and pulls back the sheets to examine her feet. He is pleased to discover that Jacqueline's feet are fine. Earlier in the film, he rejected a pretty woman named Christie (Lela Rochon) because her feet had corns. Interestingly, Marcus does not check the feet of Angela (Halle Berry), his eventual right partner.

A fourth convention is a "neurotic sidekick" who makes the other characters appear normal. Neale considers Tony Randall's character in the Doris Day-Rock Hudson films a good example of the neurotic sidekick. Marcus' buddy Tyler (Martin Lawrence) fills this role in *Boomerang*. He sees racial prejudice in everything, including the game of pool because the white ball knocks the black ball off the table. When Tyler learns that Marcus has not had sex with Jacqueline and three weeks have passed, his response is "yo, man she is a lesbo . . . ." When Marcus insists that she is not a lesbian Tyler concludes that something sexual is wrong with Marcus. Tyler reverses the neurotic asexuality, which some have seen as coded homosexuality, of the Randall character.

The last convention is having fun. "Playing together, having fun together, are key elements in the ethos of romance . . . " says Neale (292). In *An Affair to Remember*, Nickie and Terry leave the ship to visit his grandmother and have a wonderful time enjoying music and tea and each others company. In *Boomerang*, Marcus and Jacqueline attempt to dance but she does not like his bump-and-grind style and wants to leave the dance club in New Orleans. Engaging in sex is the only time that the two have fun. However, his true partner, Angela, enjoys cooking and watching *Star Trek* with him. They share a nice Thanksgiving together at his apartment with his friends. Marcus also enjoys himself when Angela takes him to the children's art class that she teaches. Here Murphy is not the oversexed black male without a real partner.

In the adventure films which made him famous Murphy's partner was usually a white male—for example Nick Nolte or Judge Reinhold. Murphy was physically active, running and jumping and car chasing to apprehend criminals. He often affected disguises, such as a stereotyped gay man in *Beverly Hills Cop*, or an African exchange student in *Trading Places*. When in 1986's *The Golden Child* Murphy was given his first romantic lead, "he was still not permitted to have explicit love scenes," as Donald Bogle has noted (431). In these roles, Murphy defied authority and solved problems with his own wisecracking style. He was the more dynamic one in his partnerships.

However, in *Boomerang* Murphy is a dog with little bite. The company where he works has been acquired by another cosmetic firm. He loses his position as head marketing executive to a woman, Jacqueline. He does not understand the power structure at this new conglomerate and makes a foolish ploy that backfires. He is used by the elderly Lady Eloise (Eartha Kitt) as a boy toy. Perhaps some critics did not like this film because Murphy seemed too vulnerable. Here, he has no gun and he has given up his voice, the voice that made a crowd in a redneck bar in *48 HRS* take pause and notice.

Marcus, who markets perfumes and cosmetics for a living, does not see the connection between himself and the products that he hawks. Like a perfume tester in a department store, Marcus has been sampled by many women at the company where he works. His method has been to come on to them strong and sensual, only to fade or retreat after consummation. Marcus slowly begins to realize that like a tester he can be sampled by Lady Eloise and Jacqueline and then discarded.

At first glance, Marcus and Jacqueline seem to be the ultimate power couple. They are successful executives. They are physically attractive. They are stylish and intelligent. However, the film shows us a woman whose career is still growing and a man whose career is in decline. Jacqueline has his former position as head of marketing. Whether one sees Marcus' position as a traditional male role or an untraditional male role, he has little to offer Jacqueline beyond sex. In fact, the viewer knows that Jacqueline thinks he is pathetic because he slept with Lady Eloise.

It is Angela who saves him from being emptied or totally discarded. Marcus is more than just a beautiful package to her but he is also a sensitive and fun person. "Central to romantic comedy is a learning process, a process in which the members of the couple come to know themselves as they come to know one another, and in which, in doing so, they come to develop and acknowledge compatibility and mutual love" (Neale, 292). As Marcus and Angela come to know one another they learn they have much in common such as creative interests, culinary interests, and *Star Trek*.

Murphy is quite good as a nurturer in this film. He coolly and adroitly handles the firm's eccentric client Strangé (Grace Jones) after her temper tantrum and rowdy sexual display in front of the marketing team. He appeals to her ego and suggests that the new perfume be named after her because it symbolizes her essences such as beauty and strength. Earlier the viewer witnessed Marcus smoothly support but also tone down

*Marcus (Eddie Murphy) and his "right partner" Angela (Halle Berry) in* Boomerang.

Nelson's (Geoffrey Holder) lewd sexual perfume commercial featuring cherries and bananas. Murphy here displays a level of sensitivity found in very few of his other films (*The Golden Child, Coming To America*).

His stature is diminished in the film even when he's in the company of his male friends. Murphy's slender frame is overshadowed by the taller David Alan Grier (Gerard) and the bulkier Martin Lawrence (Tyler). Since Murphy's portrayal is quieter and calmer, he lacks the macho outbreaks that were staples in his adventure films. Perhaps this diminished power had the devastating impact of reducing the audience's identification with his character.

Murphy's former film personae are however present in his male co-stars, particularly in Martin Lawrence's character. Chris Rock (who appears as the obstreperous mail clerk Bony T) and Lawrence have comedic styles that are similar to Murphy's old stand-up delivery. Marcus' buddies are an insightful reminder of two of the male types available to women: Tyler, the oversexed crude male who is racially paranoid, and Gerard, the sexually repressed male whose wife left him because he had a low sperm count.

"*Boomerang* is a stagy, high concept comedy of manners. It aims at being a screwball comedy with Marcus as a Cary Grant-like leading man, suave and debonair. Instead of succeeding in this goal . . . Marcus comes off as a gigolo, pandering to ladies' wishes throughout and without direction or will of his own" (Langdell, 75). Unlike Murphy, Cary Grant had plenty of opportunities to fine tune his suave ladies man character during his long film career. He offered movie audiences a safe sexual appeal. "He brought elegance to low comedy, and low comedy gave him the corky common-man touch that made him a great star," said Pauline Kael (624). Grant, like Murphy, occasionally had to maneuver beyond the grip of a sexually strong woman like Strangé; in his time, early in his career, it was Mae West. Yet, he never harassed or pushed a woman too far, save perhaps in a rare drama like *Suspicion*.

There was a playful and at times innocent aura about Grant's acting style. Grant performed somersaults for Katharine Hepburn in *Holiday* and as a CIA agent in *Charade* he pulls a face that astonishes Audrey Hepburn. "What makes Grant such an uncannily romantic comedian is that with the heroine he's different from the way he is with everybody else: you sense an affinity between them" (Kael, 624). Grant became the Sir Walter Raleigh of the cinema, gallant and chivalrous, setting a high mark for future romantic comedians to achieve.

According to commentator Ed Guerrero, Hudlin's attempt to transform Murphy into a Cary Grant-type romantic lead was cinematically retrograde. Using Grant as a model, he argues:

> recalls the early, imitative black cinema practice of conceptualizing the persona of the black actor in terms of contemporaneous white stars, dating from the early black "auteurs" who billed their actors with such titles as "the black Valentino" or "the sepia Mae West" or "the colored Cagney" (Guerrero, 195).

The fact that Murphy's benchmark as the star of a romantic comedy is Cary Grant indicates that inequalities in Hollywood films have seriously hindered black actors from developing exciting and possibly iconographic images beyond typical racial stereotypes. Screen character and craft are important elements in romantic comedy. Opportunity is also important to refine and highlight one's talent.

The quote attributed to Murphy by Will Smith—"'cool and funny,' don't mix"—is both astounding and sad. There is no hint of acrimony in Murphy's tone but there is a sense of resignation about what is possible in film. Equally sad is the fact that Murphy, now viewed as an elder statesman, is passing this message to a potential future black romantic lead.

Murphy's work since *Boomerang* has transformed him into a clever comedian not afraid to submerge his identity in special effects and make-up. He disguises himself in *The Nutty Professor* films and film audiences do not have a problem with his many impersonations. His characterizations have both vaudevillian and minstrelish aspects to them. In *The Nutty Professor II: The Klumps*, Murphy creates five obese family members whose relationship suggests an updated and feminized Amos and Andy comedy. Some critics, such as Anthony Lane, find the impersonations offensive: "an eye-rolling, tongue-lolling parade of appetites" (Lane, 76).

Since *Boomerang* Murphy has steered clear of romantic comedies in which he might again be compared, unfavorably, to Cary Grant. In doing so, however, he has succumbed to what bell hooks called "stereotypical representations of black males" that in Lane's words have "people in the theater roaring at sights that would have flattered the prejudices of their grandparents." Murphy may have abandoned the romantic comedy field too soon. A recent profile of a newly popular young comic, Chris Tucker, mentions that "no one disputes that the black middle class is growing, but no one in Hollywood— that is, none of the white executives who make decisions about which movies and television shows we get to see—is quite sure what that means with regard to mass culture" (Hirschberg, 37). In times to come, *Boomerang* may not be thought of as a failure but rather as a harbinger of great comedies to come.

## Works Cited

Donald Bogle, *Blacks In American Films And Television: An Encyclopedia* (New York: Garland Publishing, 1988).

Ed Guerrero, *Framing Blackness: The African American Image in Film* (Philadelphia: Temple University Press, 1993).

Lynn Hirschberg, "How Black Comedy Got The Last Laugh," *The New York Times Magazine* (September 3, 2000), 34-39ff.

bell hooks, *Reel to Real: Race, Sex, And Class At The Movies* (New York: Routledge, 1996).

Pauline Kael, *For Keeps: 30 Years At The Movies* (New York: Penguin, 1994).

Anthony Lane, "The Fat of the Land," *The New Yorker* (August 7, 2000), 76-78.

Cher Langdell, "*Boomerang*," in Frank N. Magill, ed., *Magill's Cinema Annual 1992* (Pasadena: CA: Salem Press, 1993), 73-76.

Janet Maslin, "*Boomerang*," *New York Times* (July 1, 1992).

Steve Neale, "The Big Romance or Something Wild?: romantic comedy today," *Screen* 33:3 (Autumn 1992), 284-299.

# Introspective Laughter: Nora Ephron and the American Comedy Renaissance

Doug Williams (2001)

Nora Ephron's films deserve serious attention. Her screenplay for *When Harry Met Sally* (1989) established the pattern for a decade of romantic comedies of manners. Her rise as a Hollywood director helped to consolidate a countervailing movement of complexity against otherwise dominant violent special-effects films.

Tragedy always defends the existing rules of society. Comedy, if not overtly critical of its society, at least implicitly questions the status quo that its protagonists must escape.[1] Comedy is a combination of ancient structural design with contemporary concerns, as Stanley Cavell and others have noted. "Old Comedy" and "New Comedy" are terms that initially applied to classical Greek comedy styles. Aristophanes' social satires are characteristic of Old Comedy. His antagonist characters represented individuals or forces that he thought were dangerous to Athens. Mike Nichols' *Primary Colors* (1998) is a recent example of this style.[2] New Comedy, as characterized by Menander, Shakespeare, and screwball comedy, consists of a romantic couple whose romance is blocked by the existing social order. Where Old Comedy exposes and casts out the evil that corrupts society, New Comedy is less concerned with blame and more concerned with regeneration. In common with the romance genre, romantic comedy protagonists restore their society, sometimes including their antagonists in this restoration. In Menander, the opposition is familial. In screwball, it is external social forces. In recent comedies, it is internalized forces.[3]

The protagonist couple is potentially the foundation of a new social order in New Comedy. The couple's struggle against opposition is secondary to creating themselves individually and as a couple. Old Comedy is more concerned with the struggle between the comic protagonist and antagonist; the romantic relationship is incidental to that struggle. When the rise of feminism made the relationship between genders a focal point of conflict, it made heterosexual New Comedy couple negotiations much more complex. Old Comedy replaced New Comedy as the dominant mode in American cinema as a way of evading that complexity. Brian Henderson noted this problem with comedic sexual dialectic in 1978, and concluded that after a decade of silence, romantic comedy was dead. As Steve Neale pointed out, this was just at the time a new type of comedy, which Neale calls "nervous romance," was beginning.[4]

Woody Allen's *Annie Hall* (1977), which initiated the new type, combining Old and New Comedy elements, seemed to be a film Allen was driven to make. *Manhattan* (1979) was more crafted. It consolidated the new genre style, and resolved *Annie Hall*'s insoluble sexual dialectic problem by returning to a pre-feminist female ideal. Neale has noted that succeeding comedies of the '80s followed *Manhattan*'s longing for old times. In these "new romances," according to Neale and others, apparently deviant women cast

**341**

off wildness and return to domesticity. These films coincided with a call for a return to traditional gender relationships. Though feminist icons continued to be produced in melodramatic action films, as Yvonne Tasker has noted[5], few of these roles were in comedy. As few women were in positions of creative power in Hollywood in the '80s, the types of roles written for women in general diminished.

This is the film world that Nora Ephron entered, and she did not like it. She commented about the limited number of interesting roles for women, citing as examples the films *JFK*, *Bugsy*, and *Malcolm X*. All the male protagonists' wives in these films had the same role:

> "I never see you. You're never home. Why don't you come home?" I thought to myself, "Gee, this is great. This is apparently all Oliver Stone or Spike Lee can ever imagine a wife saying to her husband." No woman would write that part and have it that hackneyed, that clichéd.[6]

Ephron regarded this less as deliberate sexism than it was a failure of imagination in a male-dominated industry. In response to a reporter's question about the unrepentantly quirky, angry teenage girl she helped to create in her screenplay for *Cookie* (1989), Ephron said:

> As a woman screenwriter, my job is not to write some idealized woman, but to write women who are real, whatever they are like, who are lovable or not lovable, but who are at least as comprehensible and as complicated as men are in the movies.[7]

Ephron's desire for complex characters is characteristic of her comedies. Comedy usually operates as an interaction of character types. But Ephron has always worked toward an interior exploration of character in comedy, both in her early Old Comedy style ironic mode comedies and her New Comedy style romantic comedies, that sets her film apart both from the nervous and new romances. Her films express a '70s concern with self-discovery that is often condemned today as narcissistic. But a truer word to describe this theme is introspection—looking within oneself to discover what is truly one's own, and what has been projected upon oneself. Ephron's goal is to find real people under the masks society, and indeed, the characters themselves, take as their identity.

This tendency is perhaps most obvious in Ephron's non-romantic ironic comedies, in which her scripts present false scapegoat characters through which she mocks and condemns contradictions in society.[8] These screenplays—*Silkwood* (1983), written with Alice Arlin, *Heartburn* (1986), *Cookie* (1989), written with Alice Arlin, *My Blue Heaven* (1990) and *This Is My Life* (1992), written with Delia Ephron—each follow the Old Comedy model of a protagonist who attempts to construct her own society in opposition to the bankrupt social order in which she finds herself. In each of these stories the heroine discovers that the role she is given by her society is destructive of her human identity, and she breaks the rules to change her society.

*Silkwood* and Ephron's other early screenplays follow late '70s to early '80s feminist-influenced films such as *Norma Rae* and *Heart Like a Wheel*. Most of those films were structured as melodramas; Ephron, however, writes in the comic mode. *Silkwood*, directed by Mike Nichols, is the most deeply ironic of her early comedies, a particularly dark

*Nora Ephron, directing* Sleepless in Seattle, *and Julie Kavner in* This is My Life: *"Women who are real."*

Old Comedy in which the protagonist moves from ignorance to knowledge and begins to identify the flaw of her society, but is too weak to overcome her antagonists. As she becomes conscious of herself, she also becomes conscious of the network of oppressions in which she is entwined.

Karen (Meryl Streep) shares with her boyfriend Drew (Kurt Russell) and roommate Dolly (Cher) an irreverent attitude toward the work culture of their employer, Kerr-McGee, a company that manufactures uranium rods for nuclear power stations. Karen is one of many workers at Kerr-McGee who are "cooked" by radiation. But her friend Thelma and other "cooked" workers internalize the Kerr-McGee message; the worker is to blame, never the plant working conditions. When Karen protests, they blame her. Karen's principal antagonists are her supervisor, Hurley, and her co-worker in metallography, Winston. They both deny Kerr-McGee's disregard for workers' health in the factory and radiation danger to society, and are implicated in the mysterious assaults Karen suffers. In her private life, Karen's ex-husband and his wife combine to isolate her from her children. But while we are shown many antagonists, appropriately we never see who is responsible for her death. The enemy in *Silkwood's* world is not an individual but a social order in which sexism, exploitative labor practices, and fear is the way things are; alternatives exist only as fantasies.

*Silkwood* establishes a number of features common to Ephron's films. Ephron's Karen Silkwood is heroic, but she is no symbolic abstraction of heroism. Her heroine is an average person, and her motives are complexly human; here is no heroine-template drawn from a scriptwriting class. Ephron begins with a comedy writer's premise: the existing social standards are absurd, and they need to be discarded in order to allow a truly human existence. As this oppression is conceptual rather than physical, violent physical action does not solve problems in Ephron's plots. Karen ceases being a victim not by striking out at her oppressors, but by seizing control of her own identity. Oppressive people in Ephron's films are truly awful, yet they are also not really the enemy; they are less individuals than they are objects through which the social order expresses itself. Sympathetic characters lapse into this other voice, as Dolly does when she abruptly tells Karen during an argument, "you took about as good care of Drew as you did of your kids," and then takes it back as she becomes conscious of what she has just said. Even Karen lapses at times, but her growing separate identity makes her more aware of her voice.[9]

Drew and Dolly represent two different responses to the awareness of an absurd society. Drew's response is to quit the society—to move away to "someplace where it's clean," as Dolly summarizes it. Dolly's response is to defy society, notably in her relationship with her lover Angela, yet also accept society's evaluation of her defiance. She is confused by herself, and does not seek an alternative identity in which what she feels and does is positive. Karen searches for alternative identities to speak. She turns to the union as a source for an identity in which she can find herself, and through which she can find a meaning for the conflict she feels. Drew and Dolly do not see anything positive in this. "You—on the union negotiation committee?" Drew says in disbelief when Karen tells him of her becoming active. Dolly's lover Angela tells Karen that fighting Kerr-McGee is hopeless. "They own the state, they own everybody in this state."

When he moves out from their home, Drew comments that Silkwood is two persons, one he loves and one that irritates him by questioning the social order. But he and others are also dual beings, half themselves and half-possessed by the voice of Kerr-McGee. This duality of voices, which emerges particularly in times of stress, is a sign of unfinished identity. Drew begins speaking Kerr-McGee to Karen after he realizes that she may have had a relationship with Paul Stone (Ron Silver), the Washington union official who helps the Kerr-McGee workers to organize. "People're going to lose jobs, Karen." Karen speaks with the Washington union lawyer's words that fighting Kerr-McGee is "a moral imperative," and Drew correctly hears this as an alien voice. But in Karen's case, she is developing her own voice out of this pastiche.

What truly irritates Drew about Karen is that she reveals to him that he doesn't have the courage to accept responsibility for his life. "Don't give me a problem I can't solve," he says to himself. This refusal to face the difficulty of establishing a personal identity is the persistent temptation of Ephron films. It is only by escaping the prison of what other people assert her identity to be—her manager, her coworkers, even her best friend and her boyfriend—that Karen becomes herself. Achieving a *personal* identity is the common mission of Ephron's protagonists. When people dare to change themselves, the social order will be transformed.

*Fearful societies:* Silkwood *(Streep, Russell, Cher) and* Manhattan *(Streep and Allen).*

*Manhattan* has a similarly fearful society, though the upper class characters of *Manhattan* lack an external force like Kerr-McGee to account for their difficulty to be themselves and their inability to change. When Mary (Diane Keaton) and Isaac (Woody Allen) accidentally fall into a first date, there is a cognitive dissonance between the romanticized city imagery, George Gershwin's "Someone To Watch Over Me" playing on the soundtrack, and Isaac and Mary exchanging superficial intellectual babble. At the end of the sequence, after commenting on the different styles of their analysts, Mary and Isaac sit and look at the Brooklyn Bridge. For the first time they themselves seem to be momentarily released from their fear and alienation, and aware of their surroundings. In the shot they are reduced in size and shoved out of the way to the edge of the screen, as though the bridge itself and the music that is its voice is imposing its will on the reluctant lovers. Then the music stops in mid-measure as the film cuts to the dysfunctional extramarital affair between Mary and Isaac's friend Yale (Michael Murphy). This is a pattern in the film—a contrast between the seeming desire of the city itself to impose trust and romance, and the sick humans who interrupt that romance to defiantly chatter on about anything but the moment.

Neale comments on the recurrent convention in romantic comedy of "the wrong partner," who "provide[s] points of comparison with, and contrast to, one or other of the members of the couple, and . . . often represent[s], in addition, an aspect of the personality or motivation or aspiration of that member that stands in the way of [the] couple's formation and that thus has to be cast aside."[10] But really this is less a feature of comedy than it is of all narrative. The competitor is the motivating figure of drama, by whose actions or agency the hero is forced to discover his or her true identity. All narrative is a movement from ignorance to knowledge. In comedy and romance, the competitor is (to borrow Stanley Cavell's term) a False Dandy, someone who falsely claims to know the crucial facts of existence. The False Dandy is ignorant of truth, but the competition between the False Dandy and the Hero drives the hero toward knowledge. In tragedy, the competitor turns out to be the True Hero. The comic or romantic False Dandy frequently knows that his or her claims are false. The tragic hero is a false hero, but he or she is not aware of this; that is the source of the tragedy. In melodrama, by contrast, there is no concealment. The narrative drive is then to see Truth triumph over Falsehood.[11]

Romantic comedy in this century is a dialectic between false and true gender ideals, and so comedy tends to have dual heroes and False Dandies. In *Manhattan* the oppositional pairs are Mary and Tracy (Mariel Hemingway) and Yale and Isaac. Mary and Tracy also have shadow doubles, Isaac's ex-wife Jill (Meryl Streep) and Yale's wife, Emily (Anne Byrne). Tracy, the 17-year-old high school student, is an uncomplicated girl who seems a less articulate version of Emily. Emily's conversations with Yale echo Doris Day's housewifely conversations with David Niven about the virtues of Connecticut in *Please Don't Eat the Daisies* (1960). She seems unaware of the '60s and '70s, as Tracy seems innocent of the previous decade's upheaval in gender relationships. Like the old buildings of New York, Emily and Tracy seem to be part of a threatened tradition. Just as Mary tears down Tracy verbally, the post-Sixties generation in the film tries to tear down New York's old buildings. Isaac's sympathy for the buildings represents his redeemability, his capacity for feeling, if only he could be recaptured from the cant of modern conversation. The buildings cannot speak, as Tracy cannot intellectualize, the rapture that they embody. And so when Isaac in the end is stunned into a silent smile in the closing shot, that silence is meant to be a Manhattan rhapsody of redemption.

Though *Manhattan* is a romantic comedy, it evades the difficulties of creating a modern romance. Tracy does not change. Her likes and dislikes do not come into conflict with Isaac's. The compromise Isaac must make to live with Tracy is to wait for her to return, not to accept an aspect of her character. She represents sex without guilt or complexity—a fantasy. Mary is different, but the qualities of relationship that Mary seems to offer are rejected as unwholesome. The new society brought about by the romantic couple also leaves out Emily. Emily is less a voice than a presence in Allen's film—an empty presence of the sort that Ephron was to complain about in '80s films. Moreover, that character of empty presence was the situation in which Ephron found herself in the late 1970s: The wife of a philandering husband.

Ephron's ironic comedy of manners, *Heartburn*, was an attempt to bring the Emily role alive and to give it redemption. It was not a popular film, but the 1983 book and 1986 film, also directed by Nichols, were crucial to Ephron's development. Rachel (Meryl Streep), a food writer, overcomes her foreboding about marriage to marry Mark (Jack Nicholson), a perennially philandering political columnist. The film is based on Ephron's novelization of her marriage to journalist Carl Bernstein, so thinly disguised— and presumably so unfair, from his point of view—that Bernstein threatened to sue while the movie was in production.[12] Mark is, relative to other Ephron characters, underdeveloped, but he is not a monster. His infidelity is not something that he does in defiance of his society's rules, but rather as a tacit fulfillment of its expectations. As in *Silkwood* and *Manhattan*, the social order destroys rather than nurtures its members. *Heartburn* combines Karen Silkwood's self-evolution with *Manhattan*'s dialectic to produce the beginnings of a woman's nervous romance.

Ephron may have written *Heartburn* with *Manhattan* in mind. At several points in the narrative, Rachel fantasizes that her marriage is being presented on *Masterpiece Theater*. Both films revolve around dinner conversations. Isaac has Freudian analysis, while Rachel has group therapy. The film invites speculation that Ephron saw her own marriage in Allen's film; Ephron speaks in Woody Allen's voice, as Karen Silkwood speaks with the union lawyer's voice. But Ephron also takes Allen's voice and feminizes it, just as Karen Silkwood develops her own voice. The book *Heartburn* itself echoes Jill's writing about her marriage to Isaac, but Ephron does not divide the woman of experience into martyr or monster, as Allen's film does. Ephron—from her Emily-like point of view as the suffering wife—does not see passivity and innocence as the answer to the problems of the post-feminist era gender dialectic. Ephron's answer is to fight against deception and continue to have faith in the possibility of a true marriage of equals.

Ephron establishes this theme at the beginning. Mark and Rachel see each other at a wedding, and Rachel plots how to introduce herself over the words "Love bears all things, believes all things, hopes all things, endures all things. Love never dies." Mark brings up marriage during their first date. "I'm never getting married again," Rachel tells him. "I don't believe in marriage." "Neither do I," Mark says. We cut next directly to Rachel and Mark's wedding. But instead of a public ceremony we see Rachel introspectively agonize with various guests whether it is possible for marriage to work. No one can come up with a really strong statement to convince her that marriage is something to believe in. "Marriage doesn't work," she wails to her therapist. "You know what works? Divorce." Friends, relatives and analysts cannot reassure her that love *can* endure all things, as they are unsure themselves. The marriage is an ironic marriage, a contract ensured primarily by witnesses who don't believe in the words of the contract.

The community is always crucial to the teleological drive of romantic comedy; the new couple either renews a good community or overthrows a bad community. As *Heartburn* begins where most romantic comedies end, with the new couple finding its place in society, the nature of that society particularly comes into question. The house into which Rachel and Mark move serves as a metaphor for the complexities of building a life together, invoking the pattern set by other post-nuptial comedies like *It's a Wonderful Life*, *Mr. Blandings Builds His Dream House* and *Please Don't Eat the Daisies*. In those films, there is an explicit or implicit comparison between country and community, city and alienation. But the communities in *Heartburn* wander; they are less a matter of location than of quality of interaction. The contrast is between superficial and true communities. Social interactions are sincere and intimate in the true community. In the superficial community, social interactions take place in large parties in which people are isolated from each other, or small parties in which the common theme is whose marriage is in trouble. Individual relationships similarly break down between the superficial intimacy of living together and the true intimacy of living lives interpenetrated with understanding one's partner.

After telling Mark that she is pregnant, Rachel and Mark take turns singing songs about what their child will be like—as in *Silkwood*, trying to find the right voice through which this identity as a married couple can be fixed. But their somewhat manic efforts to find the right song only underscore the lack of connection between the life they live and the ideal of introspection and commitment to sacrifice the songs represent. In the society of gossiping couples to whom they break the news in succeeding scenes, the conversation immediately turns from Mark and Rachel's baby to trivialities. Surface counts, not depth. Sex is interesting, but not relationships. The songs, like the lines of enduring love from the wedding, do not fit the society. Ultimately, when Rachel has her second child, the superficiality of Rachel and Mark's marriage is underscored by Mark's late visits to the hospital. Mark's oldest friends and his housekeeper feel that they need to explain to him what type of food his wife likes.

In *Manhattan*, the chorus-voice of truth is George Gershwin's music. In *Heartburn*, Ephron's contemporary Carly Simon plays what cannot be said,[13] erupting into words once Rachel discovers Mark's affair with Thelma. This serves as an answer to the question of what song fits this marriage. Over the montage of Rachel's flight to her father's house, Simon sings of burning soufflés and screaming lullabies because of the lies of romance. But then she strikes a new note: "I know nothing stays the same/But if you're willing to play the game/It's coming around again." The song that fits is not one of celebration or of passive acceptance, but of endurance in the struggle to find a true marriage.

In the penultimate scene, a dinner party, this interior monologue becomes public. As usual, the topic is whose marriage is collapsing. The hostess, Betty, is planning a dinner party for Mark's mistress, Thelma Rice, to show support for her as there are so many rumors about her marriage falling apart. The topic of gossip switches to David and Harriet Kaiser, another sundered couple. Harriet left David for David's secretary, a woman. This echoes Jill's split from Isaac and her coming out as a lesbian that Isaac discusses at the beginning of *Manhattan*. But where Allen's film treats Jill simply as an antagonist, Ephron explores the implications of this split. Betty cannot understand how David could be married to Harriet and not be aware of her true attraction toward women, especially as they had been together for years. "How is it possible to live with someone that long and not know something so fundamental?" Rachel says that it is possible—that you live in a fantasy of intimacy. "And then the dream dies . . . . Which leaves you with a choice: You can either stick with it, which is unbearable, or you can just go off and dream another dream." At that point Rachel slaps her key lime pie in Mark's face.

In a romantic comedy the couple marries—or remarries—and the social order is renewed. In *Heartburn*, this final scene is more Old Comedy; the false social order is revealed, but the true society is not established. But the film finally is unsatisfying. *Manhattan* resolves the problem of modern romance with a fantasy romance object. *Heartburn*, written before Ephron met and married fellow writer Nicholas Pileggi, shows the destruction of a superficial romance, but not the superficial society. The film neither completes the conflict of Old Comedy nor establishes a clear path for the development of a New Comedy social transformation. In the final scene, Rachel is on a plane. She and her daughter begin singing a song about the "itsy bitsy spider" that loses its home but starts over again. It is the right song; the chorus begins singing with them. But how Mark could be changed or what alternatives to Mark exist is left undeveloped. Intimacy remains a dream, or perhaps something that someone else, Harriet perhaps, has discovered.

Ephron's first film as a director, *This Is My Life* (1992), takes up where *Heartburn* leaves off. Dottie Engels (Julie Kavner) leaves her relationship with the wrong kind of man and finds success and love on her terms. But it is an Old Comedy narrative as characters represent more the contest between social forces than they show the possibility of romantic intimacy. The conflict between true and false intimacy is between Dottie and her older daughter Erica (Samantha Mathis). Ironically, Erica is disturbed by her mother's professional success. She imagines that her father will be more interested in sacrificing himself for his children. She journeys to her father, but finds him to be emotionally detached. His new, more traditional wife is more like a zombie than a person. Each of them is an object of ridicule, not emulation. Dottie's success in opposition to her ex-husband's absurd social order (as observed and eventually understood by her oldest daughter) is the story's focus, not her or her daughter's romantic involvements. Ephron chose this story to direct because "there were things I was writing that . . . felt personal to me," and she didn't want to rewrite it in order to attract a director. "You know, if you write about women—at all—there's a very short list of people who want to make movies about women . . . and even fewer studios."[14]

Ephron's breakthrough film was *When Harry Met Sally* (1989). Though it was unquestionably her script, it was written in a catechismal interlocution of male and female stereotypes with director Rob Reiner, and benefited from ad-lib additions—particularly dialogue from Billy Crystal, and concepts from Meg Ryan. "Instead of feeling violated by it, I felt, well, this is great . . . . Someone just walked into this room and made that scene funnier."[15] But while she learned from what had taken place, she wasn't able to incorporate this immediately into her writing. Though Ephron is sympathetic to the material, *Cookie* (1989), directed by Susan Seidelman, fits more comfortably into Seidelman's *oeuvre* of self-assured women who con their way to success than it is of Ephron's introspective heroines. The plot of *My Blue Heaven* (Herbert Ross, 1990) is almost a sequel to *Cookie*, but the plot focus is further away from Ephron's interests. Both are Old Comedy mode films. Ephron's *Mixed Nuts* (1994) is an attempt to do a "nervous" version of a '30s social New Comedy of the sort in which Frank Capra specialized. But the serial killer landlord in *Mixed Nuts* is an artificial construct compared to the real threat proto-fascists and fiscal conservatives represented to Capra's audiences. The nascent new society of *Mixed Nuts* does not really have anything that either forces it to come into being, or any socially relevant problem that prevents it from coming into being. Ephron understood that Allen's type of narcissistic-neurotic romances captured a quality of her era, but she had not fully synthesized a voice of her own.

Allen's adaptation of New Comedy to its time in *Manhattan* was popular—the national identity of the United States is teleological, so there is a New Comedy bias in American films—but it leaves Emily and Yale dangling in its otherwise solid resolution, as *Heartburn* leaves Rachel and Mark dangling.[16] As Mark and Rachel are the center of *Heartburn*, what is a minor but revealing flaw in *Manhattan* is a major flaw in *Heartburn*. When *Harry Met Sally* resolves both *Manhattan*'s problem of Emily and *Heartburn*'s problem of Mark. In the process of telling how two people overcome their fears and fantasies about the other sex in the course of becoming married, Ephron created a true romantic comedy that incorporates a post-feminist address of the issue of what marriage can be.

In the screwball era, according to Stanley Cavell, the plot drive in a comedy of remarriage was not to bring the couple together, but to bring the couple *back* together. Remarriage usually meant that a couple literally remarried, as in *His Girl Friday*, or that engagements or unconsummated marriages were rejected in favor of a true marriage, as in *It Happened One Night*. Both of these happen in *The Awful Truth*. In the post-feminist period, the sexual dialectic is of identity. A true marriage enables both members to be true to their inner selves in a way that is not possible or perhaps even maintainable apart. Marriage is less of a social contract than it is a conceptual state. It is not discovered in public ceremony but in private dialogue. The object of marriage is not certifiably lawful sex or socially acknowledged companionship, but a new order of being; that is the justification for the persistence of marriage as an institution. It is not just a relationship, but a new kind of identity, in which each partner's introspective interior monologue becomes shared. In the "nervous" and other post-feminist comedies before *When Harry Met Sally*, conversations end, and even monologues cease. The Ephron comedy does not bring the couple back together so much as it brings the couple truly together, signified through monologic conversations; two people speak as one.

As *Heartburn* is a dialectical homage to *Manhattan*, so *When Harry Met Sally* is *Annie Hall* reshaped by Ephron's antagonism to Allen's tacit premises. Both films use evocative Gershwin, Rogers and Hart, and other Swing-era romance ballads as supportive and ironic commentary on the narrative. *Annie Hall* begins with Alvy Singer's (Woody Allen) introspective confessional monologue in which he puzzles out "where did the screwup come" in his life that caused his breakup with Annie (Diane Keaton), and ends with Alvy's voiceover monologue as he unexpectedly meets Annie in a theater line. *When Harry Met Sally* begins with a documentary-style shot of an old couple's duologue,[17] in which each take turns telling how it came about that they became a couple. This is the first of a series of seemingly non-diegetic documentary-style inserts of couples telling odd stories of how they came to be married. *When Harry Met Sally* ends with a final insert of Harry and Sally themselves. They sum up the film's narrative in a few lines. The audience has a privileged understanding of what their brief duologue implies, and this casts the previous inserts retrospectively into a pattern: romance is not just a moment—even if it begins that way—but a process of creating in two people a shared identity that deepens individuality even as that individuality is interpenetrated with the other.

While *Annie Hall* and *When Harry Met Sally* are markedly similar, the differences between the films are most striking. On unexpectedly meeting Annie after their breakup,

Alvy has memory flashbacks. Annie sings "Seems Like Old Times" over the flashbacks, but she is the object of Alvy's introspection. We do not hear their conversation in the last scene, only Alvy's interpretation of it in a voiceover. As Frank Krutnik notes, the song's confident romanticism is in dissonance with the romantic couple who invokes it. In Ephron's film, Harry tells himself in the penultimate scene that "you're your own best friend," but keeps having flashbacks of being with Sally. Where Alvy's flashbacks are nostalgic introspections that lead to a sad final comment on the necessity and impossibility of love—and are his alone, unshared with Annie—Harry's flashbacks make him realize that he cannot be satisfied with just being with himself. Alvy is sad, but Harry is diminished. Where Alvy loses a mirror, Harry is in danger of losing a kind of self-awareness that emerges from dialectic.[18]

*Annie Hall*'s Annie is Alvy's protégé as well as lover. When she and Alvy part, it is not so much an act of will on her part as it is a yielding to temptation; Los Angeles and the delusional seduction of materialism and hedonism seduce Annie from the spiritual explorations and physical trials New York represents. As they divide their belongings in their apartment, Annie talks about her need to "grow." But she never speaks directly about what *she* really wants, not even in the final breakup scene at a health-food restaurant—the sign of her new allegiance—in Los Angeles. Annie's conflicts are always important only in context with Alvy's struggle for identity in the world, as is the case with Old Comedy. The film does not explain Annie's desires; she apparently receives them from her environment and her teacher/lovers. Neither Alvy nor Annie honestly discuss their feelings to each other. Neither trusts the other.

Yet the film closes on a mystery. Annie returns to New York. She is living in Soho with a new boyfriend whom she is "dragging" to *The Sorrow and The Pity*. This is a sign; she is still Alvy's disciple. But then he finds that she is something worse than a spurning lover; she is an apostate, a schismatic. Though the heretical heathens of California have lost their hold on her, she remains apart, marked by his beliefs—and thus still part of the New Comedy couple—yet espousing some unknown derivative variant of Alvy to her own followers. What evil could divide Alvy from his disciple remains a fundamental and philosophical mystery that Alvy must ponder alone.

In *When Harry Met Sally*, whatever is mysterious becomes the subject of an argument. Harry and Sally are not in the position of master and protégé; each teaches the other. Their honest communication is only possible because they resolve not to see each other as potential partners. Freed of the ventriloquism of gender roles, they find a new voice. "I feel like I'm growing," Harry tells his friend Jess (Bruno Kirby) after Harry and Sally have become friends. He tells Jess that he can tell anything to Sally, and get "a woman's point of view" on what he does or feels. "And the great thing is, I don't have to lie because I'm not always thinking about how to get her into bed. I can just be myself." Because he is himself, and he says what he thinks instead of trying to say what he thinks Sally wants to hear, his myths about women begin to fall apart. The most memorable instance of this is Sally's proving to Harry that women can fake orgasms, but the film is full of small conversations that slowly break down Harry's smug presumptions and beliefs about what women are really like.

Sally also changes, though less overtly. Isadora of *Fear of Flying* (1974), the popular novel by Ephron's contemporary Erica Jong, is a more daring character than Sally, yet comparing the two characters is revealing. Sally shares a susceptibility to living, as Isadora says, "as if she were waiting for Prince Charming to take her away 'from all this.' All

*"A woman's point of view": Meg Ryan and Billy Crystal in* When Harry Met Sally.

what? The solitude of living inside her own soul? The certainty of being herself instead of half of something else?"[19] When Sally and Harry meet for the second time, as she is being dropped off at the airport by her boyfriend Joe, she tries to emphasize their couple-ness—though when he tells her he loves her, she responds, "you do?" But what she feels is less important than what she sees through other's eyes.

Sally shares Isadora's fantasy of the "zipless fuck," though in a less detailed form. Each describes their version at the beginning of their stories. Isadora's recurrent fantasy is that she yields to the advances of a stranger on a train as it passes through a tunnel. Sally's recurrent fantasy is of a "faceless guy" who rips off her clothes. "For the true, ulti-mate zipless A-1 fuck," Isadora says, "it was necessary that you never get to know the man very well." Indeed, Isadora notes, once the object of infatuation becomes a person, "he was an insect on a pin." The zipless fuck must have "all the swift compression of a dream" and be "seemingly free of all remorse and guilt."[20]

Sally's friendship with Harry begins to unsettle her romance fantasy. After Harry and Sally have become friends, as they are dancing together on New Year's Eve, Harry begins to think out loud about what it might be like to be lovers as well as friends. Sally dismisses the thought. The things that she likes about him as a friend would bother her in a lover. "I can't explain it. It's just something that happens to women after a while," she tells him. If Sally shares Isadora's belief that knowledge is the killer of romance, she differs in that she finds in Harry an intimacy she is not prepared to lose. She tries to set Harry up with her friend Marie (Carrie Fisher) so that "we could all still be friends." In return, Harry brings his friend Jess to meet Sally. Romance with a friend is dangerous,

Sally reasons, but group intimacy, with sociocultural barriers to keep her and Harry safely unromantic, can preserve their friendship. The flaw in her theory is that confessional intimacy and romantic intimacy is not a group activity, as she and Harry find out when Jess and Marie desert their group date.

When Harry and Sally date strangers, the problem becomes acute. Each watches the other's partner warily, and then vent their anxiety to Jess and Marie. They note the ways the stranger is wrong for their friend—how, significantly, each is not him or herself—in the presence of the stranger. "Sally went to a baseball game?" Harry says worriedly to Jess. "She hates baseball." "Harry doesn't even like sweets," Sally says to Marie about Harry's date, who owns a dessert business.

Passion overwhelms fear, momentarily, and they finally have sex. New Comedy forms usually had the parents as the blocking elements that prevent a couple from coming together. Screwball comedy replaced the rule of parents with the rule of society; social class or convention, including conventions of gender, keeps the couple apart. In the New Comedy revival Allen initiated and Ephron refined, the conflict is between a socially imposed sense of identity—of appropriate ambitions, of beliefs, but particularly of gender—and the characters' true identity. In Ephron's variation, the protagonists do not really become protagonists until they achieve enough of a sense of self that they can overcome these invisible, internalized barriers. Identity, not sex, is the end—a sense of self that enables the protagonists to be truly intimate with each other. Sex is in this case only a metaphor for a more profound intimacy that requires learning.

In screwball comedy, the male partner could be "captured" almost accidentally, as in *Bringing Up Baby*, or through deliberate conquest, as in *The Lady Eve*. Deception is a recurrent theme. The fact that symbolic social rules such as "man pursues woman" or "people marry their own class" could be overcome was all that was needed. In the Ephron New Comedy, the interior state of characters is vital. Accidental consummation of desire is too easy; it is like the "green world" of Shakespeare's comedies, in which couples come together in the fairy world or the Forest of Arden, places outside of the real world in which the couple must live. This dream world enables characters to realize what they want, but it must be constructed in the real world in order for these possibilities to become manifest.

When Sally and Harry have sex, it breaks down the unconscious wall between them, forcing them to new depths of introspection. Harry and Sally have talked about the different beliefs and rules of gender each has grown up with, but each now has to overcome consciously the distorting lens of gender that sex has placed between them. Harry in particular is not ready; he is feeling "suffocated," he tells Jess. "It is like he just disappeared," Sally tells Marie. "What we did that night was your idea, not mine," Harry insists later at Jess and Marie's wedding reception, denying his own desires. Sally is a woman; women trap men; therefore, Sally deceived Harry. That is the cultural gender script Harry inherits, and when he sees Sally as a woman instead of a friend, he unconsciously interprets her behavior by his unexamined beliefs.

Sally is hardly in a position to disenchant him, as what began as a fantasy night akin to a zipless fuck has transformed into its exact opposite, an act weighed down with consequences, humiliation and remorse. When he wants to resume their platonic relationship, she cannot. As she said when she and Harry first met, the attraction between them is "already out there," and can't be taken back. "It changes things," she tells him. "You should know that better than anyone because the minute it happens you walk right out the door." She knows him so well that he cannot conceal his withdrawal of intimacy from her.

Significantly, when they have lunch with each other the day after, their conversation becomes a nervous *Annie Hall*-like mixture of lies and silence. Harry breaks a long pause with a lie. "It's so nice when you can sit with someone and not have to talk to them," he tells her. "It just shows how really comfortable you are with them." His own voice has become replaced with a social homily. They finally stop speaking, as even lies are too revealing. Each feels betrayed by the fact of the other's gender; each feels the other is no longer a person, but a stereotype.[21]

In the end, Harry seems to be saved by the soundtrack that, until that point, was only available to the audience. He walks the streets of Manhattan on New Year's Eve, and we see his flashbacks of him and Sally together as he talks to himself. As in Allen's *Manhattan*, he suddenly becomes silent and listens to the melody the city seems to be singing to him. New York and its culture becomes a *deus ex machina* that leads the protagonists to self-discovery. Anticipating the role of the angel Michael in Ephron's later film, Sinatra sings "It Had To Be You" and reveals to Harry what he needs to do. He runs to the party where he knows he will find Sally.

Once he finds Sally, she does not simply understand and forgive, as Tracy does. Sally has to be convinced. "You can't just show up here and tell me you love me and expect that to make it all right. What am I supposed to say?" Harry's response is not to tell her what to say, but rather to plea to continue their dialogue.[22] Each is free of a script, but only free in their intimacy with each other.

Memory and recognition are at the core of the Ephron New Comedy. Infatuation and fantasy do not require knowledge, and sex does not require intimacy. In a society where sex is no longer restricted to marriage, and marriage is no longer simply a heterosexual contract to live together and share possessions, the meaning of marriage itself is in danger of being lost. In the final moments the film clarifies the six previous nondiegetic inserts of couples talking about how they came to be married. The seventh and final insert is Harry and Sally telling how they came to be married. They briefly sum up the events of how they met—but unlike the previous inserts, we have been privileged to see what lies behind their words. Their brief description of their meetings over twelve years describes a process of self-discovery and growing intimacy that culminates in a desire to share life experiences together—not just the physical pleasure of sex or the narcissistic fantasy of infatuation. Love, in the Ephron New Comedy, is the establishment of intimacy and identity in the face of cultural rules that promote superficiality and confusion.

*When Harry Met Sally* became the new standard by which romantic comedy was measured. But Ephron herself did not return to romantic comedy until her second directorial effort, *Sleepless In Seattle* (1993). She and her sister Delia co-wrote the script with Jeff Arch, who wrote the treatment.[23] The film's success consolidated Ephron's status as a leading comedy director, but it lacked the dialogue and character development that marked *When Harry Met Sally*.[24] In their place it had a traditional comedy pattern of seasonal metaphor, in which the desolation of winter is overcome by summer's return.

*Sleepless* begins with the funeral of Maggie Baldwin, architect Sam Baldwin's (Tom Hanks) wife and Jonah Baldwin's (Ross Malinger) mother. Sam and Jonah's period of mourning ends with the "magical" restoration of their loss in the form of Annie Reed (Meg Ryan), Maggie's successor. The narrative structure is entirely consonant with a comedic cycle of death and rebirth, but Annie becomes more the depersonalized structural reincarnation of Maggie than a person in her own right.

What saves Annie from being simply the object of a new romance mystery ritual is the plot theme of illusory and true intimacy, and the incorporation of *When Harry Met Sally*'s gender dialectic, as mediated through popular culture. Annie "meets" Sam by hearing him on a pop-psychologist radio show confessing his continuing mourning for Maggie. Annie—and women across the country—become obsessed with Sam, in part because the anonymity of the medium allows Sam to confess to emotions that he himself and other males in the film dismiss as "chick stuff."[25] It is as though the physical proximity men and women may have to one another is separate from emotional proximity. Ephron implies that this dearth of intimacy is growing, through Annie's mother's story of how she and Annie's father met, and particularly through juxtaposing Leo McCarey's *An Affair to Remember* (1957) with Annie's self-described "realistic" relationship with her fiancé Walter. But if *An Affair to Remember* haunts Ephron's film as a female nostalgic image of romance, there are several other films mentioned that serve as interlocutory counterpoints to *Affair*, notably *Fatal Attraction* (1987). The two films serve as the focus for women to discuss a lack of intimacy between the sexes, and the focus for men to discuss the dangers of emotional vulnerability and of women as active sexual beings.

This gender divide is a lie, Ephron argues. Emotional engagement is a basic human need. "I'm always a little surprised when people refer to things like *Sleepless in Seattle* as 'chick flicks,'" she commented recently. "Although women are probably the ones who say, 'let's go see it,' lots of men like romantic comedies."[26] *Sleepless* vibrates between fantasy and cynicism—usually cynicism on the part of the opposite gender (usually men) against the other gender's desire. Immediately after Annie first hears Sam on the radio, Ephron cuts to Annie meeting with her editor-friend Becky (Rosie O'Donnell) and other reporters at a story conference. One of the stories is of how Sam's radio broadcast caused 2000 women to call the radio station in Chicago to get his address. Annie tries to describe what the experience listening to Sam was like for her. "It's like what happens when I watch those phone company ads." As Annie and Becky gush over these vignettes of idealized emotion, the two male reporters look at each other blankly, and then attack. "I'll tell you what it is," one reporter says. "There are a lot of desperate women out there looking for love . . . . It's harder for a woman to get married over 40 than to get killed by a terrorist." Women revealing a fantasy of idealized emotions are dangerous.

And indeed they are. Romantic narratives are almost always regarded as inferior or escapist in comparison to realistic narratives. But it would be more to the point to note that they point out the failures of society to fulfill the needs of its members. *Fatal Attraction* was a gothic projection of fear of sexuality—the death-knell of the sexual revolution, personified as a desperate woman. By contrast, *Affair* creates an imaginary space in which the desire for intimacy is not an object of fear, but of discovery. Watching *Affair* causes Annie to think. "Now *those* were the days when people *knew* how to be in love," she cries to Becky as she is typing her letter to "Sleepless in Seattle." "They *knew* it was *right*, it was real . . . ." Romance, as Northrop Frye notes, can create conditions in which alternative realities can come into being.[27]

The Empire State Building, a monument to romantic aspiration and frustration in *Affair*, serves as the material catalyst around which a more authentically intimate relationship takes form.[28] Architecturally, it is more than just pragmatic; it embodies romanticism in a material form. It links Annie's fantasy of fearlessly vulnerable communication to her real world—as Ephron means to link the fantasy world of *Sleepless* to our world—through its simultaneous existence as a real and a narrative object. As Allen did in *Man-*

*hattan*, Ephron implies that emotional excess in architecture, in narrative, and other cultural artifacts, can serve to remind humans of our own needs. Narratives—by extension, narratives like *Sleepless in Seattle*—have the potential to call us back to ourselves.[29]

*Michael* (1996) is a much darker film. Harry and Sally discover each other through the neutral ground of friendship. Annie and Sam can be saved by the manifest presence of romance in a building. But even multiple miracles and the presence of an archangel is barely enough to break through the shells of bitterness and cynicism Frank Quinlan (William Hurt) and Dorothy Winters (Andie MacDowell) use to protect themselves. *Michael*, for all its angelic context, takes place in a fallen world in which all spirits are broken, everyone is compromised, and all victims are victimizers.

*Michael* is structured on L. Frank Baum's *The Wizard of Oz*, though its debt to Oz is seen through carnival funhouse-mirror distortions. "When they handed out the parts, you got the heart," Frank tells his colleague Huey (Robert Pastorelli) at the beginning. "Yeah, right, I got the heart," Huey says. "You got the brains, is that what you're saying?" Frank and Huey are friends who need each other to function. Their employer, Malt (Bob Hoskins) is an inverse-wizard. Like the Tin Woodman, Frank once had a heart, but he lost it, along with his job and his wife. He now is frozen in the employ of the *National Mirror*, writing stories he regards with contempt for people whom he regards as fools, the sentimental thralls of his employer, the all-powerful Malt. The Scarecrow-like Huey is, if he had the brains to realize it, the *National Mirror's* ruler. He owns Sparky, a dog that is identical to Malt's childhood pet dog that was run over by a truck. The dog is an embodiment of sentiment to Malt and his similarly damaged readers. Malt has "Millions of dollars tied up in that dog, and the dog belongs to you," Frank tells Huey, but Huey is incapable of using that knowledge to exploit others' weaknesses.

Drawn by a letter, Frank, Huey, and Dorothy journey to the prairie to "get an angel," Michael (John Travolta) for the *Mirror* Christmas issue. They find, though they are unaware of it, "home." Home is the place where all fears are laid aside, and all lies drop away to reveal the truth.[30] "Heaven is my home," Randy Newman helpfully sings on the film's soundtrack at the film's beginning, but as usual, the Ephron protagonists are initially deaf to her blunt soundtrack chorus.

Where the *Oz* protagonists are aware of deficits they don't really have, *Michael's* protagonists, particularly Frank and Dorothy, are utterly crippled by emotional wounds they try to deny to themselves and others that they have. This affects their perception of the winged angel Michael. Frank's name is ironic, as he is never frank. He is more like an Orwell bureaucrat, practiced in doublethink. Frank and Huey profess to each other that all winged beings are frauds, yet immediately insist to Dorothy that Michael is a real angel when she refuses to play their confidence game. Dorothy, fixated on the idea that all men exploit women, assumes Michael is another slick deceiver. Neither acknowledges the evidence that angels might be real. In a state of cynical despair, it quite literally takes miracles to reawaken these frozen, fixated beings to life.

The sybaritic, sugar-swilling Archangel Michael exposes Dorothy and Frank to each other during the journey, revealing to themselves and each other their own longings for a pre-cynical world of trust through things like pie. "Pie gives you the sense that you're a four-square person living in a four-square country," Frank says. Typically, Ephron uses the soundtrack to signal her characters' epiphanies of rebirth. Dorothy's song "Only Heaven Knows," and Bonnie Raitt's song "Feels Like Home," are chorus voices that the protagonists become aware of as they discard their hard-boiled shells of experience and regain emotional vulnerability. The unconscious world of the soundtrack and the conscious world of imagery become aware of each other in harmony.

But Dorothy and Frank must return to the real world where archangels cannot exist. Michael fades away when they reach Chicago. Typically in romantic comedy, protagonists who find what Frye calls the "green world" must recreate that knowledge in the world of experience. Frank and Dorothy are not up to the challenge. Though they confront Malt and unmask his illusion of power, they cannot retain faith in each other. Frank resumes his dishonest pose as a heartless reporter, and Dorothy resumes her armor of aggrieved victimhood. In this sense, *Michael* is the closest to *Annie Hall*, with protagonists who are incapable of honest communication. Deception about emotions, to oneself and to others, destroys people and relationships, Ephron's films proclaim; *Michael* declares this empathetically. "It never happened," Frank tells Huey of the whole experience of angels and romance, after building a bridge between two piles of sugar cubes, and then knocking it down. It is only through a final act of divine intervention that the couple comes to a happy ending.

*You've Got Mail* (1998) also plays on the contrast between the cynicism of experience and innocent trust. Gender is the mask that Harry and Sally are able to set aside for awhile. Broadcast media mediates gender-specific dreams and provides a confessional for desires in *Sleepless in Seattle* . The protagonists of *Michael* conceal themselves in defensive shells in a real world of illusions. *You've Got Mail* takes the anonymous monologue of *Sleepless* and makes it a dialogue through the magic of e-mail chat rooms. As in *Michael*, the real world its protagonists inhabit is filled with illusions of cynicism that the characters must overcome.

The film begins with a tracking shot over a computer-generated representation of New York. The camera tracks through artificial streets and stops at a building. The computer image fades, revealing a real brownstone building underneath. The artificial world is devoid of complex detail—a mask that conceals a messier reality. Kathleen Kelly (Meg Ryan) and Joe Fox (Tom Hanks) are e-mail friends. Each is living with a partner, but they find themselves drawn into what they regard as an illicit relationship. Hidden from each other by the computer, as Kathleen says, they "pretend that we're the oldest and dearest friends—as opposed what we actually are, people who don't know each other's names and met in a chat room where we both claimed we'd never been before." Each is living proper, rational lives with correct partners, doing what they are expected to do, and feeling lost. Between the two of them they have created a world without personal history in which they can discover themselves.

The situation Kathleen and Joe are in is very much like *When Harry Met Sally*, in which Harry and Sally were in a self-created refuge from gender-based self-censorship, and like *Sleepless In Seattle*, in which anonymity allows an intimacy too self-revealing for casual social relationships. What is different is that Kathleen and Joe know each other in another role, as figureheads of a socioeconomic war of identity. Kathleen Kelly is the second-generation owner of The Shop Around the Corner, a small neighborhood bookstore that specializes in children's books. Joe Fox is the third-generation executive of a chain bookstore, Fox Books, which sells books at a discount and drives small bookstores into bankruptcy. Each plays a role in which they are at war with each other over, as Kathleen Kelly's boyfriend Frank (Greg Kinnear) puts it, the future of "Western civilization as we know it."

It is this conflict between systems of economic relations that is the more profound mask

*Experience and trust: Tom Hanks and Meg Ryan in* You've Got Mail.

that the protagonists are required to penetrate. *You've Got Mail* is a remake of Ernst Lubitsch's *The Shop Around The Corner* (1940), in which a man and a woman work in the same shop competing with each other. *You've Got Mail* updates this theme by placing the couple in different economic entities: The old, typewriter-age world of the neighborhood shop, and the new rationalized economy-of-scale chain store. Where concern about income made the original protagonists forget themselves, Ephron's protagonists are each tugged by the cultural patterns associated with the kinds of businesses they manage.

One of the ongoing subtexts in the film is the universal suitability of lines from *The Godfather*. "*The Godfather* is the answer to any question," Joe writes to Kathleen at one point in his e-mail persona. But as in Coppola's film, in which the business destroys persons, Joe and Kathleen's businesses conceal each from the other, and each has a hard time separating their true identity from their business mask. Joe is a nice guy, but as Joe Fox, he becomes an extension of his father and grandfather, chortling over driving neighborhood fixtures into bankruptcy. Joe accidentally wanders into Kathleen's store and each is charmed by the other. But when he runs into her again at a publishing party, Joe becomes the voice of Fox Books and attacks her as "a bookstore so inconsequential and yet full of its own virtue" that he, as Fox Books, had to investigate. Afterward, as "NY152" he can confess to Kathleen as "Shopgirl" his shame: "Do you ever feel you become the worst version of yourself?"

The ability to break out of that role and see oneself and one's opponents as people is the great difficulty in *You've Got Mail*. Though Ephron's New Comedy romances are very different in tone from her Old Comedy stories, they share at heart not simply just the triumph of the protagonists against their opponents, but the protagonists' triumph over the worst versions of themselves that their social circumstances impose. Ephron's characters struggle to achieve an imaginary space within which they can construct their own voice. Secondary characters, particularly the elder Fox men and Joe and Kathleen's partners, show the danger of a lack of such an introspective space.

Patricia Eden (Parker Posey), Joe's partner, is the editor-in-chief of Eden Books. She is another conglomerate scion, but unlike him, she has no imaginative place or spiritual identity in which she is anything but Eden Books. "'You should go to a retreat, you really should go to a retreat,'" she quotes someone as telling her just before Joe goes off to get her another drink and meets Kathleen at the publishing party. "'It's a really great place to calm down.' He said that to me, isn't that hilarious?" The thought of introspective withdrawal for her is unthinkable. Patricia is always in a hurry, has no remorse, and only talks about publishing. "She makes coffee nervous," Joe says of her to Kevin, his store manager.

Joe leaves Patricia and meets his father Nelson Fox (Dabney Coleman) at the family sailboat, which doubles as temporary housing after failed relationships. Joe's family history is of shallow and self-delusive relationships. Schuyler Fox (John Randolph) apparently exchanged letters with Kathleen's mother, Cecilia. She was "enchanting," but, this elderly father of a pre-teen daughter says, "too young" for him. Nelson Fox has just married his fourth wife, and she has just deserted him for a woman.[31] Patricia is in the family tradition; intimacy plays no role in Fox relationships.

In heroic romance, frequently a wise old man or woman offers sage advice to the protagonist. In comedy, a foolish old man or woman frequently reveals by their example, and by the things they say but do not understand, what path the protagonist needs to follow to fulfillment. Joe and Nelson are commiserating. Nelson has to find someone new. "That's the easy part." Joe thinks his father is telling some kind of joke. "Oh, right, a snap to find the one single person in the world who fills your heart with joy." "Don't be ridiculous," Nelson replies. "Have I ever been with anyone who fits that description? Have you?" By this point in the film, Joe has: Kathleen. Once he sees this, he then begins the slow process to transform his fantasy of NY152 and Shopgirl into a real relationship.

The Fox world is easy to find fault with. The Shop world is also flawed, however. If Fox has no history, the Shop world leans toward stagnation. Frank is the most obviously flawed Shop world person. Any change—as in from typewriters to word-processors—is the "end of Western civilization as we know it," to be fought to the death. He is Ephron's parody of the Woody Allen characters who use typewriters and obsess about old New York, such as Isaac in *Manhattan*, David in *Hannah and Her Sisters* and the novelists in *Everyone Says I Love You* and *Celebrity*. To Ephron, the Shop world is a beautiful world, but it is also Kathleen's mother's world, a place of nostalgia. When Kathleen loses the store, she says it is like losing her mother. Both Joe and Kathleen are living their parents' lives, not their own. Each needs to find a voice of their own.

If Nelson is a foolish old man, Birdie (Jean Stapleton), the employee and friend of Kathleen's mother, is the traditional wise helper. She is a link to Kathleen's mother, but also offers support for personal growth. "Closing the store is the brave thing to do," she tells Kathleen. "You are daring to imagine that you could have a different life." Identity emerges from introspection. Kathleen begins writing children's books. "Who would have ever thought I would write," she tells Joe. "If I hadn't had all this time . . . ." With introspection, Joe and Kathleen each give up the partners who resemble their public masks, and begin to imagine the world of intimacy that each has helped the other to see through their internet personas. "Is there someone else?" Frank asks Kathleen when they break up." "No," she answers. "No, but there's the dream of someone else." It is thus appropriate that Ephron evokes *The Wizard of Oz* again when Joe and Kathleen truly meet at the end, to the tune of "Over The Rainbow" on the soundtrack. "Over the Rainbow" is a song of returning home. In the Ephron film, the romantic couple does not seek to find the past, however, but to find an identity that allows them to be more themselves than they have ever been before. Only by looking beyond the world as it is to the dream world of what it should be is it possible to escape the dead weight of past generations. From *Silkwood* to *You've Got Mail* the prototypical Ephron protagonists have a quality of imagination and courage that enables them to look beyond the language, roles and restrictions they are given. With this courage, anything is possible. As Ephron herself in a commencement address at Wellesley told the students:

> What are you going to do? Everything, is my guess. It will be a little messy, but embrace the mess. It will be complicated, but rejoice in the complications. It will not be anything like what you think it is going to be like, but surprises are good for you. And don't be frightened, you can always change your mind. I know—I've had four careers and three husbands.[32]

## Notes

1. The tragic hero violates rules that are just and is cast out for it. The comic hero violates rules that are absurd or evil. Whether the comic hero succeeds or (in ironic comedy) fails, the existing standards of society still come into question. This does not mean that there are only progressive comedies. Conservative comedies exist too. It does mean that comedy attacks what, in the structure of the comedy at least, the audience is meant to see as the dominant rules of its society.

2. Ephron's own model as a director, judging from her interviews, is Mike Nichols. Nichols, who directed Ephron's *Silkwood* and *Heartburn* scripts, is an actors' director. Nichols, with his comic partner Elaine May, was a superb improviser, and his sense of performance continues to guide his work. Nichols is temperamentally drawn to Old Comedy style; there are no heroes in a Nichols film, only the innocent and the guilty, and a society built by the latter. Ephron is more romance-oriented. She retains from Nichols, however, a desire to motivate the actors to invest her words with emotions drawn from their own lives, and a tendency to rely heavily on the director of photography for visual form. In Ephron, as in Nichols, one must look for style in theme and in performance—and of course, in Ephron's dialogue.

3. See Northrop Frye, *Anatomy of Criticism* (Princeton, NJ: Princeton University Press, 1971), 43–5, and *Spiritus Mundi* (Bloomington: Indiana University Press, 1983), 148–156.

4. See Brian Henderson, "Romantic Comedy Today: Semi-tough or Impossible," *Film Quarterly* 31:4 (1978), 11–23, included in this book, and Steve Neale, "The Big romance or Something Wild?: romantic comedy today," *Screen* 33:3 (1992), 284–299.

5. See Yvonne Tasker, *Spectacular Bodies: Gender, Genre, and the Action Cinema* (New York: Routledge, 1993), 132–152.

6. Nora Ephron, quoted in Marsha McCreadie, *The Women Who Write the Movies* (Secaucus, NJ: Birch Lane Press, 1994), 192–3.

7. Nora Ephron, quoted in McCreadie, 195.

8. See Northrop Frye, *Anatomy of Criticism*, 42–46, for an outline of this comic mode.

9. Ephron and Arlen create a world so dominated by the language and thought of Kerr-McGee that it amounts to a speech genre in which the characters are trapped. Mikhail Bakhtin's concept of heteroglossia, of words and concepts retaining "traces" or "crystalizations" of their social order, is helpful in understanding Ephron's persistent theme of people trapped in word-genres and social scripts.

In this case, the speakers are unaware that their own voice is more an expression of Kerr-McGee society than it is of a personal point of view. Only when their situation forces them to hear themselves do they begin to become aware of their voicelessness. Their task then becomes one of finding the words through which they can begin to create a conscious identity that allows them control over their words. See Gary Saul Morson and Caryl Emerson, *Mikhail Bakhtin: Creation of a Prosaics* (Stanford, Calif: Stanford University Press, 1990).

10. Neale, 289.

11. I borrow Stanley Cavell's term from *The World Viewed*, but the summary of narrative is from Northrop Frye and Joseph Campbell.

12. Bernstein apparently had some cause. In the penultimate scene in the film, Rachel slaps a pie in Mark's face as the climax of a hostess's dinner party conversation about infidelity. In real life, according to Sally Quinn, who was the hostess, Ephron poured a bottle of red wine on Bernstein's head. "Sally Quinn, *The Party: A Guide to Adventurous Entertaining*," http://www.salonmag.com/books/sneaks/1997/10/28review.html

13. Carly Simon's own publicized break-up with singer James Taylor makes her a particularly apt chorus-voice in *Heartburn*.

14. Nora Ephron, *Charlie Rose* (PBS, Dec. 1998). "Some male film executives are less interested in a film about a woman's cure for cancer than they are about a man's hangnail," Ephron was quoted as saying once. "That isn't quite what I said," Ephron commented later, "but it's what I meant." Darrel L. Hope, "Delivering the Mail: The Wit and Wisdom of Nora Ephron," *DGA Magazine* 23:6 (March 1999), 48.

15. Ephron, *Charlie Rose*.

16. Of many sources for the American culture of messianism, Reinhold Niebuhr and Alan Heimert, *A Nation So Conceived* (Westport, CT: Greenwood Press, 1963) is one of the most articulate. Herman Melville, speaking of the treatment of sailors at sea, commented in *White Jacket* that the United States, as "the Israel of its time," bore a special responsibility to transform existing institutions into perfect institutions. This messianism, informs the Feminist dialectic Stanley Cavell observes in screwball comedy in *Pursuits of Happiness* (Cambridge: Harvard University Press, 1981). Though this is a general trope of comedy, the theme of restoration of natural law over a sickly culture is particularly strong in American comedy, the last echo of American revolutionism. *Robin Hood* (1991), the underrated John Irvin film that was released on television to avoid being swamped by the inept Costner version of the same year, is an explicit yet elegant example of this. The land literally becomes healed and blooms with Robin and Marian's marriage, the morally-restorative marriage of Norman with Saxon.

17. In Bakhtinian phraseology, these duologues are "polyphonic." Each member of the couples' voice is a self-conscious polyphony of gender, self, and other. Cf. Gary Saul Moreson and Caryl Empson:

    The essentially aesthetic act of creating such an image of the other is most valuable when we seek not to merge with or duplicate each other, but rather to supplement each other, to take full advantage of our separate fields of vision . . . . Properly performed, the aesthetic act in daily life involves a reassumption and a reconfirmation of one's own place after the other is encountered . . . . It follows that the task of providing artistic form requires two distinct centers of consciousness (185).

    By contrast, Ephron's villains and fools notably lack a conscious awareness that their thoughts and actions are stereotypical. They are unconsciously imprisoned by their speech genres rather than self-conscious performers of them, crippled by their inability to inhabit other points of view.

18. See Krutnik's comments on the differences between the song's invocation in each film: "Love Lies: Romantic Fabrication in Contemporary Romantic Comedy," in Peter William Evans and Celestino Deleyto, eds., *Terms of Endearment: Hollywood Romantic Comedies of the 1980s and 1990s* (Edinburgh: Edinburgh University Press, 1998), 21, 25.

19. Erica Jong, *Fear of Flying* (NY: Signet, 1995 [1974]), 11.

20. Jong, 14.

21. Frank Krutnik, "Love Lies," in Evans and Deleyto, claims that Ephron and other romance film-makers tell the audience to "learn to lie, learn to love the lie." I think this scene suggests a more complex reading is intended in these endings—certainly in the case of Ephron's films. The whole point of her films is to get *past* the lie, to discover the real person behind the gender or social role.

22. In the original script, Ephron originally had Harry respond, "who makes the rules on these things . . . . [I]t's you and me." Someone, probably Billy Crystal, changed the beginning of his dialogue to a more lyrical list of the things about Sally that Harry loves, echoing appropriately the list of memories from George and Ira Gershwin's "They Can't Take That Away From Me." Emotionally, this is better, but it is conceptually a small loss.

23. Delia Ephron is a significant writer in her own right. According to Nora Ephron, she and Delia are similar writers. I will subsume Delia within Nora's penumbra, but with the caveat that Nora Ephron is the person who enables a certain kind of story to come into being, rather than the sole author of everything in an Ephron film. See *Charlie Rose*, Dec. 1996.

24. Terry Pristin, "How 'Sleepless In Seattle' Slew 'Em, " *Los Angeles Times Calendar* (July 2, 1993), 4.

25. "I just want somebody that I can have a decent conversation with over dinner, you know, without it falling down into weepy tears over some *movie* she just saw," he tells his brother-in-law at one point.

26. Hope, 48.

27. Northrop Frye, *The Secular Scripture* (Cambridge: Harvard University Press, 1976), 166.

28. *Affair* is a remake of McCarey's *Love Affair* (1939). In both films, the Empire State Building serves as the location where the film lovers are to unite; the building is an image-schema representation of the relative importance of love to other human concerns. Though in reality its height record has been superseded by cold Bauhaus boxes, its impassioned Art Deco style keeps it, in romance, the "tallest building in the world."

29. Ephron has also said "I'm not out here crusading for anything except the ability to make my next movie and have it kill some time for people," but in this she is echoing her mentor, Mike Nichols. And they are both lying. Ironically, like their characters, they too need emotional shields to protect themselves.

30. Ephron chose cinematographer John Lindley to shoot the film because of his work on *Field of Dreams* (1989), in which characters mistake Iowa for heaven.

31. The woman who leaves her husband for a woman, an image Allen treated more or less unsympathetically in *Manhattan*, seems for Ephron to be a sign of sincerity, precisely because it does not easily fit social genres of behavior; to come out after having been married is to be aware of social genres, to have a conscious identity in conflict with them, and to act on feelings. All of this is precisely not true of the Ephron antagonist. In this instance, then, Ephron's minor character deserting the false relationship for the real one is foreshadowing the protagonists' overcoming their own passivity in the face of social genre.

32. The multiple husbands theme supports the point of her comedies: Ephron's films are not comedies of remarriage, but of true marriage. Nora Ephron, Commencement Address, 1996, http://www.wellesley.edu/PublicAffairs/President/pics.html/#video.

# XI

# Neither Here nor There

## Gregg Bachman (1996)

For more than twenty-five years I have reserved a special place in my life for the films of Woody Allen. It has been only recently, however, through the perspective that these years offer, that I have been able to fully appreciate how my connection to the films is much stronger than merely an affection for their characters or an affinity for their humor. As I trace the development of Allen's themes across the breadth of his works, I can detect the outline of my own story, the struggle of the hyphenated-American, the assimilated Jew cast adrift between a society not ready to fully embrace him, and a religion and culture he is not fully capable of embracing. I can see the gradual evolution of a spiritual journey not yet complete, from the youthful iconoclast through the dark and troubled agnostic to an emerging, more hopeful pose. If drama, as Hamlet suggests, is but a mirror held up to life, then it is indeed my own life that I see reflected in the works of Woody Allen.

My story is not dissimilar to many first- and second-generation hyphenated-Americans. My grandparents emigrated here in the first quarter of this century. They left behind the rather cloistered society of the European shtetl and found themselves thrust into the roiling melting pot that is America. As their families grew they faced the rather prickly question of assimilation. On the one hand, they could cling to the old ways and desperately build walls to hold the new world in abeyance. For the most part, this was the direction chosen by the Chasidim, the "keepers of the faith," the ultraorthodox sect externally recognized by the men's black frocks, beards, and broad- brimmed hats. Or they could try to go in the opposite direction and attempt to fit into society by becoming "True Americans," a process that would entail a wholesale abandonment of the old ways. Both my paternal and maternal sides chose the latter route: customs were dropped, Yiddish was not taught, goals were altered.

This did not happen all at once, of course; instead, there was a gradual falling away of traditions. The strict dietary laws of kashrut would be maintained in the home, but accommodations would be made for restaurants and eating at the homes of gentile friends. Shabbat, the traditional day of rest and observance, would be acknowledged by the lighting of the candles on Friday nights and attendance at synagogue on Saturday morning, but then life would go on, commerce conducted, games played, like any other day of the week.

I was born a baby boomer and raised in a suburb in upper New York state. My house was filled with the latest gimmicks and gadgets, my life, with scouting and camps. Pork and shellfish were served at the family table, milk was drunk with our hamburgers. Friday nights were reserved for football and basketball games, and we attended religious school on Sundays, the gentile sabbath.

There was precious little room for religion. Jewish rituals and traditions become more rote than meaningful, and we followed the Jewish equivalent of the gentile's biannual pilgrimage to church on Christmas and Easter. I remember all too well the interminable holiday meals with older relatives chanting seemingly endless prayers in a confusing lan-

**364**

guage as meaningless and as remote to me as Latin. Bar Mitzvah, the significant ritual marking the crossing of the threshold into adulthood, became an excuse for exotic parties and extravagant gifts.

This is not to say that my family became fully assimilated into mainstream America. We do, after all, live in a predominantly Christian country, where everybody gets days off for Christmas and Easter, while major community events and school tests are held on Jewish holidays. Our status as the other, the outsider, was continually being brought to our attention in a variety of ways. When I was in grade school I was constantly reminded, either verbally or physically, that mine was the first Jewish family on the block. Other ways were less direct. At my private, nonsectarian high school, for example, assemblies were opened by the recitation of the Lord's Prayer, and I was forced to bow my head and pretend to pray lest I draw more unwanted attention. This subtle type of exclusionary practice continues in many other venues to this day, as "our Lord Jesus" is invoked at public gatherings.

Outsiders enter into a rather pernicious cycle. Assimilation, which waters down heritage, leads to insecurity and the attendant fear that we will be revealed as pretenders to the mantle of "True Americans," and that we will suffer the consequence of ostracism or persecution. But once we are unmasked and inevitably driven away, where will we turn?

I, for one, had lost any vestige of my own unique sense of culture, and I felt just as out of place with my "own" as I did with gentiles. As a result, I was indeed a classic product of the drive toward assimilation. I found myself in the unenviable position of not only being on the outside of society, but on the outside of my own religion as well. I was constantly being identified as a Jew, but never consciously identifying myself as one; I suffered the pains of exclusion by gentile America, but I found little solace within the culture that made me different.

I was truly neither here nor there.

My attraction to Woody Allen stems from his constant struggle with this same cultural conundrum. His films continually strike the discordant notes of "outsider," "assimilation," "discovery," and all the attending complexities that resonate so clearly with me in my life. We all would like to think that people judge us by who we are and how we behave. However, most Jews cannot escape the reality that once we are discovered to be Jews, people will forever categorize us as Jews. And if we have no strong connection with this affiliation, we then have the makings for a highly personal and difficult struggle.

Although Allen has gone on record saying that being Jewish doesn't enter into his creative consciousness (Pogel, 25), he firmly identifies his characters as Jews. Melish, Stern, Singer, Zelig, Rose, and Kleinman sounds like a Jewish professional association, but all are the surnames of characters Allen has played in his films. "Any character I . . . play would be Jewish, just because I am (a Jew)," he has noted (Pogel, 25). People simply cannot accept him as anything else (Lax, 165), and, as Mast elaborated, his very success depends upon his Jewishness (Mast, 126). But here is a rather difficult problem: What exactly is a Jew? One answer lies in the desperate struggle of the outsider.

From the very beginning, Woody Allen's films were suffused with a preoccupation of being the outsider. In *Take the Money and Run* (1969) Allen is the misfit, the castoff from society who clumsily turns to the life of crime. As the criminal outsider he is constantly under the threat of discovery and arrest. When he is finally caught and incarcerated, he can earn early parole by taking part in an experimental drug program with a dangerous side effect: He is transformed into the ultimate Jewish outsider, a Chasidic Jew.

*Woody Allen, transformed into the "ultimate Jewish outsider":* Take the Money and Run.

In *Bananas* (1971) Allen's character, Fielding Melish, in an attempt to find meaning and identity, finds himself instead among revolutionary fighters in San Marcos. Here he is definitely outside of his element in a world filled with bearded, dark-skinned men and tall, virile women, and saturated by Christian symbolism. Indeed, Christianity is so pervasive that it has even invaded Melish's subconscious—he is plagued by the odd, Bergman-inspired dream of being borne on a crucifix by flagellant monks.

Melish valiantly attempts to assimilate with the guerrillas, but significantly winds up getting urinated upon when practicing his camouflage. However, in spite of himself, Melish lives up to the myth of the successful Jew and rises to a leadership role. Then, disguised with a beard that eerily echoes his transfiguration into a Chasid, he returns to the United States to curry favor and funds from the government.

Once back in America, Melish cannot maintain his charade for very long and he is unceremoniously unmasked and put on trial. His prosecution quickly turns into a persecution, as two "expert" witnesses broadly justify an assimilated Jew's uneasiness with being discovered. One is a cop, who bluntly lumps in Melish with other "Jewish intellectual crackpots," while the other, Miss America, the epitome of gentile purity, is disarming but no less intolerant. "It's okay," she warns, "to be different, but not too different." The jury finds Melish guilty, but the judge suspends sentencing provided that Melish not move into the judge's neighborhood, an obvious slap at exclusively gentile enclaves.

The extent of the reach of this exclusion is underlined by a mock news bulletin that crawls across the bottom of the screen at the end of the film: The first men on the moon, it reveals, have erected a Protestant-only cafeteria.

Thankfully, segregated neighborhoods are a thing of the past, at least officially. But a Jew, or any outsider for that matter, must still be on guard. When my wife and I first moved into our Gulf Coast neighborhood about five years ago, I was unsettled by a neighbor who noted we were marking a Jewish holiday. "Are you a Hebrew?" he asked, squinting his eyes. "Well . . . I am a Jew," I replied, wondering if I now needed to procure a rather ferocious guard dog for protection. Much to my relief, he was not so much to be feared than avoided. He was a member of a Christian fundamentalist sect that revered "Hebrews" for their part in the story of Christianity, and whenever I subsequently ran into him he would want to explore Scripture with me on the spot, whether we were in the aisle of a grocery store or at a gas station pump. This encounter reminded me of a student I met when I was an undergraduate. Born and raised in the mountains of Pennsylvania, she actually believed that the Jews were a myth of the Bible, an allegorical ancient people whose legacy existed solely to demonstrate particular points in Sunday school lessons and sermons.

In *Sleeper* (1973) Allen confronts this issue in a rather creative way. Just as my schoolmate from Pennsylvania and my neighbor in Florida thought of the Jews as the ancient people of the "Old Testament," Miles Monroe, the protagonist, awakens to find himself out of time and out of step with the world of the future. He is surrounded by those who have been taught to fear contamination by aliens or people like Miles, who follow an ancient and dangerously foreign system of beliefs. As the outsider, Miles futilely attempts to save himself by blending in, this time by masquerading as a mechanized servant. But once again he is discovered and the government sets out to forcibly assimilate him into the prevailing value system. As part of his brainwashing, Miles meets up with a beauty queen, who Allen again portrays as the statuesque gentile vision of what is right and acceptable. To win a pageant one needs to conform to the dominant values and ideals, and Miles is coerced into believing that *he* has won the contest. Reduced to tears, he receives the requisite fur-lined mantle and bouquet, and enters a world of facile people and blind obedience.

With *Annie Hall* (1977), Maurice Yacowar notes that Allen extended his abilities to a more profound place, abandoning parody for a direct voice (Yacowar, 29). Indeed, almost from the very beginning of this film, the theme of the Jewish outsider in contemporary America is presented with little subtlety. For example, Alvy, the protagonist, tells a friend that he believes he has been accused of being a Jew when someone in fact innocently asked him if he had eaten lunch: "Didchoo eat? Jew? No, not did you eat, but jew eat? Jew. You get it? Jew eat?" And later, Alvy explains why the country won't back New York City: "Don't you see? The rest of the country looks upon New York like we're . . . left-wing Communist, Jewish, homosexual, pornographers." The coda to this argument is the most telling, for Alvy admits, "I think of us that way, sometimes."

A funny line, to be sure, but very revealing. We must remember that the entire film is presented as a series of Alvy's recollections as he attempts to "get his mind around" his breakup with Annie. So when Annie sets Alvy up by noting that he would be someone her Grammy would call "a real Jew," and we then see Alvy transformed into a Chasid during the disquieting ham dinner at the Halls, we need to keep in mind that it is not others that see Alvy as the outsider, but that *he* sees himself that way. As Gerald Mast observes, this "is an image of Alvy's own self-consciousness (stemming from) his own insecurities and discomfort" (Mast, 132).

If you are abused long enough and are not given an opportunity to develop a strong sense of self-esteem, you begin to believe that maybe you really are deserving of the abuse, and that maybe there is something to your tormentor's attacks. This thought is reflected in a sentiment of Alvy's, which he voices twice in *Annie Hall*: "I wouldn't want to be a member of a club that would have me as a member."

Another response to the abuse might be an ironic variation of the Freudian concept of identifying with the aggressor. Alvy does this when he meets his first wife and reduces her, as she claims, to the stereotype of a New York Jewish Left-wing Liberal Intellectual, thus both reducing his wife to the stereotype he himself fulfills, and turning that self into a redefined aggressor.

This psychopathology can often lead to extremes of self-degradation, as we see in *Zelig* (1983), in which Allen's chameleon like character wins access to both the Vatican and the Third Reich (Stam, 113). But the mimicry is often incomplete, and the Jew is plagued not only by his own insecurities, but by the continuing fear of discovery as well.

These fears and insecurities achieve their ultimate expression in the Kafkaesque nightmare *Shadows and Fog* (1992). A killer is on the loose and protagonist Kleinman is roused from bed in the middle of the night to take part in "the Plan." But what is the Plan? Everyone assumes Kleinman is on the "inside" and knows it, and he wanders the shadowy, fog-filled streets desperately trying to see where he fits in. Ultimately, the mob turns on Kleinman and begins to hunt him down, for, as Richard Blake so poignantly observes, the ultimate cost of being the outsider is death, a fact the Jews, living in the shadow of the Holocaust, can never forget (Blake, 63).

In both *Annie Hall* and *Manhattan* (1979) Allen's characters are accused of being paranoid, but with such a history of oppression and annihilation, who could find fault in a little Jewish paranoia? Indeed, the Holocaust is an unwelcome poltergeist, haunting even those American Jews who believe their lives were only tangentially touched by this heinous tragedy. For me, a second- generation Jewish-American, a German accent, for example, can stir the oddest knee-jerk reaction of revulsion, mistrust, and fear. The Holocaust, internalized and barely repressed, is hovering just on the other side of consciousness to spew forth at seemingly random times.

Even a cursory look at a number of Allen's films bares witness to this sad and strange phenomenon. Whether it's the swastikas adorning a guest's sweater or a character described as "Mr. White Teeth, Mr. Tall Aryan Nazi Nordic" (*Sleeper*); or California disparaged as a place filled with sycophants who will even stoop to give an award in the name of Adolf Hitler (*Annie Hall*); or Cliff in *Crimes and Misdemeanors* (1989) remembering the day his wife stopped sleeping with him because it happened to fall on Adolf Hitler's birthday; or Ike, in *Manhattan*, revealing that he has never had a relationship that lasted as long as Hitler's and Eva Braun's; or Wagner's music being a touchstone for Nazi sentiments (*Annie Hall* and *Manhattan Murder Mystery* [1993]), an Allen film seemingly will not pass without a reference, no matter how fleeting, to Nazi Germany. Even the Volkswagen Beetle, introduced by Hitler as "the people's car," makes a cameo appearance in *Bananas, Sleeper* and *Annie Hall*.

Pushing my point a bit too much, you may say? I, too, was a proud owner of a Bug in my younger days, but my joy was forever tarnished when a Jewish acquaintance looked askance at my car. "Just what *are* those seats made from?" she asked. It was an awful, ugly thought, but painfully on target in its goal of drawing attention to lamp shades, bars of soap, and window curtains.

When confronted with such a legacy of hate and persecution, where do you turn for comfort? Assimilation had so systematically undermined my beliefs that I could find little comfort in my own culture. Woody Allen recognizes these effects of assimilation in *Annie Hall* in the unique conversation he presents across time and space between the Halls of the 1970s and the Singers of the 1940s. Annie's mother asks Alvy's mother how they will be spending the holidays. Mrs. Singer answers that they will be fasting, and Alvy's father explains that this is to atone for their sins. "I don't understand," Mrs. Hall complains. Alvy's father sheepishly admits, "To tell you the truth, neither do we. "Allen is suggesting here that through assimilation, many American Jews have lost touch with the real meaning behind our customs. Our rituals have become empty and our traditions hollow, thus creating room for ambivalence as depicted in such items as the Christmas tree we see in Alvy's apartment as he breaks up with Annie.

In *Sleeper*, the resistance fighters attempt to reverse Miles's brainwashing by making him relive what they call a major trauma in his life. The trauma is a seder, or the ritual meal that marks the beginning of the Jewish Passover, that took place back in the Brooklyn of Miles' youth. That Allen chose this as a traumatic point calls attention in and of itself to the dilemma of Jewish identity in modern America. However, as the gentile actors struggle comically with their Hebrew and Yiddish malapropisms, Miles regresses even further and takes on the persona of the quintessential outsider, Blanche Dubois from *A Streetcar Named Desire*, a character painfully alienated not only from the whole of modern society, but from her own people as well. Blanche is suspended, as are many assimilated people, between the old and the new, and is truly neither here nor there.

The vast majority of the Jews I knew while I was growing up seemed to have a better sense of who they were than I did. They spent more time at the synagogue, went to Jewish camps, and belonged to Jewish organizations. I was never afforded these opportunities, which probably accounts for my discomfort among them as well as among gentiles. The older I grew, the more I sensed something was missing, so I set out to discover what it was.

An obvious course was to reject religion outright and play the youthful iconoclast to the hilt. I didn't need any prescribed system of beliefs. Hadn't the great philosophers of the late nineteenth and early twentieth century declared God dead?

We can see this same response in Allen's earlier films, which befit a younger, more invulnerable person. The premise of *Sleeper* is a wonderful example. The Great Leader (God) is dead and has been dead for some time. Those in control are convinced that if word leaks out of His demise there would be chaos and, worse yet, they would lose their power. The system, then, depends not so much on the existence of The Great Leader, but rather on the illusion of His presence.

If one desires to condemn religious systems in general, one need not look any further than Catholicism, one of the most complex religious systems of all time. Allen seems to save a special barbed enmity for the Catholic church, which he construes as Big Business. The conclusion of *Bananas* is interrupted by a commercial in which a priest pitches God's choice of cigarettes. Allen perceives the act of confession as rote and mechanized, as in *Sleeper*, in which Miles, after his brainwashing, attends an automated confessional and receives a Kewpie doll for absolution. The film maker portrays Catholics as fairly simpleminded, because they unquestionably follow doctrine and the concept of papal infallibility; in *Manhattan* Ike reduces Catholics to the level of mindless birds when he observes that they mate for life like pigeons, and the Pope's infallibility is linked with the computer that has run amok in *2001*. The Catholic church is portrayed as corrupt and an instrument of evil, and we are reminded in *Shadows and Fog* of its complicity in the Holocaust when Kleinman (played by Woody Allen) stops in at the Catholic Church to offer a $650.00 donation. Kleinman soon becomes aware that the priest and a Nazi-regime member are drawing up a list of Jewish victims.

In *Interiors* (1978), cathedrals, the monumental symbols of Christianity, are mere edifices, architecture to be admired as pieces of art, but not as places of worship. They are cold, cavernous spaces, void of any solace or love. This idea is underscored as Eve's last hopes of reconciliation with Arthur are cruelly dashed in a vast empty cathedral.

Allen certainly does not feel that the answer lies in the faith of his parents. In the first half of this century, liberal Judaism embraced the insights of twentieth-century science and began to move away from a literal interpretation of an all-powerful God. As the horrors of the Holocaust came to light in the middle of the century, the American Jewish movement continued to move not so much away from God as towards an emphasis on the traditions of social and individual responsibility.

In both *Hannah and Her Sisters* (1986) and *Crimes and Misdemeanors* (1989) characters ask the unanswerable question of where God was during the horror of Auschwitz. Cliff in the latter movie suggests that, assuming the absence of God, the individual is forced to take on the responsibilities of his actions. But the terrible burden of this responsibility is voiced by the almost paralyzed Joey in *Interiors*, when she asks, "How do you figure out the right thing to do? How do you know?"

Finding the basis for an answer can be daunting for some, but for others it is a simple matter of rationalization. For *Crimes and Misdemeanor's* Judah Rosenthal, whose status and security in life are preserved by the contracted murder of his mistress, God becomes a luxury he simply cannot afford. With time he awakens to birds singing once again, and his guilt ridden conscience seems to adjust; his father had always warned him that the eyes of God see all, but if the all-seeing, all-knowing God is powerless, what then? End of story.

Contemporary Judaism asks us to consider how we will be remembered before we act. Indeed, one aspect of the Judaic concept of the afterlife is that we will live on in the good deeds we perform in life. For Ike, in *Manhattan*, who stands accused of being too self-righteous, this is a lifelong struggle. In response to Yale's argument that humans are weak and not God-like, Ike's response sounds suspiciously like this basic tenet of contemporary Judaism. Pointing to the skeleton in the classroom in which they are arguing, he asks "What will future generations . . . say about us? . . . It's very important to have . . . some kind of personal integrity . . . . Someday we're gonna be like him . . . and I wanna be sure [that] when I . . . thin out that I'm . . . well thought of."

During the past twenty-five years, many young assimilated Jewish Americans, who, as Mickey describes it in *Hannah and Her Sisters*, "got off on the wrong foot" with their Judaism, began turning to other religions and philosophies; we had drifted so far from home that we felt we could no longer find safe harbor there. Some chose conversion. I had a cousin who became a Jew for Jesus; a friend's brother became a Southern Baptist. In *Interiors* the Christian Eve turns, as her daughter Renata calls it, to "the Jesus Christ nonsense." Late one night, as Eve watches her televangelist, we hear the televised story of Roy Schwartz, a "Hebrew" who has obviously accepted Jesus and who is there to explain how the Jews fit in to God's plan today. Mickey in *Hannah and Her Sisters*, after dodging a terminal diagnosis, begins his quest for meaning through religion. One of the religions he approaches is Catholicism. He goes out and obtains his interpretations of the external trappings of this religion (a crucifix, a picture of Jesus, a loaf of Wonder Bread), but in the end Catholicism's "die now pay later" philosophy doesn't intellectually appeal to him.

When I was in college, I flirted for a time with Eastern religions, yoga, and transcendental meditation, but Allen shows little tolerance for what he considers mere fads. "I can never subscribe to a religion that advertises in *Popular Mechanics*," Alvy explains in *Annie Hall*. But what *does* he believe in? Alvy describes life as a bleak existence separated into the horrible and the miserable, and he displays, as does Mickey in *Hannah*, an obsessive fear of death. And who fears death more than someone who doesn't have, if not the answer, then at least some faith?

Seeking religion is not so much an intellectual exercise as an emotional journey. This basic struggle between the intellect and the emotions is explored in *Manhattan*. Ike and Mary are shadowy figures wandering through the wonders of the universe re-created in a planetarium and museum. Mary becomes overwhelmed with the availability of information at the museum. She sighs over how she has a million facts at her fingertips

*"Nothing worth knowing can be understood by the mind." Ike and Mary (Woody Allen, Diane Keaton) in* Manhattan.

and Ike responds by saying that "they don't mean a thing . . . because nothing worth knowing can be understood by the mind." Mickey echoes these sentiments in *Hannah and Her Sisters*. After reading the great philosophers, he's come to the depressing conclusion that, in the final analysis, they don't know any more than *he* does about the meaning of life. In both these instances Allen's protagonists recognize that the ultimate religious commitment requires that great leap of faith, but they can't quite make the jump themselves. In *Interiors* Allen seems to be suggesting that faith can be found more in the emotions. As the lively character Pearl puts it, if you cannot know the unknowable, then you just have to "feel it."

When I got married I could have very easily turned my back on my Jewish roots and raised my children outside of any particular faith. But I was plagued by the nagging feeling that the Jewish people had withstood more than five thousand years of persecution from without, yet here I was systematically undermining the religion from within. Who was I to say what was right or wrong? My children should have a firm sense of who they are as Jews in America, and the hope and belief that there really is a God. As I set out to discover what being a Jew actually entailed, I surprisingly found what was there all along: an emotional and spiritual home not only for my children, but for myself as well.

In Allen's latest films we can see that he has been struggling towards some of these same conclusions. Although we cannot find an affirmation of Judaism, we can, for example, detect at the end of *Shadows and Fog* an almost wistful desire for the ability to accept the illusion of God, an idea suggested much earlier in *Sleeper*, as Kleinman escapes death through the illusionist's magic mirror.

In the same film, Irmy, the sword-swallower (played by Mia Farrow), and the clown, Paul (played by John Malkovich), find renewal and hope, as I have, through a child. But children are not just the hope for what may come; they *are* the reaffirmation of the future itself. The narration that supports the closing images of *Crimes and Misdemeanors* perhaps best exemplifies this emerging optimism: "Most humans keep trying and find joy in simple things like family, work, and in the hope that future generations might understand more."

And perhaps in Allen's future works, he too might come to understand more and ultimately resolve his cultural and religious ambiguity, as I have in my life's journey. I cannot say that my perception of myself as the perennial outsider has vanished completely, but there is something to be said for the old adage that there is safety in numbers.

## Works Cited

Woody Allen, *Four Films of Woody Allen* (New York: Random House, 1982).

Richard Blake,"Looking for God: Profane and Sacred in the Films of Woody Allen," *Journal of Popular Film and Television* 19 (1991), 58–66.

Eric Lax, *Woody Allen* (New York: Alfred Knopf, 1991).

Gerald Mast, "Woody Allen: The Neurotic Jew as American Clown," in Sarah Cohen, ed., *Jewish Wry* (Bloomington: Indiana University Press, 1987), 125–40.

Nancy Pogel, *Woody Allen* (Boston: Twayne, 1987).

Robert Stam, "A Tale of Two Cities: Cultural Polyphony and Ethnic Transformation," *East West Film Journal* 3 (1988), 105–116.

Maurice Yacowar, "Woody Allen in the 80's," *Post-Script* 6 (1987), 29–42.

# Self-Directed Stereotyping in the Films of Cheech Marin

## Christine List (1994)

In the late seventies and early eighties, Richard "Cheech" Marin and his partner Thomas Chong created more than a half dozen comedy films.[1] Yet it was not until 1987, when Marin went solo to write, direct, and star in *Born in East L.A.*, that any serious study was done of his work.[2] There are two probable reasons for this lack of interest. First, Marin was not credited as a co-director in the earlier films. That fact may have discouraged film scholars from looking at Marin's productions because we tend to privilege an auteur analysis. In 1988, however, Marin revealed in an interview that he did indeed co-direct the films credited to Chong.[3] When one considers that Cheech and Chong worked by improvisation, the conclusion that Marin exerted considerable influence over these films is a reasonable one, prompting inquiry as to how these movies represent a Chicano perspective.

A second reason why film scholars may have shied away from the Cheech and Chong movies is that the Chicano stereotypes in these films appear to be derogatory and counter to the progressive nationalist goals which Chicano artists and activists had outlined for *El Movimiento*.[4] Chicano film scholarship has tended to ground itself in the strategy of unmasking negative stereotypes while affirming positive counterimages. The position has been a necessary one given the long history of anti-Mexican sentiment in the U.S. Nevertheless, this approach, when applied to the feature narrative, favors films with naturalized characters who have complex psychological explanations for their behavior. Marin's slapstick, one-dimensional Chicano character in the Cheech and Chong films contradicts that aesthetic.

To evaluate Marin's contribution to Chicano cinema, it is necessary to look at how ingroup-created stereotypes might combat negative images imposed from the outside. This strategy of self-directed stereotyping has been used previously by the Chicano Theatre Movement to criticize assimilationism. Other ethnic minorities, such as African Americans and Jewish Americans have also used negative stereotypes as cultural weapons. With an adequate theory of ethnic humor it is possible to assess Marin's Chicano doper films as actually constructing a subtle critique of ethnocentrism.

### Self-derogatory Humor and the Ethnic Stereotype

Marin's films, aimed at a general audience, have been financially successful at the box office. *Up in Smoke* was the highest grossing comedy of 1978. Marin states that his films enjoy such popularity because his style of comedy makes a positive moral statement by bringing up important social issues beneath the mask of humor. "I've always said that my method is to slip the message into your coffee. You don't taste it. It goes down smooth, but later you feel the effect."[5]

The Chicano character Marin plays in the Cheech and Chong films is a doper who has some street smarts. The opening sequence in *Up in Smoke* establishes the character type he will depict in all his early movies. He awakens on his living room couch surrounded by a hoard of children watching cartoons; and, still drowsy, stumbles to a filthy bathroom. Too late, he notices that he's been urinating in the hamper instead of the toilet. Next we see him saunter out of the house. A couple of other Chicanos hang out in the front yard cutting hair. He crosses the street and admires his ride, a big old Chevy. The interior has a low-rider look to it: fringe balls, stenciled windows, chain fashioned steering wheel and crushed velvet interior seat covers. Cheech leans back in the driver's seat, a cool *vato* grin pasted across his face, and slinks ever so slowly away.

As he cruises down the California freeway we discover that this lazy, dirty, lowriding Chicano with too many relatives is also an over-sexed macho. When he comes upon two blondes sunbathing by the side of the road, he crosses into oncoming traffic, but the blondes refuse his offer of a good time. Undaunted, he soon spies two giant breasts down the road. Cheech calls out with lascivious intent, "Hey bend over, I'll drive you home, baby," and heads recklessly across traffic once again.

In these opening scenes, Marin paints a picture of the Chicano, which, at first glance, affirms preconceived negative stereotypes of the Mexican American.[6] This depiction of self-derogatory images by an ethnic group has long been understood as a manifestation of self-hatred.[7] The pessimistic position has been premised on a reductionist interpretation of all ethnic humor (both inwardly and outwardly directed) as social aggression. In most studies of self-derogatory ethnic humor in Jewish and African American communities, the aggression was viewed as evidence of masochistic personality disorders.

Recent studies, however, have argued that self-derogatory ethnic jokes operate within marginalized cultures as sophisticated means of self-affirmation. Ethnographer E. Oring asserts that the masochistic theory of humor does not distinguish between a simple communicative act and artistic expression. He adds that ethnic jokes are primarily structures of ideas to be perceived intellectually, which means they are based on the creation and perception of an appropriate incongruity or irony.[8]

A central question one must consider when evaluating Marin's use of long-standing Mexican stereotypes is whether he establishes the appropriate aesthetic distance in his films, thereby inviting the viewer to look critically at the stereotypes. Freud, in *Jokes and Their Relation to the Unconscious*, maintained that one way a joke teller succeeds in using self-derogatory caricatures without the listener feeling superior is to make sure the listener knows that the joker has only been pretending to ridicule him or herself.[9] If one looks closely at the visual and narrative style of the Cheech and Chong films, it becomes evident that Cheech and Chong delineate the text as a make-believe space.

Narrative structure in Cheech and Chong films is based on a series of ridiculous scenes clustered about an improbable premise. Plots in these films are practically nonexistent. Just as with a Three Stooges or Marx Brothers film, the viewer of a Cheech and Chong film does not go to see the movie expecting a complicated plot, but rather anticipates a string of cleverly done slapstick sketches.

The opening sequence establishes a cartoonish frame of reference for Cheech and Chong films. *Cheech and Chong's Next Movie*, for example, opens with Cheech and his partner Tommy Chong stealing a garbage can full of gasoline. They decide to pour it in their gas tank directly from the can, spilling gasoline and garbage all over. They pretend no one can see them doing this, although they are at a busy intersection. Saturated with petrol, they hop in the car and speed away. Cheech tells Chong, "Oh shit man, I'm

*Negative stereotypes?: Thomas Chong and Cheech Marin (top);* Born in East L.A. *(bottom).*

going to be late for work again, man. That's the fifth time I've been late this week, and it's only Tuesday, man." Then Chong lights up a joint and the interior of the car explodes. In the next shot, the two are covered with cinders, clothes are shredded, and eyebrows are seared. Their appearance resembles Wile E. Coyote after an explosive encounter with the Road Runner. The clownish tone serves as a barometer for the rest of the film.

Mise-en-scène in these movies is also magnified as Cheech translates stereotypes into visual hyperbole. In *Cheech and Chong's Next Movie* the two dopers live in a "vintage ghetto" house. Graffiti decorates both exterior and interior. Trash clutters the lawn, and a property condemnation notice covers the front door. In contrast, we are shown the "Anglo" neighbor's garage neatly painted and obsessively organized so that each object has a hook where it must be placed. By bringing together stereotypes associated with the Anglo suburbs and Chicano *barrio*, the two set designs reinforce the cartoonish quality of the film, encouraging the viewer against reading the stereotypes as realistic.

## Strategies of Diffusion

Any ethnic identity can fall prey to stereotyping in a Cheech and Chong film. Chong, who is actually of Chinese Canadian descent, usually plays a nonspecific Anglo hippie character. The doper personality he depicts is just as crude, dirty, oversexed, and unemployable as the Cheech character. Even more so than Cheech, Chong is obsessed with smoking and selling drugs. In *Up in Smoke* his parents are cast as rich WASPS who threaten to put Chong to work for the United Fruit Company (a corporation infamous for oppressing Latin American workers) unless he gets a job. Chong, clad in dirty jeans, long hair secured by a bandanna, and wire frame glasses, gives his dad the finger and heads out in search of some weed.

In *Up in Smoke*, other Anglo, Black and Japanese American characters are humorously presented as gross stereotypes. Stacey Keach plays a narcotics detective. His burr haircut, thinly cropped mustache, and tightly fitted polyester suit accent his patronizing, authoritarian personality. Another ethnic character is Curtis, Cheech's jive talking African American neighbor and a Hollywood-style hustler who dresses like a pimp. There is also a Japanese American reporter in the film, predictably named Toyota Kawasaki. And, in *Things are Tough All Over*, Chong plays an Arab who loses his temper at the slightest provocation, causing him to swear murderous revenge in every scene.

When one ethnic group shows another in a disparaging light it is usually taken as a sign of hostile aggression.[10] But if all characters in the films are exposed as having some sort of ethnicity which can be subject to equal ridicule, the negative effects of stereotyping are altered. This is especially true when Anglo characters become ethnicized through exaggerated speech, costuming, and behavioral traits as in the case of Chong and the detective. They are shown to be just as vulnerable to becoming the butt of an ethnic slur as the other "ethnic" characters in the films. In this context the Chicano stereotype is revealed to be as overgeneralized as the Anglo type.

Research on ethnic stereotypes shows that all cultures depict outgroups as dirty, vile, and uncivilized. This of course helps justify oppression of struggling minority ethnic groups.[11] If one looks at the various stigmas attributed to minorities in the United States, it is evident that each group has been similarly characterized by the majority as unclean and barbaric.

Scatological joking is a comic strategy found in the Cheech and Chong films that succeeds in diffusing this stigma of depravity and baseness associated through stereotypes. In *Up in Smoke*, Cheech gets the runs after eating Mexican food. He hurriedly searches for a john, holding his buttocks and muttering, "Come on cheeks, stay together." In *Cheech and Chong's Next Movie*, Chong twice tricks Cheech into drinking from a jar of urine. Later, Chong urinates out the bathroom window onto their Anglo neighbor's bald head. In *Still Smokin'*, Chong performs a comic sketch in which he imitates a dog in the act of defecation.

In *Jokes and Their Relation to the Unconscious*, Freud noted that jokes which rely on bodily degradation for their humor succeed because the listeners recognize that all humanity is equally subject to the same bodily functions. He interpreted grotesque humor in the same manner he explained the obscene joke. Such jokes work by unmasking inhibitions imposed upon the listener. In the case of the Cheech and Chong films, the precarious nature of white Protestant civility is belied by the actions of Chong's Anglo characters. Juxtaposing the baseness of the Anglo and Chicano characters universalizes the dirty Mexican stereotype.

Hollywood has traditionally shown Mexican male sexuality as either perverted or exotic and has generally disapproved of romantic liaisons between Mexican male and Anglo female. Cheech cleverly plays with the stereotype of the oversexed Latin. His character obsessively offers himself to women by making crude statements such as his comment to Chong about a girlfriend in *Up in Smoke*, "I hope she hasn't eaten. I got something for her. Tube steak smothered in underwear."

In an ironic twist, most women enthusiastically accept Cheech's sexual overtures rather than being offended by his bravado. Cheech discovers, to his surprise, that these women are sexually freer and more insatiable than he. In *Nice Dreams*, former girlfriend Donna invites Cheech and Chong up to her apartment to have sex with both of them. In *Still Smokin'*, the Dutch chambermaid uses both men and then sends them crawling away begging for mercy. The scene is intercut with stock footage of rhinos, turtles, and monkeys having intercourse. The film insinuates that Cheech can be considered perverted only if all of nature can be rendered unnatural. Any hint at violation of the women is dispelled because the women are eager and aggressive instigators. They are untainted by false conceptions of Chicano sexual stereotypes (rapist, bandido, gangster), forcing us to see these stereotypes in an ironic light.

Disrespect for authority and the law was attributed to the Mexican American personality and regarded as a cultural flaw. Hollywood films again communicated this through the stereotypes of the bandido, greaser, and gangster. Marin turns the stigma into a positive trait that the audience can identify with by molding his character into a type of trickster.[12] In *Cheech and Chong's Next Movie*, Cheech sneaks off a movie set with his boss's van by pretending not to understand English very well. In *Up in Smoke*, Cheech resorts to stereotype in order to evade the narcotics detective when both end up in the men's room. Cheech plays the Mexican buffoon, making some silly references to his own penis. When he leaves we find out that he was actually urinating on the detective's leg. We are gratified at this clever mode of simultaneous masquerade and revenge.

Freud has noted that rebellion against authority embedded in the hostile joke marks a liberation from its pressure: "We laugh at them (rebellious jokes) because we count rebellion as merit."[13] Cheech's rebellion becomes very pointed in *Up in Smoke* when he sabotages a racist movie production by wandering on to a Hollywood set of a typical Chicano gang picture. The exploitation movie's antagonist is dressed in a zoot suit and holds a knife to the neck of a terrified white starlet. The zoot suiter is encouraged to exaggerate his villainy by a bigoted director and his crew. The scene is interrupted when Cheech "innocently" advises a confused actor from back stage to make an early entrance by crashing through a wall of the set. The production is forced to close for the rest of the day.

Cultural critic Sandy Cohen in her study of Jewish humor in the U.S. asserts that by employing the same stereotypes used against the ethnic minority, the comedian can confront the fact that the dominant culture does not see either the real ethnic culture or its resistance. Old world folklore of Black and Jewish immigrants provides numerous examples: "Thus we have the Jewish *schlimazel* waiter who because he is 'inept' 'accidentally' spills hot soup on the patronizing customer, or the slave, who because he is 'incompetent' burns down massa's barn."[14]

Marin's films use similar tactics. In the Cheech and Chong movies, ethnicity is worn like a glaring emblem of difference. With the underlying self-consciousness of the trickster, Cheech's character conveys the image of the Chicano as someone who knows he is stereotyped and always tries to resist by showing he is aware of the typing. This is strongly illustrated in *Cheech and Chong's Next Movie* when Cheech sings the lyrics he's composed to a Mexican folk melody. He refers to the ballad as a "protest tune":

"Mexican Americans don't like to get into gang fights. They like flowers and music and white girls named Debbie too. Mexican Americans don't like to go to movies where the dude has to wear contacts to make his blue eyes brown, and don't it make your brown eyes blue."

The lyrics make a direct reference to Robbie Benson's stereotypical performance of the Latino youth in *Walk Proud* (1979), an urban violence/exploitation film which was met by considerable protests in the Chicano community. The intertextual comment positions Marin as a self-conscious "Chicano" filmmaker/persona, albeit under the guise of doper humor and understatement.

## Marin and Raza Cinema

In terms of style, the Cheech and Chong films fit within a comic tradition of slapstick or bawdy humor incorporated by the Chicano teatros, most notably El Teatro Campesino founded by Luis Valdez in 1965. The Teatro produced humorous morality plays called *actos* utilizing broadly played stereotypes of themselves as well as Anglos to preach solidarity and pride among Chicanos. One common stereotype employed by Valdez was the pachuco or streetwise Chicano youth. This persona started out as Johnny Pachuco in the acto *Los Vendidos* but later grew into El Pachuco, a complex mythological tragihero of Valdez's play and film *Zoot Suit* (1981).

When we compare Marin's streetwise doper with Valdez' pachucos, the differences in political messages of the two Chicano filmmakers becomes more apparent. Valdez created a character that was socially embedded in the Chicano community. He showed us that El Pachuco's identity was formed as a result of confrontation with racist social structures existing since the European invasion and conquest of Aztlán. For Valdez, the gang member becomes a symbolic Aztec warrior, an instrument for channeling political awareness to his audience.

Marin's street character, on the other hand, does not identify with the *barrio* or gang.

He mainly cruises in the Anglo world with his Anglo cohort. His enemies and detractors, though obviously racist, do not stir up anger and violence in him, nor do they revive any primordial identity or consciousness. His sarcasm, unlike El Pachuco's, is nonthreatening. In the end, he doesn't have to take a stand in these films, nor would he want to.

This is not to say that one image of the *vato* (dude) is more valuable than the other. Many critics have pointed out the dangers of adopting a mythological vision of identity. They argue that myth obscures history and sometimes encourages a utopian vision that can lull political movements into inaction. But there are also advocates of establishing a mythic identity for its ability to inspire a community in the search for its true cultural roots.[15]

In comparing Marin's *vato* to Valdez's *pachuco* I do not imply that Marin is effacing his own ethnicity or sidestepping all issues of Chicano identity. To the contrary, in the Cheech and Chong films, Marin marks himself as Chicano in a very self-conscious way. He associates himself with contemporary low rider culture, speaks *caló* (Chicano slang) and dresses in the traditional uniform of the *cholo* (contemporary term for *pachuco*): khakis, suspenders, a Pendleton plaid shirt and stocking cap.

The comedy in his films depends on foregrounding ethnicity as Marin forces Chicano and non-Chicano viewers alike to recognize his otherness. In many respects, Marin's humor is similar in function to jokes told by Chicanos about Mexican folk medicine. These jokes center on the character of the *curandero* (folk healer) whose treatments are often portrayed as absurd and lewd. But while the *curandero* figure is ridiculed for an outdated reliance on indigenous beliefs, the jokes also expose the *gringo* health care system as equally inadequate. Américo Paredes remarks on the double nature of these jokes: "In satirizing of folk medicine and *curandero* belief tales, they express a mocking rejection of Mexican folk culture; in their expression of resentment towards American culture, they show a strong sense of identification with Mexican folk traditions."[16]

Marin's humor is likewise double-edged, oscillating between assimilation and separatism. In *Cheech and Chong's Nice Dreams,* Cheech finally gets rich by selling dope. Living the good life, he has a mansion on a beach front populated by topless blond sunbathers. He arrogantly jokes about becoming a sun king (an allusion to the Aztec god central to Chicano nationalism) who throws joints to the natives. Although he dresses in the casual attire of a successful California capitalist, Cheech's character still falls back on his ethnic ways. From his mansion he orders four bottles of "fussy pussy" while he cooks tortillas to make some "Mexican pizza." Later, Cheech loses all his wealth after accepting a bad check from an Anglo who agrees to launder the drug money. In the final scene, Cheech and Chong are forced to take jobs as male exotic dancers, ironically calling their act "the sun kings in paradise."

Cheech's naive desire to fit into the capitalist mold as an ethnic results in his downfall and humiliation. The humorous effect of this comic situation is similar to the way Paredes says the *curandero* jests worked. "It releases a complicated set of conflicting emotions ranging from exasperation to affection in respect to the unacculturated Mexican American."[17]

In *Cheech and Chong's Next Movie,* Marin looks inwardly at his community in a dream sequence in which Cheech appears dressed as an Aztec priest. He approaches his girlfriend Donna costumed as a dead Indian maiden awaiting sacrifice on a Nahuatl temple monument. Cheech, with salacious desire, feels her breasts and prepares to rape the lifeless body. The scene suggests the religious ceremonies of the Aztecs were actually occasions for male perversion. By challenging this symbol of Chicano identity, the icon of manhood, Marin calls into question the sexism imbedded within the revival of Aztec heritage in the Chicano Art Movement. As William W. Cook notes, "Satire is a double-edged sword. If it is an instrument for attacking the enemy, it is also an instrument for keeping the tribe in line."[18] In this case, self-derogatory ethnic stereotypes serve as an internal monitor for the community as well as an indictment of falsehoods imposed from the outside.[19]

## Conclusion

El Teatro Campesino embraced the image of the *pachuco* (coded as gangster by Anglo media) and transformed him into an heroic symbol of Chicano identity. In mainstream Hollywood films, Cheech Marin presented a de-politicized pachuco with many of the same negative traits which have been attributed to Native Mexicans in the United States for centuries. Marin's films, however, do not project a masochistic or demeaning image because humor works to contextualize the stereotypes. Since all ethnic groups, including Anglos, are typed in equally absurd ways, Marin's broadly drawn comic technique forces the audience to consider that ethnic stereotypes are overgeneralizations. His trickster antics appeal to the viewer as Cheech subverts authority figures and institutions like the Hollywood movie industry that he himself operates within. Self-derogatory humor also provides the means for looking critically at the Chicano community by comparing traditional values with new problems.

Groups that have been targets of racial stereotyping have always been faced with the need to generate positive counterimages with their art. Sometimes this results in a kind of "image policing" by artists and critics who are quick to condemn any type of negative character depictions by ethnic artists.[20] Cheech Marin's films show that an ethnic director can take a negative stereotype and, through humor, expose the stereotype as racist (among other things), thereby initiating the process of diffusing its significance for a general audience.

## Notes

1. *Up in Smoke* (1978), *Cheech and Chong's Next Movie* (1980), *Cheech and Chong's Nice Dreams* (1981), *Cheech and Chong Still Smokin'* (1983). They also starred in and wrote *Things Are Tough All Over* (1982) and *The Corsican Brothers* (1984).

2. Rosa Linda Fregoso, "Born in East L.A. and the Politics of Representation," *Cultural Studies* 4.3 (October 1990), 264–280; Eduardo Tafoya, "*Born in East L.A.*: Cheech as the Chicano Moses," *Journal of Popular Culture* 26:4 (1993), 123–29; and Chon Noriega, "Café Oralé: Narrative Structure in *Born in East L.A.,*" *Tonantzin* 8.1 (Feb. 1991), 17–18.

3. Dennis West and Gary Crowdus, "Cheech Cleans Up His Act," *Cineaste* 16: 3 (1988), 37.

4. See, for example, "El Plan Espiritual de Aztlán," reprinted in Rudolfo Anaya and Francisco Lomelí, eds., *Aztlán: Essays on the Chicano Homeland* (Albuquerque: Academia/El Norte Publications, 1989), 1–5; and "El Plan de Santa Barbara," reprinted in Carlos Muñoz, Jr., *Youth, Identity, Power: The Chicano Movement* (London: Verso, 1989), 191–202. For an overview of current political thought among Chicano artists see special issue of *Imagine: International Journal of Chicano Poetry Journal* 3, 1 & 2 (Summer-Winter, 1986).

5. Crowdus and West, "Cheech Cleans Up His Act," 37.

6. For an overview of stereotypes of the Mexican American in Hollywood films consult: Charles Ramírez Berg, "Stereotyping in Films in General and of the Hispanic in Particular," *The Howard*

*Journal of Communications* 2:3 (Summer 1990), 286–300; Gary Keller, "The Image of the Mexican in Mexico, the United States and Chicano Cinema: An Overview," in Gary Keller, ed., *Chicano Cinema: Research, Reviews and Resources* (Binghamton: Bilingual Review/Press, 1985), 13–59; and Arthur Pettit, *Images of the Mexican American in Fiction and Film* (College Station: Texas A & M University Press, 1980).

7.  For a summary of research based on this approach, consult Mahadev Apte, *Humor and Laughter: An Anthropological Approach* (Ithaca: Cornell University Press, 1985).

8.  E. Oring, "Everything is a Shade of Elephant: An Alternative to a Psychoanalysis of Humor," *New York Folklore* 1 (1973), 149–159.

9.  Sigmund Freud, *Jokes and Their Relation to the Unconscious* (New York: Penguin, 1960), 148.

10. Apte, 42.

11. Apte, 108.

12. There is a also a link between Marin's Chicano stereotype and the Sixties counterculture, especially in the way Cheech's character taps into the "Question Authority" attitude of the time.

13. Freud, 111.

14. Sandy Cohen, "Racial and Ethnic Humor in the United States," *Amerika Studien/American Studies* 30 (1985), 204.

15. The coexistence of works by Valdez and Marin establishes a pop culture dialectic between these two essential views of the role of myth. For a deeper understanding of both views consult Rudolfo Anaya and Francisco Lomelí, eds., *Aztlán: Essays on the Chicano Homeland* (Albuquerque: Academia/El Norte Publications, 1989).

16. Américo Paredes, "Folk Medicine and Intercultural Jest," L.I. Durán, and H.R. Bernard, eds., *Introduction to Chicano Studies* (New York: Macmillan, 1973), 271.

17. Ibid.

18. William W. Cook, "Change the Joke and Slip the Yoke," *Journal of Ethnic Studies* 6:1, 113.

19. José Limón has done a study of *agringado* joking—jokes made by Texas Mexicans which poke fun at Mexican Americans who by Tex Mex standards are too "americanized." He states, "Texas-Mexican joking is not an exercise in self hatred; rather it takes account of societal differences in expressive ways that strengthen group identity and pride." José E. Limón, "*Agringado* Joking in Texas Mexican Society: Folklore and Differential Identity," in Ricardo Romo and Raymund Paredes, eds., *New Directions in Chicano Scholarship* (University of California Press, 1978), 48.

20. Consult Salim Muwakkil, "Spike Lee and the Image Police," *Cineaste* 17: 4 (1989), 35, for an explanation of how this problem has affected African American filmmakers.

# Notes on *Bamboozled*

**Gregg Rickman** (2001)

The face sings, alone
at the top of the body.
—"A Poem for Willie Best," Imamu Amiri Baraka (1964).
I hopes I shall hab de honor ob displeasing you all.
—*Life of Jim Crow* (circa 1830, quoted by Lhamon, 186).

Spike Lee's feature film *Bamboozled* was widely criticized upon its release in October 2000, even by some African American critics, who regretted its revival of forgotten imagery or felt his indictment of modern popular culture was too sweeping: Lee is making "minstrel arrests," claimed the African American film critic Wesley Morris. ("Lee has set himself up to be the biggest Big Brother of all—which is just what black people need: another cop.")

Nonetheless *Bamboozled* is an important film, astute in its argument that blackface minstrel imagery is still called on today by contemporary filmmakers. A well-received drama released the same month as *Bamboozled*, Mimi Leder's *Pay It Forward*, employs a caricatured jive-talking do-ragged African American criminal (David Ramsey) in a key supporting part. Although arguably a failure in many aspects of its dramaturgy—its third act collapses into a melodrama that seems at least at first to have little to do with its pro-claimed theme—*Bamboozled* raises so many vital questions relating to ethnic stereotypes in comedy that some comment on the film seems called for.

Lee is merciless in his critique of the blackface tradition, editing in clips from classic American films throughout his work and closing *Bamboozled* with a montage of images drawn from those films (freely intercutting such white actors as Al Jolson, Judy Garland and Mickey Rooney in minstrel-style blackface with clips of black character actors like Hattie McDaniel in stereotyped parts). Indeed, Lee's sell-out producer Pierre Delacroix (Daymon Wayans) assigns the names "Mantan" and "Sleep 'n' Eat" to the street per-formers (Manray/Savion Glover and Womack/Tommy Davidson) he hires to act out his minstrel TV show, after the 1930s-40s character actors Mantan Moreland and Willie "Sleep 'n' Eat" Best.

Two questions arise: is Lee's critique of the blackface minstrel tradition a valid one? And is his equation of the performances of comics like Moreland and Best to that tradi-tion fair? For if so, it follows that his criticism of African American images in contempo-rary comedy is unanswerable, and in interviews Lee has extended his criticism to include videos made by gangsta rappers, sitcoms like *The Secret Diary of Desmond Pfeif-fer* and the Eddie Murphy-sponsored *The PJs*, as well as many modern films. (Within *Bamboozled*, the character Sloan Hopkins/Jada Pinkett Smith, researching blackface roles for her boss Pierre, has a videotape of the 1995 feature *Friday*, starring Ice Cube and Chris Tucker, prominently on display in her apartment.)

Lee presents minstrel show imagery (including that of the show recreated within the film, "Mantan: The New Millenium Minstrel Show") as unrelievedly negative. Some his-

*Womack/"Sleep 'n' Eat" (Tommy Davidson) and Manray/"Mantan" (Savion Glover) as the minstrels of* Bamboozled.

torians disagree; there is a long-standing debate on the topic. Eric Lott, in *Love and Theft: Blackface Minstrelsy and the American Working Class* (1995) notes a tradition dating to Constance Rourke's *American Humor* (1931) of "celebrating minstrelsy for its 'blackness,' seeing the phenomenon as a public forum for slave culture which might have liberating effects" (7). More recently Robert Toll (in 1974's *Blacking Up*) and others have ventured similar positions, which Lott finds "unhistorical" although even harsh critics of the phenomenon such as LeRoi Jones (Amiri Baraka) were noting as early as *Blues People* (1963) that while "in one sense the colored minstrel was poking fun at himself . . . in another and probably more profound sense he was poking fun at the white man" (85).

More recently, W.T. Lhamon Jr., in *Raising Cain* (1998), argued that the original blackface performances of the early nineteenth century "moved toward cross-racial affiliation" bespeaking "a new underclass alliance" in a series of plays about "bursting bondage . . . the moment that knotted together the white and black youths in the audience" (150-54). Lhamon links "the commercial phenomenon of blackface performance with clowning and trickster traditions in Africa as well as in early North America" (179), connecting Legba—the limping spirit of the crossroads in African myth—to the "insistent limp" of Jim Crow performances of the nineteenth century which in turn he finds carried over into the dancing styles of Little Richard Penniman and Chuck Berry in the 1950s. Similarly, Lhamon relates specific moves in minstrelsy to the dancing styles on display in videos made by Michael Jackson and M.C. Hammer. (Lee's stated connection of the minstrel show tradition and modern rap musicians—represented in *Bamboozled* by the character "Big Black Africa"/Mos Def—is thus confirmed.) To Lhamon, "If one grants Jim Crow the licensing, backward talk of a trickster . . . he represented (a) cross-racial affiliation which was repellent to many people in the nineteenth century and seems hopelessly romantic to many people of all hues and persuasions at the end of the twentieth" (191).

It is easy to speculate that Spike Lee, who has consistently opposed interracial relationships[1] and who here ridicules crosscultural studies (an offensively caricatured Jewish woman with an Ivy League degree in African American studies is derided as a "niggerologist" by Pierre) would instantly reject, if it even occurred to him, the notion that blackface could serve to create a new "underclass alliance" in some modern format. Another filmmaker might have reworked *Bamboozled*'s plot so that the unexpected success of the "Mantan" minstrel show would allow Pierre and his performers to subvert their forum in some progressive fashion. Lee gestures at this when he has his integrated TV studio audience start turning up in blackface and claiming that they are all "niggers," but rather than using this to proclaim that race is merely a social mask Lee uses this to register another step in Pierre and the cast's downfall. Lee further divides Pierre and the duo he discovers in the way the producer passively allows to be performed (and to be cut off by his white boss), rather than actively aid in transmitting (in some easily arranged live broadcast), Manray's protest dance sans his blackface. Lee's film declines into black-on-black homicide in its final reels as Big Black Africa's group turn on and kill Manray even as Pierre's ex-lover Sloan Hopkins shoots and kills him. The impasse Lee finds himself in is gaping and irremediable.

Yet in African, Native American and European traditions trickster figures, reimaged as clowns, have often served as carriers of social protest, and, if reimagined by Lee (as he fails to do), might have done the same in *Bamboozled*. In Africa and in North America, clowns, in healing rituals, crossed "into taboo territory or experience," which is exactly what takes place when Manray and his colleague Womack first put on their burnt cork. What they are doing is forbidden; they are breaking a boundary, and their first studio audience perceives what they are doing as taboo. In Africa, clowns "do this in order to convey a medicine that is derived from dealing with the taboo . . . . Clowns bring medicine from forbidden experience into acceptable arenas, so that timid but longing fans will not need to go where clowns have gone" (Lhamon, 179-80). Healing medicine is exactly what taboo-breaking can provide, and it is very interesting to note that, according to Lhamon, this medicine is often represented by blood, sometimes menstrual blood or feces, which in turn can be symbolized by brown water or mud smeared on the clown's body or face. We are in the realm of taboo-breaking carnival in medieval Europe as described by Mikhail Bakhtin. "Burnt cork blackface is clearly relevant here," says Lhamon. "Blackface performance is a ritual that inoculates its congenial publics in motley experience" (ibid.).

Or at least that is Lhamon's argument about blackface. In practice, blackface ritual was often degrading to African Americans, whether they were being depicted in minstrel shows or were playing the parts themselves. Even Lhamon recognizes that the trend toward denigrating blackface performers was already present in the 1840s, "the links white and black common people attempted . . . turning inside out into scorn and differentiation" by the 1850s (186). This continued through the rest of the nineteenth century and into the twentieth, and it is this period that the black performers of the 1930s and 1940s criticized by Lee came from.

And yet . . . it can be argued that skilled African American performers, like their nineteenth century counterparts, used or could use their stereotyped roles to convey, at times, some form of social protest. This has also been debated for some time. Clearly Spike Lee finds the film work of Bert Williams, George Lincoln Perry (a.k.a. Stepin Fetchit), Hattie McDaniel, Willie Best (a.k.a. Sleep 'n' Eat) and Mantan Moreland all irredeemable. Clips of the first three of these are used in *Bamboozled*, Williams in the body of the film, Perry and McDaniel in the montage of Hollywood scenes that concludes the film. The names Sleep 'n' Eat and Mantan, meanwhile, are given as mentioned to the minstrels Davidson and Glover, respectively, and we see a few clips of Mantan Moreland in action, bulging out his eyes (his comic trademark). We also see clips from the 1950s television series *Amos and Andy* as well as various racist memorabilia, obsessively collected by the guilt-ridden Pierre.

Williams—a stage star of the 1910s who performed in blackface—aside, none of the performers Lee criticizes here were blackface stars per se, but Lee ties together minstrelsy and the sort of roles Perry *et al* performed into a bridge that allows him to criticize contemporary culture. Is Lee fair to these performers? A closer look at these films is necessary. Williams in his time was considered their peer by comics like Will Rogers and W.C. Fields. His surviving film *A Natural Born Gambler* (1918) humiliates the Williams character and his friends, who attempt an illegal card game but are routed by a cleverer white police force. The film also allows its star scope for some brilliant mime, a few seconds of which turn up in *Bamboozled*.

George Lincoln Perry was one of the most popular character actors of the 1930s. He lived long enough to defend his Stepin Fetchit persona as a pathbreaker for black actors who followed him (McBride); and in his book on John Ford Tag Gallagher mounts an interesting defense of Perry and Hattie McDaniel's roles in *Judge Priest* (1934), a film extracted by Lee in the clip montage that closes *Bamboozled*. ("Ford captures the spirit of a racist community . . . but Ford also suggests that seeing . . . the attractive aspects in censorable individuals and societies is more promotive of true tolerance than seeing only the censorable." Gallagher, 103.) In his book on African Americans in film Donald Bogle notes how Moreland and Best, in turn, invested their stereotyped roles with some humanity. Moreland's habit in his films of remaining on hand "until his white friend needed him," and then taking off (Bogle, 74), might possibly have been seen as subversive by some (black) audience members, even as (one imagines) white audiences saw this as a comical stereotype of an untrustworthy coward. It's useful to note that some within the African American community found blackface a useful mask. "We put on blackface when we had something really crazy to say," remembers one performer in a 1928 production quoted by Lhamon (188), and if we conflate, as Lee does, minstrelsy and what comics like Moreland did perhaps Mantan Moreland's cowardice can be thought of as wisdom.

Indeed, in many traditions there are multiple examples of comedians who employ their comic mask to veil social criticism, be they court jesters, literary figures like Czechoslovakia's Good Soldier Schweik, or heavily made-up clowns like Charlie Chaplin and the Marx Brothers. (Mark Winokur's *American Laughter* discusses Chaplin and the Marxes in detail as immigrants who used their heavy make-up to support a critique of their new country.) In this book's Introduction I briefly discussed the claims made by many contemporary critics for Bakhtinian carnival as the site of valid social critique. Yet a look at the history of carnivalesque cinema shows that it has just as often been used to reinforce negative stereotypes. Blackface minstrelsy is used to satirize peace conferences in both the Marx Brothers' *Duck Soup* (Leo McCarey, 1933) and Wheeler and Woolsey's *Diplomaniacs* (William A. Seiter, 1933), and these scenes could be viewed as representing "something really crazy." But neither do these films have anything positive to communicate about blacks. (For a discussion of these scenes from a different perspective, see Henry Jenkins' *What Made Pistachio Nuts?*, where the author redeems *Diplomaniacs'* play with a Chinese stereotype as exposing "the arbitrariness and conventionality of its character construction" [202] and by extension character construction in Hollywood films generally.)

Looking back at Hollywood's output, we find several comedies with circus or carnival settings made in the 1920s and 1930s, a period when they were a living part of American culture, passing through town after town. Racial imagery is common in some of them — Roy Del Ruth's *Side Show* (1931), the W.C. Fields vehicle *You Can't Cheat an Honest Man* (1939) — used in both instances to demarcate a firm line between white and black: for example, Fields' concern about an "Ethiopian in the fuel supply" in *You Can't Cheat an Honest Man*. A divide is posited in these films (which also include Frank Capra's *Rain or Shine*, Clyde Bruckman's *Everything's Rosie*, and the Fields vehicles *Sally of the Sawdust*, *The Old-Fashioned Way* and *Poppy*) between carnival culture and the staider society the carnies pass through, but on neither side of the gap is there racial parity, even though the carnival is presented as "A city on wheels — a world in itself" in the opening titles of *Side Show*.

*Side Show* is particularly interesting here as it's the only one of these films with a female protagonist. The film emphasizes the distance its star (Winnie Lightner) feels towards polite society. Her character's more genteel sister tells her "I don't want to be a lady — I want to be like you." Lightner later compares herself to "the three-legged boy who can't do anything but sit," and is further marginalized by her unladylike clowning. Much of this clowning involves her taking on the roles of marginalized ethic groups, as for example Princess Mauna, "the only living descendent of Hawaiian royalty." Lightner also appears in blackface as a "cannibal chieftain." In the latter role she barks like a dog, gets a pie in the face, trips and falls over her slapshoes, and is seen whaling away with a comically enlarged (phallic?) club on some white males during a riot.

Lightner also appears as "Lady Beautiful, the Living Painting," "a picture that lives" — mute, but her clowning kills the intended tableaux. The Otherness of circus life is emphasized by the Otherness of Lightner's personae, which also involves gender transgression, as with the gag that opens and closes the film. "If you don't come across with

*Winnie Lightner as "Princess Mauna" in* Side Show *(1931).*

my money—I'll shave off my beard" threatens the film's bearded lady in its opening scene; at the end of the film, the heroine's clinch with a posited boyfriend is interrupted when the bearded lady starts to shave.

These films, then, challenge conventional social and gender roles in their carniva-lesque scrambles, but seldom if ever challenge racial taboos. This is as true of the roles played by African Americans in silent slapstick comedy (Bowser) as it is of screwball comedies later in the 1930s. Even anarchic oddities like the Olsen and Johnson vehicle *Crazy House* (Eddie Cline, 1943) continue to uphold stereotypical roles. The film treats viewers to a mad "Crazy Street" sequence full of a homegrown surrealism akin to animat-ed cartoons. But in this inverted world a top-hatted African American is still shining shoes. Lee is right, so far as he goes: classic Hollywood cinema is more or less irredeemable.

Rejecting oft-repeated and in his view unlikely stories of how blackface was stolen from African American individuals by the first internationally successful blackface performer, T.D. Rice, in about 1830, W.T. Lhamon proposes instead "a process of social osmosis" to describe blackface's cross-cultural transmission in the nineteenth century and since. He

*Spike Lee, early in his career. As a performer and director Lee has consistently employed humor and satire, and in his concert film* The Original Kings of Comedy (2000), *and in the character of Pierre's father Juneburg (Paul Mooney) in* Bamboozled *he showcases black standup comics as a scathing, satiric alternative to the minstrelsy he finds prevalant in black acting, both in the past and today.*

sees Jim Crow as a "figure of surviving in (culturally) overlapped space" who plays out "contested multiple meanings in identity" (184-85). In our postmodern culture, with its rejection of the idea of a unified human identity in favor of constantly shifting, culturally determined selves, it would appear Jim Crow is due for a rediscovery. This places Spike Lee at once ahead of the curve in recognizing blackface's continuing relevance to our culture, and on the wrong side of postmodernity in protesting its return. Writes Lhamon:

Everyone is stuck in a quagmire, everyone stands around staring at the same legends, reflexively blaming the other fellow, flipping used data over and over. Every way one uses the stories of expropriation, they lock out from serious discussion the motley connections blackface performers and publics were piecing together. However good it may make us feel, a "rhetoric of blame" will not recover that motley. (Lhamon, 185.)

That *Bamboozled* indulges in a "rhetoric of blame" (Edward Said's phrase) cannot be doubted. Yet Spike Lee can be thought of as a critic of blackface minstrelsy in line with Imamu Amiri Baraka (LeRoi Jones), who in his "A Poem for Willie Best" (1964) made the connection between the antics of a minstrel and the victim of a lynching:

> . . . Give me
> > Something more
> than what is here. I must tell you
> my body hurts. (Baraka 1979, 22-27.)

The same connection is made by pioneering African American filmmaker Oscar Micheaux in his *Within Our Gates* (1918), where it is the clownish black informer who is the first to be lynched, and also by Clyde R. Taylor in his commentary on blackface in his book *The Mask of Art* (1998). He writes of the close connection of minstrelsy (whites unconvincingly portrayed as blacks) and lynching in Griffith's *The Birth of a Nation* (1915), another film whose "comic" scenes are extracted in *Bamboozled*. "By its extraordinary fusion of the two basic rituals of the post-bellum South—the minstrel show and the lynching—the movie exposed the essential kinship between them" (115). Lee's film visualizes Baraka's poem, which in turn envisioned Willie Best lynched. The multiple homicides at the conclusion of *Bamboozled* begin to make sense after all.

## Note

1  As in 1991's *Jungle Fever*. This is carried over in *Bamboozled* to Pierre's overbearing white boss, Dunwitty (Michael Rapaport) being given a black wife, which he thinks excuses him from being called a racist. The oafish Dunwitty is one of the film's most interesting characters—he claims to love African Americans, to be more black than Pierre, and appears late in the film in blackface himself. He represents the mask of racial benignity removed, and if Lee's film falters in its escalating failures of plausibility, it succeeds in pegging Dunwitty as a common character type, a white man who doesn't really like African Americans but who makes exceptions for certain star athletes or entertainers: a "Wall of Fame" of athletes covers his office walls.

## Works Cited

Imamu Amiri Baraka (as LeRoi Jones), *Blues People: Negro Music in White America* (New York: W.W. Morrow, 1963).

Baraka, *Selected Poetry of Amiri Baraka/LeRoi Jones* (New York: W.W. Morrow, 1979).

Donald Bogle, *Toms, Coons, Mulattoes, Mammies, and Bucks: An Interpretive History of Blacks in American Films* (Third Edition, New York: Continuum, 1996).

Eileen Bowser, "Racial/Racist Jokes in American Silent Slapstick Comedy," *Griffithiana* No. 5 (1995), 35-43.

Tag Gallagher, *John Ford: The Man and His Films* (Berkeley: University of California Press, 1986).

Henry Jenkins, *What Made Pistachio Nuts?: Early Sound Comedy and the Vaudeville Aesthetic* (New York: Columbia University Press, 1992).

W.T. Lhamon Jr., *Raising Cain: Blackface Performance from Jim Crow to Hip Hop* (Cambridge: Harvard University Press, 1998).

Eric Lott, *Love and Theft: Blackface Minstrelsy and the American Working Class* (New York: Oxford University Press, 1995).

Joseph McBride, "Stepin Fetchit Talks Back," *Film Quarterly* (Summer 1971), 20-26.

Wesley Morris, *"Bamboozled* collapses under its own contempt," *San Francisco Examiner* (Oct. 20, 2000), C-1 ff.

Clyde R. Taylor, *The Mask of Art: Breaking the Aesthetic Contract—Film and Literature* (Bloomington: Indiana University Press, 1998).

Robert C. Toll, *Blacking Up: The Minstrel Show in Nineteenth Century America* (New York: Oxford University Press, 1974).

Mark Winokur, *American Laughter: Immigrants, Ethnicity, and 1930s Hollywood Film Comedy* (New York: St. Martin's Press, 1996).

Postscript: See *Cineaste* 26:2 (2001) for a symposium or *Bamboozled*. In it Lee speaks of the "great understanding" and respect he now has for performers like Hattie McDaniel ("that was the only choice they had").

# XII

JULIA ROBERTS
Julianne fell in love with her best friend
the day he decided to marry someone else.
MY BEST FRIEND'S
Wedding

# Shoot the Actor

**David Thomson** (1998)

"What do you all expect of me?" Woody Allen's Harry Block seems to be asking throughout *Deconstructing Harry*. And he brings a load of whiny lament to the line and its attitude, even if he isn't an actor—so much as a block, a feeling-blocker. He shapes the climate in which he's always there ready to make a last effort to meet anyone's (cockamamie) ideas; it's part of his dogged, weary calm—never losing control, never eating the scenery—no matter that lots of the women who brush up against him are, sooner or later, made into crimson harpies of wrath, helpless incoherence, and torrential other-ness; it's the credo that lets him think of himself as an endlessly patient, tolerant man, ready to talk about everything intelligently—especially the things that were most hurtful and irrational; and it's the mainstay of his self-pity, the way in which, whatever happens, whatever charges or bullets are hurled at him, whatever tirades slip like water from his sloped shoulders and elfin head, he's ready to be the sucker, the one who sits there and takes it, the victim.

And this works well enough until, at last, you get a chance to look at him straight on and you see the bleakest eyes on today's screen, the intransigent certainty that it's all about *him*, and the passive resistance that knows if he keeps on asking in his listless, plaintive way, "What do you expect of me?," he doesn't have to deal with the question himself. But what does Woody want or expect?

I must admit a few things straight-away: I don't like to look at Woody Allen; I don't like to listen to him; but I think he's getting better all the time at that thing called filmmaking. And by now I'm getting used to the realization that it's so hard to like filmmakers—as opposed to their work. By which I mean to suggest that while Woody Allen does not just like himself so much, but can hardly see anything else with the same intensity or respect, there is an extraordinary tension rising (in me) between hostility and fondness. But is there really another American filmmaker around worth wrestling with in the same way?

After all, what do we want from Woody? In the Christmas season of 1997, just about every critic observed that nearly every movie—the good, the bad, and the fatuous—was going on too long, and slowing down to accommodate that length. But *Deconstructing Harry* came in at 95 minutes, with twenty or so significant characters and four or five weaving storylines, with characters appearing as their real selves and as they figured in Harry's chronic fictions, and everything was clear and workable, the set-pieces and the segues, the funniest lines and situations of the season, self-loathing as sharp as fresh anchovy—time to look at Elisabeth Shue and see her odd, Novakian shyness, while seeing yet again that Billy Crystal (electric and beguiling on the Oscars or in Ken Burns' *Baseball*) is a terminally empty actor (does Woody see it in others? you bet he does), and time for that riveting thirty seconds of sprung rhythm and bravura editing from Susan Morse (the code gone wild), as Judy Davis gets out of her car, as if to say, Did you ever think that movies could look like this?, so your eye wakes up again—and I was reminded of David Hockney's observation, ten years or so ago, that he gave up movies because he knew what shot was coming next—and there's now an urge in Woody as there was once

*"Now Everybody* Really *Hates Me": Woody Allen, with Jimmy McQuaid and Helena Bonham Carter, in* Mighty Aphrodite.

in Godard to find a new way of seeing—in short, whether you think it was funny or touching, or not, was there a movie last year that had more going on, and such assurance, such fucking facility, that the more was merrier, so that a little while into the picture you eased back into its serene momentum, knowing that it knew where it was going? Which is nowhere near the same as liking it or not.

I noticed in the year's roundup that several *Film Comment* writers had liked *My Best Friend's Wedding*. I was pleasantly surprised by it, too, but in the broad area of romantic comedy can anyone honestly claim that it rivaled the knowledge of people, the speed, the deftness, the formal daring, or the Parker-like (not Alan Parker) shifts of tone and voice in *Deconstructing Harry*? I mean, don't we need to admit some very basic facts of dramatic skill—like *Husbands and Wives*, 107 minutes; *Manhattan Murder Mystery*, 108; *Bullets Over Broadway*, 99; *Mighty Aphrodite*, 93 . . . or *Radio Days*, 85; *The Purple Rose of Cairo*, 82?

And when I say dramatic skill, I'm really referring to the very subtle movements of different lines and impulses that go to make a sweet, harmonious whole. If you wonder any further what that means, I challenge you, here and now, to write down a halfway adequate synopsis of *The Purple Rose of Cairo*, say, or *Radio Days* or *Deconstructing Harry*.

You won't be able to do it because, all of a sudden, you'll realize how rich, intricate, and tricky these pictures are, and how much what happens depends on how you're seeing it. Whereas, synopsize *Casino*, say, and you have to marvel that the thing itself got to be 182 minutes. Pure cinema for 182 minutes, of course. None of which, necessarily, gets close to whether we like *Casino* more or less than *Radio Days*.

But it does start you thinking, and swept along on that unruly river, you'll soon find yourself adding up some more numbers. And then you discover that, so far, Allen has directed 26.333 films—that third being his share of *New York Stories*. One does not automatically esteem a director because of productivity—Edward L. Cahn did over sixty between 1931 and 1963, and as yet few festivals have made a fuss over him as our forgotten man. But maybe festival fever does overlook fecundity sometimes; it can be its own smokescreen. So a Kubrick, only seven years older than Woody, is deemed grand just because he's in the process of evacuating his thirteenth film. Would some of us feel inclined to take Woody more seriously if he worked less often—if he was more measured, more blocked? But then think of Sydney Pollack, at 63, a year older than Allen and the director of sixteen films. (True, he has done more; he has produced and enabled, and he has acted—wasn't he that grave, vain idiot in *Husbands and Wives*? Why do people act in his films?) And *The Firm* was 154 minutes; *Out of Africa*, 161.

Still, if we ever again honor the notion that directing is an art or a craft or a trick that benefits from practice, we may regret that so many of our better directors work so sparingly (because they grow weary, or because they need too much time to make their deals first?). No one would argue that Allen has driven himself into poverty by disregarding his own deals. Still, he has done that thing most critics and teachers advise—just kept working, and never ended one project without having the next one lined up. And—whether you like the stuff or not—doesn't that steady application show? I mean: isn't he better than he was?

After all, no one gets all there is into *Deconstructing Harry* without having learned how quickly and lucidly you can show things. And just as Woody Allen went from being a kind of amateurish slapstick filmmaker (*Bananas*, *Love and Death*, *Sleeper*) to a sad impresario of the bitter comedy of emotional hope (*Stardust Memories*, *Manhattan*, *Hannah and Her Sisters*), and just as he discovered the advantage and the film language in having Carlo Di Palma and Santo Loquasto as his regular collaborators, so the "visual" in his movies has relied increasingly on talking heads and the very complete spatial relationships in shifting group shots. The films have become much more engrossing as something to see. Minus the élan of camera movements—exhilaration is all on the soundtracks in Woody's films, in talk and music—he has come to look like Renoir of the late Thirties. Not that you have to take the films that seriously, if the comparison throws you. But why not look again?

It's not just that Allen keeps working away, as if only that regimen could keep him alive or fight back the depressions that prey on ease or inactivity. He goes so much further to meet the model of a modern film director as drawn up by the most liberal and humane film critics and commentators. He never yields to the great gambles of *Titanic* or *The Postman*; he would hardly know what to do with the creatures and the hardware in *Alien Resurrection* or *Starship Troopers*. *Zelig* aside—a rather large aside, let us say, years ahead of the rest of Hollywood in putting nonentities hand-in-hand with the great—you will not find special effects in Woody Allen movies. Rather, he insists that moviemaking is a matter of real places and natural light, with no drama more uplifting and no effect more special than the turmoil in a human face—whether it is Judy Davis

*"Pictures about the people he knows"*: Husbands and Wives *(with Farrow and Davis)*, Manhattan Murder Mystery *(with Keaton)*, Everyone Says I Love You *(with Norton and Barrymore)*, Deconstructing Harry *(with Shue and Crystal)*.

struggling to hide blushing pride and self at being her sister's "other woman" in *Harry*, or the kid wisdom in Mariel Hemingway in *Manhattan* telling Woody, "Look, you have to have a little faith in people." Or is it faith in little people?

Woody Allen doesn't kid us, or himself, that he knows, understands, or is interested in real gangsters, say, or the Dalai Lama. Yet, time after time, he makes pictures about the people he knows, the city he has locked himself into, the very streets and apartments that

• • • • • • • • • • • • • • • • • • • • • • • • • • • • • • • • • • • • • • • • • • • • • • • •

are like his lovely life sentence. Ironically, more or less, that world is pretty close to ours, for just like Jules Feiffer in his cartoons, Woody Allen has regularly depicted his own audience—a world and wealth of people worried about being safe and adventurous at the same time, about being in love, being esteemed, being smart and hip and cool and warm in the late part of the 20th century. These people worry about their work, their integrity, their motives, their sincerity—and, increasingly, they have gone from worrying about Woody (or the Wood within) to being just a little restless and jittery about being near him, or near enough to become his creatures.

Call it selfconsciousness—which, surely, can as easily be stupid and vain as noble or touching. But who else in our panorama of moviemaking has had the wit, the accuracy, the lightness, and the indifference to human pain to make that uneasiness so profound a subject?

And don't we sigh with rapturous agreement when the very talented but surely out-on-a-limb James Cameron says that all he wants to do now is just two or three very small, intimate films—as if to urge him on, yes, yes, that's where art and depth lie, Jim, not just at the bottom of the sea. Study Bonnard and Monet until you've lost that young affection for comic book cut-outs. And isn't that what Woody Allen has been doing for over twenty-five years, so that one scene from *Deconstructing Harry*—you can have Kirstie Alley's multiple explosions, the Richard Benjamin–Julia Louis-Dreyfus assignation, or the conversation between Davis and Amy Irving—is enough to let a *Titanic* fan know that, yes, there are quite different decks and classes of human talk, substance, and uptake, and some people have them and some don't. Woody can be smartass, facetious, too cute for his own good, nastier than he knows—he can be like Gore Vidal, so you can't quite judge where your respect for him and the loathing meet but Woody Allen does think, does know, and can say things (even if you worry about the prowess) that so many other filmmakers are deaf to.

So all we have here, really, is just a 62-year-old guy who can't stop making movies, who makes them by old-fashioned precepts we prefer, who makes them modestly, using the camera and film as they were intended to be used, exposing us to ourselves, our foolishness and our dreams, more or less with comedy and pathos. And—let us not forget this—when he runs into the most notable "difficulty" his life has yet had; or, if you want to put it this way, when his cold, selfish manipulation of others is discovered; and when he is widely trashed, mocked, and abused by *his* people (because his people worry more than most others about whether you could and should fuck your stepchild), he does not falter or cave in, he does not "rest," he does not back down, or seem to immerse himself in extra therapy (surely, he is the great visionary and exponent of therapy sessions as just another name for story development or actors' improv). Instead, he digs in and makes not just one film a year, same as always, but makes *Husbands and Wives*, *Manhattan Murder Mystery*, *Bullets Over Broadway*, *Mighty Aphrodite*, *Everyone Says I Love You* and *Deconstructing Harry*.

As if to say, thanks skin bracer—I needed that!

Now, you don't have to *like* those films, you understand. No, all you need to do, is show me anyone else in America who has come anywhere near that run of work. And sure, you can say it's just Woody being Woody, making the films so fast that he doesn't have to pause or think them through—that his "thinking" and "worrying" are just schtick. All right, I don't like him, either, I don't want to be with him or have to listen to his justifications in person. I wouldn't want to have to watch him and Soon-Yi under any circumstances. But we see a country prepared to defy the character "thing," so long as Bill Clinton does such a terrific job playing that other character, the guy thing. Meanwhile, *Broadway Danny Rose, Hannah and Her Sisters, Radio Days, Husbands and Wives, Bullets Over Broadway, Mighty Aphrodite, Everyone Says I Love You, Deconstructing Harry*—you don't have to please me by liking them, or working at liking them. But still, throw in *Annie Hall, Manhattan,* and *The Purple Rose of Cairo* and you've got eleven films that are. . . . Well, never mind what they are, can you really tell yourself that we're not in the presence of a major director?

Take *Bullets Over Broadway,* and the moment when David (John Cusack), the playwright, realizes that Cheech (Chazz Palminteri) has killed Olive (Jennifer Tilly), the woman he was hired to protect. Olive was the gangster's moll and a showgirl with dreams of doing theater. So the gangster put up the money for David's play—*God of Our Fathers*—so long as Olive had a part in it.

I know, I'm talking about gangsters, and you're saying I told you before that Allen didn't use gangsters. What I said was, he didn't kid us, or himself, that he knew or understood or was interested in real gangsters. The Thirties hoodlums in *Bullets Over Broadway* are the kind of figures that Allen's imagination has inherited from movies, and he's only interested in what he can imagine. They're play figures, as well as guys in a play, stooges that let him do the voices and hire some actors. But their presence immediately leaves some sense of a gap, an abyss, between reality and play. You get the same thing in Hawks, all the time, where the most consistent straight-faced joke was that Howard was a man of these real tough worlds—instead of a fantasist. The same gap exists in David, between the very forceful assertion that he's an artist and his real status as an opportunistic hack. Because he's all talk and no substance.

Olive can't act (though Jennifer Tilly handles that limitation very prettily, and got an Oscar nomination for it). Still, her role is small. She's getting along well enough in the rehearsals, and Cheech just sits there in the gloom of the theater waiting for her to finish. He's there because, whatever Allen knows about gangsters, the gangster boss knows show people are too tricky to leave anyone as dumb as Olive alone with them.

There comes a day at rehearsal when, out of the dark, Cheech, in fury and frustration, throws out an idea about fixing a dud moment in the play. This is delivered in long-shot so that we see the stage, the front rows of the orchestra seats, and—with a swaying pan—the place where Cheech is sitting. There has been no one shot, let alone a soulful closeup, of Cheech listening to David's naive, pretentious play, grinding his teeth. Allen hardly gives us a closeup in the entire elegance of the picture, preferring those tricky long-distance views where people struggle for position and we have to look and see. You can say that's because it's a movie about a stage play, but in fact Allen has always been drawn towards the detached, problematic point of view, and the crowded stage on which everyone has his reasons, and his chance.

He feels no need to reveal or underline the artist in Cheech, or to separate him from others in the story. But as soon as we hear the bored bodyguard's idea we know he's got genius in him, and the camera wavers—as if it needed a second to adjust to that—and then carries the idea back to the professionals as insight, answer. From that moment on, Cheech begins to be co-author of the play (whenever he can remember to be that polite to David).

So Cheech comes to the point of knowing that Olive is ruining the play—killing it. No, she's not that bad, says David; and anyway, it's a small part. She's a necessary compromise.

Again, there is no closeup soliloquy to show Cheech's brooding: though worry is Allen's great subject, he is at his best when not isolating it (framing it in self-pity), but letting it air out in the weather of the ensemble. So Cheech just shoots Olive: which isn't what a gangster would do (and it surely means Cheech's demise); it's what an artist would do—because that kind of willfulness has no choice and no truck with compromise.

David guesses instantly what has happened, and he storms in on Cheech in a pool hall. The slam of the door opens the scene and sweeps David across the room to where Cheech stands. This is the master shot, and the only shot; the single setup looks at a receding diagonal, and it plays the splashes of orange light on the walls against the squashed pistachio rectangles of the tables. Without ever giving you a shot to knock your eyes out, Allen has become one of the most graceful, and spatially enquiring, composers in American film. It's a camera style such as one finds in the best of Preminger (a great arbiter of doubt)—and it's something that has received hardly any comment over the years.

The beauty of the image is utterly unspectacular and unshowy; it's just a way of keeping an open mind and making us address what people say. (Time and again, directors intent on talk make the best compositions.) David rants at the gangster for being so callous, as he defends himself as a way of measuring what has happened—"I'm a decent, moral human being." Seen and heard at a distance, that's nothing but a bum line—one we flinch from, in the way Cheech might have done. And Cheech asks what sort of decency it is to be carrying on with the lead when David has a girl already. He knocks the "author" down and tells him, with an absolute severity, "Nobody is going to ruin my work."

*Bullets Over Broadway* is a comedy. Its framework cannot help but see the sad irony in the meeting of an "artist" and a gangster that teaches both of them what fakes they are. David takes a lesson in playwriting and in basic modesty, and he goes back to his girl (why not? she's only been having sex, sensational sex, with Rob Reiner—nothing like love)—"I know I'm not an artist, and I know I love you." And Cheech is as dead as van Gogh or Schubert; his own last line is another knockout suggestion to fix the play's curtain line. The humor here is not a matter of Woody's one-liners—it's the line, the arc, that goes all through the film, and it's what genius is all about. It harks back to the chief gangster's knowledge—that show people are tricky; they fool themselves, for the sake of it; they play around. But that leaves an impulse, a commitment to perfection, quite ready to destroy itself if the play is improved in the process. Which only helps remind us what a serious business comedy is, and how it was always made and intended for the tougher, more painful lessons about emotional life, social order, and human ambition.

Somewhere along the line, Woody Allen is a David who has absorbed Cheech's lesson—and thus a New York showperson who has acquired the concentration, the cruelty, even, that may make a genius resemble a killer. If you doubt that progress, then look at *Crimes and Misdemeanors*, which comes just five years before *Bullets Over Broadway*, and which stands as one of the most rigged, shitty, dankly sanctimonious of Woody's films.

*Crimes* was not shot by Di Palma. Its photographer is Sven Nykvist, which may mean just that Di Palma was busy elsewhere, or that Allen wanted to get himself in a Bergman-like moral trough. The results are horrible. A ponderous pan shot insists on linking a closeup of Judah (Martin Landau) with one of his dead girlfriend (Anjelica Huston) at his feet. The style is always looking to confront some of the most slippery and unlikeable of characters with Moral Dilemma. It's misanthropy with a vengeance. The group shots are filled with fussy irrelevance: the ensemble-ism this time degenerates into names like Claire Bloom, Sam Waterston, Joanna Gleason—and, let us add, Mia Farrow—doing nothing (and Allen's big casts have always offered far too much of that—he doesn't so much showcase his guest stars as humble them and becalm them in their vanity).

But in some grim contest with himself, Woody has found Landau as the only other actor around as unworthy of a lead role as himself. Landau's self-regard is unctuous and unwholesome. The thought of his affair with Ms. Huston is preposterous—indeed, the posed love matches in Allen films are often offered without the least conviction or spark. Obsessed with sex, he is terrified of looking at it. Landau's self-justification is humorless, clammy, and revolting. And when he tells his brother Jack (Jerry Orbach doing *Outlaw and Order*), "I'm not going to let this neurotic woman destroy me!," we hear a line that was waiting to be traded back into Woody's real, ugly life with merciless ease. So Judah lets Jack—a mysteriously humdrum figure, with contacts—arrange for Huston to be offed. Orbach gives us maybe the only grownup or appealing figure in the film, a glum, practical man, oppressed by a lifetime of being the black-sheep brother, the dumb one and the failure. There's a great moment when, after the deed is done, as Judah is lamenting and stroking his bad feelings, Jack tells him curtly, "Be a man!" It's as if the line had slipped through the prevailing self-pity that leaves every other line cute and stuffed.

And if Woody is expecting us to sympathize with his moral refinement in seeing how Judah gets away with it all, and even feels better as time passes, so he throws in the most woeful and childlike of his own countenances at the end—that cringe-making stricken closeup as he realizes Mia Farrow has gone off with Alan Alda (at just the time, maybe, he was longing for the real woman to find someone else).

In other words, the determination about feeling bad overwhelms life or courage in *Crimes and Misdemeanors* (the more Woody's films hinge on men, the more likely this outcome—*Henry and His Brothers* would turn out an orgy of suicide). And the character Allen plays—the high-minded documentary filmmaker who can't stop taking his 12-year-old niece to the movies or see why his wife has given up sex—is creepier and more alarming than he ever seems to understand. (There are people in Allen films way past the need for therapy; only terrific drugs would help.) There is no more glaring proof of the self-destructiveness of Woody acting in his own movies than this film, and no more grisly moment than his monstrous reaction to the story his sister tells of the lover who defecated on her. He howls and covers his eyes—the exaggeration loses her experience. That's not just bad acting, it's a level of performance that derides the art and community of acting, and undermines the pretend reality of the work. It's what got Olive shot—and any one of us would be ready to squeeze the trigger. *Crimes and Misdemeanors* may be as bad as he got—we have to hope so—as a study of self-adoring cowardice dressed up as moral discrimination. Of course, it also got Oscar nominations for Best Director and Screenplay—so it's up to you about liking it.

Much as I like *Deconstructing Harry*, I don't support Allen playing Harry—nor do I really believe that he tried desperately hard to find someone else. (Though I can see a wonderful film about a director like Woody, going through actors endlessly, and being "dismayed" because in the end only Oscar Jaffe can play Oscar.) Imagine Harry played by Richard Gere, say, or even Alan Alda (an actor who evidently holds a dreadful fascination for Allen), and the implicit poison would leap into view. Imagine Chazz Palminteri—he deserves more. Imagine Gore Vidal—he likes to act. But finally, Woody, just give us anyone but yourself now that you've found the hard, sure distance and the necessary resolve to stand back from human beings and just watch their tricks.

Of course, we don't have to like all these films (he makes enough for hits and misses), just as we don't have to forgive or forget what happened with Woody, over there . . . in life. Do we? As it is, in the last few years, the hero-worshipping stance has had to come to terms with the unequivocal report that Capra, Hawks, and Lang were all shits. The same sort of comeuppance may be on its way for Clint Eastwood and all the others. It's just possible one day that we'll grasp the need to be a pretty awful person if you want to be an artist. In which case, I'd propose, *Deconstructing Harry* is an indelible lesson along the way, with that shameless last view of the zealous clerk to his own imagination, typing up life as art.

There's stuff I haven't even mentioned that I never want to have to see again—*Interiors, Alice, Shadows and Fog, Another Woman,* and those early films where people said he was so funny. But I do want to say that I think Allen has grown up, devouring his own poison, and being tougher because of it (it seems clear now that the events of the early '90s strengthened him—okay, left him no alternative but to be a bastard). He has found a deeply impressive style and the habit of making one adventurous film after another. I mean, we've hardly touched on *Everyone Says I Love You,* which came out of some side-pocket, filled with authentic whimsy, creating a race of song-snatched people, with Goldie Hawn never better, and with that odd, awful, sly trick about the secrets of therapy being used to advantage, so long as it's all for story.

I'm not sure what we should make of such numbers, but at the age of 62 Woody Allen has been nominated six times for Best Director and eleven for Best Screenplay—that's in the Billy Wilder class, and Wilder is an untouchable. More to the point, let us offer the thought that in *Bullets* and *Harry* there's a style and an intelligence akin to the way Renoir regards Jean Gabin's showman at the end of *French Cancan.* This is a filmmaker whose journey exceeds that of any American working today. His sense of the great untidy group of acquaintances is, at its best, a vision of great originality and importance. It makes his contemporaries seem narrow and old-fashioned; it lets you believe still that movies might address our modern-ness better than other arts. This is a great filmmaker. And if we've never liked "Woody" less, well maybe that tells us something about filmmaking and art that we are still too young to take hold of.

Still, I'd shoot the actor, given half a chance.

# Notes on David O. Russell

**Dan Sallitt** (2001)

1) One encounters immediately in David O. Russell's films his desire to affront, to transgress, to violate social standards of gentility. This inclination begins with the plots: *Spanking the Monkey* (1994) uses incest as the central plot device, and beyond this unsettles us with its genuine dislike of the parents; *Flirting with Disaster* (1996) similarly pushes generation-gap humor too far and ends up calling the parent-child bond into question; the story of *Three Kings* (1999) is built on an uncomfortable vision of bloody chaos caused by U.S. intervention in the Gulf War. Along the way, Russell crosses as many boundaries as he can: sexual (the oddly matter-of-fact depiction of masturbation in *Monkey*; Ben Stiller's erection, and the licking of Patricia Arquette's armpit, in *Disaster*), political (Stiller's discomfiture at the Reaganism of the San Diegans in *Disaster*; hundreds of anti-American salvos in *Three Kings*, culminating in the U.S. Army playing the mustache-twirling villain as Mark Wahlberg nearly dies of suffocation), familial (Arquette playfully using her baby as a sexual prop in *Disaster*, the montage of parental sex at the end of the same film), racial (Stiller being fingered as a Jew by his Michigan parents in *Disaster*; Spike Jonze's institutionalized anti-Arab patter in *Three Kings* being censored whenever it veers toward anti-black sentiments), hygienic (introducing the mother [Alberta Watson] with a bedpan in *Monkey*; illustrating battlefield injuries with frightening simulations of internal organ damage in *Three Kings*). Many other instances of transgression are thrown away and non-diegetic: the infidelities of the father (Benjamin Hendrickson) in *Monkey* aren't referenced in the dialogue and don't affect the plot; the mother's destructively selfish reaction to Jeremy Davies' acceptance to the medical program in the same film is abandoned after she acclimates; American soldiers casually overpower untrained Iraqi troops, turning action scenes into satire in *Three Kings*.

2) As implied above, Russell has a penchant for tipping characterizations toward malevolence and selfishness. Each parent in *Monkey* is a monster; parental evil is softened by the comic conventions of *Disaster*, but Mary Tyler Moore's edginess often becomes harsh and hostile, and Russell enjoys evolving Alan Alda's character toward sociopathy. Minor characters are often frightening in their hatefulness (the pack of friends in *Monkey*; the bed-and-breakfast hostess in *Disaster*; the soldiers fraternizing over a dying enemy at the opening of *Three Kings*); at times Russell perhaps shades into condescension when he directs too much bile toward a minor character (the lady on the bus at the beginning of *Monkey*; Aunt Helen in the same film). Most strikingly, even the protagonists often veer into unsavory behavior, while remaining our identification figures: Davies' treatment of the neighbor girl (Carla Gallo) in *Monkey* is often casually contemptuous, and his careerism is expressed bluntly; the dishonesty and sexual opportunism of Stiller (and, occasionally, Arquette) in *Disaster* goes a bit beyond genre expectations; the outlaw soldiers of *Three Kings* look on passively at a number of atrocities before the plot moves them to protest.

3) Russell's distaste for political correctness is sometimes extreme enough to be edgy. The psychology-based ideology of the neighbor girl in *Monkey* is presented as a tool for

**401**

• • • • • • • • • • • • • • • • • • • • • • • • • • • • • • • • • • • • •

victimizing others; Russell turns Tea Leoni's counselor in *Disaster* into a psychobabbling clown, and, deviating a bit further from convention, depicts Lonnie (Glenn Fitzgerald), the product of Alda and Lily Tomlin's liberal parenting, as a vicious hysteric.

4) As a balance to the above tendencies in Russell's films, his taste for transgression is generally presented in a mundane context and counterpointed with humanizing psychological detail. The mother makes a convincing feint at discretion in *Monkey* before giving Davies the unsettling news that his father didn't want children; Davies' interest in the neighbor girl in *Monkey* is revealed through two point-of-view closeups, one of her childlike red sneakers, the other of her breasts; Moore is introduced showing us her bra in *Disaster*, all the while hectoring Arquette about the importance of wearing the right bra size.

5) The monstrous behavior in Russell's films is likewise scaled down with psychological detail and placed in a

Flirting With Disaster: *Tea Leoni and Ben Stiller.*

mundane context. The father's awareness of his role as family villain in *Monkey* is presented with a nonchalance that is both grotesque and psychologically persuasive; the mother in the same film makes a token, half-hearted attempt to stop Davies from badmouthing his dad before she joins in; Alda and Tomlin's behavior during their flight from the law at the end of *Disaster* combines callousness and vague humanitarian gestures, the latter always abandoned without much struggle. Central to the impact of *Monkey* is the way that Davies is shown, in persuasive detail over the course of several scenes, to collaborate with his mother's attempt to seduce him, his teenage lust subtly vanquishing judgment and taste. (Russell is one of the few American directors to be convincing in depicting characters in intellectual pursuits: the mother editing Davies' paper in *Monkey*, the preppie hoodlums in the same film posing math problems to Davies.)

6) Another way that Russell balances the depiction of malevolent and grotesque behavior is to juxtapose it with moments of undisguised empathy. The mother's depression in *Monkey* is depicted with an early, startling close-up of her crying without provocation, though her controlling nature shows through as soon as she becomes verbal. Leoni is dismissed as a lunatic through *Disaster* but gets the summarizing line of wisdom at the end ("Every marriage is vulnerable—otherwise marriage wouldn't mean anything, would it?"). The Iraqi who tortures Wahlberg in *Three Kings* is not only given the more cogent political arguments, but also makes a precarious emotional connection with his victim.

7) Psychological observation sometimes shades into appealingly abstract dialogue: in *Monkey*, the father's bizarre, complicated instructions to Davies to use the father as a scapegoat to manipulate the mother ("What do I know, the hell with me, etc."); Davies on career choices ("I wrote about children with AIDS" "Why?" "Because people say that's where the future is"); the father's hilarious attempt to calm his office mates as he hears on the phone about his wife and son's incestuous relationship ("It's just a little family matter"); in *Disaster*, Moore's reply to being asked not to smoke in front of her infant granddaughter ("Whatever happened to the Constitution in this country?"); the establishing absurdism of Wahlberg's post-cease-fire encounter with an enemy soldier at the opening of *Three Kings* ("Are we shooting?" "What?" "Are we shooting people or what?").

8) Russell always builds his stories and stages his gags using established entertainment conventions. *Monkey* can be seen as using a familiar comic structure, that of a character whose life goes wrong in every way: in this case, from the dog interrupting his masturbation to his friends habitually beating him up to his mother trying to sleep with him. Russell transforms this conventional framework by pushing all the plot elements toward extremes instead of toward resolution: unhappiness, capped by incest, leads to poverty and attempted suicide, resolved only by *Five Easy Pieces*-style existential flight. *Disaster* goes further, and sometimes with mixed success, into comic convention: Stiller and Arquette are a sitcom couple tangling their relationship in a string of lies and losing all perspective with each new story twist. The plot has an old-Hollywood symmetry, as the couple works their way through three outrageously different, caricatured sets of birth parents. *Three Kings* suffers the most from Hollywood conventions, with its mandatory enlisting of the protagonists in a sentimental moral stand, and its manipulation of our sympathies for the helpless Iraqi refugees; but its stronger scenes are also built around well-worn war-film riffs (the cynical soldiers whose horizons are broadened; the small unit making a foray into enemy territory; breaking into the enemy stronghold to rescue a comrade).

9) Russell's most exciting moments are three-layered: a familiar narrative or comic convention is exaggerated into a transgressive act, then grounded with a flurry of humanizing psychological detail: Davies telling the father about his incest in *Monkey* (old-fashioned melodramatic confession heightened by the discomfort of the incest, counterpointed with the father never being fully distracted from the business situation in his office); Alda and Tomlin's flight in *Disaster* (cheese-it-the-cops comedy paired with

the outrage of the near death of the policeman [Richard Jenkins] and Alda's callous reaction to it, fleshed out with the couple's bickering and Tomlin's half-hearted compassionate gestures and reflexive stabs at parenting); an imprisoned Wahlberg finding a stash of cell phones and calling his wife in Detroit in *Three Kings* (the familiar escape from enemy headquarters, effected via the technological loot from a prosperity war and couched in inane domestic chit-chat). *Disaster's* reliance on comic convention is both its weakness and its strength, leading Russell to the edge of genre cliche but imparting a narrative momentum that caps the film with a barrage of dazzling multilayered scenes, one of them (the parental sex sequence[1]) after the credits start rolling.

10) As Russell's budgets grow, his films show an increasing flair for art direction. Kevin Thompson's production design for the different birth parent houses in *Disaster* is brilliantly satirical, especially the San Diego location; even more impressive are the crazy-quilt bunkers of the Iraqi command in *Three Kings* (designed by Catherine Hardwicke), concrete labyrinths festooned with inspirational political posters and Arabic carpets and crowded with piles of electronic gadgets and household appliances looted from Kuwait.

11) After the relatively functional camera style of his first two films, Russell took an entirely new tack with *Three Kings*, destabilizing the story with a barrage of MTV-like visual effects: disorienting zooms, tilted camera, telephoto closeups, trashed film stock, pixilation, and slow motion. The principal effect of this style is to erode the force of the narrative line and to rob action scenes of their clarity, fragmenting them into unheroic mosaics of blurred motion and bloodletting. Though the visual tools are more varied, the treatment of action in *Three Kings* calls Peckinpah to mind; one scene, the cease-fire-breaking shootout with the Iraqi army, almost seems to be quoting *The Wild Bunch*.

12) The medical theme of *Monkey* (Davies is a medical student, his mother a would-be doctor who gave up her studies, the television in their house usually tuned to a medical channel) returns in *Three Kings*, heightening the physical, unheroic quality of the action. In a winking homage to his character in *ER*, Special Forces officer George Clooney is able to diagnose any war injury, and even to insert a shunt into Wahlberg's bullet-damaged chest cavity to prevent air pressure from crushing his lungs; Clooney's explanations of internal injuries are accompanied by graphic visualizations that force us to experience the film's violence in an empathetic and concrete way. Bullets in *Three Kings* are fearsome, flesh-destroying objects (their impact enhanced with sickening ripping sound effects), not signifiers of power or victory; a gas attack leaves the protagonists' faces dripping with tears and mucus.

13) After two decades of hoping for little from Hollywood entertainment film, we are disoriented to realize that today's most promising young American director has the temperament and ambition to make a beeline for the heart of the entertainment industry. *Three Kings* demonstrates that Russell can work with undiminished inspiration in Hollywood, but also that he is vulnerable to the pitfalls of industry filmmaking; one hopes that its commercial success increases his bargaining power without diluting his individuality.

## Note

1. This scene, originally showing only the three married couples in the film's theatrical release, was expanded in the video release to include footage of Leoni and of the gay couple (Richard Jenkins and Josh Brolin).

# In a World of His Own: *Rushmore*

## Jonathan Rosenbaum (1999)

*Rushmore* has a good deal of content and human qualities to spare, but what makes it such a charming and satisfying experience is its style. Its segments are introduced by parting curtains, each labeled with the name of the appropriate month, which serves as a chapter heading—a neat way of calling attention to the broad and attractively composed 'Scope frames and of parceling out the story in bite-size seasonal units. Less obvious and functional but unmistakably style-driven is the fact that the curtains come in different colors, giving another kind of lift to the proceedings. All the scenes are short (at least until the film moves into its homestretch), and director Wes Anderson also films these scenes in long and medium shots; in general he indulges in long scenes and close-ups only after he's earned them. Because this is a studio effort that knows what it's doing—a rare breed these days—it makes you wonder how many close-ups and long scenes are squandered in other studio releases.

The film is a comedy about Max Fischer (Jason Schwartzman), a 15-year-old student at Rushmore Academy, a private school in a small town, who's too wrapped up in a bevy of extracurricular activities—hilariously cataloged in one extended montage sequence—to finish his schoolwork.

Max develops a crush on a young, widowed grammar school teacher named Rosemary Cross (Olivia Williams), befriends a local millionaire and Rushmore graduate named Herman Blume, gets expelled, enrolls in public school at Grover Cleveland High, and writes and stages elaborate plays at both schools. (The first one we see him staging is derived from the 1973 movie *Serpico*.) He's always a bit ridiculous, and so is Blume, but everyone in the movie is accorded a certain dignity that keeps him lovable.

Significantly, the character initially introduced as Blume—played by Bill Murray at his most inspired, with a characteristic mix of quizzical distraction and terminal world-weariness—eventually becomes known to us as Herman, and even Max's father, played with amiable sweetness by Seymour Cassel, finally registers as just plain Bert.

This dignity is often revealed in small but precious details. The bond that develops between Max and the millionaire degenerates into a protracted feud when Herman also falls in love with Rosemary after serving as go-between for his teenage pal. One of the comic grace notes in this feud involves Max's friendship with Dirk Calloway (Mason Gamble), a much younger classmate at Rushmore, who spies Herman emerging from Rosemary's house, blocks his car when he's leaving, announces, "I know about you and the teacher," and spits with fury on the hood of Herman's car. Another comes soon afterward, after Dirk reports his findings to Max and Max arranges a meeting with Mrs. Blume to report on her husband's infidelity; before they get down to business, Max offers her a sandwich and she accepts, choosing tuna over peanut butter. Dirk's loyalty in spitting on Herman's car and Max's civility in offering the tuna sandwich are two good examples of the kind of gifts offered by this movie to both its characters and its viewers—an act of piety toward passion in the first case, a respect for simple courtesy in the second.

Comparable gifts crop up in almost every scene. Some involve Max's father, whose

**405**

doting and nonjudgmental affection is undiminished by either Max's horrible grades or his defensive claims to Herman and his wealthier Rushmore class-mates that his barber father is a neurosurgeon.

Some involve Rose-mary's gentle negotiation of Max's infatuation and her own guarded affection for him; some involve the fluc-tuating friendship between Max and Herman; and still others relate to Max's shift-ing relationships with Dirk, with his worst enemy at Rushmore—a Scottish bully named Magnus who's much older, played by Stephen McCole—and with Margaret Yang (Sara Tanaka), a classmate at Grover Cleveland who likes him in spite of everything.

Adolescence is a big comic subject in American movies, but it's usually squandered—along with close-ups and longer scenes—with strident acting and other telegraphed effects. But Anderson, who wrote *Rushmore* with Owen Wilson, never allows the audience to lose its dignity either; the coolness of the comedy—like that of Buster Keaton, Jacques Tati, and Albert Brooks—respects us

*Love in Blume: Bill Murray and Jason Schwartzman in* Rushmore.

and characters alike. The pain and cruelty of adolescence aren't avoided, but the short-scene construction and gliding tempo prevent us from dwelling on them; the calm objectivity of a Keaton, Tati, or Brooks gazing at the world qualifies as a kind of mea-sured wisdom, and *Rushmore* emulates this sane equipoise throughout.

Treating quirky adolescents with affection was already central in *Bottle Rocket*, Anderson and Wilson's only previous feature (in which Wilson played one of the leading parts), but for all that movie's style and grace, it bears the same relationship to *Rushmore* that a watercolor bears to an oil painting. This movie goes further by creating something more than a milieu and a circle of friends, widening its span to encompass a little world to contain them. It also dissolves the usual distances between characters of various ages (including not only Dirk and Magnus in relation to Max, but also Herman and to some extent Rosemary), creating a utopian democracy of concerns that purposefully rejects the automatic and often unconvincing generational solidarity that underlies most movies about teenagers. This is perhaps the movie's most inspired wild card, though it also means that the world of the film begins at times to become infused with magical realism.

Even if we accept Max's becoming best friends with Herman, the disaffected father of two of Max's classmates, we may balk when Max subsequently persuades Herman to spend eight of his ten million dollars on an aquarium designed to win Rosemary's admiration. At this stage the film's comic invention gets stuck in a groove; the adolescent grandiosity of both Max and Herman expands only because it has nowhere else to go, warping the world that contains them in the process.

These occasions aren't the movie's finest moments; they indicate that the filmmakers became so smitten with their characters that they got carried away, much as the characters themselves get carried away with their infatuations. Yet even this flaw is seductive—as it is in the fiction of J.D. Salinger, another sympathetic chronicler of adolescent overreaching whose eagerness and attentiveness can lead his fiction into equivalent forms of fantasy projection and hyperbole. To their credit, Anderson and Wilson share none of the class snobbery that subtly infuses much of Salinger's work, and though they don't harp on it, they seem to understand some of the less articulate forms of adolescent anguish that arguably make Booth Tarkington's *Seventeen* an even better evocation of teenage nightmare than *The Catcher in the Rye*. But like Salinger they harbor a protective gallantry toward their characters that becomes the film's greatest strength and its greatest weakness.

For all its lightheartedness, *Rushmore* reeks of mortality and historical traumaa paradox made possible by its stylistic fleetness, pumped along by snatches of nearly a dozen British pop tunes of the '60s. (Anderson's nostalgic and lyrical employments of this music often recall the more extended uses of Simon and Garfunkel in *The Graduate*, a quintessential pop expression of the '60s.) Max's dead mother, Rosemary's dead husband (another Rushmore graduate), and Herman's stint in Vietnam may not be equivalent points of reference for these characters, but the movie gently treats them as if they were. (The movie never really furnishes an explanation for Herman's boredom and alienation, apart from his wealth and his conventional jock sons; Vietnam is Max's hypothesis for the root of Herman's problems, and by default it becomes the movie's as well.) Max's climactic and hilarious play about Vietnam—staged at Grover Cleveland with elaborate special effects in the movie's final and longest sequence—is dedicated to his mother and to Rosemary's late husband ("the friend of a friend"), pointedly bringing all three together. It's Anderson's way of hinting that all three characters have suffered irreparable losses without hitting us over the head with them, and it seals the past's ongoing claims on the present that locate the entire movie in some kind of temporal netherworld that is neither. (The traditionalism of the school itself, so central to Max's sense of his own identity,

Rushmore *director Wes Anderson.*

is clearly part of this period ambiguity, along with the importance of Watergate, *Serpico*, and Vietnam to Max's career as a playwright.)

The play itself is about reconciliation; it ends with Max, playing an American grunt, proposing to a Vietcong guerrilla played by Margaret Yang, his new girlfriend. It also leads to other reconciliations: between Max and Magnus, Rosemary and Herman, Max and Rosemary. There's even a reconciliation between Max and Rosemary's friend from Harvard, a young man whom Max drunkenly castigated as an interloper at a dinner after the premiere of his previous play. Unlike the madder schemes of Max and Herman, this optimistic ending bears some recognizable relation to the real world: not only has the past become integrated with the present, but the invented world of Rushmore has become wide enough to encompass our own.

# "I Just Went Gay, All of a Sudden": Gays and '90s Comedy

Robin Wood (2001)

Cary Grant's famous line in *Bringing Up Baby*, now inscribed in history as the first unambiguous use in films of "gay" in its modem sense, may eloquently stand as epigraph for the current influx of gay characters (mostly male) into contemporary mainstream cinema. The phenomenon is obviously the result of the undeniably immense advances of the gay movement in recent decades (if anyone had predicted them to me when I was thirty I would have been totally incredulous), Hollywood being more a barometer of progress (in *any* form) than its instigator. We have now reached the point where (in Canada at least, and in certain areas elsewhere) gay and lesbian couples have full spousal rights (short of the right to legal marriage, which will surely follow), and where the annual Gay Pride March is among the most popular spectacles in the major cities of western civilization, its "cast of thousands" drawing even greater crowds of generally enthusiastic spectators. It is time, perhaps, for some new statistics: on what evidence was the traditional estimate of one-in-ten based? It can hardly have taken into account the multitudes of closeted gays secretly indulging their "sick, evil, disgusting" desires, or the many who refused to indulge them at all, leading (at great psychological cost) "blameless" heterosexual existences. Such people have much less reason today to fear the horror of society or to feel a corresponding horror of themselves. One can rejoice that the demeaning stereotypes of the past (fully documented in *The Celluloid Closet*, both book and film), the "sissy" of classic comedy, the sadistic minor villains of film noir, have been replaced, by and large, by attractive, likable figures, positively viewed. Before we get carried away, however, a clear and critical look at the limits within which gays are presented in mainstream cinema seems appropriate.

## Gay Movies

As starting-point, we should note the continuing distinction between films primarily for and about gays, and films containing gay characters but aimed at straight audiences. *Trick* and *The Object of My Affection* are both light comedies, yet the audience for the former appears to have been almost exclusively gay, for the latter predominantly straight. (I am speaking here, of course, of audience *proportion*, not size: obviously an expensive mainstream film with well-known stars will attract more people than a very low-budget film with unknowns). One answer might be that "gay" movies are thought to be about gay concerns (the fight for liberation, protest against oppression, etc.), yet this is clearly no longer the case. More to the point, I think, is the crucial matter of sexual frankness: in a "gay" movie we might have to see gays not only kissing (occasionally permitted now in "straight" movies, if not too passionate or sensual) but making love, with at least simulat-

**409**

ed sexual activity. Even when men kiss in straight movies we don't have to take it too seriously, because the stars are known (or at least assumed) to be heterosexual: they are just *acting*. When Tom Selleck kisses Kevin Kline on the mouth in *In and Out* it is funny not merely because of the situation but because they are Kevin Kline and Tom Selleck, who *of course* can't be gay (if they were they wouldn't be major stars, would they?). But what of two unknown young actors embracing? It might be real, they might actually be enjoying it.

This already tells us a great deal about the limits of gay representation in mainstream film: even in these days of partial and precarious "liberation," straights find it difficult to face the realities of gay sex. This seems to be so taken-for-granted that its logical oddity is never recognized: gays do not, on the whole, appear to experience the same dread of watching heterosexual sex scenes. When a film invites me to watch a handsome man and a beautiful woman making passionate love in the nude, while it doesn't strike me as something I would wish to indulge in myself, it doesn't strike me as in the least disgusting or distasteful, and I feel no impulse to leave the theater or avert my gaze. The answer to this apparent conundrum is simple: gays have not been *taught*, since early childhood, to find such behavior "sick" or "evil."

## Why Comedy?

It seems at times as if no '90s comedy is complete without at least one gay character, however minimal: every Adam Sandler film (except, unless my memory is at fault, *Happy Gilmore*) has one or more, *Blast from the Past* has one, *There's Something About Mary* has a whole gaggle (or giggle?) of them, and even the otherwise entirely unadventurous, lame and reactionary *Forces of Nature* has its one mildly amusing scene set in a gay bar. Though gay characters are rarer in high school movies, there is a prominent one in *Clueless*. On the other hand, gays are scarcely more visible in dramatic films today than they were fifty years ago: aside from *Philadelphia* (essentially a Big Theme movie about AIDS), the only distinguished (and undervalued) Hollywood movie that comes to mind is Mike Figgis' *One Night Stand*, of which a gay man is the positive center, its spokesperson for sexual freedom, *even though he is dying of AIDS*. There is also the British *Hollow Reed*, written by Paula Milne, directed by Angela Pope, in which a divorced father who has come out as gay discovers that his young son is being physically abused by the wife's lover, perhaps the first film to suggest that gay men might be responsible and appropriate fathers. The reason why gays have been largely excluded from dramatic works is implicit in what was said above: in a comedy a gay character, even if not himself a comic figure, would be rendered "safe" by the film's overall tone; his relationships would not have to be taken seriously, and there would be no necessity to show him in an erotic situation. A particularly clear example is *Happy, Texas*, a film I found moderately objectionable despite the fact that I would travel miles to see anything in which Steve Zahn appeared. The resolutions of the various "affairs" fully confirm what is implicit throughout: that straight relationships are "serious" (even when comic), while gay relationships are comic (even when "serious"). It is not the fault of William H. Macy, whose performance would, in another context, have been very touching. I saw the film at a press screening during the Toronto Film Festival, and the "Gentlemen of the Press" (the phrase here requires the inflection given it by Rosalind Russell in *His Girl Friday*)— and, I suppose, its Ladies—laughed aloud when Macy weeps in his car at the loss of his projected lover. In isolation, the scene is not in the least funny, and Macy plays it (if one may say so) straight. It becomes funny (I suppose) within a context that presents the amorous attachment of a gay man to a man he believes to be gay but whom the audience knows is straight as essentially funny in itself. So, at the film's end, with all the threads wrapped up in a neat bundle, the two straight men get the women they have fallen for, but the gay man is shown to be perfectly satisfied with a somewhat grotesque replacement: for gays, anyone will do—after all, it's only sex isn't it?

One can discern a similar strategy in *There's Something About Mary*: the one scene in which gays appear takes place in a layby; the police arrive, whistles are blown, and dozens of men in various stages of undress rush out from the bushes. The scene might have been funnier twenty years earlier when this was about the only way in which many gay men could have sex (it should have been, at that time, very sad). I should say at once that I see absolutely no moral objections to promiscuous and/or anonymous sexual practice—indeed, as I indulge in them myself about once a week, usually with great enjoyment, it would be extremely hypocritical. The objection is twofold: one, that it is the *only* appearance of gays in the film and therefore stands, for the general audience, as "the way that all gays behave all the time"; two, that promiscuous/anonymous sex is presented as *automatically* funny. (I have found it a great many things, but only very rarely "funny," though there *have* been occasions . . . .) Ben Stiller gets Cameron Diaz for life; gay men get (if they're lucky) a quick and furtive blowjob.

*Gay relationships are comic, even when serious: Jeremy Northam, William H. Macy and Steve Zahn in* Happy, Texas.

And what of lesbians? They remain virtually invisible. The heroine of Araki's very dis-appointing *Splendor* has a lesbian sidekick. The only *major* lesbian character in a '90s comedy that comes to mind is the Amy (Joey Adams Lauren) of *Chasing Amy* — and she is "cured" somewhere around the midpoint. Lesbians have never been quite as shocking as gay men (they even turn up in straight porn films, and gay men never). It seems that, however likable, charming, sympathetic a gay man may be, there is still something rather titillating about his appearance in mainstream films, and gay males (or heterosexual males pretending to be gay, as in *Happy, Texas*) can still be presented as intrinsically funny.

The remainder of this essay will examine some more positive ways in which gay men have been presented in '90s American comedies.

## Survival of the Buddy Movie

I discussed the homoerotic content of the '70s buddy movies in *Hollywood From Viet-nam to Reagan*. One result of the new awareness of gayness (hence of possible implicit or ambiguous gayness) has been the careful purging of the genre of the kind of under-tones that were especially clear in *Thunderbolt and Lightfoot*: no one must be allowed to have suspicions about Mel Gibson and Danny Glover, and if any traces survive it is despite scrupulous surveillance. But one highly idiosyncratic (and irresistibly charming and funny) buddy movie seems quite unashamed of such implications: *Bottle Rocket*, the debut film of Wes Anderson who has subsequently confirmed his brilliance with *Rushmore*.

The film might be described as a love story between one young man who isn't gay and another too naive to know that he is: this is never made explicit (how could it be?) but the traces are clear enough and it seems to me what gives the film's wry humor much of its charm and poignance. (An additional, extradiegetic, twist: the two actors are real-life brothers). Dignan (Owen Wilson) has sublimated his feelings for Anthony (Luke Wilson) into a constant desire to impress him with elaborate and eccentric plans for rob-beries which they will, of course, undertake together; Anthony's brotherly attachment to his friend is evident in his readiness to go along with them. The relationship is beautiful-ly established in the opening sequence, where Anthony feels that he must *pretend* to escape from the sanatorium from which he is in fact being released, because this is what Dignan had planned and he can't disappoint him. Dignan shows no interest in women throughout the film; problems develop when Anthony begins a romance with Inez, the Mexican housecleaner at the motel where they hide out after a robbery. The humor of his attempts to interfere in their relationship (interrupting their encounters in the swim-ming-pool and on the steps beside it) lies in his total inability to understand the nature of his disturbance. When he finds Anthony lovingly sketching his beloved, and Anthony retorts to his disparaging comments, Dignan's response is, "Don't treat me like the jeal-ous friend who's envious of you, because that's not what this is about." What it *is* about is, of course, that Dignan is envious of Inez.

## A Girl's Best Friend

One way of obviating any threat the presence of a gay character might pose to straight sensibilities is to detach him from any contact with lovers (actual or potential) and cast him in a platonic relationship with a woman: the strategy of, for example, *Blast from the*

*Past, My Best Friend's Wedding* and *The Object of My Affection*. This can be seen not merely as an evasion but as acknowledging a very real and positive phenomenon of our times, boldly established long ago in *Victor, Victoria*: the strength and mutually supportive value of friendships between women and gay men. *Blast*, while pleasant enough, is negligible; the other two films are, in somewhat different ways, very interesting. The interest of *My Best Friend's Wedding* is grounded in the fact that, unlike *The Object of My Affection*, it is a quite wonderful movie, among the most intelligent contemporary rethinkings of classic screwball comedy. Its director, P.J. Hogan, walks an extremely precarious tightrope without a single stumble, the film's comedy continuously threatened by undertones of genuine pain and the possibility of loss, the plot setting up a classic screwball situation in order systematically to reverse all the conventional expectations this implies: the heroine Julianne or "Jules" (Julia Roberts)—what one might call the Katharine Hepburn role—does not end up with the man she loves, her rival Kim (Cameron Diaz) does *not* turn out to be either a "bitch" or a "bimbo" who can be ousted from the narrative without qualms, and the Cary Grant role is divided between Michael (Dermot Mulroney), who marries the rival, and George (Rupert Everett), who is gay. If it's possible to "steal" a film from a uniformly perfect cast, Everett steals it. He has the great advantage of being an openly gay actor who (despite the requisite looks and charm) has explicitly renounced the possibility of playing traditional romantic leads, so that the usual "of course he isn't really" safeguard doesn't apply. The intimacy between George and Jules is the greater because free of sexual complications: he can lie beside her on the bed, pull her back down by her hair when she tries to get up, speak to her with total frankness, so that when, without his permission, she passes him off as her fiancé, he can enjoy himself by hilariously overplaying the role, with thoroughly goodnatured oneupmanship. Comparison with the parallel character in *Blast from the Past* is illuminating: there, the character's function in the plot is simply to bring Brendan Fraser and Alicia Silverstone back together, the typically subordinate role of "sympathetic" gays in Hollywood movies. But George remains securely himself, a person in his own right, with his own life (even if we never see much of it—he is not associated with a lover, unless it is the silent baldheaded guy at the opposite end of the table at the dinner party in George's home). Everett's ironic detachment is the perfect representation of the intelligent gay man surviving (and even flourishing) within a heterosexual-dominated social milieu, belonging but never *quite* belonging. It is intelligence, above all, that Everett conveys, the intelligence that permits him an awareness superior to that of those around him. His advice to Jules, as they lie on the bed together, clearly comes from within: "Just tell him you love him . . . Tell him you've loved him for nine years, but you're afraid of love . . . afraid of needing . . . ." (Jules: "Needing what?") . . . "To belong to someone." So much gay experience within heterosexual culture is summed up in that moment. And the entire pre-wedding day party sequence, culminating in the communal performance (led by George) of a Dionne Warwick song, can stand beside the greatest scenes of classical screwball in its intelligence and complexity.

*The Object of My Affection* deserves a little more recognition than it has been given: for once the gay character is also the leading character (aside from the very broad and farcical *In and Out*, the only occasion I know of in a mainstream comedy where this is the case), and his need for lovers is clearly enough acknowledged. This makes it (I suppose) something of a landmark film, within its context. If only it had been better! The film is a reasonably faithful (*too* faithful?) adaptation of Stephen McCauley's splendid novel—or at least of its plot: it makes little attempt to find any equivalent for the pervasively ironic tone of the novel's first-person narration. It needs a somewhat younger Rupert Everett in the lead, and it gets only Paul Rudd, who is likable enough and gives a passable performance, but that's as high as one can put it.

## Adam Sandler: from *Billy Madison* to *Big Daddy*

At the beginning of his first movie, *Billy Madison*, Adam Sandler establishes the basis of his comic persona, his essential good nature: Billy, in the bath, squirts foam soap on to each nipple, then adds a mouth to create the familiar "smile" face on his chest. In the course of the first ten minutes he associates himself with children (his own infantile behavior anticipating the major plot premise, his enrollment in school to complete each grade in a fortnight, starting from the 1st); animals (the giant penguin he hallucinates when drunk, and wants to send either South or to the zoo); blacks (his mutual love relationship with the family maid, whom he treats on equal terms: subsequently, when he asks for his "snack-pack" to take to school, she remarks "I thought *I* was your snack-pack"); and gays. Billy is in a bar, drinking with two buddies; one asks "Who would you rather bone, Meg Ryan or Jack Nicholson?" Billy considers the question seriously, then asks "Jack Nicholson now or in 1974?" He is told "'74." Again he considers, then (having given the matter careful consideration) opts for Meg Ryan. One does not have to find this unambiguously gay-positive to find it surprising in a film aimed at a primary audience of teenage males and young men; one could hardly expect, in such a social context, that Billy would opt for Jack Nicholson. The gag introduces a whole series of gay jokes (there are at least six) that runs through the film. Most of these involve the comic stereotype of the school principal, middle-aged, grotesquely fat, thoroughly unattractive, and gay: apparently a totally negative exemplar of gayness. Yet, surprisingly, though giving in to blackmail in a plot to disgrace Billy, he is permitted to redeem himself and is brought back for inclusion in the film's almost all-encompassing generosity, from which only the determinedly malicious arch-villain is excluded. He is last seen hugging Billy enthusiastically and exclaiming "I'm still horny!" (The film offers another quasi-gay character: Steve Buscemi, in an uncredited cameo, the former school loser whom Billy used to taunt, reacts to Billy's telephone apology by delightedly applying lipstick).

No one will wish to claim (I hope) that the Sandler films prior to *Big Daddy* are unambiguously gay-positive. Yet they seem to me, considered within their social context, at least interesting. The stereotype of *Billy Madison* reappears (in various guises, but essentially unchanged) in *Bulletproof* and *The Water Boy*: one supposes that it seemed to Sandler (who has, one must assume, considerable control over his films) about the best his assumed audience would be able to accept without feeling alienated. If even this seems too strong a claim, the reader is referred to the films of Jim Carrey, and specifically to the extremely popular *Ace Ventura, Pet Detective*, Carrey's debut movie hence directly comparable to (and scarcely more ambitious than) *Billy Madison*. The "hilarious" scene of Carrey's hysterical reaction to the belief that he's kissed a man by mistake is perhaps the most extreme instance of the kind of casual, prejudice pandering homophobia one has come to expect of films directed at the teen audience. And isn't *The Cable Guy* singlemindedly dedicated to equating homosexuality with psychopathology? (I should confess here to a prejudice of my own: aside from their attitudes to gays—though one cannot separate that aspect from the whole, it is clearly a part of it—I always

*Adam Sandler's "essential good nature" on display in* Billy Madison.

enjoy Sandler and find Carrey unwatchable. I cannot stand his face-pulling, his aggression—always directed at the audience as much as at other characters—his sheer "noisiness," whereas I am drawn to Sandler's generosity, his good nature, the essential gentleness that somehow survives the occasional manic outbursts. I would agree that it is a matter of temperament as much as politics.)

Two of Sandler's films deserve detailed treatment, both for their particular distinction (within the limitations of his ambitions, so far) and for their treatment of gayness. *Bulletproof* is notable as the one film in which Sandler's character can be read as gay—given an additional "kick" of miscegenation in that the "object of his affection" is black: though the progressiveness of *Big Daddy* is more obvious, this may be Sandler's closest approach to a "radical" film. (Is this why it appears to have been his least popular? It might well make reactionary teenage males uneasy in ways they can't quite pin down, hence can't deal with.)

The complicated plot has Rock (Damon Wayans), an undercover cop, betray his "best buddy" Moses (Sandler), who is mixed up with a gang of drug dealers which Rock has infiltrated. Rock (whose name carries obvious overtones for movie audiences) then has the task of taking Moses across country to trial, pursued by the gang they have exposed (inadvertently on Moses' part), who naturally want revenge. The key scene occurs in a lonely motel run by an unattractive and apparently ultra-conservative man called Charlie (the film's variant on the school principal of *Billy Madison*). With Rock within hearing, Moses leans across the counter and addresses Charlie confidentially:

Moses: (indicating Rock) He says he's not gay, but, er, I'll see what a few drinks and a back massage'll do to him, huh? That might get him up a little. Look at him, the way he's standin'.
(Rear view of Rock talking on the phone, bent over, his ass protruding.) Waitin' for you.
(Charlie looks somewhat interested, then shakes his head, but indecisively.)

Moses: Say, is that your wife back there? (Closeup of photograph on Charlie's desk: his wife appears to be a man in drag.) Goddamn. She's hot.

Charlie: (humbly) Thank you.
(Rock, phone conversation concluded, asks for a room.)

Charlie: The only room we have available is the . . . er . . . Honeymoon Suite.
(Enthusiastic wolf-call from Moses, offscreen; he addresses Charlie again.)

Moses: Me, you, the old lady, a little sandwich action? Come on, you're a piece of white bread, she's a piece of white bread, I'm the salami.

Charlie (innocently): She's not eating sandwiches, she's on a diet right now.
(In the Honeymoon Suite, Moses sings in the shower while Rock lies on the double-bed, covering his ears.)

Moses (singing loudly): We both know/ I'm not what/ You nee-ee-eed. I'll always love you I'll always love yoouu . . . .

Rock: Shut up.

Moses: You'll always be my bodyguard, you know that.

Moses then tries to escape, naked and covered in soap, through the shower window, and gets stuck. Charlie passes by outside with a wheelbarrow. Cut back inside to Moses' bare ass. Rock sticks the barrel of a gun up it. Moses screams. Charlie watches with great interest.

Rock: Let me guess, you dropped the soap.

Moses: Please take that out of my ass.

Rock: I want you on the bed, now.

Subsequently, we see Charlie on the phone to his wife, trying to persuade her into a "sandwich."

Obviously, the scene could have been played for crude homophobic laughs, but it isn't. After Jim Carrey's relentless and tiresome mugging, Sandler's understated acting style (he delivers all his lines "straight") comes as an immense relief. As I see it (and this seems borne out, or at least nowhere contradicted, by the rest of the film) the implication is that Moses is indeed gay and aware of it, but knows the man he loves will never see him as anything but a "buddy," and so falls back on a gentle, offbeat, ironic humor that at once acknowledges and denies his commitment. Later in the film, when the rift between the two men begins to heal, Moses tells Rock "I'm not going to get mad at you. I'm falling in love with you all over again." And Charlie, the comic stereotype, suddenly springs into life as an action hero, saving the couple's lives by rescuing them from an assault by the drug gang: the film is full of little surprises. It's true that, in the final sequence, Moses (now a bullfighter in Mexico!) is surrounded by sexy and admiring young women. Yet his ambition to become a bullfighter (who, on his own admission, would never dream of harming a bull) seems centered on the attraction of a fancy, flamboyant costume, and his female admirers are abruptly dismissed when Rock turns up (unable, apparently, to keep away, and now expressing his real allegiance). The film should logically have ended with the two happily in bed together, but obviously that would be too much to ask just yet. Perhaps one day . . . .

*Big Daddy* makes Sandler's commitment to the acceptance of gays quite explicit. Critics have noted this in passing, as one point (the *only* one, apparently) in the film's favor. The most recurrent objections seem to be: 1) The film celebrates irresponsibility, in that Sonny (Sandler) teaches the little boy to urinate against people's doors and trip up skateboarders by placing sticks in front of them; and 2) That its humor consists largely of pissing, shitting and barfing. Both seem to me totally misplaced. The former can logically have been made only by those who walked out before the halfway point.

The basis of the Sandler comic persona (the man-child) is established at the outset in Sonny's behavior, then succinctly summed up in the telephone call with his father ("You act like you're a six-year-old"/ "Very well, Dad, I'm a six-year-old"). It is Sonny's childishness that enables him to establish an instant rapport with Julian, the little boy who turns up at his door, and the irresponsible behavior quickly releases the child from his timidity and sense of abandonment: he has lost a mother but acquired a supportive "buddy." The turning-point comes in the sequence of the parents' day at Julian's kindergarten, where Sonny is confronted by another small boy with splints and bandages, his injuries caused by Julian's skateboarding trick. The film's leading theme is of Sonny learning responsibility himself and transmitting it to Julian, without sacrificing (beyond the necessary compromises) the child's freedom. The film offers, in fact, some salutary lessons in child-rearing: Julian is allowed to choose how he dresses, and even to choose his own name ("Frankenstein"!) in preference to the name bestowed upon him by others. Sonny also finds ingenious ways of making study and responsibility interesting and attractive. As for the second objection, if you are disgusted by a child's natural functions (and the inconvenience they may cause), then, yes, you will be disgusted by *Big Daddy*. I find its "toilet humor" charming and very funny.

If *Big Daddy* is about education, it aspires also to being educational. Surely no other film addressed to the youth audience (an elastic concept that would appear to include myself) has been so explicit and direct in its project of educating teenagers about gays. *Bulletproof* can apparently be read as homophobic (I was rebuked by my thirty-four-year-old heterosexual son for liking it, and no doubt he is more in touch with the way in which young people receive the film), but Sandler makes this quite impossible in *Big Daddy*. Sonny's best friends are a gay couple, an ingredient not in any way required by the plot. A few minutes into the film Sonny attends a party during which various plot threads are established. Before they leave the two men kiss, onscreen. Another of Sonny's acquaintances expresses his unease. Sonny tells him "That's what gays do." The acquaintance says he preferred the old school days, when the couple were their "brothers." Sonny tells him, "They're still our brothers. Our very, very gay brothers."

Having made his statement, Sandler could easily have dropped the issue, and the characters. In fact, although the explicitness of the opening statement is dropped, the gay couple (who happen to be lawyers) return in five more sequences:

1. On a bench in the park, Sonny (who has decided to keep Julian—not, initially, as a means of winning back his girlfriend by demonstrating responsibility, but because

he wants to) asks his friends for advice. Knowing Sonny's habits, they try to dissuade him from something they believe he can't possibly cope with. Sonny's response: "You two want to get married, I support that. But leave me alone."

2. Sonny and Julian meet the couple in the little parkette on Christopher Street and 7th Avenue, where the statues of same sex couples (gay and lesbian) figure prominently in the decor.

3. While Sonny goes out with his new (potential) girlfriend Layla (Joey Adams Lauren, from *Chasing Amy*), the gay couple babysit, watching *Thelma and Louise* on television. One exclaims "Look at Brad's body," then hastily adds, to his lover, "Of course, I like yours better." Again, we are given a third party, looking embarrassed and disapproving, as an unflattering reflection within the film of anyone in the audience who might be reacting with hostility or distaste.

4. The gay couple turn up as Sonny's legal counsel for the trial to decide adoption rights. During the proceedings one wipes a smut off the other's brow, a gesture of intimacy in a public place.

5. The gay couple participate in the final celebration, completely integrated in the company.

One might also note (as further evidence of the film's progressiveness) that the suggestion in the courtroom (if Sonny secures custody) is that Layla will be the breadwinner while Sonny stays home and raises the kid. I wish I had had a father like that . . . .

## Equal rights

The gay couple of *Big Daddy* function within certain limitations: they represent a somewhat sanitized (bourgeois-respectable, well-behaved) version of gay culture, and their presentation is self-consciously pedagogic. Such objections cannot be raised against two brilliant comedies in which gay couples also figure prominently, the second features of two of the most interesting among the current generation of directors: David O. Russell's *Flirting with Disaster* and Doug Liman's *Go*. Both amply fulfill the promise of their debut features (*Spanking the Monkey* and *Swingers*, respectively).

*Go* offers the more immediate comparison with *Big Daddy* because it also seems directed primarily at the youth audience. It is, of course, an altogether more sophisticated and complex movie, the virtues of *Big Daddy* being dependent on the absence of such qualities. Its (relative) commercial failure seems at first sight surprising: is the tone too caustic?—were teenagers and twenty-somethings disturbed by an uneasy (and well-founded) suspicion that they were being satirized? But, unlike the *wholly* caustic *Flirting with Disaster*, the film is notable ultimately for its generosity and good humor. What finally distinguishes both films from *Flirting with Disaster* is that they are ensemble movies in which the gay couple, instead of being subordinated to the lead figure, is given equal prominence with the other characters. The films are remarkable in that they take gayness absolutely for granted, without the least self-consciousness: their gay characters are neither demonized nor idealized, they are just people. If the gays in *Flirting* are objects of humor, so is everyone else; if the pair in *Go* are lacking in moral awareness and even simple common sense, they are no worse (and no better) than the other eight young people who figure in the film's three interweaving plot-lines. Despite or because of their human failings, they seem to me the most fully acceptable representations of gays in the Hollywood cinema so far.

Interestingly, given their totally different tone, milieu, and the age bracket of their characters (and presumed audience), the issue of infidelity is central to the two films' presentation of the gay couple, but there is an important distinction: in *Go* the gay men represent the *only* couple in the film (aside from the older, corrupt and manipulative cop and his wife). *Flirting*, on the other hand, is singlemindedly concerned with "the couple" as an institution: apart from Tea Leoni's adoption counsellor and the disturbed and disruptive son of the aging hippie parents, all the main characters (parents and children) are organized into couples, all hopelessly dysfunctional. Russell appears to be establishing himself as the nearest approach to a radical working within contemporary Hollywood cinema: *Spanking the Monkey* is an assault on the family, *Three Kings* is the first Hollywood film to expose the basis of America's involvement in the Gulf War (it establishes that Bush urged Iraqis to rise up against Saddam then left them to be massacred; the notion that the United States was motivated by a noble and disinterested concern with the fate of Kuwait is explicitly challenged). *Flirting* attacks the very basis of our culture, its obsession with the couple, with marriage, with biological parentage, though its underlying seriousness is perhaps "covered" by its frenetic humor (it has in common with *Bringing Up Baby* —if nothing else—its exhausting nonstop comic invention). Its gay couple (which, if anything, seems marginally more stable than its perpetually warring heterosexuals, despite or because of the apparent incompatibility of the partners) consists of a middle-aged, conservative gay and a much younger and more obviously attractive man who is self-professedly bisexual and ready to discuss intimate details of sexual behavior with anyone eho will listen. All they seem to have in common is that both are cops. The older man appears to have resigned himself to the fact that the younger will always want other partners; the end credit sequence (where they are not only shown in bed together, in juxtaposition with the various heterosexual couples, but are allowed to kiss) reveals that they have adopted a baby, a somewhat desperate means of sustaining their relationship.

It is a pity that the gay couple of *Go*, Adam (Scott Wolf) and Zack (Jay Mohr), appropriately playing television actors, while given a whole episode as its central characters, do not interact with the young people of the other interlocking episodes: aside from brief contact with Sarah Polley, they remain essentially separate, and the justification for their presence (necessary to the plot) at the "rave" seems somewhat forced. Despite their serious imperfections (they are ready to drive off and leave Sarah Polley to die), their relationship is presented very attractively and quite without fuss; especially refreshing is their quite unhysterical attitude to infidelity. Their discovery that each has been unfaithful provokes no more than transitory tension, and when they discover that they have both "transgressed" with the same young man from the television studio ("Jimmy in makeup") they are able to convert the tension into the shared enjoyment of confronting him together. As the film's only young couple, there could be worse relationship-models, gay or straight.

### The Daytrippers

*The Daytrippers* merits special attention here, both for its excellence and its significance, despite the fact that the issue of gayness is neither introduced nor hinted at prior to its last ten minutes. Its premise could be precisely that of a classic screwball comedy, even though it is never "screwball" and, by the end, no longer even a comedy: After a tender domestic scene and the husband's departure for the office, the wife finds what appears to be a love note from someone called Sandy carelessly dropped under the conjugal bed; she tells her mother, who promptly organizes a trip into town to track down and confront the husband, recruiting the reluctant father, the younger daughter, and the daughter's boyfriend for her miniature army. It's the perfect fusion of the classic marital comedy with the classic family comedy; it would end, of course, after a series of hilarious misadventures, with the discovery that "it was all a misunderstanding," and a joyous reunion all round. The wife would be played by Myrna Loy or Jean Arthur, the husband (if his part were expanded) by William Powell, the parents Mary Boland and Charlie Ruggles. Our sense that the ghost of some such funny and reassuring movie lingers throughout in its background only adds to the film's disturbance, as such expectations are systematically thwarted. The action moves from early morning into middle-of-the-night, the narrative progressing along superficially traditional lines, with various delays and complications: the husband is not in his office; he is to be out all day, but is expected at an evening reception for a currently fashionable novelist; the family track him to an apartment building where they watch (from a distance, out of earshot) as he leaves and says goodbye in the street to an attractive young woman; they lose him again and are distracted by other mishaps and encounters; he is not at the reception . . . . We could still be in familiar territory, except that, with each episode, the tone darkens, the humor becomes more edgy and disturbing, the day/night movement underlining a progression into disintegration. Specifically, each encounter illustrates a different tension, disturbance, disruption within family relationships: a delinquent father is living off his son in secret while failing to pay his ex-wife alimony; two sisters, both high-strung and neurotic, bicker over possessions. This progression is counterpointed by the steady deterioration of relationships within the family on whom the film is centered, and the escalating collapse of traditional values: most notably, the younger daughter (Parker Posey), abruptly attracted to a handsome and intelligent young man (Campbell Scott) at the reception for the novelist, even more abruptly abandons her somewhat absurd but very vulnerable fiancé Carl (a characteristically wonderful performance by Liev Schreiber)—who has the mother's fervent endorsement as ideal son-in-law—on the pretext of forgetting her handbag, returning to the reception for a quick and passionate embrace and exchange of phone numbers. What we have is the "family comedy" brilliantly updated and culminating in the family's total and apparently final disintegration.

Instead of the traditional "it was all a mistake" ending, the film moves not merely to the revelation that the husband (Stanley Tucci) has indeed been unfaithful, but that "Sandy" is a man: the final disintegration of the nuclear family coincides precisely with (and is precipitated by) the emergence of the "spectre" of homosexuality. The movie ends, quite logically, with the two sisters walking off together into the night, abandoning their parents and their own (actual or imminent) marital ties, presumably to try to sort things out and think.

The current right-wing assault on gay rights is firmly entrenched in the belief that "family values" are being threatened. The gay response has been, overall, that this is not the case, the gays form "families" of their own. Both are absolutely correct. The point is, surely—and this is why *The Daytrippers* is, in its implications, one of the key films of our age—that gays do indeed constitute a threat to traditional family values—that is, to the values of the patriarchal nuclear family whose repressiveness and authoritarianism the right is committed to restoring. That there can still be "families" in some sense of the

The Daytrippers: *Hope Davis and Stanley Tucci. "One of the key films of our age."*

word is not open to question: families no longer dominated by the figure of the Father (actual or metaphorical), no longer preoccupied with biological parentage, no longer tied to notions of permanence, "fidelity" (in the purely sexual sense), or "correct" roles. Above all, no longer defined by principles of domination, subordination, control, manipulation, coercion, guilt, punishment . . . .

A final word on this marvellous film: I would like to celebrate its generosity. It could so easily have become merely cynical and negative (a charge that could be made against, for example, *Flirting with Disaster*, which has a similar agenda and an utterly different tone). It expresses neither disgust nor condemnation toward the gay relationship; neither does it blame the wife (Hope Davis) for leaving. All the characters are treated with consideration rather than contempt. Superficially the mother (Anne Meara) might appear the exception: many of the tensions are exacerbated by her hysterical need to "manage" everyone and everything. By implication, however, her position is thoroughly understood: like so many traditional mothers, she has been compensated for her total disempowerment beyond the home with the assumption of power within it. She is finally more pathetic than reprehensible. Even Carl, the center of so much of the film's humor, apparently smug and pretentious (especially in his political commitment to the restoration of an aristocracy to remedy all society's ills!), is allowed his moment of grace, the revelation, not only of vulnerability, but of an authentic generosity of his own.

It is good news that the director, Greg Mottola, after two years of (cinematic) silence, is making another film. One looks forward to it with the utmost eagerness.

# Notes on Contributors

**Gregg Bachman** is Associate Professor of Communication at The University of Tampa. Dr. Bachman writes screenplays, publishes short fiction and is an award-winning video producer. His screenplay *Out of Place* was a finalist in the American Cinema Foundation and Santa Fe national screenwriting competitions. His scholarly interests range from oral history and silent movie audiences to contemporary filmmakers such as Woody Allen and Spike Lee. Dr. Bachman is co-editor of the book *A Slightly Different Light*, forthcoming from SIU Press, and is a regular contributor to *Creative Screenwriting* magazine.

**Charles Barr** is Professor of Film Studies at the University of East Anglia in Norwich, England. Since writing *Laurel and Hardy* in 1967, he has gravitated increasingly to the study of British film history: his books include *Ealing Studios* (1977, published in a new ediution by the University of California Press in 1999) and *English Hitchcock* (1999).

**Ken Bowers** is a longtime silent film fan who works in the Hollywood film industry.

The late **Andrew Britton** was the author of *Katherine Hepburn: Star as Feminist* (1984) and several powerfully argued essays that deserve a collection of their own. He was a member of the editorial boards of *Framework and Movie*, and of the editorial collective of *CineAction!* .

**Frank Capra**, who as his essay "The Gagman" states entered cinema as a joke writer for Mack Sennett, helped shape Harry Langdon into one of the most popular comics of the late 1920s. In the 1930s Capra became one of the most important Hollywood filmmakers, directing such landmark comedies as *Platinum Blonde* (1931), *Lady for a Day* (1933) and the seminal screwball comedy *It Happened One Night* (1934). *Mr. Deeds Goes to Town* (1936) marked a decisive move by Capra into the realm of social commentary, where he remained for the next decade. After the commercial disappointment of his masterpiece *It's a Wonderful Life* in 1946 Capra made a few less ambitious films, mostly comedies again, before retiring in 1961. His compelling autobiography *The Name Above the Title* (1972) helped restore his reputation as the master of inspirational dramatic comedies. He died in 1991.

**Kathleen Chamberlain** is associate professor of English/ Film/ Women's Studies and Associate Dean of Academic Affairs at Emory & Henry College in Virginia. She has presented papers on the Three Stooges at the Popular Culture Association. Her published scholarship focuses on juvenile series books and has appeared in *The Lion and the Unicorn*, *Children's Literature Association Quarterly*, the anthology *Nancy Drew and Company: Culture, Gender, and Girls' Series*, and in two forthcoming anthologies, *Defining Print Culture for Youth* and *Scorned Literature*. Her essay on Lizzie Borden appears in the anthology *Pioneers, Passionate Ladies, and Private Eyes*.

**Aneta Chapman** would like to thank her dogs for allowing her to finish her essay. She lives and works in San Francisco.

**Richard Combs** writes for *Metro*, *Positif*, other European periodicals and other publications. He is collaborating on a book on art cinema with Raymond Durgnat.

**Raymond Durgnat** has taught film and aesthetics in England, America, Italy, India, Finland and New Zealand. His books include *Films and Feeling*, *Eros in the Cinema*, *Jean Renoir*, *Bunuel*, *The Crazy Mirror*, *A Mirror for England*, *Sexual Alienation and the Cinema*, and (with Scott Simmon) *King Vidor, American*.

**Chris Fujiwara** is the author of *Jacques Tourneur: The Cinema of Nightfall*. He writes frequently on film, music, and literature for *Hermenaut* (www.hermenaut.com), the *Boston Phoenix* (www.bostonphoenix.com), *Feed Magazine* (www.feedmag.com), and other publications.

**Brian Henderson**, Professor of Film at the State University of New York, Buffalo, is the author of *A Critique of Film Theory* and the editor of two volumes of screenplays by Preston Sturges, *Five Screenplays* and *Four More Screenplays*. He most recently co-edited (with Ann Martin and Lee Amazonas) *Film Quarterly: Forty Years, a Selection*.

**J. Hoberman** is the senior film critic for the *Village Voice*, a contributing editor to *Sight and Sound*, and an adjunct professor of film at the Cooper Union in New York. He is the author of a history of Yiddish language cinema and the co-author of *Midnight Movies*, a study of cult films. His writings have been collected as *Vulgar Modernism* (Temple University Press).

**Buster Keaton** entered film in 1917, as a sidekick to Roscoe "Fatty" Arbuckle, after a childhood as a vaudeville performer with his parents and siblings. He began starring in comedies filmed at his own studio in 1920 and for the next decade released what are now considered some of the greatest of all comedies, most of which he directed. They include *The Playhouse* (1922), *Sherlock Jr.* (1924) and *The General* (1926). His career declined with the coming of sound but he continued acting in film and television until his death in 1966. His autobiography *My Wonderful World of Slapstick*, as told to Charles Samuels, was published in 1957.

**Frank Krutnik** is the author of *In a Lonely Street : Film Noir, Genre, Masculinity, Inventing Jerry Lewis*, and, with Steve Neale, *Popular Film and Television Comedy*. He is a Professor in Film Studies at Sheffield Hallam University.

**Christine List** is Professor of Communication at Chicago State University where she teaches film and television. She is the author of *Chicano Images: Refiguring Ethnicity in Mainstream Film* and a member of the editorial collective for the Democratic Communique. She has directed several independent documentaries including *No Nos Tientes* (*Don't Tempt Us: The Students of Guatemala*).

**Blake Lucas** has contributed over 100 essays to *Magill's Survey of Cinema* and *Magill's Cinema Annuals*. His writing has also appeared in the reference works *Film Noir, American Screenwriters*, and in *Written By, L.A. Woman*, and, as a regular critic, the *Los Angeles Reader*. His monograph on John Ford was translated into French for the 1995 Cannes Film Festival Retrospective. His essay "Saloon Girls and Ranchers' Daughters: The Woman in the Western" appears in *The Western Reader*.

**Jim McCaffery** is a free-lance writer now living in Brooklyn. His work has appeared in *Monkey Flesh* and *The San Francisco Review of Books*. He fondly remembers summers spent at his grandmother's house, The Old Castle, an eighteenth-century farmstead in the Long Island town of Peconic, where he befriended the ghost of a twelve-year-old boy named Nathaniel. He has no curriculum vitae to speak of.

**Leo McCarey** entered film as an assistant to Tod Browning. At the Hal Roach Studios in the 1920s he worked closely with and helped create the screen personalities of Charley Chase and the team of Stan Laurel and Oliver Hardy. As a director of features he worked with many more of the greatest comedians, including the Marx Brothers in *Duck Soup* (1933), W.C. Fields in *Six of a Kind* (1934), Mae West in *Belle of the Nineties* (1934) and Harold Lloyd in *The Milky Way* (1936). His other comedies include *Ruggles of Red Gap* (1935), *The Awful Truth* (1937), *Once Upon a Honeymoon* (1942), *Good Sam* (1948) and *Rally Round the Flag, Boys!* (1958), as well as important films in other genres. He died in 1969.

**William Ian Miller** is a professor of law at the University of Michigan. His most recent books are *The Mystery of Courage* (2000), *The Anatomy of Disgust* (1997), and *Humiliation* (1993). He is also a student of the Icelandic sagas which form the subject of his *Bloodtaking and Peacemaking* (1990).

**Malcolm H. Oettinger**, author of the 1923 profile of Buster Keaton published here, interviewed many other silent stars, including Norma Talmadge and Louise Brooks, usually for *Picture-Play* magazine.

**Louella Oettinger Parsons** (1880-1972) began her journalistic career in Chicago in 1910, creating the first movie column in the country for the *Chicago Record-Herald*. Early in her career she scripted such features as *Chains* and *The Magic Wand* (both 1912), going on to author *How to Write for the Movies* in 1915. Relocating to New York in 1919, she began her long association with William Randolph Hearst's publications in 1922, and for years was one of the most powerful women in Hollywood, famously attempting to suppress the release of *Citizen Kane* in 1941. She appeared on the radio and in several films and has been portrayed, in films depicting Hearst's doings, by Brenda Blethyn (*RKO 281*) and Jennifer Tilly (*The Cat's Meow*). She retired in 1965.

**Donald Phelps** has, over the past forty years, contributed some quantity of essays and reviews to a plethora of magazines, a few of which—*The Nation, National Review, The New Leader*-remain alive. He regards his "home base" as literature (mainly American) although he has written at some length on movies. Those seeking a path through the small wilderness of his published work may be piqued to know that an edition of his collected essays, *Reading the Funnies*, was published in 2001 by Fantagraphics Press. His thanks to a variety of friends, editors, sponsors, and teachers of many descriptions, would require at least one additional page.

**Gregg Rickman** co-edited *The Western Reader* with Jim Kitses, and is the author of a number of books on Philip K. Dick, including *To the High Castle* (1989) and the forthcoming *Variable Man: The Lives of Philip K. Dick*. He has contributed to such journals as *Film Quarterly, Science-Fiction Studies, Wrapped in Plastic*, and the *San Francisco Weekly*. He teaches film at San Francisco State University.

**Jonathan Rosenbaum's** books include *Movie Wars, Moving Places, Placing Movies, Movies as Politics, Andre Bazin's Orson Welles: A Critical View* (as translator), *This is Orson Welles* (as editor), and

• • • • • • • • • • • • • • • • • • • • • • • • • • • • • • • • • • • • • • • • • • • • •

*Film: The Front Line* 1983. He also authored BFI monographs on Erich von Stroheim's *Greed* and *Jim Jarmusch's Dead Man*. He is the film critic for the *Chicago Reader* and has contributed to magazines including *Film Comment, Film Quarterly, Written By, Scenario, Cineaste, Trafic, Vertigo, Meteor, Bianco e nero*, and *Close Up*.

**Marty Roth** is a professor of American literature and film at the University of Minnesota.

**Dan Sallitt** is an independent filmmaker (*Honeymoon, Polly Perverse Strikes Again!* ) and a former film critic for the *L.A. Reader*. Sallitt has also written for the *Chicago Reader, Wide Angle, Chemical Imbalance, Cinema Toast*, 24fps, and the Toronto Film Festival. His e-mail address is sallitt@post.harvard.edu.

**Richard Schickel** is the author of biographies or critical studies of D.W. Griffith, Douglas Fairbanks, Harold Lloyd, Walt Disney, Marlon Brando, and Clint Eastwood as well as collections of his essays such as, most recently, *Matinee Idylls*. He is also the author of the BFI Film Classics monograph on *Double Indemnity* as well as books on other topics such as *Intimate Strangers: The Culture of Celebrity* in America. He also reviews films for *Time* magazine and has written several documentaries on film.

**Ben Schwartz** is a comedy writer living in Los Angeles, California. His latest screenplay, *Damned If You Do*, is to be produced by James Cameron and directed by Stan Winston at Fox. Besides hunting down any all information Boasberg, he has also published in *The Carl Barks Library*, the *LA Weekly*, and on-line with the satirical web site Suck.com, under the name "Furious George." And yes, he thinks Al Boasberg's should be the fifth face on Mount Rushmore. What of it?

**Bob Stephens** wrote a laserdisc/DVD column ("Lasermania") and covered genre films for the late lamented *San Francisco Examiner*. He has contributed articles on horror, film noir and science fiction movies to *Filmfax, Films in Review, Five Fingers Review, Sci-Fi Entertainment* and *Science Fiction Age*.

**David Thomson** was born in London, England, in 1941, and now lives in San Francisco. He was educated at Dulwich College and the London School of Film Technique. His books include *A Biographical Dictionary of Film; Showman: The Life of David O. Selznick*; and *Rosebud: The Story of Orson Welles*. He has contributed regularly to *Film Comment, Sight and Sound, The New Republic* and the *Independent on Sunday* (in London).

**Ruth Waterbury**, whose 1925 interview with W.C. Fields is included in this volume, continued as a Hollywood columnist into the 1970s and co-authored the 1964 book *Elizabeth Taylor: Her Life, Her Loves, Her Future*. In his book *The Kennedys in Hollywood* (1996) Lawrence Quirk describes Waterbury as "one of Hollywood's prime interviewers and somewhat of a mother figure to stars she interviewed."

**Paul Willemen** is the author of *Looks and Frictions* (1994), edited *The Films of Amos Gitai* (1994) and co-edited *Questions of Third Cinema* (1990) and *Encyclopedia of Indian Cinema* (1999).

**Doug Williams** is the author of "Pilgrims and the Promised Land" in *The Western Reader*. He has taught at UC San Diego and Mills College, and is currently a technical writer. His scholarly interests are in the interactions of cinema, culture, and conceptual metaphor.

**Robin Wood** is the author of a number of books on film of which the most recent are *Sexual Politics and Narrative Film : Hollywood and Beyond, Hollywood from Vietnam to Reagan* and *Hitchcock's Films Revisited*. He is a founding editor and frequent contributor to *CineAction*.